Spiralling Inwards, a collection of verse and things

Spiralling Inwards, a collection of verse and things

Published by The Conrad Press Ltd. in the United Kingdom 2022

Tel: +44(0)1227 472 874

www.theconradpress.com

info@theconradpress.com

ISBN 978-1-914913-68-6

Typesetting and Cover Design by: Charlotte Mouncey, www.bookstyle.co.uk

The Conrad Press logo was designed by Maria Priestley.

Printed and bound in Great Britain by Clays Ltd, Elcograf S.p.A.

And we too can work to form a pearl,
out of our own grit guts experience;
we too have a hard craggy protecting shell
yet are soft and tender inside as well. (Sometimes needing to quell
our clinging hard like hell, to our known rock as well)!

Dec. 2021

8

A simpleton's close reading of!
(Mathematical Operators of ♂+♀=he+she=her=male+female
Female contains male bivalent and ambivalent)

No holds barred -
this is number 8
but if it lays on its side
it's snoozing 8
and I can't type it
'cos it's nowhere on my laptop -
as it is the mathematical
sign for infinity
nothing less;
an identity unknown
stopping all further thought.
And as it is infinite
it isn't a number
as numbers are finite.

Take a blank sheet of paper
and pick up a pen and
imagine a snoozing 8..
Infinity is asleep
and the blank sheet
is Nothing – there's nothing on it.
Snoozing 8 is beginning to wake
with an image in his head
to start something – the Universe. So something has come out of

nothing, so far.
Amazing So put your pen down
with a dot on the sheet -
something is beginning to happen now -
you can choose how to continue -
say – up,around, diagonal-down then
up, around, diagonal-down
and you come back to the beginning.
This can continue repeatedly
without lifting your pen.
So the beginning is the end if you stop.
The beginning; and end of the Universe
which is said to be happening, where everything
disintegrates to nothing or photons only, dead stop -
a freeing relief – no need to leave stuff for posterity.
As Carol said, 'it must be tiring to be infinite;
that is a fun thought. So the infinite can have a rest.
I think Science would squirm in their seats at all this.
But Maths is very keen on infinity as it lies near the core of it all
even at the finite vicinity of 0.
Physics isn't as it felt to be unnecessary, stops thought, is incomplete
and is
never-ending and is not sensed. World without end. Amen!

June 2021

∞ !

Modern Speke

'Right now
find your happy
which ticks all the boxes.
We're talking –
                    um?
               mm
          mm
     um mm
ummmmm?

head to head and neck and neck.
Job done.
Get it in. Happy days.

He was sat and she's a shero.
We're shipping your item'
from a UK town to town!
(there must be a river to cross!)

Laptop and mobile language
is gobble-de-gook on Gobblebox.
Never use XXX – it's now sexual.
PUK number, verification code
SIM code PIN.
Option 1,2,3,4,5,6 for what?
Scrambled egg is my brain now
and SIM disabled. Sod the lot.
I had thought LOL was lots of love.
It isn't. It's laugh out loud.

Mar 2021
AKA a nice round 0 (also known as)

Music Sound Word

To be a poet you've got to be deeply stupid - not as a criticism but a truth

O my being – Sibelius Symphony no. 2
transfixed transformed
within without all
magnificent amazing sound
by a being sounding god
who is God.
The heights depths
that a human can reach
above within below around.
All these words inadequate
that elevate me wordless

into a heaven profound -
past present and future all one -
such a range of feeling all one –
now and not now -
from its despair gentleness
greatness magnificence -
a triumphant exuberant exhilaration
rising, rising above the mundane.
Music sound is primary beyond Word.
Sound reigns.
as I struggle with words.
I give up, sparkling alight now
as I wept and shivered in awe

Aug 2021

A Wild Garden – a continuing environmental saga

Mine, here now – to keep up with the times.
Trees all round, large ones
and none of them mine -
their leaves fill gutters fast
which overflow – flood, aghast.
Bees and wasps buzz in the loft
so be cautious there, go quickly off.
When it's warm midges swarm.
Mouse holes are all over the soil -
2 entered my open back door
and 1 blocked a downpipe drain there
costing hundreds to kill and repair.
Imagine seeing a mouse
scuttling round in your house.
Aphids suck and prosper killing growth.
Foxes poo on the grass which I loathe.
Fat wood pigeons waddle and shit everywhere -
their unblinking white rimmed eyes stare.
Squirrels break the bird feeders to bits -
the nuts scattered to the ground and gobbled up

so that the poor tits have none at all and quit.
All in all – a flamboyant mess
so that I'm sure I don't like this stress -
at all, at all and utterly pissed off at best.

Are people not part of the garden scene? -
disorder, a big part of the 'green' scheme.

Apr.2021

The Meeting Room

This bright place, chairs, cushions, plants
and low coffee table -wait – now, new again,
expectant for us to give birth to the word
under the care of a wordsmith midwife;
to then build blocks and knock them around
or on the anvil, to forge and hammer steel shapes
under the sparks of laughter and hidden tears.
Creation is always violent in its birth -
we are pushed and pulled in sweat and pain
and blood and tears in rain, in ice, in thirst in gain
and not all is in vain.

But near bubbling streams
there are smiles as well.

June 2021

1 & 2 letter Words
A Faint Hunch ? autonomous self

No I?
No. M is
So I am he
I am we

I am us
I am it
I am me
I am.
Lo - it is so.
O go to it.
An as-if
a no-no
ah me o my. No
Oh - I am in he
he is in me.
Do. Go to -
on or in or up -
on he, of he, in he?
Us. Ye. We. co.

Re - ex ma by pa?
no - ta.
A pp cf. cc.- a.m & p.m.
Oh no. Ay - it is so, um.
Ha ho hi la-la
ad e.g ed. my id ?-
ah um, um, um.
At it, at it!
Ox. On & on!

O - I am ok
So be it. No IT. NO
So be it so
I am me. It is Me.
I am - Us - We.
he is. Is He?
It's M.E. ME
'It's E'.
It's me
It's We, Us.

7.5.02 Canterbury

There are some 43 two letter words in English, including some uncommon old ones and 8 or more abbreviations. The New Oxford Dictionary. All are included in the above - except pi po and oz. There are 3 one letter words I.O and a. E is my initial. 'It's' is allowed = it is. ? & is. Ox indicating 'you clot' or 'idiot'. M is a friend.

'16 Tons'

to the American Western folk tune of the same name
Apologies to overweight people and old people. I too am an OAP but with a new Black belt in Shotokan Karate

lub-dup, lub-dup, lub-dup, lub-dup
(the sounds of a heart). is the chorus
'zits' are boils. 'Cottage cheese flesh' is that
fat irregular skin surface from large fat deposits

19 stone and what do you net?
A second days solace and a hangman's bet.
Fat and a coronary, blocked heart tubes -
so why do you bother with the stodgy greased foods.

Chorus.

Cottage/cheese flesh and dewlaps with zits.
Lots/of/bulges, squigges and cellulose bits.
But, and a but looms large and set -
so maybe a death from a stroke and bad debt.

Chorus.

But who am I to talk like this.
A blown old medic who is taking the piss.
Wait/a/bit your turn soon - a few more years;
that's/all the grace allowed you till a doddery old dear.

Chorus. then ending in - Dum...

Canterbury Nov.2002

A Child, The Universe and Time,
'The truth is in the depths' Democritus

Time is running out – not jogging
but running fast with swift feet.
I must swivel my eyeballs
and reassess the situation
as I'm up to my ears, going round the bend
and all over the shop - all over the place;
at 6's and 7's; running round the houses,
at the end of my tether, end of the rope.
Out of strength.
If I am at the end of my tether
then I am about to become free of restraint!
Flippin heck - what the hell.
Hello there Speedy. Stop.
Stopping is very good;
in the Universe scheme of things
time does not exist – my quiet self.
There is no past, present or future.
Kids are quaint and brilliant -
they have to learn clock time of adults
but intuitively know of no time at all.
They know of 'schooltime',
'goinghometime' and 'timeforbedtime'
but not what the hands of a clock are saying.
Clock times are different all over the Earth
and below and above the earth
and different on the ground
to up on the mountain top.
At heart, the Physicists now say -
the Universe occurs as Change,
Happenings of Events, Relationship.*
The Universe is a child - I say, where is no time,

no space and is full of mischievous events
and out of that comes our adult prejudice
and blurred particulate knowledge with dull eyes -
'everything in the world becomes blurred when seen close up'*
not particulate enough - our eyes fail there.
The child Universe has been and is growing into
adult stuff out of a blurring soup
but we and it are at heart a Child.

It seems an invalid is invalid! Or -
'This is what I have in my purse' ..
'but I have to do this' … -
different emphasis in both.
Language is quarkish, quirky, unpredictable idiosyncratic;
like 'accommodation' as well - with its letter waste.

July 2019.

*The Order of Time' by Carlo Rovelli

A Couple

At a cafe corner
a middle-aged couple sat.
She at first mobile engrossed,
typing in the numbers
to make a presumed purchase cost
of her shiny credit card.
He, day-dreaming, wrapped up -
thoughts away and afar.
The next time I turned to look
they cuddled close
arms around, quiet.
It was not a time
for inadequate words.

My tension eased.
It was so good
though a knife pierced my heart -

my mate had died
some years ago,
yet not alone as I somehow
sank into their oneness so.
Somehow also I was now
warmed yet struck thus so
I can know…

Nov 2019

A Dive In

under the influence of affluent influenza

I dip my bucket into my deep-within well -
so many superfluous words;
no one sit near me, give me space -
water everywhere in my well,
not life giving but drowning in a 'flu place.
There's a frog in my throat bucket
dear Liza dear Liza, croak croak croak
quark quark quark – which is my second name.
I love you quarks – the scent of the transcendent;
like God you're everywhere and in many places
all at once; and in a quantum vacuum nowhere all at once.
Time is a practical illusion in our brains –
past present and future are all one -
the past is in the present and in the future,
the present is the past and the future.
The future is in the present and past.
I could hug you Einstein, your Spacetime
for this transcendent wafting whiff.
There's another immense reality, counter-intuitively, outside
our small, but so far the highest, brain-heads inside.
Life is just a temporary home for gluons, quarks -
the immortal elements of the universe.
There's a hole in that wall dear Liza, dear Liza
where someone tried to picture-hang as you do.
It turns into a long Loch Ness monster dinosaur
raising his snake head above the gloomed greylake.
We have a knack of believing our illusion-vision

trying to make sense of nonsense but making nonsense again.
Nessy swims up to me with a flaming 'hello' and
'you all are a bunch of blockheads to believe,
to believe I really exist outside of your brains!'
Then he disappears in the morning mist rains.

The Quantum vacuum is not empty despite its name -
it has fleeting electromagnetic waves
and particles popping in and out of the universe.
Mass comes from virtual quarks, some who never die, and gluons,
fizzing, quivering, some annihilating, in a bubbling
quantum vacuum.
Within nonsense there's sense and within sense there is no sense.

Mischievous immortal quarks -
their 'counter-intuition', 'togetherness-in-separation',
and their 'superposition'.
Matter is merely vacuum fluctuation -
glorious Icons – their 'colours' and gold and all 'colours'.
Hurray.

Mar 2018.

P.S. In Quantum Physics a particle can be in 2 or many places all at once! (superposition)

However once we do a particle measurement of say its energy or position this superposition is lost. One could say particles interact with the observer and his measuring! Yippee.

A Little Dog

A mum, dad and 2 kids
sat snacking round a table-bench
in 'Shakespeare's' garden pub -
cool under huge parasols high up.
A French bulldog, pop-eyed and tongue half out -
his face too blunt to hold them in, squat
is lead-harnessed to the bench leg
and so tight he can only stand to eye-beg

while sniffing the food smells above
with eyes following delivery of delicious stuffs,
waiter balanced, to other groups fast and rough.
The mum was nearest him and so busy
being beautiful while the kids eat, delight dizzy.
All are too busy – a culture sad had
of ignoring their dog. So bad.

I can stand it no further
and rise to tell Mum her dog
can't lie down therefore together.
She apologises – though why to me!
then unties the dog to the care of her mate, carefree
where he can lie down and wait
under the table, cool while they eat.

I can't believe this happened at all.
A pack of such insensitivity, lack and gall.

Sept 2019

Just Bubbily Doodeling

A smug bug
in a rug
jumped into a mug
and swam
then turned into a grub.
A pug cub
snapped it up
and got into
a fug hub
then rubbed down
in a tub
and lo -
became a wee white Westie dug.

15 Nov 2020

A/Cross Dressing
The problem of the English language

A large man and plump
walked past in the street
bulging muscled legs, short frilly socks
ahead of a lady group of plump pink bunnies -
all of them dressed in frilly short
sleeveless pink and purple floral frocks
and pink sashes shoulder slung.
But he had an bursting large ruc-sac
and even bigger brolly up
and a short shaven hair crop
with just a front 'unicorn style' blob spike up
and 2 pink bunny-sprung bouncing pommels atop;
were these supposed to be ears? - I mused.
I couldn't resist bursting out with a laugh.
Was it a wedding they were off to
aiming for the cathedral or not?
I hoped it was – an anti-dote
to its snooty stuffy upper-class

He was certainly not cross.
Cross is angry or here more accurately -
dressing gender across
or maybe cross at it not being acceptable
to dress boundary across.
Anyway it was great fun
and female he most certainly was not -
his legs said that out loud.
This – a 'Hen Party'
dressed as bunnies now, hot -
and food for thought.

May 2018.

More Info. on Ants

I was tickled pink today to learn
that a Scottish ant the size of a rice grain,
the largest ant of all here,
builds dry nests over several decades,
2 metres high, out of chopped down,
gnawed grass stalks on the sunny side of a trunk
which have a waxy coat so repel rain.
In addition they have central heating, ventilation -
if it gets too hot they open up air vents
and if sunny but too cold
they troop out and sit on top of the the nest
absorbing sun's heat then go back indoors
to share the warmth throughout with all.
But I don't know what happens
if it's too cold with no sun – no sun-bathing.
And if the nest is snow covered
the warmth of their bodies inside
and heat generated by decaying grass
would melt the snow to water which then runs off.
Clever – eh. Brilliant I say and most sociable.
So you're lucky – no large mounds in your house
at this stage.

June 2020

An Apple Bit

This bit of raggedy apple reminds me
that things fall to the ground Newton-like
and die and their seed dies, cracks open
and new life springs forth.
Give thanks to this apple bit giving life
to my sense of sight touch taste and smell
and the sound as I bite - nectar of the gods.
O ye of little crunch, crunch down
and let my senses flow in trickling cidered juice -

death and life intertwined around.
The apple has died that I may live a bit -
so mourn and rejoice in this apple bit grown.

Oct 2013

Basset Hounds. Bodies of Beauty
(from French bas - low, Latin, bassus – short)

So ugly in disproportion, the 2 dogs are beautiful!
Superb splendid gorgeous handsome grand soulful.
On my scooter I went the wrong way down Burgate
to follow them, on leads under 2 owners, old.
I stopped to ask them across the road and their kind was told.
I laughed in joy and they grinned. 'They're beautiful', I called.
Not your ordinary beauty though – a new one, piebald.
One was brown blobs on white, the other dappled black and white,
both friends jogging jaunty- bouncing slow,
their blanket skins bouncing floppy on their backs
with every move, rippling wrinkled loose and low.
Large in every respect except short wrinkled legs;
overall – the size of a large labrador,
deep bodies near 2 foot long somehow;
long ears trailing ground as they sniffed the smells;
large doleful droopy eyes, neat perky pointed tails
and firm, plum-tight ripe balls.
But then surprise – their willies just touched the ground
with each bouncing step on their 6 inch little wrinkled legs.
I wondered what they hounded – not with speed though
and too large to go down burrow holes. It's hares on foot!
Long noses and wrinkled heads to catch and reflect all the scents.
Scent detectives second only to bloodhounds to boot.
They sniff out unseen in low brush/grass a rabbit or hare,
bay out low, flushing out their quarry who escape and are shot
and because they are slow they are far from being in the line of a shot

They had to lie down for short rests for short legs perhaps
and I learnt they love being on their owners laps!

and love to go their own way regardless, obsessed with
following scents
And I chuckled and marvelled. They had made my day
and off I went content on my way.

A pram passed, full of a cuddly chubby blanketed babe.
Yay oh. Cheerio.

Dec 2018.

Beachy Head Cliff Deaths

Today a 42-year-old mum
with her 5-year-old son
jumped to their deaths;
what went through them, intense
as they flew through the air?
A few days ago 3 bodies were found
also on the shore below.
Such unbelievable driven despair -
wrenching gut
breath stopped,
stopped in my tracks,
stopped short.
A chasm blank
as I heard the news.

How does it feel
to be in dying thus?
No record of this
that we all have to go through.
Shall I wear a smart phone
when dying conscious
that I can convey, record.

Near death experiences -
light at end-tunnel cries O God -
did she murder her boy or not?
It looks like she did

but at what age does his consent
and understanding legal become?
5 years is very young, too young
for such.

The police record nothing suspicious -
not even the murder moment thus - silent -
even if they had – so what as
conviction beyond - she too was dead.
What would have happened
if she survived but he died.
Murder surely would have been the charge
and in court she - tried.

June 2018

Black Holes

Never seen before, have now come out
from behind the Universe curtain
with a shy demure debut. Sacred before
that is feared.
One was seen not long ago
for the first time ever – a donut shaped ring of light
surrounds the black abyss of M87 behemoth
in another galaxy, 6.8 billion times
the mass of the earth's sun -
picked up by 8 earth telescopes
on the tops of the world
then computer interpreted in sense.
Black holes so hungry they gobble up
stars and dust and even light - nothing escapes
possibly to create new stars planets worlds
in fearful awe as their gravity is so great;
light outside is bent into a ring.
No-one knows what goes on inside the hole
but light disappears 'forever' it is said
yet who knows what happens to it then,

maybe all is transformed to what then?
Our galaxy's black hole - Sagittarius A* is small
and not yet 'seen'. His name means an archer
represented by an arrow and bow -
our black hole.

I want to give M87 a nicer name -
perhaps his highness Holy Hole HH.
Who knows – maybe HH is stirred
by my simple warmth for him!
And yet so feared
just as I am so fond of Quarks.
Who knows? We don't know everything.
'ydoan o nudn' much.*
you don't know nothing!

*from E.E.Cummings, ygUDuh' - you-got-to.

Apr 2019

Blackbird

Once blocked to write I come alive.
He is just and only that – a black blackness
and by his sharp stab yellow beak
marked by movement from his dim surrounds.
We're in the back beer garden courtyard
of 'The Shakespeare' pub with such renowned presence!
But Will's gone out shopping as I tell passers by -
stopping to take photos of the pub sign.
The bird searches for 'crumbs under the table'
which we are 'not worthy to gather up' but he is.
Scarce of any pickings as it's midwinter
and peoplefolk don't sup outside
but he is persistent, searching low and high
and stopping to suck up sups
without throwing back his head
to let the water trickle down as most birds do -
except pigeons and him. There he sipped

from the water handle sunken round cups
of the square steel cover of the drain,
coming back often to sip for more.
Two large old clean metal milk churns
stand solid guard
below the old rust bicycle, wall-slung, well above,
with its crossbar ad 'The Shakespeare,
Purveyor of fine meats and game' -
this the street of 'Butchery Lane'
once filled with butchers shops in old times.
There's an old fat five foot coopered slatted barrel
with 4 metal rims to hold them in place –
the lost complex crafts of old.
He has a wooden plant box atop his tub
with a frondy spreading light green plant -
his style - hair cut.

The blocked black spell is broken – a bird has flown free.
Thank you Blackbird – wild and free.

Feb.2019

Blue Tit on a Flower

Just a second's spontaneous glance
caught a Blue titlet -
alighting on a floret -
one of a spray
of Canterbury Bells –
a fresh light blue,
blue on tit blue.
So sweet, then
the bell dropped
under his light weight
and did not break -
that's all.
He was his mother watching
a nut to crumbs snapping
from the food tray

crumbs falling -
but him weaning,
she his chirp pleas ignoring
and wings fluttering
fed herself now.
He - a ball of short feathers,
a fluff ball
with no neck
so puffed up and plump – ooooh!

June 2018

A Blue tit
Haiku

Who else would sit on
the tip of a pink rose bud
but a cute blue tit.

Ordinary

Who else would sit
on a pink rose bud tip
but a tiny blue tit;
near his foot -
a dew drop sip.
He drops like a bullet to feed.
So pretty - he jumps and flits.
He and his friends share table food
but robin scares others off.
The tits sway on the hanging feeder in gales.
I would be dizzy by now.
They can fly in high winds -
the wind has no effect.
The wind parts to allow their flight.
So many popping here and there
like tiny blue-grey fleas.
little cheeky cheery chappies.

Who else would sit
on a pink rose bud tip?
Why yes - a shy jenny wren.

Canterbury Dec 2002

Brexit. Since the Referendum Unsolved
The Talk

Now 3 years on, the most mostest
hated word
is Brexit. You say it to folks then there's
groaning, moaning, sighing, fighting
in Britain, Brexit, the Backstop -
a giant trug load
of complex negotiations back and forth,
hargy bargy –
UK and EU standing their ground unbudged;
a President of some European something
wishing Brit MPs in hell
and Juncker, President of the EU Commission
saying 'I'm already in hell' here now.

Oh – Oh – Oh.

The E.U. stubbornly doesn't look at its faults
that caused a lot of the UK to want to break off
from its domination in the first place.
But there, omg, Theresa May is apparently compromising
and is persistent and dogged, well done -
back and forth to Europe like a jack in the box.
'Keep Calm and Carry On'.
Only God knows what next will be done.

Jan 2019

Bzz. Thump

A bungee-jumping bumble bee nuzzles nectar,
buzzing among tiny slim yellow hawksbeard flowers.
He stops, lands and under his weight the stems, slender -
bend, bow right down, even to the rich brown ground altar.
But Bumble zooms off to the next nectar-cup-
bouncing-back-bloom lifting, springing back up.
He buzzes and I chuckle in delight and fun
and so we fly free round the round orange sun.

July 2006

Cadbury's Chocolate Ad
And the music of the Stars

A little girl, serious comes to the counter
in a corner shop, her head just above the counter.
A serious older bearded Asian man looks up
from his counter-laid paper work.
She hesitatingly, quietly asks
for her mum's birthday - a chocolate bar -
mum squatting down outside
with an eye on her child inside.
He gets a large bar and puts it down.
She slowly puts down an old 2/6 coin -
he waits for more and up comes one grey button
then one red one, then a ring with a pink plastic gem,
hesitates then her favourite special little plastic elephant.
He slides the bar to her, she slowly takes it and makes to move off.
'You've forgotten your change,' he says and returns her elephant.
She gives the chocolate to her mum, so pleased and touched
as I was.

'There's a glass and a half in everyone', not just one, says the ad.
in the bar too made of cocoa and milk.
All so moving and sadly sweet and happily sad.

I watched BBC's Horizon 'Cosmic Dawn -
amazing scenes of the Universe.
The background music Preisners 'Lacrimosa',
'requiem for my friend' - oh so beautiful, no words;
before words – comes unutterable sound.
At one point 'I saw heaven and earth' - 2 images side by side -
the telly Universe and the little girl chocolate ad.
Utterly complex, utterly simple alongside -
so beautiful - and wept, tear cried.

June 2018

Christ!! ??IT? Wait

Mantra Common Sense.
Just get on with it.
Life is just this.
Not our images, dreams.
Perfection is junk.
The future is not. It's now.
This very now. Nothing else.
Get that in your stormed head.
Hard cold ruthless.
Concrete steel lead.
This sheer bolt from the Black.

Urgent phone call 7pm. What?
Hospital appointment 2 days for what?
Consultant Urologist. 1 hour wait.
GP has said nought.
He knows me of years ago
when they first settled in our road
and I took around my home grown,
as a neighbourly welcome, my sweet peas.
A good nice man. More of my pee required.
Squeezed out a few drops. Blood negative again.
7 mm shadow on my bladder UltraSound.
Cystoscopy by urethral tube now required.

Stunned. ? Cancer. The big C.
The primed guillotine waiting to drop.
I maybe old but it appears not ready to die yet
though glimpsing of this, I've now had enough -
the chattering monkeys doom.
Urgent new GP appointment 1 hour wait
shuffling in my seat. She is good.
What is IT? Could be a common benign polyp, cyst
? will take it out at cystoscopy –
then again wait path lab report.
He and his department are very good.
CT scan of before, only good for 1 cm. blobs not less.

So I leave to flounder on my own -
an eternity of fear run riot – shaking, unsteady
to the Red Cross shop to sort bags -
restless - a distraction welcome.
Notice little things blazing out.
Christ
what next.
It's the not knowing - but why should I control
and why should I know?
Simple. I can't.
Just Wait and Wait and Wait and wait...

Aug.2018.

Clock

The clock
quietly ticks,
so confidant and proud;
with insistent clicks -
seconds, minutes, hours,
days, weeks, years;
hands jerk, he has a face.
So pleased with himself,
omnipotent – he controls all

hanging high on the wall -
his pendulum swings
almost as if no-one or anything
can stop him except Time itself.
Hypnotic persistence -
I laugh and sway in time with him
'cos you know what -
absolute Time does not exist – that's the fun -
in the deep order of things.
But he doesn't know that
'cos we made him
and times everywhere are different -
in the beginning
which was also the end!

Sept.2020

The observable Universe update Dec. 2021
with thanks to BBC2's recent "The Universe"
On dropping fixed ideas and taking on Counterintuition
Yes. The Sun sings Sound

The Cosmos is an enigma, a paradox – magnificent and beautiful.
I am not up to this; it's so mind-blowingly impossible Possible.
It seems there was darkness before light in the face of the deep.
Before the dawn of time, there was no space or time.
Before the Big Bang, Cosmic Dark Ages ruled – a time before time!
where only Energy was – the mother of all and the big bang
where violence and dark before creation exploded into light.
Without darkness and violence there is no creation and light.
The energy God is both dark and light implicit in all.
When stars and supernova die, they explode in light.
Black holes exist at galaxy centres and give rise to creation
through Information, inherent in the heart of everything,
to a new being state of no time or space.
They are black, as any light and matter at their entrances is
gobbled hungrily
and can't escape as gravity dominates -
as they need delicious food to swallow in order to create!

They are a part of God; they are black holy holes, in truth.
All in existence must die to give rise to creation.
Death and life are one and both are transformation of Information
Black holes are the Heart of Darkness, the Ancient Monsters –
angels of God!
We are wrong, at a deep level, that space and time exist. They don't e.g. time is different at different places and heights; and we make the clocks.

When I die, as I said before, I hoped that God would take me on a guided tour of the Universe but as space and time don't exist – it would take no time at all
and as space does not exist, I would not need to move!
What is at bedrock - is that of Energy (c.f biblical Spirit) before anything and all, and that Energy (which can't be seen) conveys Information before any big bang. And linked to that is "Consciousness" where all things are aware and responsive to their surroundings. Consciousness integrates Information. All things are aware and responsive to their surroundings, not only human beings (e.g plants and tree roots and leaves, the Black hole Event Horizon etc). Consciousness and Information are puzzling. We intuit that they exist – but how do they work?

What, not yet seen by current telescopes, is beyond the "observable Universe"?

Dec 2021

Light travels at a constant 186,000 miles/second, Quantum/ Astrophysicists are now the new priests.

Cosmical Waking
Listen up children with all your ears

At night Sun was fast asleep.
Moon had taken his watch
but she was not yet fully full up
as she hadn't finished

her 'Crunchie' meal of Stars
and 'Milky Way' bars.
Dawn made her entrance
between their shifts.
Sun rubbed his sticky eyes
and yawned and stretched
under his Cloud bedclothes
in grey misty Dawn.
Slowly sleepy Day stirred and stretched.
Sun felt he had to remedy this slow start
so he jumped out of bed
and Cloud's covers fell to the ground
as rain, then lo and behold -
as Dawn had gone a.w.o.l -
Day was shining sparkly, sprinkled
with diamond water drops
and he was going full steam ahead, fresh.
A Cockerel crowed
and all of us little People woke
in the sun-tide flow
on this side of King Universe.

But no talking till after breakfast!

Apr.2018

Some Cheeky Potted Scrambled 'Counter-intuitive' Creation Quantum Noteicles
The Soul of the Atom! Intimations of Divinity! Tommy Cooper's universe
I am confused but more importantly chucklingly, twinklingly amused

To be confused, confounded, baffled, befuddled, mystified, perplexed, perturbed amazed at 'our wonderful Universe' is now good – it's so far the 'truth' and it leads to more curiosity and understanding so there is no final 'truth' - yet.
Probability, not certainty, rules – like tossing a coin. So far that's the best physics can do.

'Where our conceit that the workings of Nature don't necessarily accord with common sense' and prejudice - the sun is said even now, to rise and set even by the BBC weather app. It doesn't Perhaps daybreak and dusk would be better. Also our prejudice that sea waves flow to the shore. Wrong. It's the waves of energy that do, not the sea water. The water may do same-place somersaults. Wavefunctions can 'slosh' back and forth.

We need more of an uncommon sense now.

Physicists dislike extrapolations of their findings to other experiences. If they disagree with somebody they can call it 'tripe, rubbish, shit, holistic drivel' so herewith out of rich compost comes life. And out of idea energy, come word particles! Within the macro is the micro. Within the atom is all sorts. We are made of 'up and down quarks' – and electrons. All of us – there's no particle racism at root. I love the beautiful amazing, the mischievous, the antics. So herewith.

In the beginning which wasn't, there was Something
but not a thing = no thing = Nothing Who/which was there, who was not a who or a which; who! was nowhere and everywhere before the beginning which wasn't.

From nothing in the beginning comes a Universe which was
squashed to the size of a pinpoint where 'angels' jive in an
unbelievable enormous Energy storm burst neither created nor
destroyed. Energy, the Ultimate, before 'anything' else at all.

Then different forms of energies split off
to form 4 forces and fields. Word particles come from the soup field of ideas!

Only common gravity, the weakest force (yet holds the earth in orbit round the sun
- (that's pretty strong to me) is a problem and has no quantum description; a graviton is posited but not yet found.

And out of these fields comes mass and particle condensates.

in a soup swirling where time does not exist.

Mass is not a primary property of the ultimate building blocks - just

$E=Mc^2$ –

energy and mass are interchangeable.

Quantum from quanta – energy packets. We don't see energy only its effects, but we do see Mc^2 as e.g in the energy in all sports! 'A ball flying through the air knows which path to choose because it actually and secretly explores every possible path'. Electrons 'know' about and 'talk to' each other! And when they move in semi-conductors they leave 'holes' for others and 'holes' move around. Electrons and holes 'meander'. Particles talk to each other. Electrons avoid each other. Atoms and quarks love each other.

Einstein - 'The eternal mystery of the world is its comprehensibility' and 'the fact that it is comprehensible is a miracle'. Despite the intricate complexity of the natural world there are not many rules and laws.

These initial combining energies, corresponding to temperatures around 10 billion billion billion degrees, would have been prevalent a fraction of a second after the Big Bang. Then the Universe cools and Higgs bosons form like water cools to icicle condensates. Hot atoms 'jiggle' faster than cold ones and they share electrons – love sharing to stick together. Fuzzy electrons love orbital movement, like the earth round the sun, and only 2 electrons, no more, can be in each energy orbit level though why only 2. 'Every atom in the Universe is connected to every other atom'. And they love sticking together – a result of sharing their electrons. And quarks love branching into gluons who love gluing particles together.

It is so difficult to pin down the impossible possible. One of the great mysteries of physics is that the electric charges of the proton and neutron in the atom are exactly equal and opposite. Why don't we fall through the floor? – because negative charged electrons repel each other in the floor and shoes. Electrons like to avoid each other. c.f quarks who love each other. But it appears there is anthropic fine-tuning in the universe - all this it seems, by random mutations, to drift towards the origin of intelligent life, still going on in juggling genes too.

There's this 'weird' and 'spooky'zoo' of hierarchical particles - whose names even physicists can't remember – which are frustrating - the 'God particle' = the .god-damn particle', the 'Oh my God' large particle, exquisite maths, awesome findings of 'spins, orbits spirals jumpings hoppings leapings jigglings flittings' of 'particles' like folks in our rock/ pop dance; leptons, bosons, massless gluons which glue quarks together, anti-particles which 'shuffle' backwards in time; positrons which are electrons with instead a positive charge and are anti-matter; some with

varieties of positive, negative or neutral charges, and an electron can have several different energies all at the same time; baryons, muons; neutrinos which can pass all the way through earth. Whoopy!.
Quirky quarks – 'top and bottom', 'up and down' kinds, 'charm and strange' kinds
and kinds with colours which aren't really colours at all. Colour could not be seen as nature demands that all observable particles are 'white' but physicists are running out of words. So there is a spectrum of 'real' colour but not of particles
Quarks taken from James Joyce's 'Finnegans Wake' from the first 'quorks' a nonsense word against pretentious scientific language. Symmetries and breakings, changing and swappings, anti particles annihilating yet not – just forming new
out of old. Masses becoming massless and vice-versa. A proper improper soup.

Energy bundles of quanta and vacuums which aren't vacuums and
particles which are virtually there but are not, and are real and
'surreal' -

a continually changing fluctuating primordial soup forming and unforming ceaselessly. Language is being stretched beyond its limits. Particles which exist and don't, as points or waves or both. The very act of measuring something introduces a disturbance – that means we are relating to subjects not divorcing them into objects. There are no objects – us/them, them/us. Sizeless pointless 'angels' hopping in a pin head at the beginning of the Universe. A light photon scatters off an electron sitting in an atom of my eye and that will trigger a chain of events leading finally to my perception of the photon as I become aware of a flash of light in my eye. 'It is one of the wonders of life that we can see anything at all'. This the quantum measurement problem. This also relates to how our past might influence the future. So there's a school of physics that says 'shut up and calculate'. Nothing exists in isolation. All uncertain and particles have different spins. Two quarks close together relax and are at rest – how sweet is that – like love! apart they are agitated. An isolated quark has energy infinite - almost as if desperately searching for a mate. (Like God has to create, not liking to be on his own!) And no-one has ever seen a quark on its own – like the unseen God!. 'Things' seem to love the lowest energy state. Don't we all after much thinking and activity. But a state of unchangingness is non-survival yet even death/annihilation has some 'life' to another state.

Now at last has been found the fat Higgs boson 'God-damn' particle – (Higgs, who worked out the maths nearly 50 years ago) whose field is there to give mass to the deprived massless – food to the poor! Particles 'bump' into him on their way in the Universe and 'zig-zag'. Empty space is full of Higgs in a maelstrom.
Did that start the big bang origin or cosmic inflation of our universe?
And a particle can be in many places all at once; and 2 are together even when separate. The trinity 3 in 1! We are at root, bundles of quarks so laugh and love your mischievous and unpredictable self!
Life is just a temporary home for quarks and gluons – the immortal elements of the universe. Quarks quack the scent of the transcendent.
Quantum theory predicts that every particle spends some time as a combination of other particles in all possible ways. Tested. Like trying on different suits for size. Temporary reduction of conservation of energy so that 1 particle can become a pair of 'virtual' evanescent unseen particles which quickly rejoin to the original particle as if they had never been there. Tested.
Quarks are particles like electrons but different as they also react with the strong force. 2 lighter quarks bind together to make up protons and neutrons in the atom – constantly flitting from one form to another. Hurray! All this sounds like us.

Massless elemental particles cause matter to have mass.
Higgs bosons are quantum fluctuations in the Higgs field pervading the entire Universe, visible in experiments only when energy is injected into the field.
The light photon (they have spin) does not interact with the Higgs field, it snubs it, and continues to move unhindered at the speed of light, (they are light), remaining massless.'And let there be pure light'!

At bottom so far! the fundamental Universe building lego blocks are not discrete particles at all but they are continuous fluid-like substances called fields spread throughout all of space which is not space at all.
The ripples in these hectic fields get turned into bundles of energy quanta.
A vacuum is space devoid of particles, boiling and bubbling and frothing in a soup of changing 'virtual' particles and anti-particles constantly created and destroyed. Mass is just the resistance to acceleration
Even 'nothingness' is being investigated as it is 'dark'.
We only know 4% of our universe; 96% remains unknown and is called dark matter and dark energy. Perhaps 'love' is like all this as well!

Maybe you can say anything and it might be true
as 'counter-intuition' is important in the quantum world.
Even though Einstein said 'the only really valuable thing is intuition'.

Einstein - 'in this effort towards logical beauty spiritual formulas are discovered necessary for the deeper penetration into the laws of nature'.

'Nature has no problem with infinities' but we and maths do.

Einstein - 'The Lord is subtle but he is not malicious' but with the enormous time and cost (multi-billion pound Cern Large Hadron Collider paid for by 54 countries) to find a Higgs boson particle 'it is reasonable to accuse the Lord of possessing a certain mischievous wit'.

About Einstein in a biography, physicist Pais 'Subtle is the Lord' - says 'his reasoning was mad but his madness has that divine quality that only the greatest transitional figures can bring to science'. And also why do physicists write of Nature and the Universe with a capital N and U but science with a little s? Capital letters - 'the best way of dealing with things you don't have a good answer to' in 'The Hitch-hikers Guide to the Galaxy' - Douglas Adams.

So far the quark is Lord, making up protons, neutrons; electrons are in all and us too but Higgs boson is King. Without it and its field and the interactions, there would be no Nature/Universe. Quark masses come from it slowing them down. Perhaps God is an enormous massless Quark in 3 places all at once as 1. And also a Higgs boson - giving out gifts of mass in different ways to form, create the cosmos!

When I die my quarks will live on in eternal life! I hope God will take me on a a guided tour of the Universe and as time doesn't exist it will take no time at all and I would like to meet especially Sibelius, Brahms, Shostakovitch, Mozart and Tommy Cooper with the background Universe music.

I've had enough now. Have you? So 'shut up and keep musing' as we can't 'shut up and keep calculating' unless we are advanced mathematicians. Quantum mechanics is in computers, transistors – the most important invention in the last 100 years and has saved millions of lives. Transistors in a mobile phone - a million of them; a hundred thousand of them cost less than a grain of rice.

How on earth did man come to have this amazing capacity for mathematics out of the blue. Is it our Quarks jiggling Bachian counterpoint dances in our brains!
Physicists talk of time and then of it not existing. Also of particle probabilities then later of particles per se! Everything is and is not.

Thinking of the death of stars and black holes – we too die when we can no longer generate sufficient energy and pressure to resist gravity, we fall in on ourselves like stars and the massive star Supernovae explode in death - but do our quarks go on immortal? We are made of star dust. Black holes continue to fascinate researchers and whether they emit radiation; and also how gravity rules - there is no quantum theory of gravity as yet. Death hits a dead end. Though gravitational waves have now been detected. Our galaxy's biggest black hole is Sagittarius A* far far bigger than our sun.

Don't panic.
Here endeth my 'holistic drivel'!
But I hope it's got you fascinated
curious, amused and confused.
Just now I better 'shut up'.

June 2018

With thanks to Brian Cox, Jeff Forshaw for 'The Quantum Universe, where anything which can happen does happen' and 'Higgs' by Jim Baggott.
Etc. Apologies for any inaccuracies. It's the gist.

The Creeping Crab Sentencing to Death
Cancer

Sentenced Now – not in time but always
as we somehow all are – mostly unaware.
Though for most, not knocking loud on your front door -
but then coming into your house – a few found cancer cells;
a black-robed scythed skeleton in your front hall
then the surgeon burnt, slashed and sucked him out -

and blasted him with cytotoxic squirts.
Once cancer even if out, always so, but now not;
yet suddenly or slow, the guillotine hangs ready to drop.
'I had not thought death had undone so many'
-'The Waste Land' TSEliot.
it has flattened them, now numbed, stupefied.
A swatted fly splattered on a wall - discovering who you are -
never ever the same as before -
struck dumb blind deaf and in survival, rage
and waiting for the sun to shine again
from the Hockney brilliant abbey window stained glass.
As the best medicine, laugh in Death's face.
Like Neolithic man had exuberant festivals
to salute Death; and like the Irish wake -
the senses and mind-sensing numbed to celebrate.
Change (that is 'end') means finding a new latitude
for a new direction. We actually don't walk in a straight line
which isn't straight at all but curved in spacetime..
Dying and Death is change. Strange.
Death should be, not a skeleton but obese, the glut of his kills,
forever ravenous.
No room for the British 'stiff upper lip' - 'stiffs' a plenty dead.

Silly/Simple/Stupid/Wise Delight

I saw a little plump ole' lady.
She brought in for auction to 'Flog It'
4 small coins not thinking them much.
She found them under a bed -
her father had died.
They sold for £760 as gold
and warm, her simple surprise delight lit up.

I've discovered I'll nurture
my own 'silly simple stupid' self -
drop brains and thought.
And chuckle and laugh.

Now nothing I know now.
Wise -
laughter – medicine - the best.
Like seeing some ladies bum cheeks waddle like ducks
when they're aiming to be tres chic.
Folks smile at me in Butchery lane
sitting sipping coffee – I guess it's my jaunty cap
cocking a snook at brother death who laughs -
'I'll get you in the end – just you wait'.

Sept. 2018.

Cystoscopy K and C Hospital

Urology suite sharp, dreary gloom -
no wall pictures, Patients mute, staring up -
just lists of things to do and not
for bladder health – no caffeine coffee,
carbonated drinks, smoking, alcohol.
Yes to antioxident fruit and veg.
Called in quickly, undress and wait -
lay down, legs akimbo -
camera tube in via anaesthetic cream.
Told to look at the magnified screen
and there wafting in the tide, a coral polyp with fronds,
ominous delicacy and beauty, thought after I return home;
'where are the fish' I asked -
a beamed response woke the glum surgeon and nurse -
'there', first aliveness pointing to a few swimming specks.
10 minutes it took. The leaden faces returned.
He wrote notes and 'I don't think it's cancer' quietly said.
        Have I heard right?
To return in 6 weeks time for pre G.A assessment
then back for tumour resection cautery, 2 nights on ward,
        maybe more if worse so how to pack a bag and
bladder catheter bag to carry around; 2 weeks later path lab back.
        Shit,

I had hoped it would be done there and then.
Mental turmoil goes on and on and on.

My glass is half empty, drunk with dead drunken doom
reeling. Drinking in 2 litres fluids a day, 9 large mugs full;
so bloated stomach gurgling swishing round
till it gets to my bladder – down - peeing often.
Troubles eased, sharing with friends
    the first true ones I've had.
    Drop, float give up the fight.
How to be comfortable with being in uncomfort! -
    in 'co' – with and 'fort' – strong.

Aug 2018.

GP says of the polyp - 'they're now taking everything out'.
I hope they leave me with something inside, not just an empty cavity!

Death

Kadunk out.
This life stopped.
Cremation arranged
to be consumed
in bright fire
and heaven will sense
my incense haze
to a new dimension
unknown, transformed
or 'brief candle'
'out out' -
just that.

Apr 2019

Destruction of Dinosaurs
The tip of the Iceberg!
Written for Suffering People

Appalled at the asteroid hitting earth
fire bomb blast explosion shooting fragments,
rocks dust to the atmosphere;
thousands of Hiroshima blasts
shrouding the entire whole earth,
going grey, dark, no sun, massive temperature drop.
All life killed except tiny mice -
a few insects and greens survive – small things
repopulating earth, large predators extinct
then millions of years to evolve anew.
Without that extinction of dinosaurs
humans could not appear. I wish we,cursed, had not
The enormity of the event at that moment -
a few seconds later that asteroid would have shot
into the seas from the earth's rotation
and the destruction less.

Where was a God. Sitting on his backside
allowing this satanic force and doing nought
if not ending or preventing it.
The slate was wiped clean at such suffering cost
to start again. Well why mess up in the first place?
He must have known this would happen,
omniscient,when he first created the universe.
I hate him with all my deformed guts
with a vehemence unknown
A good God. Fucking hell.. like hell.
He is Hell as well.
And he it is who should
creep and crawl at our feet
for forgiveness – not us.

Sept 2018

Disorder

If you want an ice-cream scream; Screaming gets a reward!

A bad day of strife
for this garden pub life.
A screaming young lad
held by his distraught dad
is carried out to the street.
The boy turned back, his cries increased
when he saw a choc-ice ice cream
given to his small sister, it seemed
who was being held by his mum
who gave scared glances along
towards her son overcome
probably expecting more scream surges strong!

A wife smiling took care
of her husband, very obese
with a limp who just managed
to sit with a stick in release
through the table-bench seat -
as is the fashion, trousers down somewhat
but no Calvin Klein underpants for his butt
so there's an apparent half bum crack.
She fed, she watered him, she smiled non stop.
It took him 10 minutes
to squeeze out of his bench seat prop.
Her smiles persisted towards the sky and crowd
as she waits for him to succeed, bent bowed.

The screaming boy stopped,
returned to mess with an ice-cream -
his parents glum. Silence all round
except the munched cracking of dripping cones;
an infected bartered peace, unsound.
I couldn't wait to leave the scene
to find elsewhere, my honey-hole spot.

Sept 2019

A Dog and Bare Bones. The Horror

Sometime ago
a man and his faithful dog
went climbing
among the mountains of the Lakes
but the man fell to his mysterious death.
off a narrow iced crag ridge edge
and 3 months later a shepherd heard barking
then found the man's clean skeletal scattered remains;
with his steadfast dog, fat and well fed -
standing guard and scaring ravens away.
The dog had also given birth
to a nearby dead pup -
she had eaten her master's body to both sustain in vain -
that 'maternal instinct supreme.'
The dog and his master,
in devotion, constancy, loyalty - became one in all ways
Was this a savage wrong - severe, extreme?
or a crucifying, excruciating, dreadful racking Right -
utterly proper, honest, correct, exact?

Dumbfounded – I cannot speak
except with the Psalmist 'O God
Thou hast laid on us a heavy burden'
'You have put us to the test'
The horror of it thus -
and at what price paid?

Feb 2021.

I saw this TV documentary on The Lakes recently and this true story was mentioned in passing and passed on quickly. I couldn't do that. You may already know of the story. The dog is called Foxie. 2 poems were written (Walter Scott and Wordsworth if you want poesy and no dead pup told of) and a beautiful Landseer painting of it hangs in the Royal Academy but no dead pup there.

I don't want to get into poesy taking away the deep 'moral' impact. I can't find out what subsequently happened to the dog. There are 15 dictionary sections for the definition of Right!

Some bare facts without sentiment – comparing this with human cannibalism – in law cannibalism is not illegal, but killing for it is illegal. Complex. It has existed through the ages, and in tribes, including as a ritual. Some tribes eat human flesh to literally introject that loved dead relative. In concentration camps, emaciated prisoners have eaten dead corpses.

It is commonly found that dogs eat their isolated dead owner who has died from whatever cause. They stand nearby the corpse, have not been fed and try to waken the owner by pawing, nudging,curling up beside, licking, nipping then biting him awake and after 2 weeks eventually, starving, they have to eat him as an instinct to survive.

Some mother dogs of puppy litters, neglect, then kill weakling ones to allow the others to survive. Incidences known of father's sacrificing their lives for their children and likewise to save their comrades in wars

Dog on dog cannibalism rarely occurs in the wild and in poor townships.

Notes on **Charles Gough**. (see poem 'A Dog and Bare Bones.' The Horror) – the 'man' in the poem was not really a man yet at age 21, fell off a deep precipice to his death. An aspiring artist, he became immortalised as a martyr and icon of the Romantic period. Gold watch and silver pencil and Claude glasses (artists painting implement) and 2 fishing rods found at the site of death with his hat split in 2 – what were the fishing rods doing at the top of a mountain! A martyr and icon rubbish – he was said to be an impetuous impulsive youth who knew little of climbing. Admittedly his guide failed to accompany him due to other duties. Which owner would take his pregnant dog perilously climbing?

I am angry at this. His temperament meant he was bound to get into trouble climbing and you could say he got his just deserts of death while the dog got full meals and dessert!

But he became a martyr and icon of the Romantic movement – God knows why while the dog became anonymous – no one knows what happened to her after she was found yet there are 2 poems and a painting of her. I feel she is the 'icon'.

Perhaps this is the end of the story.

Homeless persons street squat
rug wrapped, bowl far out
with scribbled notes
'I'm hungry, God Bless'.
They must see many shoes pass.
There's no people about. Not now.
Crunched by the virus in large chunks.

Gravity and Time. A Conundrum

In Physics thing last longer if low down
where time passes the slowest.
Higher up, time speeds up

Little do we know
that we seek a place
where time runs slow
and gravity is low
to precipitate that;
where everything falls down not up.
And where we live longer than on high up.
But we have an inborn fear
of dying - yet dead we fall low
down to earth
and can't go lower more
except under 6 foot.
Yet strangely up to 'heaven' we long to go
tired of down below
and time running slow -
to perhaps where there's no space or time's inflow ?

If you aim high, you can crash;
Better to find what's within – low.

April 2020

Smiles or Yuks? Finding your Way

A grape to us is yum – to a dung beetle yuk. Each to his own.
A little critter who messes in dung – a bulldozer in reverse,
a top recycler above all – 'scarabeus sacer'
sacred - is the Egyptian Khepri, god
of the rising sun with a scarab face;
a dung beetle, humble, of transformation, rebirth.
Who travels from east to west like the sun in a straight line
(well it's the earth that revolves nowadays round the sun)
and emerges fully formed from a mess of dung.

At his antics, I am tickled and amazed – he sniffs out
then urgently forms a fresh dung ball carefully shaped
with his powerful front legs, paddle-shaped
and hurriedly runs off in a straight line at speed, up-side-down
away from his mates who try to steel his treasure;
he does Kung Fu and throws them off in measure
then heads off, face to ground, and back slender haired legs up
controlling the ball for miles which can be 10 times his weight
where he digs a hole and buries it, pear-shaped in a safe spot
to come back to snack or for his mate to lay eggs
in the 'brood ball' with food 'sausages' ready to hand
and new beetles then emerge fully formed withall.
Larger birds can pick them off – like cockles to us.

How does he find his way with such dogged drive?,
not put off by obstacles which he knows how to get around
and not put off by falling down a high sand dune,
tightly holding on to his tumbling prize. He can even persist
in getting back up or if not then he stops, thinks
and climbs on top of his ball and proudly does a little circular dance
(the ancient Egyptians said it was for pleasure, joy);
to reorientate himself as he uses the top half of
his upside down little eyes to find the sun,
or if a nocturnal one – the moon, and if no moon as compass
then the Milky way the only animal to navigate. If no light, then
he's lost
        and maybe sleeps till a next time and that can be long.

He can fly, helicopter-like, and has tough wing-cloaks for all
the falls.

There are 3 main kinds of dung beetle -
'tunnellers' in, 'dwellers' on, 'rollers' of - dung.
Amazing variety of colours – metallic blacks, opalescent blues,
aquamarine greens, iridescent purples all mixed in.
And now we know they are vital in land enrichment,
removing sources for pests and flies and removing
run-off of toxic substances to water sources.
The New Zealand and Australian governments
have imported millions of them as they had none that worked.
They save North America, yearly, billions of pounds
All from a little critter who loves dung.
So my many smiles of delight – not yuk.
Tumblebug, I love you with your mucky face.

July 2020

Draft Dying and Death

Mind numbing, it deadens my thought
contaminating - it makes me die.

I am stunned to write
yet somehow I must – gutgrabbed.
A wise friend after dementia years -
trouble to his son and family,
then a care home, came to his end at 94 -
or at the beginning of something unknown else.

He was decreed 'comfortable at the end of life'.
And was not responsive but he 'tried' to talk.

They brought him a little tree for his birthday
which they felt he really liked.

It was scary to watch him gasp
but they felt he was waiting for them to leave
before dying which they did and were relieved.

This was just pre-pandemic
so he died in time – well.

Life it seems is decreed physical only and nothing else.
But it's clear that the mind heart soul whatever, go on.

It's like a baby is totally different to an adolescent
or to an adult or an old man
but they are one and the same person
within their physical state.

Person is my favourite word.
And who knows his person
may well be living on to another state.

We Just don't know
as dying and death are all over the place.

What is this 'after-life'?
Quantum physics gives a hint
whether you call it God or not....

2020

Electrons in Touch Sight Smell and Hearing

Yes – our little quantum particle friends, like electrons.

I can be stunned dead by an Amazon electric eel's
600 Volt shock
and an Egyptian thunderer catfish likewise stuns prey
and likewise a torpedo ray
who is so muscle bound with electric producing muscle stack blocks
he cannot undulate his wings so tail-only flaps.

Electron from Greek for amber – you rub hair with it and it sparks.

Plants move. Yes…
A Venus flytrap closes fast on an insect trapped
not by muscles but by electric charges changing the pressure in the sap.
Brambles grow along fast, flowers open and shut.

Bees hover over flowers -
they have a +ve charge, and flowers -ve, so bee is drawn to collect nectar and pollen,
that cancels the charge so he buzzes off. Pollen is actually a -ve charge and is actually drawn out to the bee.
Another bee pops around but there is no charge now – come back another time for a sup – so he flies off, ignoring the flower, quantum message received.

Flower perfume is from 400 chemical compounds and bees can scent those 1 mile off. Chemistry is physics at heart

Leaves
can be chomped by caterpillars and grubs so they give off warning chemical alarms to other leaves who develop nasty tasting chemicals to other grubs who yuk. Also a chemical that wasps recognise to come and eat the grubs. True story.
Trees talk-scent to each other.

And roots can talk and hear. Sensitive equipment picks up crackling sounds underground. It's not known for why.
Creeping, crawling, crackling, chemicaling, communicating,
- the forest is so alive.

Aug 2020.

Final Marathon Run. Cancer
Appointment Urology Nurse for result again after an hours wait. Some had been waiting 2 or more hours. I came in, heard this and started a

rebellion. All of us asking who what where when. Good.
A photo in my folder of the cancer lumpI tell her I dread this. She is good. Tells me Grade 1 TA uroepithelial cancer = transitional cell carcinoma – the lerast least malignant of them all. Histology checked the removal at all levels – the tumour the epithelium the muscle underneath. Checked by 2 Consultant Histologists. Cofined to the tumour – a few cancer cells. The cancer can flare up elsewhere in bladder so 3 monthly cystoscopy check ups that this was a knock out blow or if toxins stimulate more.
Exhausted immobilised shattered sleep forever. That bastard came into my house.

Think

It was caught very early. Other diseased can be worse – heart attacks blindness deafness arthritis lameness etc. etc. can be debilitating worse. Why have people put cancer on a pedestal as the most feared? Rubbish

I don't want to talk of this anymore but 3 people want me to phone them about it.
The nurse said 'just put it out of your mind now' and 'this is not going to kill you. You'll die of something else'.
I phone 2 of them – busy. The 3rd avoids feelings. Sod the lot.

Just funny silly stupid people now are for me the best. Just kick disease in the face with hob-nailed boots.

4th Oct 2018

Flash Camera Shots

A little long low black Dachshund stopped and wagged
only the <u>tip</u> of his tail, mind - no more. Rationed -
like cheetahs, leopards, tigers long tails do too, when relaxed.

A long bulbous beagle dog I swear
wagged his whole tail without a care
in constant circles, <u>clockwise</u> complete, fixed fast.
There has to be a large range array classed

of muscles controlling dog tails amassed
as they can change their wags fast.

A pavement pigeon picks at crumbs,
stops and shakes his tail feathers
from side to side, - fanned out ones.
Then he struts and puffs up his chest and woos
a disinterested lady bird with coo coo coos.
I sit on the bench and likewise louder do -
he stops deflates, puzzles where and who-who-who.

Words! How much quicker
a video picture!

Jan 2018.

'Flu Silence. To Clear the Air

Left ear dead – large old T tube drum hole, R ear reduced
then flu – ear ok – later tele goes dumb, mouths words
increasingly unheard. Bad – urgent GP wax block,
drops, clean out. Not supposed to but nobody else. Still deaf.
Antibiotics 8 tabs. Sudden total sound cut off
then inverse loss – no low tones at all only squeaky highs.
Stop antibiotics. Rage. Gallons water drunk to wash out.
Next day sudden clear. 2 more episodes so it's not meds.
Urgent GP, audiologist – refer urgent care.
Hospital can't see me so to a consultant, private.
Effect – world's sudden change, Isolate.
Sounds are eerie squeaks, no low tones at all
(usually low tones ok, high tone loss).
So totally cut off from folks
Drum now good, ear clean. Do nought, wait. Can hear.
Later repeat audiogram and new tympanogram – recovered from 'flu.
Stressed out. Max. Wait.

Dammed Up

Stress of deaf. Guts then seize up, constrict for 7 days.
Left side pain – long standing not the usual
frontal yearly cramp and I didn't click
but GP had given me a sudden clue – ahh it's the old IBS.
Urgent GP again – soluble fibre antispasmodics lactulose.
Utter relief – it works but L. pain persists
whole body and me released. Whew.
What goes in – some must come out.
We have to create, put out -
so much is that in life -
art, poetry, thought, craft
so even more mundane – the bowel -
a baby's first gift.
A marvellous poo 'purse'
of St. Julian of Norwich.
Or a bird taking away faecal pellets
of her hatchlings from the nest.
Never in my life have I needed
so much urgent GP help.

May 2018

Two Forgotten Heroes

An African nurse – night duty
in a care home for the elderly -
strong big shoulders, blue gear
left on a night watch to care
for a Covid dying man,
no help or advice at hand.
The man in great distress gasps for breath,
the nurse is doing his best, forced to search the web
for help. No back-up, crack teams, consultants anywhere.
Tears in his eyes and down his left cheek.
I was struck to the core by his compassion and quiet distress.

My front doorbell rang at 8pm.
There was a box full of bags on my doorstep.
Bending down over them, clutching a paper sheet
was a tall man in grey shorts and shirt -
Tesco it was and he stood up with the sheet,
fine features and stature, intelligent face -
he seemed out of place and more rounds to go till midnight.
It struck me he'd lost his job - this viral plague
and had to find any job he could get.
I winced at so many without work
and families to tend.
God faithfull ! – I doubt. They're left in the lurch,
dying and distressed.

Aug 2020

Fur and Things

Parked by the river, I watched passers by
taking themselves and their dogs of all kinds for walks.
And there before me 3 very large 'beauooful' ones
side by side in a threesome chariot-walk pulling their owner along
on short black leads and black harness straps.
I think they are Russian Samoyed chaps
And I mean large long and very wide, 3 foot long, 2 foot wide?
pure white fluff balls with legs, all very thick fur, black eyes,
small faces, black lips, perked ears.
They had to be reined in, their owner leaning back, to cross the road
after just squeezing through the pedestrian gate.
I would have gone amongst them, knelt down, cuddled them all,
sinking myself in their lovely thick fur.
Like I wanted to with fat woolly sheep -
those with small side pointing round ears, (not the large top vertical
pointy ones) -
of Herdwicks, Romney Marsh and Ryeland ones.
I was once told that golf balls shot on Scottish greens
get lost in the fur of wandering grazing sheep unforeseen.

Pigeons and Town Steps to the Citi Terrace Caf

There are 22 steps up to this caf eats retreat.
I was about to descend them to get to the street
and there before me were 2 pigeons plump
plopping sedately down all the steps more or less in time set
one each side of the central hand rail; yet
the plops such fun to see.
No flying down for them free,
their legs too short to step down one by one.
And there was an odd coo or two as they went along

Dec 2018

Gliding 2

Today I flew in the heavens -
blue skies and cotton-wool clouds -
flat bottomed meaning thermals abound.
Hauled up by a sturdy wobbling
engine propelled aertow plane,
racketing around,
wind turmoil engine roar at front.
Sudden silence, release, tow cord cut -
spiralling tight now on her side
and we don't fall out.

There's Essex, The North Sea,
Thanet, Thames Estuary,
Ashford, Canterbury.
O yes – and a red kite nearbyi.

Oh – so glorious, forever so free.
No – down steep sharp to earth
landing fast with many rabbit hole bumps.
No more words
then I savour deep and quiet stunned.

Perhaps we're born to fly
though it's not in our bones -
not descended from birds
though from a common stock root.

July 2018.

Graduation Noise

C and C beautiful and handsome, tall long legged
so well groomed and dressed
and so excited and in a hurry
to get to King's school to log in on time -
Little ole me left behind
walking as fast as I could.
I gift him his mortar board.
The tassel to keep off the flies in days of old.

Zapped, sledge hammered,
cathedral cacophony
trumpet fanfare blasts,
long unheard speeches -
us clapping for over an hour
as each of 300 graduates
come up for a green/gold gowned
capped chancellor handshake.
I remain polite and listen
to catch as much as I can
yet the cacophany blasts my ear/s.

Weave our way out of the black robed mass
to Wagamama meaning naughty child
for Japanese food. Heated talking again loud
in this reverberating kitchen pot clanging caf
and we try to talk but I hear bad
and am a loud speaker, badly heard -
a simple fool in no glad rags
but they goodly said 'come as you are'.

It's a funny feeling when you tell a snippet of yourself
and it's not taken in. I forgive – it is their day
But this, the main thing, is a big moment for both.
And both very pleased I came. Invited so honoured - so

So many impressions achieving basic degree success.
So much noise, so much.
I still reel blasted out of my deaf depth.
I feel so much out of life
but is all this pomp and ceremony a bauble
and really part of real life?
I feel so small -
my life and being of little worth.
        Yet is it.
I have many degrees diplomas membership,
helped many many people,
big academic success -
what's not to like?
Now retired on the junk heap. Scrap.

July 2018

A Drab Grub
An inelegant portrait of metamorphosis

I am I
metamorphing
to a butterfly;
a catkin caterpillar once,
(French from shaggy-cat,)
a worm larva
nibbling leaves in arcs
but now driven by desire
to fly in colours sky high
anew to see, to see and scent
and touch and feel the present
with two aerial wires intent -
antennae bent.
Thought drops stops

as I need to chrysalis crack
hanging thread-strong back
while I change my clothes and me -
shiver sublime fast
sudden - at last flitting free up.
So my one I is three forms -
3 in 1. I'm a trinity. Yes!

May 2019

A Jumble of Mumbles
Haiku.revisited

Chubby baby glugs.
She's held safe and soft and close.
Warm breast, loving eyes.

I saw a sick man
in winter sleet, creep slung low.
His sad slow eyes – teared.

Canterbury bells
Cathedral peel ringing clear.
Old Harry deep low.

Silence impacts in -
imprisons in block struck force
then a sung chord sings.

Crockery pots sit
well used, proud, ancient, serene.
I have feet of clay.

My red breast robin
flits fast to my feeding spot.
His kind eye looks deep.

Tiny ladybird
being bounced 'oooh' on a leaf
by falling rain drops.

Gales rip my roof ridge.
Phalanx winds hurl gusts at me.
I reel and stutter.

A moth flutters stuck -
gutted in candle light wax.
Life ends in death – dunked.

Oh – pot bellied pig,
your tummy touches the ground.
You make me chuckle.

Crisp green grape strung taut.
I bite once and crack sweet juice
and firm flesh bursts forth.

A blank paper page
is better than useless words.
I like clean white snow.

Infinitesimal
stem cell; such healing queries -
pluripotential.

A little boy chucked
a hunk of bread at a duck
who turned full turtle.

Unstrict Haiku

The morning square is empty
and a shop sign squeeks -
wind hanging.

The street lamp tingles with light
the leaves silver. And the trunk in front
tries to hide the straight iron post.

A long coat lady, old, twinkles her little legs,
her pudding hat pulled down
firm above her nose in the street.

'Have a Nice Day' -

as they say in the U.S. of A
and now too here.
I parked my scooter -
the proper 2 wheel one
and not to be mistaken,
undertaken by the disability
buggies 4 little wheels -
at the motor bike rank in the square.
And there to one side was a dying pigeon
faced flat out to the brick wall
at a large shop refuse bin,
flattened, flopped down
panting like hell, a dying sign,
not moving at my approach.
There was nothing I could do
but feel concern and alarm.
Along comes another pigeon -
I thought in compassion!
to be with it – but no;
it forcibly mounted it for a fuck
taken as a submissive female
so I shooed it off.
I've never seen a dying pigeon before -
there must be thousands daily in the UK
though we don't see them die
as they go to a hidden spot so to do.
Pigeons can't gauge others it seems.
They can't even put a foot on a crust

to hold it still while pecking the other end
and 2 can't even share a crust.
I was then bumped into by a gang of youths
unseeing of others then I ordered a coffee,
sat down and was joined straight off
by an old nattering hag whom I ignored -
wanting peace. Coffee was brought
with 'have a nice day'.
I went back to my scooter, and surprised
found the dying pigeon had gone -
nowhere to be found under bins or cars.
It was not old. It was not injured;
was it taken by a tramp to cook for food?
Was it diseased? Had it flown
hundreds of miles exhausted
and panting had recovered?
Or was it panting for a male to mount?
Pigeon shit is dangerous -
histoplasmosis
that spreads to people
so they are often culled. Good.

Apr.2019

Have you Noticed. Micro-'observation'

I hadn't seen in all my decades of living -
a 3 ice-cube glass of non fizzy orange juice
made from 100% juice concentrate
after half way through my sucking straw, not bothered before.
I suddenly noticed tiny tiny bubbles fizzing sizzling
at the outside meniscus of the fluid level in the glass -
to begin with, sometimes a complete bubble rim right around to start
then confined only to where the cubes touched the glass sides.
Starting bigger bubbles only seen from inside the glass, not outside
and they disappear first before the littles seen only from the outside
Bubbles to me are when fluids boil or in fizzy carbonated drinks
where carbon dioxide is released when the bottle is uncapped
or when juices ferment from bacteria and yeast, a slower process.

Ice cubes made fast trap unseen air – the larger bubbles released on melting
and the rough surface of ice-cubes is a nucleation bubble source
I became excited and fascinated – the street and I lit up;
who was making the juice 'boil' against all of my common prejudice.

My friends had come to say hello here and now – before my eyes
quantum (that packet-magic) word, quantum particles-fields,
fields of 'grains' – growth. Real, not only in books.

I must experiment as to what was making the juice boil/fizz.
Check the juice ingredients – not carbonated,
pure juice, no preservatives, from the fridge, screw-capped -
expiry. Jan 2020 – it hadn't fermented, gone off.
Wait till the ice had completely gone – no bubbles now.
The cubes melted and bubbles fewer and smaller and still only there
where the cubes touch the glass side but only a certain cube/ glass interface
or between cubes sometimes. Then bubbles went except for an idiosyncratic few -
sometimes no bubbles at all to start or end.
Try ice in water alone, there's no bubbles; try it in other non carbon juices;
it's there in apple juice; it's not there where preservatives have been added.
It's there in fresh fridge orange juice
I could detect no scratch faults in the glass where bubbles can form.
Even next day I watched with a magnifying glass
as the bubbles were so small – ? small coming from big.
I think perhaps the bubbles are from the juice and its sugars
allowed to ferment now – opened in air but surely not as fast as this, so not -
and the warming! but only of cold glass/ice bubble interface!
and with mocro-organisms around, micro-bugs – that takes long.
But why and why then only seen outside the glass
then disappear and stop when the ice warms and melts?

Go find a friendly bubbly deep quantum physicist. Usual folks won't know.

I spent ages looking at that glass, inside and out and all round.
Yippee – I felt happy and round.
Bubbles – a lovely word.
The word looks like what it is and sounds.

Oct 2018

Attitudes to Health, Illness
2 icicle cubules please in my glass

Death knocking on my front door.
Riddled with fear. Possible cancer
awaiting cystoscopy, resection and path.
Yet I have no symptoms, don't feel ill.
Now I know how those WWI men felt
going over the trench top -
hitting that blasted bloody mud in droves
wounded or dead.
Fear. Drop. Nod head in Yes, not shake in No.

So – just let be.
No need to understand or why.
Not judging self or others -
stepping back, being aware.
Patience. Trust. Trust the staff.
A wood staff helps you walk in rough climbs;
Staff in hospital places there to assist.
Not striving, not fixing.
Accepting.
Letting go. Breathe slow.
Chattering canopy tree-top brain cell apes
It's ok to feel fear
but now, take a break.

Death – it's not my life to give up.
I didn't make me nor did they
then who did?
Knowledge is not power – it's something else
and the less you know the less you worry.

Every line crinkle crease tells a story.
Recall some good.
And give, not in duty forced but in 'love'.

Now I feel as if I'm in courage – brave!
A very hard place.

30th Aug. 2018

Hearing Sound Yes Observing No. Macro-'observation'
yet observing can be hearing too Macro 'observation' Ob – towards,
servare – look at

'Observing' hints at being attached to objective, detached.
'ob' – in the way of 'jacere' to throw in the way - of the mind
All in the quantum Universe and with people is relationship
and everywhere where you 'observe' you change
what is 'observed' in relationship; contact
in subjective mutual, co – together, tact - touch

'In the beginning was the Word and the Word was with God and the word was God'
an oft quoted text and 'word' – quite catchy tricky, oblique
but rubbish to S. John. In the beginning was feeling, idea, thought, sound
(and where was a god? - as usual wordless mute!).
Sound, also the particles of words
Listen to the sounds of letters – formed by the lips, tongue, glottis, breath.
Aay bee cee dee, ee ff gee,
aitch I jay kay
ll-mm-nn-oh-pee
qu rr ss tee,
Uu vee wuu, (double u)
xx ywi zzz.
Have you noticed, in 9 out of 26 letters the sound ends in ee -
except in the US of A, instead of zed they have zee -
the only english speaking country to do so, though why?

Sound first then words.
Like a baby's sounds before his words form
and the first man's gutterals around the fire, tunes songs,
yellings on facing a lion. Then scribbles in sand,
red ochre scenes on cave walls.
Gutterals and uh uh. Yes, the first solos -
before the symphonies of still inadequate words.
Check NASA - even the centre of the sun sings, vibrates - not talks.
For now, I hear, here rest my case.

So in the beginning was Sound.
Vibrations, that is sounds, are all in the Universe.
There is nothing – no thing except in relationship.
'Thing', 'objects' don't exist except as relating, as subjects
in the Universe, the earth in it -
and it is 'finite yet with no border' -
an electron doesn't exist except when relating to other fields -
there is no beginning and no end as spacetime is curved.
An ant walking round the equator of an orange
starts at a point – the 'beginning'
and 'ends' up at the start – the 'end'
and goes on and on looking for the 'end'
which never comes till it changes course.
Yet vibrations-sound-music is at root maths.
So now in the 'beginning' was immersed-in-Maths.
Again I rest my case!

Sept. 2018

Heat Wave Drought

Nettles have got the best front row seats
by the riverside stage show
but the show of its flow
has come to a green gunk halt.
No rain water feature plays
in the drama sludge schedule now
so they bide their time
and disappointed droop.

'Let there be Light'

Have discovered I have neglected light
in my quantum noteicle research -
photons who at the beginning used to zig-zag
but later travelled and travel in straight lines
so the Universe then became transparent -
the shortest distance between 2 points
at 186,000 miles per second
and faster nothing can go.
Due to pressure waves inside
'the sun rings like a bell' vibrates
in a low tone too hard for human ears, like elephant speke
and so did the early observable Universe.
Photons it is, are massless, are light
and they are an electromagnetic force,
one of the 4 forces, the others -
gravitation and forces strong and weak.
An electron changes orbit
and emits a photon starlight flash
which is a basic quantum energy packet;
and is not made of anything else, it's pure.
It is its own anti-particle too, ignoring the Higgs Field
which to the massless gives mass
and it can be both a particle and a wave.
How's about that -
but we too are our self and anti-self.
In the deep deep sea
bioluminescence is the norm
'and let there be light' -
to deceive, talk, alert.
Darkness is the absence of light
and nothing so far can travel faster than light
in the observable Universe
though why not? 'cos it would need energy, infinite.

July 2018

'The crazy rules of quantum physics'. Tiny electrons swarm around the atom's nucleus and atoms communicate with each other via their dancing electrons. Randomness is a fundamental feature of the Universe.

I am an Old Woman Now – not When I am one
'kiss my pixels'at the High Street Xmas market
Helter Skelter

A red and white pepper pot core 60 foot high

wound by a helical spiral down-fast slide;
a Helter-Skelter harem-scarum -
hesitation, disorder, haste, confusion
round and round, whoosh zoom,
and silent, utter free delight
sat on a small coir doormat.
O yes, I'm young again though eighty three years
and bum-land fast so the crowd shout 'wows'.
I put my hand out to be hoisted up in style
and the attendant does with a very big smile.
I felt like skipping away but too old for that
though I go to a gym to work at and remedy that -
my return home wobbly, achey reviving, plonk sofa-sat.
Now I can say 'Yes' to all life in fact;
a mat-splat, begat a wildcat.
Wooeee.

Skelter ME skelte=haste
Jan 2020

humans of the earth hum in both senses, humus rich earth, hummus chick-peas Arabic earth.

Here and There. West and East – under the influence of deafness

How do you raise your one eyebrow ?– looks learnéd, noble.
A child's ash cry amongst bombed concrete rubble
then TV's shallow dross. Is that all you can do - untroubled?

Later may be too late.
Here in the UK couples migrate to country route estates -
straight for costly homes, nit-picking, ticking boxes,
room numbers, shiney plumbing chrome, perfection of kitchens,
room sizes,
while millions are without a home. Shoeless alone, a child lugging a
back-can
blanket-strapped, walking miles for foul water panned, more than
barefoot. A man with bomb blasted legs and wooden stumps
grabs the rails learning to walk. No start no finish – over cramped
humps -
starting the impossible unknowable; stay naked brave clenched.
Murder torn Middle East toxic death, the fly swarm swelling stench.
We all fight as we think we are right, the other wrong entrenched.
The Cathedral memorial garden where the dead sing
silence and still the wind; wilt-sprinkled roses strewn, sad songs
- fling
while males have sperm millions to spread rife and rape
but women have just one egg so carefully choose a mate
and if you fear women – to abuse, you pick on a child;
rutting stags squirting their zillion seeds inbuilt, wild
in the kingdoms of spermed animal and pollen plant compiled.
I utter out word seeds while machine-gun bullets rapid stutter.
The homeless forgotten world of world's children, gutter
street sleeping, big dark pleading appealing eyes
and you blink an eyelid, that's all, unwise sidewise.
Here - a posse of prams, street phalanx abreast defies -
barge passers by; procreate at all cost earth lost, overcrowded.
And soaring age, violence propels insurance funeral costs shrouded;
litigant lawyers sprout. There - starving people, the boned ribs of
kids cry
then, with their sunken eyes breathe their last beyond a cry
while obese people here waddle wobbling along, fuelled,
gulping battered beef burgers obscene pulled -
but devoid of deep content - and they also deep starved.
Now I feel my world has broken, secure supports moved,
kicked out from under leaving frail fear flailing in a flood -
now quite deaf full blast - this poison, and life also, of
unending change.
There in the Middle East a donkey whipped lame

carrying massed loads of rubble, brick, 4 times his weight
collapses in the worn track – silent pleading, maimed.
The face of suffering - dark compliant eyes bereft,
forced patience, broken-in obedience, no fight left -
this the hurting. All. Downfall to Hope and back again bound,
but the story of life itself is at root, the story of temperature, sound.
Time is an illusion; there is no past present future only
Einstein's Spacetime.
Life is just a temporary home for the immortal universe elements -
this the sun's hydrogen to helium then to a lessor extent
other elements,
elemental fundamental particle probabilities. No need for the gods
        as quarks quack the scent of the transcendent.
But oh that donkey – I cringe under its load. The universal hero
- awed
        and that child it's Christ's!

Mar.2018

<u>'Home is so Sad'</u>
by Philip Larkin

'Home is so sad. It stays as it was left,
Shaped to the comfort of the last to go
As if to win them back. Instead, bereft
Of anyone to please, it withers so,
Having no heart to put aside the theft

And turn again to what it started as,
A joyous shot at how things ought to be,
Long fallen wide. You can see how it was;
Look at the pictures and the cutlery.
The music in the piano stool. That vase.'

Home is so Glad

(with thanks to Phillip Larkin for 'Home is so Sad')

Home is so glad. It waits as it is now,
Forged to the troubles of all who are low
As if to let them know. Entire in vow
To those there who disturb, it prospers-so,
Having every heart to remember how

And to remain as that it always was,
A safe accepting hearth of how things are,
True to the mark. You still see why it is:
Look at the faces - and the reservoir
Of patience; understanding love. Those eyes.
They're yours. They're ours.

Canterbury

An Outburst. Humans and Animals
the end of the Planet?

Animals kill, eat, survive, defend their territory,
make herds, procreate excessively; ant swarms on earth's face'
Humans kill meat, kill their kind in wars, murder,
try to get dominance for territory, form races, religions, tribes, -
procreate excessively – so humans, stop;
doing exactly the same as animals but more.
So now there's global warming from fossil fuels
and methane gas from farting cattle and herds;
the seasons are being shuffled, temperatures, climates altered.
There are more tsunamis (a relatively recent word),
more heat waves, fires, volcanic eruptions, earthquakes, floods,
As there are no natural predators on humans they go on procreating
ad infinitum so things will get worse.
Perhaps natural forces will control in the end?
Nature can be terrible as a virus is backfiring, killing
old folks and young en masse.
God works in mysterious ways his destructions to perform.

The old testament knew that.
Why on earth did he create this way.
So although we think we are cultured, love arts, music, books etc.
at depth we are animal and worse.
Destruction and procreation are universal
and nothing to do with a god
though he must have pressed the first button
to fart it all off.

What drives evolution but the need for food
so mutate and change our life style.
How does DNA mutate driven by need?
Just random DNA change by chance -
a lot fails as useless; one might not.
Stop climate pollution, stop carbon emission,
stop increasing population.
Stop irresponsible fucking. Stop.
It appears it's 'so good to die for'!
'The wheels that squeak get the oil'.
Saves all the pfaff, din'it.

Now all this has, for the while, stopped.
A non-living virus DNA mutates
to slaughter the world -
Covid-19 its officially called.

2020. The start of the Plague.

I am a Particle!
Well I am in the Universe scale of things!

Walking between rooms
for this or that or the other -
it comes to me that I am a quark,
a very large one, the size of a Googol perhaps.
That name was coined by a 9 year old -
a mathematician's son.

One Googol is 10 to the power of 100
or 1 followed by 100 zeros – crunching the numbers -
1- 000000000000000000000000000000
00000000000000000000000000000000
0000000000000000000000000000
0000000000 – now I'm out of breath -
not the giggle of Google for internet search.
But quarks are mischievous cheeky
and like to go round in company of 2's or 3's
and like being in many places all at once (superposition)
or none all at once; or togetherness-in-separation -
that is if you separate a pair and nudge one
the other will simultaneously jump
even if at either ends of the universe!
All making up life itself - as we all are;
cider brandy scent for the angels
who definitely are quarks!
God has a sense of humour
as well as tears perhaps!

Apr.2018

It is as It is
Can it Get Any Worse?

I don't want to write this -
it's boring and gnawing.

Gutters flooding,
kitchen roof leaking,
door leaking rain,
TV pixelating,
PC mouse dying,
my place at the Red Cross stumbling
managers changing;
calls can't get through, incoming;
scooter faltering
new one questioning faulting.

I dilly dallying undeciding -
old one loyal, me guilting.
Whole roof felt faulting.
2 gym sessions missing
as cough/cold flu vac effect taking;
grass overgrowing needing cutting.
Too many appointments making
for fixing.
Me shaking.
There it's done.
So what – it doesn't help -
just let go and wait. Dumb. Numb -
wait wait wait pondering mulling.
Roofers round massive cost -
2 back roofs rotten wood and ancient felt
due to collapse under snow;
3 vans in drive and 5 workers,
mess everywhere. Will take a week of chaos.
4th van then 5th Openreach phone engineers
spend 4 hours with this and that fiddling;
Phones fixed but no internet connecting.
They're still fiddling.
'Bite the bullet' said the roofer
he wants to stop the done-before bodgings.
A medic said 'if you can't fix it, learn to live with it.
A older man said he was preparing for his mortality.
I say 'bite the bullet' and live now.
I can do nothing but clear up some mess
and try to get in and out of my blocked house.

Yes it can get worse – now Pandemic Covid-19 virus strikes
so the world is in Lockdown and comes to a halt.

Nov 2019.

Legs and Things

There's a lot of people in the streets today

a forest of shapes, sizes, legs – an array,
rushing round shopping for Xmas goods -
a forest, like trees - short tall round - in the woods
or aged with wrinkled skin bark;
but these trees move on legs in this street park.

Marvellous legs, man or lady, in skinny jeans,
legs creeping along knock-knees bent, running legs,
good legs walk-spoiled as they land bent-kneed,
legs with splayed feet quite common, or pigeon toed,
bandy legs, very fat legs but firm
and carrying lots of weight;
some limp with a sore hip, knee or foot -
some with one leg shorter but managing well
and of course tiny toddler legs so stumbly sweet.
Then the rare ones well built, macho in cold shorts,
sandals, even in East winds, short sleeve shirts.
Some trunks are wrapped up so bulky-warm
from top down to ankles then surprise forms, transforms -
the feet have no socks – just sandals, a cold sharp alarm?

And of course secondary legs – zimmer ones, trolleys, frames,
sticks, some tapping, some white ending in a roller ball
for blind folks. Is this a universal kind for all blind ones overall?

Trousers so varied but the commonest in teens and ladies
are the skinny tight ones with fit slits and for air though why in
the cold?
There are country corduroys, flannel, flared bottoms, padded ones,
three quarter length ones, Turkish, ethnic bloomy ones
with numerous folds and crotches near the ground, no slits
and rare very high fashion ones all glimmer and glitz.
Trouser types in M&S labelled 'slim, high or medium rise,
superskinny, jeggings, slim bootleg, leggings, straight' size -
all new and no slits seen yet – buyers it seems do home scissor cuts.
Then there's this older tub man regularly passing for his pub pint,
with short little steps. He takes in a breath – he's not short of it
then breathes out and blows out his cheeks into ruddy balls
regular as clock work then out comes his tongue tip to wet his lips

then his dentures move and settle anew often and again in grips.

But best of all are plump legs in skinny jeans
with knock knees and marked splayed feet.
I'm serious and not taking the mick.

Dec 2018

Legs

A bunch of bronzed, loose-limbed lasses
flow past in bum tight short shorts, frayed ends
splitting buttock cracks – ouch, sore.
Some, you even see the bottoms of the bottom
where they peek cheeky from under the shorts
where they join the thighs.
How free and easy is youth,
few burdens of cares except such tight shorts.
I used to be like that -
that forest of legs -
Olympian superb
now wasted and weak,
walking with care.

Tumbling Dandelion Seed

A fluffy silk thread ball parachute
with a tiny full-stop size middle
rolled gently and lightly
down the gutter
with the faint breeze.
Suddenly it took off in the air -
whisked above the shops off,
off anywhere.
Hardly visible so delicate and light
except to its friend the breeze
who knew where it was everywhere.

Maybe only 30 soft spikes -
the less and lighter the better.
Such a marvel un-noticed.
I hope it finds a home
to settle and sprout anew.

No it can't,
it has dropped its stalk and seed -
just the parachute buff ball left
        to disintegrate.

July 2018.

Letter in the Post. Sudden News

Of a copy of a letter to GP from the cystoscopy Dr.
who'd said to me quietly of my bladder
'I don't think this is cancer'.
Now this letter says
'...the 7 mm lesion looks like a possible TCC...'
and writes he explained to me about the finding.
        He didn't.
What is TCC or don't send me a letter copy.
Googled TCC – it's transitional cell carcinoma.
What the fuck hell is going on -
a reversal of what I was told.
Is this surgeons flexing their
omnipotent power over patients -
gods of life or death
or are they preparing me for the worst in case it is
when it isn't and scared so they can't do it face to face.
        O.K God kill me fast
but not with a long lingering death.
        Bastard.
    Accept it.
  You are near dead.
Under major threat, knocked about, splattered to bits;
TCC transitional cell carcinoma not TLC tender loving care.

Courage – going over the trench top shell splintered.
Bite the bullet. Dead.
Hold onto the word 'possible' not probable;
perhaps this is all to prepare me for the worst
in case it is. Yet it maybe not.
It's how to tell people, share, would stun them,
sharing shit not anything good
Yet maybe it wouldn't.

Anaesthetics department have been phoning all day
then get me. Date for op Sept 7th- earlier than I knew.
Nice lady phoned Ruth taking me to hospital.
I have to have O.P pre-anaesthetic assessment soon -
will phone tomorrow. Phone Ruth. She's not stunned
but understanding – a relief.
Eventually told they would give me an appointment for next week.
Community association meeting
and the consultant urologist I had seen professionally
said he would give a friend and me a lift to it.
Only social contact and that meant we avoided each other.
I was brimming over with questions but couldn't ask.
Hardly social contact at all.
But met a 96 year old who drives and we got on.
I learnt from him a lot – making good out of bad.
And I backed up his suggestions for improvement
for better member support. Again in turmoil. Shit.

21st Aug 2018

Life seemed new for a few moments
after being in Hell
and still there
Scythed Death still Knocks on my Door

Away from town for an eternity
now back down steps there slow
and then a tubby man, shorts peaked cap
yawns. I chuckle.

Young men don't do their hair in the morning;
tousled in bed is the fashion.
A little pretty girl gives me a smile, a passing wave.
I too. That's all. My writing is now dead.
I have been slaughtered strangled wrangled -
life crushed out; like a water rung out cloth
twisted in knots; or like being trapped in a burning bombed tank on fire.

Hospital drop off - walk miles to the ward – mixed sexes waiting ops.
Greek cons. Surgeon tells me of horrific op risks for my consent.
Theatre gown freezing 3 rugs 5 hours wait wheeled to pre theatre by a mechanised trolley, 1 porter long wait to theatre and tipped onto table via a slide.
Knock out man (anaesthesia) needle in my hand, stuff in doesn't work - nurse giving me oxygen in mask. I natter on is this nitrous oxide? Given more knock out and out for the count.
Wake up in a new 2 bed ladies ward.
Foul food so soups and ice creams. Always having to give pees and bloods.
I've made it. BP often. Try to sleep. Got a couple of hours in 2 nights.
Surgeon sees me for 1 minute. Tells me, 'it was tiny' only took 20 minutes'
He smiled sat down – a hope sign perhaps. 'Major op' all bladders are thin walled easy to cut through = a leg bladder strapped for life common. 4 weeks appointment for path result ? Cancer or not.
Return of fear.
Wait and wait and wait and wait.
Lovely surprise – Amy visits – cake, roll,, favourite peaches, roses, 2 books.
Have to drink 2 litres a day. Avoid constipation. More bloods and urine taken. Little sleep. Discharged – me, Amy, John slowly to his van – great. Home and Amy gets coffee and roses in my bedroom - 'nice to wake up mornings to' and she keeps in touch by mobile text.
Sleep on and off for days at last. Extraordinary care from Amy and she says 'You're brave'. Peace.
The day after return massive projectile vomiting 3 foot out – unbelievable amounts of creamy fluids, bits. Why? Danny tells me its the anaesthetic – happened to her too.
Little amount stools passed, bits – no bowel action for days, rectum

empty so take large amount lactulose and cosmocol for faecal impaction. Gripes for 3 hours then massive dam unblock solids and diarrhoea. Hurray – cleaned out. I've done it. Relief and peace, bed and sleep – cleaned out top to bottom. Now can't eat in case it happens again. Phone surgery can't get through. Phone 111 2 nurses awful questions 'is anything hanging out your bum?'. They phoned surgery to phone me. Got a good GP – Dr. Jones (think I'll change GPs.) - told me all this is complications of anaesthetic and hospital. It had happened before when I went almost totally deaf – stress a huge factor where my gut goes into total shut down.

Now to take 1 or 2 sachets with food and eat.

Town next day and relax in my usual pub outside seat but tension and hand shaking marked – do I have cancer or not; some shopping for food and relearning how to walk. Topped up mobile near run out. Jon had brought me fruits and lemonade and milk. The largest blueberries I've ever seen

Wait and wait and wait. Remember good things – Amy and Jon.

This is happenstance. In a lessor hell.

To every struggling street person in wheelchair, crutches, limps, hobbles, pallor, suffering eyes, to myself say 'well done you'.

Hoping for no further hospital/GP contact – next day letter in post ? Appointment 4 week s? No. Letter from surgery to make a phone appointment with GP within 1 week. Shit – what now? Phone and told Dr. Jones will phone next Wednesday between 2.30 and 6pm. I ask what for – told its about my pre-assessment before op. For Christ sake what the hell – just leave me alone. What complication now?

Wait and wait and wait and wait.

Is there nothing right with me?

2 days later – near normal stool. Surprise, surprise. Hurray for how long though?

Phoned Amy to thank her so much.

Wait and wait and wait and wait.

Sept 2018.

Little'uns and Old'uns

Yemen India Africa
little emaciate bodies faces
abused girls.
Blind kids stumbling.
So many, so many.
Ribs, limb-bones, skulls
prominent, gaunt.
Fear in large eyes
or just blank-cut-out
waiting the next assault.
A little brown boy
long shorts, large sandals
striped T shirt stumbles
careful steps, blind
across rocky ground
eye-tears silent plead.
Trachoma he has.

Covid-19 has not yet come there much
while fit kids here, if at all,
get no symptoms or mild if that.
Why so virus safe?
Why so unfair. Why so unfair?
While us old'uns
die like flies, Covid crunched,
loved by the virus
as mature wine.
or we shield in solitary cells
to flood protect the NHS
while the young congregate
on marches and beach and park.

Back-line workers stuck -
heroes too, we are.

June 2020

A Lockdown Prudent Lift. A Risk
? Light relief

The sun is out,
The birds will sing.
Daffies bloom
and snowdrops bling.
Hooray, hooray
for doom has gone
and hope is king
'cos millions
are jabbed -
arms all bared
and they are glad.
But gleeful now
Covid rubs new spikes low -
'O goody, goody
we'll silent spring
and blossom beautiful
in peoples' lungs again'.
As jabs mean life,
our immune response
will smash them down
as Body/Science is king
and nothing else -
not poetry, art -
not anything else.
But schools are top
for a lockdown lift
still cautious of body health.

No body then nobody,
no mind heart soul self.

Feb 2021.

Logistics of Living

Diaries dates times
getting from a to b to c to d
phones mobiles PC trawls surfs

messages weather checks.
What to wear for rain and snow.
Getting fixed house faults
housework and cleans.
Getting up and making the bed,
shopping, news and on and on.
Where is anytime left
to just be alone
without doings and things.

The logistics of living
but the water of life is giving
not forced and by will -
the religious 'good' -
but in warmth and joy'

1 Item for Example

2 TV's collapsed with messages
'no signal', 'no service', 'no video', 'no programmes'
over Christmas and the New Year. You can't make a poem of this.
Being alone, old and isolated the telly is vital for life contact.
So local engineer in to fix I aerial socket plug. It works. Hurrah.
Fails so google Freeview and outage several times.
E-mail them then phone 08081000288.. Radio/TV 03709016789 -
they tell me to phone 034 56505050 to get help with manual tuning
as autotuning has been done on both. Freeview gives 2 further numbers
014181712292 line dead, 01481740310 in Guernsey! and astonishment.
Electricity Board as unplugging and replug gives something
combined with flicker lights 105 emergency
electrician comes same night – no problem external/internal supply.
Local engineer 01227765315 says contact aerial engineer
at 01304813964 – leave a message to contact me. Hasn't.
Freeview again and given another local contact 08081611424 -
number not recognised. Freeview is useless.
Phone original installers of the 2 loft aerials 08003165928 and at last
get some clarity. He will come in 2 days time
as he feels it is an aerial problem in both and not the Dover transmitter.

Maybe I'm on the right path now. Wait and see.
Meanwhile find and fit a new plug extension to my sofa seat
to unplug when the signal goes off often and not have to get up.
This has taken me all day.
Where is life apart from the drudgery of logistics?
Are you frustrated and bored? I am.
But there is a child walking miles

Jan 2019

Looking Forward to ?

Am clawing up a steep mountainside
loose falling rocks nothing to grab hold.
Awaiting cytoscopy biopsy and path.
People are thick stupid incompetent, dull.
I am old, somewhat deaf, lens implants,
unbalanced walk.

Look forward to sleep's escape
or my laptop and card games
TV Room 101, Flog It, Antique shows,
QI and Have I Got News for You
A vodka orange and lemonade and snack.
Pub daily for coffee, orange juice, coconut prawns
and reading – especially Hitchhikers Guide to the galaxy
where I can actually chuckle and laugh out loud.
The greatest loss to English literature
was, at 49, the author of the Guide, Douglas Adams died.
My special scooter at 30 mph
weaving between cars.
Week-ends to the Red Cross shop
to sort donated bags and rubbish.
Now my house and garden are finally fixed,
looking good except for a garage door lock.
My apparent purpose to write.
Such a vibrant life!
Yet the garage door lock is now fixed.

Then I lost my hearing aid -
it was found at the pub.

Let go. Give up,
can't control, can't know.
To my imagination 'Shut up shut up shut up'
to scenes of gloom, doom
Don't even wait.
Turn into melt lead.
    Drop.
    Let go.

Aug 2018

The Lost Cap and Death

For 15 years I've had my Cap -
grey black corduroy and peaked -
a pinned on red pom-pom atop.
It's always on my head except indoors
and except when my scooter helmet is on.
Then it's folded and stuffed inside my jacket -
so one day the routine I did
before shop take-off to town
then got home and it was gone.
A panic vacuum gasp,
a gasp insuck for more oxygen
to deal with immanent threat, loss.
  I went back,
searched the road sides, streets, shops
but it was definitely lost.
This Cap is me, I am it. 2 in 1.
Mourning, I felt bereft,
half of me gone.

The next door's neighbour's wife had died -
a long slow Alzheimer death.
The windows of her bedroom opened wide

to let the stench of death waft out;
there are five chemicals involved -
most repugnant warning avoid
but one is a sweet smelling perfume
though for what – that death can be sweet!

I prepared to go out, put on my jacket -
one arm of it was stuffed, blocked.
I pulled the stuff out. It was my Cap.
Cap on we jumped for joy
and me shouting 'I've found it' three times now.

Loss had gone, new life was born,
    and death was destroyed, done.

June 2018

Luscious Lady

Luscious lady walking -
'*Juicy*' in big bold letters
written on her T shirt front
over big boobs bursting, bouncing.
        Happy days!

A hunk of a man
crew cut hair
in an American football top -
large letters and numbers
over enormous shoulders
shoving and bullying his way
through the force countering air!
His glasses strap
sunk in the fat muscle folds
of his thick fat neck at the back,
just visible now.

There's an almighty battle going on
between String theorists
and deep Loop Quantum Gravitists
about Gravity and before the Big Bang start
but just now again trying to merge
into one and trying unifying
Quantum mechanics and General Relativity
both opposing but tested true
into 1 TOE – theory of everything – the big toe.
        Good luck I say
to Man's urgent urge for oneness -
        to unify
as in love's need to come together
in difference – not the same.
The Grand Unifying Theory
is GUT – and TOE!
        Hurray.

Oct 2018.

Me and Nonsense An Exercise and I apologise
of the person I know best -
a person of short sentences
In Chaucer's Prioress' Tale in Middle English London sub-dialect
I found stanzas in 7 lines all rhyming or alternate line rhyming
(various beats but all less than 5)

Beats 4. I walked into a town and fell into a well - (heptaplet=7)
I had dreamed of heaven but found I was in hell
so I splashed about with a full swell yell
and to many gathered people I said farewell
but I needn't have bothered as they sounded a bell
and as I swallowed a frog – my yell was quelled.
After all was said, there wasn't a well.

3. So I dusted myself down (tetraplet=4)
and went my way in a frown
to the final edge of this town
all covered in earth, brown.

2. The grass was sown.
Hedge hewn,
Job done
and poem blown.
1. I
sigh,
my why?
is high
but I try.

Finally discombobulated – disconcerted and confused, wrangled and mangled
I'm out of this rule and recipe prison.
Happy is my heart;
I can now cook my own hot-pot.
Hurray.

Jan 2020

A Merry Midday Buffet

A snapshot of folks at a garden pub table

It is hard to smile
at a small group joke
with cheeks food-full
chewing prawn salad awhile
but sparkling eyes say it all
as dark wine free flowed
under a sparkling sun mode.
Even harder to laugh
as that is open mouthed,
teeth glinting lips apart;
food, unplanned, might mush out

Yet it is done somehow?

Sept 2019

My Fridge Freezer

Nearly 30 years old -
no trouble for years
then last year the bulb went
replaced by an engineer
in difficult access ok.
Then it went again -
replaced and he left off
the bulb cap shade
so I could get easy access next.
I came home, opened the fridge -
no light again
and the whole fridge gone -
no fridge engine hum
and the bulb blown black.
I turned down the thermostst -
the whole fridge freezer worked
with another new bulb
but I had already ordered
a new fridge.
They took away the old
for crushing. I patted him out -
so loyal – very sad in thanks.
So sad. But sad
his particles will return to the Universe
to make new shapes.

Apr 2019

Near the End if not at -...In Limbo
Is there anything good inside me at all

I was well before all this hospital, GP stuff. Now I am unwell - exhausted, drained out, lethargy, leg pain upstairs, weak unsteady, knackered after a shop. Back ache. Then home sitting, not lying down or walking – pain in left side - ? muscle spasm Dead tired, fed up with living.

Drag self to GP appointment - dare I ask for path. Results? She asks what? Shit.
She browses computer. Results out. Tiny growth and bladder muscle out in bits,
cut out, burnt bleeds. Bits sent to path.
A few Grade 1 Cancer cells found, the least sinister – muscle clear. Checked by 2 Consultant Histologists. Caught easrly
I was dumbstruck. 2 friends of friends had the same polyps – benign ok, go free.
I let rip in self defence – attacked by death. 'You've had cancer and now are clear' - she says. See the urology Nurse for any further follow up plans. But bladder tumours can pop up again.
I had deliberately kept myself sitting on the fence – you have it, you don't. Terrified anew – shaking hands +++. Death had come in my house. Though probably less terrified than I would have been if I had denied that I could have cancer
TV of worse off kids in starving countries gives some proportion. I love stupid 'idiot' folks on tele. And laugh. Laughing is so good.
The nurse might tell me something different to GP and doubt if surgeon took it all out. Want to see full reports. Maybe GP. down played it all. I have to and do trust the surgeon – then grateful to him and the process for the first time – called him Democritus Socrates Papadopalous. - saved from a horrible bladder cancer death. That was worth it all. Accept I had Cancer – that creeping horrible crab. What would you feel and do?

GP deals with dying people daily and cares and supports them and it's common for older people to want death. All finished and done with. 'You're not dying' she said.
I was told by someone that God was in Auschwitz – maybe in me too now for a change. Well why did Christ let out a cry 'eloi eloi lama sabachthani – my God, my God why hast thou forsaked me?' on the cross – God was not in Him or Auschwitz

And thanks to Japan for saving me twice. Many years ago when my partner died I took up Shotokan Karate which saved me. And now a meticulous Japanese lady found a tiny bladder shadow on Ultrasound scan where others wouldn't and may or may not have saved me – who knows. So it is hard to trust.

29th Sept. 2018

Night Driving

The world is void and black
And stretches miles away
Out to the back
Yet presses in on either side,
Squeezing and thrusting the engine on
Into the blinding span of light
Where, in the bleakness of the night,
The verge with stippled gilding gleams
On deathly dark leaf spears and spikes,
Edging the rushing road which streams
And merges into shade patched hedges ...
Then, colourless infinity ...
And, further on, an entity
Of glaring light sweeps up the road.
You cannot see. The wheel is gripped
With sweating hands
Only the sight of sparse wayside plants
Saves us from eternity.
The danger past,
The shaking hands unloose the wheel,
And tautened backs,
Relieved,
Relax.

Oct. 1956

On Off Things

Switches, 'buttons', locks.
Home lights, door locks home and car;
Central heating, laptops, printers, mobiles,
TV and remote controls -
no doubt many more.
Pedestrian crossings, train doors.
Shop check-outs,
lawn mowers, strimmers, cutters.

We spend a lot of time relating to them
important always.
If they go wrong - 'damn it, fuck it' -
woe betide. Woe galore.
Provoked I say -
'don't push my buttons anymore'.

Our Profligate Language

Wasted letters in
command, recommend,
resurrect, accommodate -
too many mms and rrs and ccs.
Occurred – I c wasted
but 2 rrs ok; if only 1
then it would be cured – wrong.
Double meanings in sound -
u, you, ewe -
refuse, ref**use.**
Ton or tonne.
So you 'step up' now
and find many more
All sound makes sense
but often letters don't – so!

Apr 2019

Pandemic Ads
And apologies for TV's undiscreetness

Have you noticed
telly ads are populated by Life Insurance for fears of death
as death is really alive now!
and gambling gung-ho ads to die in debt; so what!
and animal and human charity appeals amass -
animal more profuse than human ads. -

interspersed with manic ads for goods
like 'erectile dysfunction clinically proven
discreetly delivered to your door' -
what on earth?
and multi-people zooms for query what.
And junk food ads despite government's threat
to banish such before 9pm. -
UK brexit folk the fattest in Europe Ex.
No-one knows what's really going on -
all wobbling around like scalded pigs..
'But what can we do?
We have to do something'
says an ambassador for UNICEF
so we fiddle with poetry, pounds and pence.

Aug 2021

note on 'undiscreetness' should be indiscreetness but it's too close to 'in discreet' = being in a position to be discreet.

A Pot Plant on the Coffee Table
In Celebration of its Renewal

Not any old plant
but a special
who says so proud
'look at me' out loud
'in full bloom
of sky blue
and my large green leaves
predominantly two
luscious and long
curling, my arms akimbo.
I've just been re-potted
in deep rich dark soil
in a big blue-grey pot.
A Cape Primrose Ice Blue.
Streptocarpus my family name

as I have spirally twisted fruit -
strepto-spiral, carpus-fruit.
The more leaves I have
so the more I fruit'.

'My name is Confidence.
I'll give you some too
as we all should feel thus
given a new lease of life
as long as we're cared for as my owner does -
as faithful my owner is now
so Fido my name for short.
But do you know
for some years
I was pot-bound, unloved,
shrivelled deprived,
a ghost plant
hanging on
by its sparse root threads
but whoopee,
look at me now endowed unbowed
blossoming full proud.
A miracle we survive anyhow
against all the odds so
care is that miracle 'Miracle-Gro''.

June 2018

Parody
A Potage Poem - June on the Farm

The summer morning brightens up
With whiffs of eggs in frying pans.
5 a.m. The sleepy rise.
A lighting day of sunny plans.
And now a heavy downpour wets
The joyous pets
Of dripping fur around the hall.

And feeding pigs bucket slops.
The showers fall
On sodden plants and growing crops,
And in the middle of the stall
A clump of brown-cows chomp the cud.
And then their plodding in the mud.

9/10/2019

P.S. A Take off of Eliot's Prelude no.1.
This pure technique gives
scrambled brains not eggs.
Imagineering it is not.
Scrambled I am.
I usually write from inspiration
to technique and not rhyme/rhythm
technique to domination.
But a useful exercise.
Tortuous.

Pre the Big Bang which was not a bang
but more a 'Stretch' or a 'Swelling cooking Cake'

There was this tiny subatomic patch of space before any Big bang/stretch. It was relatively cold and without particles who have zero dimension. Space was expanding extremely rapidly – any particles at all there were moving
at high speeds away from each other and in a tiny fraction of a second, being as far from each other as 20 times the distance between the Earth and the Moon.

This is called the Epoch of Inflation.

It was filled with the 'Inflaton' field like a still ocean in all space, and tiny ripples appeared in it, maybe observed today as gravitational waves – the seeds for galaxy growth. It became melon sized then inflation began to slow as its driving energy converted it into a sea of elemental particles.
And its cold became a hot gas of elementary particles which included the Higgs Boson massless field able to give particles mass for galaxies stars, planets and people.

This the Big bang stretch

Virtual particles and anti-particle pairs emitted out of nothing only exist for a short time before annihilating each other. But with inflation each was separated and blown apart by the rapidity of it so they could not come together to annihilate and so become real material particles. 'Inflaton' particles then decayed to produce a bunch of lighter particles. 'Inflaton' particles have never been found as yet – maybe all used up so long ago.

This theory is not proven but is getting more and more acceptable amongst physicists. And maybe it didn't only happen in one small subatomic space but all over – a vast number of bubble universes - a Multiverse each with its own laws.
In the search for the Theory of Everything, TOE, bringing together Quantum theory and General Relativity, String Theory is dominant in the search for this holy grail. Strings are 1 dimensional (particles zero dimensional) and a hundred billion billion times smaller than a proton, part of the atom's nucleus. And posited to vibrate in 10 dimensional spacetime, whatever that is, but far more than the 4 dimensions we have known today, So a near infinite variety of possible worlds, bubble universes – so the Creator likes blowing bubbles and cooking cakes, just like our child selves.

June 2018.

Thanks for this to Brian Cox and Forshaw 'A Universal Journey through the Cosmos'.
Compare it with Douglas Adams 'Life, the Universe and Everything' of the series 'The Hitchhikers Guide to the Galaxy' and Roald Dahl 'BFG' - all very similar!

In Prison

The cell was slowly dark and the barred pained window was
scattering rain and isolation in sliding sleet river drips -
thunder and light concomitant and consistent:
Earth is slower than we'd like it.

Earth is deranged and less of it than we think
uselessly simple. I sup and slurp
the soup gruel, scraping the last drops up.
The boredom of things being the same day in and out

And the cold freezes with a crackling sound, for Earth
is more drab and cruel than one imagines -
in taste, in sight, in sound and in the fingers of touch
there is more than bars between the rain and isolation.

May 2019

A Question?
(transgender - a recent new word)

To take a bigger picture, a faltering attempt
of all the info on homo, lesbian, transgender
flourishments nowadays, A rapid rise
in children seeking a transgender state
and all the info on children
starving and abused in the world
with Western child mental illness' rapid rise
and all the info on world populations soaring,
babies born here there and everywhere
regardless of whether the earth
can manage to food-support all -
and the rich get richer and the poor poorer
and vital forests smaller and smaller.
No overall rational World planning so disasters ensured.
And how ancient species of man
like the Neanderthals got wiped out
and how species of animals
who couldn't evolve likewise.
Current man is due for extinction if - - - -
so the rise in alternative sex. Transgender children,
a universal attempt to stop the birth rate explosion later and now,
child deaths likewise. All this a deep world undercurrent control.
Children are the first to suffer and die
in all the universal conflicts and wars.

The world is brutal, the Universe immensely indifferent, aimless,
a blank mystery, the will to power to survive, ugly, callous,
the prodigal waste and destruction, and pain promoting evolution
matter and anti-matter, rampant particle creation and annihilation.
Why oh why create it this way.
You know what - God needs to be held accountable for this
so therefore it's not us so much who need to creep and crawl
begging for forgiveness not worthy for the under-table crumbs
but God himself and by whom? - the Godhead the first before the trinity's god!
If the Universe had been created with only creation, no destruction
there would be no need for compassion. All would be in
comfort, complete.

In deep physics – space is granular, time does not exist, neither does place -
to me this could be placeless heaven – an understanding
unfathonable, new, true -
beyond our limited comprehension, language and thought.
When his great friend Michele died, Einstein wrote to Michele's sister -
movingly - 'Michele has left this strange world before me. This means
nothing. People like us, who believe in physics, know that the
distinction made between past, present and future is nothing more
than a persistent stubborn illusion.'
I think I believe that too as we have more illusion than we know
as we disdain, neglect this new deep physics like ostriches with
heads sand-buried -
still thinking a flat earth and a rising, setting sun of aeons ago,
of old belief and thought – disregard of the new.
No wonder, awe too.

Nov. 2018

A Story in the Repair Shop

Two short plump persons, well bundled up -
on crutches, simple, an old man and his wife,
trundled in with many chins in great hope.

He was clutching a precious case
housing his Hoffner broken guitar -
its neck snapped long ago when they moved house.
As a youngster he'd eyed it in the shop front,
daily determined in time to get a job, save up;
one day it was gone, so forlorn, he went home
and his mom asked 'what's up luv?' He sadly told.
She left the room, returned with it to his great joy
then long days spent in learning The Shadows sounds.
Decades later they returned concerned, to see the repair -
its return to former glory unveiled with gasps, wet eyes.
His round face and chowks and dewlaps
wobbled in delight. His blue eyes sparkled, lit up -
he became so vulnerable and young again.
I warmed and softened with both of them.

Chouks, chowks Scots for cheeks
The Shadows – popular rock group band of the '60's

Feb 2021

I Vote the Best Shop Window in the U.K

M and S in the High Street.
At the front door side
stood 2 slinky black models in pride
placed on tippy-toes facing us shoppers outside
one with her right hip hitched up
just like models on the cat walk rut.
Each had lacy small bikini briefs on
and gestures of matching flimsy bras -
one in black, the other tan brown.
But below them on the window glass
in big bold black letters – it said, first-class -

'DRESSING THE NATION'.

More like 'Undressing the Nation' -
for Ann Summer's sexy self!

I was entranced, amazed and laughed.
Shoppers walked past ignorant of the fun -
        downcast.
Less is more - but it was a cold NE wind
so more clothes help the less warm
but we're outside and they, nearly naked are inside warm.
There's no other shop like this with fun.
The telly ads. have fun
so why not shops with none?

Sept 2019

Soul

In the beginning was Nothing and out of this came Everything -
beautiful, ugly, glorious nothings and somethings
Everything
has soul

A loo, toilet, privy -
see in curve, its beauty
and comfort it gives for all.
An old armchair and tatty
formed well and well worn.
Restorers make it come alive
and keep alive its old soul
retaining its age, some defects as well.
Animals have soul, a personality
or animality, no 2 the same -
even 'identical' twins are different.
Everything is individual unique -
from planets to pebbles in the universe.
People now seem to be
yearning for the old -
old crafts have sprung back up
which happens when there's enormous change -
to restore the old, fresh, and its soul back alive again.

I don't know what is soul, its undefinable.
If it was defined it would be gone – like god
    all the twatter and blurb.
It's something unknown yet deeply sensed-known.
Perhaps a 'happy' for some and to others 'trash' told.

Dec.2020

with thanks to tv's 'salvage hunters', 'antiques roadtrip/show', 'the repair shop', 'classic cars' etc.

Special Animals

    I love elephants, eles
galumping sedately along
on large sponge feet,
sometimes holding the tail
of the one in front -
wafting large leaf ears to cool
and for flies to swat.
    I love little robin and his orange chest;
when he, puffed up, dips down, I do too
and we have a dance of 12 dips or more.
    I love plump woolly sheep – especially the ones
with smaller ears pointing sideways not up
with short thin legs and black knees.
So woolly, I was once told that golf balls
get lost in their fluff on a golf course.
    I love beavers building craft dams for larder and nests -
their long teeth, iron brown, to cut down trees -
they have to keep beavering away at wood
as their teeth keep growing fast
then their diving slapping paddle tails to trouble warn.
    I love bulldogs – their blunt flat snuffing faces,
doleful eyes, bandy short legs and waddling gait
and docked stump tail, now no longer allowed.
    I love wise owls with those enormous eyes,
radar-dish faces, asymmetric acute hearing, silent ghost flight.

But mostly I love pigs, fat pink or pied
with floppy ears that cover their eyes
so they mostly only see down to ground
and very good for snuffling truffles out
and for that, a stubbed moving nose -
their flopping ears gather all scents.
They are actually very clean and only poo
outside the mud wallow. And the mud is to clean their skin
and protect against sun.
And then the clumped bunches of musk-ox
with clouds of steam-breath in warmth;
so large with long trailing skirt fur
that hides stick legs and hang dog heads, small horns.
Woe betide if they charge their tonnes.
And then those low slung, doleful, friendly, wrinkled
Basset hounds.

I'm just in love!
What ones do you love?
There's more but not to bore!
Did you know that zebra stripes
dazzle and confuse hyenas, lions
who don't know where to quite strike;
the same with annoying biting flies.
How about that for clothing against midge hordes?

Mar 2021

Steam Engine
A Simple Pleasure

An old black and white telly video
popped up on the screen.
A magnificent living hot shot
of The Flying Scotsman -
in his shed built specially for him
and full frontal face on.
He was alive and puffing out steam

from every orifice jetstream agleam -
from down by his giant wheel rims,
from his sides and from his chimney, proud -
steam filled the shed in crowd clouds.
He was pawing the rails
straining his being
to get going to break record speed.
I couldn't stop doing the same -
huffed great puffs from all over me -
sides, chest, ears, nose and mouth.
Then laughed and laughed
in chuffed delight in him and me -
both - magnificent machines.

Canterbury July 2020.

Strange Encounter in Butchery Lane

In the heart of Canterbury, an English town -
me, on my favourite outside pub seat sat down -
saw an Asian couple, she a modern black haired lass -
he squatting on a bench outside watching tourists pass
with a round bald head, big smile
at the next-door Eastern food 'Happy Samurai' caf.
She takes a photo of him, he grins.
I could swear he is the bald Buddha re-incarnate -
in black track suit, little, plump.
I was impelled to get to meet them fast,
instead they slowly ambled past.
'He looks like the Buddha' said while I stopped the lass
and they both laughed a hearty big 'Yes'
and I too was blest
as he went his jolly beaming Buddha way
so happy to have that role place.

I had done a bit for relations between East and West.

Sept 2018

Summer High Street

So many people massed -
large tourist lumps here, there,
talking, standing fixed
blocking highway streets.
Or dithering shop groups
blocking the aisles chatting -
flicking the clothes
standing back.
Or persons impeding corners
when all I want to do straight
is get from simple x to z not irate.
Instead, I predict, rate and wait
their potential moves and when -
weave, speed up, slow down then -
I could scream.
So I walk past them and nudge
their bulging packs, bags - to budge.
But now instead I see them
as atoms, molecules, quarks -
or unpredictable chattering macaques
who natter, natter, squeak and squawk
so I chuckle easy now.
I must be a boson king somehow
That's something. Wow.

Smart Mobile Phones

Never before have thumbs been so mobile
in our evolution of the race;
we, a race, race towards extinction
hunched over, mobiles clasped,
focussed squint-eyed while our thumbs
intricate moves, 3 joints, dance to type fast.

Sept. 2019

Surprise Delivery
a sketch in a beer garden

a small lump
of moss
fell off a dried
roof

rich green with
a dark mudmaze
of roots
tiny copperlike stems,
light green sporecap tops
all pointing
oneway.

I picked it up
and placed it in
an old planter bed

as something so finefrail
deserved
not to die yet

in this harsh Creation
happy to destroy
all it has made
like a child
knocking down
his building blocks.

Later its capsule tops
pointed another way
signalled by the sun
        that day.
        It's alive
            Yay.

Apr.2019

In medieval council votes, all those in favour shout a jubilant 'Yay' just like youngsters today.

Teeth

A trekking couple,
not on mountain scree
but on the cobbled streets,
pause and stare up to this pub sign -
'Shakespeare' - it always gets a tourist look;
I was impelled to say but didn't -
'Shakespeare's not in today -
he's gone to shop'!
Hers - a small cropped head, up-turned
had very large upper teeth -
the first thing I saw when I scanned -
so much so she can't shut her lips
and she mouth breathes. Her loved one? -
I wonder how they kiss. Well done.

A Determined Toddler

A young toddler one and a half feet small
in joggers with knee patches and peaked cap
could actually push the slight pram
his mother usually pushes him in
along the gutter slab strips.
It comes to a sudden stop
jammed against the pavement side.
He investigates the cause -
he already knows the physics of 'cause and effect'
and his tiny trainers stamp on one slab -
and it's given a thorough look
and the cement around touched
and tasted with a yell from his Mum.
He rights the pram
and careers off full blast -
Mum running after him fast.

All toddlers I've found
love the different shapes
of street cobbles and stones.
There are 5 different types each side.
And they taught me that - to detail look.

In India a tiny toddler
sits in a cardboard box
on a pavement
in a busy feet street
waiting for food or a coin,
head bent down
looking at his feet;
so sad and sweet --- aahh.

May 2018

The Alien in Butchery Lane

Over 6 foot tall
but very slim overall -
a lass sidled
slowly by-bye
in a full length
black skirt;
a tight little jacket, awry
and small wicker-basket worn -
handle-cradled on her arm.
But most surprising of all
her long pale face withal
focussed ice-eyes
into the dark pub sidewise;
her great top-knot,
hair built, bundled
up atop,
bound by a small scarf
increased her height in part.
She was dealing out

non-stop
leaflets into every shop.
She did not look
as one of us at all;
maybe of some occult
esoteric coterie cult.
It was those haunted
full-size
ice-blue ashen eyes;
a shiver squirmed
up my seat
to find my spine
to slither up -
yet a person she is
so it stalled
in its tracks
and froze.

Oct 2019

The Gym

Now I belong to the earth again -
on scooter flying through town
after an hour's muscle tussle
on the gym's black armed robots;
effort and sweat and will
to try to keep my old body on;
other young were going full tilt
so are we all afraid of decay
and a desperate dying death.
Sweat pouring, towel wiping
water bottles sucking guzzling,
keeping up with machine speed running,
running for life
escaping decay.

But after I felt grounded, earthed -
belonging to this world.

Language depends on time
in common words like was, is,
present, past and now
but the Universe doesn't.

July 2018.

The Muse!

How I find I write. How do I?
Today I have just thought.
I didn't think. It thought me. Yes.
I get struck with an inner or outer scene
as utterly right – a bubble with a light bulb seen! -
a penchant for a paean poem -
or wrong, disturbing, jangling bad;
awesome or awful. So common, I write. Sad.
Then important the idea to catch -
and notice I have been struck back.
Then to note details, a pencil word sketch
and with discipline write a quick draft;
slow -(a shaky hand I have)
then discipline back home -
sofa-settle down and type it out rough,
feeling for rhythm, less so rhyme
and word order, length and time.
Then come back to it often to correct
to notice where there is a jarr
and work on it deliberately – to expect -
till it feels somewhat better now and I accept.

I hate the discipline bit.
It's all training in being aware.
Most of our lives we see
yet don't see enough.

So common, I mostly write!
When I'm busy on all this
I am shut to new delight
Yet goaded there's so much more -
out of sight, indefinite,
a delight precise, that's exquisite.

Sept 2019

The Woman behind the Bar
(above the basement beer-well)
A modern scene of 'The woman at the well' (Jn.4:7)

A tad bit more than four feet small -
in a tubby long puffa coat -
well it was cold outside
and she has a cig break
sitting on the opposite steps
up to the terrace cafs.
She had well-worn plimsolls
and no socks.
Such a sweet face
smiling above the bar -
shining eyes welcoming
new-leaning, pint-beer folks.
She was pulling a pint
from one of those lovely row
of wooden handle pumps,
like upright rockets.
and tending the dripping froth.
Just a simple young lass
who has got a rare job.
Such humble-ty, grounded earthed
(not a machine) -serving us.

I had no other way
of expressing what she shone -
exceptional, remarkable, wonderful -

(such flat words) -
in her ordinariness
or if you like – to some in the west,
the woman at the well;
'she is Him' to myself I said -
except the woman at the well
watered Christ who, unrecorded, I hope said 'thanks'.
'No problem' she would reply,
like in these days, meanwhile she had
many relationship ones
of 5 husbands past -
so he helped her there
as well! ♫

Now she has found her man,
sitting smoking up those same terrace steps -
a chef from the same pub in their break
and she has become transformed and 'glam'
in love - with a hug and a kiss.

Apr.2018

The Word

We're in a row
of boats and we row
then row
as to whom
came first
or last
and each other splash.
English
is troublesome to foreigners
and us.

Dec.2020

Record Thirst Ever

Distant thunder mutters -
grey skies are looming from the SW;
cross winds are trying to stop them
coming over our parched earth -
record high temps recorded today -
of 'record', a double meaning there!
A magpie and coal-tit pant open beaked -
I have never seen that before – a first;
leaves droop thirsty, drooping bad
crying loud for rain but none comes down
so I water them urgently bare foot.
The sky drops a few rainspots, thunder mumbling.
The skies are in labour pains groaning rumbling.
I continue watering – these drops are not good enough.
Finish - then dark darkens; among the black, lightning strikes.
Sky's waters break and she sighs, at last giving birth -
a ten minute rain burst full and astounding,
large water globules pour down, running flooding.
I go inside and watch it suddenly stop
and sigh relief, wet.

My cup of tea is now empty
yet marvellously full of air -
space is not nothing -
nothing is not
it is quantum field 'grains'.

July 2019

Those Eyes The Hours

Metaphor is a luxury language in starving countries

Sand veers and sears in eyes, lungs phlegm -
from harsh scrub flatland seen through dust;
their bank cash - as penned goats condemned,
their water bugged with filth and thirst
behind a thorned, rood-fenced requiem.

The young for the old - investment shrouds,
mothers die fast before and giving birth;
flies zoom down dark, quick stung, in clouds,
but war has stopped; loud tanks quiet rust; bare earth;
kids shit and vomit parched, wounds rot; language - bed rock.
Scrap. Folk count as little worth.

They walked three days for hospital help -
the child screams tears - his compound fracture realigned -
tortured, ligatured, sutured - without drugs.
Those eyes. Bright burn. And shine.
White bone through dark skin - bloodcrust fear.
How can you not crack and cringe
at such shuddering hurt - unhinged?
Under windflood - gusts thud.
Those eyes - sear through - as winds sheer.

To survive, to accept, to go on - proud.
He makes a spade from tank tin rust,
she makes charcoal, hallowed load,
he works till he slumps in deserted desert dust,
she gives spare wound swabs and crusts.
A baby is born.
And we give scorn.
And small concern.
An aid forlorn
from our full bellies - robust
and carping mouths unjust.

In this - (vertiginous rage) -
to us who wait and assuage -
and unsharing fiddle, and fractured flutter
while simple unbowed people die and suffer?
But the essence of us knows and can restore -
The hours. Those eyes. They're also yours.
They're ours.

Canterbury

Time, Change and the Acorn

I was a seed in the acorn. I wasn't asked if I wanted to be conceived by a bit of pollen and a flower, then born, dropped into the earth bed in 'Rhodesia'. But that I was; when any creativity is going on all effort is in it's creation without asking if it wants to be that. I was raised, fed and the youngest of 2 saplings and steadily grew gaining in girth and knowledge. My tree was a very quiet tree, obedient and compliant. Research has shown that trees come in families and they communicate with each other. My father tree died when I was 2 years old – from what who knows, I don't and my family didn't communicate much apart from practicalities. So my mother had to raise us and keep up a job (cycling 7 miles to work and 7 miles back).

She was a tough Scotswoman with a sort of calvinistic background from Falkirk Scotland – all in black and scowling. I had about 20 relatives from both sides who emigrated everywhere and were pioneers in Zimbabwe – shop keepers in the bush, silver miners, bridge and road builders.

At school I was very good at sports, biology, physics and chemistry but hopeless at maths. Mother suffered innumerable illnesses and hospitals so I was inwardly driven to study Medicine – got scholarships bursaries grants etc after completing degrees in Science at Cape Town University. In 2nd year medical studies 5 of us had breakdowns after a whole year stuck around dissecting smelly dead bodies – a massive change was occurring. And my tree had to withstand lightning strikes, thunder storms and harsh drought but it did get some rain to survive. This showed me that real change comes through suffering and that all evolution has to die to give new and altered life forms. The real me was being formed. So my winter's dying grew into a new spring and high achievement in my career.

Now is the time for growing old and the loss of physical freedom and activities but an increase in creativity, new an exciting ideas and mental/ emotional strength. But bits are falling off my tree which must be a preparation for a sometime dying to an unknown state. I don't believe that all this massive universal creativity is eventually for nothing. The universe may eventually end in a whimper having started with a big bang as one reality, but I am learning there are several realities outside our own brains.

This acorn has grown into a tree and is making numerous acorns – over

500 poems and has treated, helped and healed numerous people – who in a sense are my descendants.
This other universal Reality, apart from our little local brain reality, amazes and fascinates – like time passing is a brain-made illusion as in Spacetime there is no past, present or future – they are all there together everywhere. Also like quarks fundamental building probability blocks – they can be everywhere and nowhere all at once. Language fails.
This constant pressure in communication, in condensing codifying contact – in all experiences.
We certainly are all connected, watching and wondering – even trees do it!
It is easier to have our personal stuff read by a distant reading public than to read it out loud.

Canterbury Feb 2018

Time. Note Sketches T,T,S,S,H

'Dum spiro spero' - while I breathe I hope.
I saw a young lad wandering along backpacked. He talked to someone out loud. He had no mobile in sight or out. Were his inner voices busy?
I saw a young lass walking along with 2 boxes of take-away food also talking out loud to no one. But she had mobile white wires to both ears.
I asked at the phone shop. There are microphones in the junction of the 2 wires.. Both talks were real – one classed as abnormal the other 'real'.
I saw a tiny puppy in a puffa jacket pocket 'going for a walk' his owner said.
I see men's hair styles are different now. One with a severely shaven head and small tufted tuft atop. Another older man again with a shaven head, bald top patch and a thin front fringe top combed forward over his forehead like President Trump.
Another with a ginger curly mop, ginger full beard, black crown top fading to brown with a blonde forelock. Men are into dyeing their hair now too.

Love cannot be given. It can only be received. True love expects nothing. It only waits – there maybe indifference, response or rejection.
The internet is abysmal. People are out of jobs. Books are of less value.

The paper written or spoken word is being strangled. The Internet causes spam and phishing and fraud and buggers up its content from time to time. I am furious with it, have lost several files, got buggered up by microsoft who apologised.

Am so enlightened in reading a short history of myth. Early man worshipped the Sky, River, Animals as he was so open to their magnificence. He expected nothing in return. Later he made gods and expected and prayed for help. He lived by hunting with the danger of death. Initiation was vital to pass from one stage of life to the next. Man has always hoped for a better life and finally after the last trial of death, a hoped for a 'heaven'.
Development, growth is always through passing through danger – dying to the old self. Heroes, heroic in living/dying through like the god myths.
The degree to which one 'falls', breaks up, 'fails' is the degree to which one has not had. I can hear and taste tears running down.

Rarely in a shop foodhall do I laugh if at all. But at the top shelf of M&S I found a pod of 'Quark' cream cheeses – my favourite pranksters in physics. Of course I bought one and continued chuckling down the aisles. And there in front of me was 'Dirty Fries'; it seems to mean with flecks of herbs and cheese.

To hand over control where indicated is to be in control.
T.S.Eliot 'On Margate sands I can connect/ Nothing with nothing. The broken fingernails of dirty hands. My people humble people who expect nothing.'.True meditation. And compassion.

My most useful word is 'ok' – firmly, strongly said it indicates a definite stance. When softly said – you give over control where indicated and that is to be in control!
My favourite word is 'person' – a round soft special precious word; 'people' is too general and 'humans' too objective, technical.
The moon has a menstrual monthly cycle!

Feb 2018

Time?

Einstein. 'the dividing line between past present and future is an illusion'.
So reality is ultimately timeless. Time is relative and flexible.
We often use past word forms to talk about the present or future – after, if, unless, supposing...Past present and future exist simultaneously.
Once events have passed they continue to exist somewhere in Spacetime.
Everything is ever present. Time does not pass or flow.
There is nothing in the laws of physics to state that time should move in the forward direction that we know. Time is a human construct – a practical delusion.

Our being, brains, consciousness tell us time exists, passes, flows –
that's our reality. But out there there is a different reality -
Spacetime where past present and future are all one.
The past remains present and in the future,
the present is in the past and future, and the future
is in the past and in the present. Got it! Dizzying, mind boggling.
This seems the reality of the transcendent, universal –
call it God if you will. I am excited and thrilled. Einstein –
I could hug you for this signal of transcendence
so much more thrilling than any doctrine or creed
I hurry to get to town to give me more time there.
No need. Time does not flow, pass. I chuckle, giggle like I do
with prankish quarks who can be e.g. in 2 places at once
even at the observable ends of the universe.
We never need to hurry! Hurray.
There is no physics of time, only of Spacetime.
We it is who made the hands of the clock and the clock.

The Big Bang at the origin of the physical universe (Polkinghorne)
is being equated with the mythos of Christ. That's wow but exclusive.
So I lost my special scissors searched everywhere but lost'
They've gone lost for me but still exist somewhere.
I die so am lost gone forever but 'my'quarks
are still present in probability, reconstructing, getting up to pranks,
being everywhere and nowhere all at the same time. Watch out!.
'Quantum theory as the basis of understanding the physics of the mind'.

(Roger Penrose) My quarks are at it again.
Dual aspect monism – only one stuff in the world
but it can occur in 2 contrasting states (material and mental phases).

Life is just a temporary home for the immortal elements of the Universe (B.Cox).
We let out ideas but ideas come back at us - they're transcendent.

Feb 2018.

Town Oddities
some portraits of

A black curly Labradoodle dog
with back knock-knees bent! Indeed,
slowly strolls under a very long lead.

Her long hair fell over her right eye;
she walks head drooping to the right
to clear this eye. It's permanent forever, cricked
unless she finds a smart little clip to back-tie.

A bouncy brown brindle dog
with a white chest patch
has a stump dock tail of 1 inch -
and, blow me down -
a teeny bit it can wag -
his bum worked hard for that -
it's a bit cruel so
now they don't do that.

Man beer-bellies and large
like the bow of a stumpy barge
parting the air waves afore,
arms out to balance like oars,
shoulders back and back arched back
to counter the for'ard front mass;

and trouser belt low slung
snuck under wobbling
collops of fat hung.

A lass with a bum-freezer leather top -
but her fleshy butt
cling film wrapped
in skin-tight chequered jeans -
        judders
with each step she takes;
her hands fold demurely
in front of her pussy
camel-foot front.
Is this the height of fashion
or just a bit odd?

Apr 2019

UltraSound Scan

The morning after the blast
of Graduation noise,
I had to fill my bladder
with water – 2 pints of it
to highlight it 1 hour before;
managed it and was praised;
conducting gel on my tum;
a dark room and breathe in and out -
an instrument panel and knobs.
Done – over now – relief -
I could now pee like hell.

7 pm an urgent call from surgery
to see GP next day plus bottle of pee.
Panic rose in my throat – the big C?
Death sentence given, the axe guillotine -
sleepless – 'mindfulness' call up,
aware of only breath, nothing else.
Accept. No control. Drop not tensed.

To surgery and wait 1 hour.
'What can I do for you today' GP innocently asks.
I'm stunned. I explained. She computer checks -
'oh, they've put you on the urgent list.
Ultrasound is not an accurate tool so always follow up -
a routine, with further tests.'
Stunned again with relief.
I get another red capped bottle to go and fill now.
I can't as I am still collecting it in my bladder -
for any urine blood. I don't have any to see.
'Trust me' she says
so I have to wait 1 week for result.

I have twice been severely hammered
in 2 days. Down and out. Done.
But the pee bottle tested ok a.t. GP -
sigh again in relief.
2 days later get a call from KCH
to arrange appointment in 3 days
with a Consultant urologist
as I was referred by GP.
What the fuck hell is going on?

July 2018

Up There
The Sky and I

Sky – blue, black, red, orange -
such a short little word
for such an immense.
Tell me what's in it and beyond.
Tell me of stars, moon and sun.
Tell me of the planets - their names, their how.
Tell me of black holes, tell me of the Universe.
So learned men give me names
and deeper men give me
of quantum physics and particles -

of the deepest quarks, fields,
bosons, forces, photons
and all their mischievousness -
like they tunnel through matter
and one can be in many places all at once
and a pair being separated and one nudged -
the other jumps even if at the other end of the Universe
and observation alters what is observed;
all counter-intuitive tricks.
At root fields and probability is what we get.

Knowledge and understanding
thus lie in words in part -
an immense universe in itself
and like evolution they develop and change;
How do we see things;
differently with difference -
it's all in our brains so what is real?
so we, so much, do not really know;
faith develops by way of doubt and
knowledge comes by way of ignorance
which as yet have no words.

The smallest word is I
yet a person is so great.
We indeed are made of stars,
the very particles that were born
over 13 billion years ago
and passed down the chain to us.
So who and what are we now?
There is knowledge without words.
Just lift up a fold of your skin -
        that's stardust.
So - we were conceived as stardust seeds
long long long ago.
So – pinch up your skin - awake - like so.

Oct 2019.

Warms

Tiny round fluff ball
critters – zillions of them
invaluable to us all
'cos they keep us warm
throughout our earth.
But we need to find them, feed them
unless you're an otter or polar bear
with double fur coats -
outer for water, rains,
inner for all kinds of colds
like our ski coats.
They are life-giving, preventing death
against frost, ice and snow.

You can see them in fire
but they hide within
our boilers for heat -
that is many, many warms.
And they're deep from the furnace Sun Orb.
I love yeull.
Muchly thanks.

Apr 2019

Waves

Energy can neither be created nor destroyed

Waving a hello or goodbye across,
the arms are propelled back and forth;
then there's hair wavy undulating curls;
the Mexican wave in football crowds -
the people don't move out of their place
but the wave energy undulates around.
Not just like them - we are waves.
Sea waves are not water flux and flow -
sea waves are Energy that flows,
the water just does same-place somersaults;

near the shore they break as underneath the shore slopes
so its water falls back under the coming energy wave
so under-over curls and its energy dispersed
in the sound down crash and sand soak-up.
It's energy never created nor destroyed
as Einstein so famously said.
Put some plastic bath toy ducks in a water glass tank
then shoogle the end water with your hand,
the water energy wave moves to the other tank end
but the ducks stay virtually put.

Form and Shape are defined – undefined Process, within this,
changes form.
You could say God is Process within and Christ his form, shape.
A piece of good music always comes to an end -
if it went on interminably, repetitively we'd be meaninglessly bored.
And being bored means our loss of interest, involvement
as by nature we connect
Music is superb, beautiful because it also ends, dies.
We too are thus – grow old, entropise, energy released,
diminished form.
Form/shape has to have a beginning and end giving its
energy elsewhere.
Death gives form and shape closure – that is its meaning, our Energy
continues on.
We are Waves - in the sea storm or calm in life seas and their earth
shore end.
Waves would not be if there was only sea and no earth shore on
which to break.

Painting shapes, writing poem forms
are in an energy process -
they come to an end, die
but live on to be other enjoyed.
We too are a painting, a poem, a wave;
every one of us.
In death our Energy is given back to the Universe.

Aug 2018.

What to Write?
On being personal, reflective and honest

I have absolutely no idea what to write now in terms of it being in journal or memoir form following the form of the presented articles recently – Oscar Wilde's impelling feeling prison release letter and the fine objective journalism on local Chinese society (where the author doesn't seem to relate how he feels).
So currently I'm in a vacuum. Regarding the former I have ideas of my own past, in being in a kind of prison in South Africa many many years ago and written in poem form – descriptive and feelingful and I feel they're quite good though I'm not the best judge. But perhaps they're not ready to share on their own. The problem is what and how much to share and what is acceptable to others, mostly unknown, unless we all know our past kinds of prisons - which is the process of dying to the old – a new self forming. There's a time and a place for everything.
Regarding the latter China piece, I have travelled to Japan, Russia, Morocco, Egypt – that was in a group to see the sites with little involvement with their peoples. What struck me most apart from sites of interest was the absolute thrill of aeroplane flight and its intricacies written on, but now age makes me stay put in Canterbury where I also love watching and writing of street people and reading. All my writing (over 500 pieces) is mainly in poem form and to me it's like a journal and memoir of sort, some of them clearly are.
I would like to write something now but cannot seem to draw up anything currently, equivalent, out of the depths, heights or surface of my being or experience. And I'm feeling it vital to be as honest as possible - hence this.
Apologies if this causes some problem but maybe this too is part of a journal or memoir as maybe poems can be as well.
Perhaps this can be a turning point and I can now feel free to write without poetic freedom and restraint! Perhaps do both. We develop in catching our ever fluid thought and evanescent emotion – in expression. It is our creativity and our life. So we're all artists and heroes – all creating e.g in cooking, gardening, making things, writing – not just the elite of painters and writers.

Jan 2018

When will it Stop?
Dare to Know Emmanuel Kant

Got home from hospital and the marathon to get through op.
Home and projectile vomiting and faecal impaction'
That's it – can try to settle and wait for path result.
Next day letter in post, maybe appointment for that.
No – letter from surgery to make appointment for GP to call me
Emergency, urgent or routine? Phone surgery arranged.
Mess up with my prescription – call in to surgery.
She asks if I have a letter for urgent appointment. Not again.
Remonstrate. What the hell – another.

Wait for phone call from GP. For hours. Have to go to loo. Miss call.
Phone dead. Again phone – remonstrate. Well you missed it.
Phone again for another next morning 8.30 till 12.30.
Wake at 10. Alarm clock on bed. Phone on bed. Failed.
Missed another call but message to phone back.
Did so. 8.30 till 12.30. Wait. 12.45 GP calls. Its my hesitant GP.
Pre-assessment had told her my slight anaemia and kidney.
She and I already know that.
Is that all. Relief. I let loose what I had to put up with..
She understood.
The process of getting to op is worse than op. Many refuse.

Then Letter for appointment for M. Jones Urology in Nov. What the hell is this for.
Phone OP appointment person. Who is M Jones. He says gynae/ oncology.
So I Have cancer 'oncology'. He says new computer system being set up
but will phone surgeons secretary who'll phone me back. She does.
NO – Mauna Jones is Clinical Nurse Practitioner not an oncologist
who'll phone me next day 2 till 4.30. So have to wait the whole day - first for the GP call then nurse. 1 Hour to get to town to shop between.
Nurse phones before 2pm then again at 2.05 when I've got back.
Her Nov. appointment too far away will speak to her secretary for sooner

in 2 weeks. No she and GP haven't got results yet but better face to face when she has. Will get another letter appointment for 2 weeks.

I cannot tell you the utter complexity of all this. Disastrous.
So if I am lucky – will get it sorted in 2 weeks.
I don't care if I've got cancer. Sod the world. Sod people.
Sod everything.
I've had enough.

20th Sept .2018.

2 more appointments – 1 for ear wax, 1 to see ENT surgeon for skull bone op for hearing aid.

Still wait appointment Audiology for special new Cross hearing aid for bad ear., GP says forget about all that for now. Town next day – I'm off. Leave me alone. Get out all you bastards and idiots.

Then another NHS letter – my ENT surgeon appointment has been cancelled – will inform me of another date. Don't care for more surgery – just give me my other special Cross over hearing aid for defective ear. So more chasing up Audiology Mon. for an appointment for that Please!

Wondering And Some Whys

Cows udder-milk churning to butter
when they run or walk?
horses heads bob back and forth
when they gallop?
Ducks heads do too when they swim
and pigeons too on walking.
Walking gulls don't head bob.
An executor and executioner do the same thing -
carry out death or something else.
Pigs don't poo in their mud or sand pits -
they deliberately leave the scene, even piglets too.
Why do lambs jump so high and even twist mid-flight -
to me that's a living joy.
And they tail-wag fast when suckling – the first content.

Happiness seems to be tail wagging in animals (or fly-swatting).
Cows skip and jump too when let out to a green field
after a long winter in sheds. Sheer freedom and release.
Cows mourn the death of their one - like elephants
and can comfort a grieving person as if in compassion..
Stroking cows and dogs drops in both both BP's and pulse.
Cows lie down to get warm especially their tummies.
They don't have 4 stomachs – they have one divided into 4.
And they have a varied diet of grasses and eat selected tree leaves
and avoid poisonous plants.
They don't have top front teeth only a pad. Their tongue curls round
a grass bunch and that and lips can pull
whole grass up to swallow then regurgitate.
Why do cheetahs have marked black stripes down the sides of
their nose?
It's where tears would run! Camel means 'beauty'!
Large tortoises hiccup in mating though how under their
huge shells.?
Do 'jumper' jerseys jump?
Highland cattle have fringes covering their eyes so how do they see?
'Please trim my fringe' they moo out.
Why do bulls and bison kick back dust with their foreleg
? to dust-soothe their horny hot under-parts.
'Murmuring' starlings in their thousands whirl in dark clouds
at dusk.
Goshawks don't seem to blink at all. If you blink you miss.
How and what provokes evolutionary change – a chance 1
off mutation
that helps survival that takes on? But at a molecular level, how?
Why do moose and bison and billy goats have beards and men too?
Goats have rectangular pupils – the wider to see you with?
Sloths hang slothfully up-side-down
so do they see up-side-down slowly?
So many why-whys I ask-ask
so I'm like a child - the basis of science.

Dec 2019.

A Few Special Word Sounds
An exercise in sound (not ideas) for fun

Perhaps say each of these words fast and pause between them –
they're super
Cricket
Rivet
Pivot
Divot
Privet
Give it
Cricket
Fidget
Midget
Ticket
Wicket.

Then make a story if you want. Our stories will all be different.

A chirpy Cricket
said to the small cat Civet
under the Privet
as a Midget
buzzes and fidgets.
'Shall we pop along
to the Cricket -
and watch a falling Wicket.
We have an entrance Ticket' -
as the bowler makes a Divot
then Pivots
and, his all, gives it.

'Where is my place
in the scheme of things?'
sadly said the rusty Rivet
from all his tears dripped.
To make something of this
is all very difficult.
Try it.

April 2020

Go to red pdf icon at top line.
Click on that. Save. Is in 2018 vol. 6. with red pdf icon
and the original is not lost (as in Soda)

World Word – Update
That little letter l – el not1 one
as type doesn't much distinguish; hand writing does

New technology lies in the skies – hence the www 'cloud' -
data storage space for all our images and communications
on the internet waves in space which can sharing 'stream' out.
Now our selfies, mobile images, tablet stuff
could be stored in DNA ? in life's chromosomes
or perhaps concocted in a lab.
Quantum computers with amazing powers
could use qubits, tiny particles magnetically suspended
in just above absolute zero -275 Celsius or centigrade
where the roles 0 and 1 states coexist – i.e.
1 and 0 and also superimposed both together -
so computation can be massively speeded up,
not ordinary computer binary bits where 0 and 1 are separate.
Full stops are bursts of heavy metal chords -
you can hear them on a Radio Kent rebel cheeky chat show. True.
So if you hear or see an unattended full stop
report it to the police! A tingly word,
'Antiquities', - is the department that tickles antiques!
Virginal – vaginal. Yes – born of man.
So assent or dissent in ascend or descend – no, now inscend.
Easter should be banned!
as we're eating our baby bunnies and chicks!
Have you noticed ice-cubes massed
in a bucket on a pub bar shelf?
They snuggle together to keep cold!
Put one cube on a plate
and it will melt fast - not so in a crowd,
whereas animals huddle to keep warm.
'Problems' anymore don't exist
only 'issues' atishu – 'bless'.

Dung beetles – 'yuk', roll the specially moulded dung balls -
backwards, their sturdy front legs push them back in straight lines,
their slender back legs cradling the ball,
their faces down navigating with an eye on the sun
or at night on the moon and if no moon then on the Milky Way.
How good is that – not 'yuk' anymore.
Nonsense can make sense except where both dung ball and beetle
tumble backwards down an unseen sand-dune.
'Oh no!'- all that work – it's too much to go back up the hill
but maybe he doesn't need to as the idea was just to
escape fast from thieving mates
and to bury the hidden ball as a future food store.
'Information' is the in word now.
'Happy days'.

Apr.2018

Worthy

Sitting at a pub table outside,
a little fluffed up robin
in all his full red chest dress
swift flew down
to me nearby
in a twinkling eye.
Street fallen leaves had turned gold.
A cold day it was
hence his feather fluff -
he wasn't full and fat.
I asked and got some crumbs
from the pub boss
and sprinkled them table-under.
He came again and fed
then flew up to the chair opposite
to look me up with a cocked eye.
'You're so worthy
to gather up the crumbs
from under my table' I said -

I was talking to him now.
'Am I not'?!

From then on he often perched near;
I think he was really looking for little worms
between the cracks of the ground bricks
but none to be had
I was happy and sad.
How we all struggle so

Nov 2019.

YgUDuh

ydoan	you don't
yunnuhstan	you understand
ydoan o	you don't know
yunnuhstand dem	you understand them
yguduh ged	you got to get
yunnuhstan dem doidee	you understand them dirty
yguduh ged riduh	you got to get rid of
ydoan o nudn	you don't know nothing
LISN bud LISN	LISTEN bud LISTEN
dem	them
gud	god
am	damn
lidl yelluh bas	little yellow bas
tuds weer goin	tards we're going
duhSIVILEYEzum	to CIVILISEthem
e.e.Cummings (1894-1962)	[interpretation] E.W.

A Gift

A little present dropped
at my feet -
well, 3 foot in front
on the cobbled street;
I still know the exact spot;
a bubble, a fist size squat blob
blown from a high street shop
from one of those bubble machine pumps
wind pumped dumped;
a rare one to land this far
of all the thousands blown flopped.
He must have danced
atop over the roof tops.

He settled there and did not pop
but showed his spectrum colours in
swirlings mergings on his atom thin skin,
shimmering opalescent glowing.
Quantum particles-waves-probabilities all in
spins, doing a happy merry jig
in perpetual collision destruction, creation
and the energy within involved therein
showing me of what the universe is made
(and not in a sand grain conveyed) -
the law of transformation and change
and the 'Uncertainty Principle' famed.
Then his colours clear and stop - strange
and colourless, he then pops disarranged -
and unknown, has gone into a different subatomic state -
a something else, of what I know not – like us, bubble-like at
death's date!

Amaay-zing
Whoopee.

It doesn't mean
that if you can't see it
it doesn't exist.
The visible light spectrum

is only a very small portion
of the total light wave stratum
which is a small part system
of the electromagnetic spectrum
so far as a whole known.

May 2017

We know so little of our universe -
only the 5% of the total, with unknown unseen
dark matter 23% and dark energy 72%.

A Little Gem

'the sweat of the sun is gold',
and 'the tears of the moon is silver' - Inca sayings

A pudgy baba
in a rattling pram
on the cobbles being juggled -
couldn't see out
as his woolly cap
had been wobbled
down over his eyes
atop.

Blandly pushed by Mum behind
he didn't seem much to mind -
just continued drawn in prattle
to feeling his gangly rattle
with no attempt to push his cap up.
Chuckling – I enjoyed closeup

Perhaps he hadn't connected
what had stopped his sight
and the remedy thereof outright.
There was no need defined,
indeed he didn't mind.
He was content with just touch.

Apr 2017

A Quiet Vacuum.

Nothing has struck me this week – that is, if I am waiting for a flash of enlightenment or a sudden image of truth and beauty. It's just that the hum-drum ordinary is all around like a haze so I plod on waiting. I'm sure it's there – maybe the eyes to see and the ears to hear are muffled blurred – a pot simmering gently, not cooked yet. The trouble is I am unaquainted with paragraphs and prose so offer
The eye of the ego I.

A day of balm.
A warm wind wafts and greets
down the petunia hung street -
refreshed, loosened calm.

Tiny puppy
Just off breast paps -
his little legs working blurred fast
to keep up with his watchful lass.

My present pre-occupation is with change and uncertainty. All is change – from a tiny quantum quark to the cosmos - sandwiching us; and with what is truth?
'I would be unstoppable if only I could get started' says a fridge magnet while I coffee-sit at a street caf watching. There's a lot of I's in this so it's probably boring.

Oct 2017.

A Side Street

The quiet comfort
of older couples
hand in hand
disturbed by the
high pitch excited chatter of
hoarded little scholars
squeezed from a local school
in a Roman museum,
cardboard swords keen.

This street gives me
quiet content

watching passers by -
all different, unique;
confidant in themselves;
their looks, hair, dress
but especially their multicoloured shoes.

I don't know what date it is -
who cares.
It's the morning of peace instead -
the year, two thousand and sixteen plus.
The sun is shyly shining here -
and no cold east wind blows.

Elizabeth Webb

?Abstract Nothing in Winter

My world has been chock full of bad mundane matter somethings,
and so oaths -
a list as long as your arm and in font size nine, in recent month
paths -
all outgrowths strengths depths myths.

Now I need not even words
just utter quiet peace, no guards
just repose hush still calm towards ?
no TV racket word batter
no movement clatter
no mind monkey chatter
no feeling, no knowledge natter
no reading, books. Simply just still eyes and looks..

'I've got plenty of nothing and nothing's plenty for me' - the song
and 'why is there something rather than nothing?' some
ask headlong..

Only 4% of the universe is composed of matter such as planets,
galaxies, life and stars.

That leaves 96% of the universe unknown uncomprehended unseen
undetected and impossible to mathematize.
It's called dark energy and matter. Dark but why not call it Dark
Nothing? I ask.
But that so called dark nothing therefore maybe something great as
it has - gravitational effect on what can so far be seen now with the
highest minds known.
So apparently that unknown nothing really does contain unknown
something far greater than we own, know, are shown.

But we can image something from nothing as well,
and breathing aware dwell
in just a look between people -
understanding the root of all! -
maybe only quiet sound, a small call;
as matter is full of vibration, crowned, ground -
the proposed string theory of the posited multiverse unfound -
strings vibrate giving sound, the ground.
'In the beginning was the ...' sound. Not Word.

Then perhaps the sound of laughs, so good.
Wow – it's cold! Cold-something stood, relative-nothing warm hid!

Nothing can be very fruitful.

Nov 2017.

Our African Cook

Charlie Ndiweni he was and he had a small room with bed and shower at the back of our house on the ground's edge in the suburbs of Bulawayo (the place of killing). He was about 5 foot, wiry, trim and very strong – a quiet person with greying bubbly hair whom we trusted with our lives - emotionally that is. He cooked, served at table and house-cleaned for us for many years and we could always go to him for support and protection when our mother was being aggressive under the affluent influence of whisky 'sundowners' – a common custom in the colonies.

We moved house many times – mother having many affaires (a moustached man from Arizona who bought us cowboy chaps and gear, a man from the Canary Isles called Pav - a lieutenant in the R.A.F and a man from Reykjavik Iceland) finally marrying again a teacher from Huddersfield England. Perhaps all the world was emigrating then. My father had died age 50 from God knows what, I don't, when I was about 2 and a half years young.
It was Charlie we turned to – there was no racism in us then. Finally he retired with his many wives and small kiddies (formerly piccanninies) and my mother bought a little farm for him to settle in. Did we mourn our loss? He hadn't died!

Oct 2017.

Age

A little ole man,
a five foot high gnome,
old, with careful steps
walks alone
and stops at Aztec silver shop
for a handmade trinket
for his mate at home;
who's not with him -
is she dead perhaps?
Fully alive
he lives in hope.
Bravo -
he hasn't given up.
I now love the old.

One, I am too.

May 2016

Ageing Growing Old

The old are very prominent these days
as life is medically prolonged.
You know what -
they're the bravest most courageous of all -
the front line troops going 'over the top'
then the death pall calls, picks them off and one by one fall.

There goes one in pain – a hip joint -
for a replacement but no funds left
after the expense of others dialysis, coronary by-pass.
There another, a bewildered man, his brain cells packing up.
And another – a sad one looking longingly
at the window trinket silver shop -
his family somewhere unknown, wife dead?
Then an old lady cocking a snoop, two fingers up
being trendy dressed like the young
but not drab like they and full of colour and flare,
'sucks to you, death' implied -
living every last minute to the full inspired,
the black scythe always overhead.
All us taking just one step at a time,
careful, full of care in case we fall.
The young don't have this at all -
no need, they just live full.
'L'oreal infallible Sculpt', face cream pores clog, botox
grimace face-lifts,
colours, hair dyes, luscious lipsticks pout, eye-liners lashes
camel length,
nourishing hair with false vitamin CG (there's no such, hair is dead).
The scant clad lady walking cross-legged in the sea in J'adore –
Dior scent.

The young are terrified of growing old.
But we can be as young as we feel, now bold -
it's how we view age whose aches and creaks can be outweighed by
its gains.
Recent research on ageing has secrets being unravelled.
Growing old can be great. The old are more honest and usually tell no lies.

They are slower as they have amassed a lot of knowledge which
takes time to sift.
In brain function they resemble children more,
new neural connections and their right and left brains are more
closely linked.
For instance smells bring back old memories – they synesthize.
They care more and can be more creative as time goes by.
They are more loving, have more compassion and empathy – they
are wiser.
They have joined up thinking and are better at conflict resolution.
They are less susceptible to colds as they have experienced most
viruses past.
And they care less about what other people think.
They are more in touch with how the very young think
and feet get longer, arches flatten. We lose height.
Is this overdone? Some of us are cranky narrow threatened
closed hunched.
The emphasis is on '<u>growing</u>' old, not going to pot. And coffee is
good for us.

So we need to believe in ourselves and raise a glass. Cheers.

Jan 2017

'Amputee'

A man in shorts
with metal legs of the sort
of deep green of the military force
of some Asian stock perhaps
2 young sons
and steadied by one,
hand-held - won;
he also has a graft arm scar gap.
I intuit and catch his eye
and ask a shy
'Gurkha?' and gently point to his legs,
he nods; Himalayan Nepal;

I sign a thumbs up, a sign small withal
to his and their courage,
and smile and he nods -
'great' against all odds.

His whole family joins -
wife, mother, 2 pretty young daughters
and 2 small sons.
They all move on.
He has provided them with life
at great cost to himself foregone -
          so Dad-proud, all one

Aug 2017.

'Beauty'

A tall blonde passes
crimson lipped -
a lacey white skimped top;
skin tight black jeans -
and open knee slits to breathe.
She wobbly walks
on six inch high heels,
landing in each step
bent kneed.

The high heels don't permit
a straight leg.
Here's 'Beauty' at what price.

I am reliably informed
that highest shoes
can be eight inch max.

April 2016

Open Behind Bars Broken
(With thanks to G.M.Hopkins)

This concrete city grey-high, hard grown
ramned straight to a small soft sky square,
light cramped, columned-cut against nature,
against all - lunged against natural curves known
thrown cutting angles axis-marked, deep scored,
strained dark slanted sharp, no green, no grass at all -
proclaiming proudly puffed for more and more
money the magnificent summit of steel, the all
that struts confines restricts incarcerates despoils -
and vision is tunnelled out of touch
to this pinnacled monolith of lost truth
Under such hard thwarted growth
souls shrink shrivelled squashed,
minds bend-broken, break crushed;
hindered shrunk heart stops, stops.

Look up high, the hampered sundered sky.
Storm heaven, a blue sky shower defies purifies.
Spittling trillion rain drops cry
dazzling little diamonds of liquid sun,
skittling cowering people to shelter-scuttle run
popping umbrella mushroom handguns.

Then high voltage from out of nowhere -
a peregrine falcon falls ease-shot-sheer
plummets two hundred miles per hour,
vertiginous, free from out of nowhere
but then from a concrete overpowered tower
bursts that silhouette, quickset-shadow, jetthreat-ramjet
and behind him the air snapps shut - and smells sweet wet.
Tiny greens, daisy grass upsqueeze outgrow
between the trodden pavement-crack-feet below.
This calcified zero town - yet wild is not undone, now.
and concrete has become also, Hhis clifftop echo.

June 2016

Believing in Oneself

Queen Elizabeth I

'I have no master,
I am childless.
God give me strength to bear
this mighty frightening freedom -
I am myself'.
'And I am married to England'

Gerard Manley Hopkins

'As kingfishers catch fire ----
what I do is me: for that I came.

Hannah Hauxwell

'Whatever I am and wherever I go ...this is me'. (her Dales farm).

Best of Britain

Mahatma Gandhi - 'a nation can be judged on how it cares for its animals'

In anger I turned off the news
sick of hearing disastrous stuff -
it seems they go out of their way
to dig with relish all the bad and dark
and leaves us groomed in gloom.

I turned the car down a side path
and there was a police van
and a man looking, scanning
the road up and down -
waiting for what?
And there on the tar

a young swan
huddled and watched.
I winced.
It was 'beached',
had crashed off-course
for the reservoirs.
Then the RSPB arrived.
I wept in relief.
And two lasses
gathered the swan up
in a holding bag -
wings safe - and I joyed.
This is the Best of British -
good news.

Nov 2016

Bits and Bobs

Infinity
Eternity

Wordless
What's that,
these, nothings -
possible in the impossible.

Tiny puppy
just off breast paps -
his little legs working blurred fast
to keep up with his watchful lass.

The eye of the ego I.
A day of balm
A warm wind wafts and greets
down the petunia hung street -
refreshed loosened calm.

Sept. 2017.

Bits and Bobs

Lads hair cuts, several styles
but the cutest one is a top cut quiff -
very short back and sides, even bald shaved

with thick hair, groomed oiled on top -
just a little left and a side path part.
Like a plain cupcake
cream dollop splurge atop.

A Smart Woman

A smart woman passes, business-like
in grey-black striped jacket, tight skirt
and a shiny slung shoulder bag.
But her high heeled black shoes
clopped along rough – was it a horse?
They were too big with an inch gap
at the back between her shoe and heel.
But she bravely clenched her toes
like you do when trying to keep flip-flops on
so they unbelievably stayed on -
most of the time, apart from a hobble, wobble here and there.
All that effort to keep up with the times -
targets objectives business executive stuff
and jargon time-wasting board room speke fluff.
    Is it all of worth?

Dec.2016

A Bonny Graduate

Canterbury - full of students capped, gowned.
One made me chuckle aloud -
as she walked unsteady along
on 6 inch high heels long, all wrong
with a clicking song -
her gown billowing
had slipped down, drooping -
her just-on-hood hanging
over one shoulder nearly off;

her mortar board angle-cocked
and just off her specs-sight somewhat blocked
Dishevelled long curly hair -
one lock over her glasses and fair.

Knowledge's pursuit
does you thus - acute to boot;
gives you turmoil en route,
and makes me twinkle -
with a rekindle - Yes.
Giggle. Tingle.

Sept 2017

A Bubble Bath

I poured too much Imperial Leather bath cream
into the water and left the hot and cold running
coming back in the nick of time to stop a flooding
of frothing bubbles oozing over the edge falling.
I dug a hole in it and eased in and washed
then lay back gingerly to soak and bask.
The bubble mass quietly popped down
and left a bit of froth at my ankles and feet.
Waiting, I watched.
In colder air bubble skin pops.
If I were a dog I would hear those pops
but I'm not. Do you hear the pops?
There were two large bubbles at the edge.
I carefully observed one, one inch across
and there a little square reflected light,
the light source from the ceiling above
had travelled at 186,000 miles per second
and no more than a couple of millimeters wide
had settled on the bubble side.
But then to my utter delight
the tiny white light on the bubble
changed to green then blue-green

then briefly a red spot then back to a square clear white.
This cycle repeated itself several times.

My friends had come to say hello,
on a miniscule scale - photons and quarks -
basic building blocks of the universe
and something was making them change -
was it the rising heat of water's challenge?
I did not care. I had not noticed it before
in countless baths.
I was just so chuffed.
O what a delight
for me on earth.

May 2016

A Winter Leaf

A winter leaf from a bare-boned town tree
in frost bright white light, bristly
missed by the caterpillar street-sweeper-car's spree.
Rustbrown crackling dead delicate, earth-scent
curled veined skeleton in the light bent-spent -
no soil to enrich, dead in vein, in vain;
just dead on hard tar, no soft earth present -
again inhumane.

My soft boiling eyes – emerald tears.

Winter Buds

Camelia bushes and anywhere
fragile buds surge in below zero.
Surprised, how so? as harsh weather
spurts their presence further.
But yes, shielded in essence

by hard bracts and scales in balance.
Perhaps our hard cold lows clothe
and promote new growth
within a safe shield below -
waiting spring blossoms' warm soft glow.

Jan 2017

Butchery Lane Canterbury
Adagio

The summer morning rises up
from its sleepy dreamy bed
with wafts of brewing coffee
to be sipped unsaid,
from Cafe Turquoise with ginger jar,
window treats, sweet delights to be had;
horn gramophone, clay clock teapot displayed.
A tousled student T-shirt says
'Things To Do Today
1.Get Up. 2.Survive. 3.Go To Bed' -
the beginnings of busy days.
Now nearly nine o'clock
and here are no smells of slaughterhouse.
Outside The City Arms rennaisance
'Real Ale, Real Food, Real Pub'
a gentle breeze baffles a paper wrap
who tumbles and skips
along the street about our feet
greeting 'I too am here - pick me up' complete.
And lazy shoes cobble-clatter
on their way to work,
reluctant to be roused.
There's a gentle hum of talk
in the muffled morning walk
and a flimsy top on rounded boobs
says 'Get over it', double meant.
A van delivering stops

for fresh greens, boxed, for lunch dropped.
A Postman, steadfast, bagged work-horse,
strides trusty with weights of letter post.
And a pair of slit smiling jeans wobbly walk
on six inch high heels knees bent,
stopping a straight landing leg intent meant.
A summer lass 'PORK & CO.' on her back
bumbles past, bright floral tights
round a plump piggy rump butt -
to lusty lads as prime cuts
The meat merchants are back!
The town slowly wakes.

May 2016 .

Poetry, Oxford English Dictionary – 'literary work in which special intensity is given to the expression of feelings and ideas by the use of distinctive style and rhythm – (no mention of rhyme). In early use the word was used for creative writing in general.'
Adagio (slow, restful)Andante, allegro, largo, lente = slow variations.
Vivace, scherzo, presto - fast

A Cantonese Ivory Fan

A Cantonese Ivory fan,
over a hundred years old
and bought for £1 sold
at a car-boot sale job lot,
sound and perfect it was
then auctioned for nearly two thousand pounds
to the Chinese who value and love their past
at the other side of the wide web world.
I weep as the bidding goes up, up.
And I weep for the little old carver
who, to make, so long working - brings
this intricate beautiful, stunning thing.
He is at last rewarded well.
His bent hunched back dwells

but straightens now, in joy, uncurls;
immortal, his fan is loved well, still.
But now, please
stop slaughtering elephants
just for their regal tusks.

Oct 2016

Change

The house sat
heavy on his back -
now instead a ruc-sac.
He's free at last
to wander
and wild wonder
sizzling with spirit.
Tomorrow he'll set out
to discover
but today,
a last old day -
feet up, pipe lit and puffing
and dreaming.
Momentous – a new life,
gut amazed, frightening.

April 2017.

Celebrating the Coccolith Story. Over 250 relevant c words distilled to 130

A cliff page chapter of the crumbly chalk cliffs of coccoliths
Their cute minute stone berries are called coccospheres made by coccolithophores
Now called Blue Planet Plankton

245 million years ago they first appeared – the Cretaceous age

(but fossil forms are found in the Cambrian about 500 million years ago)
as blue-green sea bloom communities of phytoplankton chloroplast algae,
grass of the sea in high concentration seen now from space,
the top plant oxygen maker for life; causing constructing the continental shelves –
underwater handshakes from UK to Europe, connecting Britain to France
formed by these coccolithophores colonising congregating
the clearer 50 metre sea column top.
They are the calcium carbonate crystal-coat outer skeletons of chemical calcite
around a tiny cell; a capsule case cave. A single coccolith is 5 – 10 millionths of a millimetre.
Countless coats in company, 60 trillion per square metre,
sink to the deep sea-bed sediment carpet, cumulate, compress
cluster clot coagulate conglomerate
and different shapes cohere configurate
like basket, disc, bowl, horseshoe, wishbone,
or overlapping plates stacked one on top of another, in a sphere,
like sections of a football coccosphere – of placolith type.
Classified as Calyptrolith cancolith ceratolith cribrilith cyrtolith etc.
Why this enormous variety and shaped by what for what purpose -
over 100 different clever shapes, sculptures - even honeycomb, star, cap, arrowhead, football
bagel, umbrella, cube, necklace, bun, tennis-ball, starfish, mushroom, jellyfish.

Whoopee.

But they create the coast crust chalk cliffs
crucial to our planet geology and who knows, the cosmos.
And they are now in cement concrete, marble, clay china, ceramics
lime, limestone, mortar plaster putty - the basis of civilisations
and in the white, red and brown chalk paintings in caves, and 5,000 years ago;
in Egyptian pyramids of agglomerate limestone concrete made in situ.
Without them we would have no current buildings, pottery,
no giant hillside cast in a white cut pagan horse -
the earliest carved 3,000 years ago, or potent man figures,
no chalk for blackboards and teaching of and

understanding our world – Einstein teaching his equations
although we have pen and ink. No limestone underground caves.
No chalk Channel tunnel, no Blighty's sign – the White Dover cliffs.
No gymnasts hand rub to better grasp, ant-acids for soils and medicines, tailor marks for material cut, no plaster casts for broken bone care, no pool cue chalk.

Now, little coccoliths this morning cleaned your teeth in toothpaste. Hurray.

We are confounded on the question of their function -
no one knows – possibly defence against grazing zooplankton,
or infection by bacteria or viruses, or controlling buoyancy,
or releasing carbon dioxide for photosynthesis,
or to filter out harmful UV light or in deeper species,
to concentrate light for photosynthesis in chlorophyll.

Of living coccolithophores – these little gems have a strange life cycle.
A coccolithophore may have one type of coccolith or more than one coexisting;
they may move around then become settled. Sexual fusion may happen but is rarely seen
In one moving stage they have 2 wagging flagellae and between that
a flagella-like but curious curly spiral haptoneme, and in another, none.
It takes 1 hour to start constructing a coccolith and 30 hours to construct a coccosphere
and the cell sugars control the growth and shape of their calcite crystals of calcium carbonate
so they seem to be important in climate change, acting as a carbon sink.
Inside they contain 2 golden brown chloroplasts which can move
to collect optimum light for photosynthesis. Clever.

Little miracles -
they are a marvel so vital yet so lovable charming, cute.

Feb 2017

Cosy Things

Cosy things, warm things,
glowing twinkly smiley things -
these I love, above all else.
A plump labrador ushering
a blind lady to corner turn.
My sheepskin slippers neatly placed
waiting patiently for me at home
for my feet to slip in.
A blind man's white stick ball
cobble-clicking in front of his step.
A dog with a cosy jacket – winter-warm;
milk froth on top of my coffee
made like a snowman
who sinks inside the jug
when poured.
My cap down – red pom-pom atop -
unknown people give me smiles and stop;
the different-sounding shoes make on cobbles;
six layers of clothes, the shortest outside
so you can count - in some.

Comfy faces – a few rare people have
and smiley twinkly eyes
welcoming and warm to themselves
and open to the other across gaps.
They tend to be the well fed plump
with round pink cheeks. Aglow, clean, bright.
Oh – I've found a little thin lady
with pink cheeks and twinkly eyes;
and small people just like dwarfs;
and a fat lady whose legs
could hardly get passed each other
as she walked, so wide-based.

April 2016.

Waiting a CT Scan

Anaemic for a decade
my GP begs me to have it done.
I've refused tubes, afraid
evaded as a diagnostic aid -
stuck down my throat dismayed
and up my bum - an invade -
no gut symptoms have come.
So before , I have no food
for 36 hours then on -
take strong laxatives
and to sit waiting at home
near a loo all day.
It's not all this syndrome
but it drums up further fear
and the fear of fear;
having to face life threats -
possible surgery of cancer, the big C,
gut bags, chemotherapy -
slow dying with a big D.
I'm many decades old.
How do I die and from what?
Best is unknowing in sleep but
I have no control over that
and deceive my self that this is so!
We're in the hands of Fate,
meaningless life bait, an end date
as a bottomless pit to this fear
which writing fails to absolve anywhere near.

Detach. Don't fight. Let go.
See good. Breathe now - slow.
See good. Live this moment. Now.
Others have been here before. Allow anyhow

July 2017.

The CT Scan (abdomen and pelvis)

Complex – 3 notification pages for a quantum physics scan.
4 days before – for 2 days no bran
then 36 hours before – no food, only sweets and fluids
of quarter pint on the hour every hour now on.
8 am.the day before drink powerful laxative
dissolved in quarter water pint. 4 pm. Repeat. On both occasions
massive purgation and gripes – floods leaks and mess.
Instructions to be near home toilet. Washing and more.
Understatement of the year
8 pm. 50 mls. opaque contrast media in 300 mls.water.
On the scan day – 500mls fluid. Now not a person -
just a sewage outlet and water tank.

At the hospital CT/MRI scanner unit wait subdued, blank.
Instructions to take all clothes off and don
shorts with a back slit, coat back slit and covering coat
then there I am before a 7 foot high white donut - stunned
I lie down on the movable trolley to go into its hole.
Before that I have a tube stuck up my bum
to blow up the colon with carbon dioxide gas.
Joke about floating up to the ceiling above
and an intravenous cannula in my arm
for an antispasmodic and further opaque media
to show up the vascular system plan.
Allergies to iodine/opaque media and asthma unallowed.
Then the machine is turned on and buzzes -
that's my friends - accelerating electrons and photons
in the centre of the donut which circles round and round -
the bees my friends buzz. The technician is surprised I know
but sadly he doesn't know about unseen little quarks.
There's an imoji picture on the top of the donut -
electron I ask? He says it could be a photon light
but it's to show me when to breathe in and out.
In 20 minutes it's all over so I pat the donut then dress and wait.
He brings me a sandwich and biscuits and tea.
He is nice and tells me the scan is ok so I go. .
As per instructions I don't have to wait 4 hours.

Still leaking but far less and blowing out the colon gas -
I could blast off to the moon.

Food Food Food, glorious food. Sleep.
It's all over. Sighs of relief.
Next day feel light, good and better all round.
(In colonic irrigation maybe there's a point?)
I've been through purgation, purgatory to a quiet paradise.
A kind of catharsis. Now the long wait for the results – Jesus.
Haunted, black thoughts invade. Have I got the big C?
2 days later I'm informed the Scan is fine. Phew. What was all
that for?
A dying encounter bottom up! Which persists ? Is this PTSD.

July 2017

Dark Matter and Energy in the Sea Hell Deep

(with thanks to BBC's 'Blue Planet'). (Apologies for inaccuracies)
If you want your mind bent and opened and strangely glued and appalled then see this!

Miles below the surface of the sea
where no sun is
so our Blue Planet is black
the dark matter there is unseen
as in the outer universe.
But here new findings show it's there,
the Deep is our planet's largest living space
revealing itself as unknown creatures
who communicate by light flash and cannibalize
and many are transparent jelly ghosts with inside eyes.
One creature can clone itself - so strives
and everlasting forever lives.
The sea floor mud covers half our planet 1 mile deep
and sea dark makes up half the same and in twilight sleep
yet there is more unimaginable alien life, and life,
astounding, than on earth above and its known life.
So much of it depends on a sudden light flash

to communicate and to defend; a light screen – an octopus squirts,
spurts luminescent fluid to hide unhurt from predators alert.

Its a hell, gruesome life bent on devouring and sex crossed -
there's no love and compassion here just surviving at áll cost.
It's a grim underworld and in the abyss, utterly dark -
one meal can last a year for a strange sixgill shark;
even dead bones are food and here's
corals that can live for 4,000 years.
Some scabbard fish only upright swim, exist.
Cracks in the sea bed go to the centre of the earth and tear
in violent flare.There are enormous pressures down there
yet seapigs, fragile translucent fish, seatoads live 6 miles down
under pressure equivalent to a 50 jumbo-jet stack crown.
On the ocean floor, the abyssal plain, tectonic torn, pumps
high stacks that boil and one fish walks on transformed fin stumps
and strong salt brine thick sludge kills any life there
which on contact convulses burns and twists. Elsewhere
methane gas exudes in bubble torrent bursts –
riddled with decaying matter slum sludge ooze;
this where hydrocarbon life started 4 billion years ago.
So we perhaps have the remnants of all this base gross
in our DNA and unconscious flow – ancient, aglow deep below?

Astrophysicists take note and learn.
More is being known of the dark sea depths,
twilight zone than that of the dark outer universe.
What is appealing is that light flash, large eyes inside jelly or
prominent on tubes
even at this prime-evil, primaeval stage – the plea 'and let there be
light' is!
I wonder at a Creator who dreamed up all this mystery and marvel -
amazing terrifying horror dread grim awe, also beautiful.

Nov 2017

Dog Trots

A little white Shih-tzu dog along plumps -
compact woolly, legs like stump logs -
no demarcation of elbow and wrist
likewise the knees at the back -
and trained to trot in this town street
next his owners legs and feet discrete
in a jungle of the crowd
of leg tree stumps.
He has to weave in and out
never looking up
in this maze of flesh woods
all around.
A dog must wonder, drawn
to 'what the hell's going on
and where are we going
and for what reason'
in this sunny spring season
along.

Some dogs wag their tails
side to side, some even in circles round
and some in time with their gait
some as if beating drums on either side
and some with tail flops straight down
also in time with their gait
and the co-ordination required is great.
I wonder what muscles are there involved.
Some don't wag at all -
their tails hanging limp beside -
which takes the least effort around;
some, tails between legs, hide
or just tail-tips wagging limp down.
Unhappy or relaxing, just tired?
are their owners less loving as guides
implied?

Apr 2017

Face with a Cold

Some peoples' faces are all squeezed together -
that is the eyes, nose and mouth - the threesome star
as that is how we read recognise another
not the surrounds which are
the cheeks chin forehead and line of hair.
One slim small lady's squeezed centre face
was covered in a very large spectacle space
emphasising the threesome even more
as did her red cold nose and chubby bubble cheeks.
What fun to the fore she wore!

Unique.

Nov.2017

Fatness

How do people become
so gigantically fat?
In ladies it all goes
to their boobs and bums;
in men, to their tums up front -
significantly
altering gravity
and gait somewhat.

May 2016

Fashion

Big woolly rainbow pom-poms
on the tops of shiny high heel shoes.
Lace is back, a must, around jean bottoms
and shorts; and there's lacy tops -
not real lace to see, of course

Long brown hair suddenly turns
to bright blond at the tips,
blending nicely, splayed over
a lime green top at the back.

Now back-pack ruc-sacs
are being worn on the front
and cradled like a new born babe.
So now you can easily get at your stuff inside.

A lovely podgy Afro woman,
black and in black and grey gear,
arm in arm with her white mate.
She jauntily wore a black woollen cap
with 'SELFIE' emblazoned in silver,
a new word not yet in the OED.
She didn't need a mobile stalk.

A woman dashes out
from the Aztec silver shop,
clutching a little parcel bag
for a silver trinket she'd bought.
Her trainers were worn,
her toes almost through;
her dress skimpy -
it wasn't hot but cold.
But there was a toss of her head.
Yes – a trinket treat or present
instead of new shoes
and from me, a warm – why not
and my low mood was put in its place.
A carrier bags says
there are 'good things inside'
which reminds me – and in me too.

Today the economy is down
as there are a lot of worn dirty shoes
and tousled heads just got out of beds.

She stoops and kisses on the nose
her summer shorn splay-footed Shih-tzu dog
then straight away kisses her man on his lips.

Sept. 2016

FIRE
No More
Tower block 'Inferno'

I can't take more - now
cancerous invading -
three tragedies in a row;
Manchester bombing,
London bridge stabbings,
now London tower block burning.
Awful, awful, awful beyond words -
blood burns and the fire of hell hurls,
worlds swirl whirl.
I shut my ears and eyes blur
yet folks rally round and aid -
heroes emerge - firefighters
daring raging flames afraid -
all give regardless of place weighed,
religion's case swayed,
colour race grade or shade,
or creed prayed.
News is never balanced with good
so I change channels and search
and find the delightful amid a nice piece
of 'Secrets of the Zoo' - lost
amongst murder, sci-fi, serial killers, police,
community breakdown at any cost,
competitions, prisons, the obese, the holocaust.
Even nature documentaries
are about struggles to survive -
killing, predation, devouring alive -
the strong on the weak – the worst.

I curse the god for this 'divine comedy' outburst
an unholy disorganised mess.
gone so terribly wrong – the distress
of hopes loves dreams deprived, lives
all charred in melting pot graves
        Yet -
from the black carcass body burnt
will phoenix rise the 'inferno' immersed
to 'paradise'? Burst.

And now another arsenal -
a terrible forest fire in Portugal
and a van rundown on Ramadan Muslims
outside a London mosque.
All this in a short time space.
        Enough.

June 2017.

Dante's 'The Divine Comedy – Inferno, Purgatorio, Paradiso.'

Foreign Foods in a Food Hall Canterbury. (over 170 of them)
Why oh why don't they have dictionaries on the walls there to
describe these foods;
e.g ? are chickpeas peas from chicks,
jerk chicken – chicken that has been jerked about,
jumping jack beans;
does salsa dance and
does emperor Caesar lead the salad?
is antipasti totally against pasti?
Where are the countries from where food names are from?

There are so many names for different curries, rices, lentils, sauces, pastas – what are their tastes? What's the difference. I even doubt if I have got spellings right from scribbled lists – taking me many hours to list. Different dates, even different haggis, different olives, venison, dips, pizzas – there's even a demerara sugar salt smoked bacon.

Feta, harissa, felafel. malagueta, pulled meets (?pulled through a hedge backwards), New York deli,
focaccia, ciabata, bloomer (is the bread blooming or is it being sworn at), wasabi beans, dirty fries (? mud on them), ricotta, halloumi, frites, edamame, beef wellington (Wellington's boots?). Mud pie yoghurts.

Quinoa, cajun, chipotle, manchego, jalapeno, amarillo. Terryaki, nacho, tortillo, taco, posh dog (? a sauce made from poodles), pitta, pretzels, chimichurri, pina colada, maroona (is it marooned?), creole, kalamata, tapenade, stiratini florentines,
ciraldine dorotea, cacaosuyo fajita,, enchelada, mauka, granola, passata, periperi, rogan josh, tofu, tarilli, argan.

Goujons, celeriac (not like celery), chard, spatchies, tenders, eton (a high class schoolboy) mess, sunken (not risen) cheesecake, parma-cotta, compote, amontillado, sundae, kalamota, pimento, piripiri, tapas, salami, coqamuin, chorizo, ingliabella (beautiful english),
carbonara, jambalaya, ragu, arrabbiata (arab), peperonata, mornay, chili con carne, empanadas, majo, alioli, galangal, satay, dimsum, wantons, charsin dahl, prosciutto, porchetta, pilau, pancetto,
kabanas, banoffee, pavlova, roulade, beer battered (battered with beer!).

I now understand that Quinoa is rich in protein and is from Peru where the locals had it as a staple diet. Now it has become so popular in the West that it's now cultivated primarily for export and that the locals are become malnourished as a result. I look at the foods on the food hall shelves and feel amazed and guilty at such extravagant choices available. If a tomato has been dropped on the floor by a careless shopper, I gently pick it up and put it back with its friends.
Food sacrifices itself to feed us.

Medallions of pork and bacon (they're round medals), panpiettas, chipolattas, lardoris, spatchcocks, flatties, posh puppies, sliders, blinis, terrines, gruidlox, bucatini, fettuccine, tagliatelle, penne, fusilli, girasoli, linguine, proseco, cannelloni, peppardelle, frittatas, empanadas, alforno, primacara, lightly dusted (with a feather duster)!, tzatziki.

I have found a ‘sweet and buttery olive’ which is neither but at least it's not salty.

Most mixed foods are so highly herbed you can't taste them e.g prawns under lemon. At least I have found 'chicken provençal' which is good.

Aug 2016

Catching the Air. Gliding in a Sailplane. A First
Falling upwards – glider falls by gravity against stronger
rising thermals
like trying to go down a rising escalator!

From the recent CT scan-hell I am hurled to Life,
thrust propelled launched slung flung
into the Sky – such a little word but so full
a joystick near my legs to give me such joy
nestled close like a little egg inside its big mum -
my safe cockpit nest.
There's the Windsock. It is an airfield.
I felt the presence of WWII pilots around!

Briefing before, some theory, controls, safety, rules of the 'road',
plane body, dials then off to meet the bird
resting one wing on the ground the other up,
great length of wing but very slim, sleek-styled.
Parachute strapped on with 3 locks, and in case – a sudden
release bar;
4 seat strap belts, many dials and knobs,
speed about 80 mph, aertow height 2,000feet when up
No engine, rising air-dependant, the force -
like Andean condors soar. My instructor behind and
towed by a control-wobbling engined plane,
an abrupt pull then bumping across the field.
Take off into wind then rapid release of the umbilical rope.
You can also go up from a heavy vehicle by winch launch
at the other end of the field – a quick remarkable ascent
but only to 1,000 feet – cable shot, release like a catapult. I am told.
We rose up with lift off. Thrilled, as if on a racehorse I crouched.
Up and extreme wordless exhilate glorious and shout arms up
then sudden silence from the roar of wind on wings behind the plane.

Borne-up. Released. Born. We graceful soar.
There we are. A silent heaven. Breathless. Enthralled.
Now circling and I disorient. There the club house, Challock village, green forests everywhere, neat fields, Canterbury cathedral, Ashford, Whitstable, Isle of Sheppey, English Channel, French coast (they also have White cliffs – we were once joined), South Downs hills (good lift) in a circle tight
Rising air can come from hill tops and dips in the land, ripples in air and thermals
anywhere where hot air rises. Best indicator are cumulus clouds - flat bottomed cotton-wool ones the best.

I was given control – joystick by tail elevator forward/back for down/up;
bank left/right stick left/right - aileron control. Position crucial guaged by her nose.
Bank, centre, up correction, - she likes going down. 360 degree circle twice.
I am praised a bit. The joystick is so sensitive – slight moves best.
Come back to land into wind – airbrakes rise on her wing tops.
Bump to earth. Many fast bumps – I laugh. Stop, one wing rests on ground.
The cockpit roof lifts up, people unleash me from all the straps.
I hard-heave myself out, bum then 2 legs – a tight squeeze.
In karate days my arm muscles strong now disuse of weak age.
I kiss my plane on the nose, hug the organiser, handshake instructor warm.
Oh ----- glory grandeur grace, honour great.

July 2017

God and his Kenosis. (his self-emptying/altruism)
Kenotic theology

Apparently this is to explain suffering; he laid down his omnipotence to create creatures of free will to have a say in their nature to evolve and this entails suffering, the catalyst for evolution, as he desired their free choice to love him or not.

That is not true altruism which expects no reward – like a goal to be loved for himself in return. Was he lonely?

You witness gross suffering of neglected abused animals, unbearable and you turn your eyes away. The only thing left good of them is their soft deep suffering eyes in their emaciation bones and dirt.
I shout out to god - ‘what the hell are you doing about this. You just sit on your witheld omnipotent backside watching and don't lift a finger. Just waiting on us imperfect creatures you made to do it all.

Process theology says its impossible for him to give up his omnipotence in self emptying as that means he has omnipotence possibility retained – still retaining the potential for omnipotence. Their thesis is he never had omnipotence in the first place – a metaphysical impossibility for creatures with free will.
Free will is over-rated. There's genetic and biological mechanism determinism.

Dec.2017

Hacked

Snug on the sofa -
laptop atop my lap,
where else!
Playing all the bright icons
desktop
and doing Freecell solitaire
and Googling quarks,
often following NASA's Universe.

Suddenly an urgent message
from nowhere pops out;
I forget the warning length
but contaminated I am now
and to phone this number
and not to turn off, get out
or I could lose all I have.

So I phone and immediate get
a London Indian
of Windows Professional help -
my heart racing,
my brain roaring in focussed fear.
He connects to my computer over space
and for three hours on the phone
I watch him plunge
to its inner cauldron depths -
where all is black and
white word lines flash.
A list of 602 times hacked
out of 19,000 connects
in over 5 months
by a hacker in Atlanta Georgia
U.S.A.
My standard Microsoft and Windows
protection has been by-passed.

Dumbfounded at what lies
in a computers brain and heart -
as if going
to the centre of the earth, dark.
He smashes the hacker
and installs four icons,
new ID and password contact
to him and him alone,
no one else.
A superprotect
at great cost.

I struggled with his accent
but he's brilliant my god.
And next day, a red alert -
a new Malware detect
but my new icons smash
in a flash.

I am not to touch these icons

but daily check and upgrade -
so my PC runs slower – so what!
I feel safer having been
on a whirled journey
inside and round the universe.
I don't bank and buy on the Internet,
never had for years,
always aware of viruses and bugs
but never hackers - now hacked off.

April 2016

Was it 'cos
NASA me suspects?

Honoring Hannah Hauxwell of Low Birk Hatt Farm, Baldersdale
a poet said 'as kingfishers catch fire'... 'what I do is me: for that I came'

Howling blizzards, thigh deep snow -
too long a winter for this lonely daughter of the Dales -
isolated, working a remote farm for 60 years, in the North Yorkshire Pennines;
blood inbuilt to stand firm after her parents, relations died
having farmed for generations – a solitary survivor, the only child.
Extreme poverty, life stripped back to bare essentials and even worse -
no electricity, no running water. Water for her cows
collected in buckets and for herself, breaking thick ice
on the stream below; often repairing dry stone walls,
wearing rags iced over, mended, patched often and again;
an old army coat lasting 40 years over her dead uncle's kegs*
and gumboots.
Speaking to no-one around for near 3 weeks
yet her words poetry, music, ancient. Animals her family, friends -
hauling large bales of fodder on a sledge or on her back
to feed her beloved 'beasties', Rosa her old cow.
If water froze solid she'd milk Rosa for thirst
and sleep in the warmer barn against Rosa's side

who was 'served' yearly to produce a calf, driven to the market by a neighbor
as women were not then allowed there to barter and sell;
sold for around £250 - a years income, at £5 a week for food, fuel.
Old tins, boxes, bags never trashed,'yan never knows' - she hoarded all.

Yet rich in her indomitable spirit, tranquil acceptance,
translucent innocence, sheer wisdom serene, broad shouldered, white-haired.
Her love of animals, love of her farm, it's beauty stark.
'At night the moon plays on Hunder beck and to me, the waters sing a song' -
the memory of this is eternal, hers and herself; the two are one.
No fertilizers, pesticides used on her land;
a meadow has been taken over by a Wildlife Trust, an SSSI now -
for its original grasses, flowers – 'Hannah's Meadow' it's called -
rare species which have been there since the Ice Age.
She puts perspective on our paltry complaints -
changes our entire relation - profoundly moving, impossible to pin down.
A passing rambler met her and told Yorkshire TV,
documentaries were made, she became internationally famed -
as people were so deeply moved, drawn.
Eventually drained-spent by unending hard toil,
with much reluctance selling her farm, white and in tears, cradling her little dog,
settling in a Cotherstone terraced cottage nearby
with bath, tap-running water delight, radio, heating and light.
Worldwide funds helped her to travel Europe, the States – a long desire.

There is no doubt where the heart of Hannah lies -
'Whatever I am and wherever I go ...this is me'. 'Nowt else. Who be thee?'

August 2016

*kegs in N.Yorkshire are trousers

Head on
To death

An insurmountable task
Ageing – bits fall off
eyes ears balance strength
memory sleep feet chest.

Face it – look him in the eyes,
skull holes but a bone toothless smile
my centre ground has gone
it's dying not yet dead.

Free up imprisoned imagination,
give it a say instead of it ghosting around
inside your head, surfacing often unwanted.
So imagine I get cancer or a stroke
they want to keep me alive
surgery chemo/radiotherapy
medical gear attached fails
palliative 'care' now on.
Paralysed at home can't move much.
Would fear much the 'locked in syndrome'.
No one else 'cares'.
Can't eat, mess bed – lie in the stink.
Squalor degradation desolate alone.

Trust has gone. Belief gone in folks
relief through the agony to die at last
be dead. The bubble has popped.
There – it is done.
Let God be God who doesn't exist
but who Insists, who Calls
who himself has died
and who therefore knows ours.

Maybe out there in the real world
people might care and are 'good'.
The future is unknown.

It's Now, now, now -
that little word 'Now' – a world.
The sun shines.

July 2017.

The Honey Pot
No. 10 Butchery Lane

Old ladies
and kiddies
always go after -
lured, inspired, stirred
by cakes and sweeties
in the shop window
show front -
drawn like bees-ies
to a honey pot treasure hunt;
their glowing face-ies
and smiling mouths
quiet murmuring songs
        of 'Ooommm'
or something that has a word tang
        to go along.

July 2017.

Hot Air Rises
hearing the poetry of John Donne

Having, with aids, poor hearing,
I sit on a hard high chair, undeterred,
stirred and intently listening;
low soft sofas for others heard.
The warm breath air of words
rises for me to catch them assured, like rising birds,
or like many rainbow bubbles of soap stirred
with a lot of background clatter and popping
        I've tested it out -

it's true, it really is – calming.
Sitting low, words are lost
and I can't catch them rising
from a low seat at any cost tossed
in the cold air which is denser
and weighs more so sinks -
their molecules huddle together
as if for a warm wink
which doesn't come -
there in the cold low-zone weather.

Mar 2017.

I am

'I am that I am' – says God
so me too is me
and that is to welcome myself -
come well, reunite insight;
bright, lightsome, light.
To welcome all – invite
anger, irritation,
annoyance, hate and hurt -
as guests who can teach
and who allow me
to say 'shut up' -
under my breath.

April 2016.

Images

Then I was, now I am.
Sigh. I am letting down
my bucket in the well
and drawing up air.

Maybe, apart from water,
there is a fish
or frog there
somewhere
I don't know -
wait and see;
don't spill,
lift slow.

I do know I'm decrepit old
with few years left,
digging rich peat
finding a mummified corpse.
Blasted by images
too rich and mixed;
a kaleidoscopic blur -
image unresolved -
so empty the bucket out
now. Fast

No – I'll be dust for the stars.
Stardust.

April 2016

Little Things

'Sufficient unto the day'
are the little things thereof
and for all days in love resolved.
No grand thoughts,
fantastic images, symbols, myths.
No more amazing sights, smells, sounds
which frenzied hide
the significant small
but they,winking, find me, 'I'm here'
under the rubble of them all -
a little plant, there are no weeds,

surviving concrete pavement cracks
        and rock walls

Accept it – dying comes and goes.
Dust, rubble makes glinting stars
in the black night sky above.

April 2016.

Manchester Suicide Bomb

What meant most - fore-
cutting to the core
was a shot of a mother
whose 8 year old daughter
had been murdered
with 21 others unheard
and many injured
in that horrific slaughter -
triggered bewildered -
of young innocents incurred.
A little tubby woman intervenes
in floral blouse and blue jeans,
alone hunched and crying
then contained, held by many arms
so utterly distraught in pain
and so utterly vulnerable, harmed.
I gasped and sobbed;
why this robbed and why
an innocent pop concert
to a mass massacre cry.
Mass compassion defies.

June 2017

March

March is marching fast.
In it, it has an r -
doesn't that signify something?
I've forgotten what so far, past.
O yes, you're allowed to eat shellfish
plenty of oyster, mussel dishes, clams
all the way from their programme
of September through April
but to stop in May's timetable.
It can be stormy like the god of war Mars,
March now stars, healing winter scars -
breaking it's shell into spring.
The first day of spring sprung.
Daffies and narcissi thrust
and the Sun's beginning to peek out past
those dark looming clouds.
It's not the black dark death purple of lent.
It's bursting out of its socks and buds are rent,
wanting to explode in growth.
It's not dying, not death, not death
but new life and life coming -
the son of man - us becoming, humming.

March 2017

Substance Soul

Let your body be -
you can never be dispossessed
of its riches intricacies miseries
as you grow old; see -
that's your substance soil and toil.
It can reveal it's depth essence soul
if you open your inner eyes, whole.
Most of us are closed off so
then groan at lack, low -
the past long ago.

Jan 2017

Metaphysics

With thanks to 'The Work of Love' ed. John Polkinghorne

Usually we are masqued defending, protecting masked.
And some do very well thank you very much;
some struggle but just manage and I feel a fondness
and wonder if a Creator cares at all in solace kindness oneness
but shared then in his care, wondering astonished at that.
Some suffering people are more Christ than christ is – at -
their pain goes on long, not 3 days short.
And some don't manage at all and maybe sometime that was us.
Or maybe they are something of christ-god! - plus
or maybe they just are, just, and that right.
You just takes your changing choice to discuss in delight.

Yet now urgent. Suffering whether of extreme torture pain
is also and together of mind and heart;
profound psychosis of disintegration
or the weight of a broken heart. Now I see maybe the Cross had all -
bearing the entire suffering of the weight of the world - indeed
the universe.
Babies need 'all-knowing' 'powerful' parents in control;
they then grow into mutual relationship without power
so our adult 'belief' 'faith' likewise has grown
as God in his emptying 'kenosis'
of his omniscience omnipotence and power
wanted all creation to take root -
room to be itself and form itself – like parents of their children -
does love want puppets or relationship?
with of course deviations, mistakes as we are not God -
to learn from and change, progress and develop. Evolve.
And thus God suffers with every creature –
and changes too, even dies if it was God incarnate who died on
the cross
as he cares and waits and patiently hopes.
Only patience gives and forms time; violence doesn't.
(from latin patientia suffering – as it hopes).
Out of primary suffering can come secondary
so called judgemental 'sin' of mistaken turning routes.

Yet violence exists – the Big Bang of the origin of the
universe. Volcanoes
or the violence of lions at the kill. Violence essential to survival
and birth.
Essential to grabbing a child from the front of a coming car or
near fire.
So – what now?
I learn from post-modern – an evolution of classical establishment
theology -
that 'suffering must arise from God, it must do so, not as intended
by God but as necessarily implied with the sort of universe he has
created ...' and 'evil arises from the divine nature that can ultimately
be overcome by goodness' - the Satan/God split dichotomy has
resolved. A parent seen as witholding becomes Satanic in his child's
screaming of fear and rage. That parent was once omnipotently good.
And if Christ was god incarnate we'd have no hope as he was not
truly one of us
'Jesus had the form of god by being a perfect image of God' as
a person
so Christ is not God incarnate but a perfect image of God.

Nov.2017

More Clothes

A very old man walked so carefully
his loose clothes hardly moved at all
as he'd shrunk so much from before -
small withal overall
He seemed to be apologising to them
for moving and being alive interim.

Women are wearing long slinky tight frocks
with various long slits sides or fronts.
Usually with such material, thin, scant
you see the outline of their underneath pants.
I've now seen several where I swear no pants were worn.
In the streets it's called going 'commando' with scorn

so no bum-pant outline there shows -
just for their mate - all strokey smooth, aglow.

Sept.2016.

Muscles

A six foot man, his handsome amazon wife
and pram-pushed kid, pass.
He, so muscle pumped up, encased;
his neck bigger than his bald shiny head,
neck skin thick, bulging creased
all this excess testosterone, perhaps.
He walks splayed legged so muscle full -
his thighs are wide, they're pushed apart.

And so content they all are. Relaxed.
And dad's the one to gently push.

June 2016

The Brain

'And the brain locked...'
No the brain is free -
it's we who lock it in
with chains, dead bones and bolts.
But it's beautiful and free
and ordered in its spontaneity.
A complex jelly outside the skull
it's nest.
I'm now loving my brain best
and asking it, she and he as one,
what it would like this moment, now.
A sigh out released – it says
'a writing rest', 'phew' -
'at last' and 'thanks'.

April 2016.

My Heart

What my heart is like...
Well, it feeds my all, every cell -
faithful and loyal.
Hard working at seventy beats a minute,
a hundred thousand times a day,
thirty six million times a year – that is
under conditions of rest.
The trust pulse of my life. Trust.
If it stops, I stop, dead.
But love survives, ahead?

April 2016.

My List of Attitudes for Health

Simple. Yes. Let go.
Detach. Drop. Trust.
The now – say hello.
Allow. It's ok. Soften.
Give up control.
Vulnerability is ok.
I am. Less is more.
Let it be. Give.
Space to be.
Thought isn't facts -
Breathe -
softening uncertainty.
The only certainty is uncertainty.
Not judging. Patience.
No need to be happy.
A beginner presence -
Accept. The essence.

Dec.2017

My Mundane Tooth – A Current Preoccupation

Preoccupation is usually about worrying stuff and this keeps us mulling over it. I don't preoccupy with the good – it just comes to mind in intermittent memory. image and flash. Most older folk do worry about entropy, dying and 'the Box' but it's rarely mentioned, just shoved in a cupboard with a door bolt locked. So I'll veer off from that to this in a fast shot!

After some months of things going wrong – house roof leaking after the flat garage roof crumbled and it and its door fixed, the old printer failing and having to get a new one, the grass mower packing up, lights fusing 'cos the kitchen bulb pops, the water fountain causing the fridge to cease, a large wall picture suddenly crashing down and smashing the wall plugs below, carpet moths eating my Afghan carpets for Rentokil to squirt them dead twice with total furniture upheaval access, a CT scan to successfully rule out cancer at total disorder, clamour to my con<u>tent</u>, <u>con</u>tent and guts, and to crown it all - a bad tooth ache, pain like a boring, burrowing - so to dentist and bad prognosis and wrong antibiotic prescribed - so to GP to get the correct one at last. Then scooter breakdown. Shite.

Now exhausted and before you're bored and groan - Bed escape – Still - Sleep and sleep - Food slops – Wait - Dreaming of Nothing – lovely and great. Glorious. Yay – the pain has gone. And things are now all fixed. So I'm sure this rings bells as with most of us 'it never rains but it pours'. Perhaps too much bad somethings makes nothings and good nothing becomes something hopefully good – the eternal cycles - as we tend to be creatures of hope.

The energy of hope, like gravitational force, keeps the world going round on a tightrope in scope! Nice bit of metaphysics this I hope!

The current fashion of jeans' knee-slit open tear holes. 'Isn't it cold there' I ask but fashion might be more important than comfort, I muse, as no-one says no or yes.

And have you noticed what peoples fingers do when they've got gloves on? Some fingers seem to want to escape or snuggle down. Her jellied double chin wobbled with each step footfall on top of a plump tum so no more sweety cakes now as the sweetmeats in the tea shop tempted her in. And how they have their mobiles in, to and on hand – their always present best friend to keep some command.

Where am I going? Just some somethings mumbling on. Full stop – and ...

If you want to observe – just look! Let nothing have a say, so I now 'shut up and close this book'. Amen.
My favourite word is simple – persons.

Dec.2017

My Tree

A magnolia and one of the most primitive trees,
along with the ginkgo and monkey puzzle,
has grown 3 times its original height, now 30 foot
and it houses bird feeders for blue tits,
occasional ravenous starlings, a red spotted woodpecker
hanging on the nut feeder, tail anchor under flexed
and green ones too, an occasional blue jay and
flocks of long tailed tits and a few great tits.
It provides two nests for collared doves.
And chaffinches hoover up the nut bits falling from above
also three pot-plump waddling wood pigeons
slowly waddle for the crumbs on the grass ground.
Nuisance grey squirrels have given up getting at nuts.
I've won.
Robins are now learning to copy at the hanging feeders
though unused to dangling down
and on New Years day two chaffinches have at last done it. Hurray.
Evolution under my nose – needs must.

This tree is to me a pain in the neck
shedding its thousands of pink flowers
then hoards of seed pods with red berries
then billions of 5 inch diameter thick leaves.
I spend my life raking all this up – in winter 7 times or more
the leaves are the worst -
they keep falling and are slippy to walk on.
I had it pruned but now it just grows higher than broader

in defiance.
I have grown to hate it.
Get rid of it now.

This morning, leaves all cleared, work done I looked at it
from the kitchen window. It was ghost like, stark bare,
in the winter mist, gradually becoming aware
that I was growing to love it, not only the birds.
A skeleton tree with two old nests reaching for the stars.

It gives me oxygen, takes up my carbon dioxide,
I can hang a hammock from it, it gives me shade
and work exercise throughout the year
and 2 weeks of glorious pink white petals, large.

For the first time it has been valued in 15 years
and I said gently 'I love you' - - -
but for how long.
I love it when the tree is in winter rest best.

Jan 2017

Natural History Museum London

A cathedral to life's beginnings
and survival of the fittest
where Darwin is worshipped -
an easy reclining eight foot marble statue
greeting you as you rise with the easy stairs.
Where fear and struggle are the catalysts
and if you don't have these
you don't survive change -
like the dodo and the near extinction
of the kakapo owl parrot, fearless,
large, delightfully stupid who is near wingless
and now can't escape introduced stoats.
The world is an amazing place

of change upon change upon change.
Yet the dragonfly has the most developed eyes
covering his whole head to predators detect
but his brain is undeveloped
to sense all what his eyes tell, say.
What's gone so right and so wrong here?

When I enter the hall of this sacred place
with its enormous dinosaur skeleton in the dark
I feel at home and in awe at last!
not alien as in religious cathedrals, churches flat.
But in the street outside
the learning disabled are pushed in wheel chairs
to survive and early die without descendents.

It's all about survival of the physical and mentally fit.
Where's the emotional and spiritual element, evidence?
None at all is provided there.
'Spiritual' evolution of birth control,
a must and yes; at least I've done that!
and the necessity of compassionate balance
in this overpopulate earth.

At our rate of mental evolution
all work will be done by robots -
all will be unemployed except computer geeks, engineers;
so wars will increase and the 'fittest' will die,.
Survival of the 'fittest' ends in death -
gruesome or otherwise as it usually does
and something else takes its place.
And it's called 'Reality' harsh, relentless
which is what is and the why unknown, regardless.
There must be a better spread, concern for our planets health
and concern for number-limit persons must evolve, develop
in balance.

Aug. 2016

New fresh Thoughts

Dying is being going into Being-Itself.
Faith is a venturing courage to be. Paul Tillich.

The world is sacrament.
Being doesn't exist but calls/insists. John D. Caputo

Smile at me .....as I smile at you
I love you and am smiling at you. Caputo – modified as ...
Prayer of (God) to Caputo
and Caputo to (God).

Newborn

It's summer and the temp is high -
a young couple pass by
wearing crushed shirts, flip-flops, shorts
and a slight breeze lightly cavorts.
Dad is carrying on his front
in a shoulder sling – deep asleep, sound
a baby, tiny, new born just born
like mammas carry in the African continent:
unbelievably sweet, small -
such a delight over all for all.
Mum is now gloriously free
and walking light on top of the air
after nine months extra load born.
What growth is surging on in there
under closed eyes at such a life's new dawn?

God – we waste words in monotonous floods
or scattered, 'broadcast' like a sower of old;
how many seeds will grow?; the soil is dry and poor;
the seeds dead, old.

But here is wordless bursting life, so full and bold.

Aug. 2016

The Lord Oak

He, for it is he, is massive strong with a stumpy fat solid trunk the width of 4 large hugging people's trunks – then his vast branches shoot out to the skies to catch eternity. I cannot word him in delicate gentle exquisite detail. He is all robust strength and pride, impressive thrusting. An immense colossus grand mighty towering. He has 10 tons of wood. 'I am King here' he says in deep bass booming 'and in my arms I have a whole nation of creatures - life living off my life'.
He fills my window even from far off and now it is his season of dying his leaves – masses of them swirling off in the winds to feed the soil below in all its life; lovely autumn changing colours, the physiology of which is more pleasing than the aesthetics. You can even put a stethoscope to his trunk to hear his sap rising in faint bubbly gurglings. And in the low evening sun the dappled light of him catches your breath. And his cute acorns drop in their little green cups so beautifully made. But he also annoys – I have to rake up his millions of leaves often off my sloping drive as under frost or snow I slip and skid. (actually 1 oak makes 700,000 leaves)
But he gives me oxygen enough for a year as I give him carbon dioxide! (actually he uses it in photosynthesis to make his food) - so he depollutes our air. His wood the great stuff of the great galleons of old and he survived the horrendous hurricane of 1987 with cyclone winds of 130mph; and he doesn't need gardening at all. He bends for nothing and no-one.

<u>Notes.</u> BBC 4 Dr. George McGavin 'Oak Tree'
Oak from O.E 'ac'.
6000 oaks in HMS Victory – winning the battle of Trafalgar
800 year old Salisbury Cathedral made of oak – tallest spire in Britain.
Oak gall permanent ink used for all document writing for 1400years e.g Shakespeare, Mozart, Bach etc.writings.
He can outsmart caterpillars from eating his leaves in then making unpalatable bitter tannins.
Warming bark and antifreeze sugars allow his life in freezing conditions. His best underground friends are his root fungi whose threads bore into rock for phosphates and other elements. His roots spread 30 metres and if laid end to end would be 5 miles long. And his fungal threads if laid end to end would encircle the world.

The oldest oak is at Bowthorpe Lincolnshire and is over 1,000 years old. He is completely hollow (a rumour that 39 people have squeezed inside) – his heart eaten out by fungi yet he still lives.

And there's much more. He really is a living responding being to whom we need to bow to with our arm boughs too!

Oct 2017

Overlooked

A family of four,
two young kids -
ruc-sacked the lot;
the littlest one
has a toy duck
clutched
but she spots
the bull head
in Butchery lane
atop a shop.
She pulls back, stops,
points, calls out
for the others to watch
but she's dragged on
in her mother's hand
with no complaint thereon;
Mother looks down -
no interest at all -
no fun, none
'Look see' delight shunned.

This deeply, I recognise.
People wanting me to see their stuff
and not join me in mine.
The fabric can tear of space-time.

May 2016

Stopped in my Tracks

Petunias in the crack
outside the HSBC bank
in the wall
behind the fruit stall.
7 blooms from 1 plant, small
and of lavender blue
or light purplepink hue.
It has survived the dry heat
of 30 degrees, complete
in the street discrete
squeezed in the crack
of hot concrete set back,
        desolate
yet thrives so delicate.

Hundreds of business
and busyness feet pass
blind, crass en masse.

O – the posy is love-ly
she's so sweet, fragile, comely.

I took a mug of water
and poured it down the wall -
a thirsty drink for her.
And no-one saw at all.

July 2017

Poetry

Poetry is not a code
though often you'd
think it was.
But a condensate of notes

simply said with
stark breath intake
from a brilliant eye.

Though not a cure
it is a lifeline
giving creativity -
a blow hole.
Though most would not think so.
It is - vital to life.

April 2016

Polly

Polly is dead. I'm stunned sad;
a fourteen human-year old Border Collie
who ignored sheep on his Lakeland holiday breaks.
Despite her 104 dog years
she barked and bounced
around my neighbours house
as lively as a young pup.
But most importantly
would dash out to greet me when I arrived.
And jumped up as if to give me a hug.
At no time have I felt as welcome
even if it was only to lap up
the rest of my sugared tea cup.
Her owners must feel so empty now -
from her, split up.

I'll remember. And wonder. And love ...

Poppy, the Book, Simon

Next day, low, I coffeed at a town street pub

absorbed in an amazing kids book -
a story of an osprey and the children who cared -
the most amazing wholifying holy book
with no religious language at all;
I lived in it with no glance for the outside around
and wept and joyed.
Then young Poppy rushed down the street
and threw herself at me with a hug
then little Harry then their Mum and Dad -
my adoptive family – all hugs.
Polly, in Poppy, lived on – glorious and now.
Then Simon, the pub man behind the bar,
so welcoming, friendly again -
smiling - I was indeed rich gained,
here below and above.

Oct 2016

Proud
A Graduate

A family stop
in front of me and a sweetie shop -
much talk and mobiles out.
A lass has her mortar board tasselled cap
and her basic grey gown graduate.
Finally a decision to take shots snapped
of her tossing her cap air-up
with a shake of her locks, set-up close-up;
a graduate student, she poses
and a sexy wiggle does
and all laugh – 2 brothers and Mum
but especially Dad in sum -
3 shots of cap and her in air -
cathedral back-up there
then into the pub to celebrate without a care.

Their fun, is mine second-hand too as
I don't remember my parents presence

at my graduations years ago.
Especially when I was very little, oh -
father was dead, out, below
though under earth low; so...?
sweet and sour I here know.

July 2017.

Puddles

Little street puddle pools on the cobbles
are being tickled by tiny fine rain drop bubbles.

If you want to see if it's beginning to rain in mist
look and you won't see it straight off, you may have to persist
or try putting an outstretched hand out
to feel it - is not easy but
just look for a puddle being tickled instead
if there is one somewhat spread.

Mar 2017

Putting Off

I have been delaying writing
of the most central problem -
that of growing old
but perhaps it's not confined
to numbers of years held.
Yes 'bits fall off' - eyes, ears slowly fail -
lens implants and hearing aids
and teeth decay and break.
Like desert dunes, skin dries up
itchy and wrinkled and slack.
A mild unsteady gait makes me focus
to walk without a fall, neuritis night foot pain.
Life constricts, travel cut down,
trusting only the knowns which then change.

Veins balloon at various sites;
sleep a struggle. Not enough exercise
in body and mind; on effort, muscle cramps, pain
and fatigue easily sets in, constrains, drains.
The memory of so much done before -
such a full former outer life remains
and a lot no longer possible here, now.

Doom and gloom loom large, writing shakes.
Visions of difficult dying,
undiscovered on ones own – the worst;
my beloved safe home
full of worms, flies, death's stench.

But in not travelling this outer world,
inner riches are revealed, unfold.
The answer is not future's thoughts;
it's living now with what simply is, in ages
and making more of it than before; riches -
my cut rose, deep red in a blue vase, sweet scent;
a jam buttered bun on return home
after drenched rain and floods
which my motor-bike sailed through
without breaking down
then dry clothes warm changed – utter delight.
And vodka-lemonade-orange sigh sips -
sofa sitting, settling back pain
Teenagers don't relish these simple things
to this extent. Their time is overfull. But kids can.

Christ actually died alone, no mother, friends there so I have
company here.
There – I've confronted it here so it's done but ? for good
without fear!.

c.f. Waldemar Januszcak BBC Hans Holbein
'The Ambassadors'.

Sept.2016

I've just discovered you. Hurray. Tremendous. What a relief. At last after 6 decades of searching among the different christian tribes. Here in conservative Canterbury the ethos seems to be 'don't rock the boat' – understandable as trying to save political unity at too great a cost. But now I have found your writimgs that I can click with.

I am not a christian – that just adds to the divisions like Jew and Gentile, slave and free etc. but I realise we need to base somewhere. I believe in persons not religions – but I am a 'secular' non-theist Yeshua enquiring follower. John D. Caputo put me on to that name as Christ's original name and he put me on to dropping the overworked misused name of God. Richard Dawkins is right to be an 'atheist'. Both words 'God ' and 'Jesus' have stuck in my throat for all I have heard of them – they just do. I can't make them not to – but it's a bit easier now with your work. And Meister Eckhart's 'I pray that I may be rid of god in order to find God'. I like Elohim.

I can't read the bible – it can be a dangerous book e.g christ condemning the man to hell or something for not using his talent. My gut feeling rejects that as also God's astounding violence in the O.T. I go by gut feeling as my guide! e.g the wonderful 'abide in me as I abide in you'. I realise discernment is needed. I've given up going to church.

And I just love contemporary knowledge especially the sciences and especially the cheeky antics of quantum particles which make me laugh in delight but are 'spooky' or 'weird' to some physicists. But now their antics, like passing through walls and being in many places at once etc. are found to be the base of life e.g photosynthesis etc. I feel the awesomeness of 'God' in the universe but not in church which bores and angers me. Apologies but it does. What amazing stuff will quantum physics next find, I wonder.

Great that 'supernatural' is out. I cringe at suffering in Nature, in people, while god sits on his backside and does nothing. Caputo's idea that it is we who do the 'heavy lifting' of doing something about it. 'Jesus wept' and 'I thirst' are very meaningful. And 'I am'.

It would be good to see a short book on your goodly 'living fully, loving wastefully and being all that one can be' expanded as this seems to be the crux. I realise this might be difficult to generalise as it's so individual. That's why I love the great 'I am' ...me too!

But now importantly a further question. How would you dream

of the Eucharist being celebrated in church or do you accept it as it is with its various differences but still the same and go along with it but saying something different under your breath? But without 'we are not worthy', 'I am not worthy' and the confession of 'sins'..I love the story of the prodigal son – the father rushing to greet his returning son and celebrating him. Parents don't make their kids confess any naughtiness returning straight from school and make them take a bath before celebrating them home. It's better to understand 'sins' and their causes I feel. All this unworthy and sinful emphsis is damaging and destructive. The word 'sin' needs to be to given a rest as it stops us trying to understand what lies under. Other words are better.

Another question – can you enlighten me on 'The Lord's Prayer' - our father which art in heaven! thy will be done! 'Will' to me indicates coersion doesn't it? and 'lead us not into temptation'? Did Christ say this? I prefer 'Abba Father' - simple, or Mabba (= ⚥).

In the Beginning was the Sound!...word is made of sound like the profound immense symphonies of Sibelius and Brahms. I would love a church filled with that and art and poetry amongst its services! - contemporary. Great music is awesome.

Sorry about all this – I don't want to put you in a difficult political spot which may irritate.

A poet said 'As Kingfishers catch fire ...'what I do is me: for that I came'.

But mainly great thanks to you for being and writing.

Elizabeth Webb, retired medic.

Quantum Fundamental Particle Noteicles

If I could -I would love to meet
my friends, the quarks
and be at one again
in creation
as I first was.
They live in 3 families in pairs -
'up and down', 'top and bottom'
and 'beauty and truth'
now called 'charm and strange' quarks -
and they, with muons and taus too

(heavier than electrons),
with electrons and neutrinos
are fundamental building blocks
of the Universe -
part of protons, neutrons
in the atom's nucleus.

What's amazing in all -
is that they can burrow and tunnel through matter
like a ball through a brick wall;
and one can be in many places all at once
and if a pair become separated and you nudge one,
the other one instantly jumps -
even at either ends
of the observable universe.
In general, they can 'hop, pop
and fizz in and out of existence,
sniff around, walk, stroll, get excited,
claustrophobic, bubble, have flavours, colours,
coherently dance to a choreographed beat,
spin in different directions all at once
and their polarisation angles
point in different directions all at once'.
And they have no need of time, none at all.

What's more, they prefer doing these things in secret
as when observed or measured these things
sometimes don't happen or change or revert
to the behaviour of classical physics.
They are real, lively or ghostly, lovable characters -
vital to life – the vital spark
but frustrating to quantum physicists
who can call them 'weird' or 'queer' sometimes.
As with energy which is 'neither created nor destroyed',
my little friends are eternal with no need of time at all.

But they are me and I am them so 'eternal' I already am
my body is made of them from the origin of the universe.
I am made of them - 'stardust'.

April 2016.

Rendevous with Death

Have you seem Hans Holbein's scene 'The Ambassadors'?
with the foreground elongated distorted shaft -
which turns out to be a human skull – appalling and real
if only glanced at, sidled up from the extreme right side.

The table contents signify earth below, like the world globe
and a mandolin's broken string. And heaven above
with a celestial globe and astronomical things.
And two people, the rich man and the poorer priest -
ambassadors to King Henry VIII.
The distorted skull aims at all in the scene.
All are temporary and perish. It's final - at first sight
only if quickly glanced at from the extreme right side
where the skull takes on its 'real' 'true' shape.

But the distorted skull of death is an illusion
if confronted and pondered long, head on, centrally from the front
it indicates the same illusion for all that is seen and unseen
in heaven – all religions, and earth- all matter and form.
But if the skull is glanced sideways from the right side
the exact skull is revealed, that is, it is not an illusion -
it is 'true', 'real' - the death and perishment final - of all things.
We usually live most of our lives from the sides, sideways -
not as well, pondering them from the front, reflect on, straight on.

But again hardly seen unless searched for
is a near hidden crucifix symbol, sign
almost concealed by the rich drapes, green and fine
at the far left top corner of this scene..
This the symbol of transformation
from death to new fresh alllife.
An inexplicable allusion to the principal of transformation
to unknown being, beyond vision or word.
Simply perhaps there's no gain without pain
without current 'religious' focal intent
and 'there are more things in heaven and earth
than are dreamt of ....' - more than we know, meant.

But some prefer to just die – that's it,
with no further meaning implied.
Both the head-on wondering confrontation, reflection
where even death is an illusion
and the sidled sideways glance where it is not -
occur in our lives.

Sept 2016

Roots in Brexit

Here, as white as a snowdrop,
yet I, an African too – country hopped.
And came from there 50 years ago
but then also deep aeons long ago
as the beginning of time flows, knows -
the first humans spread wide,
colonising the world astride.
So I have no need
to wonder why I left there
to come here.
I am both here and there
and everywhere.
And dizzy in this fairground
on this merry-go-round.
It's fun but nice to get off.
England is my soil now -
Europe falling out and off.

Mar 2017

She Rests

I collapse and sip sitting in relief at a city caf near a tree,
gentle wind leaves falling day dreaming - now free;
a woman comes settles softens in respite rest ease -

an old worn T-shirt, a scruffy puffa jacket squeezed.
Hunched, she takes out a cig, lights up and sips latte inbetween -
her head bowed and intently aimed strained, hair screened
towards her cup – a wave of peace spreads over her face
and down her body. She leans back and sighs in grace -
then her cig hand shakes, then an expression worried worn -
she carefully counts the notes in her purse; again torn.
Privileged - I had glimpsed a life deep in her without a word heard,
yet seen.

Nov 2017

Shoes

Fashion allows now -
(not only impossible high heels)
but squishy low,
flat, slip-on trainers anyhow -
all rainbow colour souls,
thick rubber white soles
full of slits and little side holes.
No body weight
can squish them flat, deflate their fate;
an easy gait
squeezed out all round.
So comfy sound.

Sept 2017

Simply

Simply – just this -
no grand thoughts, ideas.
I just table solid sit
and write code -
ancient hieroglyphs
like this.

April 2016

Yes

Yes, earth, you opened
amazing today, seeing
and trees birthing
and No and nothing, no thing;
everything's gay
being something.
Now I, now, what -
but how?
It's yes.

April 2016

Snapshots

Puppies

A buxom woman
slinkingly dressed with
low slung top, high heels;
'She's showing her puppies'
a man said as
she wobbled along proud.
'So sweet' I said.

Shades

Ways to not wear 'shades'
which are sunglasses.
1. On the back of your neck -
   stalks round neck or stalks over ears.
2. On the top of your head.
3. Slotted in your jumper front,
   folded, hanging by one stalk.
4. Hung by strings of various sorts.

Sucking

A toddler not toddling
but in a pram aloft holding
a baby bottle of milk bubbling
and to get a suck struggling
as the pram on the cobbles
is wobbling
and the liquid milk
is jumbling around
quite a lot.

Fragility

A little girl
pram-pushed
by her big dad.
The pram, basic, just metal struts
carries a tiny person,
keenly scanning -
delicate, fragile
with a floppy straw hat.

How do dogs tailwag?
Lots of muscles there involved -
quite a job to multi-task
with co-incident walking lead asked.

Aug 2016

Town Street Snapshots
If you want to observe just look!

A plump roundy tawny buff bulldog, wrinkled roly-poly skin
plonked himself down and sat not on his bum therein akin
but askew on his right haunch in a clever endeavour -
I s'pose that's the most comfy with the least effort ever

with however, his back legs loose to one side
not under squeezed and wide.
His chowks dribbled, his tongue hung loose to the side -
content he was as all round he watched on the kerbside
puffing occupied.

A Chinese lass in graduate cap gown and hood,
lovely loose long black hair flowing around and coy
as she was cradling for comfort her favourite toy with joy -
a big Bagpuss pink and white striped pussy cat
so famous on kids TV of long ago that
I pictured her receiving her degree
in the austere Cathedral ceremony
with Bagpuss taking her scroll
from capped gowned Chancellors, high-ups
with open mouthed distaste and scowls.

I saw a real Humpty Dumpty today.
The cold weather snap has brought out in play and gay
an epidemic of quilted puffa jackets and coats.
And woolly caps with furry pom-poms atop – well most.
A short dumpy man waddled stocky along -
a very large roundle bloated body but strong
in an enormous puffa short coat and stocky
no neck but a pimple of a bald head atop like an egg
with sticking out little arms and bandy legs.

The current fashion of large jean knee-slit holes.
'Isn't it cold there' I ask and guess
but fashion might be more important than comfort
I muse, as no-one says no or yes.

And have you noticed what people's fingers do
when they're wrapped in gloves around?
Some fingers seem to want to escape or snuggle down.

Her jellied double chin wobbled with each step footfall
on top of a plump tum like a large ball
so no more sweety cakes now

as the sweetmeats in the tea-shop window
mesmerised her in with sugary info.

An old lady limped along and daily I saw this unchanged
with a massive grey birdsnest hair-do arranged
in piles of long hair uncombed unwashed atop.
I looked for baby birds nesting but saw none in that mop.

Dec .2017

? Stupid Humans; Us
The evolution or destruction of language and us

Hi guys, you want it – you gotta have it.
He was sat, never sitting -
somebody must have sat him down,
with his oiled quiff going head to head
scoring many ghoals from many schances foreign managers say..
Subwoofers were on thumpfull blasts
It was wicked and so cool yu know -
like .... like .... like ..yu know.
No I don't! Well listen up. Can't I just listen?
We're talking...Talk me thru' it. Get it in.
He squirted himself with Diesal Brut after shave
but pollutant diesal cars are now being banned.
There are many issues these days, never problems.
A's have become up-side-down V's as in SΛMSUNG.
Showstoppers are everywhere -
ding dong, phishing, syncing.
The showdown, the footfall, gigs.
Bring it on. Selfies nerds geeks.
We're talking. End of. A no brainer
It's iconic but a lot are this so they're not -
it so is. Absolutely. Emojis now.
So now I'm going to cook my heart out -
well don't get it in the dish. High Five ok?

We're not the highest in the evolutionary tree.

Animals and plants are far more related than we.
They don't overpopulate the earth -
they only kill for food not in mass destructive wars (population control covert).
Humans are always keen on competitions - the basis of wars.
Knights and Damehoods are given to sport heroes and pop-stars -
what has the world come to – where are writers, thinkers, scientists
and those who do 'great' others great good.
Water and soil are the best – in food they made and make all of us.

The oil-slick of loss and grief. 'I'm filling up'.
No river ever ends in the place where it began.
The whole of our lives are lived inside ourselves – our rivers -
a smidgin is shared in words and words are rarely dug up
in the soil in a later age. Our little rations of experience.
Others reflections in this life of the river appear and pass.
The long stream of being flows back into the dark past
and we become more alive with the energy of others bog-rich death.
    Dying can be the only thing to feel left
    that gives others life. Perhaps the era of a new dawn at best
    Ding dong. Deliveroo, Caffeine shampoo. Going head to head.
    Thanks – no problem. Check it out. No worries.
    I could die for this. Eat your heart out. Listen up. Wha'eva.

Jan 2017

Surprised

I was investigating
packets of spinach leaves
in no hurry
on the supermarket shelves
then felt a tap on my left arm
and thought no more -
there was no harm alarm.
The tap repeated itself
insistently now.
I turned and there below
was a little lady

perhaps just over 3½ feet small,
a sky blue summer coat and shawl
and fair curly hair overall
and perfectly formed withal.
She pointed to the top shelf
and gestured for me there with no word
to a small overhanging packet preferred
which I reached for and passed down;
the smallest packet of cut onions around.
'This one' I asked. She nodded
        and disappeared.

What a coincidence -
I had just been reading
a kids magical story
of Knockers - 'the little people'
who help us in Cornwall -
'my little friends' it reads
so my turn to help them now.
And mischievous quarks too -
my little friends, due.
Enchanted, I still am,
And muchly bemused.

May 2017.

P.S. I have never again found a similar small cut onion packet so was I in a delightful dream! Perhaps it was a tiny potato one.

Taking myself in hand

Today I must take myself in hand -
my inflated shadow is blowing up.
So it needs some light shone on
this black hawk pecking my good self
into bloody torn chunks.
We sometimes exist
as if the present doesn't count.

It dawns on me to be severe with my shadow, firm –
I had allowed it to run wild, supreme -
to stop these crap negative thoughts
that like a black cloud of brain flies swarm -
of who I am and of how little worth
against others elevated being selves.
I swear at the self denigration, doubt
and shout and curse it to shut up, get out.
        I bare my claws.

This stand is good - wherefore
now I am restored, worth more.
I don't need to compare myself with others might.
I am me, like a kingfisher catching rainbow light.

Now I want to be delightfully dim and doltish.
I laugh and love at TV's silly ads,
'Have I got news for you' and 'Q,i'
with Stephen Fry's rare questions
provoking the panel's made-up free range, simple replies.

Religion has no humour – its greatest fault.

Sept.2016.

Tele and Current Cool Kids Speke
where U=Λ

'We're talking'... jobs.
So 'check this out'. 'Like'
He 'was sat' and 'she's a shero'
'up close and personal' 'yu know'
with 'good vibes' and
going 'head to head' -
earphones for their 'stuff'
'selfies piccies' with
'betta technologee'.

So go 'neck and neck'
'find your happy' -
'get it in'. 'right now' -
as 'it ticks all the boxes',
'a no-brainer' and
'what's not to like'.
'Job done'.
Here's your 'cuddily' toy.
'It's a win- win'.

'No worries' now -
just a 'tickily, bubbily' cough
so 'take this off of me'.
Thanks - 'no problem'.
'A showstopper'.
'So cool'.

Everything's 'iconic' so they aren't.
But 'chill out' and
'happy days'.
'End of'.
'High five' -
'Mwah, mwah'. with a kiss-kiss peck on both cheeks
'Have a nice day'

Nov. 2017

The Body

The isolate body isn't -
without mind and spirit.
It is the temple
housing those two guests
at the East end altar -
top of the world – the head,
in its essence.
That brain -
the most complex thing

in the universe;
abuzz with
singing neurons
in choir, most magnificent;
all to move my big toe
in time and tune
with my foot,
my leg, my hip
to a tune to time tap.

April 2016.

The Call

'What is calling you?'
I was asked.
To be honest
I hear no clarion call.
But feel an inner impulse
pounding through -
what to do to make sense
of my little experience;
my old curiosity shop inside;
the fittest survive, preside
so it is said
by transforming self instead.
An unamed focus,
a nothing specified
which is the bed rock
of something.
The bog soil
from which all springs, bouncing.

I wait and write and knead
letters, the dormant seeds.
What will spring forth - freed -
the great I AM and so, me too
and we are us and not only what we do.

Love wastefully and true -
not in some grand passion caprice,
though that would be quite nice -
but in little things left instead
like one's cosy welcoming bed.
Live fully, unbroken -
aware of the smallest event,
all senses open
as age takes away much
and then gives much
as one becomes intently aware
of each moment spare -
like the clarion call to pee
and how that feels – to be
of worth
and so delightful
as warm water pisses forth.

Be all that you are and so can be.

Jan 2017

'The Cloud'
Pooled services of the internet

No longer fluffy clouds
but WiFi networks, 'the Cloud' -
like electricity, gas sub-stations -
this the wireless internet;
no pipes, cables at all,
they're just waves
zooming everywhere
all over the universe.

No longer sky -
now stuffed full
with many zillion peoples'
computer photos, waves, files;

twittering, face-booking, flick'r-ing
nattering, jabbering, tweeting
mindless, often malicious stuff
accessible from anywhere
on earth's globe from any of your IT stuff -
tablets mobiles smartphones, iphones, PC's, laptops.
Cyber-terrorism, hacking rife -
spam, junk, virus, malware.
The universe is no more -
pristine untouched of our human dirt.

Not much person to person contact -
instead people, mobile-hunched,
fingers crooked
to scan the apps
and tap thru' the texts
from tiny alphabets.

No more birds, sky, virgin clouds.
The once happy moon
now defaced, has clod foot marks.
And space trash circles in arcs;
our planet is beginning
to live in a rubbish dump park.
Is this progress pumped out -
I suppose it is but the sun goes dark!
There is some good got? -
more knowledge, wide bought
and robots to do the work -
to leave us aspiring geeks unemployed.

Oct 2016

The Farm For Fun

In Southern Rhodesia as it was then, visiting Rhodes grave on top of a kopje (little hill) of granite in the expanse of veldt (scrubland). The worn path up, lined with resurrection plants, dead that come alive with rain.

A farm nearly the size of Wales – 3 kids on 2 horses cantering, two on one, in the bundu (bush) – they suddenly swerve and stop. We fall off then climb back on (at 10 years one is supple) and this repeats often – hoopoes cackling from the tree tops where their massive stick nest nestled along the dry river bed.
Or climbing haystacks and rolling down in khaki shorts, bare feet and tops sunburnt.
Or catching heifers tails to be swung around and thrown.
Or trekking to a rock cave, shouting and singing to scare any leopard off and give us the necessary courage – to see a few bushman paintings there on the walls.
Or at night sleeping on floor mattresses when a cobra slithered in through the top of the window. The farmer, a lovely buxom warm homely woman who pioneered the running of the farm on her own, slashed at it with a long cavalry sword swearing. Bona Huntley her name. Bed legs sat in tins of water to stop ants climbing up and all had mosquito nets against malaria.
This was our 2 week holiday away from our distraught mother.

I first got a degree in the Sciences then worked as a research assistant in kwashiorkor (protein malnutrition in African toddlers) but got fed up with the wall of chemical glass's daily greeting so got grants, bursaries, scholarships to study Medicine at Cape Town University medical school - a 3 day train-trek down.

The Anatomy Class For Hard Work

Second year medical Students of 7 years study before graduation at last

A large dissecting room with about 40 marble-top high tables strewn with 40 cadaver corpses, formalin grey-brown supine, 2 students each side peering over the top, half a body each to dissect through layer by layer through the year; every centimeter and millimeter of every structure meticulously dissected to learn what was anterior, posterior, above below, fore and aft - like the brachial artery in the neck. You can't do surgery without this detail like fixing stab wounds or removing lumps. Much latin involved in the names therein. Someone dared a group of us to hide then get locked in overnight in the corpse dark. Scarey it was.

One student committed suicide in residence down the corridor, took an overdose and hid in her room cupboard, found curled up dead. Five of us then had nervous breakdowns. Later I won the class medal in Chemical Pathology. I have it still. Training now is not as detailed as it used to be – perhaps more on relationship.
There were great times, camaraderie – giggling at jar pathology specimens of organs like a liver with a deep crease caused by tight, boned corsets and all agreeing how good it felt to do a good pooh. Sometimes you laugh instead of cry.
That training was invaluable as a junior houseman in an African hospital doing skull burr-holes with a drill to relieve brain pressure of a cerebral haemorrhage or sucking out fluid around a heart or amputations for cancer or carefully cleaning the TB gunge around a spinal cord, the patient walking now, out of hospital after leg paralysis. Stuff only consultants would do in Britain. But a patient died under my anaesthetic care as I couldn't intubate her within 3 minutes as she was so grossly fat. And there was no senior to supervise. After all these years -with experience, degrees diplomas, membership - what do I do now. Nought. Except write. What a waste!

Sept 2017

At Café Rouge
The New
Menu

Oh -
what's with this though -
'topped sourdough,
tomato,
smashed
avocado'? -
not mashed!
A sad 'oh no'.

A crucified avo -
that we may have life's flow -
smashed here below
and have it

more abundantly so.
Death gives rise to life's show
ever since life first began
4 billion years ago
although tentatively slow.

Oh!

June 2017

A Sudden Meeting in the High Street

A figure emerges behind a van
beige summer suit, tie and panama hat -
the tie, the striking point
yellow and orange paisley type swirls
with a blue-green touch.
I greet him ceremoniously.
Exuberant, the Professor waives his arms
and tells me he is to conduct around the cathedral
a high Indian dignitary from St. James's palace
and that he, the prof. has been around
the largest Hindu temple in Britain -
in Neasden North London it was.
I note his tie is very suitable.
'I know, I know' he said
not 'o thank you' to my compliment.
But how to greet the high-up was his problem -
a bow, shake hands or pressed together hands
as if in a prayer and what the Japanese do,
bowing very low the higher the rank.
The importance is the importance of both. Prominent. Top.
The first not the last.

I had sent him an e-mail tending
my resignation (from his originated problem-filled.
christian house group) without a reply.
He totally ignored that or perhaps forgot.

My presence was only to receive his importance
which I gracefully did. There was no mutual relationship.

It got my goat like a worm burrowing under my skin
so I had to spend puzzled sad time working this out.
This is it. I am no longer recognised as important.
My profession once was. And I wish to dominate,
to know everything and be listened to
and make others see my point
So he is my shadow side.

But I had openly received him on his level
and he had not me. He sidled off. He decides to end contact.
So I wished him the best.

Why have I taken such trouble with this brief meet.
It's the haunting shadow perhaps.
Or have I made it all up?

Why is he so scared of being vulnerable and ordinary
like most of us are and not a cut above the rest?
'The first shall be last and the last first'!

Sept 2016

WATER
The River Roar
over the top

Swollen waters, rock and rapid
tumultuous, down a fall hurling -
bulging turbulent torrents surging
a gargantuan impulse liquid rabid
of salmon spawning
driven resolute blind;
red muscle powered, up-leaping
flying tails propelling wagging

mid air flailing
thrown back down, prevailing,
falling back, failing, flung, flungdown.
I can't help surging shouting
I'm on my feet jumping
urging them, up-welling -
a few of many winning
leaping marvellous, 10 feet up -
mass impulse effort immense
power driven intense
against all the known odds.

For what? -
to spawn their milt sperm milk
spurt shed spread to dregs
over frail little lucent orange eggs
twirling in pebbly eddy beds
in the still small quiet water spread
above the rock wall, down downfall
then they, exhausted, drained
die in shallows spent strained;
dying-to-give-life had flowed
having given their all, utmost -
sweet precious hallowed
honoured cherished
entire life-loved.

June 2017

Breakfast

Would you like
your Brexit
hard or soft boiled?

EW.

Don't We Often Do This?
What is real?

A real grey big umbrella
swanned regally past
fully expanded
unfolded extended
but covered in, downcast -
a large rain water
downpour of dribbles and drops.
Puzzled.
I knew there was
and had been no rain at all
so I carefully looked
and saw its dribbles and drops
were ordered, symmetrically styled
and thus man made, false and applied.
I had been tricked and duped
into seeing something shaped
that was and wasn't
and is and is not.
In this, is 'is' only nature
and of humans 'is not'?

May 2017

From Stephen Hawking 'A Brief History of Time'.
'Imaginary time may sound like science fiction but it is in fact a well-defined mathematical concept.'
' There are, however, special numbers (called imaginary numbers) that give negative numbers when multiplied by themselves '. (whereas ordinary or 'real' numbers when multiplied give positive numbers).
'So it meaningless to ask: which is real, 'real' or 'imaginary' time? It is simply a matter of which is the more useful description'.

The Throstle's Song in th … notes
The Thrush's Thinging Throngsong
(threshed thyme - to th… Thou the divine)

Thou thinkest that this thin thief-thing
thirsts thy thought thrust through thick
and thin, though thrashing themed theory
that thronged those thirty thicket thorns
threaded through thy thermalled thundered throne.
That thorax throbbed,
thereafter the three thumped thuds thawed.
Than that this throat thrilled,
that then thou thoroughly threw
thyself through their threatened thin,
thonged theology theme.
Thrombosed thanatos thugs they;
their theist thoughts, throes,
theories, theses - throttling thorned.

Thence Thou thrived that theatre -
there thrown - thwarted them thus -
that this thin thing, that thither thereby therein,
this third thief, therefore thrice thanks thee,
thousandfold - thanks thine.

These, Thy Thee Thou
Thyself Thine. The. Thing.

Canterbury June 2002
modified Sept. 2017.

This is about metanoia - transformation, the essence of
all crucifiction
Apologies for 'to', 'divine' and 'and' as non-th... words.
A throstle is the older word for a song thrush.
'Thinging' refers to singing the 'thingness' (Heidegger) of a thing!
'Threshed thyme' smells sweet.
Apparently the Sanskrit tat.h for that and similar english words
have divine implications. The th... words found seemed to dictate a
theology.
It is about the obfuscation of r/Reality by theory, preconception,
creeds etc.
The three thuds refer to the sound made by the three nails of the cross.

It is neither ‘evangelical’ nor ‘liberal’ nor ‘catholic’ nor ‘anything’.
It’s just experience that everything suffers then dies then transforms -
epitomised in the historical crucifiction.
In Yorkshire folks still address another as ‘thou’.

Thumbs Up

A passing unknown man
trailing behind two women
gave me a smile
and a greasy thumbs up
amidst his mouthful of fish and chips -
food on the hoof backup supped.
Pleased, I returned a thumbs up
as two ships passed on their way
in the clouded crowded day.
Then a young toddler lass
aloft on the shoulders
of her dad swiftly passed
but she gave me a most
penetrating long-lived stare
so I likewise, then 2 shops down
she waved and smiled – now no glare
so I, genuine, likewise.

Two pigeons passed at my feet
looking for tasty crumbs.
It seems they have to bob their heads
forward and back
while they walk
and very fast when they run.
Do all birds do this*
and is it for added impetus
or an effort waste?
A crowd of legs came along
and one stretched his neck tall
in acute observation and fear
as he walked fast, small

and out of the way
but there was no gay display
order of the day
head bobbing now!

Next day a tall thin man walked past,
small face and large beak nose.
And he, pigeon head-bobbed somewhat -
a habit not a disability
which I liked a lot!

*The answer is no so even moreso 'why'? 8 out of 27 bird groups do it including magpies, cranes and crows. A lot of research is going on and in one a pigeon was put walking on a treadmill and it was set at the same pace as the pigeon's walk who then ceased bobbing. His surroundings had stopped moving.
There are 2 stages to bobbing, lasting milliseconds - of thrust and hold. Head thrust forward then held while the body catches up. The aim to stabilise vision, it appears.

May 2017

My Toe

I stubbed it on the concrete floor,
unhanded, trying to get a slipper on
and yelled in pain. Yes reticent pain -
am I not allowed to admit it, fragile.
But it soon swelled till
I couldn't get round the house, immobile -
without shuffling short unsafe steps -
while planning ahead to cut down moves
as if a hobbled elephant in chains;
I went to bed for two days,
leg up to fluid down drain.
Slowly it improved so boots on, donned
I gingerly got to town
for necessary food and it bettered
as the day and motion moved on.

I've done it, I've done it -
hurray, in spirit -
I've survived
but what would it be like
if I was really ill, deprived?

You've no idea
how a painful toe
cancels me out as invalid -
an invalid. It's scary now
Yet I bounce back better -
so go slow,
even fuller in simple life
than ever before
from all that strife!

Oct 2016.

(e.g.Transiting transport translate transform transfer)
Trans = across
Over 1,000 words start with trans. Numerous others have trans incorporated in them
so trans is the most prevalent state on earth e.g in evolution

Transients

I have discovered that we are all this -
as most of our time is effort spent
in trying to arrive with little time in being there in content.
Think of the long time in preparing a meal
and the little time in eating it real well with zeal
and in getting some transport from a to b
by any means not yet arriving carefree.
Or in preparing to go to bed with a sigh of relief.
Everything we do is mainly how we get to do it in belief -
transiting doing is long in transport athwart
and doing is the process of done and done is short.

Dec 2017

To W.B.Yeats

It's fashionable in the streets
to carry a ruc-sac
full of nothing much.
To the Irish it can be
boring to be happy -
as also to a lot of us -
despite our cries.

But you were overflowing
with immense, intense dreams
that tore you apart – sometimes mad
and left us, our neurones singing,
whirling in dance.
Your furnace Ireland's hurt and legend
and Maud Gonne spurned -
the love of your heart.

But, at bed rock, your memories as a child
had nothing but its burning pain;
an ice-burg mother's misery, inaccessible, withdrawn
'locked and frozen in each eye'
and to her paralysis, madness decline;
a haunting spectre within.
So you became women obsessed -
drawn to the opposite in Maud,
a warrior woman, auburn haired, fierce eyed
then many lovers thereon where you came alive -
penetrating their 'labyrinthine beings' within -
not the cold mother cruelly warmth-witheld.
But still never content at all -
your Mother, the first prime fuel -
that image upon inner image gushed out,
sometimes dangerous, a lifeline hurled -
in immense courage, honest to yourself.
Homeless, even in sad death -
living on in us.

Let us rejoice and give thanks -
a noble, Nobel laureate
not only for Ireland but throughout the world
in the great struggle of mankind
to understand
in one, beautifully drawn.

April 2016

Walking Round the Earth in Time. From the book of Revelations

As I walked round the future earth
top to bottom and from side to side
a tide of orphaned children
stumbled across the desert blind, denied;
born for nought, hungry and starved.
Sand storms whirled in trumpets up
and rivers had cracked, caked and dry.

As I walked round the earth
everywhere I saw conflict, wars
across African states, Syria Afghanistan
Libya Iraq Israel Palestine
and many more - ancient cities rubbled spoiled destroyed.
It's about tribal fights for poor resources poorly deployed
and corruption at the top for riches of underdesert oil.

As I walked round the earth
I saw ravaged forests human done
and jungle animals and plants gone
and savannah elephants and lions none -
nowhere to be seen – trapped and shot
as the earth became overpopulate
regardless – with procreating human rats and rot.

As I walked round the earth
the ice-caps had melted south and north

great crashing ice cliffs sea-falling
through human greed burning
and polar bears nowhere to be seen, nothing.
Low lying islands had sunk
beneath the rising seas dunked.

As I walked round the earth at night
the cities lights burnt bright
even in empty business high-rise blocks.
Skyscrapers clutching the sky, riddled the lands, choked
crawling with overpopulate ghettoes, slums gridlocked
and rural space left mocked, deadlocked.

And here buildings inside at the last
are no books left, the Word has disappeared -
destroyed, replaced and filled by numerous waves -
computers, tablets, iphones, ipads, androids.
Their god – the Internet, World Wide Web slaves.

As I looked up at the heavens -
man's space junk rubbish deadens;
20,000 pieces circling
at 17,000 MPH hurtling
OMG. Oh my god darkening.
Where are true stars?

Jan 2017

What to do Today

(About our spiritual evolution Spiritual is a yuk word now but there is none other)

To see if anyone has discovered that
Christ was a man of the highest depth.
What top scholars have recently done
is discard traditional creeds, doctrines
and their literal mumbo jumbo spun
which are much later gentile additions after Christ -
and shown him to be a Jew - but is that all now?
The new testament stories are stories
made by Jews, wrapping his life

in their old testament liturgy, history, heritage
ignored by the Roman hierarchical church
and even now a 'gentile heresy' in fact.
The stories are not historical fact.
In the modern world virgin births, body deaths to life
and people walking on water etcetera don't occur
and are less and less believable by more and more.
The crux is to sense the stories profound deep heart
unwrapped from the later wrappings – put aside.
So to me he was a great person crucified.
He lived fully, loved wastefully, was inspired
and was universally conscious of the whole
with the courage to be who he truly was.
No-one knows what he really said.
The gospels are several decades after he died.
Can you remember what someone said
to you 30 to 50 years ago? I can't;
and it is well known that different witnesses
give varying accident accounts.
But I have a gut feeling
he was the deepest human
of all time, a person profound -
neither Jew nor gentile,
of no race, religion at all at depth
and beyond all our words -
untrammelled by fancy myth -
compassionate above all,
mysterious, like his God yet revealed.

Is this gut feeling right
or it just is, neither wrong nor right?
I now have a feeling that theology, religion
boil down to psychology, therapy, analysis
with a true ineffable Presence
That maybe 'evil' is illness
as Georges Simenon said.
I have come full circle now, here.
And plus.

Aug 2016

Winter Warms

Yes,
not the adjective but now a new noun
like colds so why not warms, earth brown.
They're glumpy and round and soft,
secretive, hiding in my cave depths.
If you look after them safe
they give their glow in passion puffs;
you need to feed them in winter, fuss
them with many layers of clothes bound
so you too look glumpy and round -
and nourish them from top to toe.
But woe-betide if you don't though -
they yell, sneeze, shout and shiver
till you run for cover
for a scarf and jumper
and gloves discover
oh glory – now cozy
and glowing snug, drowsy dozy.
Warms – it pays well
to care for them -
of growth the groundswell.
In summer they take
a well earned rest
basking in the yellow sun, blest.

Colds - walk out, leave, squirm -
you're unwelcome and do harm.
Sometimes a warm will take a cold
and nestle it under a fluff fold.

Jan 2017

Words

Reply to Robert Graves 'The Cool Web' and 'Warning to Children'

Forays in and out, foraging for word-food -

wonderlands, world meadow words,
jungle tangles, drowning sea depths
driven to make sense and form of chaos and void in word.
Genius and madness spring-up, flood from the same within place -
a deep dark cavern within us, death and lifefull -
mindless mad speech – unrelated to the real
and sparkling genius moulding image and thought from formless mud.
$E=mC^2$ - a tiny lump mass m mixed with huge C light speed squared
gives enormous energy converted from mass; E and m are equivalent -
so you and I, being large lumps, are near energy infinite.
How strange is that; also the action of quarks – Einstein's 'spooky, weird'
but these altered the scientific world, our age evolution's spurt.

Universal night phantasms, dreams -
images flooding from every sense it seems
become mad in daylight act – the I, its loss -
'I am God or a miserable sinner' ... – reality unfaced;
an inner theatre lived out that ends in inner death.
But words are essential to survive and relate to the outside world,
and to our inner deep chaotic core which we all share unaware.

Words are poison or life-giving food;
it's not they that can be mad but the cavern chaos is
and they can befriend and understand us
from disintegration's breakdown in psychosis.
A child can have simple unprisoned words
within the family's warm care.
Babies, not yet, but they have actions, sounds – early words.
Yet stuttered, general, vague 'spoken-speech-language words'
can dumb-down, drown-down, throttle-clasp.

Now it is said that babies have multiple perception
which as we grow we lose. Some people have synesthesia,
a sane fantasia – seeing sound, tasting colour and word,
time projected as colours around, numbers and letters scent
and some even see numbers as personalities as well;
loud tones are brighter, dark liquids smell stronger.

Some have more crosswiring neural connections -
brains are plastic, active; so metaphors, images make sense.
Light is not colour; it is fundamental photon-bit waves -
it's our brains that make the colour, adaptive to survived life.
Colour is seen in the context of what's around, like bees, like us.
A blind man can 'see' to cycle by tongue-click echoes like bats.
And we see the world in the lens of the past.
So let's synthesise rich and keep the I, synesthize wide.

Nov. 2016

HRH's Visit to Riding for Disabled School, S.Augustine's, Canterbury

She dropped in a red helicopter. I was a volunteer.
A rumour had it arranged by a major general's word in her ear. Later, I
returned a Council letter to a nearby unknown couple. 'Who do you think
I am' - he asked. 'A major general' - unthinking, I replied. The penny dropped; it was Himself.
His wife continued to iron her pants.

Evil hides and They Bomb Red Cross Huts in Kabul

She is completely veiled - an Afghan under Taliban rule.
Women may not read, write, work, make-up, paint their nails.
Un-named atrocities in the soccer stadium as spectacle. They have the
highest child death rate in the world; they starve.
But there is courage left among the weak and poor.

30.10.01

He is a person well known for his beard, spiky left eyebrow and a fluffy crown of hair (from taking off his mitre often - that must require practice so that the 2 back flaps don't get stuck). He said he would be terrified of the responsibility of the job on his own but consoled to feel his Christ was with him.

I saw him at the Enthronement (the principal of an Archbishop as well as the person).The 2,400 assembled people of all faiths and hierarchies and government and crown waited in silence. You could hear a pin drop. Then the 3 knocks with his horizontal staff reverberated awesomely around the cathedral with 10 seconds delay from the nave to the farthest east end chapel - and he was let in - no fanfare as is customary - just a solitary lonesome figure. He is welcomed and welcomes.

He loves Psalm 100 - 'let us make a joyful noise unto the Lord'. African drums and dancers cavorted and beat. I love that too.

I saw the tabloid photo of him bending low to kiss the 5th C. £50 million Canterbury bible - he looked immensely frail and vulnerable but not brittle - with such a weight of responsibility.

I saw him approach the great marble chair of S. Augustine; he and the chair were lit up, his face flushed against the behind dark - a childlike and awed look as if to say 'Wow - is this mine?'- in delight.

I shook his hand 3 days later - a wet fish was not offered, just firm and resolute. He spent over an hour shaking 2,000 people's hands at the back door! (the West door). His right hand must be sore and bruised now.

He writes poetry and is painfully aware of people's struggles and sufferings in earthed sensual language - a human being. He wishes to 'listen' and be 'open' and is capable of embarrassment at his almighty list of titles. He is also a scholar and former Professor of Divinity at Oxford University.

I am initially impressed - a person of some depth - though his books are complicated.

I checked the great West door for pits in the wood. 104 Archbishops have knocked 3 times with their staffs. A total of 312. Pits are definitely there even though the wood is oak. That requires some strength. But which pit is whose is unknown. 'How good and joyful a thing it is to dwell together. It is like the precious ointment...upon the head that ran down into the beard' in psalm 133 sung in the Chapter House after - with 'I will not leave you comfortless; I go and come again to you,

And your heart shall rejoice then, Alleluia.' Yes - that suits and can comfort him.

Shall I read you some fragments of his poems? - they are not easy.

Canterbury Feb 2003.

A Mother

A distraught woman quietly weeps
red-eyed tears
clutching a little soft toy
of her dead child -
kneeling at the flower covered spot
where he died.

I, who hated my mother,
in compassion, choke.
One mother is caring and good.

The Cold

Fat peoples' cuddly clothes
are their warm layers of cellulose..
I have a puffa jacket.

July 2012.

A New Voice

Lately, over points in time I am knowing
there is a voice - new new new it is,
a compassionate warm voice humming,
fresh through all the mould of dark thought rotting;
but which is not a voice at all
but flickers of quiet surprise;
a sense of being by a warm fire-glow

and the cold wind whistling outside now
through frantic bare branched trees -
the shivered temperature zero.

It said - 'you're ok, feel my warmth with a sigh
as you have felt cold fear of dying-growing old;
both are you but know kindly amongst both
among embers of the gentle fire flow
as darkness depends on light
and the light on dark.
Let go, let go, let go'.

Feb 2013

Psalm 151, Cantate

(with apologies to King James and to those past and present
and after those who have said it before).

'Sing unto the Lord a new Song' (Psalm 149).
'Make a joyful noise unto the Lord' (Psalm 100).

1. Our Father which art Nourisher Guide Protector,
beyond and before and in all gender.
Incarnate, immanent, immense, the Now eternally forever;
the Beginning In the Now and in every now, without before or after.
The Being above and in all being, being before becoming and time.
The toward and with and in and inbetween all creation.
The thingness Thouness essence of all essences.
The I Am of all our I ams. Thou art therefore we are.
Thou art so I am. Without any journey or ascension - we are.
2. Protect us from all minishment, diminishment
Who was and is now, and is forever, who both is and is not.
Who shuts and opens the door of our understanding
according to his desire; who is unitedly diverse - the universe -
as a body is one yet many its parts.
3. Behold uncreate Him who creates the theatre cosmos

for his and our amazement, interest and delight;
the director-producer Alpha and Omega, the cast - angel comets,
asteroids, shooting stars, the flaming fire of sun and Son,
fractals, galaxies, infinitesimal particles; matter because it matters.
The shining ones - costumes designed by Light.
4. The replenishing terror of volcano, magma magnificent -
and awesome storm; nebulae, space and time, so immensely grand;
the changing quakes of earth's fearful crust,
ceaseless unchanging change with no end.
Incomprehensible - He garments it all with dark and light
and showers us with songs symphonies and lullabies,
rippling streams and white water rivers. O see - ah.
Even the tiny cased pupa metamorphosing to a butterfly, lifted up.
In nature's most secret folds - the God plays. Everything is God.
5. And more magnificent than all these - our consciousness
before and in the convolutions of the brain (which receives our mind)
and its galaxies of neurones, millioned - above all angel splendour;
the small spiral of a snail, helical DNA somersaulting.
And in our slow snail spirit in our littleness, feeling, spiralling -
resonating the evolution of the universe slowly becoming.
6. Bless the Lord O my being, who answers my turmoil
with the slow response of his patient people;
who understands my roaring rage of a lion
and impetuous haste of an unreined horse.
Who hears my cry of desolation in silence.
His tender mercy comes like the Samaritan - and as gentle dew -
and not that of a false judge. He gives thoroughly in pardon,
and in forgiving - gives before. Not the experience - but the Event.
7. Who hast the power of thunder, the speed of lightning
and the grace of flowing water - superabundant;
behind and in all bubbling, laughing and moving,
the twinkling of an eye; in all sadness and weeping magnanimous.
The music in all things resonating in Thy people -
their resonance between - of sweet sounding strings
singing bowls, rippling flutes and thunderous drums.
The wind in our face, that very wind which blows where it desires
and cooled the countenance of Christ - the same, the Spirit -
in the parched desert sandaled dust. Divine disclosure revealed.
The very wind who brushes the grass hair
on wild dune tussocks and moorland slopes.

Who is the soft innocence of morning sunshine
and the evening sunset of evensong wisdom - blood red.
8. Our God is Comfortable in the temple of man's soul,
the ground of existence, Prompting us to be free
of fear - hidden or open - as naught is free,
Nice Naught, as nothing is, and God in his Something
with his hands outheld to hold, safely and gently holds
as Christ clears the clutter of fear of our strange withing guests;
the labour not ours alone but shared in the meeting of people - real.
9. The Father who came down to meet us, His family,
when we were far, far off. And we who are made in his Image.
Who loves us before we ever loved him - as Friends not servants.
Whose delight is In us, who bends down to feed us and takes us up
In his arms and lifts us up as a little child to His cheek;
who crowns us with his soft mercy and lifts up the light
of his countenance for us - In the very same of people good.
10. He takes our yoked burden when we stumble and fall.
The Inbetweeness of the Spirit between people.
The Betweeness between the smiling eyes of mother and child.
And In our fragile soft weakness and rainbow tears
before our true strength and power. We are not known to ourselves.
Who is the Word, who is Truth which is one,
who is Light and Delight and Life and Love.
11. The redeemer of the past through the present presence
of love, trust, faith and hope in and for us - of good people.
Before we loved He loved us. The Eloi * - a vulnerable God
and In the very Cry of crucifies Christ on the cross, horror, Nought -
the purity of untransformed horror - absolute;
and In our cry. The Christ - the only incarnate
passionate living God, the only bound God.
The only vulnerable nailed killed God - who knows Ours;
the soothing Balm to our pain - healed; and through
his decreed Ascension, so our Transformation - ours.
12. Our weakness is as the still reed bending in the breeze,
pliable with vulnerable strength; and woven strands
together are rope - strong.
The straight still lithe bamboo - waiting for the wind
to touch and enkindle among its leaves and stems - whispering song.

After such Love and Truth and beauty and Goodness
and Light and Delight and Life and beyond all understanding -
and with no end to the things to be said,
He is and was and shall be the only ultimate Peace and Rest.
The All in all. Real. Free. Profoundly Simple.
The One.

Canterbury Jan 2003

*'Eloi, eloi lama sabachthani' - 'My God, my God why hast Thou forsaken me?'

A Question

I have enough anxiety
To live
And to think of dying,
But not
To do either -
To live or to die;
In no mans land
Split inside.
Effort to act either
And not think much.
In my house of many mansions
A bigger people room required.
Yes - I chose life -
I will - frightened;
And I must laugh
And cry.

O wise ones of the land
What is the answer?
'I am wise' - say
Effort, Will and Can -
Laughing, lounging on cushions
Drinking wine in the sun.

7.11.67 Cape Town

A Time Past
(monosyllabic Short and Sweet)

It was good to flee our mum's rage.
Those breaks on a farm
in the third world near Rhodes grave
where dead plants grow green in the rain
and great quartz and grey glint rocks
make strange scenes in the low hills -
and the suns rise in white heat.
Storms flash quick
to set fire
to thorn trees
in the dry dust haze -
then all goes quiet.

The dust wind whirls in tubes
up to the sky, the clouds loom dark
and there's a warm rain smell before rain -
a scent to come for the parched earth
of peace and thirst slaked.

But we, in shorts and nil else
at 8 and 10 years of age,
climbed domed hay stacks,
chewed straw in the sun
and caught young cow tails
and were swung round and round
in the bare foot dust.

Red breast birds, grain birds and long tailed ones in black -
and gem birds (such as are not seen here)
built large nests in trees
by the brown rain beds.
And the sun birds whirred
on top the sweet blooms sipped.
My horse threw me, bare backed both,
time on time, then kept still
while I climbed back.
We crept in the rock caves.

On the walls, a sketch here and there
done in red dust paint
by the bush folk of old.
Caves - where large cats with spots
slept at mid day in the shade.
We shout to scare them off!

Our warm farm host
killed a large snake
whose 'bite' spelt death,
with yells and a sword,
as it slid to our beds on the floor
through the gap in the door.
Farms were the size of Wales.
Those times were free, and good
as the sun burnt our brown -
so long gone - and long lost,
long in the past.

Canterbury 11th Nov.2002.

Words which had to be avoided in order to retain the monosyllables are Rhodesia, resurrection plants, granite, silhouette, lightning, rises, acacia, heifers, Bishops birds, long tailed Widow birds, Paradise flycatchers, Hoopoes, river, remounted, Bushmen paintings, leopards, python ...

A First Abseil for Kids Cancer Charity

A sponsored sheer-plummeting vertical drop -
though I am seven tens young and old -
harnessed helmeted steel-hooked on top,
a single thin life-line hold, splits a small life grown, hung bold
from the dark won chasm and fall of done death cold.
'Don't look down' - a sharp given askance command -
brave back turned, heels beyond the sharp sheer edge
feet flat out, legs tense straight - a horizontal stand,
the tripod stance strained confirmed to descend -
but one foot slips - a body wall crash to the ledge.

Spinning mind blanks out - no past, present or future -
nothing, slung shell-shocked, not even terror;
my automatic flung feet fast recover -
a clear rung army order - 'go' and I go
belaying down with clung care, - small, slow.
Wrung reliance comes - large sprung steps now -
then I found my hung dizzy-feet - on flat fair ground.
It's like being born torn - a birth cord bound!
I had navigated one abyss if not my inner own.
I long to jump far out, rebound - exuberant, fly down;
a spider on a long-webb nylon-thread unwound, blown
harness unleashed - to profound earth found -
briefly sound and firmer.

Sept 2006

Trilogy

Arranging Shard Scraps of a broken Stained-glass Word Window
Latticed Mullioned hidden-hinted Damask Rose!

The Sorting in ABCD

a. The aridly avid age aborts, autistic anarchic and absurd;
anathema - an acid absence, acutely alone -
anguished aliens, the abused austere abyss again.
But ah, the apt arms arc, atone at-one -
absorbing the ache, and are an aimed arrowed axis ace
acting aeons ago In all the after and at and and,
and across and almost and already and around
and about and any and also; the all - I am, thou art;
a lap-altar alters, anchors aids, amends
assuages, anoints, - not at, apart -
but in and with and for, affirmed -
amid an anthemed amen.

b. In the between beside behind beyond;
in the balm of best blest bliss our bereftness burnt -
in the brute brunt barb of the bent branch beams

crossed in a blazed blood-burnt brow, bond blown
by a before body broken; the bread bitten back -
and the brimmed base bitter cup not passed -
that we beg and bite the belt, being, breathe, bridged
by a bright babe bud, bold bare born - both beaten and bound.
He blossoms and becomes our beauty, brilliance and being.

c. Can the 'can't' of cold core care of a cursed crib child of clay
catch, cut and convert the chaos of the clotted city - cloned,
competing confused coerced complying, clogged?
The canker of 'can't' is caged and captive culled, cured
in the cross-costing charmed cascading chalice crowned
'It is done' in the cup and cragged crux of care caressed.
A candleflame. We are called, and we 'can' -
compelled to come.

d. In the do does don't did done, division, down,
in divorce, deaf-dead death, in the dying dumb.
In the delight of a dove dawn, dew day dreaming.
Now deeply discerning a descending desolate dereliction
in the drudge of a disabling demon of doubt and despair,
drowning in the desert deluge of dust and decay.
But we depend on the duet of our distilling dialogue dance
where dogma and doctrine are defused disarmed dissolved
in the dignity of the divine dream - done
distinguished by dominion's diadem
in his delicate damask design.

AD, BC - before Christ -
anno domine - the year of the Lord.

<u>The Place</u>. with a.b.c.and d.

I am in the dark confines of deafness, dying, being dead.
I am in the clarity of concord comfort calm delight,
not I am deaf or dying or dead
not I am content delighted calm -
but Being - in all these corners of above before, I still Am
and abide held as I Am, even despite dying and death.

But for what, unless the complete whole, unknown -
perfect undivided, awareness complete - not only the part.
Before and Now - not only the abyss of anguish abuse
not only banishment bereftness -
the craving; not only confusion chaos,
not only deprivation despair.
Not coitus at any cost - but at-one, combining our creation.
And behind beyond between beside, before all -
our centre, chubby dormant child -
a baby cooing, angry afraid crying, or asleep calm
or beaming dependant; bursting blossoming
cell-dividing, defenceless, breast drinking deep -
and bosom content. A close couple and child crowned,
cradled caressed, adored admired
at the altar-affirming circling-arc of arms.
The divinity of this trinity, beloved we are now -
and being - become; cocoon and butterfly.
Am I being conned or crowned?
Whose will be done? in this colour-shot rose window -
fire-flamed flared, light blazing dark, radiant brilliant.

The Waiting. neither. Crucifiction by Baegert, Derick the Elder.
The greater the struggle, hung strung, the greater anguish and gash.
What is - is - nailed down done. Rage blame escalate pain as
thief-limbs loose-roped, try to tear free, they thrash, harsh -
one lifts, writhes stunned-up; the other droops, blinded down.
He inly looks, 'silent' With and In Passion Between begun won.
It is the giving action of Waiting - nail-held taught firm, unshunned.
Thy autonomous will be done. It is. Thus it is. That is - acceptance
hammered in, nailed down. It is done.

No answer - the answer - the bread lump of doubt
I AM - a stone, thunder lightning, sound of snowfall
flowing river. Kiai. - perfect imperfection.
I am a chickling returning to Mother Hen.
The onslaught of my rebounding sound voice
in silence - sospiri.

Sospiri - plaintive
Kiai -a shout of spirit together

Lent 2006

Addendum to Creation Evolution Mystery Question Mark

Volcanic eruptions spew out replenishing mineral rich earth.
Leaves fall to the ground and replenishing rot.
Our cells die throughout our life.
A seed falls to the ground, cracks open and dies to a new tender
shoot - like splitting earthquakes and shifting tectonic plates.
Ash to ash, dust to dust. Everything dies and renews.
Tsunami volcano tornado.
That's out there. What about inside us?
Anger grief sadness turmoil suffering pain, the cracking equivalents
with amazing energy - that crucified Christ, death force release
to one with God to new life. We are shown what death is.
And we die daily in adjusting to ourselves and to the world
with insight..

He did not die to save us from our sins -
only a violent abusive god would demand that paid price.

'Don't you want to be with me Elizabeth?' now and after.
It's not the death It's the horror of the dying
that I fear often and most.

April 2015

Adonai Prism

Thick black night splits the headlights
as intention focuses on what might appear
out of the dark unknown ahead.
Unknowing - waiting, might be the real known -
white light unbroken in the prism.
A great beamed sweeping crystal arc
dumbfounding a pair of caught eyes
glowing stunned, gunned down.
I have a few words ignored/returned
with white barred teeth - spat back -

a blow across the mouth -
trust blood hurt, spurts.
Rock bound carbon undating
the ageless song.
The white light of the sky
rests on our ploughed furrowed brow
in a spectrum of life colour Christ.

*Yeshua - the soft found Aramaic Word.
'Yes you are'- slow. And I am heard -
my ear drum clicks unblocked.
I have waited decades for that voice.
Adonai - Lord. Word.
White light breaks, melts
to soft rainbow tint tears -
the prism - the Christ.

*the original word for the

now hard, contaminated word - Jesus

Canterbury April.2004

Afghan Women

Women of the world arise -
you have nothing to lose
but chained veils.
Cloth woven prison bars
over nose mouth and eyes.
Blue draped Marys
mothers of babes;
squatting in dust,
a limp hand outheld
to beg for their child -
confused beside. Quiet.

Or shot in the head behind
by a coward male gun.

En-masse
in an execution ground -
a lost forgotten stadium
given by the UN.

Identity assaulted and raped -
so anonymity to survive.
Too terrified to emerge
the blue covered crysalis
enveloped crust.
We have it better
in the West.
And that was earned hard.
Even that - still ...

Such a sounding name.
Afghan.   So proud.

3.4.02 Canterbury

Age? Redeemed

An older couple emerge from the steps, hesitant, hand in hand
and he leads. He with a ruc-sac, she with slacks falling down
but just, just held up. They wander round the arcade shops
then settle for a Morellis snack.
A frightened bird, she sits scared
while he gets coffee, croissants
and plastic pot portions of butter and jam;
he lets her struggle to open the pots and she can
but her knife falls lost to the ground.
It is left as his she shares found.
Slowly they eat and stay silent bound -
spreading, chewing very well and long.
Fulfilled, she sighs and smiles at last
and they look up at the sky and chimney pots.

This is all too delicate and fragile and I wince.
But it is so simple - so few joys left apiece?
Still hungry he searches for a few coins
then munches toothless a large current bun
and more butter and jam then
just able he bends and collects
the fallen knife found.
They leave slowly - in respect
and he goes to inspect
round the corner for the lift down
but she stops, noticing two young men
in coat tails having their photo taken
outside the mens' hire suit shop for weddings.
She smiles - old memories arise, safe then.
They walk slowly down, hand in hand -
probably been together for decades long
and closer than we'll ever know in silent song.

I think she is dementing slowly, demeaned -
and wished I hadn't seen this scene -
most don't have eyes to see this sort of thing.
I suppose it is pure simplicity and love -
bound to be cut short in death from above -
but timeless and everlasting.
But what of the other - then?
Perhaps age wearies them
and the years do condemn;
at sunrise and sunset, we can't forget -
as we all grow old and lose, from the beginning
but remain always a simple child within again.

Canterbury Oct 2010

Alan - a lesson

Alan - the driver of the coach
stopped at a roadside caf
and let us off for a pee and break -

one of many pit-stops.
he was unashamed to roll a fag
and puff in their chatting presence -
unashamed and confidant of who he was -
outside, none of them smoked,
some had given it up.
I - in hiding smoke a cigarette peace-pipe -
a pariah, as it's not done. Not him though.

But simply, I am my own company and friend -
no need to crave more all the time;
yes - be with others some of the time.
It's now different - not the future or past.
This moment set down. Now here. This now.
But for how long?

Nov.2014.

The Alien

to town in need of company after 2 weeks illness, isolate

A three foot small, spider-fingered figure,
thin pale spindly arms and legs -
malnourished, pot bellied, enormous eyes -
sad, hurt, a large head.
Seeing but no ears, hearing nothing,
bulbous drumming deaf.
It has landed on earth -
a fault in its mind machine -
off course.

It grew up in neglect and has lived on its own, deep isolate.
But here now on earth - strange creatures move and stir and shift
and have their being with each other inter-communicate.
It has found humans who change, budge around, strangely talk -
that it too was once a person, it recognises deep
in the secret places of the heart. Its eyes widen wider with water
but it can only wait and watch and try to silent comprehend -

skin ridden with antennae hidden, up full volume to detect, predict -
past deep wounds safe encased in fear, mistrust
against the greatest known threats -
contact isolation, absorption in death.

But somewhere sometime it finds, is found, is welcomed -
person-held, discovering where the hard enemy within cries silent.
Empathy as the scent of a rose, sun-warming,
wounds as medals of courage, a hospitality place;
faithful tenderness transforming - the ultimacy
of being understood, to be loved and so to love,
the slow gift of rejected self given back;
pain increase - resurrection rare.

May 2007

It's Hard being Allah

Light a tea-light for God -
feel for him
in his loneliness and aloneness
midst our hate and indifference
of each other -
and so longing for our love.

Nov 2006

Amber - Pause

Christmas '98, Amber
St. Martin's Psychiatric ward
Overdosed - red light -
To know - that i know -
That i am not .
Near sectioned under Mental Act
by GP negligent

the social - and duty
Consultant pomp;
saved by a Senior reg;
All night nurse watch.
A no-one, nothing, nowhere;
All days nothing to do
But baths two a day
Set to fill 2 inch;
No drowning here, but
Discovering you can run
the hot water 3 times
To get a decent fill -
Though you can drown
In the bullrushed pond
Unfenced - if you will.
Smoke non-stop,
tele and pace up and down.
Schizos confront -
Violent behaviour below boil.
Wood cross held aloft
Jumbled jargon like this
Sermon monotoned.
Pills queued
tight fist bureaucrats.
Let out a few hours
then alcohol breath test
in the public passage.
Nurses know all.
Shuffled around beds
Confusion increased.
Locked doors, doors locked -
two breakdowns in 40 years.
Not bad - at all.
Being paid for my sins -
each hour - infinite hell.
There is this unsaid. There,
cedared circle of old trees -
Winnie the Pooh, Eeyore.
Quiet. Green light.
Let go. Go.

From nothing comes something.
Not amber forever.

31.1.02

An Appalling Event in Spring

An older couple
browned from
a recent Costa del Sol tan
and fat from fish and chips
and full of glaring scent
sit finishing coffee
and their sandwiches
from triangular plastic
crackling wraps.

A tiny house sparrow
whom I know to be feeding her chicks
hops on the chair top
and scans their table top
for a possible crumb given or dropped.

She looks aghast
and glances at her mate
for 'what now' in disgust.
This glancing between bird and mate
her lips snarled up
goes on many times.
The answer is simple -
throw the bird a tiny crumb
and not too large or messy
as is commonly done.

Instead, she gathers up
all the leftover crusts
and tucks them in the plastic box
now firmly shut.
No crumbs -

not even ‘from under Thy table’
from the two heartless mean ones.

early 2009

What is an Angel?

I sit in the cold sipping coffee
from a cup with a plastic top and a within-it hole.
‘Coffee of the day please, tall, in a cardboard cup
with room for milk’ and sometimes a raisin twist.
Do I love or do I not? And they know me well now
with their pavement tables in that coffee shop.
Those in the street pass by, one by one
to the toll of the bell clock
with clicks of heels and rustles of bags
and downcast looks. Fraught eyes, wrung dark,
scanning wide for this and that.
It’s shopping for Christmas and lights for trees.
Their eyes are tired, sad, but impulsed along -
drugged by what others do and don‘t.
I go to the Red Cross shop further up.
So many fag ends at the entrance -
wedged between paving cracks.
Me and my broom sweep away
the trash of people because folks
have been trashed in the past.
They walk, stand and ugly talk
because they have not been loved.
Re-entering the shop, I swing my broom
because I am happy to have done a job well done.
It seems full of poor people searching down.
The room and me suddenly glows; a shining one -
an unseen angel has come amongst
and three true Bruegel* folk
are set in the midst - gently holding in tiny hands
the trash cheap bric-a-brac
now turning to gold in their eyes;

*Flemish painter of cartoon people

little people hunched by burden
and round from many layers of clothes,
squinting through bottle-bottom glasses
slung between their eyes,
scared to be seen, hiding to be bold.
One peers at me (who am tall above)
between the rails of clothes,
frightened and scorned before.
Warm flushed now, my eyes say -
'it's all right, you're safe here, no need to fear'.
The angel set down three golding uglies
who are Beauty, Goodness and Truth,
three little people above angels and the heavenly host
Do I love or do I not? I don't care. Care cares us.
Words speak us - not we speak them.
And they too are little creatures.
Waiting to be found Words.

Canterbury Dec.2002

Anxiety

This tyrannical punishing mind
that's come from my mother
persistent 'nagging' - her word
still remains with me but it's not me -
the nagging about past neglects and dead father;
the nagging about fears for the future
all of neglect and loss and isolation and dying.
Old patterns of mind on auto-pilot
so let all this float by.
This gap between the way things are
and the way we think they should be.
It is not our fault
that we get frightened and depressed;
what if there is nothing wrong with me
and an inner voice is pleased with me
This is all training, some discipline

as in karate. Black belt stuff.
Growing old is not for wimps.
Our mind has a mind of its own.
The relentless commentary of our thoughts -
just to see them as mental events
as clouds passing across the sky;
a judging irrational tyrant.
But death is the final healing.
The answer is to be together
through relentless change.
A relentless rationality in all this -
- creation is detached. But people can and do care.

Now my arms are tense and shoulders braced -
a beating immanent; stomach clenched
a vacuum inside - the horror of hell.
Yet outside as if normal.
I have to hold still - coiled unsprung
in case I go mad. But I don't.
Perhaps mad with rage back.
And it goes on and on with a tightened chest.
Just breathe - a terrified child
let it kick and cry and hold
and hold it gently now. It's not my fault -
maybe there's nothing wrong -
so accept all this with compassion. But this is hard.
And now a neighbour has died
feeding into my nonsense of doom and gloom.
We have no control in the end
and delude ourselves if we think we have.
Utter detachment now - clinical reason -
we are born and live and die and that's it.
Detach detach detach.
There are good things in my mind
which I don't notice -
so search the nooks and crannies
amongst the dark caves.
Nobody is normal when you get to know them.
Obedience (from the latin audiare - to hear)
discipline (from disciple - a pupil)

and detachment - keep my cool
all things learnt in karate.
And this inner journey
has the same principles as the martial art.

And now kindness towards myself
and allow things to be as they are.
We carry burdens that don't need to be carried.
This is it -
this is what is.

And give of myself where I can;
see an inkling of gratitude for who I am -
the hardest of all.
And above all for this time -
have patience
and practice and practice again and again.
Working to see my mind
as always 'there' over there, the future
or 'then' back then, the past.
It's the NOW now.

A simple life.
And simply to allow the experience
of each moment to be just as it is
without needing it to be any other way.
Did you know an amoeba
can build his house -
minute grains of sand
with an entrance hole
and a few spikes around -
the whole the size of a full stop.

Just trust. Just as the breath if left to itself
naturally sorts itself out.
The unstoppable juggernaut of mental chatter
has been stopped for a while.

May 2013.

Anxious about Anxiety

May I be free from fear -
becoming sensible - balanced in sense.
Trust. Let go. Aware - the breath,
detach yes even in dying death;
non-attachment - Yes
to simplicity now, and then.
Breathe into anxiety - cradle it Held.
All things new - beginning again
not judging but trusting; letting go -
Neither young nor elderly
accepting tenderly;
watching and patient - not striving to fix.
I am not my pain - I am not separate.
Just be as I am - the only moment now,
the only moment I really know,
not the future or the past.
Whatever it is, it's here. It's ok.
A process proceeding
hold myself, as I was not held safe
at the age of two years
with deaths, major illness and separations;
doom and gloom now
belong to that past unheld
but no need to dwell there
digging more dirt or picking
the scabs and scars from the past.
Feelings are just my feelings -
neither good nor bad; accept them because
they're already here, whatever they are, it's ok.
Soften, befriend myself -
a warm uncertainty, not cold and harsh -
with gentle compassion now;
I can't do the things I used to
but I am good enough and can be more than before
Having been and am, troubled -
I have a lot to be and unique, give (but where?) -
through pain, wiser I am

but not so unique as to be alien-alone.
Whatever it is, it's here. It's ok.

Having never known a father - dead when I was two
and a harsh mother 'absent' in surgery and ill health;
this new word - 'Father', quiet and simple speaks -
the still small voice -
'I am coming to find you', 'You are loved - rest in me
at home at last as I am at home in you'.

June 2012.

Inscape Inspace in Apollo 12

God transcending -
Shot dark night -
The far earth side.

Then sudden sun white light
Strikes sharp
Shot bright
Blind height sight.

Blazed dazing
Retinal glare gazing -
Astronaut daring
Universe bending
Earth sphere curving
Stardust ascending
Floating ellipsing
Infinity unending.
Gravity gone
In awe - mind blank.

The mind's supernova born -
New feeling, thought, idea.
Galaxies, gas clouds,

Constellations, satellites,
Impact lunar craters,
Orbits, planets eclipsing
Black holes sad sucking -
Even space and time.

Again - slow dark
Transcending god
The far earth side.

Out there subsiding -
Is greater here - selfed
in the neurones - of mind.

22.2.02 Canterbury.

2 Separate Seconds
He them Distinguished joined

A small circling fly, shoulder alights
knowing dying looms of the within child
as the before of 'hide me', not heard, nowhere to lay its head.
Dereliction, annihilation, desolation - all 3
sat on the sunned bench squeezed side by side -
imprisoning each other as is their want -
near that great honey stone cathedral house
holding them together - in a shell - just
but it's night dark despite a blinding sun.
The fly, hand swatted, jump-jets fast -
faster than the hand reflex.
A boy chases a cheeky blackbird, games on the grass.
His thick glasses fall as he flying plays. And -
I, sitting quiet - a slow silver car, chauffeured comes
darkened window panes. Blank fear scans inside
and there a bearded face forward leans
and gently waves and smiles bright.
My heart lifts. Out of facelessness I have a face;

I become am - seen through the glass dark
also face to face and met when still far off.
Our archbishop - honoured, fear not.
I knew then - He lifted
the light of his countenance up
and let his face shine on me then
giving back life first, relief, some peace.
Cracked - a foundling was found blest.
The new '*and yet*' out of the dark,
out of the before of ITs upsurge, the past -
had transformed; a moment's good -
at that sacred narrow place
at the 4th rung of the black loop chain
around the grass where the car passed
on the grey cobbled stones, four foot from my face;
two long stones mark the spot
as I sat, moved, not wishing to budge.

A careful dustman meticulous thin
knocked my arm and emptied the bin
and a soft sorry spoke. I looked up
and there his head ringed by the sun
blinding white above, imperceptible in a haze.
A second - I am. 'The hand, the burn, the touch'.
Amazing ordinary, mysterious, meant;
these 2 moments, within 3 persons - sent.

outside Canterbury Cathedral June 2004

The Astounding before Christmas

Street people passing - spendthrift;
hums of many voices, low, soft -
broken salt-ice crackles underfoot
hum-drum people - few well off;
young small families, ordinary things;
gift wrap rolls, glitzy bits, boxes, bags -
shopping, shopping to give

and give more and more;
there is a giving love under
a cloud of frantic rushed air,
The giving underpins
the 'secular' life at this time, now;
maybe motives are mixed and intricate
but there's nothing sophisticate
except for a rare expensive snooty fur, elaborate.
'Secular' yet bursting with the giving desire -
that - the spiritual core.
Different faces, dark clothes from cheap shops
except for the colours on kids - galore.

And what is coming? -
the God-Child is being borne in all
through that well-worn nativity scene of long ago -
but who knows? -
God deeply loves them all and most don't know -
perhaps I as well.

Jan 2011

Baby A & - beginning and the end. Blinds on the Unthinkable,
Drawn or Opened. The Ordering principal -
an aspect of the creator God, the opposite - his chaos, both
effusing from the void. 'Slaughter of the holy innocents' - more
than 3 children a week die from abuse in 'developed' Britain**. A
'fundamentally sick society' where love is last or lost

Dvorak's String Quartet Nr.12 Lento. op 96

Nameless, 17 months, yet 8 of known horrible, brutal abuse evolved-
unbelievable in this fair, curly haired, blue eyed boy's radiance.
Could they not stand the contrast, lighting their felt bad ugly selves?
Sweet - with his 2 older sibs, good. In essence - beauty, innocence.

The Unimaginable, Incomprehensible

Later he became thin and drawn with red eyes, a shaven head -
swung round by his feet, his head bashed against floor and cot

broken tooth swallowed, blood spattered clothes, 8 broken ribs,
full of lice, his face pummelled like a punch bag,
chocolate smeared to cover over his bruised gashed face -
blue with cold then fevered meningitis ruled out,
finger tip and ear lobe cut off, nails pulled out
hospital discharge and his broken ribs missed;
a gouged head then a missed broken back.
All mother thinks, is this day is her birthday.
Death. Died abandoned. The father gone. Broken. Dead.
After a massive blow to the head.
More than 50 injuries, wounds and seen by 78 'carers' in 60 events.
Do as you have been done by - children can taunt pigeons and bully
those smaller than themselves. Born life to quick death

<u>Clues Lost in the Long Grass Trying to Comprehend the Incomprehensible 'Eyes to see, ears to hear'</u>

Carers careless, care less, and the public cries-out for witch hunts;
overworked social work 40 page reports, married to their lap-tops;
real alarm over-ruled by managers, as were the waiting police -
their hidden horror making them dumb, blind and deaf
because it cannot be felt - unable, the unthinkable, to think
in the chaotic looking, blaming - clues missed
but they are there and therein lies understanding a solution in part;
little is known within of the 'mother'! It's all about
independent inquiries into the London borough and hospital work.
Mother initially admitted under the Mental Health Act
as either a cover-up let-off or psychotic as a result;
her boyfrienw imprisoned, liked breaking frogs legs -
both possibly survived in psychopathy,
themselves tormented as babes -
though this maybe denied and denied by any grandparents and so on in history before that. Unhelped - it has to be - it is unbearable to confront, alone, such experiences in borderline states, leaving them mentally and emotionally undeveloped detached, unfeeling, walled off, just surviving, protecting against further hurt - with no empathy, no sense of others suffering, alarmingly indifferent to it, chaotic with no ordering principal within, often with numerous inadequate, aggressive or fathers, absent. Disturbed mothers are compelled to be drawn to such and fearful of revealing their presence.

This is not the borderline diagnosis between neurosis and psychosis
but possibly borderline between psychopathy and insanity, sharp.
And diagnosis gives the initial order - a start, but not the end stuck.
There is no quick psychological fix. Help is long term.
Maybe there were some good times in a few previous months
with a few playmates and their mums in a park;
one such cared for him for a few weeks undamaged respite,
but he was then returned 'home'. Maybe he was welcome born -
for a few months before his real father ran off and why? -
and it all badly slumped soured.
Being loved stimulates all growth but vital for hippocampal, orbito-
and pre-frontal cortex development in integrating living together,
crucial for an awareness of the other and feelings and self.
Being ignored neglected abused can produce breakdown hormones
of stress with blocked brain growth - 'she's not all there' in more
than one sense. Total invasive involvement can lead to death and
total emotional neglect can lead to slow death - 2 extremes of hands
on and hands off. Good hands bring a living life, not a dying one of
neglect. Young children are suffering as Mothers are being forced to
go out to work. But the child abuse has to go on - compulsive rituals
of it to expel the dangerous and the terrible within, trying to kill off
the unloved abused baby within, which screams for love and was
never satisfied or calmed; and so, devious and threatened when their
victim is to be removed, adept at covering up with co-operation that
is false. The mother concealed the presence of the 2 males in the
house, which was not a home, and concealed the toddler's bruises
with chocolate smears around his mouth. If confronted -
aggressive menacing fierce denial, evasion, lies, distortion result.
The stakes for discovery, too high. If the victim dies or is removed -
breakdown can occur to insanity, suicide -
as the unloved, therefore now cancerous bad child self, is destroyed,
that which was so fiercely trying to be walled off.

<u>'Sins'. 'Evil'. Obedience Stultifies. Following the essence of a
trusted father and mother by example is the finest</u>

A 'diagnosis' of 'evil' gets nowhere and understanding is blocked.
It is a total failure of a loving good enough family echoed again and
again in the past. It is not a 'diagnosis' of sins and that's the end but
moreso 'and there is no health in us'. No health means ill-health

or illness and what do we, now, do with that? Confession without understanding just perpetuates and glorifies the strength of the bad. Early on we need to try to understand, try to comprehend the depths of deprivation involved, to attempt to give long term support, containment, treatment which may involve a family split to save.
Too late and imprisonment can be felt as relief at last.
The penultimate front - prison becomes safe.
At last firm action, the ordering principal, begins, long term.
No-one likes feeling out of control and lost.

Blind, Deaf. Publicly Abused as 'Feral' and 'Dysfunctional scum'
The warning bells need sound if numerous workers are involved and without firm co-ordination - their hidden anxieties supported revealed, gut feelings allowed when meeting fierce denial and aggression at the defended dangerous mixture of psychopathy and insanity, veiled. It is easier to forget, to pass the buck around - in neglect. No-one wants to 'see' this stuff. Just as there were only 3 who could be-with in Christ's dying and therefore in a sense, their own; the rest fled. The workers have become borderline, on the borders, edge; the family pathology rampantly infects the caring system and flares out to the public who send abusing threatening e-mails to staff with no 'comforting staff'. The ordering principle has been lost. It is easier to 'witch hunt', sack, demand resignations ; easier to fill in forms and tick boxes and have to write long reports - to defend against turbulent emotion, to stop thinking the unthinkable - than to painfully connect and to understand, and in attempting order, to stand firm. How can you understand another while computer clicking with a lap-top screen on your lap, both screened off? A minority of cases are this serious but a large proportion are so concealed that they are not picked up by the community and social work. Those that are unthinkable, unimaginable, incomprehensible may well need new experienced specialist task teams, within child care, the last pass of the buck, to allow both to function better; to come to the front-line trenches and not to command or stand back behind the troops. After all, a heart transplant requires a specialist team to work. Support, direction, counselling are vital to enable all concerned to withstand, understand the chaos (chaos has potential), the tumult. A paedophile lodger was also involved; was there sexual abuse as

well? All 3 abusers were charged, imprisoned and are still probably
blocked; if not they might be well impelled into deep insanity
or a suicidal end. And God, as Christ, wept.
The house now an empty bruised shell with a door chain lock hung,
symbolic, strung closed-ajar; the squalored life removed.
God help the two siblings, remote.
As winter dreams of spring - may 'dark sentences be understood'.
His ashes were scattered in some unknown piece of ground,
a paupers plot; a few playmates left flowers and a lonely Pooh Bear;
nothing marks his grave, there is none - the brutalised body burnt;
a public outcry, a newspaper put up a plaque. Flowers grew
and cuddly toys which he never had, left on the spot.
Neighbours must have heard screams but fearful,
they'd gone to ground.

<u>The easy believable Unbelieved. The Unthinkable Thought. No God.</u>
All art music, faith and belief spring from Imagination, the image,
which is in the likeness of God - where ultimate values are shared.
God of Tinsel, you better love him more than your baptised named
Son - an adult able to chose, accept death, for only 3 days crucified.
The God whom Christ had known first within his holding Mother,
and Father holding Her - gave love, order, stability, sense.
Ordinary fathers and Joseph are marginalised in religion and now.
The Father God above all, transcendent now, not immanent.
That ordering principle within comes from
both parents' essence and presence, given and received.
This baby had none - tortured, tormented for many months on end -
with no loving parents (Christ had a mother, where was Joseph?, and
two close friends at his death). Who here was really there for him,
in the squalor of that battered house?
And no father, let alone God known to whom to cry out.
in his many gethsemanes and golgotha, the end, cut.
And Christ wept.
This baby's 'parents' relieved, possibly cringing, hollow-laughed;
the cancerous inner and outer screams had stopped.

<u>The Incomprehensible. Why do You allow?</u>
What price that said defence of our freedom? The defence that You
allow free-will, choice - the ransom, the sacrifice of death for us of

your Son, set, allowed- to 'pay (you) for our sins'; sins, a bad strong
penultimate cover-up for our primary vulnerability first. Is His
sacrifice Your love? The emphasis on sins and sacrifice rather than
his death and resurrection showing us ultimate humanity, full real -
that is, a dying to our unreal, defended 'false' selves in maturity
and so able further to understand, help others needy, known.
And human Christ, too, had such, sorely tempted high on the Mount.
So this baby died to galvanize caring institutions to save other little
ones and to show others what all are capable of if given love or if
love is withheld yet cannot face and the result! Is that Love and
life for him? Those forms filled in, boxes ticked, multi-disciplinary
meetings with no true leadership, trumped up statistics, targets met -
all to defend against the trustworthiness
of intuitive feeling, under-standing - the real work.
The massive vulnerability of this non-family, walled off.

<u>The Unfeelable Felt. Giver of Free will -</u>
that You maybe worshipped and loved by choice
but do you love us?
Someone said 'if just one little one suffers there is no God'.
or he is a deranged one. So we cry out that we may be rid of this god
so we might find the unknown love of the God of Love.
If he takes leave of God for himself and for God
like the maturing of the father and the prodigal son, -
that is the highest, dearest leave-taking of man, with mixed hearts.

<u>The Imaginable Imagined within the Unimaginable</u>.
A burst of light midst the dark - from music and art -
this baby - a Caravaggion violent crucifiction.
Now he has been borne aloft winged fast,
propelled straight to the arms of God.
His ascension, his transfiguration - Him - up to God.
Not an El Greco assumption or Madonna and Child in the clouds
but God and Baby P enfolded up.
No madonnal coronation, no angelic annunciation.
No. A coming down to meet, not a having to go up.
A saint above every saint and they're all adult.
Not the pentecostal spirit dove's descent down -
No - not a part of god but the whole of God down;

not 'knock knock, knocking on heaven's door' but
the gates of heaven flung wide open, known, won - God descends
down to him, comes to him like the Prodigal Father comes,
runs down to meet his now suffering Son;
the prodigal father - wasteful, lavish in creation-evolution-
procreation, sperm millions where winning through is only one.
His annunciation down, utterly special, not by angels but by God.
A tremendous Bach Johannine passion surrounds within the sound
and high lifted up - 'o weary, broken body, farewell' - unbound
released from every grief and pain at last - and, shining, found.
The tortured Word can be transformed and can transform.
Young buds surprisingly appear in winter frost, cold blasts. Why?
This baby's essence, energy*vitality, cannot be destroyed or lost,
now a whole healed babe and child.
Within. Beyond. 'His understanding cannot be fathomed'.
His intimate doors closed on us grown children
trying to understand his procreation - the world, the universe.
'Silence,like a cancer grows', can be absence loss, the fear vacuum.
But if you know being-with, the other of language is also silence
listening to real essence, not cheap chattering metallic tinsel-talk;
an ineffable enfolding strong presence -
the silence within presence;
here God is said to enter with his all.
Stillness - the depth below word, image, sound - fired white, fired.
Not the harsh silence of thou shalt not, but thou shall.
You are loved so can You love, before all -
and Baby P was not and was blocked -
but maybe he now is and can, in the quiet stillness, warm.
The depth below word where we cannot speak and need not.
'Safe at last' - the paupers plaque, beyond bent time warped.
+'Goin' home, goin' to fear no more' Dvorak's largo New World.

Dec 2008.

etymology 'prodigal' - L. prodigere - to drive forth/away, wasteful, lavish.
Baby P is ? Paul Phillip Peter Patrick Percy. **See Article 5
Universal Declaration of Human Rights.
*$E=Mc^2$ energy can neither be created nor destroyed. +Cotton fields
slave song.

Baptism

perfection is a curse
promulgated by the church
a thoroughly horrible shoddy word
unless it means trying and not trying
to be whole. Names are our seeds,
our essence special place, heard
though words can confuse.

days have always been uncertain
between the landmarks signposts
trace elements - of skin and bone -
iron for the substance soul
singeing lemon peel's sharp hum.
But we're mainly water-made life blood
given a place by a name hallowed
within our water and under the water shelled
silver trickle on our head, once safe-held
maybe within grace of the white alb fold;
aeons - before time's dawn - head thought,
though why not trickled on our
heart bare baby breast felt? A child -
and welcomed well, the well spring
for sparkling life - once amoebic silt.

Thousands of poignant pansy faces smile
to be seen, scented, named in the park
tinkling at our ankle stiffness
beside the running river - poured down
on the deep heart sound of earth.

Canterbury Westgate Gardens April 2004

A Grotto Bath

it's in our real nature to be happy, whole - a blueprint inbuilt;
we, short of life breath air, gasping for perfection as

fishes in staccato groans evolving to walk on parched land,
ungainly folk, like wildebeests on helium out of control -
stampeding round in the arid dust of the herd -
no easy elegance of whale or bird;
as if also buried alive above ground, unheard -
bruised by the bloody blessing of insult and anger
hounded by numbers and by time itself a number -
in chattering multiplicity and argumental tumult
drizzled frazzled bits - the tinselled bling of the town,
the twizzlesticks of my candy floss mind down.
I've come to look at nothing - a whole lot of nothing
I want to be an unmoved stone finding its place despite the river
but I am muscle made to move and falter
on the last lap of life and stumbling through somehow forever;
mind bleeding from insult - the great penultimate mover;
fear like a mallet arced down on metal, nails hammered in flesh,
the white flame of fright searing through tinder bodies, unable -
can I be saved - if not, the acid pain unbearable.
I begin to sift through the polluted water of desolation
aware that my illusions are unreal, hard human work, good sweat.
I want to be flowing smooth in the places of people -
like I am on the sea under clear sky and sighing clouds
or among the wind-waving rustling grass.

A deep bubbling stream from round rain pebbles
a cheerful noise - this, the running bath
solid rocks round the base to step over -
mind and body perhaps like perfume of the flower.
I see my hurt clear to the bottom of the deep pool
like dull steel hammer blows to my heart's centre;
for years I have fought to love my life, but a tiger said 'no'.
A soft smile means everything - without teeth's snarl
The sponges of my lungs moisten back
to fish gill-feathers from the dry fumed town;
the burden of the great body bones lighten -
as I wallow in water reaching to far off hope -
the voice within drumming insistent that there is only bad -
then a slow dawning that this is delusion -
aware to do the only thing I could do -

to become aware - attempt to rescue myself;
aware so I don't even know who I really am.
Laying down a current flow of words, the sharp knives of words;
my only children are these words also
in the deep green scented herbal blest water;

also He knows to ask 'why' and I...
as the secular talks to the sacred.

Pink body wallow - pink feeling, I sink in the glow
rose blush flow - the evening sunset of candlelight low,
ferned, bullrushed, cream soap shell, scallop shallow
shells round the bath as the sun cascades light shafts now
through coloured bottle-window glass, shelved in rows.
I become a dolphin, a fish at home in water
from whence I came a million years ago -
muscle stretching - in hot steaming bubbling green water -
the cramped stilted stifled
gravity drowned, embattled
upright weight encased
defence eases - for a moment gives way

and a voice maybe says my name,
be held small and undoing, let go, stay

Oct 2006

To write on 'Be Here Now' – (as we're trying to create!)

I'm sorry but O gosh

my brain neurones are in a flashing
non-stopping scatter and skit,
randomly in clicks, firing
all over the place
without words yet.
That's where I am now -

being asked to write -
are others the same?

Table pens paper silence chat.
Do we know each other yet?
Then out of this chaos an image forms and boils.
Thoughts copulate conceive gestate -
sperms all over the place
aiming for one big ball of egg -
frantically fighting for first place;
to twiggle and wiggle
through the soft shell
and then wham, the Big Bang
the Universe is create.

Small simple things - that's all we've got as yet
but from out of the simple comes big.

April 2013.

Beauty Spoiled

Have you seensome ladies bottoms;
they have tight short pants
under their trousers
as they walk past -
dividing two beautiful buttocks
into the ugly four;
that must be sore.

Nov.2014

Bedevilled. Discovery. Lions and a Lamb

Pigeons haven't learnt to use one foot to hold a piece of bread on the ground steady to peck and eat. Perhaps I Can!

The Interminable propaganda of Depression.
1.bedevilled by negative images flashes and thoughts

waking wanting more sleep to escape myself
two words 'THE VOID' appear
or an image of a woman in black
with a pudding hat
carrying a metal thermos flask
like the one I have
on a motorway bridge;
she intends to jump to her death
but walks toward me - she doesn't jump.
I am full of fear - thumping heart,
stomach a knot, shoulders clenched.
I am forced to get up
perhaps a way of saying 'you're alive if up
dead if not'. Yet in the day I am always
fighting the fears.
A battle here between inner life and death.
        Simple! as that.
Or the TV ad for a mouthwash -
a glamorous woman undresses
and takes off all fault cover-ups
to reveal a toothless gap;
horrific the contrast - the siren song ad.
And now the doom precipitated
by the doctors quarterly investigation
of my constant slightly low haemoglobin
and kidney function tests - unnecessary repeats
without my choice - to cover themselves.
2.The old doom and gloom
and dying disabled paralysed desolate
        a slow disintegration.
I write this to give it space.
3. And obsessive tunes in my head.
A fear of insanity looms, some small medication
but it has side effects on my gait;
then I neurologically ruminate.
Yet many are on pills for this and that.
        So now I have caught
these now just passing mental events
not besieged by tigers in the jungle
but holding a pen down on paper

there to welcome them in a gesture of embrace
and to give them space.
Whatever it is, it's here and it's ok -
myself, my gait, gloom, my kidneys, my bloods
and now the tunes in my head as possible lullabies.
4. I am now aware of being constantly critical,
down-putting of people and of myself
and oversensitive to ordinary knocks;
unkind to others and to myself.
Driven in whatever - shopping cooking
cleaning clearing gardening
to finish in the fastest time.
So in a shop I see all the colours and shapes
for the first time in good time slowly -
        and with care;
there a proud pineapple sitting tall
with his mates, bristling and sweet
and my chuckle seeing him so -
so I soften. I am always too hard.
These small nice things and
a helpful shop assistant with her smile there.

This curious awareness embrace -
whatever it is, give it space
    with my life breath.
But this of no avail on its own.
But then I have M long years -
steady faithful valuing affirming;
In him is the grace of God -
growing old, full of grace
and where lions lie down with lambs.
That thoughts become written in water
not as true dogma cast in stone -
    let them float past by,
    they're not my real self.

Can I be a contented cow, warm and soft
in a warm field, chewing the cud instead?

Better that life's knocks are seen as a challenge
to become hardy, resilient and robust -
that is the meaningfulness.

Mar 2012

Before and After
Nocturne

It's raining after a great wind.
The dry days have broken
and black pools tell of a simple quiet
reflected in quartets of yellow light.
Short puffs tender ripples of tickling gusts
and grey mists tripple drizzling bits.
And water slits trickle and cut
on window pains thrown oblique -
watching drops join and fall fast -
a flattened nose pink against glass
reflecting a regression and sudden
rebound out of mist.

4.5.68 Cape Town.

Beginning Again.

Under the clown mask of my mind capering
The warped remains jingle
And I run with time under subways
Down urine stained steps and stairs -
Porcelain tiled and gummed with immense breasts
And groins and nightmare dimensions
Of coloured pretensions and signs and stares.
Drink long and tall John join the men.
The drummed hiss and charge
And tack of trains cracking

Blue flash shocks
As steel lines converge.
And bowlers and umbrellas
Sit erect and glazed
Looking at the white eyed gaze
Their eyes dazed in time and space.
And time runs in tunnels
Black pipe-line pumped
And up steel wells and shafts
Machines scream from metal throats
And people untalking commute pulsed
Through gut and city blood in corpuscular crowds.
Trains pass below and above
And soil is choked concrete
Where no grass blade cracks
And the cracked angle of mouths
And crackling laughs.

I walk on pavements
On edge stones thinking -
This shell of deception -
A compression of dimension
From a once noble conception depthed -
Jingling - as I run with time along corridors -
My boots come covering cracks
And gaps between gaps
And we meet stare and pass
Looking from empty eyes for a touch.
Watching under scaffold nets
A plump man haired -
A fat paunch and braces parting
Stir with quiet eyes and tongue sucking
A copper orange cauldron, drummed
Of liquid hot tar.
And buckets fill blue smoking
Dripping, slung swinging
Swinging up into grey sky.

I press an ivory button among moments

Under black names on a black door.
And the door opens
And I wait for wisdom and the years to pass.

25.11.68. London. -
for my assessment interview for a Jungian analysis

That Bird Dying

A little blue-tit on the road,

no blue but a winter coat -
lay quietly on its side
immobile as I passed
by its still side.
But its eye blinked once -
all that was left of its life.
I didn't like seeing it -
fear in my heart
and nothing I could do
to make it all right
but remove it from sight
which, repulsed, I didn't do.
We all have to die, but why?
a long dying perhaps
of illness or slow age -
relentless, nullified.
Just leave it for a predator -
cat, hawk, fox or magpie
to recycle fast - devoured thereby.
So few dead birds seen
out of the millions alive.
This, its birth labour
to a new life somewhere -
the labour of done death
dared bare - in precious care.
Its the fear of becoming nothing
that is, inside, killing -
all that living

for after nought.
But in dying -
it's the trust of an afterlife
that lives alive.
That the given grace of God.

When I returned
the bird had gone.
It's over. Recycled.
And with sore relief, I sighed.
Maybe it had flown released
special to new blue skies.
Beautified. Beatified.

Feb. 2012

A Flavour of Busy Boho's Caf-Bar Eating-place

Double alcove-fronted, panelled, embellished window glass -
a table two seats each side in a cosy corner recess
where you can drink your coffee almost on the cobbled street
next Eastbridge homes above the river Stour, south east beat
and watch people pass of every shape size colour and creed -
like being in a bubble without noise - strange but good indeed.
A young lad climbs an old lamp post there. I do appreciate that -
something out of the ordinary, walk-along, beaten track.
'Chestnut roasts £1' from an ember-barrelled barrow, rising steam,
a man and his dark daughter, gypsy-like, tend and roast; she seems
as yet too little as she has to bounce up high to help to stir;
sacred twigs of kissing mistletoe for sale, hang down there.
Across - the familiar patch where good homeless folk freeze
and peddle their 'Big Issue' mags and I often think they sneeze
when they call that name out fast; and their happy dog - knapsack
bed and blanket wrapped, tail wagging out, rolls on his back.
Boho's good boss, nice staff, welcome us and them in their caf,
likewise, allowed for the loo, the wriggly, young dark lass.
People glance in, wide eyed, but it's full, so they rush past.

Inside, a painting of a plane dropping six bombs in high flight -
of microphones down, - we must listen to the war torn plight.
Brocade papered purple walls, and some in a sage green coat,
paisley black and white tablecloths, tables of solid iron wrought,
van Gogh wicker chairs in rainbow colours of paint blocks,
tall lamp-stands with awry shades, nine art deco sunray clocks,
adjoined, time's props - and plastic candelabra light glass drops;
a green reindeer head hangs next three black swallows, not ducks.
An elaborate gild mirror near a Gainsborough print duchess -
someone has added pink novel specs thru' which she stares hapless
at an heraldic coat of arms and blackboard with 'roast parsnip soup'.
A digeridoo corner-stands, waits; and piece de resistance, a scoop -
on a candle-lit slim nook - a plaster incandescent gleaming Christ,
all lime-green, shows his shining heart, a new startling slant is cast.

Outback, the covered patio awning of lemon yellow shade,
a growing bamboo and on the back wall too - sage paper brocade;
a wicker chair in yellow paint, wall hung, suspends in quiet space!
And among the green plants, a statue of a pregnant woman placed.
I have a coffee with milk from the list, don't know its name -
Americano, the same? and a white plate of three hunks of tasty toast
piled under juicy cut mushroom buds and a soft poached egg blob-
(I once said 'me no like shush' as a kid so I leave the same crust)
-while I pour over poems under my green-pompom black-cap nob
which often seems to give a twinkle and a warm smile back.
It's not hackneyed. It's unique. Boho - Bohemian south bank.

St.Peter's Street Canterbury Dec 06

Coxed, Boxed and Foxed

A sermon for a time for not being so but to be being!
(? a modern Western Dhammapada!)

Don't let yourself by yourself put yourself in a box
or even moreso by others, branded sizzling as this or that.
There are trillions of boxes - diagnoses psychiatric, ethnic groups
religious types - and categories of soul, sinner, of social class
poor, rich - often the rich are poor and the poor rich.

or clever stupid shy bossy over the top, psychopath.
Mostly in the West, it's the 'I am what I spend' box
and the restless couch potato of the tele box
Not even box yourself with 'do' or 'don't'.
We all are - I am - persons, in the divine great image
of 'I am that I am' as also the 'couch potato'.

Go deeper than this box or that
to the ultimate within
where out-there, inhere, gently dissolves
and the All becomes clear ... er!
    of 'I am that I am'
        and
Yeshua says 'yes you are' as I am.

Openness to the ultimate unknowable but feelable real
in a moment, in an hour, day, year - pregnant emptiness;
the originary naked self , a placeless place the true experience,
shared with another - making room for ourselves.

But we also need the cash box
of even a 1p copper coined piece - and locks,
keys, to live in some sort of order unmocked.
Boxes containers can be convenientbut,
watch your whole holy holey socks -
this pronounced coxing and boxing
demeans - flummoxes, foxed.

No - not even, 'a watch it' box
(look at the multifarious meanings of 'even')
or even the life-coffin-death box
Accept the question of why? how? what? box!
as much as an answer box - the box job lot.
And that includes me also, tight intucked.

The divine hand is a devilish ticklish Puck

May 2007

London '78

A Loaf of Bread

Someone long ago, stone-ground
dry grain seeds to pulp on granite rock -
moulding barm-froth to dough-pulp.
The floating zinging yeast cells, raised it -
rising secret on the simple cindered fire.
A loaf was born, leavened to lift us up; -
and 'ground' us; a fragment bread, fermented
from a full within, whole loaf.
All the world knows the staple food,
a broken bit from heaven's hearth heart,
earthed, opened, felt and loved.
Dipped husks, soft chunks, mouth melting;
nuggets, crispy hunks and crunchy rusks;
steaming shapes sit solid waiting, cooling quiet;
round square oblong oval bulb-lumps, plumped;
pastel creams and scented brown blobs, dumped,
light flour, spray scatter misting, oozing warm inside.

He broke it - 'This is me for you' -
to those gathered round -
the simple table fire.

Canterbury Mar. 2004.

Breakwater

what is broken changed - a world theme?
but here in this fractal - an island coast
are spans of flat tan sand

fresh sea tang salt hidden air
gulls swoop and easy rise
the bay grey hazed - but the tardy
North sea south channel tide
creeps in imperceptibly slow
and a few bored herring gulls patient
bob with the facing tide -
they can live 30 years or more,
no rush, and can smash drop mussels
from a great gouged height;
their intriguing beak red spot
for the young to peck
soliciting regurgitated food up.
A flock of fifteen sanderling
wave chase and scitter in centipede steps
knowing the rising water will ease the sand soft
to peck the snap fleeing sandfleas hopping smart.
There should be no shortage of chalk in schools
from the falling frozen and thawing billion-year crags;
little goblins built the cliff chalk bricks
huddling neat beside each other in stacks
but chalk snapsticks now are not most commonly used
as our inscape defences computer crumble fast.
I made my mark with chalk rock 'I love..' irrelevant
on a concrete wall sure to be erased by high tide.
A marble real pigeon edges close,
black grey white superb swirled
his tail quivers wanting a thrown crumb.
I hadn't noticed that before; have you noted
babies also tremble when food comes near?
The bay is well kept tidy, very English -
senior citizens, prams, beach huts, toilets and a caf;
bungalows, greengrass, many notices and dog pooh bins;
once we were wild simple primitive unkempt.
A flock of foreign students lose their ball
to the flat sea bed below. I crunch over mussel
rocks, retrieve throw and bow and they clap high
one says 'I'll never forget' in thanks.
There's bird foot trefoil valerian wild carrot -
lush sea spinach for the wild soup pot.

I walk the tight rope breakwater into the sea
marked by a candy striped light pole
just beating the coming-in tide. This was once
a working harbour for beached boats.
Rag worms crawl and cockle shells burrow
star fish walk, dogwhelks snorkel and someone
makes sand tracks on the rocks, who knows who.
Barnacles grip, winkles close their trap doors
and mussels are mean tight - not food for the birds.
Lugworms make their sandcasts like themselves
not quite in the image of god - burrowed -
eating watersand and excreting it in coiled tubes -
tiny above-level ropes; two lug holes like us
paired, a pit ear for in and a pile cast out. Squishy -
best bait dug by fishermen within their deep U tubes.
God is an artist painting the world-shore in strokes
parallel sand wave lines weave among white chalk fields
and the millions of black mussels, last years crop.
He has a sense of humour - strange 'aliens' from seaspace
dead men's fingers, bootlaces, sea mice. And sea squirts squit
and zipping scuttling zebra cuttle-fish dart;
rock boring mollusc piddocks also use
their sharp edged shells to drill holes.
I didn't see all these. And no doubt
they prefer our laughter with, not at.

The breakwater breaks our turbulent mood low
our broken tide comes in lapping relentless slow
filling the sacred scared, rich nothingness, now.
Our waters have broken new birth to grow.

Westgate on Sea April 2004

A Breughal-Within ButterMarket Mass of People.

Squat, dumped fat.
Knee knocked, bird toed.
Beamed broad, lamed, jowled.

Ring-pierced runts sored.
Lumped, bent, squint
glassed, hobbled.
Skewed stuffed -
tramped shuffled
Chubbed Buddhas pram pushed.
Wheel chaired, bumbled.
Hunched, spine curled.
Bald scruffed cropped.
Frowned grinned gargoyled.
Weighed by bags low bent -
Yoked curbed braked crawled
Vexed sighed teared grinned.
Butts burst, bellies bared,
boobs sag, bulged lunch-boxed.
A Brit bag-pipe drones
Deaf, dumb, blind in-side
Dazed and gagged,
pugged on the snout.
'Wheels that squeek get oil'.
And there, it's so.

They hum
sing sweet. Swear
unheard in word.
A race apart, a part.
I, Inchoate, blurred -
Friable, fragile fractioned
Infinitely finite,
Febrile, imprisoned chained -
I, not they -
Beyond the fold.
And it is so.

And it is so.

Broken Beauty
(with thanks to Gerard Manley Hopkins - 'Pied Beauty')

Glory be to God for broken things.
  Cracked pots, plates, bones, bottles, bruised brains;
    branches, shells, shards, glass. And grounded wings.
A beaten child, toy limb-torn, shaken brings
  sad hearts, sheer broken minds, cracked asylum schized-sing
    to shuffling, shifting shadows sick-wrung, in cells cage-kinged.
And thunder-split sundered skies cathedral-peal ring.

All things counter, common, re-ject, strange;
  Whatever is discard, cracked (who knows how?)
    With blast-blown past, sacrificed, slow-decay, fast-change,
He fathers forth whose brokenness surrects
      united-diverse, parts-whole. Him pray-praise.

Canterbury.

Broken Bridge

Someone with cancer of the throat

Stalactites of frost ice
picked cold as hell,
crystal in the clear white air -
drip cooling crisp down
the real red relieved
dammed cancer throat;
life cancelled by 'growth' -
a meridian cut to the quick
in out, out in -
from South to North.
(Also tumourous -
our greed to increase, advance,
progress, succeed.)
But rocked in the hollow
of the arm - infinite.
Dew diamond drops
evaporate -
tears down the face -
slow - the face, a bridge

between folk.
Eyes talk, ears see.
Mouths are silent - mute
blocked - by a broken bridge.

Canterbury Apr 2004

A Broken Reed

She went down to the waters edge and peered in between the long reed strands.

It was a footpath along the Regents Canal in London near Marylebone at the height of winter. There had been a snowfall. It was cold and her breath was as smoke in the air. She was a beautiful woman with fine features and fair flowing hair taking a slow walk in the crisp air to reassemble her self-pride to comfortable proportions. No other person spoilt the white delicate scene or shook the powder snow off passing branches, neither were there footprints behind or before. She was troubled. He had left her with no word, everyone loved her; she just couldn't understand. A ripple in the water caught her eye. She stopped sudden and short; and another and another - like rising bubbles. She knelt down and peered between the reeds. She could see her reflection and admired it again as she smoothed back an aberrant lock. But then another appeared. It was no reflection. She was Ophelia again. It was Ophelia drowned.

But Molly, a dishevelled drug addict, her personality almost obscured by inner pain, had been sleeping rough under a bridge in a cardboard box further down. She woke from a turbulent sleep, rose sore afraid, and stumbled, shuffling to the canal edge. There was no other person present at this early hour. She knelt by the water, drew up some in a heroin ready syringe and prepared to inject her raw sore covered arm with a belt tourniquet. But a bubble rose from the water. And another. She peered in and saw the image of her dead mother Ophelia.

'I'm late' - Molly said, and threw herself into the pale arms of the reflection. Re-united. A broken reed.

Canterbury Oct. 2002

Bzz. Thump

A bungee-jumping bumble bee nuzzles nectar,
buzzing among tiny slim yellow hawksbeard flowers.
He stops, lands and under his weight the stems, slender -
bend, bow right down, even to the rich brown ground altar.
But Bumble zooms off to the next nectar-cup-
bouncing-back-bloom lifting, springing back up.
He buzzes and I chuckle in delight and fun
and so we fly free round the round orange sun.

July 2006

English Buses

Double decker tall ships of the road -
they used to be red but rarely now -
trundling humbling, bundling
people cargo
over the bumbling bumps
of potholed tar below;
tacking and swerving in great arcs
with their flat-face bows.
But that was a narrow near hit though as
our bus, through the old Westgate arch tower
(Canterbury's Scylla and Charybdis -
between the rock and the monster),
held its breath, drew in its tummy
and squeezed through snail-slow
with a long sigh. Bravo.

Others take for granted that captain's skill -
sitting upright, uptight staring straight on.
But not to be sneezed at - my own
unknown smile unshared known.

I chuckling changed tack - my small sail,
now from half empty to half full.

Early 2009

Buttermarket 1

The morning square is empty
and a shop sign squeeks -
Wind hanging.
Only the lonely read poetry.
The refuse man in yellow bright jacket
swerves his caterpillar machine -
Front whiskered suckers awhirr
in gutters for fag ends.
I drop my papers carefully
in the black bomb bin
specially aside set.
A couple come
and open mouthed
Stand staring at the starved stone christ
above the cathedral gate;
My old teddy bear with open arms
is so much softer and warmer.
A fresh lass with pink cheeks detecting my aloneness
asks me the 'things that guide you through life' -
Her bible firm clutched to accost -
'things' don't guide, so
I wave her on her lonely search.

I sip my coffee at the round caf pavement table.
And my cigarette smoke rises -
Incense.

17.1.02 Canterbury

Buttermarket 2

Workers dad, steel-eyed mate
Wheel push chair
Chubbing child, cobbled street.
Little 'uns judder in prams -
'a bone-shaker i'n't it' - joggled.
The old pub sign - a twenty degree angle shift
Not a corner wind lift.
You can paint a picture in words
if you stop and see.
Not seeing - I can only see
if it first sees me.
Guys and gals young, spiked hair
Pierced nose, lips and ears
Tight jeaned bums appear.
Pigeons settle on crumbs -
They clatter, skit-skeet, flick-fly fast.
The mountain wheels of a bike-
a nice sound on wet street -
between quiet people hums
And cobble heel clicks.
Held packets russle swing.
A long coat lady - old
Twinkles her little legs -
A pudding hat pulled down
firm above her nose
She peers through pebble rims -
her shoes bochel, rocker bottomed.
Everything happens unnoticed;
Nothing happens in the square -
It's all a between.

'Everything handmade here'
The potters shop squeezed between.
A peppering of thought masks
come out of cracks
from their houses
And disappear fast -

where to meet?
I'm intrigued.
The seasons colours in shop windows
Are lilacs heathers and blues;
For men - its khaki in all hues.
'Fashion tops and trousers tailored - best buy'.
No-one in the street looks pale model-like
Though they desire, aspire.
The street cleaner
And his chariot of fire
Sweep past me fast
And I smile and fondly point
To his tickling brush wheels.
His grey eyes smile wide
And he greeting meets.

31/01/02

Buttermarket 4

There is a soft hum in the muffled square,
humming mumbling, humbling murmuring
happy as crickets singing chirping, no crickets about,
of quiet rosy folk after Christmas and New Year
the air gentle after snowflakes and light rain clear.
My shoulders loosen lax, drop down here;
people can be sweet and gentle there
from a deep distance in the cobbled square;
double chin dimples and happy twinkles, debonair -
some crippling along in winklepicker stilettos
another sad, doddling with bladdered drunk woes
A little old roundling lady, spine curved
in many directions went her way, fine, observed
with a twitch, country hat pulled down, beige;
bags, rocker-bottom shoes, long mac -
into Hawkins bazaar she neatly popped,
suddenly skittled, stopped, side-stepped,
to a shop for small kids and toys; strange -

toys for herself? - yes, full shelf ranged -
happy as a cricket singing and chirping.
I chuckle to myself warm watching
from the window of the old pub across.
Trifles of little beauties; tickled pink gloss -
light as sweet candy-floss spun tossed across -
circling curling stick-twirled, whisked.
This - the little lad's two fishes and five loaves
the peoples hunger somewhat stilled -
a butter melting moment, lulled filled.
The sound of one hand clapping - mine, is the sound
of laughter - there is no another hand heard.
Daily dying, singing spinning these shaped words -
the meltscent herbs of sent grace shed.
No trees here - but somewhere, arms spread
their falling leaves return to their roots -
detritus and dust to dust contributes
to - earth to earth underfoot; soil transmutes.
Yet I have many selves, that darkened child shoot
crouched cornering in a corner deprived abused;
without a family you're a nothing lived.
But love is not love at first sight sighed.
I sneeze, spinning words on a paperscrap
and from the bar-lady 'bless you' quiet.
A second hearty sneeze - I giggle light,
another 'bless' in accord, gently heard.
I chuckle and turn - and she grins, broad.
Eyes meet   bright eyes.

Jan 2006

Summer in Cafe Rouge Longmarket Square

Notification! Civil Rights?

a. Heartless insensitive talk is now not permitted in enclosed buildings as it is far more polluting and damaging than smoking and rife in its spread of related dis-ease and ultimate disease - of human

pain, the prime mover and thrust cause.
b. 'Outdoor caf tables and chairs are barred to non-smokers - they have to eat and drink in the dark inside'.

so we twinkled together under sun-shades
over tea-cups tinkling with spoons
in strata-ed cheesecake neatness, ice-cream,
hearts melting and strengthening -
the musings of mystical mavericks
with our peace pipes
in the within of things.

By nature folk are lovers
who create in order to love -
bursting the wineskins
of old categories - the current kilter
and of ecclesiogenic neurosis
of thought and heart -
or of those who row
with one 'right' oar -
or the walled 'great stare'
of meditation, schizoid
or the jackboot of callous talk and act -
cigarette craving's roots.

And we, free-ranging
over the universe
soared in the thermal
updraft of resonance -
where below stared
war and drought,
carbon foot-prints
and carbon sinks -
in the new need
new language arose
then we plummeted to earth
to the lips of our wounds
through dark parachute clouds,
lightning zig-zag streaks

and the belly rumble bursts
of thunder, black and deep
as we carried sunlight shafts
in our mesh-net bags -
a requiem for a dream.

June 2007

A Navy Woollen Cap in Pantellis caf

The cap is eating the cake -
a little lad's eyes hiding under;
only his mouth nibbles -
sticky crumbs all over;
bigger than his face - the pepsi mug
an inch away, for a small hand gulp.
Muffin disappears deep in a
minute's munched meditation,
then cap is raised - wide eyes around look.
'Come on son' says strong Dad -
both wiggling from squeezed seats -
and off they go for the next adventure.

The cap loved the boy warm, in the cold
the cake loved the boy who loved the cake
and cap and pepsi likewise.
Everywhere, things say they love you,
however little loved.
But first - Dad loves the boy.
'Come on daughter'!

Canterbury, Feb 2004

Casualty

Longing - a catastrophic

burst of recognition
in this suffering
most society and self
induced.
In explosive paraesthetic
liberation of self
Resolved.

And I laugh in my depth
Empathic, full
at the scream of a child.
And the drunken, drooling
vomitus-ridden poliotic
who couldn't escape
metal-real impact.
That is what makes us
creatures of a god -
paralysed by paradise
Blind
As it cannot be got here
in the smell of vomitus
or incense. Near
I saw what god sees
in a flash -
a mass of muddled
human matter - a part.
And softened.
hand washing with carbolic soap
the measles crusts
from a Cheyne-Stoking child.
And those polished benches browned
velvet - by black, ill shod starved.
The thread of pain
weaves bodies bowed
Acne eaten
Slukking slime
Cracked and stabbed
Groan and cry of
Children dried

Or burnt to bone.
And dust -
to dust return

That was my glimpse -
flinching at the automation
demanded by a mass of medicine
And not being steel
Forcing steel
Into child cast
Which burnt and stuttered.
I play it cool - the cast
Opisthotonic in imprisoned anger -
Asking for release or answer.

It was resolved in that carbolic glimpse
And omniscient became soft and close.
The yellow moon is there
netted by silvering leaves of gum.
Tendrilled taut
at an unadaptable pace -
in this factory of pain
pills plaster
And no peace.
The deeper questions of living
have no place in chaos.
But yes - sharp, when that is resolved
And a cup of coffee is passed.

'66 - Mpilo Hospital 'Rhodesia' as a Junior House Medical Officer

Magnifi-Cat on Cathedral Spring Grass

A puddle of dappled fat cat, a squat tump*
contrasting enchanting, incurled paws, plump
nesting in the cropped lush fresh green grass there,
the rare ancient-garden-stone-walled-square;
a place of peace and space, the interface pass -

day-closing, sun coupling, basking,
eye blinking in comfort, quiet, apart
smiling silent in the warming spot.

'Do I sleep or not?' Cat asks, shut-eye
'or just relish being admired
but undisturbed by strokes by
tall strange humans, high
two-legged passers by' -
an occasional returning shy
slit eye-glance out, the land to spy;
so an odd purr responding
for sun-warmed fur suffusing
pressed down to skin tingling
'feels oh - so good now'
and Cat and I became the Purr.
Bundle of dappled furr -
relational - to satisfy to sanctify, simplify
Cat never purrs on his own,
animals never let you down
except when they die
so smiling too - I delight and sigh and reply
with a backward-gurgling-glance good-bye.

day-dreaming, dwelling grounding gathering abiding, sun-courting,
soaking loving nestling, evening-fading, absorbing-warming;
being, doing-nothing, being offered, living - alive entire,
and offering everything in the Now;
I learn in this waiting somehow
that it isn't waiting - as waiting is thought -
about what I must do and need next anyhow -
as Cat shows me what is already here to edify
that my eyes right before me require.
'All real living is meeting'*, an opening afire.

Canterbury June 2007
*Tump - a small mound
*Martin Buber.

Cathedral

It's all so high here
And we so low.
Swing high soul
Swing low.

As the man with brass and chain
Swings sweet incense
Incensed to fame
In the eyes of god.
Swing soft soul
Swing low.

Pure song reverberates
Reaches the earth-end echoed;
And solid sandstone
Stops the spread of depth.
Sing sweetly soul
Sing deep and low.

You whom I stabbed last year
Up there,
Murdered in mangled pain
Smothered, fractioned, chained -
Did you know I was cutting cord -
Cut deep and wide and free, Lord
And give me aim.

The candles, christ
And cross and priest
Are all so high
Up there and out -
Dig with it man
In deep concern -
Swing fast, swing doubt.

And there the people
Part but cut,

Dressed in Sunday best -
Dark -
Corsetted in what will
Have its say;
The fat will out
And fry with floating flowers
From hats high and proud
At judgement day.
Frizzle fast soul
Below.

Confused - I need it all;
It must remain
But new and old.
Swing high soul
Swing low.
The pendulum arc
Struck sharp -
Depth, deep concern
The ground, the rock
Of my meaning marked -
Where total isolation
From You as well
Is faith absolute.
And God saw it was good,
Not now.
Swing deep soul
Swing low.

25.3.67. Cape Town Cathedral

Cern and Particle Physics And 'Perhaps'

'What we need is imagination'... Richard Feynman – physicist being in the onset storm-depths of our inner core universe. The great physicist Niels Bohr said 'You're idea is crazy. The question is: is it crazy enough to be true?'It takes the biggest to discover and look with the smallest in many fields of knowledge. Too much knowledge cohered is dangerous.

to myself

I am convinced there is a co-relation, equivalence - of mysticism, particle physics, psychoanalysis, metaphysics. Each hint at each other. Each could learn from each other. The same principles thread through all. The surface tinsel-talkers of this and that are now afraid - say Cern should be stopped. They cannot look at their hidden 'psychotic' equivalent depths for fear they, not Cern, will blow up or collapse to a black hole under massive gravity pull. There is 10 times more dark matter with no light, than the visible light stuff -
the world has always been in troubled dark.

Going up, not down, to Fresh Earth

Today the early town is happier for me because I heard the sound of the universe in bird-song peeps of my life-line phone check; because a caterpillar double-circling-whiskered street-rubbish-sucker cart stood stopped, chuckling sweet, in front of a plate pile of leaves set down, his meal to suck up; because of the Bank and soft hum of people and the ding-dong ring of 'next please' in the queue and bleeps from the wall money-regurgitating machines for 'take your money' and 'take your card' and the wall ad. 'do you own shares'? with a little fat pink pig, specs on his nose, a bowler hat and tight

pin-striped grey suit with lapel rose. And because a quiet pram babe is still while Mum and Dad have a chance to catch a snack, eat, talk; he has been snuggled down with a loose blanket and, face to face, a cuddling soft fat cow with ears and soft horns and striped feet and behind that a dozing tiny hand and roundy head - sweet. The babe stirs with his feet, Dad pram-rocks as if to say 'we're still here'.

Often today I chuckle with myself - no particles to share. To know the essence of a jug, the jugness for a first time with care.

Father, Son, Holy Spirit = Nothing, Form, Energy-force = Action, Passive-Passion, Creation.

From the hidden idea in nothing springs the wish in me to make some home-made crusted scenting bread from particles of water, flour, cells of yeast and to watch it expand; a bread universe creating from particle stuff. Deep down things are simple and beautiful - like an early glowing pregnant mum, with her hand held on her tum.

For the time, chuckling, I see hear anew, fresh. Perhaps it all ends
in a whimper. Perhaps n/Nothing is found!

[as a T shirt says - 'I started out with nothing and pretty much still have it'!]

Sept 2008

A Chant for Advance in Retreat
Bishops retreat House
Island of Iona. Argyll

Centred
On the Christcarved
In pearwood on oak -
Inseparate inscape of a silent whirlpool
we saw the morning windsoarer, a buzzard circling, in his gliding on the upcurrent shearing Dun I, the highest point, where we stood - the centre of satellite islands with magic names like I Lagh - the Island Bent like a Bow. A skylark called high and dropped as if shot to its rock. The salt sea air seasoned the reeds of the chanter and drones - my sounding pipe - and together we had found our home. Though the old chiefs must have turned in Reilig Odrhain, the burial ground graves of kings. A fishermans boat, Iolaire - Eagle, beat against currents to Staffa where the bagpipe and I, in Fingals Cave, first found resonant root beneath the basalt dome, transferred on return - as the skylark plummetted to earth and forgot to put out her wings to brake -

to the rock cave of S. Judes London at high tide where sound and word

can surge like the sea against its walls - in all Triune conflict and force. 'Iona will be as it was' S.Patrick said and it is. Gashglint of heavenhint, the sword of the Son, stormcross SoundGodWord and the
within-seasurge rock.

Fireside talk, stories at mealtimes, homecooking, haggis, some whisky and porridge - not in that order - gave comradeship with the folk from S.Judes. Marsali, Muireall, Daibhidh, Seumas Micheil and Rob - tapadh leibh, tha mi a tighinn a rithist - sounding phonetically for me as well as, with short a's - tapa layv, ha mee a chee-ing a ree-isht.
Thank you, I am a coming again.

> 'That the closer I move to death
> One man in his sundered hulks,
> The louder the sun blooms
> And the tusked, ramshackling sea exults'

Ealasaid. 3.6.83

Love Warmed

Few children hear the story of Cinderella these days - but they know harsh reality without. So this is a little up-side-down, in-side-out, topsy-turvey story of that fairy tale. We fiddle with words while Rome burns; but now it's New York and Kabul for real.

Icen, for that was his name, is 9 years old; he's a small ugly lad with sticky-out ears and a pointed chinned puck face and scared manner. He lived with his old father and two elder fine strapping brothers. They had no mother; she died when he was 2 years and his father was ill, though still able to give him beatings. Stiff upper family lips got entrenched and worse. Mothering and othering were absent.Sibling rivalry was the penultimate thing there; the deep thing was that no-one loved and understood the other.

Icen tended to the Aga stove which had to be kept going day and night and he did other menial jobs around the house as well. It wasn't a home; he couldn't go to school as he was his father's carer. His elder brothers roamed around and truanted and hung about the night street lamp in the dark road and smoked hash to dull pain.

Icen felt isolate and derelict as if he didn't really exist at all, while his brothers seemed, on the surface, to flourish. His father steadily deteriorated. Social services were too low staffed to help and when they did, they had to keep to forms and time tables.

But Lottie, the corner shop lady, sensed his hidden desolation and phoned a lovely childless couple yearning to adopt another youngster; they had already adopted Cinderella who was about Icen's same age. They had a simple terrace house near the corner shop. Yes - the news was good and Lottie arranged with his father that Icen should meet his 3 new friends. All five gathered themselves in front of the glowing fire. It was winter. Good simple food had been prepared, that well tempted Icen to eat his first fine meal in years. He sat on the large enveloping sofa and at last - a chance at being held and quietly cuddled. Cinderella glowed with him. His real self, in cold storage, had now been found and warmed for the first time - but not the last. He was a bit scared of this new cherishing and understanding acceptance. His handsome brothers grew cold when they heard; they had had to remain at the house with their father. But for Icen, this new place was no house, but a real home with a hearth.

They had all been deprived of a good mother for so long. But good Lottie had saved the day - for one - and for one day...

Aren't we concerned, not only for Icen, but for his father and brothers as well?

12.11.01

Cinquain Fugue in B flat Minor

(Fugue - flight from Reality)(5 lines of 2,4,6,8,2 syllables)

me doh -
iambic, soh -
te trocheic, re re
soh anapaestic, doh - la re
dactyl.

I am
a trachea,

stuttered thick, and now dumb,
an archaic pterodactyl
on ground.

Spondee
hallowed pumpkin;
a serendipity,
now monosyllabic mute struck;
agree?

October, 2002

Suggested tune in B flat minor with your rhythm –
Lento dolce mp !

me doh
fah me re soh
te la soh fah re re
soh fah me re me doh la re
me doh.

Spondee - a word with equally stressed syllables.

Clearing Out

I'm already here so have done the clearing out
as I'm here in this now.
No going back through the door
of clutter and junk
of this annoyance or fear
and their boringness dumped.
I live with them and know them well
so no more for this now.
Begone dull things
for this the empty clean white page -
this moment in time not set down.

I don't want many doors -
I just want an open space
clean and cool and white;
no frames on the walls,
no sofas and seats and folk -
just a white diaphanous curtain
billowing in the breeze.

June 2014.

She walked down slowly and leant wearily on the cold metal railing of the promenade edge above calm sea; her heart was full and sore and her handbag hung limply at her side. Her name was Dawn but the weather was dusk and dark. Bournemouth was the town, usually a bustling seaside resort, but not now in late autumn. All gaiety had moved on, and within her as well. Her white high heeled shoes and large bead necklace seemed out of place for the seaside but she had left the last party music above to find her real self within - without knowing it.

Where was her home and who did she belong to; she did not know and a great sense of alienation and desolation down dragged her. She thought to throw herself over the edge as the final act that she was in control - at last and at the last. No-one would miss her - nowhere.

But Old Chris was taking his evening amble along the promenade to allow his oft-sitting creased trousers a chance to relax. He was a tall man, much stooped with the cares of many years and fattening with hip flabs of fat - and walking was good for that. He sensed, as he passed her, that something was amiss in that lass leaning on the rails so heavily. He retraced his steps and gently approached her with what a good evening it was and was everything all right. She turned with tears and a sad look and that was sufficient for him to know that words were, as yet, redundant; only an arm around would do. And it did. They leant together and could talk deeply now - deeper than the sea. Chris was Christopher, carrier of the Christ.

The setting hidden sun broke through in shafts the black impending clouds and the sea lit up in a smile at their togetherness; the dark lollipop promenade lamp did not shine - it had no need now; for Dawn would have a new day ahead perhaps. Someone had cared somewhere.

22.10.01

Cocklepickers

('..crying, cockles and mussels alive, alive O') !

Bleak stranded flat sands
of Morecambe Bay, North West.
Dangerous fast and ten foot tides
engulfed stick Chinese pickers bent;
unheard cries, twenty, drowned dead.
One pound cash a shift they were paid;
unpapered aliens, unknown and afraid -
- searching asylum, hidden in dread.

A tiny bunch of daffodils laid
against a stone walled house made.
A bunch atop the rescued pile
of orange cockle-full gathered sacs
collected with heavy broken backs.

O little people polite, quiet;
little England is stunned aghast;
cruel Gangmasters beat uncaught.
O Angelus* ring a gentle requiem.
Cry for those cocklepickers
and beare them up - high.

* Millet's paintings - 'The Angelus'
and field workers
Turning over the Soil.'

Feb.2004

Coffee by the Wayside in Butchery Lane

I have a large round coffee cup
all glistening white

with the tan brown fluid inside
and a small snowman jug of milk
with a fullsome fluffy
cream head atop jutting out,
brought to me by Simon
the architect of delight..
I pour the jug
and poor snowman's head
sinks slowly inside
and he is lost
but his hiding fluff
is warmer inside
and he keeps the
rest of the milk warm
from time to time
to top up my cup.

And I am loosened
and I too am warmed.

Feb. 2015

The Common Touch

I would like to share some thoughts and feelings about the Crib outside Canterbury Cathedral - as the nativity seems a central Christian belief and all sorts of people come there from all over the world. Cribs are not only for kids, it seems.

The figures and setting are beautifully crafted and a fitting size for that place.

And it has improved on last years' crib in that the manger and Mary have been moved round 45 degrees and the 3 wise men are now coming from the East. Last year the babe stared at the roof rafters; maybe he still does but there's now a chance of a sky view. There are now two fine fat fluffy chickens roosting on a rafter, an egg on a haystack and an eager lamb escaping from his shepherd boy's care towards the manger.

But my one criticism is that all the figures, not one excluded, remain in transcendent isolation, and are not truly immanent - as none touches the other. I would suggest that the common touch is so important and ordinary and human - so I wonder at its absence. Mary, for example could have a hand on her babe; and maybe they could look at each other; and perhaps Joseph could have an arm round Mary's shoulder and not stand behind the babe out of sight; and the shepherds, a kindly calming hand on their animals. The soothing healing power of touch and eyes that love.

A second point I note are the, admittedly loose, but constrictive swaddling bandages and know this from Luke 2: 7 and 12. I hope that is an accurate translation of the original. It raises important psychological issues, if not theological. What mother today would dream of constricting her baby like that. But it is further emphasis that He might understand our childhood abuse. Arms constricted at birth and arms constricted on a cross at death. Powerful stuff.

E. W. aka Ian Brown. Canterbury.

'Communication'

A fat woman who owns a turf club
Said to me from bloating lips
'Your face is nice pet'
'Breathing from pendulous breasts' he said.
'I don't dream of drowning anymore
My mother is dead'
Woman weary he said.
In broken pain
We talked of a drive
And a knocking exhaust
On the chassis
Malaligned.
Corridored, confined
Correlating kinds of people
And broken wishes -
I am angry and upset
At the anarchic uncertainty
In a stream of sermoned word.
One word

No word.
O burst and cry
Echoed from metal to metal
meshed
And neuroned only,
Action synapsed -
You can watch it working
Trapped.
O let me be - intact.

'Yes, I meant to thank you Dave
We have in part shared.
These things shan't go unsaid'.

The brisk whirr of forest fir
And rock dove croak.
I am whole again
Dodging down outcrop of rock
And flinging on fallen pine slopes.
One could do worse
Than be a flinger
On pine needles.

Stringing together lumbar spines
And the bones of burnt out men
O - I laugh at last.
And Lesotho mountains close
Chipping wedges of nail toes
Cleaning ears with cotton buds
Watching a rain drop on rose.
'You're off your rocker, deluded' - he said
'I can't talk anymore, you misunderstand' - we said.
Smoke rises and the cigarette tip glows red
Incinerate ash.
Her malicious chatter alarmed
'What do you think of him -
He doesn't belong'
Snuggled whisper - warned
I judge and lie as well

The adrenals work overtime you know.

Across the road
Loss in death
Loss in death
Candle flickered life
Mortuary mutilated.

So you turn on your back
Rub your face from the forehead
Down in slow massage
Squeeze your eyes in sockets
Shooting zig-zag lines and spots
In vision that is not.
Whose eyes are wide watching
A dung ball beetle scuttling.

I go for walks in the rain
And watch the traffic brooding
Concealed by a church and dark.
Action relieves indecision.
I go for walks ....
Yet because you take
A cry reverberate
Stabbing convulsed
At the christ.

'O my people, why have you transgressed' - he said.

Tired you rise from
　　　　Your writhing
　　　　To pick to peace
　　　　A black bloomed grape
　　　　From a bunch
　　　　Bowled bursting
　　　　In brown wood.
Judgement on a high seat
Resplendent throned.
A million people crushed

Like sea snails
For one royal, repentant robe
Shelled purple domed.
But the prisoner in the dock
Is absent -
In his cell
And the tossed about king in every man
Blows as a cut blade of grass.
'O judge not that ye be not judged' -
The thunder said.
'O spit not that ye be not spat upon'.
It's not that - in restraint.
I spit and judge more measure for measure
Within and with them
And from them to themselves
And back again.
Ping-pong -
I'll take their hand and mine
Wisdomed warmed
Ping-pong, ping-pong
Ting.

The wind sucked
As she opened the door
And the chinese pipes
Crystalled music
As the wind vane
Turned, gently touched.
Copper glowed in a candle flame
Twisting a spiralled strip
Of burnt smoke.

Hitching the buckled blue pants -
They strutted stiff coated
In earnest importance
The intercom corridor
Oozing assurance
From each hot showered pore.
That night the reflex chatter
peeled off the onion whorls

And my eyes teared -
I couldn't share.
And the girls tittered
Suitable o's.
The comments lifted
Sand lightly whirled
And cars droned past
Cold.
O people leave the herd
Leave the road -
It runs to the swamp
And the leader's gone mad.
But I follow the road
For the donga is deep
And my leader is dead
In the depths. Bold.

Cropped Nefertiti
Blue glittered lids
Black ringed eyes
Purses the corner lips
And sucks a cigarette
Urchin wise.
The watermelon's anaemic
And shoes have blunt toes
Paranthropus kills at a distance -
The new all purpose automatic
And protons pop from an Oldowan hand axe
So change my jackal wail
And from the wheels of regress
The pop star croons
Jerking black hips drummed
Under sorghum moons.

Do I follow?
Do I follow?
A shoot veined
Thrusts the earth shivering.
I am happy riding

And looking -
The Levallois point -
The peace of understanding.

20.2.68, Cape Town

Compassion

There was a donkey limping slow
along a heat baked dusty village road
carrying a large load of bricks
packed full on either side of his back.
He stopped, heavy burdened -
his head hung low
his eyes deep and dark.
He took another step -
again stumbled, stopped -
the painful leg bent -
its hoof off the road.

O god I jerked in tears.

There was an old woman
in rags and a large black coat,
badly bent legs.
She hobbled along, a survivor of the guns
the war torn deserted ruined road and looked back.
She and thousands of others
are paying the price
of ended 'omnipotence'
along with millions of the gassed camps
from the Nazi Reich
who were then beaten by final good.
I jerked in tears.

I don't know what it is
about Compassion;

it seems most marked
in and for the silent ones -
no spoken words.
Those who simply plod on
in the profound unspoken pain path.

July 2015

A Small Simmering Compost Heap
(in the manner of Finnegan's Wake)

My pen is going for a walk and he's lame
because words are stuck in his spinal cord
down, down there in the sacral spine -
the sacred space, by the basket of oysters
waiting to ripen out loud.
'O Lord how long' cries one oyster in song
as he lets go a rock unlimpeted
where the tide takes him out,
kicking against the pricks of a sea urchin
of bristling thoughts spiking out.
O I see this is the trick - limping feelings clam up.
Pssst... your heart's got a puncture!

Oct 2013

A Compromise

How would you like me served?
I surmise too much, minced
to fine pieces or a rugged cut?
We're going into the grammar of living;
Can I take my shoes off?
It means I value your company.
The dots to i's are diamonds
And I am being burnt.

And children born
deformed, mongoloid.
Oak leaves toss on tarmac swirled
And motor eyes dust-coned -
focus on a long haired girl blown -
Clouded out of a grey mist wind.

The enormity of hurtful veneer
clucking from choked throats
guga cuckhold, slander hurled.
A cry rises from larynxed cords
And the singing wind zones high
in overhung wires strung taut.
Gutter water trickles
And black dribbles, scummed
dark from dead depths.
There are limited words unsung, despaired.
Shadows mix, fixed stunned in concrete;
a clay cup cracks -
cut incommunicate.
And hope infarcts, circling to opiate sleep
And pain cuts the sine wave
of season - flickered out.
That clip of metal heel
tripped tombed without time
on a scarred still mind.
That unflinching child look -
Stoned blind in teichopsic dark.

1.4.68, Cape Town

A Concept

Quiet please
for I have just
been conceived.
A sacrament.
A tail wagging sperm
has penetrated

the world's orb egg,
kick starting
a division profound.
The 'bridal' bed.
The priest has raised
the host of bread and wine
to God.

I don't think I was wanted -
eight years they were married
before I came in the form
of a fertilised cell.
Two years later my father died
or something. I grew in the womb
or the force of growth grew me,
then at size I blocked a ureter -
a stone staghorn kidney calculus formed
so a maternal nephrectomy later
thousands of miles away up north.
I existed born in a vacuum abyss.
Was there a sacrament in that? -
a cord placental anchored cave.
Hold your breath in awe
at the dark holy chaos
of a lost life fought.

Then this tadpole formed -
ontogeny repeats phylogeny.
I have a tail to swim
cocooned in crowding warmth.
It grew me, I didn't grow
till nine months passed -
a birth down dark canals
to a hostile world.
A pristine unknown self
and the Other unknown.
Dark. Glass.

Canterbury, Sept.2002

Confusion - from, to pour out together

Confusion - diverse inflammatory cells, defending mending, surge to body damage.
Harsh disparate Differents, slurping merging,
clashing confounding, black hole sucking;
the chasm - past and future debris impacting
the perpetual present-past and striven-driven future;
haunted by time - the first cause of suffering
grinding down to grit; inflamed-explosions tinder.

Such little words but so much - hurt pain, sad, angry
together clotting; injured seared desolate fusing fury,
bad violent, destroyed agony, frightened, dead -
like me non-existent-loved-loving, unwanted by god.
That of a terminally hurt being - terrified, in rage.

Afraid, control hard, on this razor's edge -
this - a consistent undercurrent
drumming repetitive consistent -
the spectre of dying isolate - the gauge,
as alien inhuman unbelonging, not of the tribe;
no movement in and around, paralysed
or surrounded distant unlistening
ignored by people uncomforting
unconcerned uncaring - as in the past.
Or the death of him when the 'work' is unfinished,
the past incompletely known, unredeemed
and massively unknown untold unsaid - the past
or known as mad, shunned, isolate, lost.
Lucky are those dead, done dusted, dust returned to dust,
struggle and pain over, stopped, cut, consummate,
and withheld, concealed - we cruelly won't know it!
'It is finished', no more searching-unfinding, our the-end, at last.

What is - is, a change plummeted down;
the best is done - with little rest, calm;
spot-light-pain-stark-sights of that which I am deprived;
crushed between a hard place and a rock - I am;
I give up; raw; laser-skinned alive.

Oh for a kind word, welcoming 'You're lovable, ok', balm, calmed.
The hearts inherent wholeness from giving smiling eyes;
some glimpse recedes of a simple mind-quiet place realised
where everything together comes, within a real home at last -
in wholeness, unity - a vast inbuilt dream, miscast.
The power of wound-weakness glares, decimates,blasts
but can I watch this debris as distinct, as me and mySelf first? -
as the invading future-'there' and the tyrannical 'there'-relived-past,
to be known, set aside. It's the good in 'Here' honoured now, a start.
'You're not only broken'. 'You are being breathed ' in deep heart -
a moments sigh, I don't have to, alone, apart.

Jan, 2008

Connie 2

She's back in the Red Cross shop
buying many bags and bits
of this and that and not.
Little, fat from many clothes
a lovely restful face, old.
'I'll pop in to say hello to the Lord'
she says - to the church opposite:
For her, I open the door
and off she trundles and bundles
with a new bumping wheelie bag
and four little bags inside.

YES.

like a soccer star I leap in thought
and punch the celebrant air.
She has scored a goal - the best.
But others look askance.

Canterbury, Mar.2004

A Fictional Character
Faith

Hope hobbles hunched into the shop
to buy a small something quite often, each week,
a little old lady with bochel rocker bottom
shumbley shuffling shoes
and a pull down pudding hat
and her trolley shopping bag
which clogs the narrow channels
between the rails
of sorted second hand, steam cleaned,
colour co-ordinated clothes;
and the shoes and hats
and books and bric-a-brac.

Charity is gentle and loves time to talk.
She comes for company
and gives us warm smiles and twinkling eyes
then buys for instance, a mug, of Pope John Paul two.
The charity shop is areligious
so as not to offend - exclamation mark.
Her few pounds go out to the afflicted,
but she loves you to drop
whatever you are doing
to attend to her. I did that once -
nearly a broken plate ensued.
Sometimes she drives us round the bend
but customers smile at the open banter talk.
We know little of her yet she lives alone -
somewhere near.

Connie - her name,
only she is that,
not charity faith or hope
though these three as well;
and she's well known
to volunteer and manager staff
in this flourishing driven
Red Cross Burgate shop

where you can hear
Cathedral Great Dunstan
toll the hours.
Content. Real -
she trundles out.

Canterbury Oct.

Contrast

The little people in the street -
bent burdened backs
sick cancered lame deformed
simple in being and form.
Chicklings -
My heart melts,
impossible pain somewhere -
their sufferings.

The well-healed cultured, complex
haughty, puffed up, proud
'intellectual', 'lyrical', 'genre'-d -
nit-picking books in armchairs
in well oiled unhesitant natter, not words -
of this and that of no substance and guts -
listening to no-one. No ears to hear, no eyes.
More lamed than ever the deformed.
These crowing cocks.

He who is well has no physician need
as he doesn't know himself indeed.
The cutting know-alls, soul-thin
form-fat, self-satisfied.

Nov.2014

Hymn to Creation, Evolution, Mystery ?Question Mark

In the beginning was Nothing - no time, space, matter, sense, word.
Before God, god was, as were sublime, ultimate infinite -
all before words. The word God is not God. It is a word -
language flickers out. Query? was beyond everything known unknown.
No after or before, no boundary therefore; even no Nothing as nothing
has a boundary; and god was in the Nothing in
every thing and God was wasn't; here we get beyond words.
Query ? relates to Nothing - an eternal law. Out of nothing explodes
now something, out of indescribable density and smallness -
the Big Bang, apocalypse orgasm explosion
that shot out time space wonder! progressing quarks, matter, us! -
the universe began - expanding joining conceiving form and form
multiplied. Riverdance - of energy water glycine
(carbon nitrogen oxygen hydrogen) earth-scattered by millions
of the meteorite impact process until pre-man later became - slowly
out of transformation of all that was but we had no words
only gutteral grunts and a drive to survive as a safer herd
immersed in danger, anger, fear -
the first speech breath intake 'uuh' - vowels first with motion -
danger 'look-point-kill-fire-cook-eat'- consonant stopped words.
Something had made our world - we had not (gravity determines the
universes' evolution) we did not make ourselves so fear became awe
and sunrise wonder - exhaled 'aah' and the stirring energy within -
within intuition hunch - like something exploding within
from all we saw - our creativity now in evolution development.
The human had become a relating person drawing on cave walls -
few words; a microcosm from cosmic god; for long incomplete
till a Person came 2,000 years ago - the full expression of God.
Humankind gave this energy, force of love creation - names - Atman
the gods, God, Allah, the sublime, Ground of Being, Brahman, Tao.
But earths' tectonic plates move - collide separate -
collision destruction tornado volcano earthquake
renewing by destruction creative events. Love has to renew.
Maybe even in our inner cosmos by anger sadness grief turmoil
suffering, pain - the amazing energy, who knows but Christ did -
the final agony - death force release to one with God to new life shown.
Is this bad? And is this good - an abused 'crucified' child?

How is it to be fully human, a Person ? our forbears still in us.
Only this found - aware of our inner landscape, our inner universe
like the outer universe, expanding as the cosmos does
to who knows what. Spacious awareness - curious awareness
to sense, feel, think with compassion not judgement
and watch sense, feeling and thought with insight
anchored in awareness of the breath and body and the other -
till detachment comes with sweet soft eyes. Then all becomes now -
the moment imminent. And in Nothing God was/is!
Language flickers out.

April 2015

A Game of Canterbury Cricket

I went to watch a county cricket match
scarred, scared alone, an alien unknown
to stop thoughts of dying and death.
Forty years ago I saw the last live game -
now my eyes were wide with surprise again.
There the cool greens and green and whites
the far off shouts - the English at their best.
Boozers on brown beer, retired business men,
thin thoughtfuls score cards intent, curled down
over knocked knees supporting sheets, splayed sandalled feet.
Middlemen, a scattering of upper class. Insignia of cricket in hats,
badges ties and lunch packs, marquees. And joined to their men -
a few alongside wives and gals.

The fine old dying tree, that end, in place of third man -
ivy enfurled, tall, watching close and proud.
I walked the spongy moon-bounce field, green velvet loved grass.
The crease with bowled holes - a popping one,
a pea-pod bowler pops his ball at that point
with his last thumped-down footholes holed -
at such torsion body angles but no ankles twist.
That near-round cherry ball with white stitched seams
so busily polished on red stained, green stained white clothes.
The speed of bowling down the long precision pitch.

Crack of ball on willow bat -
those hard hit shots rocket past - so fast.
A fielder flung full length to stop or catch.
Running returns and stops.
A whisper thinness of varnish coat
between a nick or not - ball to bat.
'Silly point', silly so close, has dared to catch.
Loud shouts and all arms raise -
A finger points up to God. Out.

July 2002. Canterbury

Feed the Children First
Mark 7:27

'Let the children come to me , do not try to stop them, for the kingdom of heaven belongs to such as these' (Matt 19:13)

He called a child and set him in front of them and said 'Truly, I tell you; unless you turn round and become like children, you will never enter the kingdom of heaven. Whoever humbles himself and becomes like this child will be the greatest in the kingdom of heaven' (Matt 18:3)

'Truly I say to you - except a man be born anew he cannot see the kingdom of God' (John 3:3)

Crumbs and Tit-bits
Scraps under the Table
Mark 7:27-28

What concerned him greatly was the practice of feeding the men first. It seems women and children customarily got the collected up bits. It was for several thousand men that he had found and multiplied a few fishes and loaves (women and children were excluded from the count) but quite a few baskets of left-overs had been collected up from the ground. For who? - possibly the women and children after. Crumbs 'under the table' on the ground for the women and children. Food, and also what it represents as care, has so much meaning and where and how it is given or withheld then and now.

He had also been thinking as he walked that he was on his way to a foreign sea-side town where the culture and religion were different to his own. His were equivalent to sheep and the foreigners to dogs, in common parlance. And he knew that generally dogs were creatures of contempt and loathing - they scavenged the streets and in packs could be dangerous. Yet scavenging was a useful job not dissimilar to the refined service of our valuable street cleaners. But his tradition was also to treat all creatures as of the divine. Some dogs were useful to protect the flocks and camps against wild animals. Others to keep the granaries free of vermin.

He was tired - had walked a long way - about 35 miles as the crow flies - from an inland lakeside village where his compassion for the hungry thousands without food for so long, had prompted the fishes and loaves feeding, and also the hassle with those traditionalist religious leaders who paid him lip service but tested him out about the fine detail of the letter of the law, doctrine and tradition and their tunnel vision dogmatism on the writings of their sacred book. He was tired of them and knew deep within his heart he had to come up against them time and again. He had walked miles in the heat and dust and reached a coastal village by the cool sea - had found a foreign house - there to escape to for peace, quiet and recuperation - again breaking with tradition.

A persistent dominant troubled woman kept hassling his close friends to meet him and they in desperation told him to get rid of her as she was not one of them - tradition again. But she got through their barrier and pleaded with him, called him by his tribal name, fell at his feet and begged him to save her disturbed daughter. He was the foreigner to the area and she knew that but she must have heard of him from elsewhere and sensed deeply and in despair - that he could help her.

He remained silent, said nothing - just looked steadily into her. He had wryly and wearily told his friends that he was apparently only to help his own lost people (sheep) not others (dogs). He didn't really believe that - he couldn't - because of who he was. He knew he had come to fulfil the old faith and beliefs, not to destroy them - it was a bit like warming, relaxing and then stretching cold rigid spiritual muscles.

Her utter determination and despair resonated in him and he could see she would accept anything however little (like the woman who managed to squeeze through the crowd to touch the hem of his cloak in her belief of his compassion and help - small and little is beautiful).

His silence was that of a process of deep intuitive understanding of her. It was no good talking in concepts - only pictures would do. So he said it wasn't fair to take the children's food and throw it to the dogs. Children had to be looked after first. Yes - her child and the child in her came first. He knew 'suffer little children to come unto me' in whatever condition - for there within is wholeness and fulfilment however hard won. Perhaps her strength of persistence and dominance were also weaknesses - excessively controlling and dominant of her very own daughter and the troubled child within herself - so much so her daughter was now rebelling, destructive, aggressive and unmanageable; maybe even treated as less than human, deprived of love and respect in her own right with little chance of developing well. (nowadays put under ASBO and even Borstal).

At last she knew that someone understood her own deprivation and so that of her daughter. This was a private talk between her and him, she was pouring out her distress - after all it is only respect and consideration that she should be heard privately. Probably more was said than we know. His friends had only heard a few snatches of what passed between them. What he was giving her were juicy tit-bits to a favourite. She saw that he knew and responded in the same manner - as if the dog herself was being fed the best bits from her master and Lord and she called him that. He had overridden convention to help her as he often did. What dog would feel it was only getting the crumbs from under the table. What dog would feel it was unworthy of such. Crumbs, scraps, tit-bits - all are good to a dog and worthy of gobbling up with much tail wagging..

She felt whole and understood and she couldn't have done so if she hadn't recognised her little small hungry self. He had integrated her and her daughter's lost hidden unloved aspects. She felt a weight lifted off her shoulders. It would be better from now on and the relationship between her and her daughter was on a new fresh warm level.

Maybe now for him, there would be a bit more rest under the cool sea breezes before the long journey back to the lakeside village and more thousands of hungry and sick folk and those religious hypocrites who kept hounding him and checking him out with superficialities and whether he was breaking tradition yet again. Men again would be counted first. It seems clear that women had to be very persistent to get through others to his help.

Lent 2006

The Current Eucharist

In the beginning was the Word. And in the beginning
is the confession of sins near the start of the gathering.
I do not need to confess sins to a possible ogre god
like a child returning home from school to a scolding dad
as I am aware, my potential essence, of being short of the mark.
I do not need 'Lord have mercy, Christ have mercy
Lord have mercy' - pleaded six sequential times.
I need encouragement and not 'sins' again and again.
These words are so heavily, depressively sad -
we're seen only as sinners and servants, not friends.
I do not need to repeat my unworthiness for under-table crumbs
after having, happily, been counted as worthy just before -
and elsewhere, not here, 'made in the image of God'.
Does God really need to be told who and what he is above?
and to long praise him to the skies - if this is between friends.
I do not need will and obedience and judgement and sacrifice.
I don't want Christ's anatomy for the forgiveness of sins -
given 'this is my body and blood'; not dying for me
to add to my guilt but living dying then living transformed.

But I do need 'This is me for you' instead -
the Way, not 'will', - often, often quietly said
and I do need, in special recognition receiving, my name heard.
And often that 'love casts out fear'
and worry not - 'do not be afraid'-
a song of water for the dry earth
like the lilies of the field
who toil not neither do they spin in the hot sun.
We do need one fresh new day at a time -
as each day has sufficient trouble but enough good
as a fresh breeze cools beads of sweat -

and not the dominance of the forbidding future, the parched past.
It would be sometimes nice to hear
'come unto me all ye who labour and are heavy laden
and I will give you rest' at last - unafraid in the cool shade, found.

And specially do we need 'that when we were still far off
you met us in your Son and brought us home' enfolding
which is rarely said;
as a 'mother tenderly gathers her child' now safe
and like the welcoming Father of the Prodigal Son - home.
with a repast, robe and ring, given, before forgiven.

Instead 'Talk to me' says God
written in the children's corner
of Rochester Cathedral nave -
and quietly 'trust and rest'.

July 2010

D and D

Were first real neughbours -
through their thick and thins, highs and lows -
of leavings, separatings, departings,
violences and rows.
Silent Dave, alcoholled and overdosed
- psychiatric ward.
Denise - voluble non stop,
non listening, promises unkept.Volatile.
She gave me her pottery mouse -
A Beatrix Potter one - to sell at the shop.
She made it long ago.
I keep it safe, unsold.
Their love of walks, birds,
home building, busying, burrowing
Snuffling, scurrying.
Their house gutted rebuilt -
between numerous paying jobs.

Their bumbling, broken down car.
I saw it all - and remember.

They've gone - now -
for a caravan life -
gypsies in Europe.
A new life.
Beginning now.
Their house empty, silent.
Dark. Still. Unfed birds.
Gutted sobbed bereft -
I light a candle -
Rising sandalwood smoke.
Frau says -'people come and go
Just so. So what!'.
They seem snuffed out, dead.
And I am dead now.
Stuck stopped
in this tomb
next door

Bewildered - deep pain.
It must be my loss lost past.
So tired of this
First and last
But to remember -
I have a little mouse.

2.4.02 Canterbury

A Dark Place - She not I

You may not like to come with me here -
a dark place - in the morning and night before
but lets see if we can rescue
some wreckage from the wreck
and maybe a speck of treasure too.
This slow loss of body bits -

hearing compromised with aids
communication hard in groups
or with people who speak to their boots.
Loss of vision - lens implants
and stuck denture plates
and veering weak legs,
old alone where silence inflates, annihilates -
the house clattering in anxiety's fear -
fearing dying and its mode in pain
or conscious paralysed - the void
then undiscovered dead
maggots and flies, recycled inside
but that I won't know
as I maybe elsewhere.

This the wreck - the fear of fear;
ask gently 'What is this?'
then enough of doomed gloom
which may well not be true.
This now is what is
this moment now
each day a new gift
one day at a time times 365 times a year.
so say 'It's ok' - she's ok -
fear doesn't last,
it comes and goes.
And she has a roof overhead.
Wait with no force - accept
with shaking hands and pounding heart -
gently breathe it out
no need to habitually fix -
just stay and say 'hello fear, it's ok'
'and now you've had your say'.
See the ordinary good
not the extraordinary bad.
Soften, be gentle with compassion
anchored steady inside.
She too has courage.
and is loved of God held.

All have a capacity for inner healing -
new life; and in dying and death
precious in His sight.
She can, not can't, now
and every little good thought counts
and every movement slow or strong

and every relaxing breath helps.
Drop down with feet planted
ground firm - solid as a rock
not made of flight fear
Trust in the good, just trust.
And medicines not taken but received,
are a gift of God
Make the most of what you have -
a glass half full not half gone.
Say yes to life with a nod of the head -
open to the now and see -
the Samurai fight in defence
to overcome their fear of death.

The mind settles
from monkey chattering, scattering
mental events - the doing
and if we don't force it to be fixed
in somewhere else
we become anchored in the being breath.
Better to wonder than worry.
Let it go, practise often -
let it go, the thinking you,
let it go the worrying you,
let it go the fearing you, bullies need a firm hand -
and want to dominate. Let it go Now. Let them go.

The above piece represents a good days work;
the first time in my life I hold good in myself.
Well done in being.
The penny dropped on the bell which rang!

This is me - here I stand and am
just as, unforced, I am.
Even a tiny bit of awareness helps
to stop the downward spiral -
no need to strive to feel rest.
Accept myself as I am.
There's nothing to fix. This now.
This moment in time.
My life and death,
I and she - the mirror is me with a smile;
this the treasure, precious
in the sight of God. And in one M.

Mar. 2012

Dialogue of 2 Inanimate Dead Objects
(the order for holy communion!)
(a President is one who has been ordained priest)
(? has the powers of the president of the USA!)

(No welcome for the people then all say, they just can't wait to get into the sins/sin bits...)
'cleanse the thoughts of our hearts'.
President says. 'let us confess our sins in penitence..'
All say 'Almighty god, our heavenly father, we have sinned against you and against our fellow men in thought and word and deed, through negligence, through weakness, through our own deliberate fault. We are truly sorry and repent of all our sins ...'
President says '...have mercy upon YOU, pardon and deliver YOU from all YOUR sins...'
President - 'Lord have mercy
All - Lord have mercy
President - Christ have mercy
All - Christ have mercy
President - Lord have mercy
All - Lord have mercy (All this sounds like begging to me).

(Much exhortation to praise goes on for the god but there is no praise

for the people.
Often there is even this appalling piece:-)

'We do not presume to come to this your table merciful lord
trusting in our own righteousness
but in your manifold and great mercies.
We are not worthy so much as to gather up the crumbs
under your table...'

(The words sin and sins appear often. We have to feel guilty that Christ died for us to save us from our sins and so to grovel more.)
(Creeds maybe said or sung with this in them):-
- 'we acknowledge one baptism for the remission of sins'...
(Rubbish. There is no biblical 'original sin' etc). Man was made in the Image of God .

'Let the dead bury their dead'.

May 2003

Middle Ear Deafness. Sound-Drowned and Sound-Starved

Recipe - 1 glue ear, 1 perforated drum ear, Add and mix

Bone conduction reinforced, enhanced
in the cavernous crags of my skull
pit-caves dripping stalactites
which echo rampant my voice
booming back relative, unresolved.
Air conduction clogged, barred,
that people's speech is down damped.
It is hearing in underwater, blurred,
hazed, fogged, masked, mumb obscured
in this deep dumb green-lake immersed.

As if infected, sight dims as well -
the rippling effect - a stone thrown in a pool.
I feel encaged in my blocked self,
contact cut within this bubble isolation zone
so I speak loud, or so it seems in this twilight dusk

as I cannot gauge, adjust; alone -
I cannot get free and out, yet must.
Yet deaf, I 'hear' words of that which
is hidden or mostly by-passed
in forms of the other's body, face, hands.
So many superfluous words and nonsense -
just one key one will do to get the essence.

And silence was upon the face of the deep - to be alone.

And heaven said
'let there be sound'
and the earth
opened in thunder
and sudden sound was heard
through the deep dim dull dark water
of shadow bubbling murky words
from the faint face across the quiet room
(but all around outside sounds hissed, boomed)
as through glue gloom, I opened my ear...aid.

and the voice was clear, crisp, light, understood
and I said - 'this is good'.

July 2008

Deformed Life
A Pigeon

Wry neck, one giant wing shoulder,
the other shrunk -
a pin neck, slit eyes
and a tiny head contorted sunk.
It provokes revulsion repulsion
not pity attraction compassion.
This meant to be - heart hit -
the creator's survival of the fit
to ensure the very best -
the aim of all to aim for the perfect.

Outside gargoyles in cathedrals
balance the good within
and deter evil by being evil in sin!.

Early 2009

Design

Pink flesh flounders, scenting the sun sea surface,
signalling scattered sharp loud shots of notes -
deafening a torpedo shark - his horizontal lines, stream-lined
sensing meat and blasting sound beats;
silk speed shot, screeches through deep blind dark,
saw-teeth, jaws gape, clamp-struck, one crack,
torque-twist, bone clean cut, crimson blood gush.

A colleague has an artificial leg-limb.
He and she - sheer beauty of design, intricate -
the one in water, the other out.

Canterbury Jan.2004

Dialogue of 2 Inanimate Objects
(Shoe-sole and Drawing pin)

The shoe-sole said to the pin
I have to be very thin, (dear-skin!) -
to feel more the world
than if thick, no foothold -
he told, worn old - therein.
I know the world I walk in.

The drawing pin said in reply
I was dropped on this spot by the by -
not wanting to be up side down -
it was fate who came rushing along -
my future - in things make a hole.

So just put your foot down
and, squit, through your soul,
eeouch - you groan and frown.

I too am the world underpinned
disciplined, doctrined, grinned,
tox-sinned.

May 2003

'Fog Everywhere'
from Bleak House by Charles Dickens
(put into verse form!)

'Fog up the river, where it flows
among green islands and meadows;
fog down the river, where it rolls
defiled among the tiers of ships and tows,
and the water side pollution
of a great and dirty city.
Fog in the Essex marshes,
fog on the Kentish heights.
Fog creeping into the cabooses of collier-brigs;
fog lying out on the yards,
and hovering on the rigs of great ships;
fog drooping on the gunwhales of a barge
and small boats.
Fog in the eyes
and throats
of ancient Greenwich pensioners
wheezing by the fireside of their wards;
fog in the stem and bowl
of the afternoon pipe
of the wrathful skipper,
down in his cabin close;
fog cruelly pinching the toes
and fingers of his shivering
'prentice boy on deck.

Chance people on the bridges
peeping over the parapets
into a nether sky of fog,
with fog all round,
as if they were in a balloon,
and hanging in the misty clouds.
Everywhere -
is fog'.

25.2.02

'I Stood...' A Dilemma of which Path to Take

I don't stand and dither;
also not 'I was stood'.
And not 'I was sat'.
(What's happened to
standing and sitting these days.
who sat you and who stood you so
and why has A become
an upside down V?)

I just dash about
on this and that
uncertainty masked
by floods of thought
on this and that and those
and which way to turn next
and what to ferociously fix.

O shit the lot
neither way
will I go
slow
or hot foot;
but I can go backwards -
far better - retrace
or even turn

upside down
on handstands -
an upside down clown.
'Tut tut' they mutter,
'not done in public' -
unacceptable this.

So off I go
and lie down
   and doze
   and snooze;
to dream 'outside the box';
the real hopeful hidden me
simmering the solution
in the snoozey soup
of my true self.

Feb 2013

Discard

A south wind blows
and a piece of paper
dances and skips
along the cobbled street
and no-one sees;
nowhere and anywhere he is blown
no mind of his own -
blown somewhere unknown.

What are the laws of the universe?

Nov.2014

Doom and Gloom

Why do I suffer?
Why do I torture myself?
Why do I inflict punishment within?
    interminably thinking
of the worst future and bad past.
I am not these destroying thoughts.
But Christ feared at Gethsemane -
fearful, human and alone;
he took up his cross
and in pain, felt abandoned by God
then it finished in trusting and letting go
        and he was free
    to live completely at last.

But still a voice tells me -
why fear dying and death?
You are not Christ.
(Yet in a little way I am
as He is within and I am) -
so no need to suffer in yourself so much -
live in the world now -
soften in your real self
and say 'Well done'
for each step done.

'Whosoever shall seek to save his life
        shall lose it
and whosoever shall lose his life
    shall preserve it. (Luke 17:33).
  So Let go and Trust

Mar.2012.

The Dove

Benedictus -
'Blessed is he who cometh in the name of the Lord'

A dove, known so wary and scared,
startled apprehensive alarmed
(no brave bold robin red) -
he flies off at my distant intent.

Peace too does that,
a rare remote glimpse -
but when he lands -

his feathers float
in the breath of God.
And we are teared wet with sweat.

Canterbury Mar 2004

Dress

Buttermarket square before the tourist hordes arrive -
quiet - few about, just the chatter on cobbles of a trolley case
and an older couple pass close by;
she is plump, a cosy smile, curly grey hair, hobbling gait,
muffling along in shuffling shoes beside her mate -
a summer nearly-long homemade frock with whorls
squiggles zig-zag lines and flowers faded in the wash -
an uneven puckered hem, her favourite comfy dress,
not deliberately made but fashion nonetheless
from children's smiling curtain cloth, cut-price.
Her pink blob cuddly arms, out as wings;
so very unusual - she freely moves and sways
not squeezed corseted in lycra plastic slacks
and pastel tight tops of the sameness crowd.
Her whole self warm - the making of chuckles and smiles.

'Thank you, thank you' - in my heart, as I was down and out.
She proudly poised by the Cathedral gate next the trash bin, black
and he backs away but snaps a photo of the starved gate
high christ instead. I cry inside.

My little curved old lady who loves the kids toy shop
nearby; sidewindes by and gives me a smile and a twitch.
Two lasses pass exploding in colour out of the drab mass
in patches of lush greens, sky blues, bright yellows, vibrant reds.
I have to say 'so colourful, the best' - in return they beam and pass-
a stark rainbow in the dark. Maybe I was being given bads
so also these little good gifts - unnoticed by most.
Then a jaunty man passed, broad yellow trouser-braced,
marked boldly in inches - two large tape measures, shoulder-crossed
and a yellow broad watch-strap to proudly match -
angels can fly as they carry no time and fear - zero weight released.

It is too noisy now - people don't talk, they shout to hear;
they might be heard if they were quiet, near and clear.

So I must go now. What is - is,
the sticky long fingers here of fear.

Oct 2006

A Drive

A dance of hands on the wheel
And intricate feet -
With deep mechanic comfort
And lone peace.
The pipe of a bird
Seldom heard;
A cathedral leafed in oak;
No limit to eye nor ear
And whirl of wind hair.

Soaring above and on and up
Thermal fired; towering rock.
Sea tang salt and glare
Crusts and cuts.
In the bay below
A misted whirl
Shrouding soft and whole.
The gentle crescent moon
Whispers on glist'ning dials
Through the mist;
And speed o'ercomes
And I belong
To earth and god - at least somewhere;
And on...

6.11.67 Cape Town

The Drumchasers and Dancers
Ancient and New

at the new ultra-modern Marlowe theatre standing near the old Cathedral of Canterbury - the mother church of all - to a show of drumming and dance - drawing you in and coming out to meet you in mist and spotlight and encouragement to clap in different beats for the three levels of audience seats and finally, showers of red shiny paper bits snow-flaking down. I caught one and have stuck it to my djembe drum,
reminding me of the poppies of Remembrance Sunday as involvement of all through the spirit of those who have gone before. The communion of a deep story, religious in effect, by sound and dance, more meaningful than I have heard in a church or cathedral in words. The high coming down to the low, transcendent to immanent.

The scene - scaffolding and stage door, an old back-stage man dusting a wicker basket of toy props, discovering childhood. He sounds a shiny gold trumpet and mysteriously, people from another world appear and drum. The old man tries to get involved with the youngsters but has no place until he dusts their drumsticks and drums and is allowed. It becomes an alien spirit world as interstellar space with a background Aztec or Egyptian pyramid - the young aliens led by an Avatar spirit woman who inspires their beat.

War is raged by opposing factions in competing drums and movement and the love between a couple - by a small drum and toy xylophone; drumfights by drums not guns. A community - not the former isolation of the old man cleaning backstage in the near dark alone, but now serving by dusting their drums. It is African, Red Indian and Aztec with modern youth. Drumageddon - the last fight where bad youths dominate and demand the contents of the toy basket. The old man pulls out the toy trumpet - it is blown - they fall to the ground in worship - as their history is of a long lost gold horn which holds the secret to life; the secret is in fact childhood held in the gold horn. The old man collapses in all the chaos with a heart wound and dies. The youngsters mourn his loss as he has become loved by them in himself and in his service to them. The old contain youth within. The youngsters as spirits from another world have become, of earth - human. The long lost gold horn is now redundant.

Then the doors open and the old man comes alive, resurrected in mist and bright light.

The youngsters are overjoyed and in love, recognise him instantly unlike the stories of Emmaus and Upper Room. His old cloth cap reversed like the young, his dust coat gone - he leads the drummers in a final burst as central and important - he has become as the young, old but transformed from the old.

In a sense this was the old worn theme of death through love for others

and resurrection to new life - the Christ story anew.

I was inspired. For me - there is hope for the old, - me; hope for those who are the lowest of the low - me cleaning and sorting donated Red Cross bags, some filthy and unusable; hope for those who live alone - me at home. But he is loved, he finds childhood and community and through all that he dies and relives and leads them all in the drumming group and as well, the audience loved him most of all.

This was an old Christ - therefore hope for the old.

The Marlowe is my Cathedral now. The last shall be first - the first last.

The least serving - first.

Maybe God became human for us but also for Himself to fulfil Himself as well.

Fulfilling Himself by creating - not just a transcendent spirit above. He has to create - out of His nature, out of Love. He is constrained as well as free, as we are too.

Canterbury Dec 2011

Dud Avocado

It was a hot peaceful sort of day in September and young Cas sauntered down the street in lower Burgate near the Buttermarket Canterbury, when in the next instant some bits of refuse were unbelievably thrown out the window of an overhanging timbered house, just as in medieveal times. He could hardly conceive the mess that dripped from his head and he yelled foul abuse back at that open window as the culprit fast retreated inside.

There on the cobbled street, amongst other sloshy gubbins lay sploshed browned avocado pulp, its pip and skin - obviously over-ripened on the hot sill above so given the nudge by its owner. Cas picked up the large shiny seed and it lay well in the palm of his hand - ready and inviting to be hurled back up full force to its owner - when his mates appeared.

They had formed a rock group of lead and bass guitar, keyboard and percussion recently and Cas was their lead singer. They had long diddled about unsatisfactorily with numerous names for their group such as Spiked Hair, Ringed Nose, Bare Belly, Cool Clubbers, Wicked Breezers, Brill Bangers - names of that genre, and they were soon due to give several gigs in the local pub. They all wore the same stressed dirty coloured flare jeans with frayed bottoms, old Nike trainers, bare bellies and ring-pierced noses, ears, belly buttons and unmentionable what elses. And, of course, spiked glued hair. They were, on the surface, proud that you couldn't tell the difference between them and other youngsters.

Cas's mates rang out with laughter at the sight of him but here lay the answer before them all - on the cobbles - a 'Dud Avocado'. They yelled and jumped for revealed, inspired joy. It was 'wicked' in both the current young and usual old sense of that word. But it was a name that could stand proud against the famous real 'Bananarama' pop group.

Cas took the wet shiney pip back home, stuck in 3 sharpened match sticks 'as you do' and set it in a jam jar of water on his digs window sill. The 'Dud Avocado'. The group had found its growing identity at last. They would wear avocado green T shirts with a sploshed logo on the front. So he stripped off his gear, bunged them in the washer and took a 'cool' shower.

17.4.02 Canterbury

'Doesn't Everything Die at Last, and Too Soon?'
(The Summer - Mary Oliver)

Yes, scared but dying already is now
and every moment.
Yes, relief at being dead. How so? -
Dead, I won't know unless in another mode/form.

Yes - and ruminations of how I'll die -
the worst horrors gnawing away
like a locust swarm zooming down.

The tunnel vision of pain,
the dark soil of distress.
What antidote to this navel gazing
doomed gloom stuff?

Perhaps learning how to acknowledge all this -
accepy gently, then to let go
in patience, openness
and trust in my simple breath -
as we don't control even now,
even in this.

Sept.2014

Dying - to Live
a mixed message -
I'm dying to be loved, to love
or is it - I'm dying in order to be loved, to love

It's about dying to future dying, death, annihilation -
dying to the future - anyway, there's no way to know it
and dying to isolation dereliction
and dying to no another, desolation
and dying to mistrust, despair
and dying to non-acceptance of acceptance,
dying to gloom and doom - constant comrades
habitual partners, consorts associates mates.
The devil you know is maybe better
than the devil you don't.

It is - living in holding with another
living in Now, shared together
living in importance, acceptance,
living in basic trust and of value, enhanced
organically growing in and through another
and not that 'I must, must, must'
of a clenched fist defence.

I *feel* - in the now - open hands,
O god of beginning trust;
I *think* - in the - my end, the next hour -
in hope but feel it will be smashed as in the past.
Thought is in the future leading to a sour
secondary feeling heart, but nevertheless, still thought.

My head belongs and is held in my primary originary ultimate heart
and not that of my secondary heart in my top heavy penultimate
head.

June 2007

Dying to Live
the frontiers of the familiar go - the Way chooses

He hurried the pavement, his shoes fast covering the cracks,
hounded by rejection of his encounter-innermost -
of man made in the image of the divine God - this ultimate,
first known with another and 'welcomed into the world'
through compassionate understanding relationship, resonant;
attacked by both main sides - the pharisee false 'religious' -
and those rejecting - in distanced 'objective' analysis,
isolate, 'intellectual', penultimate - of the 'psyche' in us,
theoretical - on the intellectual couch with the void
of the silent behind chair or even when face to face;
spearheading his deepest imaginative experience -
and like M, speaking for the ordinary common folk
hungry, thirsty for a healing personal relationship
before, no wide spokesman, evaporating out, voiceless
from many a dry place of wrecking worship.
Under this back-Atlas weight his heart flutters, fails,
fibrillates - the pavement cracks split apart, gape
beneath his stumbling faltering foot-fall-step -
about to be engulfed to a yawning hole, ground-grave.
His agonised 'heart' bursting, his brain hurting hell
in oxygen lack drowning, in horror collapsing -
'angor animae' - the terror of doing-done-death.
That shadow scythe angel shot premature, precipitate -
out of the dark, imperceptible ahead, black, cruciate -
with his zoomed-down, swarming darts stung stark, secret.

But a near Samaritan appeared out of the far tunnel light
and summoned the siren scream rites of ambulance might.
Outright technology took its long labour course in bursts
with clicks and bleeps and waves and drips and masks
machine-filled, in hospital intensive coronary care units
and tending masked, sky-blue-cap-crowned and gowned angels -
to resuscitate, repair, give new birth - in a major wound delicate
down the central breastbone sternum opening chest - intricate,
his heart gently bypassed, tube pumped, renewed; convalescence.
(It mayn't have been as this is - but something close).

And now he lives many good days - deeply aware
that his God 'yearns' for him forever, felt intermittent -
a long time-deep, in so great a love place, like the Fathers
welcome of the Prodigal Son's return, derelict -
that death has now no fear here, there - in quiet moments
surrounded by earth-warmth-care of his family friends, intimate.
This God who 'yearns' for us to respond, resonant.

She, deserted in a parched wilderness, furnaced in raging dread
or swung frozen, pain brittle - the purgatory summit of a hell ahead.
Out there, she has known much of death and in here in the past -
in desolation annihilation dereliction - thudding fear.
Her breath fails, brain-gel dies, limbs weaken paralysed
speech falters, words struggle, ears deafen, touch hardens,
tears clot, blood sluggens, tissues sludge disintegrate in bits.
Isolate alone in a room, struggling to move, shuffling slow
to get a cup of tea between rooms - kitchen and bed.
No-one phones. The phone is out of within reach. The TV blares.
Curtains unpulled, closed. The route to Nothing has begun back.
Dirt and stench survive and thrive and circling gleeful, dance.
Death - terrifying as so unknown, uncontrolled, unspoken of
and often these days, dying so ward-packed, sterile, faceless.
Deterioration of body, mind - an entropy drawn out in stillbirth;
cancer corrodes her soul, growth blasts, devouring her central Self.
Control maybe taken by harsh untrusted others, feared
or she may die unknown alone, very separate unrelated -
a rotting corpse alerting the curious about - concerned astounded.
Yet perhaps, in break-up, her candle-wick smoking spirit
could light despite, because of, everything else. Already decades -
cell on cell life-spring - growth drawn toward the infinite.

I am *in* the *places* of dying, being deaf, being dead
Not I am all these places, boxes, coffins, of deaf dying, dead.
But I remain as I Am - *within* all these places - here, there.
Abandoned, she feels rejected by a remorseless God -
this - a conscious uppermost feeling, dominant -
of surface wave surge and crash, incessant
yet maybe He is the underlying lightsome iridescent,
calm blue-beamed, beneath-deep, translucent;

suffering with, but strong unbroken as well, constant.
His dying before had dunked-down-death-done-dead;
the Rock - when all about collapses, misled into dread. Disintegrate.
let go, integrate into death
held in hoped palliative care -
hypnotics analgesics relaxants,
oxygen whiffs, sweet clean scents -
tiding over the passage
within others tenderness.

let go into death - held.
A Gentle death
greets her, sensitive -
and takes her in his arms -
dark compassionate.
At last - rest.

this, as I go to visit death before he visits me -
now perhaps a confounding beautiful awefull, awful confusion.
Our within glance can only be - the I am - dance entrance -
first in relation to others best resonance.

May 2007

Clay Modelling

Grey glorious sodden stuff.
This and hands heart and head
The only tools to pass time
Pleasurably and at peace.
Upright stance, tall table
A large leaven lump
Of death cold clay.
I held my breath
In high hope humility -
Suitably clad
In the oldest clothes I had.

Now brave bold enthusiastic.
An initial attempt.
Tune in to the spirit -
Dig in ten fingers
Mould prod smoothe and slap
Soothe swing in and soil.
Yes - boldness
But basics first
Then hen pecking
Determined detail.
Busy and absorbed
Out curls my tongue
At the corner of my mouth.
Arms akimbo
Eyes narrowing
In observation and planning.
Self talking
About the pros and cons of scooping
A centimeter scallop
From the temple of my man
In one scoop.

The minds image -
Perfect but pliable.
The value in all this?
The process of production.
Formless matter
progression and evolution
Through all stages
To a likeness and perhaps
To a complete satisfaction.
The mechanics of hand movement.
The nature and feel of the basic material.
And getting grubby with a lawful excuse.

1963

Conflict

Coming down concrete steps -
Head lamps blinding
Through thick night fog.
Arms hugged around
One pound of tea
For flat mates and me.
Broke, two cents left, no fags
Two cats company.
Black night passage lights -
The others are out
Close against cold.
New found guitar chords, minor key
Hum and strum to coiled smoke.
Day dream. Dream.
Shrunken heart bursting in minor key.
Saturday and Sunday confined to four walls
Struggling to learn - and yearning.
Shall I go to you -
me - duffle coated cold.
And dream at your yellow light warmth.

Now back - they chatter
Sharing experiences of their boys.
Laughter and courage and gladness
Giggling joyful and young.
Different, a medic - they expect great of me
Chronic, cold, contact incapable
For life - crippled.
'Good night, sleep well - ole bean'.

early '60s

Farm Life

Outside -

Sun drenched, ripe golden fruit
Clusters of dark, green cold leaves
Dark scaffold of knotted stems
Burnt arms, veined hands
Reaching through leaves
For round fruits.

Inside.

They continue their youth and childhood
Unbroken to adulthood
Whereas I have broken it off.
Theirs pleasant and quite easy going.
Whole solid parents, farm life, wide open.
The father - khaki longs, old boots
faded shirt, thick leather belt,
Sun dried, well set
Bright blue crinkled eyes
Greying hair.
His battles with weather
Water and soil -
Variable, dependable.
His office - make shift
Rough wooden shelves and drawers
An old expansive desk
With numerous drawers
And secret hiding places.
Hammers, rifles, shot.
Old pictures of the family
Speckled yellow with age.
The continuity of things - inheritance.
Such as I have not.

early '60s.

A Game of Squash

'Red Devil' racket swoops
on black rubber small sphere ball.
No time passes between the instant
of hitting and return.
Rapid resounding retort,
Quick clever cold calculated shots.
Till outmastered, outrun
The ball dribbles to the corner
unreturned. Pace slackens, stops.
Pause and peace returns.

White clad, brown burnt
Anatomists delight
Top muscle meated specimens of mankind.
Action and reaction automatic
Conditioned almost reflex
Two minds versed in cunning strategy -
Boxed and cloistered within four walls -
Spot lighted shots, red lined confined.

Head bands and shirts
sweat dripping delighting.
Ball centred concentration -
almost unending.
Last deciding shot -
Point, match and game.

1963

The Microscope

Severe sombre black
Precision steel tube
Silver adjustment screws
And tripod lens pieces
Geometric shapes
Clean cold calculating.
Precision cylinders spheres

Parallel lines focussing for infinity.
Refractive indices microns
Microcosmic organisms -
Marvel of man's mind.

A drop of stagnant water
On a clean cut
Green glass slide.
Near new worlds -
Inside deep fearful
Strange slime cool green
Transparent forms
Primitive persisting
Filtering feeding
Fittest surviving
Fission multiplying - competing
Ceasing to and dying.

Chemically controlled compelled
To feed multiply move
And finally to die.
To what purpose all this?
Existing for predators -
Predator for predator
Up the scale
From pyramid base
To pinnacle peak in man.

? 1963

My Gift

I carved my cross from cedar wood
collected by myself from the mountains.
Rough - but I chiselled it
for long hours.
It left cuts in my fingers
and my soul.

And yet memory of mountain moon and rock
good things these as well.
I kept it in my special box
with my donkey, sphere of wood
and solid stone.
Precious cut core close ripped in ribbons
I tried to give it him - he refused.
A double offer of my cut and Christ's
Refused.
But he has it
Though his is higher, pure, more understood.
My motive perhaps impure to him - misunderstood.
'I must have an early night, am tired'
So he said. Time is crucial to me
Only that it is important
in essential, deep and simple things.
And yet, as always, I ask too much.
Michael, Michael - you've hurt.
Soothe the wound. Schubert knows.
I thought you were close -
now you've gone again - I've gone.
Trust gone.
Smoothe soul gone. Sweat. Turmoil again.
This toxic unendurable state.
So he phoned to placate
his guilty state - to ask my pardon about the cross.
He hurt me with my offer of a cross
Tossed.
Was aware enough to know I hurt him
so it seemed
When I flippantly talked of splitting hairs
about his poem that meant most to him.
Yet I cannot feel I hurt -
people just have excess armour
Nothing hits.
So I sand papered his sensibility.
Hardly so - if so
Too good to be true.
If so - fair enough.
I hurt you - you hurt me.

But precious enough - this
That I should be cared for enough
to be asked to forgive.
Concern whether he should keep on
Taking me on.
Gone December the first.
I've been living long enough -
Imprisoned perhaps - but through
When all the people I've needed
Have failed and gone.
Therefore no great concern this.
But hope raises its weary head again
To sink back tired again.

This complex simple I
Rejected thrown - the Cross tossed.
Not mine - yes - yet me.
The giving motives impure
But all I know.
I am - what I am.

Early '60s

Optimism

A glimpsed experience -
no fear for the future.
Enjoying a game of squash
and a good guitar.
Phoning a friend up
for a chat and coffee
at a caf over a cigarette.
Moments to ease
and relief from fear - stone alone.
A day by the waves and sand.
And a bunch of grapes for lunch -
aglow and tanned,
gently and at peace.

Sketching.
More aware and open
to people and paintings.
To others and scenes.
Not looking too much
to the future -
previously glimpsed
as a series of breakings -
tearing and searing at self
Stone alone.
The day when my cat goes -
the cat must go
but enjoy her now.
Likewise the rest.
This life is a series
of makes and breaks.
Not a galvanic current.
And also my friends
which were not my friends
but now are.
Because the common run of experience
and 'what shall we have for supper?'
and 'a happy New Year'.
The little touch
are now valuable
at least for a while.
There are times for these
and such as these
are most of the time
between day dreams of otherwise.
And times for sorrow
and a broken heart.
Of things remembered
in the past - motherless
and mothered.
Also now and in the future
but somehow surpassed.
At least distraction distributed
through an aggregate
of friends and intrinsic talents.

Weight not thrown
on one alone.
Panic now reduced
to manageable fear.

The cat scratching,
the droll of the
local church bell.
And the clamour
of cups in the kitchen.
And cigarette smoke
and a cool coke in glass.

To suffer - is -
Present in time present
Future and past.
Not closetted in cell closed
to oneself and those.
But - the great but -
to take and accept it
and go beyond.
Not stopped
Stone alone.

You do care for me - don't you?
Very much?
How one haggles at a piece
of biltong* in one's teeth.

*biltong - sun dried wild meat strips

Early '60s

On Specialling a Plump P.E.T. Patient
(Pre-eclamptic Toxaemia in Pregnancy)

This mammoth mass

With arms thigh sized
Balanced on bloated breast
And bloating pouting lips
And jellied triple chins -
Prognathic jaw
Dilating nares.

Rhythmic respiration
Not cerebrate civilised.
Just flesh alone.
One reflex lump
Throw back
From primaeval past.
Phlegmatic porcine snores.
This mammoth mass.
And to crown it all -
An elephantine fart
King size.

Probably washerwoman by trade.
Arms akimbo
Scolding her sixteen kids.
No face of peace - this.
Engorges to escape.

Twenty four weeks pregnant
Blood pressure
Two-nought-nought
One-seven-five.
Urine pure blood.
Caesar too early to save.
In spite of all this
And more -
Compassion difficult
Hardly mine.
Readings repeated each
Five minutes for three hours -
At a time

When all are sensibly asleep.

early '60s

A Rare Adventure

I don't feel very much pain now.
Last night it was bad
after you going - and
reading a book
of human chaos and struggle.
Desertion by God.
So buried my head on my pillow
and in asthmatic spasm
tried to get out in tears
a great choked cry
that would echo and
roll round the earth
and rebound from the dark universe.
But it wouldn't come.
And instead I dreamed my mother
slowly dying then dead.

But I want very much to tell you -
To confine myself to the expansive
mystic, mist-like feeling - rarified
that grew out of
the Mountains of Cedar.
Pleasure becomes so painful
that you want to crush,
Like the feeling when the cat
is on your lap -
Fur fluffed out in ecstacy
with rumbling purr
in response to your stroke.
And her fur so soft to touch
that you have to tear
at your hand

with the nails of the other
and refrain from crushing her!

The feeling has passed
but it comes again
as a soft white silken mist
low lying, caressing me gently.
The smoke it is from our fire -
delicate, with an aromatic scent
of burning cedar.
Five bright lit faces, dark eyed,
Silent, staring, hypnotised to the fire
linking us with our ancestors.
Forgotten the egg boxed cities, atomic age.
Now - round, complete, whole.
Like the wooden sphere I carved years ago.
Then heavy with responsibility -
that the weight of myself
must be upon myself - unshared.

We've stopped for refreshment
at last - on our way up the mountain.
I'm standing on a rise
about 5,000feet up -
arms akimbo
gripping my hips that
every accessory respiratory muscle
might be in action;
every accessory respiraory muscle
at maximum voluntary effort.
Vessels pounding at my temples -
sound transmitted through
the bones of my skull -
magnified to such
that I think the others must hear.
Because every step up
required that I forget my mind
jagging me to the state
of my physical exhaustion.

And instead become automatic -
sucking in and out the air
in time to my step.
To stop meant the decision
to turn back.
And looking up at the journey ahead
meant also a final crack.
So my vision narrowed down to a cone -
picking out each step ahead.
And all else became a haze.
And I found I could carry on
as long as I listened
to the rhythmical sound
of my breathing -
coinciding exactly
with my steps.
It must.
Booted feet, leather thonged -
Two pairs of Norwegian socks
Fur lined anorac.
Thirty pound rucsac
on my back.
Sweat stained, dusty -
Tearing at an orange
sucking the sweet liquid.
Finished - I shook off
the heavy oppression
round my sockets.
And the haze cleared.

And I saw beauty.

And it was tenfold moreso
because of the cost.
It's difficult to get meaning
from well worn words
that have lost their significance
of expression.
But we were high

above all the world - I felt.
Behind me were still
the loose slate slopes
on which we rested.
The sheer sided, solid
pudding of Tafelburg.
I think this type of formation
characteristic of
many main mountains
of South Africa, Arizona, Arabia.
Looking down - my booted feet
rudely parted Restionaceous tufts.
Below was expanse upon expanse -
Range upon range of mountain
and I didn't know the names.
The lower nearer ones
were blue and bottle green.
The distant high peaks - lilac
misted demure.
Mountain names always have music.
There was Sneeuberg, Crocadouw
and Maltese Cross just discernable
which none have climbed
except two with pitons and ropes.
The sun was rising
so you could look at it
frank - without protection.
The near mountains were dark
almost black when in shadow
with gnarled twisted
silhouettes of cedars
outlined.
But bright and glorious
and Tinus de Jongh orange
In light.

Again onward - we passed the slate
and came to the leeward side
of the sheer solid pudding

inverted.
And there was my first ice and snow
which I ate and drank and rolled
and threw and slid about
and left myself behind
for a few hours before it melt
in purposeful foot prints.
Something was released in us -
going crazy with delight.
And I learnt that it was wet -
someone had shot me in the neck.
And painfully cold to prolonged touch.
Suddenly we were over the ridge
between Tafelburg and Consolation Peak
and there towered the Pillar Box.
A massive isolated block
several yards from his parent.
'a chip off the old block'
suddenly stubbornly standing alone.
And beyond - new horizons -
the Kaokoveld.
Now the work becomes interesting
no more slogging but proper rock.
Going through the gulley
sheer sided in front and to the sides
for several hundred feet up.
The base strewn with boulders
around which we dodged
like goats.
Then the ropes were needed.
This was my line.
And my moanings
about having no lungs
ceased.
The others said
'she's a fly on the wall' -
my balance and intuition for grips
surprised even myself.
Every muscle in action now -
not just my overworked lower limbs.

Then we were on top
and it was the moon.
A surface like sulphuric acid
bitten into corroded cork -
and a strange moaning wind.
That was all - and the five mile
Journey had taken us
Four and a half hours
To another world.

Coming down the slate and slopes
we ran - for each step,
less time spent on
knee braking with quadriceps
than if one walked.
And it took us two hours.
Back at camp preparing food and beds
ravenously thirsty and hungry -
slangbos as mattress
ground sheets, sleeping bags,
cover sheets.
Three jerseys, three jeans
and a fur lined anorac.
Gloves and a Balaclava
all snuggled down -
packed together like pilchards.
Then I brought out my binoculars
and peered at the planets and stars -
the Milky Way, Orion and Southern Cross.
Sleep was disturbed -
cold and incontinent
from the liquid we'd drunk
to slake our thirsts.

Next day was up to The Cracks
about 3000 feet up.
Evidence of leopard and baboon spoor -
heavy going as well but
over in two hours -

aided by many glucose sweets.
Near the top
crawling like ants
between sheer cracks.
But just wide enough
to fit our packs -
three foot across -
through dark tunnels
and fantasy splitting
rock arches and pillars
like nothing I've seen
in my dreams -
or reality in pictures
or actual experience.
And orange coloured as my jersey.

Coming down to base
we passed a stone cottage
nestling near shredded oaks.
A coffee coloured matron
with kiddies clutching
at her apron.
A mongrel dog, some few hens
and a fine pussy cat
sitting regally at the window.
Washing on the line of
mauves and greens, reds and yellows.
And chimney stack of stone
broadening to its base at the ground.
Through the stable door -
a dark interior framing
a knobbly kneed
grissled urchin
grinning from ear to ear.
A soft human touch
to all this starkness
of feeling and sight.

After broth, stew and pears

and steaming coffee
and cursory wash in the river -
we chatted long hours
and sometimes just stared.
Or laughed at the very English
Englishman's parody of his race.
That night I slept
a foot from the fire coals
undisturbed.
Not making the mistake
of drinking excessively
to slake our thirsts.

Next morning entailed
an overland walk
to the Stadsaal -
a large colonnaded
sand stone cave
with perfect acoustics
and platform
where the farmers of old
used to meet and discuss.
The soil in these valleys
is sandy - not fertile.
The farmers now are poor
and poorly equipped.
Names on the walls
dated 1880
D.F.Malan 1920 -
prickling with history.
Then hunting for Bushman paintings
in caves by the Olifants river
and on the plateaux.
And easily encountered.
Some well preserved
but little known.
Strange figurines
deftly stroked
in tans and oranges

ochres blacks and whites.
The latter indicating
recent origon
and good preservation.
The Bushmen I've seen
have never had those
enormous calf muscles
so depicted.
Wishful or old reality?
Figurines with phalli
fertility scenes?
A nomadic hunting people
But never crop minded..

Then my first encounter
with Egyptian geese
amongst the reeded
banks of the river.

Stimulated now to go
forward and out.
To know
the geography and history
of this country and its people.
What do they feel?
when I as a stranger
feel strongly so.
Afrikaaner, African, Bushman
folkways and custom.
Arabia, Mexico.
Anthropology Archaeology Astronomy
Biology Geology.
But with just one mind.
I need a hundred -
and Medicine to follow.
The spark is kindled
in this new thirst.
It may die down
but can never go out.

The odour of cedar.
The wild solidarity
And morning mist.
And fire dappled faces.
These remain - rekindled
Whenever the wind blows.
And whenever the heater
in this room
reflects fire in the
dark dilated eyes
of my cat -
staring at me
from out of her depth.
This whole experience
has flared off
two ends of the scale.
Something primitive
molten ancestral -
moulded now by
a cooling keen
'civilised' mind.
The intermediate
aching emotions in me
in knowing love
have yet to grow.

You see - we didn't do much talking.
Burning cedar is strangely penetrating.
And in that mist and cedar
your presence was continually
And not isolated to this one experience alone.
But sharper.
It was not your presence in form
as you are strangely elusive that way.
But the knowledge that the essential 'goodness'
that I have experienced from you -
Is part - you are part of me.

21.7.64 Cape Town

Eckhart 29

'Drawing the mind (and heart) to what is most simple and essential'

'God is the inner reality of each thing.'
'He alone is One' - real, as undivided one.
He is Love itself - love which unites -
so I am loved and can therefore love.
And heaven is where there is
no separation, distress or pain
which are division and not one -
something that does not belong
to things in their real nature, unalone.
We are dependant intuitively
on the unity, the true, the real -
and the good already before we can
know what they are.
They were there already
as we sensed them before
the threshold of feeling and thought.
All things seek unity in themselves, all one unalone
and in unity itself - the source.
Disunity creates fear - not love or trust.

'God is the inner reality of each thing'
created, given. Only He can show us this;
that is he comes to find us, through ordinary folk -
like the allegory* of the lost hidden coin found by 'him';
or the lost sheep, thicket-stuck, lifted and held;
or the lost son welcomed home by his father with delight, joy -
all three parable levels - mineral animal human found
from the severest disunity-loss to the least -
as all three are us.
Separation-loss; the widow from her little coin,
the sheep from the shepherd and flock -
the father from his son.

Belonging; Being; Becoming; - all in trust
all these in order are at or in Home first -
united, safe at last.

All things are ordered towards God
and in this they have their own order within.

Ascent to, and through a scent, of 'heaven' - as Home
without forcing it into object form.

July 2011

*allegory - a description of one thing under and through another
My gratitude to Joseph Milne for his 'Reflections' on Eckhart XXIX.

E.C.T.Echo - from 1960
(electro-convulsive-therapy)

I cannot write - blunted, stunted, jerked and hurt.
Eight years ago I learnt ECT my brain blasts
aged twenty five cracking, - cadavers cutting, cracking -
Around a resident student's suicide
Hidden dead and curled in her cupboard dark
The corridors concrete - echo-ed, echo.

Taken to a psychiatric ward F2, fifth floor
I don't remember how and why and how
Then transferred after an unknown time
To a high wired asylum, jangling keys, locked doors;
Doped unconscious in an ambulence
Waking in a dark moment, zonked
To glimpse ghost faces in the dark -
Waking in a moment.
What did they do to me, a zomb?
What was I being and what diagnosed?
Dishevelled in hospital grey gown
With a bandage as belt, blue beetles in my head
(my mother hooked on a scarab brooch and clasp
She's now query demented and definitely dead.).
A plasticine cross above my bed
and my mother's face of disgust.
She brought no clothes for me
What had she discussed?

I went blank and have gone blank -
Now. Now.

At the asylum I had ECT, it is said -
Polished wood floors, aspidistras, a boiled egg;
My cotside knee jerks banged -
Why ECT and no consent?
Or my mother's consent and I twenty five?
Was it she who refused me to see?
And how was I discharged?
What hit me then and before?
How long was I ill - in- then, how long?
And why was I knocked out, knocked out?

Blank, I have given ECT, an SHO - +
I know the wood box and dials,
'not made of wood';
And temporal electrodes like ear phones,
Soft spasmed arch - that sudden body jerk.
And am appalled that I didn't recall mine -
In shock. In shock.
But no-one told me after or then
And I - didn't know
Till my final life span, that
There was a conference - when I sat
Regressed - dishevelled
On a platform before all -
some gutless gits who can't stand their hate;
They were - like carcassed flies;
And fate was stamped -
So I later learnt. The switch flicked.

I am trying to remember -
I have lacunae in my brain,
And I stutter and stumble words.
And ECT gives neuronal loss -
Petechial haemorrhage, gliosed;
shot a 100 volts in 2 seconds max.
Existence stopped - restart. Stopped.

This is what it's like in my mind black hole
szz crack zap, buzz frac
zap buzz crack, zap arch, zac sag
Zonked zomb.
Falling floating unending infinite -
Endless universe - dark.

The continuity of who I am - cut.
But my heart still beats, beats.
For love denied, denied -
Blights the soul we can give to god.
No love then and query now.
It's so nice to look on a card
Of a warm mother and child -
Reaching out - at last, at last -
'Beginning in the now', now.

Let thought think you and
'Be yours and I too will be yours!' *
Let feeling survive now
As I have someone now to share.
And it's not electrodes - when M holds my head;
Though I am severed, cut in half;
Longing for blue sea, white sand and sun;
And a dolphin to swim with me - through,
Through and through, - and in -
A question mark.
'For it is that what which is sought.' *
All that you love - you are.

Jan 2002

* Nicholas of Cusa. 15th Century mystic : + SHO - Senior House Medical Officer

Eggs

An egg is born - straw nest, white-plopped,
a special clean shape to stop it rolling out -

and ease for hen to homely doze and brood,
that's all there is. That's it. Simple. In quietude.
(And there's no pure round egg -
only an ostrich one the nearest, biggest -
no matter to roll - on the shallow ground dust).
Fragile delicate, like us - waiting to hatch;
it has to be that; a chick can't pick, through thick rock.
Duck blues, warm browns, plump pitted whites;
so good to crack the domed boiled top -
and finger breads sweet dip -
the oozing orange yolk.

But this was once a little life -
also, given for us.

Canterbury Mar. 2004

The Either Side and the I of us Is

Going in the dark of the after-past
we are also those who touch us now
we are then who we care for
because we are held
frayed in the small trust it is love -
in the sun baptised in the heart -
once unique and loved before time;
it is not to compare one with another
and none other fights for us but thou -
he alongside as yet waiting,
thy friends, not servants, to be given
that peace which his world can give also.
Once anointed royal, a personhood blest -
a little person of value ordained manifest -
but that hidden lost in the chasm dark of IT
the after-past, disqualified for life -
after our pristine essence given first -
then mostly disfigured spoiled scarred.
We have to believe that though it's hard

as he wise believes the same -
lief-love, constant loyal;
he stands waiting sunset-still
and comes to meet me under
the magnolia tree petal fall
when I am yet far off - small
walking slow over the counted cold stones.
The ever insistent IT of before - the after-past
wells up thick, a dark mire bogging down
or a sudden tidal wave thrown.
But yes he holds me around firm -
we together can stand under, understand
wrestling with the misfelt now of IT before.
I am also a babe within his basket warm
his basket mine. 'Remember this' - constant held;
remember - to simply mention so again
to re-call the image within the heart, felt.
I am the forget-me-not squeezing
for life between concrete cracks.
I am also a pupa, butterfly.
I am the toddler playing with
my shadow in the sun
I am my essence helping another.
Little is the most, tiny unnoticed gifts
within the void. The petal blossoms fall;
wedgewood blue is a flint stone cracked
or orange-rich and lava opal black.
The past is history, his story, my story,
the future - mystery unknown
and the present presents itself as a gift-present now.
The secular world flails in fear and drifts -
the spiritual world fails as religions dictate,
insisting on the negation of our I,
saying 'see, not me but Him' misunderstood -
as only the transcendent other, not the whole, full -
so much of our essence obliterated before and again now.
His disciples apostles followers had it simple -
without symbols of wine and bread, the whole Christ -
then we have each other remembered in him most.
'This is me for you' - simply said.

I will go on now given no other real choice -
uncommon as it is, precarious rare and precious;
again - it is not to compare one with another.
But he too - can ignite my fired faggot mind
and also bind up safe the bundle knot
to be carried home.
Imagination - before cut-off, cancelled,
cancerous, twisted, isolated thought.
Please set this also in your own sight
the same within you the person we simply are -
as grown, the little one sacred scarred,
the chasm between of IT - the past,
our essence hidden real, warm-stored safe -
waiting to unfold emerge
if the ground between us is sound, profound,
gentle firm; or two in one - none between.
He and I will wait for you
as we part - held under the going gate
as the latch drops quietly shut.
When will you come along-down the same way?
it has to be down to be lifted up -
the spring rise of trust
the needful life spirit of some need met
slowly bit by bit
rage at what was not then
yet now tear refreshed -
of our meeting eyes and arm-held -
as water for parched burnt thirst.

he the strength of fatherhood found firm
the wisdom of motherhood gentle warm.
He - blessed love
and He was a babe once. Within chaos.

Canterbury May 2004

The Established Office

You wait for me to grow old and burn
and my heart yearns
through pages of a book.
And a gentle song sung
across still water
Humming rippled thrown.
Can we live while there is yet time
in a hundred left dying days?
or is this an imposition
of a parched dream blown?

You put your hand in a packet
to make sure the papers are there;
one has been given packets empty before.
And you offer an apple in place of one day more.
Intimidated by the impact of your
own intensive dimension,
and responsible, flat and utterly mature.
Must I be collectively composed?
There is one avenue open
in an uneducated decision -
an extension of horrible despair.

Most of his cranial nerves are intact
but his *trache tube is blocked.
Never mind - la la
His electrical lines are flat.
Kick in the bucket porcupine
and put on your teniquoit hat;
we're going walking on our hands tonight
while the moon turns his tilted head.

A little authority hiding
under the towers
of a chiming bell.
And a parched country pipetting
dew morning -

her peoples' tears
crushed succulent
for a resurrection plant.

Documents declared
Work permits, passports
Papers, paper money
Customs clearance
Principally resident and principally kept;
Insurance, concessions, reservations and deposits
Exempt from tax.

Vanish.
Nothing water,
Water nothing across.
No-one. Unknown.
Cut.
Hold.
Holding tight.
Tight around you.
Untaught to
Survive.

Words must pass the customs
Accustomed words become unknown.
Questions asked of another gently
Presume a power
Where the answer is known.
Freedom of all choice is false.
The agony is of beginning decision -
It is easy to speak in sanctioned words
labelled last when gone.
Deep feeling awkwardly offered -
Untalking is fashionable, the established office
And depth reserved, fulcrumed gravity -
Inhuman. And utterly alone.

*trache - a medical short for tracheostomy.

2.4.68 Cape Town ? arranging a migration to London

A Gaunt, Starved, Wide-eyed Child in Ethiopia*

Those eyes which still tell
the world of terror,
torment hell,
fear horror -
crucifixion eyes,
large tear-glint eyes,
in glimmers of hope in help -
a hope in hell;
hope which cuts to deep despair
in the absence of help - bare
and if he only felt in desolation -
the only hope being release in death.

And around those eyes flies hone down, dark stung -
sharp myriads around the ragged camp dung.
But one solace - he is held by his Mother-starved;
here is not loneliness, of all poverty - the worst deprived.

This awful world is ruled by a malevolent god
whose Mother couldn't hold the dying Christ on high
where winged angels were droning flies.

Aug 2010

*a TV programme first alerting the world to Ethiopia's plight and subsequently to others.

Evolution

I, a creature of routine and habit,
get scared of any change, tensed and braced,
because change, when I was little,
was unheld and therefore bad
but the bad too can change -
as storms come and go.
But change and chance are here to stay
changing all the time,
repetitive, relentless.
So living evolves dominant -
with nowhere to escape.
Let the good take the hand of the bad -
both teach, however hard - accept both;
a cup half empty or half full -
half full is best
Breathe into the body's response held,
Widen the horizon - take a chance,
sometimes live outside the box
and break out of the narrow mould.
The only certainty is uncertainty -
harsh or soft.

July 2012

Exercises
(nearly a true story)

She had dropped arches from too much weight on her feet so I showed her an exercise to strengthen those arches by screwing under the toes - a hand towel, and scrunching up the towel progressively under the arches.
But she was already doing screwing up pelvic pinching exercises for secret conjugal pleasures and peeing control.
Also exercises to stop flabby chin and neck folds developing by sticking out your tongue and grimacing broad.
I told her 'well, do all three exercises at once in front of the tele'.
later she came into casualty in a state of spasmed toe claws, pinched

up pelvic floor and grimaced face with stuck out tongue - a screwed up lovable round ball.
The nurses and I killed ourselves then I gave her a smack on the butt and the spasms melted and we laughed forever.

Ilfracombe Jan 2003.

Exile in the Desert It's

I've been through the syllabus
Of desolation, decay and dying
But it's now; thoughts are just thoughts
So put them in a box –
They're only a bit, not all;
Let their anguish calm.

'There you are, I see you – fear' –
Anxious striving to be elsewhere;
A vacuum of aimless worthlessness.
So – it's here, whatever it is,
It's ok – it just is;
It's ok not to know – it's letting go
It's what minds do –
monkeys chattering and screaming
in the dark or light
Always craving for otherness.
It's just thoughts, just the mind.
It's not me now.
It's now, not the future or past.
It's worthwhile to be not do.
It's the hour glass of
Thoughts, feelings, body sense
Funnelling to
The anchor breath
Then out to body feeling thought gently renewed.

The hour glass is turned.
The bad – it melts.

Have compassion. Just trust.
Love myself.
'You're ok as you are.'

October 2014

2 Person Post card Dialogue
(Existential Angst)
To hell with the dictat - 'show not tell' Both are important

Dear Nowhere,
A card of my neighbour's garden here over the back hedge - in full spring brilliance of oriental colours - azaleas, rhododendrons, magnolias - a dazzling splendour of sight. I have cut the back hedge to see it better. It gives me some distance of vision instead of this closed in existence. She is 82 and due for a heart op. I fear for her but she is tough and may surprise. She made her Magnolia Gardens - forms of magnolia have been named after her world wide which she has bred. So my eyes water. She mustn't die.
I am a nothing as usual - misunderstood by most and made to feel wrong a lot or ignored. A small flicker of good has to come rarely and I am training myself to be obedient and quiet and non watchful - blank of mind. A piece of flotsam washed up on the shore. But that could be good for carving. I wonder often if I understand people's language and words.
I hope you are well - our contact is real and honest - no fluffing over
Keep in touch. Touch is so important and so we say 'keep in touch' - that's where it came from originally.
Yours, Nothing

Dear Nothing,
Thank you - a lovely view. Things seem more beautiful than people. I survive as you do by acceptance of reality. 'Living the truth of oneself can be seen as a creative act - perhaps *the* creative act'. Real feeling is shunned by most, however absurd it may seem - the stiff upper english lip. '...the development of the self, which happens only very slowly as 'islands of consistency' of experience gradually over a long period of time, coalesce into a sustained sense of self'.
This card is a still life of a stone by the sea - it has a serene stillness

about it; I feel no person met yet has this quality. They and I are tossed about as the waves are on this shore. A stone is a bed-rock on which living things can grow - anchored well.
Yours, Nowhere

Dear Nowhere,
Thank you for keeping in touch and thank you for thanking me - strange to say that. But far too often simple acknowledgement is by-passed, glossed over. How vital it is. It acknowledges the others presence. The little things are the really big things ultimately.
Do travel down this way sometime. It would be good to meet face to face with hugs - real touch. The manner of talking is worth more than the words themselves. One doubts a god with so much world pain. Yours, Nothing

May 2003

Extremes and betweens

A pupa simmers in metamorphosis;
a tiny within turbulence,
cracking its case, unfolding, it struggles.
A butterfly flickers, lifting to the Infinite.
Penultimate chaos ordains a small flight
and sparks alight a humming black hole universe.
That small form flips over the singularity point
and that brave flight is sphagettified in shreds;
matter - gobbled to nil, timeless. Yet now
not known - who knows? - the other side spat out?
Nowhere is there not the blossom -
the Transformation of turmoil (towards ...

the Ultimate…?

Canterbury Feb 2004

Warming Up

On this occasion
Words don't want me
to be, crouched-cowered,
squeezed-cramped
in a small cage
of doom and gloom
and of rhyme and line.

A not usual Inversion -
The Content
is greater than
the construction Form!

The piece is on
the prosaical prose and new poem
borderlands
in neither one nor the other -
where winter sheds his frost coat
and sleepy Words
rub their eyes
wakening in a spring dream
where the Small resides abides, dwells -
at Home.

You too can encounter
other spun yarns
and afterwards Silence at the edge
sits down with a deep smooth sound.
Light and dark
always let you know
there is more to come.

In honour of the Allegorical Faery - a divine Chuckle
Island Folk-lore returns
'There lives the dearest freshest deep down things' G.M.Hopkins
Soul is personhood, our is-ness essence and from Meister Eckhart

c.1260 - 'Know then that my soul is as young as when she was created, in fact much younger! And I tell you, I should be ashamed if she were not younger tomorrow than today!' So also ...

Once upon a long-ago-time in market fayres were special people but some tall stallholders made them swallow bags of salt so they suffered, lost most of their water and wither-wizened, shrank-small, diminished-dead-down. The Chief sacred inalienable ultimate primal Enchantment Being-itsElf rose them up from the crackled dead leaves through Compassion, understanding suffering, dying to new vibrant life here and now of his right hand Complete expressive Person and they lightsome flourished. Oberon the Noble bear and Titania born of the sky-heaven planet and mother earth, who helped shape destiny of old, were once two of his minor disciples. Fairies light up the light in your eye in simple taken for granted passed-by small things in the immediate world. Their playmates are children, the child in winsome grown-ups won. They are in all and all around whether straight, 'gay' or mixed - if you have eyes to see, ears to hear and feeling hearts. *Elf, Self, one's own true very self-hood-spark with a catch in the breath.*
They are the tiny people in all little people, children, our child self; they have been banished in and by rich famous and powerful people; in false inflated intellectuals and celebrities who talk non-stop, whose words don't remember without any ideas.
Creativity's source and in fair-play - their kitchen studio-kingdom is in the spontaneous soft brushes and leaps of intuitive imagination and not in the steeled workshop striving sweat of hard objective thought, the desk-drilling grilling of the 3 R's missing out the fourth R Relationship, or in hoicked up DVDs CDs TVs and IPods.

Of old their coats and fleeces were spun from shed bits of sheep-wool in the fields, small leaf clothes and fair-enough shirts of snake-shed skin, shoes were carved half acorn cups, laces were cobwebs and their leggings and scarves were woven of the same, infused and instilled from the rainbow, all these now in cool gear styles with painted faces - each in exchange for a stamp, ring, bead or fly-wing.
Fairy simply means *enchantment* like you feel in the fun-fair and the world wordless circus of the amazing little people who deLight charm dazzle enthral entrance and not only in the best real circus clowns who are Us as well - poignant lovable club-foot creative bumkins who turn

a new airy-foot world sideways, up-side-down.
They are not aliens but very much here within. The best of them chant profound poems in movement picture song and word *and they come to you in an Alone to sit as engaging words the table around.*
Slipping now into the clothes of my mystical mode - transcendent singing Enchantment becomes immanent incarnate in imagination image - a half way house between image to idea to an embodied personified manifest form.
Awe and Wonder on seeing great things for the very first time are borne elsewhere; fairies find these too big and deep to carry.
An elf is a little sprite, a spritely spirit, holy spryte - and they all fairly do two year stints of National Elf Service. People thought to be 'insignificant' like bumkins became important when they became, came-to-be, ripened into pixies and clowns.
A leprechaun is small mischievousness making you fall in love, idolise idealise with puckish willy puppetry, heart throbs and they have rings in their noses and ears. Impish ones latch with love-juice, graft glint and glee in the eyes and rogueish ones get up to tricks antics quirks and pranks in huts and stalls - also as goblins and hob-goblins known. All these tribes of fairies, elves, leprechauns goblins pixies sprites imps, cupid and clowns *can show us our hidden selves.*
Fairies hide in pepper pots, and in sneezes and they make cream bubbles in dark black-beer, the fizz of sparkling water, beaded bubbles in a wine glass brim, they throng in troops in sips of peat malt whisky, in mustard seeds and chillies that water our eyes, in gem-glints, a blob of ink on a pen tip, rain drops on cobwebs snowflakes, surf-spray, sherbet, icicles, floating feathers; they sleep snug in flower petals and vivid blankets of fallen autumn leaves, and zoom down the sun-rays of sun-rise. *They teem in tickles and mostly in laughter and deLight - a true laugh is an immediate revelation of the self and is wordless; laughter together is intimate.* They touch your eyelashes to help you sleep, crackle in winter wood-fire sparks, *they appear from Nowhere which is a great Within beyond space* and flit, hop gamble and dawdle to make the scent of blossoms, the small moths round night lights; they spin sung lullabies, stand sentinel in the twinkle of your eye, in starlight, wand away warts and spots and collect from under the pillow, your first milk tooth out; they hum in falling petals and push up the tiny forget-me-not buds peeping between concrete gaps and we don't walk on pavement cracks, do we! They're the delight in the eye of a toddler in the first wobbling steps but vanish in the sudden bump-downs; they

pop up fresh in bubble baths, in the pin-point, spot-on, sparrow beak's, precise-pecking an exact sugar-speckle-crystal, grain-fleck spot; we can't do that. They are in the purrs of a plump clumped pussy cat and in astringent tingling after-shave and in the sound of the wind, running water *and the shapes of clouds in the sky*.
There are legions of them in sudden hunches and in the flash of an idea; in moonbeams fanned in our eyes and in sparkling tears.
They relieve heavy honey bags from humble bumble bees, do courtesies, carry messages - little love child-cupids, so *tread softly in our midsummer night's dreams where dreams don't fall off.*
Some elves who were once fair and light can be dark fairies who weave in nightmares, dare-devils, haunted spirits.
Hurtful mean elves are hooked on salt and you can throw it over your shoulder to wilt their power. Grown ups like a bit of salt to savour themselves and their food *and some of them have learnt to understand their dark elves-selves.*
They are shrivelled oppressive stiff folk like some bullies who suffered deprivation of big-good-thing words - like Love, when they were small. They become large demons and form abundant lesions in power hungry fighting people starved of love and regard. But they can catalyse our growth thru' fear pain suffering, sometime shared in shared Compassion, and so are transformed in respect.
The light in holy spirit sprytes shines in the dark sprites and the dark is not overcome but through welcoming giving wisdom can be *redeemed given a second chance and the chance then can dance.*
In a twinkling of an eye something will come to us, will happen in us; now you feel it now you don't, like a wind-gust. And in a twinkling of an eye Enchantment can be gone - the coming, the going, feeling things in ways, different, where words do somersaults.

Inspired ideas images from fairies can be breathtakingly tickling, wriggling and excitement-jumping. The trick is to expire, breathe them out slowly, in a puff-powder-mist for moments of peace.
Nowadays people try to catch enchantments by cameras but it's not the same - mostly they vanish to blank memory or are bland lost.

They are fragments forming a whole for Life's sake. *They a-Bound and Bounce inside anticipation. They cling to the Hands of hope.*
Knowing he is, so I am, so You are. True thinking is also to thank -esse

unum verum bonum - being unity truth and the real, for-good.
We love because we were first loved - as a babe grows in love as he is loved within those who love him first *where whisper-words wake.* Let our children and the child within come to us, don't try to stop them for theirs is the *kingdom-of-heavenly-being-truly-at-home.*
You are the reason I am through your love; knowing she is, so I am, and You are. Fairy faces are you and I in simple Innocence where innocence opens wide-eyed. They are wings to lift us up. Stories are reality, the embodiment of concept truth and *words dance where you can discover how they grew up with their brief feather-shorts on.*

We are all sons - a son is one, who is begotten, a child.
Quoting Meister Eckhart 'Verily I say, the soul will bring forth (our) Person if God laughs into her and she laughs back to him. To speak in parable, the Father laughs into the Son and the Son laughs back to the Father; and this laughter breeds liking, and liking breeds joy, and joy begets love, and love begets Person, and Person begets the Holy Spirit (flame-spark)'.
And me -Verily, I say, feel on these things, study if you will, don't if you can't, enjoy if you want.

Canterbury Oct 2007

A Morelli's Family Tea
'More than Just Coffee since 1932'

Two kids, Mum and Dad -
loud 'dysfunctional',
settle at a round table
with a large homely tea pot
as the centre piece of peace
with milk, cups and saucers,
sugar and cakes.
All become quiet in the sun -
the honey brown brew is poured by Mum
holding the pot aloft,
elbows out -
her back straight;
then spoons tinkle

and faces munch.
They're at one
amidst sustenance
  received
which is soft love -
doing and done.

early 2009

Cheap High Street High Fashion Now

with a large slug of sloe gin! Town and street market fashion comes
before haute couture. The Kings Street and Soho flea-markets'
individual design is copied by French fashion on international
catwalks and costs a bomb, an arm and a leg
and TopShop copies them cheaper again. But fashions fast change

Any colour will do in no order, un-co-ordered, mixed
and tartans are back with the economy down turn,
throwing us back on what changes not and lasts -
that is - country style and the unchanging Queen, fixed.
So, rise tousled in the morning, don't comb your long hair
or wear a raggedy hair-cut with longer chewed side bits;
spend time on greased eye lashes, blacked eyed starlets;
grab some creased un-ironed clothes; in winter UGGs are in
or dirty old holy plimsolls or small slipper shoes, trim.
Rifle the medieval trunk for floppy tasselled toe-point boots
stocking tights, mostly garish; ladder design runs will suit.
Your 8 year old dress will nicely do, now very tight
with hem coming to the top of the thigh in light delight
or cadge your brother's rugby circle-striped top
or an old piece of raggled ruckled blanket as a cloak
or a funky floppy cardigan - yes cardies are back
with sleeves extra long to cover your cold hands, cracked
or rag strips together strung, mid hung on a belt like fairy clothes.
Belts or ribbons must not be waist-placed but under the boobs
going back to earlier times of whisping long lacy frocks;
or a short thigh petticoat will do in summer for a dress;

and a car boot sale for an old tapestry bag, shoulder slung.
Some bits of large junk threaded together, strung
for many bracelets, trinkets and jewelled necklace bling.
or tartan tight slacks. Wha'eva. Girly girly funk.
I love it, laissez-faire - chaos to order, don't give a toss.
Youngsters are saying yaboo yahoo 'I am me' - unique.
This little or much - to care about a little or the fuss of much.
Older women now with tight bras to spillage of 4 boobs each,
low cut dresses nesting a cross to a teasing tempting cleavage.
If a cocky young man - crinkled worn jeans or stove pipe legs
slung down low, nearly falling off a tight bum, which beg
to be hoisted; I am still puzzled as to how they stay up -
with frayed ankle bottoms, water puddles to soak up,
slouching along mobile hungry; a 'swagger' is a must;
old plimsolls fluorescent laces or long pointed shoes upthrust
with a curved cut shirt out and grand-dad's old cardigan -
or hoodie trainer top and floppy canvas bag like a postman.
An Italian stripe hat, pin stripe black like the mafia gang -
and glue-stuck spiked hair-on-end-fright or the style of just born
rounded off with a loose scarf in a hangman's noose slung.
I chuckle love it. All this - what fun. All these, you can
buy at charity shops often over time.

Nov 2008

UGGs - ugly; Australian, for fur lined chunky boots.

A Father's Funeral

The dark of vision frozen, fast
Alone with shadow, in fear - vast
Sand duned, a desert
A vision from the past
Groping in stabbed eyes
Wet, closed.

A mother, bowed and gentle curved
Watching the coffined wood
And gaping ground hole

The flap of parsons gown and hood
And men in dark watching, gripped.

The wind breaks
And sand blows low and soft
So immeasurably alone
Waiting a velvet touch
And vast
The iron future
And past
Churns the urn.
Reason and belief
Muffle the sound
Of sand on wood
A coffined hope slides
And death is dead.
But love screams impotent
And god laughs
With a doomed thud.

Weary of death and its cloth
Birth and betrothal
And the rip of pain untouched
They say it is she
Who must bear, crushed.
In death life must live -
In the wake - drunk.

3.12.67

Death of a senior colleague's husband, Cape Town

Instructions to write on 'Feeling Warm'

'Glow' said the glow-worm
in the forest dark;
'tingle' said the embers
dying in the grate.
The god said

‘there shall be neither hot nor cold
but just nice’ -
then He said
‘it is good’ for some
as we wrap up warm
with long scarves
woolly caps,
furry boots
and long socks.

Then the fire is lit at home
and I said
‘Oooh’
all safe and snug.

Dec.2013.

The only decent word here is ‘oooh’!

Feet

Babies curl, toe sucking, foot praying -
we can’t do that, grown up!
They know six senses whole, we have one lost.
Our feet - so neglected bubuckled worn, whelked -
calloused cramped, drop arched - made to stiltwalk -
so - stilted, shoed, shod, confined - we are.
Without feet, we’re just stumps.

Foot - a little lovely word, important in ages past -
so used as a measurement sign - now dropped
to centimetres long and scurrying centipede steps.
27 bones, 32 elastic articulated joints - one foot;
an elliptical marvelled, bowed sprung arch.

‘How beautiful are the feet of them that...

bring glad tidings of good things' - to boot.

Rom.10:15
Canterbury Feb. 2004

Fever

This moment set down
From a reel of ticker-tape time
In a square room
This section set down
Filled with unrecorded gems
Of no use at all.
So much activity outside
So little within -
Sucking a thumb
And the pearled bubbles of spit
Under a crescentic nail
And blue black moments
With eyes watching black.
A small cool sun on ice
With swords of glare
As I close my eyes -
A medieval man looking down
With the sky at his back.
A tramp in the train
Dying and white and incontinent.
No one cared and avoided
His closed eye stare.
A row of trees
With the sun inbetween
On a lane to nowhere.
A woman's face contorted in rage
Like a dried prune
Because a child threw his shoe
Down the stairs.
A jungle of grey people
Surviving in a civilised way.

Lord - let me end
In Napsbury when I'm old
Where there's grass and space
And autumn oaks and demented minds.

Children shouting, milk bottles toppling -
Two hundred chimney tops.
I tracked in tall yellow grass -
In streets and empty mind labyrinths now.
My guide has gone. Hospital beds
Transfusion sets, closed eyes.
My mother said 'You'll be the death of me'
From the depths of her shrouded sheets -
She is still alive.
The week end closed in a crysalis
And planktonic forms, shapes and scenes
Welled up from a black sea
In the centre of coned eyes.
A silicate diatom beer glass
A silicate rasquedo sun sea.
It's black now.
I'm going to the centre of the earth
In the red centre of dying embers
In my centre charred -
Footprints to show my journey
And not returned
In the soft yellow glow -
No shadow cast. No thing there.
If you look past a point, like a star
You see it better.
With vicious ferocity the end comes -
Life is unbalanced and untimed
And people cannot stand
Too much silence
In steel ribbed tunnels
Of underground trains - stopped
Stirr, russle their bags
And flutter among noise.
A crysalis cracked to crystals

From the dry dust of a moon world.

Oozing from my being
Like lemon oil
From skin squeezed pores
Not you alone - I alone
An aromatic tang of Thou and I.

I had an ambulence letter
In the form of a dead black boy
Strangled by the muscle nooses
Of his breathing tubes.
I turn things to stone.
How can you confine an immensity
To a few words
When the whole world suffers
And music hurts.
The pen drops. Then perhaps.
A blind old lady
Shuffles across the road
Her stockings crinkled
Around her shoes.
And opiate flowers on the roof of a hearse
Say there is life after death
As their cut stems wilt.
There are gaps where are no words
A sadness that oozes
From my eyes and sweat and hair.
A full stop of affirmation of an end
Where blood stops flowing warm and eyes close.
The only affirmation of a known fact
In an uncertain haze
And we have so much jargon to fill the gap
To block the screams and hunger and tears
Of an agonised world.
A sphere with lacework
Of a myriad holes and gunshot glass
Shivering into fevered fragments -
Frightened by the face

Of a skin covered skull
Agape on the cupboard door.
And cries of mine never heard
From the attic tomb
And orange crysalis
Of my blanket bed.
The shivering stopped
As I had been
To a little hell and back.
And I slept -
The orange point of a paraffin lamp
Glowed and kept watch
And morning dawned
With crystals of snow
On the window pane glass.
A cup of coffee passed
And I am held together as I hold
And brown sugar crystals
In an earthenware pot
And brown cushion soft.
A green grass blade grows
Between grey pavement cracks.

25.11.71
Primrose Hill digs and Child Psychiatric Registrar,
Belgrave Hospital for Children London -
before that at Napsbury Mental Hospital as a register

Fire -

with thanks to Meister Eckhart

this trinity of light and sound and heat of flame -
fire begotten of fire, flames borne of flame;
watching detached - a hearth fire, dream-entranced,
no before or after, caught in a flickering dance
dying into the dance - no before or after won;
dying into the dance - mesmerised at-one

skin, glowed eyes conformed warm, lost-found.
The heated hearth where raw food can transform -
naked baked bread shared, broken-With, fresh born
or a bubbling pot over, or mud ovens brick brown
body and heart fed, heartened softened - balm.

Fire-With is Ultimate, mingling colours of warmth glowed
and giving quiet light first then heat follows, delayed;
light is penultimate - from fire or across spark;
light's sped photons forth have no felt heat out -
fire's spectrum of oranges yellows reds and, white-hot
yet light needs no medium to travel in and about
like sound needs the carrier of air or water wave;
that air powers fire's flickered hunger to breathe, saved,
flamed-fervent, impatient incandescent, reckless brave
then without time's urgent thought, happy in the present.
    Fire formed from the friction or strike instant
    of hard against substance hard - violent
    the spark to flame happy abundant,
    the roar of its delight in freedom
    to sound born, exuberant.

Fire as heat is given to air to own as its own for a time -
light is taken back, only loaned as 'the sun goes down'
yet not - it's the earth that turns away then towards around
yet its gift-warmth for us for a time lingers, remains,
Sun's 5 mega-tonnes per second changed to fire-force, sustains,
warms or burns, light and heat's primal source, maintains.
Wood gives itself up dying from a tree once living -
wood's nature to feed seeds leaves, fruits and us in being
with essential forests, the lungs of the earth sustaining -
dark wood that carried the cross, borne transforming
and our little fire is born out of tinder-splinters, lit kindling.
A sharp spark takes a split heart - and stark, sudden bursts -
sparks dart up to the dark to mix with specks of light stars;
smoking contention effort, crackling, violence between
till fire transforms wood also into itself known, serene -
then the connection of fire and wood become one inseparate;
logs sigh and snuggle and recline together, red hot, intimate -

now settled, simmered-down, homely - quiet alight
heat, free after the fervour, destruction of creation, bright;
spark and tinder delight in birth - both changed in correlation
just as our heavy damp-cold woodenness, deprivation
and spark's passion-to-flame-to-fire-warmth radiation vocation.
While something is becoming something else, defenceless
it always has unlikeness troubled struggle, brokenness
avoiding change's risk, but when transformed it has rest, stillness;
giving birth likewise involves great disturbance before newness;
fire and change, like birth, involve the danger of openness -
both needing someone relating stoking understanding
like our slow transformation growth-tending, encouraging.
Fire, like crime unattended unmanaged, in fury destroys -
the storm-agony of passion that can't light another steeled cold;
the confusion and pain of hurt before anger lights-up, sparked
can only be transformed in real relationship, well worked.
Fire lights, shines first, before warmth results,
and not vice versa.
Then, glowing embers die-down after,
colding to the grey ash after-birth;
dust returned renewing us-earth -
dying in transformation.

As far or near as or not,
fire the father, spark the spirit, son the wood.

Dec 2007

Fertile Flames

Tiny flames dancing
within the apple log burning
hope, intent - flickering.
Life is meant to be burnt -
a reverie hypnotised
in the vision quiet,
seeing unseen
wood-worm riddled rot.

In Ikons, christ looks at us, somewhere -
his mother looks nowhere, sad -
downturned mouths.
What mother-baby bond that? -
his cross? - so heaven is half full
but only with those who've
seen beyond, within,
deep, down and full.

So many browning blossoms
so much fallen fruit
superabundant.
Sperm millions lost in the race
to be the first the strongest the best
to wriggle within the shelled queen egg.
We have so much to say - sperm words
which fall by the fallen fruit.
Maybe the fragile one is the best;
a butterfly reborn within
a gold chrysalis thorn of his brown crown.
The dark pupil dilates.

A heart stops alive
within the pounding dead.
The dead nourish life -
our sticky clay feet.
He does play and experiment!

Canterbury, April 2004

Flying. British Airways Boeing 777 BA 5 and 6 flights
a view out of a little rounded corner window -
if it was square the plane would crack up - fact
Eleven hour International long haul flight to and from Japan

Two low slung Rolls Royce engines
the diameter of a man and a half - inset whirlwind blades -
the best in the world and universally deployed

hanging beneath the wings by not quite a thread;
searing like an Albatross, soaring above waves, unlanding two years.
But this is a gigantic bird so thrilling and metallic heard.
Many line up in queue then taxi to a stop; the green light goes
so our engines in crescendo roar and throb
and then uplifted we are thrown back in take off -
the unleashed energy of the universe.
Wingspan 200 feet, 200,000 litres fuel in the belly and wings
I quiver, chill, shudder and quiet weep in awe absolute.
The marvellous mind of man infinitely creative - the mind of God.
Due simply to simple physics turning complex -
of wings with a greater convex surface above
and therefore faster airflow than over the flat underface -
the faster the airflow atop the lower the pressure there, so giving
lift, vacuum isn't tolerated, pressures try equalising-not the
whole truth
as some planes can fly upside down though how I know not -
it's the vital 'angle of attack' Many movable wing bits fore and aft -
ailerons spoilers flaps tabs slats, wing skin metal a few mms. thick -
and on the tail, elevators and rudder, in some airbrakes
with reverse thrust. Roll, yaw and pitch the sacred trinity of moves.
Oh - I tingle when ever I have flown. From a wing seat I watch
the pilot tickle and juggle the wing bits in turbulence.
Best of all, the landing and take off, which bits and why I know not,
out of the main wing other bits too can move in and out;
bits shoot up to the sky and down to the earth to brake
or to give more gentle lift - more curve, more convex;
I swear the whole wing tip curved up in flight. Now I know why.
A mind bending 38.000feet up, - 50 degrees C below out, 600mph.
We fly over Siberia for hours and hours at the top end of the earth
then down a bit to Japan as that's the shortest distance done -
the equator is the fattest and longest way round the earth's orb.
Back home inbound - Thames Estuary 260mph -
ailerons right down, we soundless glide, I pray not to stall and drop.
Wobble, float - over the Shard, Gherkin, London Eye - Heathrow -
land roar maximum - flaps hard down and up, brake stop.
My God. Wow.
To be curious, to question, to wander, to wonder -
that the very yeast to lighten-leaven the lifeless dough

of the commonplace,to life-giving, full bodied bread

May 2015

100,000 passengers are boarded daily - Heathrow U.K

Flying

Ian gasped water and yelled for help. His glasses had stayed put somehow, but water clogged his sight He had capsized in a Mirror dinghy in a sudden strong gusterly South Easter off the harbour at Whitstable. And he couldn't swim but he had a life jacket. Sailing with wind filled red sails was the nearest he had been to flying and the little boat was called Skipper 'cos he skipped across wave crests. But not now - he was in dire trouble.
A low grey mist hung thick and dark and visibility was poor.

But Ian knew a certain Beth - a frolicsome, mischievous, cheeky, short cropped curly haired lass. She was often off school wandering, to watch gulls on the shore's flat mudlands - a deep magic in their flight and their aerodynamic brilliance and they called to her.

One angel gull called Chiang was her companion and guide and he often circled around her and alighted near her on the low dark wet wood poles struck straight upright on the shore.

Ian and Beth knew each others thoughts without words.
That cry for help rung across the mists to Beth who was skimming lovely, flat round shiny stones across the water. She had got up to 3 bounces over the crests but 8 was her record and that only in fresh smoothe water.
That distant deeply heard cry sent a shiver through her.
'Jesus, Ian is in danger'. She abruptly froze.

But Chiang too had heard that cry and he plumetted down to Beth and circled her with a strange power.
Beth rose in the air with that strange power. She flew without flying to where Ian struggled and landed on the small keel of the dinghy which lay on its side - its mast held flat on the water by its air filled red sails.

Her weight on the keel slowly righted the boat and she hauled Ian on board gasping and coughing up water.

The foul weather stilled. Beth was dumb struck at the magic of that flight. She had often dreamt of flying. Ian shivered in a daze.

Chiang circled the little boat to safe harbour. It skiffed like a skimming stone across wave tops.

Ian and Beth hugged each other and warmed up in each others company. They knew a 'hot dogs' barrow lady, who would see them dry and fed - those steaming red bursting sausages with thick squeezings of tomato sauce -squijjes of it glugging out in squirts between the soft white rolls. And they vowed to keep the story a secret.

The little boat bobbed happily at mooring amongst his kith and kin as he told them the story - spellbound. Ian and Beth looked up in awe as Chiang dipped his wings in salute and flew swiftly into the mist.

13.3.02

Mother Teresa - 'Loneliness and the feeling of being unwanted are the greatest poverty'

Forgotten (remembering Egypt)

Forced birth by forceps grief -
flailing, purple-stamped
peripheral, in limbo - feet-hung, hauled;
light is near God - our being imbued,
but the darkness is where God Is
in the full pharaonic splendour
of turquoise scarab symbol rebirth
where sun-scorch strikes sand and stone-rock;
or the deep Blue Hole underwater magical silence
of the Red Sea blue sea sapphire coast,
where friendly fearless fin-flicker fishes
multi-coloured, brilliant, little - say hello
in the dappled rainbow lustred light -
shaft-piercing down dark-darting depths
to deep silence whirling upon its swell
resounding cavernous between the coral reefs
in swirl and seething surge.

Yet not even that - something new,
begins - a tight rope walk - difficult
(the golden gossamer thread breaks)
as waves break on the rocks -
vaguely true and precisely untrue
an acquired innocence
a way of unsaying in the saying
and in saying - the unsaid -
Pinter-prize theatre's sad-surface arcane talk.
Words about me are the failure of words
as I am more than words.
In the tension between the saying and unsaying -
that discourse becomes blindly
meaningful, and hearingly deaf;
seeing with ears, hearing with eyes;
silence can be seen felt and heard;
(my sub-atomic, faint god-gene soul!) -
that inherent hum within the buddhist brass prayer bowl.
The universe is hidden sound not word
awaiting resonance - low and heard -
the string plucked, the drum deep struck
the brass bowl circle gently stroked;
silent vocal chords, no sung voice.
Words said in silence and unsaid.
Words hidden within words
sound within silence; silence groans
in pangs of birth to sound - to wild-word.
Language moves rather than defines, blurred -
a slow-seeking which seeks deep rest.
God is more within myself
than I am to me. That is called hope
and rest is the magnetic core
within motion's copper coils before.
I do love - as I so desire to find and know -
but no - rather to be found than find
as I am flailing lost - flailed around
waiting watchful - an un struck chord
having searched deep and high and broad.

A place to where you've not been
but are in, where who you are is what? -
a vacuum under a cloud - no sun behind
yet bursting, full fathomed, full-unfound.
Word-wounds breakdown. Unknow.
A state so contradictory, impossible;
without meaning, sense, nonsensible -
labyrinthine lost. Unknown - remembered not;
where the old hoary past sucks down
ground down, sludged down; spits out.

No leader from whom to learn, to turn
who has been there before burnt spurned
as all known are remembered well;
'do this in remembrance of me' also.
He was crucified dead echoed low slow
with loved ones at his dying feet below -
but before - he had company, friends
family followers - and he said at supper shared,
and he said 'do this in remembrance of me'
but then they didn't after he died decreed -
so he returned walking through walls
and with them, broke and ate bread -
and then they remembered well.
They remembered and knew at Emmaus.
He had a 'good enough' childhood
and parents in the past - I am told;
again the thread snaps, wanders in the wind
and floats, blown into the long grass.

The Unknown Soldier is remembered; like the great;
the Isolate are not - when they are alive dead desolate -
to them no cenotaph statue or tomb made.
But 'blessed are the Poor' for they shall see God.
Yet God is the remembered Christ, he wasn't there poor.
so God is not one of us destitute needy, raw.
Yet he kept my Winnie the Pooh card more
where Piglet says 'I love you' - a thread of hope.
Known people don't see in the street

as they knowing pass by; or encased -
the congealed identity of hard boiled eggs fast
so I fight to find any good in that - dashed
and the giving up and going blank - ricoched back.
Another says that he'll remember
from one point of view. Caveat.
A vast fear of indifference.

Being nothing leaves me free -
obedient, doing what they want
chipping away at it day on day
saying what they want -
a water bucket in the line of fire
a purse for hidden coins lost.
I don't matter - yet being imbued!
Maybe I waste my time, devalued,
thin, cheap-tinselled like this. It's all there is
except unseen dreams, boundless, otherness -
not built for this world, default guilt.
Matter is substance salt stuff dealt
so I am not, matter not, the result -
finding now that nothing, blurred
is better than anything; absurd
a world without colour warmth -
hurting struck at being passed by, no worth,
wide-berthed, reject, resonant dissonant.
I am to say good things which aren't
and people become mantis nerds
of sparse dry thirsty surface words.
Opening and closing the curtains - taut,
the days circle caught, into barren vacant slots unsought...

A plastic human chameleon guise
colour changing, moulding to fit
to merge undifferent camouflaged;
eye hearing blind, ear tinnitus deafening deaf,
crawling carefully along a thin thread -
swivelling disjoint eyes, coned around ahead.
We know more about the past - unsaid

as we have lived longer there, hard cast -
there, little considered welcomed admired
vital for a child - but commanded, beaten, nagged
'do this, do that, this to be done' with force
so 'do this in remembrance of me' obscured;
seen not heard, not 'seen' not 'heard' across
the saying and the unsaying, the word and no word;
a deep sea darkness dread
past words of good or any word.

We seek the face of god
yet 'none may see me and live'
except in warm soft eyes, seeing, significant.
A seeking which seeks rest.
A search for what I know not.
Light is near God - yet he is In darkness
but there is neither light nor dark.
Disentangling the knots of words
only with another - touched.
Yet I am not words; kernelled -
my alpha essence, ultimate,
my being before being, is good -
being imbued, the hope - felt-not, not hoped.
Yet not even that - as being is not imbued.
It simply is. This-emphasis-amiss
anti-thesis-dismiss. Sheershot -
the warm gun; heartfruit pain pips burst, clot.
Anything else is a defence, carapace.
I say the words, steel-shelled, compressed
hearing this deaf clenched oppressed
You say to me you are present - expressed,
though I feel to you - not? - blocked
or to myself, many selves shrapnelled,
or one self; stewing in the pot
homeless at home in a house -
a little curling to wait on sleep, withheld.

I am - in the midst - and it is I
who don't remember and can't; cut-clipped roots -

waiting long a new remembrance, mute.
How long? is the silent cry - chords struck,
the watcher waiting - and the watched
yet no deep resonance - a heart so vast.
It is not that I have it or don't -
now or in the past.

Shade, rest, peace, oasis, quiet;
underwing - a shadow bright;
murmuring - a clear cool wind.
Consuming or contemplating -
life insured being held; a little now
and little goods multiply five thousandfold
like the two fishes and five loaves.
The low known moment now held -
not the time of the disjoint world.
It is an unfolding, a sound slow spectrum.
It is what is now - simply is...full stop dots...
pug marks left in the shifting dunes…

Dec 2005

Fragments as they Fall

I went for a walk and found a cloud and a rainbow. I took out my plastic sample bags and just managed to collect a bit of each but they protested - their cries muffled in the top-knotted prisons.
Triumphant, I went home to study the objects under the microscope. Surprised - I found that they had disappeared. Then I heard laughter in the sky.
A cloud's life is 10 minutes - true - it has been measured.
The cloud and the rainbow had ascended into heaven. And I was left on earth.

I am an apple in M's shopping bag. He will eat me then I will be inside him safe, always - a part of him.

A baby in a push chair turns its head to watch a moving pigeon on the ground. The baby's head overshoots the mark so he jerks it back to a focus. All babies seem to do this. Desire is greater than control.

In the street she was straining forward to get out of her neck. A lot of people do that.

Heaven is @bbc.co.uk. It's true. The tele says so.

You are out of your mind-tree.
A place where the pain goes. Please. Please.
Flat ears don't listen.
The dark milk of sleep.
Mystical nautical accoustical - tumtitty tumtitty tetumtitty. Got ya.
I unravel into fragility.
It so isn't.
Shreeking Heavy metal pub talk.
Take the hand of the jugular and squeeze.
Don't expect less than more.
Before rain is like the smell of silver tinsel in the air.
Butter brained she said we're closed - without a sign. I had wasted my waiting time
Just wait a picking cotton second here.
Day of the GP. Day of the Trifid.
Cortisoned courteous.
Where do duffle coats go when they die?
So many bent people. So many fawn and pastel bag-jacket clothed OAP's. (I am an OAP too). Most women don't wear bras - their large ones joggle quiver and bounce together and nipples burst through in bumps. They don't mind. And that is great. Naked underneath layers!
Nourishment not punishment.

I am not what I am. (I think that's also said of Satan or Lucifer - bringer of light). But God says of himself 'I AM THAT I AM' - no split - whole.

Classic FM - of an opera singer. 'She will give a talk on her passion for a CD'.

Shipping forecast. Humber-Thames blizzards good. Lundy - snow flurries moderate to good. Hebrides Fairisle -? So dry bright quiet weather is bad.

Why don't toddlers in push chairs put up a hand to shove aside an offending eye covering hood or hat - while they gaze at a toddling pigeon? maybe it doesn't offend them to see through one eye or none at all. Why does it us 'grown-ups'?
The contented soft clucking of fat chickens at a fresh corn broadcast breakfast.
Shedding their shrouds of silt - skeletons smile.

Of Euros - come on you little ones, jump into my pocket. We're going to spend you in Brugges.

Golding leaves on falling earth.
A solitary tree grows tall and strong. Not so a crowded one with bits of this and that around.
Chew barbed wire. Put that in your pipe and smoke it.

I'm re-inventing myself from nothing. These are the fragments. The falling leaves as they fall. The Fall - Autumn. The Fall from the most ancient age of man - primal and primordial. That primary knowing by revelation inspiration intuition to secondary knowing by reason and planned thought.

Bench mark. Niçe words. Wood and a gnarled great hand.

As much faith as a fish in a chip shop. And fried to hell.

You large tub of suet - you.
Embalming memory in a drop of candle wax.
Underwhelmed.
Broken person. Made to dig and fill his grave over and over again.
Who owns the moon? Nobody. So I sit down up there.
Finger sucking good. A pacifier, dummy and dumb struck.
Sand sirocco sears between my eyes - then veers off only to return again and again, suddenly.

A Topsoil Pumpkin drinks Hemlock - Serendipity.
Agree. Apogee. Trochee. Spondee .

'Suffer little children to come unto me'. Suffer means allow.

Circle. Fragment. Flint. Void. Freewheeling. A fragment of a circle freewheels in the void and becomes a flint stone tool.

Kebab boobs. Sounds nice. Though how and why?
A harvest of amber liquid in a hop.
Piecemeal. Flexible. Robust. Fragile not brittle.
A tenement haiku in a deprived estate. Yes.
The variety of incarnation is the manifestation of Him. The one and the many.
Wisdom is love - love is wisdom?
Knowledge is being - not information.

The golden thread of imagination - greater than anything visible in the outside world. I saw that in a dream - once only. Stupendous.

Get on your laughing gear for that - a pint.
Walk on the wild side. Walk on the child side.
'Grief is the price we pay for love' - the Queen said.
Wallow in warm words say I!. They blow in the wind.

He raises his can of Guinness and talks to the starved stone Christ above the Cathedral Gate. He too is thin and through hell. Wildwood. He's seen a lot of what the world can do and its breaking his heart. Forget about today until tomorrow and down it.
Everybody's talking and not listening, everybody's looking and not seeing. I've lost the plot. My fear amazes me - clouds my mind out.

Dead people can't smell flowers - so why at funerals? It's to wipe out the death stench - by more dying flowers. Death wipes out death for the living dead. 'Let the dead bury their dead'.

I get out of bed and say 'I am the divine me now'. And everything in the kitchen is done cos I am divine. And cos I am in divine not clock time.

I will do what I want and when I want. I am in divine time not clock time which is there to keep some semblance of order and harmony under pressure. But both times seem to end in chaos and disorder.

My tank 4 by 4 H car is called Chou Chou meaning sweet little cabbage or cauliflower. I forget which. It is Chou Chou or Choutie in endearment. I used to say 'Sweetie' to GCH as I looked after him in his dying. Not darling cos that was what he called his divorced wife. I have never had the luxury of saying 'darling' to anyone. It is not a nice word. So it is Choutie as a special word which has taken me years to find, that wasn't Sweetie. It's not very sweet looking after a dying person especially when there is the torture of hospital negligence. So it is Choutie. I say good morning as I get in - and are you autonomous today cos I am. I AM. She Is. You'll take me to town whether you like it or not. That was what my mother said - whether you like it or not. NO - says Choutie. I WANT to cos you're my friend and I will be with you always as my friend Scootie is also. Little Scootie and Chou Chou are so loyal - with me always - as no person is or ever has been.

Nauseous - I buy a 'red delicious' from the Gulbenkian caf to relieve the nausea. It has been stamped with a small sticker saying '4015 Washington' with a picture of an apple on the real thing! I crack tears and crack open the dripping white flesh. 'Take eat, do this in remembrance of me'. So I do. That is my holy communion.

Chou Chou's tyres are checked. They're way below pressure of 23. So sorry Choutie about your feet. I didn't realise 10 up to 23 of pressure made such a difference and meant so much to freer turning for you. I give her a pat as I pass.

I have found a name for Christ. The word Jesus I hate. It has been so contaminated by churches and their people. Now I said spontaneously - Jes (pronounce quietly chees). Yes. Yes. You can't say it in discourse about - you can only say it direct.

A fat wood pigeon 'ready for the pot' as they say wrongly or rightly if they're hungry - waddles about outside my kitchen window - picking elegantly at this and that stray seed blown in the dark. He is so handsome in his nice new suit.

I waddle up and down the kitchen figuring out how to swivel my butt as he does and as fat lasses do in tight jeans. And I go pigeon toed as he does in his essence.

A rejected strawberry lay near the curb on the pavement outside the bleak Inland Revenue. I so dislike that road and concrete closed buildings with night neon signs. I thought to kick it out the way into the road. NO. It was perfectly formed with a tiny green leaflet crown (of thorns). NO - it would not get crushed under tons of metal traffic. I lifted it gently and laid it later in the car. It is wounded on one side - a blood mark under where it lies. I will wash it and eat it gently in the name of the Father, Son and Holy Ghost. That is my Holy Communion. The destiny of all things. Who will take me in and absorb me?
I crack. And I have no idea of time when I'm nothing.

c.Elizabeth (Oath of God!) Webb Canterbury.

All of This has Possibilities
The Five minute Free Flow Scribble

I don't want to speak another language
it would be good if I could.
I need a universal one -
by and with and from and in all.
Something called the world-word made flesh
dwelling among us - the Word without words.
Tongues speaking babble; the tower of Babel.
Yes, he who has, dum dum zunk zung.
I am tired. Why is it not possible to share
except divorced from one another -
except at a distance, back to back
and not face to face
even though we are face to face
Death has no dominion; death is dead.
Roll down your stockings
we're going for a swim
amongst lemonade orange, sand and sun.
Float like a jellyfish without his sting -

translucent shining at peace with the world.
Dive like a gannet - an arrow spiked sharp
to its mark - that elusive fish word;
now now and now again
this moment this timeless time.

I do know that I don't know
but I know that I don't.
How amazing is Life.

Universals are instilled from the complex multitude of art, music
and language
down to simple colour and sound but none from word.
Yet abstract colour and sound
are compelled into music and art
but abstract word has no form.
No wonder St. John 1:1 said
'In the beginning was the Word ...'
which meant the All.

Feb 2013.

A little French family

of four. Mama Papa
and two young girls at a caf -
very poor, cheap shabby clothes
yet clean. They'd specially saved up
for the trip to Angleterre.
All happily talking together -
a few words each, yet enough.
Simple - 'non' goes down -
and 'oui' goes up in tone,
up and down
and others which
I don't understand.
A union jack is waved in delight
over faces and the table top.

Cakes, panninis and coke
and one shopping bag
with sales shoes in a box
from a High Street shop.
Mama is in charge of bags
which she rustles through,
arms deep in stuff.
Papa - an older man with
white curly hair, young face -
beams in all this content.
And because of all this -
this little French family
is both poor and very rich.

Chuckling to myself
I so enjoyed them all -
making up for past family loss -
for a moment - yet not.
C'est la vie. la Francois.

Sept. 2011

Double Dactyl form
(with thanks to J. Hollander and A. Hecht for it and to John Whitworth for teaching)

A Frog in the Throat
A Throg in the Froat
(a very English idea of French haute couture cuisine)

Pingery pongery
President Pompidou
Liked to eat frogs legs at
Smart little bars.

Jerkily jumpily
Borborygmusicly*

Sticking in gullets so -
Washed down in jars.

Jar - a pub quantity of beer.
*Borborygmus - tummy rumble
could use sphagettification - what happens to frog in the black
hole tummy.

xenotransplantation - transplanting tissue of one animal to another (in this case, frog leg to human tummy)
sesquipedalian - using long words
cryptozoology - the search for, as yet. unknown animals - where have all the frog legs gone?

Canterbury Feb 2003

The Gargoyles around New Year

'I tell you, when you were young you put on your own belt and walked where you liked; but when you grow old you will stretch out your hands, and someone else will put a belt round you and take you where you would (rather not) go.' Jn. 21:18

sleepless, silence' dull thud - provokes
electronic voices the second hand sound of folk;
uneasy, she's impelled to move nearer town
isolated with no transport on the home road.
Violent or vacuous programmes -
doughnut people as if empty in core space -
some sweet some surface sour outside;
silence bursts reverberates rebounds
in machine gun-fire A new year message
wishing absent nourishment for body, soul.
In bed she snuggles nest-down under covers-sunk.
Her back pain dissolves, melting like ice -
a sigh - she shuts her eyes - images appear,
bits of distorted faces here and there,
coming going tossed, turning in fear.
In sockets of skull the upheaved hours pass;

why this now then? - not even under the shadow of god;
what happened before at the child Xmas, New year;
she cannot remember a semblance of a family tree around.
The dread of being old, ill, dying alone,
at seventy, staring down the barrel of a gun -
house-trapped, veering off, camber reversed
within her broken body, in mind worse,
disaster's red wax stamped and sealed done.
Or being in hospital or nursing home
in a small room without her things at hand -
control taken from her for forever and the rest,
her white pills to let go of a life of living hell.
You take what you can bear, give up what you can't
in acid beads of sweat - there is no choice.
She wanders lost among the clutter of the house,
how to make it sell for others taste in case -
a paint out refurbish which she has done
many times before in many moves, impelled down a route
but now? and her old scooter is old and the car;
things cherish us as we can them - something somewhere.
M might die and slandering neighbours next door -
others have family friends, the norm and more.
Distorted broken images persist - sleepless for hours.
She has to force finding something good - the empty air,
the devil in the detail - heaven in a small sand grain;
maybe M's unseen face and her name said in joy.
Terror - the chasm between the little and grown self.
Pills for peace to get a few hours sleep.
Morning comes, she hastens to town - a safe place;
where people are and move, the hum of talk.
All pubs are closed but the cathedral remains at hand
with all the doctrinal apparatus and religious paint,
and concomitant crudities of ages past, not the now.
A restless nomad harrowing in hell - (harrow, to turn the soil).
Mind images like leering gremlins there and gargoyles.
Yet a central cathedral Compass rose on the nave floor -
an orientation out of lost, giving the thought of where.
The altar cloth sun burst golds and reds -a concealed cross flare;
and the south windows of rich colours - one sun, singing
through the suns-in-many-splendours deep-bursting,

life in full force. The rose said with its pointed thorns -
'The truth shall make you free' - she wanders drawn,
torn grave to know what truth means - spiked outworn.
What is her truth about the past-in-now and now.
A Place of Safety dark crypt - myriad candles glow
but tears to give their gold and silver treasure to the poor -
then she stumbles to Greyfriars gardens for peace -
greets a known screwed up man who ignores - the last straw -
needing rescuing from the pit by just a 'hello'.
One cafe open - again, again she reads her words;
tries to understand people hurting, why and her.
Someone disabled approaches, greets - an event rare;
she is utterly grateful even if it means
hearing a poured out story at length in care.

She waits to see M next day. It is hard for her to hold,
incarnating the christ through presence and absence,
a mute prisoner in her own personal past.
She has a nose for nectar but the desert is parched -
a metaphysical itch but absence abounds.
Her being-skin longs for a kind gentle touch -
what is within is unmatched without -
the sun does not rise or set - it's the earth that turns.
Grant her Thy salvation that she exists
sometime if not now. Is she here where You are -
the question yet unknown, unasked
sensing in a tear a sip of peace but not there.
Sunk in delusion - know not thyself as 'knowing' is false.
Opening to other thought and heart - mute, unknown -
a clean white sheet waits, tossed, wind-blown.
Maybe all this and a house, food, some 'work'
and M - a great privilege for a few, and BR -
though not the norm; and Lizzie, Austin - 'few associates'
and a little of Jeremy, Heather, Rosa - the rose and thorn -
no need to wish for more. 'A holi-day trek with Him, perhaps now'-
the thorns said, around their rose. ('...and someone else will put
a belt round you and take you where you would love to go').

Jan 07

A Gathering Moment

Stupendous in all dreams and decisions -
It depended entirely on what the weather said.
I think now perhaps you
should know I am growing -
A feeling overestimated in past.
It was hard to deconvince -
Now hearing you wonder
And corner skip at my approach.
But you know and I know now
You are strongly letting me
strongly grow. And this is it.
I will, tender, go
and accept the mass of malleable impact
compliant and incorporate,
Distilled from a manipulative instigate.
With a twinkle in one
open, observing eye, the other
reflecting, resolving, feeling -
discarding gently disordinate depth.
It doesn't mean to say
I'll never break apart -
The pieces are available,
not by sheer effort or force -
But an experience passed.
It's short and unsure,
It is there,
A gathering moment.

4.4.68, Cape Town

'In the Gift Box of Darkness'

In this gift box of darkness
seeds sprout
beneath our grief, loss, anger
and damping despair

wrapping them in water tears
and warm anger's cloak.
So they grow and grow.
Seeds of hope surprised by
flickering surprise and joy -
creative imaginative sparks.

If the gift box remains closed
those seeds wither and die
starved of air.

Twaddle - dum-de-dum
So be it. Amen.

Girly Fashion and new Words

She minced along,
strutted her stuff
in her boob-tube with
ruched, ruckled puckered up petal hem -
strapless to avoid tan lines
with her girly glitzy gladiator
style flats -
all to bring out the rock chick within.
Her slender pins
in the briefest of
stressed jean shorts
giving a glimpse of pink roundels within.
All her essentials, gear -
mobile, iPod, eye liners, make up -
safe in her soft suede slouch-bag
shoulder slung
and layered chunky bangles
to pull off the chilled out look
clutching a vintage style clutch,
cool, funky and glam.
Her black lashed
coy cat eyes
street scan

with sun shades
astride the top of her head -
a sniffed pert Pinochio nose -
her hair with a nibbled uneven cut.
Girly laughter blossomed
among her gang mates
all just able to read
the latest chick-lit;
the scented giggles
invite scanning boy bees
to nuzzle among the pretty petals
in the High Street.

early 2009

Gladiatrix

A Roman amphitheatre
surrounded by Stone Pine
to staunch the stench
of battle blood and bodies died.
She, for it was she -
hard trained in schools -
came from humanity's dregs
in honour to survive
Admired by thirsty cheering crowds -
Courage cremated in pyre.
Remains laid to rest
in an exclusion burial zone -
An outcast.
Fame dangerous
without self-faith
and that only
from faith in her
from another.
But then - a deeper love
than faith alone.
Her epitaph - her martial school -

Mine - on stone
'Gladiatrix' and 'Shotokan' -
The place of the pine.

Shodan. Black Belt. 22.2.02 Canterbury

Glimpses of Shapes
They so are!

Old biddies in bingo
are not to be sneezed at as
accidents and mistakes can be gifts -
seeing nice things in passers by
not pathology or judgement.
A lop-sided tea cup
with the potter's pitted glaze -
perfect in imperfection,
the sacred in the simple.
God is ever so nice, cool, brill,
wicked, like ... yu' know. It so is.
There - a tendon spun rope
with a nose stuck on
all made of mind muscle - she is;
a nuzzling nozzle of a nose,
a snizzle of a drizzle.
Another hunking around
round bulges of cellulite buttocks
but play around with your proportions
and street strut your funky stuff -
rock that runway catwalk.
Another - a jolly plump person bouncing along
with her hammocked cosied bra boobs oozing swung,
belonging together, cloven in union sprung;
and there - a short woman with large roundy melons
of a butt gloved in soft pink tight slacks, all woman -
she would be prized in Africa, chosen
by a heavy tonned chief
all shining and black

in smiling celebration -
then for a tea snack
her butterfly winged white hand
takes a cream puffed cake
to her red lips that pout and wait -
the little finger cocked
for that morsel's fine flaked sake
baked in delight; and delicate.

It so is. It so is
ribald with rhyme and rhythm,
all happy human!

Mar 2009

Gnomes

Cheeks stung with cold
Fruzzing biting icy winter
and folks transform to

Puffa duvet coats
Michelin tyred rings sown
even long boots now are so
different stitching design pattern
diamond figure of eight

side underarm and shoulder and upper arm stitches.
Gnomes with furry Russian caps, arctic furry roundel caps
Gnomes wear woolly caps with pom poms atop
and some with hoods and some with ear muffs
colours have come out of hiding.
Chief gnomes are small tumpy tubby
puffa fat and scarved galore.
Bent gnomes, eared animal caps
a few special gnomes all the way from Mongolia
ones with curly up pointy shoes
long coats with hands hidden deep in the sleeves

baby gnomes with caps slipped over their eyes -
they have not learnt how to push them up off
gnomes with specs on the tips of their red noses
and eyes peering over the tops.
slim gnomes with trousers half off their buts -
must be a cold gap.
Glug glaikit people, caps fallen over their eyes, mouths dropped vacant open
staring at street menus; in groups they block the pavement and shop doors
When it rains and stops you don't look up to the sky to confirm;
the best is to check puddles for the tell-tale drops ripples.

I have a snowman coffee milk cream jug with in words
clangers
cucumbers and their creeds c.f human creeds.
absolutely person eye liner pink mud face scarlet lips everything is iconic so that iconic ceases to mean. emanate every thought, they're so thin you hardly see them.

Round people we all are and can bounce around together. Ok to have square rhomboid hexagonal triangular people too but not if they have sharp edges to puncture the round ones when bumping around which they can't easily do.

Beaches squeek when you walk on them, the sand sings if all the sand grains are little round grains sliding easily over each other.

Gnomes in Dead Winter

Cheeks stung with cold
in biting icy winter -
puffa duvet jackets and coats
like Michelin tyre rings sown;
even long boots now are so -
coats a multitude of different
stitch design-puff-blobs.
Folk transform to gnomes

with furry Russian caps,
arctic furry roundel caps
and woolly caps with atop pompoms;
and some with hoods and some with ear muffs;
colours burst forth from hiding in the dark
Chief gnomes are small tumpy tubbies
puffa-jacket-fat and fullsome scarved.
Bent gnomes in long eared animal caps;
a few special gnomes all the way from Mongolia;
and ones with pointy-up shoes,
long coats with hands hidden deep in the sleeves;
baby gnomes with caps slipped over their eyes -
they have not yet learnt to push them up off -
mothers do that bent over the prams;
gnomes with specs on the red tips of their nose
and eyes peering over the tops;
slim gnomes with trousers half off their butts -
it must be a very cold gap.
Glug glaikit gnomes, eyes near covered by caps
mouths dropped open vacant
staring at street menus; in groups they block
the pavement and doors of shops.

There are 'absolutely' gnomes and 'iconic' gnomes -
those words emanating from every unthought word
and they're so thin you can hardly see them unfelt
and some have black eye liner, pink mud faces. scarlet lips.
It would be nice if we were all round people -
we could bounce around together;
but there are rhomboid hexagonal triangular folk too -
a few of them have sharp angles puncturing the round folk
and they can't bounce around even if they would.
When it rains and stops, best not to look up to the sky to confirm,
the best is to check the puddles for the tell-tale ripple drops.

Feb. 2015

Good Things

It's the surface, Elizabeth, or chasm between you and Beth enfolded by His heart - not the real you. M said so.
I talk to stay alive
M says ''Vulnerability gives true strength'.
M says 'we'll hold your Barnado's little one together'. She's not on her own cowering in the corner, her hands holding her ears. - that lost desolate child you.
M says Love cannot be given, it can only wait.
M says people learn from me - BR, Lizzie Greyfriars not met someone like me.

Matins prayer John O'Donohue - 'Home of belonging, Embrace of God. Intimacy of Touch'.
Eric James says Thomas doubted and questioned. So did Christ Eloi. So can I.
He says he is thankful for all those people who in this world are called to scream and shriek and cry - in words or paint or music - to unstop our deaf ears. So me.

Basil Hume says: -
hear Christ whispering in my ear
hear him say 'Come unto me'.
and that I'm most pleasing to God
and that I can take 2 apples not one - not feel bad.
and that he loves me so much he can't take his eyes off me
and that the Father comes down and picks me up and carries me up the stairs
and that He whispers stories into my ears as I go to sleep 'I have something good for you later on'.
And he is that which is most lovable (And I belong to Being)
and into those hands, safe hands, stretching out to receive my weary self.
Christ, the Man of Sorrows knows and understands mine (and deeper than I do).
and to gently weep to rob my sorrow of its agony
and if I feel abandoned by God - so did Christ
and that Christ was the only friend of the one thief who wanted to be remembered

and if I know utter desolation, so does Christ.
He says there's a sacrament of the present moment.
he says I can ask God to come and sit by my side.
He says God says 'I'm pleased with you. I like what you are doing, enjoy it and do (it well) your best.
A sheep wanders away and gets caught in a whole heap of briars. The more it struggles to get free the more it becomes entangled. A great fog comes down and the sheep is lost lonely and unhappy. It is exhausted. Then through the fog it hears the sound of the shepherds voice. It does not see him but knows he is coming in search. The shepherd approaches disentangles it from the briars and sets it free and indeed more than that carries the sheep on his shoulder back to a place where there is warmth and light - no fog briars or cold.
He says the medicine chest talks to me - 'I have a message for you' - receive not take pills. I will never leave you nor forget you. Abba Father Rabboni
'I am who I am' - a warm friendly fire for you. And he is happy I work at the Red Cross shop and he maybe in my garden and in everything in my house - also in the work there. I am not alone there - he says - so no need to dread going back after getting out to town..
It's like Hide and Seek - He seeks me - me him.
I am precious - like the lost mite of a coin, the fog-lost briar-entangled sheep, the prodigal son. I like the lost sheep story. He comes to find me - cos I can't get to him.

Vanstone tells me all about love/creativity and the kenosis of God - I understand at last. He tells me of the precariousness of creativity/love - triumph or tragedy ('things' come right or come wrong) and the latter can be redeemed depending on the response of the other. No compulsion of the other -(that includes my house and inside and my garden and outside) - not forcing. Then that means people too. Waiting for response if any. That's a very mature thing to do. I am a child that wants 'see, see ---' shared straight off and seen like me. To take a father or mother by the hand and show - and tug if they are reluctant. But that has to be tamed like a wild filly - but that's why I have to show M many things big and small - bad and good; mostly bad. Don't feel I ever had that before Canterbury.

The Grace of God?

Sharp frosts on winter roofs -
too cold to write so I look -
and there, a flow of focussed folk
throng the straight street ahead
on hobbling wonky legs.
nameless and fat and old.
And alone, I am old and dying-ruminate.
But I am young as well
and the young are here too
dodging passionately along -
(and I should too in an inner step) -
their jeans, fashion-falling-down
walking wide thighs apart
to keep them somewhat up.

A dumpy woman weaves along
shining - out of the crowd maze -
long blue skirt to the ground
and a ribbon round her waist -
its bow tied neatly behind
nestling on her plump bum -
its long ends floating to the ground.
There's a woolly beret askew too
atop her glasses and knotted bun
and a clumpy thick jersey,
humming, warming, singing -
grey with pink and a sea-blue song -
so much colour amid the dull winter hues
and blacks and dark gloom blues.
She bustles to the bookshop
and I 'saw' her aim for children's books
to scurry back to her warm home
to cosily sit in a deep armchair by the fire
to read stories to her grand kids;
one in a million she was and is -
as I chuckle in the relief of delight -
extraordinarily ordinary and beautiful -

she so raised my low heart
and I found I could smile and love light

Being up and about is so much better
than being in bed sleepless and late.
Simple things are the real life seen fresh.
And each day is a new gift to relish.
'Those that have eyes to 'see' let them see' -
is this the grace of God?

Canterbury Feb.2012

The Great Flood
A Kid's bed time Tale
monosyllabically written in 5 minutes
(polysyllables allowed for names of people)

A great rain from God came out of the grey mist - but Noah and his kith and kin had built a large boat of wood - as he knew the flood would come one day.

And so he built - and it was good.

And he said to all the live beasts in the hills and plains to join him as he had stored much food on board for them all.

So all sorts came in twos, some with spots, some with long snouts and tails and teeth, some big with fur, some smooth and some small with shells and scales - and so on. They took their place on the ark and the rain poured on and on for days and days.

Then Noah sent a white dove to try to find land. It flew high then was lost from view. All on board stayed quiet and still. Till the dove came back with a green leafed twig in her beak, for a nest and Peace. Then land came in sight - with shouts and roars and honks and grunts and such like - of glee - from all. They were saved at last.

Canterbury 11th Nov.2002.

Can you spot the problem spots? e.g. ol-ive twig.

It's all Greek to me

ABCD
EFG
HIJK
LMNOP
QRST
UVW.
XYZ and XYZee

Alpha beta gamma delta
epsilon zeta eta theta
iota kappa lambda mu
nu xi
omicron pi
rho sigma tau upsilon
phi chi psi
Omega - Alpha.

alpha and omega
the beginning and the end.
'In my end is my beginning'.
In my beginning is my end.
The stoned Rosetta!

Canterbury, Feb 2005

The Grey Clan. Grosvenor Hotel
(where the carpet begins - lots of old people in lots of hills by the sea)

Gaumless gumless jaws chomping poker cards in organised evening games. Nine hours by coach from Canterbury to Ilfracombe which means King Alfred's sheltered valley place (and the same back) with frequent pick-ups for people along the way and peeing time for weak bladders. But light giggles chuckles and raucous laughter were the order for all time as World War II times were still there. They survived

by that and I admire them - horrors I never knew.
Meal times and a flock of people descend between arches of the old time ball room hung with cascades of green and gold drapes and puckered lace curtains. Food is paramount like you broadcast seed-feed to a flock of chickens and they all scuttle for it. After supper the slinking slik DJ in oily tones quips and encourages community. No-one of the mixed wall flowers respond so he gets sickly annoyed. A few wave arms - 'the pills are beginning to work' he slithers out. More arms wave like planes in flight to his Dambuster music - 'I see physiotherapy is setting in'. No-one was annoyed at these remarks. Two couples old time dance. Quite sweet. And there's even a muted tango. Our 'young' gang hits the high time in the town's oldest pub with T bone steaks and schooner ports or spinnaker rums.
The hotel is an enormous rambling Victorian one - passages like warrens. My passages were brown carpeted with mustard walls so I found my way by that. Other passages were dark green so I avoided those. The brown carpet people and the green carpet people. My tiny single room was partly under the spirals of a stair case - intricate joinery work. But I had a tele and beverage making facilities and a shower and loo. All room had. I amazed at what drains and pipe work there must be hidden for the whole building. The brown carpet ended at my door and inside it was threadbare thin stuff that showed up the floor boards and had tags here and there. But the room became cosy and safe overlooking the fire escape.
I roam the coast, Tarka the Otter's trails and the highest points around - for splendid wild coast views to Wales and Lundy, against icy 70mph winds which brush the grass haired tussocks and sea birds wheel overhead. I am dismayed that I have forgotten their names when once I knew.
A new theatre complex has been built at over 4 million pounds - more culture there than in Canterbury. Two conical truncated towers known as 'Madonna's bra' locally. Ted Hughes, one time Poet Laureate, has unpublished sweet little poems etched on the lower glass walls and doors - about A sandflea, flounder, jellyfish and starfish - as little people. I'll read them out if you want.
I also went on a tour near Exmoor forrest and walked by a beautiful white water river in a pretty dale - down to the wild coast of smugglers and lime kilns - there against the raging wind unprotected. I found a fishermans bubble, and lichen on a stick, as treasure. Another day - a lovely drive through Devon country and villages and past the Atlantic coast with one 3 mile stretch of beach as the 7th best in the world.

Chris was my 'chambermaid' - a mother of children who wrote poems for them and was intrigued by the slim volume of Rowan Williams poems I had for night reading. She had tried to get a copy without success. So I gave it to her and wondered if she had noticed the theatre poems and she could do as well as that.
Someone got drunk on the penultimate night and someone else had a stroke so I offered black belt medical assistance but the night watchman preferred I make a cup of tea for him and a talk so then he had sweet eyes for me as a tiny hilltop chapel alight at the harbour entrance waved us goodbye. Tarka the Otter came with me in my newly bought book of that name.
'Morning campers' the driver called. 'Hi di hi' was chorused back. I laughed and no snow held us up though it made us detour nearer London. That was my first holiday in more than a decade! and I was fed.

Canterbury Jan 2003

The Theme off Music.
(from 'Wise Words for Well-being')
The Haiyan Hurricane

There's no music in the Philippines
in the dead wake of the great typhoon;
two hundred and forty miles per hour wind roar -
the greatest logged anywhere, anytime
on this fragile earth orb
with that tsunami after - the thunder, smash, rage.
Four thousand so far confirmed dead -
the sweet sick stench of death;
eleven million folk displaced, thousands missing
orphans numbed and glazed.
Homeless with no water, medicine, shelter, food
for now a week long while the world's rescue gears;
they plead to us for help.

The sound not of music but its forerunner
of roar, thunder, rage, groans, grunts, screams.
There is no music in the Philippines

and do we and Nero fiddle while Rome burns?

and Divinity wept infinite.

Nov.15th 2013.

One of Dostoevsky's characters said that 'if one child suffers then there is no God'.

17th November -The Disaster Emergency Committee has now raised £50 million from the U.K's little people. We have seen the crucifiction. Perhaps in time we shall see the transition and transformation of redemption and healing

Hassled by High Street Tunnel Vision - Regardless of Identity at Christ-mass

I contract then boil at those who clogging chat in shop main isles
or at full street corners loll around and crowd the others off
or who go along and suddenly stop, rapidly veer to left or right
when you, at last, decide to pass their hunched 'mobile' slow walk.
Who exude from wide shop doors, scant care for the flow of folk.
Who bang you with protruding bags while they natter about.
Who plough their prams in twos and threes down a full high street.
Who chug or stop their electric buggies in tight pavement spots
and unlicensed, run the same, on the very street, to hold up cars.
And people, large, who jam you close in long till queues.
And when time is tight told, the slow dawdling young and old.
And those who leave behind a pub door a-jar, so cold the 'draught'.

Where are walking licences and pedestrian rules of the road
in driving well with due attention and care -
if, for others, there is no regard.

We have visual fields, side to side, of 200 degrees
so what can I do? but walk straight on, cap pulled down
to see my feet and a couple of 'feet' in front and to both sides
and of all fine marvels - crowds part like the water must

on either side of an unseeing barge prow in full tilt and thrust
in haste at the sudden fast freezing wind gust.
So I expand, unfold in space, respect, regard at last
that when a tree trunk comes in front - I can raise my downcast eyes!

Grumpy Elizabeth Webb Canterbury Dec 2006

Hats Off, Hats On

The Editor, Outlook.

I must write about this small event, one of half a dozen similar, that happened to me in the Cathedral I called into recently - to see an exhibition of a charity and it's work in the tsunami - but mainly to find peace and some solace in that awesome place - as I have recently gone quite a bit deaf and so cut off from people while awaiting a hearing aid. I work as a volunteer at another charity.

I wear a little black peak cap with a small colourful pom-pom atop its toggle - for warmth. I also need to dress in warm larger clothes for my scooter.
As I found the exhibition I felt a tap on my shoulder, heard 2 words, albeit gently but firmly said, - '...hat off'. I turned and saw a clergyman in cassock and collar over a foot away. He drew back - I just heard him say 'what are you?' (later I remembered Christ's words - 'who do you say I am?'). My voice would say 'what' I was and I said 'oh - well, if it's hats off for men, it must be hats on for women - but wasn't Compassion and Love more important, the outer trappings secondary?' 'What do you think?' - he said.
I said 'you should know' - equally gently and firmly. He withdrew backwards. I felt sad and hurt - especially as this was the house of God.

It seems the only time I am noticed there is when I am told off for wearing my cap. Often I take it off before entering. I also feel that we have no right to judge capped teenager lad tourists from all over the world. Who knows their deepest needs and pain masked by bravado and who knows what they might find in holy places - especially if it's a warm welcome more than a regimented domination.

Beth Bew Lent 2006 Canterbury

The Hearth
(with thanks to Greyfriars Little Chapel and Brother Fire.)

Play with the letters of the word
and juggle them about
by the warmth of a fire.
The word has within it - THE.
And -earth and heart-,
less the first h, less the last;
and art and he and her and ear
and ah and at and rat and hat
and tar and eat and hear and tear
and tah and hah and heat.
And no and, and no end

The hearth - the altar
and manger and cross.
The altar the hearth
in warmth, broken bread.
The heart of the hearing home.
The altar - a greeting God
the hearth of the Son -
sacred spirit sustenance,
warmth of our real clay earthed.

Earth at heart, ear and art, sight and sound;
he and her, tah... hear, all gender and none;
tears cry, a tear rips and splits;
hah... eat, in hungry hope hands rub;
flickering heat, fire cooking food.
Ah, the ah. - warming hands and heart.

Incandescent transcendence

earthed immanence.
The ascending and descending.
The oneness many
the nothing abundance
The betweenness the threeness
The likeness the Thouness
The thingness the essence
The warming the eating
The burning the tearing
The nestling the huddling
the hearing the crying
the receiving the giving
the looking the greening.
The watching. A watch in time without time. A guard.

Avoid a void - aah - the nothing Nought
yet again it's filled with THE -
lots and lots of the lovely nothing Naught.

Longing and belonging -
to meet us - the coming
yet a long way off - the meeting.
Our oasis home. Held.
To be holy - belonging -
belonging shelters longing.
Balm. Being home.

Revised Feb 2007

'Heavy' Beauty
(with thanks again to Gerard Manley Hopkins)

Wonder to the One for lumbering things -
for elephants trundling light their young small bairns;

grave trunks air-sniffing, unfurled touch, dead mourning;
tree trunk legs, half moon nails, solidly plod the sods of earth.
Their trumpet rumble calls, infrasound as well -
in touch beyond horizons, distances, great lengths.
For whales sea-arching and pod-circling bubbles blow
the krill and tiny shrimps to upthrust gaping gulps - heavy, slow,
sounding below the human ear - as the depth of god so deep.
Leviathans, both, of earth and fathoms steep -
awed beauty of form, and company leap.

For plump bumble bees, black, orange yellow, furred -
bumbling weighty by weight and span of zinging little wing -
plonking down on petals bent to sip so sweet and sing
nectar needled from proboscis uncurled trunk -
the elephants of all formed bees, bums white - veering heavy-drunk,
ponderous navigators among the low air;
their sound talk now a sonorous buzz so fair.

For stout char-ladies who lino-shining sweep -
their tousled mops and handled swinging trunks grime reap.
For great yellow JCBees - fearless, piston-shining steeled -
uncoiled, hungry for earth chunked in jaws and teeth, tilled -
on their trunk tips! (A pin tip might be bad or good).
They destroy - for depth and space to create afresh.
Angled beauty of form so sharp and bent. For lumbering
probing philosophical thought, arcane - unveiling.

For slow learners, giant giraffes and people, rhinos wallowing,
senile ones' simple thought, hippos running, buddhas smiling,
fat tums and faces joy-greeting. For double bases stems-curling.
Chubby babies lumped in arms, limbs dangling, world wondering -
open mouthed, wide eyed, curious, surprising.
Locked scrummages in sodden field - arch heaving,
over a flippant flighty frivolous ball, mud-grunting.
Old tortoise with deliberate lifting tardy step, dawdling.
To leave his wrinkled neck, plaqued shell - head straining,
but inside, he can curl dark-safe and beat the hare.

For all things 'heavy', slow; not odd nor counter spare -
the Many in One, inventive; they're there, everywhere.
The playful god plays and can we enjoy and somewhere care?'

May 2003

'Give two true things about you and one which is a lie'

I am a heffalump -
jacket jersey sweater fleece,
shirt cardigan arctic trousers vest,
high socks and long fur boots -
all these layers of 'synthetic' fat
galumping along through snow.
I am everything now
and nothing -
jack of some trades retired
and master of none,
not even of age
which I have become.
A fool but wise -
in that wisdom.

Apparently
I am that I am.

Feb 2013

Heifers, Horses and Haystacks

Ten and eight years old - my sister and I, on our school holiday on a Rhodesian farm in the Matopos, near Rhodes' grave on a granite kopje, where resurrection plants grow dead out of granite rocks, and burst green when the rare rain comes.Suns are huge and hot, dust storms common and lightning strikes acacia trees into flame; the air scent changes sweet - and suddenly rain thunders down and the sky is black. All is eerily quiet after - new birth meditating. Our mother was never with us on those holidays; we didn't know where she was and didn't seem to care.

There on the farm - a farm can be the size of Wales, so I am told - we ran around bare foot and brown as hazelnuts in old khaki shorts. A special delight - to catch heifers by their tails and be spun around like spinning wheels. The lady farmer, well-called as Bona, ran that farm; her husband had died. She was a round, ruddy-cheeked, auburn haired pioneering, warm woman - some women were real in those days; she was one and better if she had been our mum, but she wasn't. We had mosquito nets around beds against malaria and once we yelled in fear as a cobra slid over the window sill to our floor beds. Mrs. Huntley, for we knew her as that, snatched her husbands cavalry sword and came shouting and slashing towards it. Kiai - yell of the spirit. It wrythed silent, still. She had a warm gurgly chuckle from the depths of her freckled roundness. My uncle was in the Imperial Light Cavalry and another got an MC for taking a hill single handed somewhere. The MOD did give me details. My father had a medal for being in the battle of Mons and a Bisley shot also. He died when I was two.

There were two horses for three kids. Anne was Mrs. Huntley's daughter. No saddles, only bridles and we rode them down the dust tracks to the river where the hoopoes built their enormous nests, and where quelias nests were the size of houses; and bishops birds of brilliant reds. No colours like that in England for birds, where farms are postage stamp sizes and all looks lawn-mowed. Yes - colours like that on heraldic regiments here. Well - the two horses delighted to throw us off to the dust and would wait till we had mounted again.

Those old type-shape, yellow haystacks were climbed and fallen down with whoops of delight; and oh - to lie back in the sun and chew a straw. Then off to explore nearby granite caves, an odd tan bushman painting or two, with shouts to scare off any residing leopard. Yes - it's true. Any wild water was carefully avoided for drinking, paddling, swimming; bilharzia was rife. Such a wide-eyed joy in Britain now to put a toe in wild water and know it as safe.

A few years ago my sister was accidentally killed by white neighbours, gun shooting four African burglars who were attempting to raid her place. Such is the level of violence. But then our cook, Charlie Ndiweni, was the most lovable of all at our place. He would protect us from being whipped by IT - our mother who could not cope on her own and who had descended from black-garbed Scots Calvinistic parents.

Pioneers came in all conditions and from all over the place to start new lives from old - there under the wild white sun.

01.12.01

A Babe's Terror
The First Hells

Learning separation separateness,
time and distinctness-
a first birth cheesy babe
down the birth canal forced
in mother's pain - no choice.
A new birth - descent into hell
through a tunnel trapped, expelled;
his whole-self squeezed
to fit to tight shape moulds
down there and out cold.
Pulled by feet, head, forceps perhaps -
cries and screams his first breath racked;
turned upside down and smacked
his life-line cord cut back -
wiped down of blood and muck.
Thereafter depends...mmn...,
swathed, tight wrapped.
So much safer, so safe inside.
A crucial fraught time, open wide.

In cot or pram, he screams agape
face screwed up, face fast clenched
eyes shut tight, against out there
when there is no match
between in and out; hatched -
wholly absorbed in dark fear -
flailing limbs tremble, jerk, rear;
arms up in hope of being saved -
waiting to be picked up, held
simply fed, changed, rocked bathed.

Movement is life not death - upheld.

Does it come ... and when?

Nuclear fusion of love and concern,
holy grail golden fleece paschal lamb.
If you make it, along the deep way
forwards and back - you are exiled
with 'few associates' near or far.
The cost - destiny or fate willed, filed?
Deep, complete intense, daystar.

Canterbury Feb 2005

Under the Feathers of Hen

One little new-hatch chick she has
as she sits humptied fat fluffed -
a warm hay nest ruffled buffed
rustling round her close.
Her speckled feathers soft -
layer upon layer cuddle loose -
composed. Repose.
She breathes quiet, her heart beat
gently heard. Keeping easy watch -
her chick knows calm-still peace, and rest.
No word is said. No word.

The cathedral crypt Hen breast -
an old stronghold;
stone-chiselled secret feather threefold folds;
but dark-told, awed-upheld, mysterious cold -
no human there enfolds holds.
Cathedral hen is clucking chimed bells, scold -
for long lost chicks cold, untold.

Canterbury Jan 2004

Chuckles

Henry VIII sat next to me
at the pavement pub table
under a black parasol
of an ad for San Miguel beer.
He did politely ask
if the seat was free.
A large bulk, short, red-faced man
just fitting in the seat
with a tall glass of frothy beer
in a little podgy hand;
a flaming red beard and curly red hair,
twinkling eyes - a Henry of Holbein,
a sun-shining face with a permanent grin
interspersed with bubbly chuckles within
and an occasional guffaw and some words;
manic voices were talking to him
and keeping him happy and glad.
How lucky he so was
but I kept my head down in my book
not wanting a flare up of his mental state
with an eye to eye look.

His presence left a chuckle present
as he rushed off down the street
in trainers and tracksuit in hot pursuit -
if not on a prancing steed in heraldic gear.
What would happen next
when depressed dark clouds
would behead many in fortress London's Tower.

But it's not then, after or before -
    it's chuckles now.
Oh what a mixed surprise
and I was glad too!

Oct.2014.

A Little Scene with no Apologies
for a simple imaginative child
It seems that simple words can't pass the Immigration Officer
of Complexity

A clucking
quietly chuckling
stumpy flock
of feathered balls -
hens proud, strutting -
fluffy feet, free-ranging,
pecking - in the farm yard;
browns speckled, reds
black and white spots -
a colour hotch potch;
some cosy plump,
round brown puddles
of dappled puddings
nesting clumped atop
a nestling egg clutch
of oval shell rosettes,
warm-tanned, large
cupped in honey hay
in the old beamed barn.
Some hatching
tiny chicklings
care-guarded -
tended taught loved.

If you tickle them!
they lay more gems -
simply happy hens
not needing why? what? how?
I could stop now

but busy God
is doing a shuffle dance -
his face - a chubby child.

That real face, real -
a recent news report
of a two year old
strangled and raped.
Christ's young face -
god - it was.

June 2007

Hitting the Ground Running
(an addicted person in treatment)

The road is running out the other side of forever
and meringue people pop and bloat -
low flat slung jellied bums flesh drip
and the rag bundles of tramp dead -
alcohol in their throats, haemorrhaging faith -
as blistering paint stripper thick
chars to the liquorice black stuff
burnt on cardboard pavement beds;
waters of strife petrol propelled
and blows on the trachea cry glottal stopped;
old singed tissue paper skin
scalded by the fire of hope
vexed deep in the tattered heart.
The loneliness of his hand servant
written in stone smolten in iron pits
yawning for oxygen tired trust -
the hole in the heart basic fault
or drowned, stroking green lank water weeds
dank fronds. Bodies wither or bloat -
the mirage image of youth.
You raise up to throw down dumped
in the silence of an empty tomb 'home'.
Avid void stuck in the slump of a black sump.
If you're in a hole, stop digging - he says,
at all, anywhere, wherever
so fly like a hare across the blue black

star sparkling sky. The coursing hare.
Sandpapered, drop arched, flat footed words.
Silence is death down the cold tunnel underpass -
deaf to its call. Lost - that wide eyed wonder,
the trust of the warm pink babe newborn.
After - do we go back hearing
to the before all deaf past?
A camera shot kills the soul's eye.
Doing the next thing is what is mostly
and only left. One foot before the next.
Too young to die old and too old to die young.
Abandon the mocking abundance of hope -
that siren song call -
in shimmering fear, glistening sweat -
'home' is a transitory object.
Is our suffering redemptive for each other?
The only certainty is uncertainty and movement.
Kneeling is impossible
so likewise the sign of the cross
both half stories - gas on low heat.
No difference between birth and death.
The within ripening of dying to be born -
breech birth feet first born in bed.
The crux is the crown, healing sutures gape.
Grid locked jammed - the filtering hymnal.
That bow across gut strings cat calls -
wild wails of quavered insects of notes -
of an old broken down covenant.
Music - the mind of god,
sound explodes into soft light.

Shimmy along quick -
the new black is pink
and mouths now are pierced
and black lipsticked -
the lips fruit to suck;
water locks flood shut, gismos for escape -
and may-fly thoughts dart dainty
among your daisy brain cells.

But this little man passing with little steps -
his big coat unmoving except for its sleeves -
ease his shoulders from the burden -
the swan of Lethe floats serene
down the silver river.

Exhaust fumes, global heat, lagged jaws
'lighten our darkness we beseech thee...' -
lost in your pocket, lost.
The road is running out
this side of forever.
You don't need to go anywhere, stay -
as within is far wide and deep.
The night is crazed by rupture
fear tears open the pupil wide, a fractured star;
gold on wood icons unreal, unpeopled by flesh;
doors shut; take off your words and put on your nub.
Reflection makes sharp shafts in the heart.

This terrible cure - a lifelong timeless way -
bite the leather strap -
patience bites the steel as scalpels cut.
'What the hell' is way before the last point -
on the edge of no return - a thin membrane away.
The road is running out
both sides of forever - hope cracks.
The last soft rustle of sheets
at the last sighed breath.

Wine dark sea sleep. Peace. Slow.

Feb 2005

Meditations on the Holocaust
Remembering - finding, belonging again

I once was. Can you remember?

My name is the name of all people.
Today I should like it be known
I am a person, once valued, by someOne
but I have been starved diseased tortured
experimented on - an object to assault and ill-treat.
Nameless for so long. And I have died -
but my letter was found read and remembered.
A broken gypsy fiddle, a yellow David star.
'Where there is no difference, there is no space' -
I am different - Jewish Gay, Gypsy, Simple Slow
Black Wheelchaired Mentally Unsound -
a Child - I am all people abused in ghettoes of the world
and in 'homes' hidden from love and sight.

Not long ago man converted mass to energy -
chain reactions aweful, awful to know,
an equation of destruction, sudden -
not as the sun does here - sustained hot, warm
But now it is known that that equation reversed
was the beginning of the unfolding universe -
Energy transformed to mass. A slow process.
But you and I are special unique 'particles',
persons formed in the image of God -
that spirit of ultimate concern.

Those who torture in varying degree
are themselves tortured and deprived.
Fear is the penultimate of that - love lacked -
in us all. The plank in our own eye known, unknown -
a torture repeated the generations down.
The holocaust within, our within small self -
a Lamb for offering - burnt holy, whole.
who, from ashes risen - leads us
in our shards of courage and concern.

Can those who have been found and cherished warm
share that deep and long? We are in the body of God -
eyes hands and hearts - remember there the Lost -
then found, and that within us - also.

Canterbury Feb.2005

Holy Week
The Nothing of Nothing.

I hear many sermons
(like taking a bat to a beehive) -
of God and God and God
up there and out;
of repentance judgement
obedience adoration,
praise worship sins fear
to the above all Lord;
high flying words
buzzing empty in the sky
rising to cathedral heights
and lost - unearthed
in my simple need as a child
to be valued and loved
without sin and death strings tied.
There in those worship places
winter's sharp teeth, pitoned and ice-axed
snap my skin face. I am a stray.
while a weak sun tries to shine outside.
I hear hymns of a sinful child
saved by Christ's death undefiled!
and willing himself to love - meek and mild.
Enormous crosses tower high.
They seem to see only unworthiness
under the influence of affluent guilt -
tight on terror, sin-trapped.
Broken clay pots spill shame, penitence.
Their Lord doesn't appear to love and adore,
we have to do that to him in remorse
to please and beg from the boss;
he reinforces old bad pasts -
the dull dance of cursed dust.
I have lost faith - did I ever have it? -
and can't remember where I left it.
I am tone deaf to this divine. No faith at all.

The streets outside - and singing well
the soul busker and his guitar;
a mother sharing loaves
of pink ham and brown bread
with her many quiet kids,
her purse for precious coins
carefully shared - spendings logged.
And hookers suffer to feed
their drug habit fast -
to feed a love starved past
but a woman and her van
tour their streets with safety
against violent clients -
and chocolate and coffee drinks;
condoms and warm chats
hospitality to strangers - sacred, bare.
The sweet balm of compassion, rare -
a brightness in him - 'remember me' there -
There is Christ simply sharing
wine and bread - and we remember.
Now the green blade can rise
'a light to my path' - light
and the light slants in, in incense
through early dappled leaves intense.
Benedictus benedicat.

My essential self exists
under this church crap piss
and of how I was raised -
but a pearl somewhere,
in the shit of this and that.
I am happy to inward hear
and now muddled, begin to know.
I am right, not unworthy, not wrong.
A kingfisher flash of insight
and self belief - selfish selfness -
coming together -
valued, precious.
Evanescent.

Canterbury April 2005.

Home is so Glad
(with thanks to Philip Larkin for 'Home is so Sad')
with the same 10 beats to a line and rhyme

Home is so glad. It waits as it is now,
Forged to the troubles of all who are low
As if to let them know. Entire in vow
To those there who disturb, it prospers-so,
Having every heart to remember how

And to remain as that it always was,
A safe accepting hearth of how things are,
True to the mark. You still see why it is:
Look at the faces - and the reservoir
Of patience; understanding love. Those eyes.

They're yours. They're ours.

Canterbury Mar 2003
=2002

A poor piece - to G. M. Hopkins
(who consistently affirmed Nature but rarely himself so I will try)

The dazzling mastery of the man -
a buried deep unfound jewel found
brilliant in brimming-over
bubbling-beaded-word-bursts,
stunning impelled, invincible in sound-
and-image-to word- bound;
  like no other, unmatched.
A lionheart valiant bold, bared
in his dark depressed unashamed, shared
and through that a diamond light shines
all the more immortal bright
against the velvet jet-black
of his 'Jackself'joke, poor potsherd' set.

Neurosis transformed to genius -
living woven as damask finespun.
Dangerous dared depths dived, done
'no man fathomed' alone
with his anchor and air Christ lost-found..

One whose established religion
fanned the flames of his felt unworth, sad,
(how was he as a babe-child? -
comfort-starved, unloved, guilty, bad;
prevalent then and even now in
that toxin of old, the slime of - 'Original Sin'
but at heart made in the image of God -
innate great worth and tender good.
'Inscape'. Passionate, brave. Genuine.

'What I do is me: for that I came' affirmed.
Yet at the end of a young life out-drained
'I am so happy, I am so happy
I have lived' - his last words claimed.
And 'my heart in hiding' also heard,
stirred for the mastery of the man.
For his final peace (I too am so glad), and
he, now nourished, an urchin-child in Christ.

Nov.2014

To Jim.(Hopkins seminar leader)

O thee of hard sight
who hast more seeing
than ever us simple
with two full eyes blind -
our kind thanks bind
from one of some deafness unrefined.

Monologue of an Inanimate Object written in 5 minutes
Humpty Dumpty!

I am so round and fat and trim
sat proudly on this wall so thin.
Do come and see me - stupid, grim
fall elegantly down - so dim.

Pride doth come before a fall.
And we do see pieced Humpty pall.

(in defence of Humpty - this is absolute nonsense)

A Nursery Rhyme without e's written in 5 minutes

Humpty Dumpty sat on a wall.
Humpty Dumpty had a big fall.
All a King's stallions
and all a King's chaps
Couldn't put Humpty -
as round as some baps.

(yeah - what about the Queen. She'd do better.)

May 2003

Hymn to Orange.

I love orange.

Just squeeze a citrus peel -
and - tang - a squirt squirts.
Mind the eyes though.
That warm orange glow -
between red and yellow;

red for vitality, excitement and power.
And yellow - for light, inspiration and hope.
The freshening scent invigors up my nose.
The mouth waters - and - zip - all juices run,
for a sweet, bursting-segment,
crescent curve.

And such an orange sun -
the great globe aglow;
but hibernating now -
in rain, mist and snow.
My life down that hierarch
depends on his power.
See the sun-bird whirr
of metallic greens and blues
and his long curved beak,
deep dipping at dawn into
orange aloe.
The before - I remember.
And orange marmalade
on hot buttered toast.
I remember the before.

Flickering, orange-crowned fire flames,
whisper from the warm coal glows,
and my heart is hearth-warmed here.
And those browning, bubbled,
spiked marsh mallows.
And from where stems the orange word?
it grows from the French 'or' meaning gold -
a metal most precious and beloved of old.

I have orange in my room -
a persian carpet, african throw
and orange in the painting
of the Prodigal Son by Rembrandt,
lots of orange in the son's rags;
reds in his father's robes -
a someone running to greet me,
me - dusty and dishevelled with dirt.

My tiger picture leaps orange,
burning bright,
striped black out of river waves

running free - to meet me.
And he matches the pain-staking yin-yang
and hexagram,
embroidered long ago
for my cushion cover on the sofa below.
'Think orange'
for mobile phones, they say.
But I say - feel free.
And satsumas and clementines
and tangerines tang me.
Orange enfolds - Orange loves me.
Mind you - my bedroom
is shrubbed and green-leaved;
and my kitchen brown
and pots copper-rose;
my dining room now
is bamboo-japanese.
So you see -
many colours love me.
But I wear black
and a Black Belt sensei;
the negation of all colour,
ergo - colour exists;
so orange must save me;
orange does - he loves me;
with me - he happy sits.

Amen.

21.01.02

I am Done ... and there are still those ...

I am done with word picking now.
It is, it augurs the deepening light
of Octobers nights and sleep, not work.
But there are still those unpicked,
unknown hiding-deep-in-the-tree words

and I feel the pressure of straining
upwards to heights and depths
of stunned studied insight down.

Nesting ripe apples basket straw-strewn.

Oct 2013

I am

And God said
'I am that I am,
Alpha and Omega,
the Beginning and the End'
and so am I
in the image made.

Whom do you say I am?
I have taken too much heed
of who you say I am -
now no more.
I am - and like it or lump it -
to dress, think, eat, feel
as so urges my depth.

Yes - the world opens its arms
with all things new.
Eyes wide -
the deep pools of dark eyes;
simple things create.
Oh - a big long sigh content.

May 2014

I - ego

The weekend -
The prunes have frayed
To pieces steaming
And my little world
Has broken cold.
That necessary needle glitter
Where rats squeal and scamper
And sink incisor in soft soul.
Piet a shepherd and shearer
Of Karakoul lambs from Kakamas -
Waiting with riddled bones
While we fight.
And Vivaldi cavorts
With lilting flute.
And I cry out
My heart hurt;
Resolved to nothing
This chaotic cross
And senseless dream
Of a real world shattered.
Because we strive
In a herd.
A crowd of pithless
Mammoths - tusked -
Waiting to gouge
The nearest lilting Autumn leaf
To fragments as it falls.
The pumpkin pith of my soul
Dried to a vacuumed calabash -
Cracked and tossed to river bed
Dry and parched
To fossil and carbonise
With each fissured layer of mud.
An end of the story;
The screaming I
Does not die
But snarls and sniffs

It's soul to shreds.

11.4.67 Senior House Officer,
Groote Schuur Hospital Cape Town

I Have

'the positive, accentuate; the negative, illuminate' or see the light in the positive that enlightens the negative - with another in trust. Half a glass empty - or full and sometimes a few drops, if at all, but at least a glass - fragile

I have a roof shoes clothes food,
few teeth, arms legs that work,
loneness silence, half eyes half ears,
books, three quarters person, half a person
and a bubbly duvet cosy bed
with toys wedged in the two-pillow cleft;
one-fiftieth and one-hundredth people,
garden space, sparrows, toast tea pain,
sleeplessness and a broken tooth,
running blocked nose, blue-tits, cough cramps.
A secret garden-gardening in the early quiet;
sorting charity bags and the rubbish plight,
and making good shop window shows in delight.
And said here and there, an odd word -
mostly mid sentence cut below in flow
except to one and to half.
It wasn't before as a norm
but my house has become
more my safe home
sheltering me from cold, rain.
Roses music scents and
moving in the garden, birds.
Movement is life - even plants
yawn, stretch and unfold grow; and
quiet from chatter, dogged demand.

So what now? - I am so I have -

no such thing as more nor less,
large small, little big, worst best.
Nevertheless little is enough! manifest.
I am. This I have. They, 'toys' and myself.
None other. That is what it is. Itself.
So it is, no elsewhere to escape.
And I have words to write and shape.
All for my sake's inscape
in the dark daybreak.

Thank you roof shoes toys words BR
and NB - M.

Sept 2008

'I Will Find Time to...' what?

I will find time to
have a fine meal;
then time to sleep,
then time to stay with myself
as I am now
and how my body feels;
accept with warmth
my dark side
as well as
the sun outside.
It's winter
and the clouds
loom grey -
accept that as well
till the next day.
Be grateful that the bad
passes like dark clouds
over the sky.
Moments pass by
and nothing remains
again the same again.
And please stop trying to fix

Time to know dying time and
dying of the inner tyrant who dictates.
I have too much time
with elaborate dark dramas
of failed ideals and thoughts
so then have time
to have no time at all.
Time seems man-made
        not of God.
Simple things -
not hopeless strivings
and grand ideals for my past and age.
What you have is what you've got
less is more
and that's a lot
if you really look.

Expect nothing, cling to nothing -
I do not need to be happy; cravings destroy
accept your wilderness. Surrender.
It's space.

April 2013

'The eye with which I see God
is the same eye with which God sees me'.
Meister Eckhart.

An Icon Experience

I painted an icon of M,
held by a halo of gold,
within a three day course
in a high street church;
sheer concentration, effort,
absorption, intense focus -
my shaky right hand
steadied by my left.

M has held me steady
through thick and thin',
shown me of value -
a father and mother
        in him
unfolding me within.

And out in the street again
I felt a cross eyed alien
re-learning with new sight
        yet again.
    Beginning again.

June 2012

Real Identity Virtualed Do-u-do Yahoo?

Defined by new detached language, not love, for logging-on nerds;
what's your name and first line address shared and post-code;
anti-virus, firewall, a secret greater-than-6 letter password
and Yahoo boohoo 'virtual' tears, search engines, downloads.
Not belonging to the square-eyed goggly Google eye gang
gobbledegook www dot internet dot slash slang.
I am a 'real' Geek - computer illiterate, not with it and shamed -
no common identity, humming PC with the rest claimed, named
and with his mat carpet (no cheese please), a pip mouse is a must.
Credit crunch, chipped pins and neurotic stock markets crash;
strange, you can buy money with money but at a price, rash.
A new self by downloading some poor person's dead spouse'
certificate of death at the circling click of a pipping plastic mouse.
Feared viruses roost-rule and Viagra spam is for potent paradise
and now Spam-Hacker invasion, identity-fraud surfing, trapped -
info spread world wide in a sec; so far, ha-ha, my I is safe untapped.

Face to face yet ears plugged with MP3s, iPod toys, texts, DVD's -
eyes low, an epidemic addiction to mobile-phone-hunched expertise
HD TV Plasma! (no red cells please); laptops wireless GPS Sat
Nav Camcorders, modems, Broadband, hard drives, softwares-suave

and the air is full of varied waves hard wiring into people's brains
and in the air, a brain tumour suspicion - kids beware, refrain.
Future ID card proof with thumb prints and iris lines checked
and un-smiling self photos got in glum booths to spec.
Digital TVs radios and box adds; but I have 10 digit fingers used -
many numbers to add; a press button society, greatly confused,
lost keeping up and now nationwide - audio TV is very soon out.
Heckling hackers no longer ransack recycling bag lots
but I still paper shred; so far, I am I, not someone's robot.

The new shared world religion is football, simple, plain
and there - folks identity in soul, heart is placed mundane -
joy, tears, triumph, anger, sadness - camaraderie,
mostly absent in diminishing church society.

'listen up my lovelies, love what you've got -
bangers and bad boys, the whole plump lot'
and corset and squeeze them this way and that
to new wavy shapes or whatnot somewhat.
Machines rule o.k. - new toys to play, distract -
distant instant cut-out-contact, compact.
O for pollen powdered bumble-bees in blossom scent, perfect.

April 2008

An IDS Apology*
from the tele
A Trite Ballad

'Unite or die' their leader said
in pale cool words, and grim.
No leader he and they were bled.
His face grew white and dim.

A three line whip occurred before,
it split them right and left,
it tore them all unceasingly.

A leadership bereft.

But he is learning on the spot.
His directs said quite good.
He must inspire dynamically
and gather his troops in mood.

And Kenny Clark, a large brimmed pug
with brown suede shoes, beer tum.
They said he ought to be their 'thug'
to rally round Duncan.

The country fights on box; in pub
to this and that and the other
while President Bush, a punching cub
plays cowboy and Indian power.

But Tony Blair fares just as bad
in health and trains and crime;
a poodle to George Bush - is sad;
Perhaps that's just in time.

In all of this the world moves fast
and people starve and suffer
and people crash and bomb and blast
and people kill each other

But if we all, did ballads write
and meet each as our brother.
Maybe a world in happier plight
with less a need for terror.

* IDS - current leader of the opposition - Ian Duncan Smith.

Canterbury, Nov 02

Impatience

This woman,
who sat next to me
protected by a table -
arranged all the seats
to her anxious perfection.
The man at the end
hoicked up an oyster
of phlegm from his black lungs.
Her new lover sat next
and she frantically opened bags
of this and that and the other
with numerous glitter finger rings
then spread antiseptic gel
on her hands and rubbed and rubbed it in
then a waving of hands to dry clean.
This preparation for a packet of crisps
and G. and T which once downed
was followed by more smelly applied glue gel.
Then hugs and kisses for her new lover;
so anxious she was - having forgotten how to court.
And would this couple last or not?

Then a regular across the length of seats slurred
'wha a luverly day todai' amongst her beer.
I said 'I'm deaf' which I am, partially at times
and so glad to have an excuse -
wanting peace and quiet.

I think I'll go to another watering hole.
My soup was watery
and the bread flat.

Sept.2014

In Definition Indefinite

I am trying to define
this non-being black space
that has no boundary or time,
no image picture or word
with what is left of I -
nameless terrified.
My body carries on but,
a gaping vacuum -
I don't know my heart mind.

It is a non-place of no end -
infinite awfulness desolate -
chasmed over the edge;
of an unbound vacuum void
which sucks me into itself
hurling in the dark universe;
It is a carcassed gutted incry.
It has no end. No end.
It is an ice furnace
impersonal and unconquerable.
It has no reason and no words.
It has its own life and no end.

The sour smell of hunched dominance -
suffocation by their Nan and Grandad
sharing my slatted table under the hot sun
with full fresh faced innocent kids
licking creams of ice
dreaming of what to do with their box of juice.
They leave and I breathe relief -
their talk was of teacups sugar and spoons
and dunked teabags and who owns what.
You wouldn't think they have just spewed
from that cathedral arising like a rock
out of a seething sea of people.
My non-entity takes form through their shape
and word - and that rock rising solid serene strong

out of tumult - this interminable wait -
can I be born from this - where is no-one?
Blood spurting makes fag ends float.
A bee wipes his back legs -
hovering in mid air.

August Canterbury 2002

The Sudden Incident
what? why? how? - to know justice unknown

Dead night, a forested road, dead night
curved bending, blue lights flashing
a dozen senior police, six police cars
head-lamped, torched and spot-lights slash.
I had not seen so many in a single spot
at the cost of once the bobby on the beat -
yellow jackets flash, flash photographs;
struck by the dreadful care of gathering evidence
maceration, dark death, an awful hell -
hours spent inspecting the right corner bend;
was it murder robbery, drugs terrorists? -
surveying poles, ambulance, break-down vans.
High impact implosion, a police car had crashed,
on the left, the driver hurled off? a motor-bike smashed
now on the road, oil spilled, a standing ghost;
a white test-car at speed runs at given commands,
brakes-burn-rubber, sudden-stops-skid marks -
after the incident, trying to cover their tracks
and the evidence mask? Tarmac metal lines gouge
the bike bull-dozed twenty yards up the curving hill;
was it an impact from behind or head on face to face?
no witness, a badly lit street, a danger spot,
neighbourhood Watch pushing the Council for humps.

Sitting on a razor sharp fence, trying to make sense -
do we want transparency of justice - seen to be done;
side with the victim, maybe innocent or not,

who is now probably dead
or with the police cutting crime at the cost of a life -
one less robber on the road - by the way!
the 'Incident'- incidentally killed.

Police enquiries central communications, no record
usually computer kept and they cannot inform!
Next day - an enormous incident van parked
up a new housing development road
and a white car with large apposed
red lights, externally wired.
The day after that another white van
waits and watches and leaves late
red and white warning temporary planks
criss-crossed as a cross to mark the spot -
a future warning to motorists, in part.
If you don't understand, that's understandable
as the 'Incident' could not be understood.

June 2007

Indefinition

These new heights or depths or other word
And experience of common form
Or risen to an unresolved peak
Of unknown creation
A new unknown form.
Can I make words
Which will have implication
An elevation to an
Un experienced dimension
Disordered order revealed born.
Do these realms unwritten -
Or is this a reflection of an
Un fulfilled force
Archaic and fossilised.
We have only arrived

at the beginning of knowledge
A new sublime world
Refined by the right word
Blip - - in suicidal surge -
An alien aberrant beatific earth -
Where are they, where are the words -
Or something entirely perverse
pervading expansion of creation
An expression of universal force
Raised to an infinite height;
These blasted superlatives
In the space of unspoken tone.
Music alone
Can imply it undefined.
Existing words and strokes confine.
A composite precision
Undisciplined as it is -
Inhuman ingenium
It has never occurred -
There are no new expansions
Or there are - unattained.
Common events run in the gutter -
Unstarting they believe in gods
Of intellect and activity
And what we write is unread
By an uncomfortable comfort -
Justifying each existence in reason
Each protagoran opinion is his own.
One must build on something
Confined in a vacuum securely defined
To be broken down.
And we conform, condone, condemn
According to our cloth
Hoping for an uncoming step -
A feverish supplication incensed -
Yawning at the hole in the ground in the end.

Sir, I would have you back on that platform
And because you are already there

I would have you down, Sir.
It is an easy escape in confessing avoidance
But there is this unsaid flux
Reduceable to an absurd formula -
It takes isolation and painful strength
To sit on the fence and see
An unattained beginning
To an unattainable beginning
To a boundless end.

March '68 Cape Town.

What has happened to the Inner City?
Dockland London

Pain under suede coats bell bottoms furs and electronic notes
The wails and long haired unformed moans, herds of silent browns
Massed demos and chinese chants, paradised in kicking drugs
Meths drunk, dock shot, doped, coughing clots of black spit
From smokeless zones; nose holes grit blocked, river retched
Oil drowned, wrist slashed, belched at Rotherhithe and Surrey docks
Or soaked in dirt and piss unwashed, bellies black umbilicus cracked
And caked with dirt, slutted in the sweat and pores of plugged hope.
And ivory men dreaming of moon dust from the goggly box
And phallic chocolate bars in sexed mouths
And loused heads in hospital beds from Tooley Street hotel
And homeless homes in scrap heap of cars
Taut gaunt uncombed, urine pissed tinkling
Against porcelain tube walls.
Time hiccups, time hiccups - unasked.

It's not difficult to distort with imperfect perception -
Probing in a white divorced pocket
Of a white hospital jacket
For jackels of knives and palliations
Re-assurations and pills and convulsive shocks
And worldless words diseased down the hierarch.
A lifting hand offered

An aspiring mask
Under papers and drafts and conferences and taxes
And tape and trade unions and imports and exports
And highway extensions and collapsed blocks of flats
And the shiver of tonned traffic
Blasting delicate drummed ears.

People can't say -
negations machinations conglomerations concantations
And screaming coils and steelworks
And meaning gleaming networks
Of silver tears.
Can't say -
Smog spattered acid rotted, fog gutted
In ten million hopes on metal tanks and unlistening ears
Your soul and those battered,
Wet streets, gangrened city
Spired, domed, shot arched.
Can't say -
A hand stretched down the years, across seas
Through delicious monsters and aspidistras -
Can't say -
I'm tender, it hurts.
Can't say - because to say it hurts.
What has happened to the inner city?
What has happened to inner man unmasked?
But time hiccups, time hiccups - unasked
and truth boomerangs back relative and unresolved.

Blasting tarmac, screaming, Green land. You had.
Such discrepancy between feeling
And the time to write a word -
Steeled in the dockyard of insane minds
And forgotten fear, down alleys of fractured stone.
Thermalled doves wheel in the square.
This is not saying what is wanted to be said -
Puppets pulled by passions and governments
His cohabitee and paranoid pulp
Whipped in Gestapo camps

Ulcered crusted in a council flat -
Dreaming of a kind word said.
Sucking air brakes -
Time dripping from a tap in drops.

When I have no more hope
Then I am wise - the dark world of words.
In the beginning knowledge of my end
Is that beginning conception of my beginning living
And the lack - my death.

So embarrassing dying these days -
So sterile.

12.1968
Senior House officer Psychiatry.
Olaves Hospital Bermondsey London.

Intellect
Realigned Realationship
the place of intellect - 'the eye of the heart' Eckhart

High Intellect of thought is not the light -
iced-isolate, it sheer-splits apart and kills anoxic;
simple anchored dipped - it is the wick
which needs be fed constantly
with the fragrant oil
of fresh infused Compassion
and tempered understanding;
and either alone, wick or oil
cannot glow its role and essence.
It is for both to light together
in real reciprocal correlation -
to one fire of warmth, the oneness hearts warming
of our real clay, fired, low earthing,
around the ground of our Being -
and like sharp-cut flint struck on slit rock
sparked off in a flash, split second,

and now in time's relentless history of ideas changing,
evolving mutating transforming
of a match ground against stone or grit
jagged course harsh rough
crude uneven hard tough -
outer defending natures
around our true inner essence
by the whole flame of Love listening
empathic, warm, lightsome, initiating
welcoming responding.

Canterbury Nov 2007

Is Dying Done?

And God created and knew
beforehand this our struggle -
this tired straggling people
surviving with little rest at high cost -
working long hours, hard graft,
living against great odds within, without.
  Trying to perform to targets
  intense competition, jobs lost,
  businesses going bust,
  empty deserted shops;
  the homeless tossed change,
  carefully arranged
  into corner street caps
The old alone stopped, gun crime up.
Greece rioting in slumped chaos,
infected economies -
'quantitative easing' as laxative cash!;
parliaments in disarray making deals enmeshed
and disenfranchised voters blocked
from popping their crosses in a box;
the poor poorer, the rich richer by far.
Far off children sort plastic scraps
for a few coins in burning toxic waste dumps;

dictators dictate dictate dictate, corrupt -
ruin rains down and crackling crops are guns shot.
Unjust unjust unjust.
Death to simpler ways, old and known
and the old useless, of no use the total sum
as dead leaves winter-blown.

Is dying done? - a hushed hum
and flies hone down, dark stung.
I weep for myself and all -
a choked call standing tall for all
for how long and for none.
Struggle struggle struggle, bones bent bowed.
Dying is done, dying is done, dying is done,
the chant sings -
once and for all by the One.

It's that Death has no dominion and is Done
as dying itself is never over, always around.
That is the cry echoed up and out and far
in a world in seismic shift, in quaking fear.
so, be gentle, be just.

May 2010

IT

My mother was a fat oozing corsetted slob, driven by her black serge melancholic puitannical scots parents with down turned mouths and cameo brooches pinned on black velvet chokers reining back their sagging dewlaps.

Looking back I understood she was dealing with two children on her own, my father having died of something when I was two years old. She was trying to cope with her own deprivation as she cycled seven miles to work as a secretary in the then Rhodesian Railways. I always remember the interwoven gold RR's on wooden coaches.

We were latch key kids. I once got a broken elbow playing shipwreck and had to wait in pain while she returned from work. I think she had an Opel car then called Ingulube which means pig. The hospital orthopod made a little plaster man stuck on my plastered arm.

We had numerous aunts and uncles deployed in various pioneering activities such as bush shopkeeper, engineer, silver miner, bridge-builder - all contributing to opening up the country now called Zimbabwe, now closing down. All were immigrants from Scotland mainly.

She ruled the roost, nagged, drank whisky slapped and strapped us with a 'dog-whip' which had 3 woven strands of leather - when we read books, or were seen and heard, or were not cleaning compulsively. Our gentle African cook Charlie Ndiweni protected us though under threat of losing his job.

We sat, one each end of her bed - cutting her nails and tweezing out her eyebrow hairs while she lay in state.

She is now called IT in capitals and I have her like a mill-stone round my neck. I sometimes wonder if I am making it all up but feelings are just as valid as facts as I attempt to understand. There appears to be a general taboo on vulnerability and tenderness so it needs courage to remember. Can you make poetry of all this? I ask.

Canterbury October 2002 (CAE).

Exile in the Desert
It's

I've been through the syllabus
of desolation, decay and dying
but it's now; thoughts are just thoughts
so put them in a box -
they're only a bit not all;
let their anguish calm.

'There you are, I see you - fear' -
anxious striving to be elsewhere;
a vacuum of aimless worthlessness.
So - it's here, whatever it is,
it's ok - it just is;
it's ok not to know -
it's letting go.
it's what minds do -

monkeys chattering and screaming
in the dark or light.
Always craving for otherness.
It's just thoughts, just the mind.
It's not me now.
It's now, not the future or past.
It's worthwhile to be not do.
It's the hour glass of
  thoughts feelings body sense
    funnelling to
      the anchor breath
  then out to body feeling thought gently renewed.

The hour glass is turned.
The bad - it melts.

Have compassion. Just trust.
Love myself.
'You're ok as you are'.

Oct.2014

Flighty Shaft-light Beauty

With thanks to Jenny Wren ('Troglodytes troglodytes'!)
(sequel to 'Heavy beauty' and the misconceptions concerning 'trivial' and 'frivolous')

Wonder to the One for all things light-littleweight-bright-sunlight
flighty, flirty, frilly, trifling-trivial, fizzling-feisty -
trivial, (tri via, where 3 roads meet - a commonplace common place);
for courting frivolous lads and lasses - frivolity.
Butterflies on bottle-brush blossoms of buddleia - bawdy; bright;
the drifting scent of honeysuckle and rose glows on the soft sent breeze, lent;
rustling bamboo bent; the wind tickling chimes; notes swhirl and scent.
Tasting the trappings twitter twatter. Flit flirt twirl
carousel circle cavort. Tease twinkle tousle trip-top ting whirl.
Flitters twits. Hidden hurl. A wrenching loud call -

Jenny Wren, above them all, pearl, loved by all.

One caught and in deep love unreturned palls falls stalls
sinks. Stop the rot in a creative shot there and here, stumbled words.
The shape of my heart. I have fallen for Jenny Wren above others all.

Tiny skulking skull-rattling forceful warbles noteclear under cover low.
Flits between thickets, peeks out, not seen, heard more. More than seen, heard.
Busy but fleeting outside courting - yet even then she sings above all.
Wren - a fragment and whole - as the universe tells. An accord. One accord with all.
Darkness dullness nulled pulled culled - lulled full.

Plump round-fluffed little bird, the most widely scattered overall;
the third smallest bird, (Fiery and Goldcrest before); a warmbrown wing-barred bird.
I am a hundred and seventy centimetres tall; she - a tiny nine, so small;
she makes red-brown spotted little eggs; the most numerous breeding bird of all;
with a neat stumpy tilt-tail, upcocked constant up-perked up, cocking a snook at null;
(other birds copy in spasms short - like robin who can flick his up).
A few ounces weight as light as air; and I am a lead slow two thousand and half absurd.
Her round wings trifle flight in whirr, vibrating fast over short spurts;
trifle truffle tuber - small, valuable, sweet - of the earth,
her flight path direct and swift. She knows where to go. Do I? -
the past is ever present, the present in past.

Bursting ill fell - this heart known truth peeled from the froth of false idea till
falling silent, silence falls. And I am taken up well in her song cell.
She teases - as I scan to see against the light bright burnt.

Bold summer song ticking high, ticks. An amazing strong song for one so small -
a sparkling song, high clear piercing notes of three seconds or more
with two five-ripple sequences between various notes - in thirds; wonder

amazed way-willed,
a rattling warbling song, astounding resonance and power. Emphatic explosive trill -
a stuttering scolding drill - she sings twelve months long, a wracked song quivering ,
yet the loudest of all. Astounding penetrating - size by size she surpasses a person shouting.
Tiny lungs for such massive song. A happy carefree song , nothing wrong - she trolls some notes.

Jenny Wren strains and girds her whole being, being whole - denting nil - voiding null.

Winter fast chills her tinyness toll - she sings to call others with all, to huddle close warm in a tree hole -
the sole one to call to gather, not now territorial; sixty three can cluster curl in one nesting box.
A double Troglodyte - her family name - tro, a hole, a cave - they who dwell in caves - droll trolls.

Ring out the Lord oh my wrung rent sunk soul which in Hebrew is ‘Bless Yahweh oh my throat‘.
O sing unto the Lord a new song - as Jenny Wren so ringing sings. I dream of flying free remote
about fair treetops tall; but the answer blows in the ill weird wind which flows where it went and wants.

Canterbury Sept 2003

‘Germinal’ - by George William Russel (AE)

‘In ancient shadows and twilights
  Where childhood had strayed,
The world’s greatest sorrows were born
  And its heroes were made.
In the lost childhood of Judas
  Christ was betrayed.’

‘The Transfiguration’ - by Edwin Muir

‘...In a green springing corner of young Eden.
And Judas damned take his long journey backward
From darkness into light and be a child
Beside his mother’s knee, and the betrayal
Be quite undone and never more be done.’

Karate

Shotokan karate at 65 years? Yes. Good for keeping fit, or active, keep those joints moving, or for anxiety, depression and company - an antidote for a host of things. For self defence especially for us weaker sex ! ‘Never make the first move’ and courtesy so important. And that focussed mind-empty glare that can shrivel a bully. Karate means ‘empty hand’ - that is, without weapon.

My partner died about 7 years ago; he had two strokes; the living room was like a hospital ward; I could lift his weight of 15 stone - and over 6 foot in height; I had to. I had retired especially to be with and care for him and help with his writing - a padre in the RAF awarded an MC on Omaha beach. I was lost. The local adult education centre had karate on its martial arts list. ‘Yes - come and watch’.

A line of 10 black belts surged towards me in controlled unison with resounding kiais - yells of the spirit. The hair stood up on the back of my neck. This was it - I had been found and saved.

Seven years of intensive training 3 times a week for 2 hours a time without term breaks but with breaks for various illnesses. Warm ups to start then flexibility exercises as in yoga. then ‘yoi’ ready and away at basic combinations of block moves and counters and sparring from the simplest five step, to one step, to free style. And looks and yells to shrivel an attacker. An important first precept for street fighting is first to run if attacked; if that is not possible, shrivel them by gaze and posture and if that fails, well then away you go after they have made the first move by blocking and ippon (kill) counter. Of course you don’t kill them - sufficient control to stop their attack, but you might. The Shaolin monks say there are 30 killing points on the body. We know a few.

In the dojo (training place) karate begins and ends with courtesy - and respect. (There’s not much of that left in ordinary life). If one is hit it is not out of malice. I have had a broken wrist, torn Achilles tendon, standing knock out, black eye and many bruises - bad technique and lack of good control of partners. I have a stomach that can take a very hard punch or kick - from press ups and sit ups. I have lifted a 15 stone man and eyes that often see widely. I have been trained well. Shotokan karate is not about bashing one's body with bricks. That is for brutes.

The ultimate for me in karate is the kata - ancient solo choreographic movement- forms of great beauty. 'If there is no beauty it is not worth doing'. Thunder, lightning and water flow - the 3 elements in a kata - of power, speed and grace. There are 20-30 katas in all. One is called Chinte - funny fingers, another Hangetsu - hour glass, another Gangaku - crane standing on a rock - done with all the grace and dignity of that bird; another Empi - flying swallow; another Bassai Dai - storming the fortress. Lovely names but the movements within them have deep defence and counter meanings. Breathing knowledge is so important.

At 65 this year I was awarded a black belt later made of silk and embroidered with my name and the word Shotokan in calligraphy. I can now begin to teach as a Sensei -'one who has been there before' as I had and still am taught, by those higher than me. At my age now, I don't have to necessarily do it all but must know how to do it - the business of karate. I have been there before.

Shotokan means the place of the billowing pine trees. It has given me some peace.

23.11.01

Killing Wasps

In whose image I was made
His likeness
what's that?
mind blank.
We've heard of the god
rolling sickly off tongues -
sentimental and sweet
but what about his rage -
disasters, tsunamis, quakes
natural selection -

fungus spores eating
the inside of an ant;
mad - a telescopic tube
grows out of its head.
A good god Elohim or Jahweh bad.

Yes - I too kill wasps and rage.

Sept.2015

Lass with a Pram

Bouncing along -
a lass with a pram
bulging with baby and bags -
sagging with this and that;
a mother plump
in jeans low on hips
with frayed ends -
the falling down trend.
And oozing out fat;
and knock knees bent
and above that
a short gingham frock
with swirls of bouncy frills
under a puffer jacket - fat.

I laughed in delight -
with, not at.
Is this the grace of God?
My morning became all right
as I, watching, sat.

Feb. 2012

Leaving Cape Town

This surge. This. To catch and categorise seemingly defined.
Teased apart in the synapses of tinselled cynical thoughts.
This half defined I - returned. This ill reasoned desire
To return, hidden in dark. This unknowing way to turn
And no way out. This loaded dice relapsed in a flailing
Desperate mind behind a quiet facade.
This untaken separation and therefore untaken time.
This courage but not much where fibred thongs tear and jerk
And rats gnaw in hunger of support.
This sludge and swamp slurging an open voiceless throat
Dragging and sucking down - the more effort to return.
This life in only the desire for dream and sleep.
This point of no return.

You don't want to cope. This is. You don't want to cope
And there is no one to help you to want to
In the dark of shark mouths.
You had shouted aloud as the Triumph roared
That you would live. You would live
And no bastard and no internal bastard would stop.
But the wind hushed in the currents swirled
And the dials jerked asynchronous
And the gears slipped back
And the years slipped back
And no one heard.

Your sister's a fanatic jehovah
And her lawyer husband is caught
performing with secretaries on court benches
Between approaches to counsels for divorce.
The children ping pong in hidden tears
Between Granpapa with expensive toys
And swimming pools, and their house
Which is dark at night on the hill -
While documents of mental infirmity
Are scrawled behind doors.
The Mother of all sets full sail down

To tell them where to get off
And is silently rebuffed with pagan good days -
So sets down here alone
With promises between gins of dying tomorrow.
And the documents roll and sleeping pills dissolve.
There is yet no work behind knotted red tape
Parcelling a Castle ship bobbing on oily waves.
Step sisters and cousins divorce and marry
And divorce like Hollywood stars.
Fathers die of ? blocked bowls
And step fathers divorced, remarry
From silent rocking chairs
While step brothers fuck with sisters
Behind mosquito nets, the clock ticking
As you walk towards an asylum a decade later
And told that you nearly killed your mother
For this - and rebuked between traffic jams
And radio sets and fevered shouting
Of the latest scores of the latest tests.
And coloured skin is important in a colourless world
And young men do the dirty work
Of their elders doing of shattering skulls
And blasting brains in eastern wars.
And the old titubate
Watching in rigid tremors
While the young hate.
And rotund governments condemn and pout
While people starve.
And god said it is good.
And heads of Departments
Play chess with people as pawns
And distract their evil temper
In whispered slander behind closed doors.
And a point has no dimension
And death is ill defined
Though god has these
In infinite quantities - like hell.
And god said all this was good -
You have a running start.

So you run blindly if leaving hurts and it hurts very much.
It doesn't seem you can take it - you see no way out.
And weeks more to be got through before nothing to be got through
to perhaps an unknown something to be met. You're not very brave
and you can't ask your help 'cos all are heavy laden and away.
And others block with intellect - concrete and defined
amidst ruffled hair and sheets sweated and wet. Twisted on the floor
like a kid in a nightmare. Trying to get to a solution
and wanting very much to fall and fall and fall drifting in swirls
down and free at last in air to the bottom of nowhere.
Brown and black and red and rolling and falling like a sky diver
loose limbed flying. And dunk - out. At last and no more years
ever to pass. Thud. The last lung air. At rest. It doesn't come
in sleeping and sleeping and sleeping and not knowing
the time between working and eating. And not knowing the time
as your watch has stopped because because you can't and don't want
to go on, in and to and around and surrounded by nothing. The I
is cut.
It would be all right if it wasn't so much. You will change
and you can't. A paradox to change that you must start yourself.
You will change. I will. I will. That's why I'm starting to
change in leaving. I will. I will come back. Reality is harder
than dreams but you can't let go of either and therein lies
the torture. You can't progress or regress. One or the other.
And you sleep and sleep and sleep and wake tossed and work tense
trying to decide at last in one or the other but they tear and rip
and neither wins this horrible internal fight. You can't regress
because you let down you and yourself and the social
order condemns.
It would cut you off further. And progress holds no delight.
The dilemma is clearly perceived and holds no way out unless in
indoctrination that there is life, there is light shouted across
this fight where neither hears. The more you perceive the more
disorder and torture. Continuing timeless in endless time
and the less can you alone. And you can't crack in a foreign order
liberated at last in total utter disorder.
This untaken separation and therefore untaken time.
This point with and without infinite dimension.
This timeless halted time.

This extreme effort to survive. Unknown.

?14.7.68 Cape Town

Legs and Feet of Passing Folk
(from an ant's eye view)
(dark gift)

Throngs of them - generally the same -
luminescent trainers, high heels, 'Hotters', boots
but, 'cos it's winter, sandals have ceased
but still the macho young men are in
shivered T shirts and deliberate holey slit jeans.
Someone's just crawled out of bed -
his hair awry and uncombed -
maybe that's the fashion now ungroomed.
I've just blown watery warm snot out,
out of my sneezing nose - huchee, not huchoo.
Ants sneeze! well this one does
All words are flat, the same, no sparks.
Christmas parcels galore bang against legs
and the usual tinsel and trash triumph - 'so last year'!

But there, outstanding, a pair of knock knees, pigeon-toed
and they don't trip up on themselves with woddling wobbling bums
and there, tiny feet in pointed boots
carrying ten tons untoppling fat weight, 'love handles' galore,
oozing out in rolls of dough; and there, a sartorial man in suit
with long pointy shoes medieval-like -
we used to call them winkle-pickers of old;
and there, very bandy legs in a shuffling
little old lady bent; not old rickets I hope.
There are short steps, large long steps
rising jauntily jubilant up on toes - a favourite of Afro folk.
Clop-clop sounds of high heels resound
cobble wobbling, oops a trip, but no fall down.
And without arches, flat feet plop beneath tight stretchy jeans.
Submissive supplicant tired legs - of 'let's stop at the pub for a rest'.

Wheel chairs and prams, feet and legs safe under rugs.
A new one - knock knees but splayed out feet not pigeon-toed
and some so knock kneed the legs can't straighten out -
the knees remain a bit bent on the outstep down.
Thin stick legs shivering with cold and keen to get home warm
and there, fat people who wobble and sway from side to side.
I have yet to understand why -is it arthritis in the hips?
Beer bellies drawn to the hop whiff pub.
And there people with walking sticks hobble with care.
Ooh I've found a new one, one pigeon-toed foot, the other straight.
And tiny tot scurrying feet yet to develop a rhythm of walk

What would we do without all our delightful shoes? -
and all mine are wearing out. And I'm dizzy with all this.
But there, a proper pigeon struts, his feet aren't pigeon-toed at all!
'Hotters' - comfy, wide, archstrap shoes, beloved of older folk.

Dec.2014

Lent

If I was God!
I'd be bored stiff, dim
with church hard humans
bemoaning their sins
in long services and hymns.

If I was God!
I'd be, bored stiff
at their - depressed stuff
of creeping around
for under table crumbs
and the ashing
and cleansing
there, going on;
I'd be yawning
and twiddling -
my creative thumbs.

I am bored!- dumb
with all this worshipping
adoring and praising
of me going on.
I'd say 'O come off it;
be real, true and genuine.

You'll find me in the street instead,
among ordinary persons ahead.
Outside - there's a babe's terror
with parents pram, and in error
other priorities crammed.
Can you feel vulnerability
and fear within, tight jammed?
Share it with another
in whom I am' -

and outside a tramp had sat
with a jester bell colourful hat,
chattels on his loaded bike flat;
today, he's found a mate fast -
a sweet hare-lip fine, fair lass.
He is now 'settled' back
in conventional black
and they sit at the pavement caf -
two coffees, a tray, they have -
and the Daily Telegraph.
I hope God says 'don't lose, suspend
your colour, in love, my friend'.

Canterbury Feb 2005

Lesotholand Lost

I dreamt of a poem in death by depth
walking to the world end - blue swung
over seven days in scaled sound
and lilac metal thundered delta flung.

The sweated change sectored, high raised
to a benedictine silhouette beaten
in black hills, disintegrate in depth.
A Basutu blanket loose slung
standing tall at sunset
in statued greeting immense.
The people in cities had lost themselves -
persistence strained respirate.
And Chief Nkuebe found free wheat
in the rat holes of manured huts
And rung out splendid on horse across rock.
I had stumbled in dust in a returning circle.
And this is the dreamIntricate restraint -
the dream woven indeath by dust asphyxiate
hung between dark hills
on chequered crops
in the beginning yellow moon.
A crackling growth, an eroded, cratered request -
a contracted significance -a planned correlate.
The single identity
thrown by unknown libidinous force
apraxic, complex..
A little clittering, citied people
Other pumpkin pips of town people
in a slither of protoplasmic other -
a surge of destructive power -
Ground in drilled pain
Columned in automation
and vertiginous negation.
A dichotomy patterned identified
jerked in axial dislocation.
You see - I live as yet
in preterminal simplicity
Apparently. Asking for an explanation
and an unknown thought -
that unknown word working.
An unspontaneous routine of preformed act -
an imageless world within world
extrapolated back to a therefore
known unknown point.

You can think your thoughts -
I cannot - uncorrelate. My world
turns dark dysrrhythmic.
And I am made of an indexed feeling
whom I bribe by word -
The seven of seventy seven
bartered to an unredeemed god
in the quiet, depressed realms of disparate force.
An archetypal fantasia in major depth.
This makes too much unproven sense -
This is ammoniacal uncertainty
where people accept interpretation after
and not time moment of children velvet.
That step is too confidant, too light for yours.
And the farce of important words
to feel important.
My waste paper soul whirls
in the street in treading feet
angled in the South Easter -
A piece of paper is the same
In any city, in any street.
Except here.

17-28.4.68 Basutuland trek

Less is More

As we age
things drop off,
bits of this and that -
age imprisons and constricts;
a leg won't move without pain
or limbs can't move at all -
isolate in our own house shell
no longer a home
but in hell.
The eyes don't see as well
and ears hear less.

We can't get out to see the world
as we once did.

But, you know -
riches and possessions and gadgets
and parties and cars
and senseless chat on this and that
can be empty themselves -
so then more is less.
And if you play your cards well,
age can explore the inner life of 'soul'
not the worlds of outer space;
and simple things as
sunlight on a bowl of bursting daffodils
are now not by passed.

Less is more.
Depth not breadth -
more at home with yourSelf.

April 2013

Let it be in the Fresh Air

Whatever it is, it's here now, let me be open to it, it's ok -
not forcing the outcome to go my way -
worrying, worrying - it's all just about the flux of mental events
flailing around in fear to find a fix -
what minds do, warning of danger based on the past.
The volcanic heat of ruminative thinking
is like bubbles rising from a boiling water-pot;
the aversion from feeling fragile
with oversensitive nit-picking of knots
in a body tensed; just wait, it'll work out.
Just let go, let it be - just trust; bad feeling are okay.
Fresh air coming in through billowing curtains
into a musty unopened closed dark place.
Give the fragile fear space to breathe fresh

and breathe into it all around - fresh space;
bathing it in a cool pool refreshed -
let the pain be held in accepting
gentle compassion - open not closed;
patiently holding in awareness -
breathing into the body's response and breathing it out.
Not forcing or doing or fixing harsh.
Discerning wisdom -
and a sigh in some peace
may emerge or may not.
Thoughts are not facts.
Whatever it is, let it be, it's ok.
Warm uncertainty, not harsh.

July 2012

Letter

Dear Folks,

I don't know about you all but I was not inspired to write much over the holiday; just feel I needed a good break with nothing to do. The opposite occurs and so much needs doing and to be done - my old problem of doing to avoid just being. I feel we are all slowly getting to know each other and writing is such a risky and fighting business - but inscapes are being shared. My delightful card from Jenny is up on the mantlepiece.

Well - I don't much believe in current Christmasses; suicide rates are highest at this time and third world poverty rife. I get gripped by buying fevers and lose reason! and forget the original poverty of the message. So much unbalanced substance yet no substance. As I'm only me in the house, I only have a little set of lights, no other decorations. I have some ivy though.

Last year I wrote to the Archdeacon about the cathedral crib. It is somewhat improved now but not one of the figures touch each other - all in transcendent isolation. The poor little babe is in swaddling bandages and can't put out its arms to its mother. Well - another reason to know that He might understand our troubles. There are two new nice fine fat fluffy chickens though, roosting on a rafter and an egg layed on a haystack; but there is a lack of 'the common touch'.

I had a welcome coffee in a 'workers' caf in Canterbury; there people talk and touch and help each other. An old man came in with bad Parkinsons and couldn't get down the step with his Zimmer frame so two of us jumped to help but two other old folk couldn't stand the sight with raised eyebrows and down turned mouths as they picked the peas, staring fixedly at their plates. But we got him down and settled in all of ten minutes. He counted his money as enough and ate chips and baked beans in explosive bursts - his face content as the food sank in gulps. There - was courage.

Then I go to a Christmas show put on by us all at Riding for the Disabled - folks and fancy dress. I had to hold a maypole steady and give out coloured ribbons to passing riders. So I dressed as a green pole with a tall tube cardboard ivy brimmed hat, ribbons round my neck and knee bells. You may know the myth of the Green Man - there's a stone carved one in a cathedral chapel roof. They said after I was like the green man - that was an honour as I was the only representative of a central spiritual theme; nativity scenes are fast waning, though S.Nicholas still abounds. Mulled wine and snacks after but the big shire horse refused to get back in his box. Damn it.

I continued to work at the Red Cross shop as a volunteer, hoping that my efforts could contribute a tiny fraction to the cost of repairing the three Red Cross hospitals bombed by the West in Kabul. Now the Afghans are calling on the Red Cross to help bury the masses of dead!

A Potluck supper and good talk at University; down to earth banter at the Red Cross party where they asked me to do a twirl in my first ever new edwardian trouser suit; a Christmas lunch at the neighbours without Xmas and a friend's boxing day lunch with mental talk

I had a flu' vac. as an OAP, sorry - Senior Citizen; and I can hear better after my op. But I have been in good company in all these places. To me people are the presents. That feels good.

Jan.2002

Light can be 'corpuscular' (particles) and 'wavelike'.
Make a leap ... matter can be made in the image of God!
Matter matters.
God who is light can be wavelike, the Holy Spirit - or
corpuscular, Christ.

Light can be ‘corpuscular’ (particles) and ‘wavelike’.
Make a leap ... matter can be made in the image of God!
Matter matters.
God who is light can be wavelike, the Holy Spirit - or
corpuscular, Christ.

Light can be ‘corpuscular’ (particles) and ‘wavelike’.
Make a leap ... matter can be made in the image of God!
Matter matters.
God who is light can be wavelike, the Holy Spirit - or
corpuscular, Christ.

Light can be ‘corpuscular’ (particles) and ‘wavelike’.
Make a leap ... matter can be made in the image of God!
matter matters.
God who is light can be wavelike, the Holy Spirit - or
corpuscular, Christ.

Light can be ‘corpuscular’ (particles) and ‘wavelike’.
Make a leap ... matter can be made in the image of God!
Matter matters.
God who is light can be wavelike, the Holy Spirit - or
corpuscular, Christ.

Light can be ‘corpuscular’ (particles) and ‘wavelike’.
Make a leap ... matter can be made in the image of God!
Matter matters.
God who is light can be wavelike, the Holy Spirit - or
corpuscular, Christ.

Light can be ‘corpuscular’ (particles) and ‘wavelike’.
Make a leap ... matter can be made in the image of God!
Matter matters.
God who is light can be wavelike, the Holy Spirit - or
corpuscular, Christ.

Lilies of the Field

The way is the journey as you are.
This moment. This now -
not the future dream and hope.
Just as the weed peeks out between cracks
and knows itself as a flower whatever we know!
Not even chatter and speech - what plant talks?
'It may be better to be and silent than not to be and talk'.
Sunlight brings out crowds of winter people white,
rustlings of sandwiches pasties papers and packs
and pram babies shock at their first ice-cream
gob stuffed, colding their tiny mouths
the first ambivalence - yum taste, too cold yuk.
Pigeons fearless, flock for left crumbs.
The gutters run with amber brew
and booze and drops and gout.
The old pluck the cloth
of their sleeves - huddled together
against the death of being so alone
and what is round the corner?
But moments of reflection shatter
and are shattered by a siren car call
as a father reads a story
to his son on a warm park bench.
Or the pram toddler out,
feeling the cobbles with his hands
and playing with his shadow - the Now.
Or the old woman wheeled
in her chair over the bumps;
'I'm holding on to my teeth' - she laughs.
Obese people can look much the same
claiming their lost past space
over and over again - the hidden cry of being forgot -
two seats or more for one there.
Pillar of salt - I. And there parks
a limousine hearse, a very long car
with top hats and flowers, greatly distressed -
a harrowed furrowed re-hearsal for new-life

breaking again under a heavy spiked frame -
and the brow - the clods of soil now.
Losers don't drop litter.
They have no more to drop.

That tiny forget-me-not
breaks between the cracks out.

Canterbury Burgate April 2004.

Listen O My Child and have No Fear

Be aware of judging yourself
for judging yourself and others.
Remember 'The Lark Ascending'
fluttering, struggling, falling
and the hand of God holding her safe.
Remember I may be wrong and deluded.
Remember Whatever it is, it's already here
it's ok. Breathe into it and out.
Remember the maze test for the mouse,
better when a cheese piece induces hope
and an owl induces fear.
Remember the doll with the leaden base
who can't be knocked down
but who bounces back .
Remember courage
Just Stop
Space
Open not Doing
not Fixing
just Being
in this Now.
Trust - let go
Allow
Obedience - to hear
Discipline - a pupil
Give up trying to control

No-one is normal.
Give gratitude to myself first.
Being Simple.
Patience - Practice
Kindness to myself.
Forgive us as we forgive those
Trust again and again.
Trust, held in the hands of God.
To deeply and completely accept myself
even if that is hard.
Detach - give up hope
then there's no despair.
Thoughts are not facts
even though they say they are.
I don't need to be happy;
it's ok - whatever it is
it's already here.
Let me be open to it -
soften open to it. Gentle.
The tyrannical rumination
needs to be sworn at to shut up.
Loved 'as you are' now -
just as I am now

June 2013.

Llandudno Point

where the Atlantic and Indian oceans meet at the bottom of the African continent. There is some controversy about exactly where this is. I saw it here

Stark
Wave, sun and rock
Marked in eternity.
An eternal clash
of giant granite
Crystal rounded, bald.
Solid rock and desperate urge

Erotic surge. Infinite.

Angered green opaque
A forty foot height
Engulfs, engorged in onslaught
The outer domes.
Then thunder and cannon shot -
The enraged white wave
Splits, whips angled different -
Cuts and cracks - flayed

And shot
Firework display
Of spray
Slow motion falls
Spent drenched
In sheet mist
And whirlpool of white milk
Foamed in treacherousturmoil.

More desperate
The incoming tide batters
In a cavalcade
Of crescending wave
An insistent tinnitus
Of drone and surge
Sound and sight mesmerised.
A seal plunges urgent and swerves
And a cormorant, low
Quickens it's heavy flight.
This monster arena point
No human dares, a dread coast.
And the sun dies.

22.10.67 Cape Town

London by Coach

An amazing daunting city -
sprouting high rises;
the Shard spearing the spiked sky
coated in glass
with an inner lift core spine -
the tallest building in Europe in this time.
The Gherkin just like one of that name
encased in green glass
and Canary Wharf -
the stock market hub and crash.
Lights continually on within
the empty business blocks -
a flagrant energy waste.
Modern art pylon trunks
straddling the Thames,
to carry the mayor's cable cars.
The City Airport within London Docks
surrounded by water - the flight path -
you could almost reach up
to touch the landing planes
or watch their steep take-off.
Houses and apartments
selling at millions of pounds
for only the very rich.

Then the very poor, the lonely,
and droves of tourists thronging the streets;
the homeless on benefits, no jobs -
unemployment rife; and refugees.

Such stark frightening contrasts.
Standing still
under a wisteria arch
in a yard
I gape.
Confused.
Sad.

June 2012

London Steps Retraced
(tenement Haiku - 5,7,5 syllables in each of 3 lines in tenement blocks.)

Canterbury East
railway station sizzling rain
steam rising from tracks.
A couple shelter
head on shoulder, head on head -
the heat dissipates.
Back 'home' safe. I watch
alone. It pours down drop gems
millions millioned gems.
Thunder rumbled floods
corrugated clatter roofed.
Blood red orange sun
glares down dazed, cloud hosts.
The storm strikes rage and soaks tears -
my cathected self?

Great Thames rolling down -
a timeless river wide and brown
steady and constant.
Anchoring London.
A surging tide in distant
booms abutting moored
steal empty barge boats.
I sing my song low and sweet -
paddling sore feet fresh
with families and kids
on the sandy river bank;
bird light laughter lifts
at Gabriel's wharf.

Leafy London plane trees
embankment walk subway sounds -
Vivaldi cavorts.
A poet sells poems -
pieces of paper blown for

wishes and love sown.
I called to see the
Archbishop's palace Lambeth
but he wasn't in.

Westminster Abbey -
ancestors - poets below stone;
giant marble men rise -
those statesmen of old;
but poem words swirl deeper
so fragile aloft.

O England be proud -
House of Commons, House of Lords -
great buildings so bold
yet now in recess.
So many bridges traverse
and I sing my song

The London Eye takes
us high - gazing bubbles glassed -
sight spectacular.
A bicycle wheel
powered by tread rubber tyres
like a mouse treadmill.
The old and the new -
awesome mystical, also
interlocked, woven -
calculated cold.
Yet County Hall MacDonald's
discard rubbish thrown
down a thousand times -
down plastic boxes cups straws.
Down - filth, vacant eyes.

Harsh awed eyeless Tate
Modern gigantic empty.
Stick figured people
wandering - open

mouthed. Old industry revamped.
New vision Matisse
childlike innocence
fresh clear simple colour shapes -
recaptured - old age.
Picasso broken
sundered split jumbled in bits.
The two men near twins -
interdependent.
Elsewhere enormous paintings,
sculptures - tiny heads.
Not an age of thought
but of disintegration -
or clear innocence.

Millenium bridge.
It did not sway when I jumped.
The alongside wires
taut strung steel vibrate.
A singing humming tide bridge.
I too sing my song.
The 'tiniest kite
in the world' floats in the wind -
discreet buskers sell.

Blackfriars British Rail
slate glass concourse - there St.Pauls
proud pudding rises -
untouched by the blitz.
My breath is taken away.
I must go to her
a rock rising out
of ash and back alley ways.
She whispers to come.
Climb those curling stairs.
I whisper to whom I know
not - I love you - sad
that no-one was there
to answer and whisper back.

I sing my song - sad.

Canterbury East
double checking time tables
scared I would get lost.
The back sides of homes
flashed past, some unkempt, some kept.
Proud St. Georges flags.

A black grape skin cracks
open as my white teeth sink
in its fine firm flesh.
I made it - unknown -
alone in the hot heat haze;
a little step done.

Canterbury, July 2002

The Lost Mite of a Coin

terror - the great power beyond capacity to articulate

'my soul is exceeding sorrowful even unto death'
'and he began to be sore amazed and to be very heavy'
'and being in an agony, he prayed more earnestly: and his sweat was as it were great drops of blood falling down to the ground'
he fell on his face and prayed three times to his silent Father Abba
'..if this cup may not pass away from me, except I drink it...';
three times his friends sleep, keep no watch with him and when asked, could find no answer for him because they have not yet been where he is now.

I, a Wayfarer in the olive garden of Geth-sem-a-ne beyond the bubbling stream of Cedron

I

fear funnelling down -
lost mites of words unfound

searching, nothing, words clotting
above a hole gaping, sonor words abyssed
deeper than the deep, there the echo of his voice
deeper than our suffering dread crevassed
words swirling greater than the speed of light
sucked down into a black hole space, infinite -
the searchlight of insight, minced sphagettified outright
will something come?- the something feared
opening to a vacuum void without touch sound sight
She is unheard, thudding deaf, erudite
free range scribbling difficult, recondite
She is the lost coin little - only a mite.
the toddler cowering in the corner of fright
holding herself together cramped
scared to death - scared close to the death of light
hands over ears, eyes shut tight,
mute, painful talk, evil barred, endless null in night.
In the corner of fixed forgetfulness
leading out painful memories - of a nothing blight -
so silent you can hear the earth spin fast despite
deafness so thick it can be cut with a knife.
The absolute presence of emptiness in midnight -
awful, austere stark isolate vacant - breaking under
the smolten steel rod of loss ignited alight.

II.

Remembering is also the beginning of freedom; we recall
as rain seeps to scattered strewn seeds sunk in turned soil
the passion of spring through the 'violation of intrinsic tenderness'.
The real seeing is in a mirror broken - lysis
as over the horizon the sunset-sun bleeds blood-red
treading on the sharp shards of recurrent emptiness
intimate with basic brokenness - crisis;
the hurt hound haunts lost-singing-streams in sinews parched;
the hidden ones, dog devouring time, the unclear mind.
Now preoccupied with death finding only the worst, not best;
hell's descent - He to find untransformed lost sheep;
she, in dirtdust cracks, soundless screams, dark locked bars -
under carpets chairs cockroaches sink cooker grease - vastness

upturned frantically then methodically steeled - the abyss
reined in hard, controlled, exploding with distress, nameless -
only a toddler a mite with a tender mouth in a grown form faceless
with a new voice of the young dawn sunrise
lost amiss, amidst somewhere in everywhere,
of nil within and on her back, a physical palpable presence
in spinning freefall unroped, unrecognised, endless
she did not know then the events - illness;
so much goes unsaid - the streets littered with tongues heartless
words painted with a palette of knives - a mess mindless;
the events - not told the confusion, not understood - homeless
all that memory lost, dislocated - the coin lost - worthless;
sanctioned papers 'disturbed childhood'- her birthright in smallness.

III.

Voyages from south to north, west and back south, remorseless;
money to be found for journeys for ITs severe distress-sickness,
here and there - hemispheres across criss-cross, chaos
everywhere but a steady family base and closeness;
father dying at 50 - from what foul scent of old pus - suicide?
and she, shoved off somewhere, displaced misplaced
disgraced debased de-faced, eyes averting bypassed.
She has been going on and on about 'see, see ...
as a little one - pouring out stuff dispersed -
must be now a chance addressed, not before had -redressed reversed;
resonating eyes and face when fast-glanced blest,
safe encased caressed embraced -
an uncommon commonplace at last.
Blest, yes - safe the space, regressed progressed -
years crammed into now the hours, the place.
They didn't want to 'come see, come see' face to face
unwilling immobile leaden flesh blobs morose
pulling again and again at widow IT's clothes coerced -
not like the touch on the hem of His responsive cloak graced.
As a reject - now sensitive to slight and indifference -
she must have given up - given stones not bread;
given not even crumbs but coalescing bubbles of void, dead -
trying to tug them to see and share - imploded lifeblood schizoid.
Nothing said of the toxoid-clutch, problem-overload.

IV.

Watching now babies being fed -
bottles thrust in their stopped gobs
sheer hunger-pain uncried-clear -
robbed of the meeting of eye to eye
as she looks elsewhere -
just shoves the bottle in the mouth with a blank stare
The baby gulps milk empty in five minutes flat without care
then thumb sucks staring vacantly into space
eyes like terrible crystal, horribly glazed -
then sucks its bib covering its hand and thumb;
blanket mother-object; objected - spat out; a small sob
Little pudgy fingers lost and grown too fast -
she must have given up - gone hidden good quiet, a waif;
at eight she is thin, meek in a sepia photograph.

V.

He says she doesn't have to talk - nothing to say - relief safe
She doesn't look in - in meaningful people's eyes.
Buried alive above ground, she talks to stay alive, survive -
just picked up, held, no words, no cry;
doesn't have to search for lost coin words, lost self;
will he find them - raw, carcass-skinned raw words;
he needs to talk so she knows he's there -
(in Gethsemane, his God didn't three times)
that's finding her and the lost coin words.
Not she to do it now - impelled to do it all before
to keep going - regardless to look after illness more
without much self-regard for herself
her profession and work on a narrow track..
She cracks up, down, open, living impelled in circles fast
the world's on top of her, she's on top of the world -
steering away from the lost coin, lost path
among the aging hours burdened bent down with
shadows lengthening long at the short days end length
The only word for her is smooth soft peace; truth -
calm serene, and to deeply feel - not joy or anything else -
the altar heart - just content and rest at last.
She picked up a five pence poor-piece-coin in the street.

people-trodden, remorseless - it shone to be lifted up -
like finding her lost child self; no, not now - that was the past -
unrecognised unwanted a burden unappreciated -
an un... an un....no first year basic trust
in and from the other first - so none of herself.
It feels that now as she street walks - friable unable vulnerable
amongst the babble of Babel's voluble rabble;
all these words yet it's still not said, the task impossible;
searching peace - the darkling lost coin,
searching the lost Content in the content of coffee shops.
Perhaps words are not meant here - no place -
just held - in a crushing nightmare,
burnt with bare flames that have no light there -
Way-out ausgang sortie exit - despair, no garden here;
the golgotha of dry rocks stones, sun-scorched skulls and dust.

The Gardener in the Burial Place

My name is Elizabeth, I love to hear it specially called.
I'm not only a crippled spirit, a withered plant felled.
It's ego-time-early-blossoms-the-time-of-the-spring-time bulbs
I'm right here where I was and am - a child.
Altar rock, the wall opens as a gate as his gate opens.
Time can come to me in my time - a light takes root in fireflint
it has to burn before it can transform, silent;
and eternity is born in time in every instant;
zero infinity now - the blinkwink of an eye-moment
as he waits for me by the magnolia tree;
here, the divine is not confined to quietude -
the hands that hurl sprinkling stars so wide and high;
if the hand of doom offends then deny its grip, defy, vivify.
Alone alone he rose again through the stone, the first Word
and the good wine has been left till now, the end ahead;
love shown to the loveless that lovely they are, lullaby
the fangs of hate converted - tender holy eyes shy -
unthinkable emancipation feared, dire -
personified crucified, denied desired.
He waits, comes, welcomes, says my name on the days

homecoming under the petal fall tree between black rays.
It's the chasm between my little small self and me astray
midway decayed betrayed - the yesterdays
held by an understanding his heart. I'm here 'cos he's there.
Being vulnerable defenceless weak is only possible, rare
where there is the presence of protecting safe strength upheld
which can give and is true strength. I hear 'we'll hold
the cowering toddler together' now, if I will allow
and receive, learning harm doesn't come somehow -
the home of belonging, intimacy of touch, His embrace
as raindrops from the eaves fall with easy ease, with grace.
This undiscovered country - the minute special particulars
of little loves. Life as it lives itself in all its colours -
the flavour singing through the suchness, the essence -
no more, no less and yet so difficult, in transference incoherence
perseverance endurance deliverance.
The wisdom of littleness. A nowhere without no,
being locked long ago, in in a fraction of what we are. A shadow.

'Fear not for I am with you always' -
I can take his hand and his hand lays
on my head and shoulder -
his - His - Abba.
'I won't forget you' - the great first love from God
manifest in Him through him, chiselled - now my name called
with double chin dimples and a twinkle unfurled
not the nickname Bins, rubbish, but my name 'oath of God'.
He has been waiting for me all this long while long
as I too waited long. A precarious waiting also is love
as is the responding receiving resonating salve -
not glum robotic gubbins with faces like scrotal sacs, severe.
Powerful Love gives and transforms and overcomes fear
and is vulnerable, fragile at the same time, there here, near
as it awaits its recognition and response from nowhere - now here.
Jeshua called lost Mary in the garden of the quiet tomb, shroud laid
and she saw the gardener unrecognised under the cool cedar shade
transform to Rabboni, her name given for him unafraid -
the black-eyed daisies with dew fresh underfoot, no footstep -
the quiet light of events in the early renewed crisp dawn

He can whisper stories in my ear as I try to sleep -
'I have something good for you later to see and hear to keep'
and hear Him say 'come unto me - come see, rest here'
and hear Him know I am valuable, most pleasing, precious dear
and that I can take two apples, not only one, without guilt
and that He loves me so much He can't take his eyes away
and that He comes to pick me up when I fall in despair astray;
to that chasm midway
and that He comes to sit by my side when I'm distraught
and into those hands, safe hands which stretch out
to receive my lost, and my whole self without any doubt.
The man of sorrows knows mine and deeper than I
and he tells me to gently weep - its agony robbed of its fire
and if I feel abandonned and desolate - likewise He
and 'I like what you are doing, however small, enjoy it much'.
If I, a fog-lost-bramble-entangled sheep, become -
He goes out of his way, He goes out of his way
to hear my cry, find, disentangle and carry me home
overjoyed I have been found - one wide wound.
'I am a warm friendly fire for you in the cold times unfound'
'I am in your house and garden and no need to fear
the return, returning home to an empty house here'.
The medicine chest says - 'I have a message for you -
receive not take' so the future has fewer fangs through
that gaping shark's steel jaw with evil-slit staring eyes.
I am precious to him like the returning prodigal son
the bleating jammed-stuck lost sheep found,
like the silent exhausted lost coin with delight seen
beyond capacity before to articulate in distress a cry.
The divine is within and without, we are icons of God
'Blessed are the cracked for they let the light through' thereby
through him in the spring petal-fall and the opening gate.
This the body of Christ. Amen is I am.

He first came to us because we so yearned longed loved
no longer unembodied being - seeing and watching unmoved
and not first to save us from our surface 'sins' scorched -
preached from the pulpit - reproached, smirched.
Pain horror terror anguish dread - are mankind's -

except we drink the cup - it will not pass, unatoned, unowned;
'the cup which my Father hath given me' - did not pass
our deep gethsemane called up faced clarified
terror chaos anguish - made our own, shared, unblocked
take away the bitter wine in part
from that total pool - of avail for the other heart
with whom we can impart.
Seeming isolate - we are not alone;
our desolation is representative of all shown
because we are inextricably linked together
incomprehensibly one with another
and Him, joined connected - bound.
We come down to be incarnate in ourselves - born
live, suffer, die within, again. Come alive - a new dawn
in the hands of a God who is creating what I am
by means of which I am also unaware.
Let the seed break - no more need for words here.
The present now is a gift, a present, near, dear.

The great power of Love, master poet, great heart.
Love is the name in the seed-pain somehow -
and the opening then dying flower.

Canterbury 2006

Love Divine

Love divine within all our loving,
peace from heaven to earth within;
open us your humble dwelling
to all our real true wholeness own.

Father, you are all compassion,
pure unbounded love you are;
come to us with your whole healing -
open every frightened heart.

Breathe, o breathe your loving spirit
into every troubled soul -
let us all in you find comfort,
let us find our promised whole.

My version Mar 2012

'Love is in the Air' in the side street

'Love is in the air'
in the hum and hand holds
of couples - thin and fat,
young and old;
the contented smiles
in the bandy legs
of bermuda shorts;
the rattle of wheelie carts -
pram toddlers sucking lollipops
and group debates of where to stop
for a coffee cup.
For these and all -
I can see why God loves.

Then love flies to the chimney tops
at a child's red-faced teared cry
so a mother stops with a sigh.
Old ladies all - with tight short perms
pull down the backs of their tops -
anxious - over lycra fat or flat bums.

It's September and youngsters still wear
sleeveless vests
and tiny tattered denim shorts -
'cos still, this late, it can be hot.

Sept 2014.

MAbba

Afflicted - none to here hold.
Hold me
Keep me
Accept me.
'Normal' let go. Go
Not condemned
Now, here
Slowly
Receive.

Crown me - tender mercy;
Come to meet me
yet still far off
Lift up the light
of your countenance.
Shine on me
Your face.
Water
tears
I did not ask.
He said

My delight is in you
I bent down to feed you
I took you up in my arms
I lifted you up like
a little child
to my cheek.

Precious
Loved
Little one
little daughter
You - a house of prayer

M.E. Us
It's E. M says

It's us.
It's me for you
It's Me for you between.
It's Elizabeth.

Waiting.
God hold me safe -
Give me peace.

Please...

An echo.
My cry
reverberates.

None to here hold.
Somewhere
B belongs to Being.
Belongs.

EBW

Mach II after Church!

Will you share my death lurch?
Spitfire speeding spins
At sixty five in third;
Twin carb jets gyrate
In explosive joyous torment
To beat in plight of power sent
Satan damned straight from the soul;
In mystic meeting molten
And metallic creation
of sky blue and black
Burnt off this earth.
She and I are not -
We are - mind and metal

More dear than most;
A slim steel streak
precisioned perfect
As my mind synapsed
And axoned in control
And her black and my depth
Doomed dark die -
We are one
Off this earth flown
And all the heavens ring.

26.3.67 Cape Town

Made in the Image of God

Creative God made the universe - child-like
He builds blocks and knocks them down -
a Christ child, as man-god, Christ is killed;
God destroys to better build -
evolution to better, resurrects.
Christ in anger destroys the temple blocks
of the money lenders cluttered mess.
He deeply loves, weeps - Christ wept.
He loves children who in those days
were insignificant in their own right.
He is also truth beauty justice.
Curiosity - he plays.
Almighty. Yet Vulnerable.
A lover of speed
as bits of the universe -
building blocks whiz around
greater than light's speed!
Wisdom is not a quality of God -
he has no need as he already knows perhaps
with no need to make a wise choice
between opposites.
It's to people - wisdom can be.

And there are a hundred other qualities
which we know not.
Unless you can think of more named.
Ya Latif - O sensitive compassionate one -
one of Allah's 100 names.

You know what I mean perhaps!

Nov.2012

Magnification

Just found
I'm fearful
but so what?
Accept the symptoms, signs -
shoulders raised tense,
stomach clenched -
and walk on.

Always trying to fix,
get rid of bad stuff
but it's part of life.
This - it's not so bad after all.
I magnify self-bullying bad
so magnify it's not so now
firmly underlined!
without a frozen frown.

Nov.2014.

A Meeting

My thought and primaeval integrity
Curbed within an incubator,
Or a net swung

In an arc down
On an imperial butterfly
Trapped, fluttering;
Moss and scale flake
And antennae break -
The pain sears
And she dies within
Mourning
For a depth of meeting
With herself, with one.
Yearning - a sensitivity
Sandpapered to dust -
Wind scattered for other
To bloom and seed.
A tool used and thrown
A tool used.
For a confrontation
Where the dark
Of dilated pupils wide
Channel creative depth
And fathomed integrity.
She it is, unique -
A whole, understood.

I must use at least this
Time of death.
My intellect
is left
To reflect
And trap the source
Of creative cerebration.
The thought, the jewel
Of my body crushed.
O - to leap and shout
And run and laugh
And love. The wind in my hair
Water at my feet and a
Hand in my hand.

But a lone gull swerves
And the hand of destiny
An amorphous neuter cuts.
A cry is heard.

31.9.67 Cape Town

A Mental Hospital

Still wearing that green shirt
Which has passed insanity point
Dissociate defences ripped
Amnesic, uncontrolled.
Corrugate iron souled
In shuffling blue checked clothes
Their telangiectatic blush
Of cheeks flushed
And limbs limpid lurch
Akathisic, crushed.

That green shirt
Etiolate
And ferns potted
in a gloomed ward.

High wired fences
Paced in deliberate concern
Polished with clawing hands.
Tracks cut by dusted boots
Thiazine thrashed
Striate crushed
gargoyled.
Where mourned gulls
Sweep and shiver -
huddled
In ploughed lands.
And the black river
Sweeps slower

passed these cells
Of uncultured sand.

A woman paints
An elegant egg
Joined to another.
Delirium smeared
A mesomorph breaks
Bread hunks at the table.
Brass handles locked,
Floors glitter
That the thiazine faces
may mirror
The cities disorder.

A common bath with
Dirt rings
Set in the middle
Uncleaned between.
Rows of clutched beds
Their very own
Divided by delusion
And dream.

Those three end rooms
Corridored dark
Doubled escort
Snarled.
Shocked out-thrust
Of a quivered fist
Smashed uncontrolled.
An iron bed and walled.
Through wired light
A hibiscus flower
'You swine' on blurred walls
nailed red in blood.

The Valkenburg tower
Thrusting its power

Silent
In Plein Street.

When I was eleven
The proven moon shone on my bed -
I closed the superstitious curtains
And walked toward an asylum
A decade later.

A hiding doctor
In the board room
Behind a desert desk
Seen once said
'She doesn't want you'
Then tested my knee jerks
Hoping for disintegration.
O dredge of men
Sifted to such shores.
It was difficult to get out
Through sheets of paper;
Others there
At the State President's pleasure.
It was difficult to return
But I returned
As a student resolving
And saw the suffering
And saw the suffering
Stamped in purple
On folders fleshed.
A graded abbattoir
Slaughtered
To unsure students
Those elect of men.
The great hall gymnastics
And a quiet grey man
Playing a superb sonata
On a battered grande.
And hunks of khakied men
Thundering in circles

To whistled commands.
Was I one of those? -
It was essential
And survival
To maintain
The 'I' and 'am'.

Up the rise
The domed observers
Focus at infinity.
You can always tell
Who've been there.
One leaves the gates
Shivering.

To retract to that
Contracted world
Shattered
Across the river
Where are no persons
Or possessions.
As I lie dreaming
With the sun seeping
Through brick curtains
Glowed on green apples
Refracting a jar of honeyed comb -
My pine cone bursts
With brown seeds scattered;
And a log of cedared scent
Cracks open on the sill.

Come with me there - come.
I think in terms of time
On blue checked table cloths.

19th March '65
On Valkenburg Mental Hospital, Observatory, Cape Town

Christmas Rush
and a Potted Menu at The Olive Branch Monk's Pub to be read slowly and savoured

(written by an anonymous medieval monk escaping via the underground passage from the Cathedral to the Buttermarket pub or a pint and a rare good meal).

Winter's street-slurry, flurrying, care-carrying flustered folk -
but then, for them, a few steps up to peace,
a comfy seat and glorious food.
'And He stilleth the hassled people to sadness first
then filleth those hungry with within good things to burst
and the rich superior - he sends empty away aghast.
Is it not sharing your food with your inner hungry child,
sheltering with another that same homeless poor-self, deprived -
before you can share and shelter those so destitute?'

Pineapple juice spiked with vodka and Cointreau
or lemon and humming-honey spiced warmed port
or real ale - each to quaff according to his cup,
to dream of wings and in his own thirst satisfied.

Crusty malt bouncy bloomer bread
the bread and wine, body and blood -
'this is Me for you - warmed heart'.

Jacket potato with stuffed cottage cheese and black grape spots.
A prattling prawn platter or dimple pint prawn pot,
sea-salt battered Atlantic scampi with a staple clutch
of steamed baby potatoes in a parsley sauce nest.
And drizzled with honey and mustard relish -
beer battered crisp flaked-fish and crackling chips.
Wafers of slivered salmon and tangy lime sauce
on wild flat mushrooms and, bacon, flame cooked across.
'He gives food to inner hunger and sets the self free
those many imprisoned in fear and restless anxiety'.

Beech wood or oak smoked smoky ham - pink

and pepper-pot mushrooms with pineapple rings.
Rib-eye steak, kettle of chips, new 'tatoes, stir-fry greens.
Course grain honey-mustard on chargrilled chicken wings
convened between a sour cream cuisine
and rocket salad garnish under shaved parmesan cheese
blasting off with caramelised red onions, a garlic squeeze -
beef tomatoes and red peppers - pipped diced flame-fired,
mild Cajun spicing - a kick of a tangy tease sauce, spliced.

Juicy oven steak in ale gravy, roasted 'tatoes, young peas,
chunky sweet parsnips and cracked black-pepper mayonnaise.
Home reared beef in black velvet porter malt-hops beer -
a smooth rich dark gravy and 'Look What I Found' here -
open empty arms and an unshared shout within, clear.

Scrumptious treacle waffle with creamy ice-cream.
Decadent chocolate puddle pudding, so supreme
layered with chopped brown hazel nuts - a real dream.

'Blessed are those who hunger for right relatedness -
they shall have their fill in ways yet unknown.
Blessed are they who are called to the marriage repast
for they shall be joined within themselves.
Blessed are you who are hungry now - you shall have your fill.
Blessed are the uninvited, isolated, peripheral poor -
for they are called to share, the banquet in heaven, secure.'

Wire-spliced blue stilton cheese with cherries, succulent.
'He has fed the sore hungry to their hearts soft quiet content
and filled the starving with good things - so likewise give, well spent
as we have, abundant, been lent and sent, patient, participant.'

Suffering a surfeit from a delicious word salad-bowl tossed -
I have pondered the menu long but have well decided on,
chosen, a steaming bowl of thick mushroom soup, - content
with crusty cut malt mini-bread instead! magnificat silent.
'This is him and Him for me, now resplendent -
at last some peace, home-later sleep enjoyment?'

‘He will give you strength and you’ll be like a watered garden,
like a flowing clear spring whose waters run rarely dry.
An oasis in the desert, date palms, pomegranates plump
- the pruned vine.
Once given - giving, not forced, springs free, from the fountain.’

Canterbury Dec. 07

Middle and Side States
and I as well!

Poets describe anew, as each can,
with unusual appositions grown -
world-past to present,
present to ancient past shown
and here and now, now to here;
sometimes, from a seed sown
a fresh sight is crisp mown
or a new thought open cracks
as sweet as a munched nut known-
but always trying to sound some depth
less the heights high flown -
Icarus wax-wings in fear sun-melt alone;
often stopping at mid states -
sardonic wry, clever thrown,
deprecatory, of doom and gloom
isolation dereliction, lovers lost
and little attempt at before words
and first early times that unnoticed unvoiced persist.
Or urging the giving up of all known ways
to where - unspecified unknown.
And the worship of nothingness -
or seeing nature, but not man disowned,
with new eyes in deep relationship -
or of glossy magazine poems, the ‘in’ fashion thing
or in philosophy of intellect
flapping high - unearthed down
or life being not in love faith, a new dawn

but then, trapped - unanswered where?
World weakness, laments; and all are doomed.

But where, where is an attempt
to understand sometimes the depths
of these middle and side paths?
Where, where the origin, prime mover
thrust cause of all this?

Simple - in the simplicity, cornerstone
of the babe and child with either not
or with a 'Mama Dada', good enough -
Mm - a sustained lip sound, Dd - a tongue stopped tone -
yes, those simple 'unpoetic' first child words,
first smiles, in many shared tongues, a-a spoken open
yet the origin basis ground, root, stem,
the a-lph-a opening beginning, not end;
cradle birth heart foundation,
fount, spring - wellspring of all Word
which echo down the route
and depth of adult order, disorder
and word and world; such
simple words only in books of late years found!
Ah-ugh, all human hearts are torn
sometimes or often - tiny to grown.
Other first words said -
'bad, No, horrid, hit' heard
'go, can't, naughty, shut-up'
and no smiles but glares or left crying,
no eyes, no food or hugs, away gone.

All humanity was once a child -
does it just erase, obliterate? -
it seems not - as adults
act out unaware that first hurt
forced to the first bad
as the first hurt could not be shared -
(the worst poverty is loneliness) -
with a giant unholding adult, itself a left child.

Where is written well of this,
some insight in simple formed image word
without fear described?
Where the remedy of understanding
through their own journey
in also distress, deprivation, despair -
and of a privileged given community
making up the loss in shared broken bread
with those less given - without fear?
After all - all the world's heart
has been hurt somewhere.

Wild life shows us clear
its simple essence pure
beyond title label,
baptism term word.
A rose without a name
will still be itSelf -
will still sweetly scent.
Music - the first art -
homely sound before that
of gurgles goos chuckles and cries
resonating those deep states
which poets can attempt
to also put into stories -
felt-image Word.

Aug. 2007

and the place where we are
'our' solar system, unique, possibly nowhere else as yet, known in the universe
Moon

A gentle calm, round soft sound, low hum
say it again -'Moon', try saying it again -
a person relating, Moon then becomes.
I was sad, forlorn to learn Moon is leaving,

four centimetres a year receding
slowly saying farewell, slowly saying -
but not in our time going, gone.
Moon - the chief instigator of time's reason
in the lunar months, the year's shifting seasons
and its gravity pull, ebb-surge wave swell,
the stabiliser of climatic change well.
Moon's reassuring tug like mother to child
steadies earth's 25 degree wobble-tilt mild
and keeps some comfortable climate, blanket fold
and her attraction well holds foremost fast
the protecting atmosphere around us in trust.
Yet moon was formed from the debris and dust
coalescing from the collision, devastation, obliteration
of Theia, earth's smaller long-ago-twin, in summation creation .
But Moon holds us more stable, safer in strength with
now a balanced mother of this troubled fine Earth.
Moon-moo-cow, dappled gentle cow
grazing slow, down the dark night now,
quietly munching the stars sown, low!

Earth is just the right distance from the Sun, not too near or far
and the Sun the optimum father-heat-force orb of brilliant power;
through satellite views he looks similar
to van Gogh's swirl-strokes of a sunflower.
Jupiter our guardian big brother -
300 times earth's size and therefore
with a greater insistent pulling force core
attracting the drawn debris of the universe more -
protecting us, except when he, tired, slept back
in a massive major meteor earth-shock impact -
a catastrophe again serving evolution's kick start
after the dinosaur stasis stick-in-the mud rut.
Moon-Sun-Jupiter, the trinity for us throughout.
It's not our planet Earth that needs saving, that less
she has survived catastrophes of ages of ice,
small meteor impacts and soup-oceans collapse.
She is tough; it's us - the abusing age of the anthropocene -
small reverence for each other and Nature's scene

defacing plundering, surviving, deprived-mean.

Jan 2008

More Fragments

Jam croissants oozing - ummn.
Freewheeling down nowhere
Your backside's on the bacon slicer.
Smoke rings circle my mind - the lost page - so I laugh and step inside what I'm going to do.
Fragments fragments hint at the whole, circling circling and I am underwhelmed - a broken person - this my harvest poem, embalming memory.
Deadhead dipstick dicks; absence makes the tart go wander.
White milkbottle legs.
Curlesque
Breathe - be the he eat ate beat bear heat tear rate bat bet brat tab hat her - all from the one word.
Absence vacuum gone confused pain alone sad keep head down good not got in will it return no work done have to accept what I've got.
Bewildering so utterly dangerously dependent.
Not a honey bee but a large fat fuzzy bumble-bee black and gold belly and bottom. He is be-ing; he singing be's - buzzing deep and low and slow over grass and daisies, dropping heavy and the daisy bends down to bow. So lovable. Urgent to be rescued when he flies indoors against my window. A quick soft cloth over him and a rush out buzzing free and cross.
Don't hang me on the tea-kettle.
Hutspa - Yiddish for you've got get up and go.
Piss and vinegar.
A charm of goldfinches but Jenny Wren sat atop the topknot of my Chinaman statue.
Gluggy glasses glunk. Spunk.
Pigeons aren't necessarily pigeon-toed. Their gaits are as varied as humans. They know a crust from a fag end. They know to wait for the rustle of people opening packets and sandwiches until crumbs are dropped, before dropping down from their high ledges to pick up the pieces.

An undoubled debt undoubted.
A notice on a mobile video and monitor stand read 'Caution. Move slowly'. Yes - me too.
The sun grazes across the sky.
Chaos feeds on itself like a giant inverting amoeba.
The wind that wings and wins..
A cat with cream milk.
Handcrafted people compared with factory battery people.
Stiletto wit.
You sound happy. What's wrong?
Lots of pots and plans bubbling away. Kerfuffle.
Today I found a human whose nose and lips were trying to get out of his face - and 2 with 1 arm each.
Wafer paper sunshine.
'I'm on 2 diets' he said. 'I don't get enough to eat on one'.
The Frank Bruno effect - now there's hope for mentally ill folk.
A prancing pigeon pirouettes and puffs up in circles till dizzy. He has forgotten to keep his eyes steady on a fixed point as ballerinas do. He wanted to bonk her but she wasn't having it.
Tight jeaned smiling buttocks - they like being walked and the creases smile.
The edge of heaven.
To forgive is to give more of oneself if first accepted.
'The manner of giving is worth more than the gift itself'. And I say the manner of talking is worth more than the words themselves..
Fame is immortal. Where there is no fame there is no descendent, no accepted created 'child', no immortality - for those childless.
I skip around and wander 'cos the Samaritans are engaged. Is this a bit of your brain lost? - says a passer-by.
If I were God - I'd love market people - their bunbling ways and no two the same - a miracle. And no two gaits the same. They are intent on the Now of this and that - fruit stalls and trinkets and buns. Their hum of words blend into the infinite. Baggy babes jarring in their prams - their beautiful little feet.
'Uh uh - a no warning is a universal double sound - well, I heard it in Italian as well as English.
Pumping hot heat.
The hot zone - the centre of cities where radiation effects would be the greatest. It's also the cauldron of creativity - unfortunately.
The event horizon - the edge of a black hole before being sucked into

annihilation - where I am.
Sphagettification - the process of annihilation within a black hole. 'Torn to shreds' - as IT kept saying.
The green side of the sod - alive. The brown side - dead. I like brown earth.
Stealth tax - creeping unknown unaware within.
The cringe factor.
Cosmo magazine for women found the ecstatic vaginal G spot. Women have been on earth for millenia - and only now is this known. Says a lot less for men who didn't find it - only keen on finding theirs. Not in the missionary position but as animals!
The teens are a universal time - from all countries - they dress the same.
I found a pigeon doing the side walk. I know they walk frontwards. I wonder if they can walk backwards.
This evening after chaos in the shop - I cracked under great chords of music - all those struggling little people at the shop. Linda with her stroke and angina and continuous words and laughter, values me most. All struggle in simplicity and inner pain. And I rush round creating some order while swearing in my chuckles - to keep it serious and light. My deaf fluid filled left ear frequently goes pop.

Canterbury Oct. 2003

More Strict Haiku
Crumbs to Gems

Syllables

Slippers, I love you - 5
waiting there so patiently - 7
old and used and worn 5

Cut the mind clutter, 5
chatter, natter and small talk. 7
I am that I am. 5

Willow tree bending - 5

you don't break in a storm; 7
but you weep with us. 5
(and you make cricket bats!).

Chubby baby glugs. 5
She's held safe and soft and close. 7
Warm breast, loving eyes. 5

Infinitesmal 5
stem cell. Such healing queries - 7
pluripotential. 5

Oh - pot bellied pig; 5
your tummy touches the ground. 7
You make me chuckle. 5

Magnolia tree - 5
your buds pop now, too early. 7
Will the cold bite frost? 5

My junk mandolin - 5
bought in a charity shop - 7
pot bellied, sounds sweet. 5

Crisp green grape strung taut. 5
I bite once and crack sweet juice - 7
and firm flesh bursts forth. 5

Silence impacts in - 5
Imprisons in block struck force; 7
then a sung chord sings. 5

1.3.02 Canterbury

This Quiet Place - a Watering Hole Oasis
how the light falls upon things, not only the things in themselves

This serene central place -
a garden green atrium
above High street shops;
a roman mosaic square
among York stone slabs,
tubs of bay leaf, box shrubs,
four cornered palm tree lots;
hanging baskets plump-ripe
with orange, blues, pinks, reds -
a happy colour clash
and around the square

under iron-glass slabs, the Hip-Hop 'fitness and dancewear shop'
and Millets field, trek and track,
Moss's men's dress suits, black - coat tails, pastel waist coats -
bottom buttons loosed, white wing-collar shirts
and flush-tint ties puffed up - 'for free, we dress the groom', fair.
Tousle-spikes, gels, blow-dries, cuts, Toni&Guy's fashion hair care,
- cool ragged stylists loving heads.
Cafe Rouge - all suave French with red and gold glass fronts, chairs.

And Morellis, the coffee shop where
kind staff serve and tend, the new day fresh.
Uneven warm-tiled roof tops, a few gulls atop
56 tall-stack chimney-pot terracotta tops -
the early morning quiet loved by older folk
reminding of a long-gone colonial past.
Sparrows eye me on top slidey metal chair backs
for an odd bread crumb - a real meal to them, moreover
and crumbs under the plentiful tables to hoover.
My breakfast is coffee and honey-buttered toast served up
and every 12 visits my card is stamped for one free cup.
Sparrows can beak-bite bread to bits, pigeons not -
they skitter skedaddle and scuttling, scatter toss.
A gentle pigeon does her tour - White Wing, known well
and a blackbird eyes the sky and cheerily chirps.
With no fountain of water's cool crystal spray drops falling soft -

the quiet shatters in shards -

by a lithe invading youth hoard
in the post-modern fashion fast track
of intensity, focus and regardless pack-attack,
a microcosm of the current economic world state.
If you don't keep up you wayside fall flat in fate.
broken into slithers of glass.

Canterbury July 2008

Early Morning
Respite

Dark clouds
of thunder, rain
do pass by -
some burst again
in anger and tears
so likewise us.
and why not? It's true.
No reason to condemn.

Early morning
in a city street
quiet, hushed.
The rain has passed.
There's a low hum
as the shops waken, rouse up.
Deliveries made -
a hunk of meat
to the City Arms pub.
Trolleys and feet clop on.
It's good to be alive now.

Older folk come
and consistently try
to accept their
slow or sudden death.
You see the faces etched -

life being insistently tamed out.
Younger folk? -
it never crosses their mind -
immortal, they live forever
essentially dead
except to their mobile phones
surfing the apps -
fingers crooked, bent heads.

Nov.2014

Morning

with thanks to John O'Donohue's 'Matins'

Somewhere, in the centre, the night can turn
and the storm of anguish dark begin to calm,
when the self is blown to the shore of dawn.
The heavy load can lift, contained
and the being air begin to open with light
to an untrodden day, pristine crisp; now; newborn.
Our sunrise heart can fill with bright fresh hope
and bleak chasm thought, to birth insight, transform -
as a dying seed falls to the grave-gruff-ground
and crack-bud-springs to a young green shoot.

It's I who to day can hear Him say my music name.
And I too can say 'Abba' his name
and can offer up to his hands, all the pain.
So I can rise in the name of silence
home of belonging - silence becomes sound.
In the name of stillness, longing wakens wounds
but longing is sheltered as I Belong.
In the name of solitude I am - all that I am and have and are.
I am I, unique precious earthed.
I can open my eyes today thawing grim gloom again
glimpsing the sustaining small, even a sand-grain,
the grit in an oyster forming a pearl.
Laughter's breath wings in playful nonsense' talk;

delight of eye together in the image of another;
wonder of deep talk, being mutual, the sun's warmth.
Closeness, dearness of another's touch;
urgency of imaginative thought,
as the creative chisel of the heart,
insistent, transforming dark, understanding towards.
The now, not future unknown.

Embrace in Compassion-of-God
who comes to find me through someone
and before, when I am yet far off, lost.
I am cherished comforted encouraged calmed,
congratulated crowned, loved before I ever loved.
He lifts up the light of his countenance -
and has found and is with me through another
together, and in and through himself.
His face shines upon me, welcoming
and he can give me quiet and warm rest.
So I can live this day, listening, more aware,
open to the other, steady and secure -
in calmer water toward the flushed tint mist
of sunset dusk.

Feb 2007

Soft Mouse Moments

Real moments are so soft
but others zoom down their intent
with harsh blunt words
and their staked shouts of 'me, me, sod off'
shoving the soft ones off the pavement hard
in their life speed chase. The hare.
Jagged insistent themes
broken serrated barbed
tearing ripping mangled
gashing lacerating, bloody -
at the face across. Short.
I wouldn't dispute this

having learnt - it is so.
So be it - no truck.
The soft rare moment hides -
a tiny mouse in a hole
under the skirting board -
as we skirt around
real tender need
fragile frail delicate -
Immanent.
Slow.

Canterbury Mar.2004

A simmering rushed non-poetic reply to Mr. Alexander Pope
correctly writing to his Physician Dr. Arbuthnot
Of his vicious state of Mind in reply to 'Sporus' slandering poem
of Pope

Let Popery shiver. What? That slime of filth.
Pope of popes, a purveyor of lies,
wizened, shrunken and extremely odd.
slit eyed, virulent foul-mouthed.
A writhing viper with hissing tongue,
vicious venomed, a killer of men.
Maybe you have found and realise
this pumped up snake, turns tail
and 'coupling' bites himself
with poisonous spit -
he wrythes and dies
in front of our listening eyes
to a sublime vile slug squashed.
Is backstabbing a cure for being back-stabbed?
Tit for tat, it has backfired.
I too am in guilt.
But is poetry no more
Than clever coupling and rhyme?

A warty gossiping old woman shrew, malicious slandering,

Vituperous virulent victimising and vain
A vehement vengeful vandal, a vestige, full of vice
A vampire, verbose verminous, swollen varicose, a veneer
Vulgar villainous vindictive violent vitriolic, a void.

I discovered that Arbuthnot wrote to Pope that he was terminally ill.
Pope replied to him with his vicious poem on Sporus!
Abuthnot died 6 weeks later.
Pope felt that the poem was the best memorial of friendship! and his own character - to Arbuthnot's letter to him that he was terminally ill

'Sporus' was Emperor Nero's male concubine

Elizabeth = Hebrew, Oath of god.

Jean, 14 years, Meets Mr. Tayer

She was torn by grief, her parents just divorced
so she ran and ran, running for her life
and knocked down an old man in Park Avenue New York
then picked him up - and they split.
But she walked her dog Champ, a fox terrier
and met him again so they walked together thinking.
He offered her regular times to join her. Once
he showed her a caterpillar, both of them splayed on the ground
down and he'd say to her to pretend to be one.
Then he'd giggle and both did laugh and laugh.
It's about growing changing transforming -
he to die, she to fly the world helping.
'Bon, bon, bon' - his french accent.
Then he'd say to her to
lean into the wind, smell it -
the same wind that went through Christ.
They'd play games to be people of the past.
The clouds - God's calligraphy in the sky
and they'd laugh and laugh -
both a cluttered house filled with the holy one.
He asked her what was most important -

history and destiny and any future
and how to secure that -
more specialists in spirit who lead people in self discovery.
He talked more of the future of man - the lure of becoming
and Jean didn't understand.
He believed. He believed full of wonder, astonishment
that spirit fulfils itself in a personal God.
he brought her a snail's shell - the same
spiral in galaxies and in art
and labyrinths and in flower whorls -
the spiralling evolution of the spirit becoming -
to keep true to your spiralling self;
move to greater consciousness, greater love.

The next time she walked her dog, she waited for him.
Champ whimpered. The old man never came.
For eight weeks she went back and waited.
Silence. He had died. Her pal had died.
Years later her friend gave her a coverless copy of a book.
She read and read. These were the words her pal had said.
They found the cover and there was a picture.
'O my God - that's my pal' - his name Teillard de Chardin.
Enlightened. Not self mastered.
The great mystic mind.

From J from an Internet story. Dec 2002

Mudlarks

like chaos theory's tornado, flipped up by a butterfly flight -
so everything is interwoven like these children who, given little, give
their lives for us, however distant

Worn-out, city dirt unwashed -
brown monks meditate despair,
wretched homeless hunched,
corner pavement crouched
or graffiti underpassed -
busking 'Alleluyah' without response

in blanket pavement nests.
A compliant mongrel dog
pleads - a begging bowl cap
where few copper coins nest;
statue-still sad, downcast
they watch our feet pass.

A third-world grime-smudged urchin child
suffering unjust - deep, dark-wide-eyed,
orphaned, combing rubbish, dumped -
in vacant lots, sad, stray, empty, starved.

A soldier - an abused, deprived past
now in army-safe firm charge
falls shot in trench crater mud;
given little - he gives all for us
and poppies grow where once he lay,
the old inflexible grave peace in grey clay.

An asylum woman, foetal and faecal in a corner ward,
a regiment of uniformed blankets, beds -
few possessions - yet torment possessed -
gunshot-cracked in countless mind-visions, commands
that the taunting shadows on bare walls demand.

Why? - a clenched question. Not our dross response
in sin-sodden churchianity's stopped-cross-loss.

A Skylark falls, plummets to the Rock -
his Icarus high sky-song love-spent;
as my burning eyes narrow to slits sky-shot
at the up-piercing Sun-blast sharp light shafts.

The plight of sight searing white light;
all these - skylarks all, to the unknown raised
'for whom the bell tolls'... these mudlarks marked.
It's for us. Why? ... as I stark-ask within dark.

July 2008.

Multiculturalism

Like the big-bottled sweets
called fudge - of different hues
on old sweet shop shelves -
soon we'll all be fudge-coloured.
Befuddled. Befudged. Muddled.
Or else discreet and separate -
living in closed ghettos -
unless there is a compromise on both
to a common bare humanity
with individual 'clothes'.

July 2012.

Negative Thought and Emotion
Multiple Metaphors

We're so used to living inside our thoughts;
thought - a movie metaphor -
we become the film screen,
seduced and sucked in.
So then gently escort the mind
back to its seat and watch -
not become bamboozled
and bushwhacked by it all.
We slide down the well greased grooves
of ruminative brooding -
like jumping on a train
and not stepping down
but carried along
to all sorts of dark places,
far from home.
We're taken hostage
by the thought stream
and a whirlpool, become.

But it's to become aware
and observe.

And let it all float past.
Anchor all this in each in-breath and out.
and watch, curious
and let it all drop unforced.

The mind with a mind of its own -
skirmishing chaotically
from thought to thought
like monkeys leaping in the jungle
from tree to tree above.

Aug 2012.

Rest in Bed

She pulls the covers close around
and troubled sinks down. At last no demand.
A dark cave to hide to lick grave wounds
and not wanting to be turned inside out
like an opened carcasse but needing to get inside.
The calm weaves relief thru' her spine cones
and taut strung muscles flicker ease shafts
in the breeze of rest - unwound.
Bone roots sink into deep cool sheets
and body earth settles smoothed
from vertical imperatives to a horizontal truce
and a breath sigh breathes
and makes her sighs to lightly sing
like the rustle of wind leaves.
Mind sphagetti riddled ridden unreined, unravels
and encumbrance rids of endless entropy -
a creator determined to destroy with pain -
yet not that but the past.
The sunk body weight lets go - gently surfaced
bubbles bubble up and disperse.
The essential bedness of bed.
Rest - so neglected a word - in, not on.

Some months ago a blue tit jumped
into a cupped magnolia bloom -
then flitted to a twig
to wipe his pollen nose
with not quite a sneeze.

Why this - when a warm wallow in soft down
in a winter nest encircles curled.
Cool wide-stretch-limbs awry in summer, spread eagled;
calm green shades to shift-to under the duvet leaf glades
from her wild white sun mind.
A double vacant width to sprawl unshared.
'Take a walk on the child side' + - a child again
for the first real time.
A special cushion near her cheek
and a little hand to hold -
rarely - sometimes.

The breeze of breath glides rhythmed deep -
a sign that sleep will win and fallow fall.
Painself fades slow, a small time of no demand.
The storm calms - sunk to still deeps, the sea-bed swell
but blasted sometimes by bad dreams from a black hole
inverted out - dread dead dream-screams from the past.
Only this bed tells nothing is expected. Nothing asked.
Nothing. But allows and gives and rests
so sleep can slide into her soul.
Within her-past pulsed pus, walled
destroys. But flat on her back or curled
or hyperextended on the side
or face down tummy downside -
the last resort when desperate
for mindwhirl quiet.
Nothing is expected, nothing to expect -
but yes if he is the smiling face of quiet death
who gently holds, though this too bold
as he is a law unto himself.
Only to accept the offer of this - it's inherent still rest.
She might wake refreshed after many waking times.
Action now demands inaction.

Selfweals soothed in smoothe balm.

Only a few minutes - sheet stroked
skin smoothed, sored gone.

'All you need is love...' *
Is it there? underneath?
Is it - understood?

+ 'Take a Walk on the Wildside' Lou Reed, Velvet Underground rock group.
* The Beatles - a song sung at the Queen's Golden Jubilee pop concert.

June 2002 Canterbury.

My Flame

I feel warm and glowing
above my lump of log
and little and simple and fragile.
And now I see you
lighting up another log -
the wood giving us food
and that doesn't last forever,
not even that long
before ashes to ashes
and dust to dust.
So let us glory in
our quivering colours and shapes
and we can merge -
one big flame
to lighten our darkness
not alone.
But the other is where?

My room
in medical residence Napsbury mental hospital

Quiet before rain
and sweet earth smell
Rose scent of fresh
wedge cut stem
Orange scent velvet webbed
scent threads interlaced.
Sun beams.
Orange petals
Orange sun in attic of
sloping roof and window nook.
Broken panes.
Soft english shrubs and trees
through squares and a soft
white mist and the many
english chimney pots and tops
and aerial spokes.
Grey slates, starlings, sparrows
and flickering squirrels and magpies.
My two fields - one cut
and yellow squares stacked -
the other wild and whirling
and curled in swirls.

I killed a bird with my car -
it hit my guts
and spilled them red
on tar.
Little english sparrows
puff plump in rain.
My white carved frog, filed
green glass eyed
from a whale carpal bone.
And my wooden sphere roughly cut
on which frog sits;
I carved those in the Cape.
And many assorted stones -

a flint head chipped
in the palaeolithic age;
a clay fossil bivalved;
and a stone within a stone.
Wooden desk and the yellow wood
of my mellow guitar.
An old burnt flute.
Orange hat.
Red and black
Basutu mat. Sharp leopard skin
bullet holed.
And ochered paintings
of Bushmen, a soap stone carved
from the Mountains of the Moon.
A contented clock-faced cushion
clumped on the chair.
This - my room.

25.8.69 St. Albans England

My Three in One

The Infinite, the Almighty,
Kant the First Cause,
Omniscient, Omnipresent -
Ah - now we're closer home.
The question how
To translate, incorporate
The Incomprehensible Term
To mean the most and close to me.
I and Thee -
Extremes. He must intermingle
profound and deep in me.
That word, that term?
God?
Blank wall addressed is better -
One's voice resounds, returns, at least.
God, Dog.

Father
Dad -
We have it.
Three in One and One in Three.
Fantastic figure juggling
Mathematical matter muddling
Yet forced acceptance to enter Heaven.
But see - a clover leaf
Three in one and one in three.
I kneel and pray
Yet so positioned
I am forced, untrue -
No friendship this
On hard stone floor.
What AM I required to do?

'To love my neighbour as myself'
Yet self-hating -
That won't see me through.
'To love God above all else'.
Love a term, a word, a spirit
With one's body, mind and soul?
Jesus, Christ, our Lord, my Saviour -
Jesu - better
More rhythm but antique.
John, Jan, Peter, Paul -
Why not one of these
By which to call
The Father, Son and Holy Ghost -
Spookie, the late J.C. and Daddyo.

I am ground in touch, sight, sound and smell.
No good, O God - only Spirit. Hell.

1963 Cape Town

A Simple Mystical Question in St. Margaret's Street
Looking at things freshly for us young-at hearts.

We sat on a High Street pavement curb -
me and the Leprechaun who is known
to help housewives and mend shoes.
Passersby, glued to their goods,
nearly tripped up over our cramped legs in the dry gutter
as we muse-ing sat.
"Where do shoes go when they die? - I asked
as so many shoes loomed past our eyes,
breathing tired sighs as they were getting worner and worner;
and their songs of clicks, slops, plonks and squeaks got fainter.
One desperate Shoe cried "Save us".
So we tripped up a passing strutting pigeon
who flopped flat on his plonk and gave us a glare.
Leprechaun had remained silent all the while
as he tied his long pointed green chin and tweaked ears in a knot
on account he was deep in thought about my profound question
somewhat.
But the Answer was dancing a merry jig in Leprechaun's big toe
and it was tickling and it wouldn't show itself and get out.
Pigeon yelled "Get me back on my strutters or I'll sue".
And he did via a text message on his mobile too.
The Answer stopped jigging and made its grand entrance from
behind the parted petals of a bunch of flowers on the stall behind.
"Shoes go up-side-down the right-way-up for their Soules rest
when they die" he said with zest
and his sound echoed from Leprechaun's mouth.
In delight, we threw Answer up to Air who was patiently dozing,
but missed because of our spectacles and short sight limiting.
Then Pigeon flew up to help with a 'Coo-cor-coeur*'.
All the shoes came to happily rest.
And the people came to be the right way up, up-side-down.
"Nice one" said Leprechaun - now at peace, and still,
on account of there being no more jiggling in his toe.

c. Elizabeth Webb Canterbury Feb 2003

*Coeur - French for heart! ?Matter is dual in Nature
muse-ing is musing under the treeleaves of Muse
Soules are shoes soles souls. Do only people go to heaven?

It has ontological inversion/reversion as a theme also. The right way up people and vice versa! Current theology still calls heaven up there and god on high and not on the pavement gutters - and shoes soles face down to earth and not up so when they die the soles Soules have to turn up (up-side-down!) and so people turn upside down for that (the wrong way up!).
Often when you throw something you aim somewhere. We threw Answer up to Air but missed 'cos of our 'specs and short sight.

A True Tale of a Near Death on a City Tube
(monosyllabic)

I wait still at one end and muse on the ads. stuck on the tiled walls. A girl waits near the edge at the far end. No one else is there but a guard. Sounds of a near train come down the black tube as it clicks the steel splits. Rails gleam in the false light. There's a scent of fuel and ground steel.

In a flash a meths tramp in a long brown coat and mud hair dashed down the stairs and pushed her to the rails. My heart lept to my mouth. The train ran on top of her and pulled off. She lay there still. She had missed the live rail by an inch.
More guards came and she was pulled out with care, bruised mute and shocked. I did what I could then met and heard and spent time with the shakes and shock of the tube staff.

I went off to work, told my mates and a hot drink was poured; no stiff stuff to hand. Shit.

A few weeks on I got notes of thanks from the chiefs of the tubes and was then asked to go to the High Crime Court. It turned out there was no need as I was deep in work. I hoped both she and he would get good care and just. I still have those notes.

Canterbury Nov.2002

The Needle's Eye and NOT

Hot sand where even the lizards can't run at midday
standing on 3 legs rotating, so one can cool, upheld
in that desolate furnace veldt. The eye of vision gouged.
The heart is an idiot, scratching for crumbs
the table under, which don't exist, a 'Death in Venice' -
which is the child yearning in confusion - the unclear way;
dreaming hoping for love where is none - vacant.
Adults don't hope though they think they may;
it's their scratching dust in the child desert past -
imprisoned behind empty hand bars deserted -
with big dark eyes hidden deep. Dwell not alone there -
NOT the luring chasm canyon deep cut
wide agape - sucking to gulp within its grasp
IT, the old past mostly unknown but felt -
but the inherently fertile either side
of the before-born real Essence and the grown up bit.
Harder for a rich man to enter heaven
than for a camel to squeeze through a needle's eye.
The sacred is literal, not some transcendent sky-fire
but a metal coin has replaced real exchange now;
we pay to 'talk talk' by mobile text distant.
Lazarus rich in down-out poor, sores dog-licked
waited destitute for death to get through that eye
then refused water on the tongue to Dives in hell!
Not concern or love? Justice or revenge?
Proceeding always to the East, waning resolute
where maybe we have and hold, an unknown peace.
Blindly, where no god footprint carries us on
and the water flask is void - the NO, of care denied;
a cork rammed jammed - the child is still now, shaken fragile
under the twinkling night star - impassive without personhood,
the other absent vaporised; action/passion active/passive
absence in excess makes the frightened heart die;
time has replaced presence - eventually,
drained of love-blood in the parched desert dust
not even one little arm out held, one repressed of any awareness
of all that dammed up need - damned, it now erupts and kills.

And again and again we learn anew -
NOT the staring eye-slit; the chasm gulf -
but - on either side. A repeated insistent NOT
deliberately replaced by a possible saving good event;
the expulsion of grinding persistent destructive force.
Dives had it good unshared and that meant later hell.
Where's the heaven for my little Lazarus blind?
A haven heaven with soup, warm brown bread -
for the sores. Somewhat soothed.

Canterbury May 2004.

Negative Automatic Minds

Patterns of mind that create and perpetuate suffering

Our thoughts have become words
carved in stone
rather than words written in water.

There's Dogmatic mind,
Intolerant mind,
Judging mind,
Critical mind, ought to have, should have
could have, would have mind
Hopeless mind, no good, useless failure mind
Doom and gloom mind
Punishing mind,
Worrying mind,
and Intellectualising
analysing mind
and mainly a mind Craving
for things to be
other than they are.
And a mind made
of mixtures of these

Say to them -'there you are,
let me see who you are'

and if you don't know -
say 'whatever you are, it's ok' -
and it's ok not to know.

and beneath these -
the whole gamut
of negative Feelings
linked with thought.

and beneath these -
lies that of Fear.
Become aware, gently accept -
your body will tell you -
not squash them tight
in a closed box.
All this is not really 'me'.

and beneath all these, so they say,
is mindless mind resting in Peace
in a cool breeze after scorched heat.
The real me, made in the Image.

Aug 2012

New to the Trendy

Warm and content at last
in the September sun
at BJ's caf - I see
a little lady, short and plump,
warily scanning the shop
and blackboard menu,
unsure hesitant
carrying three full shopping bags;
a mild, wide-eyed face
with a milk-like unsullied face -
simple pure like that of a nun,

free of cluttered make up -
wearing socks and shoes;
already she's out of place
in this trendy caf of students
and others of fashion
strutting their casual stuff -
proud lasses and lads
with 'must have' smart phones and apps.
To her - I soften and warm.
With courage she comes in,
tired, needing a treat break;
she asks about a can of coke
and takes it with a yellow plastic cup
from the friendly tending counter lass.
She decides and pays
and single-table sits.
Her food is brought.
She 'made' it -
my relief she has found
and has been found at last.
Sometimes I see too much and bad
but this was sweet and clear and good.

Nov. 2012

The New Born Pristine Babe. What I'd like!

A birth right - to be cherished and loved and oned first - after the wrench from that oneness before birth. No original sin. What blasphemous nonsense. Baptised with a special name - It's Elizabeth - says God - under the water of life from whence she flourished in some womb or other, somewhere.

Baptised means dipped; that's all and everything - if it's with -and in nice warm water. Unamed in the uncertainty of openness - which receives the closure of a Name. Creativity exists on the cusp between the uncertainty of openness and the certain closure of a name. Is that wisdom - that place?

But that baptismal water was to wash away original sin. Abyssmal baptism; baptismal abyssmal. No-one else said that name from thence on, till now. (My sister could not say all those four syllables). Me, she, for it was a she, was then whole fresh and bursting with growing. Her new fresh pink delicate sensitive skin. New everything, new born. Small tiny delicate. Chubby curled. A tadpole twirl. Born 7 lbs. Must have been like most babies with a large head in proportion and chubby cheeks of sucking muscles for milk.

But this real world is tarnished and clobbering. Womb wrenched bawling, grabbed by the tiny feet (those babies feet I love so much now when I see them moving them - yes they can cup them together like hands praying). Hung up side down in mid air, slapped to cry (it may or may not be necessary). That first breath inspired inhaled from an unknown battering world; bawling screaming exhaled (if not expired). Cruelty and abuse inhaled. This new world not safe, not protected - battered from the start. No laws on human rights for birth rights. Then buggered up bashed lashed nagged, a no-one nowhere. Circumstances dictated by God that her mother get ill and leave her with who knows who and where in the world. Circumstances dictated by God that her father die young from who knows what and how and why and where (no little-left-something to remember him by, special). The word 'dad' does not come easy to me. Survive by wits, passed from one to another, and clamping up not knowing even that. Dominated controlled - 'children seen (if that) and not heard'. Years later hit by desolation annihilation dereliction (dad). Shunted here and there. 60 years it took for the

d-a-d and bewilderment confusion, unworded - to word; closure that left me wide open to a dissected, disembowelled trunk

It (for now she was an it) withdrew. Her wits and words strain to protect and close what's left of that New. No-one to be one with out here. And never will. They all turn bad and she struggles like 'mad' 'dad' to keep them good. So much terror.

I cannot find anymore - on something New and Good and Pristine - as I must have been when I was born. There is so very little - as I was then and still am - so little and vulnerable and buggered up. Sound and animals, the freedom of the wild, mean so much more to me than so called sane, sanitised civilised people.

A Happy Ending. A puppy sad beginning. A beginning rending, sending, fending, pending, tending, mending - lending. A death solving. Hit, H-it, H-IT, hit by IT.

I once heard a great rush go out of a dying man's body as he rose up, his old self, and fell back dead, (so I realise now that 'spirit' is) - looking, not at me, who had been tortured by his long dying and hospital neglect, and not at his loved sea view from the wide window, which we had travelled 5,000 miles to find - as a safe place - but at the olive wood December nativity scene in front of the TV. That sound seared past and in front of me from right to left. Then gone, I wept, over his dead hospital levered bed cot-sides and gastrostomy and suction tubes and inhalers and drip feeds - and all the paraphenalia of the long dying. I lit many candles all around and the funeral men tut tutted - a fast flesh decay with candle heat. So they took the body away while the 'karate'! curate took me aside so I wouldn't see the disposal - to the kitchen. Dazed. bewildered. He needed me to die (not cared by him, but adored for him) and he needed me, for him to die cared, dared. No-one had wanted to live with me before. He - the first - and last.

I hate Xmas. Pristine secret somehow birth - severed. Dead death clamours, dunked.
The boy who saw too much too early. Was that good?

Exile Jug
The Lost One
Alien

To England and there to Canterbury 3 decades later to find my 'self'
Travelling 15,000 miles from South due North - again.
Before, long ago - it was South to North to South
and bits of East and West - here and there.
The sundered things can only groan to God who made them thus.
An 'Alien' for 7 years reporting to police whenever she moved.
Police visiting her on the wards of a mental hospital where she gave
service most others would shun; to check on her - yes, politely.
There on a chronic backwater ward
of lost 'persons' like herself. One man had stuck needles in his eyes.
Then - she wore a white coat. That was good.

Canterbury Dec.2003

Some Nonsense Stuff. True stories

There was a fine mystical tutor
Who basked in his bath; such an anchor.
A jolly, plump Toad
Plopped in for a goad
And happily blinked at said tutor.

To go for a swim in a pond -
There was a young toddler - so fond.
The youngster eye-latched,
Paddled eager to catch
But Frog jumped on his head in that pond.

There was a big Spider of Harbledown
Who frightened the lights out of Paule's frown
So she got a syringe
And pulled out the plunge
But Spider withdrew his legs, everyone.

Canterbury August 2003

NOTES

Words on Light. Ending in y -3 word lines *Roundy
word and line repetition
A Stray Postscript
The Manger The first heavens Waiting
NEW OUR FATHER

zenith the point of the heavens directly overhead.
old biddies in bingo
craftsmen crankshaft
dies irae meat not milk,
not to be sneezed at
sea streaked with phosphorescence
juggling a wine glass utensils snacks among talk
juggling a blobbed dripping ice-cream cone - you can only lick not talk

emergency escape hatch
Skate-boarders beauty of movement on street sea waves.
azure aquamarine cobalt indigo navy sapphire turquoise ultramarine
'many a mans' nose has been broken by his mouth'.
The wind farms run out of it - global stagnation
woman wife womb wonder waif wet ...wait wound wander want
A tiny tortoise going against the thunder of a crash of rhino
but because it is so tiny their hooves miss it. Aong

endurance of Tuareg desert women
sex is when 2 people suck chew and eat each other alive,
Incarnational/transcendent
Putting love where love isn't.
'I have not seen so much death and dying has undone so many'.
I have seen so much life and living has blossomed so many
Silk is stronger than steel; a silkworm's single cocoon unwinds to half a mile of thread. And woven to beauty and colour.
Waiting and writing including dying are the greatest acts of love.
Every smile touch good word/gesture multiplies manyfold *- like bacteria do and the whole becomes like all the grains in bread leavened and broken for the 5,000 - given to so many then many more. I had not realised this. It came to me, not me to it. These are my descendents.

It's like training and competing in the Olympics. I have the same emotional spiritual training. I am running the race with all 'muscle' and focus fired. Becoming old and close to the end - that is all I have.

I am alone here - none of the ordinary comforts of ordinary people - spouse family. I have to accept this. The solitude. Silence here booms loud This a cross I am given. The pain of God for me is greater than mine on my own and he takes and can take it.
So little I know of people.
grace is God giving -
light is the colour of light
simple ignorance is wise
accidents and mistakes can be gifts
doubting Thomas is questioning Thomas. Christ questioned - Eloi primal.
the return of the Prodigal Son - the return itself is a resurrection to relationship to real self- the father scanning out day in and day out for his Son to return home, not to see if he was covered with sins sores

smells - just for his son, then seeing and hugging to assuage his son's deep pain first, foremost. Reconcile the Father to the Son and vice-versa -Article 2. Such inordinate suffering and world pain - cyclones earthquakes. Why why why? The Father has to pay a price for this Sin.

I must see nice things in passers by not pathology and judgement.
Love is prime and ultimate - any being saved for 'sins' is secondary - the Event is primary - the experience follows secondarily. Vulnerability is strength.
God permits suffering and resonates with ours - to create an occasion to love one another and for compassion.
only love overcomes fear but is vulnerable as it waits recognition an response.
swale
love the questions and the answers will come
- only the earth turns around the sun and turns daily/nightly - I don't know how. We are earthcentric in thinking all revolves round us - like infants with their mother.

God is in 'ever so nice, cool, brill'
'I pray that I may be rid of God to find God' - M. Eckhart
'the nevertheless of value found in that by which value is destroyed' HAWilliams

and jesus is 1000 on a Los Angeles guru's questionnaire scale of love; an amoeba is nought
the sun does not rise - it's the earth that revolves turns around (con-ver-sation) to converse
the family jewels = male genitalia
a tendon spun rope with a nose on top, all made of mind muscle
yu know, like=Irish ?
love hurts
nuzzling nozzle of a nose

walking on air
lacework of events sun together - knits
hunking round bulges of buttocks around
the stillness intense silence booms
shaft of sunlight

honour
halcyon - serene
the wind is making merry with a crowd clump of gold leaves blown hither and thither in the autumn meadow
the foundations of the house of personality are laid in the 1st life year - the rest is superstructure. Hungry self condemning self central self

my hot babe my gorgeous babe my apples
play around with your proportions
strut your funky stuff
rock that runway catwalk
getting down to the buff
my apple my lovelies, no surgery no diets
make the most of what you've got
whacky kitch twee

a woman kneads in yeast to the dough - so too relational therapy
a jolly plump person bouncing along her hammocked cosied bra boobs being sucked and suckered
a short woman with large firm roundy melons of a butt gloved in pink tight slacks-
prized in Africa by a heavy tonned chief
her butterfly winged white hand lifts a cream puffed cake to her waiting lips
this - the age of the paper stamp size sugar square letter envelope - no bowls cubes or spoons - just tear and tip into your waiting tea cup. Grains spill. And paper bits fly-off

dawn twilight
death had picked her name out
letting go to gravity
passive wisdom simply suffers
pedalling towards the sky

Stations of (luck) love - not only the cross
the light of God in the face of Christ

Lambeth Conference discord. Bishops descend on Canterbury from the wide world 600. and their spouses. Purple fronts and ribbon name

labelled tags. Canterbury folk stare wide-eyed as they pop into shops of this and that. 10 descend on Curry's electricals and stop at the mobiles and lap-tops from the Indian and African continents. One pops into C and H for fabrics for his wife's sari no doubt. faces tell a lot fat concupiscent corrupt stern above us down turned mouths. India might be checking our markets - impassive unreadable smooth faces jet black faces and shiny black hair. One tall haughty colonial bishop in panama hat and waistcoat and light linen jacket and his proud monocled wife just stroll the streets. 2 gentle little Asian ones greet each other with bows - gentle eyes. Aware of ecclesiastical splits - at last the Archbishop and Synod have taken a firm stance - now at last women bishops after 2 millenia of Christ and Mary Magdalene the first apostle - enjoined to go forth and tell the good news of Life. 1930's at last women have the vote. What if women had ordered the world - compassion care not force power strength domination.
Perhaps the Archbishop in full regalia should take his high seat throne in the Cathedral Chapter House with all bishops lower and stamp his shepherd's crook 3 times to his flock of sheep with 'I am the father of you adolescent bickering lot. Behave and discuss your discord like adults' - with a twinkle in his eye.

Nothing (White Teeth)

Today - nothing is burning brightly.
It's everything. It's nowhere. Gone.
I know nothing of something
and something of nothing -
lots and lots of the lovely stuff.
It's everywhere abundant
between words and sentences
and sounds and movements;
between people it weaves
its coloured threads
in the interstices of silences -
between boundless gaps,
eternal and timeless. The void.

I have to hone myself

against harsh people - sharp.
A screaming ambulance stops,
round the fallen body;
curious crowds curl
the herd protecting him.
and we are impotent drawn,
longing for a resolution ultimate.
They huddle - none comes.
The hurdy-gurdy resumes.
I resent the vacuum of impotence.
A photgrapher of war
sees the dying vomit and death,
the starved abandonned
neglected. The desperate fight
to survive. I cry out.
The beginning and the end.
The via negativa - not this not that
not anything - is. It is between atoms.
Space means separation
and time separates
It is space linked with time.
Nothing is the wound of something.
God the great circle.
Death is going home.
Amen.

Canterbury Sept.2002

Nought The price of peace

Christ, son of man cries out
'Eloi, eloi lama sabachthani.'

fixed pinned on wrythedwood
movingstopped, riddled painshot
dark, ground zero, nopoint furtherword
nopoint nonholding, not held can't hold
confused in junglesay

sludged fear from below
namelessnothing blackhole
derelict desolate
so why crysay
But - no answered cry
forsaken by god.
I exist, where's the I ?
In nuclear devastate
imprisoned image
Nothing but whirlwaste
I, - I
am 'free' unsectioned
in jet flakblast and
that unheard echocry
emaciate carcassed incry
scarred canyoned earthcry
skinned alive uncordcry
scared sacred thoucry
fading faroff wordcry.
No fulcrumed rock
the nopoint desolate -
wrything blowbent gutted
held pinned, the high point,
personless scorched.
I soundcry choked
I soundcry unheard.
There is no I - drained.
the I is - sucked out -
i thirst - terrified.
Stabat nonmater.
The purity of horror untransformed -
Annihilate.

the Son of God
'Abba, Father'.
'Forgive them for they know not what they do'.
'It is Finished'.
'Father, Into thy Hands

I commend My Spirit'.

Canterbury April 2003

Oh They're All Glorious

I'm feeling benevolent now.
A lass struts past proud
boots, stockings, short skirt, loud -
her right thigh a garter high up, lewd;
what ho, a-merry O, gaily good.

A student in a graduate gown
as of old with a yellow orange hood
to match orange slacks, yellow socks,
Debonair. Brown brogues.
It's cathedral graduation day -
there are many gowns today -
reds, yellows blues, grey -
a current medieval town
with a medieval cathedral faith-frown.
Mortar boards, Erasmus doctorate caps sown -
tassels afling for the flies of old perhaps
and getting in their eyes too now.
Ajaunty ho.Congrats. Phphew blown.

An elegant woman stops to scan the menu at a nearby caf
but child-like she has turned her toes in, pigeon-wise at that.
feet-prayers, hands clasped, supplicant, submissive nourishment -
the thought of food does that to the self. I laugh in delight.
Yummy O. Yum yum.

A tall skinny woman
in summery skimpy frilly frock
of pinks, lilacs and light blues
and down down down at the feet
sling back pink shoes with very high heels.

She's come to see her child capped so proud.
Hey ho, it's winter wobbly now, chilly oh.

Then there's a bevy of little old nans
all about four foot tottery tall, wonky and sweet;
maybe that was WWII rationed food that did that.
A trundle bundle. Chatty natter O.

Who does the work in this city -
sluggish for Serco rubbish?
And there's a passing postman in a rush
in red 'Royal Mail' and black dash dash.
A pigeon pecks past and on his beak chewing gum -
wrong peck this time mate done.
Hey hoh hey, a merry-oh what now stuck?

Nov.2014

0 - Nought

Nopoint furtherword
Nopoint nonholding
Not held can't hold.
Confused to junglesay anyway
In namelessnothing addiction
So why writesay?
But - no answered question -
I exist, where's the I? -
In nuclear devastate
Imprisoned image
Nothing but whirlwaste
I, - I
am 'free' unsectioned
In jet flakblast and
That unheard echocry
Emaciate carcassed incry
Skinned alive uncordcry...
Scarred canyoned earthcry...
Fading faroff wordcry.
No fulcrumed rock

the nopoint desolate -
Standing blowbent gutted
Black personless scorched
I soundcry...choked
I soundcry unheard.

Stabat nonmater me...
Annihilate.

Oct. '98. Canterbury

Odds and Sods

Those that do not see will see
those that see are blind; at odds -
blind from near birth the clay on my eyes clogs
I wash - for a moment wisdom prods
wisdom - greater than the sun
greater than light as day goes to night
manifold scintillant turmoil immaculate
rain and wind roam distraught, divinity of light
congruence mutual resonance
the borrowed warmth of someone else's heart.
Touching the hollow of his groin
camel foot female crotches abundant
we cover the wounded self with lids downcast
our mind fills with hot blown sand
searing grains crystalled
a tiny resurrection plant is - just
a new frankness - returned as dust
and how the moments buzz around
a fly-swarm coned-down circling spun
and snow implodes to water
false even teeth glisten like pearls grit in the oyster.
A holed boat sinks in sludge on the out tide of hope.
The wind tacks close-hauled then jibes
as tossed aliens we all are - all.
Relentlessly the hours are taken out of the days,
within the swelling oedematous throat

the city wheezes its way to a halt
the back breaks, their questions, essence
and fertile fragility found then
bounced back - under cheery 'how're you - a'right?'
A'right' the reply standard when not
as a dead twig touches my cheek
and scrawny sparrows skittle bedraggled
under pavement tables - for crumbs -
struck by some sacred emptiness,
hit by hallowed nothingness,
wounds of wild wilderness
firewall of fear. O Lord quicken me now.
The child ascends in round flesh clouds
a mother folds her babe to her full breast
her hand-holds, her smiling face
he does not go to her except with his eyes
and he does not search the well-spring
from which it is given or flows
hungry he takes and satisfying sucks
the finest wind breath wraps round both
receiving and giving together in rest each both
the first welcome after the slime and blood
of being born done mutual to two, from two in one
he has stopped screaming now - quiet
colour returns to his face his cheeks glow
the light in his eye and hers so it must have been with Christ.
That rare figure who shines in the muddle and murk
within the temple of the market place us, the birth place.

I am compassed
within the points
of your cross -
compassion calls
inside you now
drawn to the cracks
and clefts of your
word-room inside words
the shadows cast by light -
the chair you sink in
aching bones rest

the empty chair;
the open book unread
the glistening plate
tap washed
It is hard to part
the hour breaks,
time speed snicks
the seconds out
chimed end - Mach 1
the cup cracks but
love simmers on
in the infinite hope infinitely intimately loved
intimacy yearned.
Horizons never end
in a round world;
euphoric gloom
the human voice;
the urgent call
of birdsong -
water the soil
with the sound
of your tears.
A squirrel squashed on the road, car hit
a ketchup squirt of splat avoidance bursting into bits.
Our fertile fragility clots, broken soil sods spurned.
Infinitely avoided - shunned.
We are the poet people, unheard seen
dreamers of dreams undone unforseen.

Canterbury July 2004

Ode to a Lost Cap

My little black beret peak cap
with elfin bud red pommel
atop a twig tweak toggle
jaunty feisty cheeky -
nice ordinary folks smile

even for a twinkly short while
despite cock-a-snoop at the withholding world.
Eight years faithful loyal,
with me wherever I go
but I and my spirit are sore lost now
hours and days searching high and low
streets verges, byways places asking all so -
whenever, wherever I go.
Now desolate I pass to - and deeply ask
the where-are-you-divine risk task -
'into thy hands I commit my cap
please take it in careful care' -
a cry in the empty air;
it kept me and my head warm -
hoping it is loved, snug-providing
to a suffering person so deserving
but I see it in vomit , wayside mud
abandoned by an abandoned drunk.
Unbearable I care for nothing anymore.
It cared and loved me more
than any two-legged-being-bore;
carried everywhere - my cap
like a child's favourite blanket scrap
or little dirty soft ragged toy;
what happened to mine in the past before?
maybe unallowed or rubbished as dirt more
What will I feel when M goes?
The precariousness divine,
the tyranny of time's time.
It is Now - not the future or past.
It is Now - held soundly fast.

Jan.2006

Old Zimbabwe

Matabele Mashona strife
Kraals round thatched
Sudza balls, eating mats,

Pounded beer, ground nuts.
Mambas and melons.
He the tall one
Chief of the tribe
Higher than a hill
Broad blade spear
A just palaver
Thorned acacia
Ndaba tree.
Mealies, maize,
Yellow cobs.
Ancestral spirits
Tall giraffe lips
Search between
Thorn high spikes.
Great Lobengula
Lives in rage
With his shield on his knees.
Izibonga - poem of praise
Under white wild sun.
Now Mugabe harsh
Rules with a rod of iron
Dictates - a baboon.
Big eyed little piccanins skitter
Me bare foot - then and now
Charlie Ndiweni - our loved cook
Saved us from the lash of IT -
our mother.
The place of killing
Bulawayo born.
Calabash - water gourd.
I am white - an African.

22.02.02 Canterbury

Olympics - London 2012

For once the TV

is free of violence and crime
and economic and political
doom and gloom.
The Olympic games have come
to London town.
There's exuberance
and joy and hope;
Great Britain is again great
and the vibes and energy
ripple throughout.

But it's the little ordinary people
80,000 in the stadium -
the energy of their massed shouts
propels the Olympians along and up
to heights never before reached.

Me and you - the little people,
the heroes, that's us.

Aug 2012

On 'U'. Grossity Atrocities
Part Objects

Numb bug bums hum
Mug-muck butts gunge
Gummed tum guts slump huffed
Rum guzz gums glurg hut
Slurp cud dumb
Dud jugs jut
Mugs must lust nuts rut
Fuck puss pus dumb
Tup lugs suck
Pug tug fug hug
Lub-dup*
*First and second heart sounds on auscultation

Canterbury Jan 2003

One Skittle Down

If they want to know
Under the armpits of a setting sun
How a gall bladder sways under beta rays
I can tell down the corridors
Of green blackboards
And i squared equals minus one daemonic line
Curled in the swirls of a black blanket
And swung under a pendulum moon.
A cow bell tinkles larva spilt dung
From a mind foamed, vacuumed.
A limitless concept verbalised
In stagnant soup
Over pin-striped confidance
Tutored and defined.
An unbelonging limb confined
And fucked from a map two thousand miles
Down a stinkwood angled route.
I said no I would not write
And hid blank pages
Under a boat trip due North;
But they said from sounds
Coming from the front of mouths
And feet well placed and skirts tucked down
That I shout Heaven and Hell open
From a sterile god.
Which was done.
But the limb wrythed
And the space became a vacuum
Filled with perspiring eyes;
And truth boomeranged back
Relative and unresolved.

You jerked bastards of saliva slimed words
Swabbing the sweat from unpractical perseverations
In an onanistic effort at an orgasmic opiate -
And pain kicks my bucking side
At so much deception to prove unsound ideas;

What ideas are sound? Irrelevance resolved.
But say this - written down
Written because confronted eyes are down -
Say it a hundred cringing times
But say it from diazepam eyes
Liberated from milligrams;
Say shit and fuck, you bastards
In an opisthotonic twist of agonal spasm
As a hawk plummets down from white sky.
A repetative gunned red rammed
Rioted in thrust rock black fumed
Blasted off from little pigeon holes slung shot.
At last - I will always -
But it is too much effort -
An honest state blinds
In the waterwheel of unmeaning given fright;
And time is pissed
propulsed up rotten acid throats -
War rawed in the gashes of gunned wounds.

There is sleep left in returning fragments -
Dreaming of a sun-bird whirr under orange aloe
With the hands of the clock at eleven
And the angle of a shadow
Angled back against echoed stone.

I will be what I am now - nothing
I have slept long under white rock and thorned acacia
I will be what I am in years time - risen up
Walking towards the sun.

? to migrate from Cape Town to London for an analysis?
I did and arrived soon after.

20-28. 5. 68

Orange Flow

I have written on orange before
so orange has gone into hiding now;
once revealed - no more;
so I drag this from the dregs of a previous zippy cup
and hope orange will forgive me some more.
Before I can eat a real fruit, there appear
several steps I must take without being too aware.
Now I have to become more aware
and I haggle, word-tussle worry and groan.
So I must look on an orange
for the first time yet again;
the mystery withdraws - of him.
Words are under the keeper of the Muse
or Puer aeternus - the eternal child - not I;
and I obedient run!; I have no choice;
so lets be brave
as I scrounge
word sounds
from sulcal cracks,
cerebrate and crystallised.
I must see an orange in the market preferably,
as that is as near I can get to one
hanging free,
fecund on a greening tree
in sunny South Africa -
and I remember well the orchards there.
None here.
Seeing and all other senses
have complex neuro paths
from receptor to brain cells -
it all adds to the old wonder of orange flow.
I see first that round bright colour
sitting snug with his mates in neat piles.
He glows for me.
So I move my limbs across the divide,
and that is a neurological feat,
to buy him and others for his delight.

I feel him first and play ball
and he loves being thrown in the air.
His thick greasy skin
has zits of bursting yellow oil
and - tang - they squirt with a finger nail tear.
That white soft pith that clogs the nails
and the aromatic zip up my nose -
so much gentler
when a skin is burnt,
sizzling on my fire.
The soft peeling squidge-sound
as the challenge is taken
to achieve a peel whole,
the shape of a star;
and the sound of my bite
in my inner and outer ear;
those crescent geometric curves
and the sweet sharp juice mouth spreads -
quiet fire, and drips down, running fast.
The fibres remaining are good gut bulk
(slugs are drawn to a gouged half peel).
And vitamins and minerals galore.
Methinks a chocolate orange
is no match for this opera.
All perception lies within
so how do I know what an orange is like
when I am not there?
He is sacrificed and resurrected within -
an ancient spring theme.
And I am refreshed now.

31.1.02

P.S. 31st Jan 02, India 99 for 2 says Henry 'Blowers'
in Dehli - BBC Radio 4
'They're selling oranges like hot cakes down there'
England 272 for 5 so far.
England won by a rare 2 (and no Dehli belly either).
And Henry had fresh orange juice -
breakfast squeezed. It's true - so far.

Our Journey An Adventure

by some different paths on how we see stories of our beginning

For all our special child selves and elves

There was a small homely bungalow by the coast, belonging to a family of a mum and dad and they loved each other so much they came together joining as one and made a baby and she grew in the warm dark inside her mummy and was born without difficulty, but Mum still had to push her out with her womb muscles working, with the help of a visiting midwife; a bonny baby, in much excitement and happiness at home. She cried a bit after coming into the new wide bright world but was soon comforted and fed on her mum's warm breast. Her parents had little trouble with her, just the usual growing pains, then teething, and the interest all babies and toddlers have in wanting to see and touch more and more of all around; then the so-called 'terrible twos' of like 'I am me' now, and many 'no's as she was finding her own real self, like dash off to investigate with curiosity all things imaginable that caught her eye, such as puddles to splash in. Her name was Bess and she was much loved and the only god she knew was her mum.

Some years on at the seashore, on a beautiful blue sky summer's day she ran down the soft white sand to the tide-out seas edge where she found a rock pool, just like an interesting puddle. She squatted down and gazed at the colours and saw her own face there like looking in a mirror. She put a finger in the quiet pool and ripples circled out then disappeared. She looked in wonder at all these riches and called out to her older friend Eli, or E for short, to come and see and join her and tell his story about them 'cos he had a story about the beginning of all this.

A few hours ago there had been no pool there, like there was once no sea, earth, sky, stars, animals birds, creepy-crawlies and us; and a few hours ago she had felt very sad as her best friend had gone to another school as they'd moved house.

Eli was very old and wise 'cos of course age and time are very fickle, old to some and young to others; grown ups had made up time to suit - he was 25 years old and a very good person. He squished down the tufted dunes in bounds and told her one ancient myth story of how the universe of all that we see and don't, came into being. That story came about in a very far country between two rivers in a desert very much like the sand dunes here.

In one tribe there was a chief god Marduk who made everything and he had a wife called Tiamat, the mother goddess (and there were other gods too and they needed humans to help them in their work) but he killed her, so all the religions then on, who believed in one god, made that god a man and lord and father like we hear now in special buildings to worship 'him'.

Another tribe of people called the Hebrews mostly weren't happy with lots of gods so, long ago, a wise very old man with a white beard, sat down by the fire light and wrote a beautiful myth story, of just one god who was very good this time, as the people for whom he'd made the story were suffering a lot as they were slaves, but the Hebrews, used to their many gods, weren't too happy about a bit of that so he left in a sentence that this one god, who they called Elohim, had called himself 'our' as if he was many gods 'cos he had made a man and a woman equally, and often he said 'in our image,'our likeness' as one of the last things he made. He breathed on all this to make it come to life like her dad blows on a little flame to make a fire in the hearth of their home come to life. He specially made light out of the darkness right at the beginning. Doesn't that make us feel pleased he liked to make us in his likeness.

Before that Elohim had taken simple lifeless clay, a bit like 'play-do', or plasticine, you get in the shops, together with salty water, as if he was a potter, and calmly and quietly made the sky and earth, plants and animals and creepy-crawlies and the oceans (like this little bit of pool here) and day lights - he didn't call it the sun yet, and night lights - the stars, but now we know the sun is a star.

After all this creative work he gave himself a day's rest - you know the feeling when you've spent a lot of time in painting a picture and it feels good to rest, and you're pleased he had a rest too, as he was so pleased with what he'd made. He'd said it was good and very good many times. All from simple without any shape to complicated with shapes like now in this salty pool. She'd make shapes more with her 'play-do' now.

Another thing Eli liked was the Hebrews love of their alphabet (theirs is alephbet, a and b). They used to leave out of their writing, letters like a,e,i,o u, as they were felt to be very special relating to Elohim and they are softer sounds than the other letters like p and t which you almost spit out. And softer is usually more for girls and women. Their story for Elohim they called bet, like Bess's b, the second alphabet letter not the first, like the grown ups call it genesis in church 'cos it was not in the really real beginning before time and stuff were made. But it was still simple stuff being made to complicated.

Bess was thrilled - goodness, beauty and writing letters meant more now. Eli's story was 'super'-'cool'- natural, like she'd heard the teenagers at school say. A 'Yes, yes' story, a beautiful risk. And now she felt better and not so sad. And she even stayed a bit when it began to rain when she carefully cupped her hands to collect the sparkling rainbow drops of water then skipped back home to their beach house to show her Mum and Dad and to get dry, have some supper then sleep and dream.

That night a storm sped across the sky with rumbling thunder, and lightning bolts streaked down to the earth as if it were in a rage. It frightened her a lot but her mum came to soothe and hold her fear together.

In the morning after breakfast she ran down to the pool but it was flooded out and the waves crashed about with much spray.

A boy was there throwing stones at the gulls and kicking the water to make them fly off; he loved to see them hover, changing their wing shape to meet the wind gusts. He wanted to fly too, sometimes dreaming of being a pilot in a plane flying above the clouds, free from earth. His clothes were dirty and it didn't look as if anybody cared for him. She knew him from school and other children called him Jaws like the scary movie of a giant shark, 'cos he could be frightening and a bully and have tempers. But his real name was Jake, or J for short. Because she had been brought up with care and love she sensed his lack and approached him carefully - most kids ran off so he was taken aback. There was no-one who really cared for him. Jumping about with excitement, he was always much on the go, she asked him how he saw the beginnings of all of us. No-one had asked him how he thought or felt like Bess did now.

He had a story which he'd heard at church Sunday school, he didn't go anymore, truanting to play in the dump yard instead, 'cos they always talked about people being naughty and sinning and having to be saved from all that and begging for mercy; but they also said some good things. Everywhere he was always being told how bad and horrid he was. The only thing he had was his real name.

Anyhow his story was of the god Jahweh, and it was told in the middle of excited people rearing to go and conquer other tribes. Jahweh had made everything and also a man, later called Adam, meaning earth, but Jahweh didn't think much of girls and women so he made one later, who Adam called Eve as she was the mother of all, from a piece of Adam's rib after an op. as kind of second rate who had to follow the man behind and do as he said. Both had no clothes and were naked.

She called Jaws Jake, his proper name now, and he was pleased, but he too was scornful of girls and made a lunge at her but she stood her ground. That astonished him so he told of how his dad beat his mum and him too in their terraced house in a dirty street full of rubbish and fighting kids but some did have loving parents there. His mum was hardly ever at home and he quite often didn't have meals.

The bible man and woman were like little children as Jahweh had commanded them not to do this and that, like pick fruit from a special tree in the middle of the special garden called Eden as they would get knowledge and would die; so that they didn't know what good was or evil - they just didn't know. But the fruit tempted Eve as she was tired of being treated as second rate and stupid. Both had heard the church prayer to this god of 'and lead us not into temptation'. And Jake had heard of a devil god, devil means temptation. 'Well' Jake said - 'why put the bloody tree in the centre of the garden for all to see like putting a forbidden bowl of sweets in our play area at school?'. He knew all the swear words, he'd heard them at home as his dad swore with every command . A snake had told them about this fruit but that they wouldn't die. They didn't die when they ate it so this god had told a fib and so Jake learned to tell fibs like his parents. Eating the fruit was a big step to take for Eve.

Jahweh was enraged, just like J's dad, and expelled them from the special garden; this was a mighty thing to do, like Jake had been expelled from several schools before with so much uproar. And Jahweh cursed them to hard labour like in prison, in tilling poor weedy soil and to have painful childbirths, 'cos he was specially worried they would eat the fruit of the second tree of life and so never die, and so be his equal. Jahweh knew everything in his head like good and evil, that means wicked, and that existed before humans came and that's a problem that still the most bright and oldest and wise people don't understand if there's supposed to be only one god; so they make up things like the devil, a not very old word, who's a tempter; well Jahweh had tempted and had a very bad temper; or they made up satan as one who opposes, obstructs, frowns. Anyway Jahweh never would die and knew everything. They didn't seem interested in the tree of life anyway, so why all the fuss. It seemed Jahweh too was as many gods. He said of humans that they might be 'like one of us, knowing' before they ate the fruit; and like the good god Elohim said he'd made humans nicely 'in our image'our likeness'. What was 'our' about?

Jahweh was supposed to be all powerful, all knowing and present everywhere all at the same time but he'd wandered around the garden calling for them 'where are you?' but he knew everything, so why?; then he'd tried to make a partner for Adam from the animals and birds but that didn't work so Adam's loneliness continued until Jahweh then made Eve, as Adam said, pleased now, 'from bone and flesh of my flesh' that was his rib. Jahweh should have known better than that. Both Jake and Bess knew that was a no, no - you didn't marry your sister as that could make children with different bodies that gave them troubles.

But Jahweh had nicely let Adam give names to all the things he had made, like we now like naming things and language; then before they left the garden, after he shouted at them to get out, he made them special clothes of animal skins like we'd seen Tarzan in the movies. That at least was good of him as the fig leaves dried out. Perhaps he was trying to encourage them to make a go of reality outside as only the fittest survived in the harsh real world, bringing them down to earth with a bump, not anymore in dreamy paradise. When they had no clothes they wore big fig leaves 'cos they felt ashamed of being naked. 'That's funny' said Jake and Bess - 'why so?'

Another important thing in Jake's story was that Adam had already thought of leaving the special garden and his 'mother and father', the writer said (but he didn't have any human ones, he only had Jahweh as that) with his new Eve, before they'd eaten the fruit and then making a life of it together outside. So the idea of leaving was already there, even before Jahweh expelled them.

Well now, they had to grow up fast and learn how to grow food from bad weedy soil and make a life without being provided for in everything, except freedom and knowing and good. Now they were free and could be curious and questioning and know what was good for the first time and also what was bad. And Eve had to give birth to their children in much labour and pain. One of their sons killed his brother. And all the people who multiplied later from all this marrying inside the family, became violent and troubled so Jahweh murdered them all off in a massive gigantic flood rage, except one called Noah (and his family) who was blameless and who 'walked with god' said the writer of the fire-light story. Noah was saved by building a great boat and he let animals come on board. That was good for Jahweh - someone grown up, who he could relate to, walk with for the first time. Bess knew if you try and force a child to remain a child you get trouble. Jaweh had tried to keep Adam and Eve in tight reins to remain children. A sort of 'super'-'wicked'-natural' story. But maybe underneath Jahweh's labour rage he did want them to grow up then he'd have company as he had specially made and given them a parting gift.

Perhaps Jahweh was god who knew in his head but he didn't have one, of both good and evil before it became visible in humans. Perhaps Jahweh was the bad god and Elohim was the good god. Who knows. And god seems to keep secrets and makes people puzzle and puzzle things out if they can. And people in church often say 'Amen' which means 'the hidden one', a word from ancient Egypt.

But Jake's Jahweh story had a good ending, if you can find it, in that humans can grow up, and know goodness which they didn't know before, and wisdom, and from Eve's taking the lead and her curiosity, to learn about the world and how best to survive in it and heal its sicknesses and have all the helpful things like ovens and phones. Knowing how to make these things doesn't come easy. It takes years and years to make new discoveries. So a No no story of difficulty and blame has turned out a good story also. Eve started it all so perhaps women and girls weren't only just a piece of old spare rib after all. Bess's dad didn't treat her mum like that. But Jake's dad treated his mum badly. Also, we can't live in dreamy paradise all the time

Jake's Sunday school didn't tell you like this story, only that humans had disobeyed Jahweh so were wicked and sinful so were expelled for this first Original sin. Yes original and creative; it certainly was original, new. But a price had to be paid for this Fall by a very good special man's horrible death about 2,000 years ago as Jahweh demanded a penalty, as they much later said, like Jake's dad did often.

Bess now understood the wretched life J had had and why he was a bully and a fighter. He had survived at the cost of his soft good self as he'd had little of softness in the past from his parents. And Jake sensed she understood and became very hesitantly less difficult with her. They did a 'high five' instead of a grown-ups handshake and went their ways to meet again sometimes. Then the sun shone.

Later they did hang out together a bit but then he had to go to a special school so she saw him no more. But on his last meeting he had carved with his new knife a small fish, like they'd found in the rock pool, from a piece of old dumped wood and specially gave it too her; it was not shark-shaped. She kept it specially in her pocket wherever she went and it got quite shiny from all her holding.

Many years passed and Bess was doing well at school. And she was learning biology of animals and plants and her favourite sea-pool life. How some animals have changed or evolved, (another big word) to survive by killing other animals for food and even killing each other and cubs, if they were males, to dominate as leader of the pack; and that a mother leopard had a girl and boy cub and taught them how to catch and kill food, then when the girl cub was nearly grown up she seriously fought her daughter cub to get rid of her, a bit like Jahweh expelled Adam and Eve.

A particular nasty story was of a fungus which lives on the ground then makes new life spores and scatters them which get attached to passing ants. The spore bores a hole in the ant, gets inside and eats the ant from inside and while it's still alive moves to its brain which sends the ant mad and it climbs up a tree and hangs on with its Jaws for dear life, while the spore now sends out a long shoot from the ants head and then it makes more spores. The ant has a slow death. Parasite was the big name for this and it had been happening for millions of years. 'A good god ?' Bess wondered. So these spores are fitter than some ants who can't cope with them. But maybe that's a way of stopping the ants getting too many; like earthquakes and starvation and human wars try to keep the very big numbers of people down. Very cruel things to happen but then it's all about how to survive.

More big words followed like 'natural selection' to help things survive dangers. Living things all have lots of cells and these have lots of tiny atoms, but more of them later, which join up to form bigger molecules, that means little spots, which form thousands of little genes, which long ago, meant a spirit in a person - or like a clever genius perhaps; and these are inside even bigger chromosomes, as they are bodies staining with colour, and these are inside barley-sugar-like twisting structures. Things so love joining up and being inside other things. But they also love splitting up to make more stuff. And these genes make you special and not like anybody else in detail; also they can be turned on and off by the outside. But basically we're all the same shape. And they give you the colour of your eyes, whether you use your right or left hand mostly, and your special finger prints which no-one else has.

This life idea or urge to live and survive, (she felt ok and safe and comfy at home with pocket money for sweets at the corner shop but lots of people are struggling in danger and poverty) - this life idea really doesn't care about anything else - just to live and progress and those who do are the fittest; and just bad luck to anything that didn't. 'Dead as a dodo' like her school trip to the museum showed.

She even was beginning to feel that anything else like love, kindness, giving to others, given to the tribe, group or gang, then gave you back security and survival.

She also learned the stuff humans had inside them, all the organs and what they do and how people make babies; and about the brain and some of its different parts and that we've got billions and billions of brain cells. - and that it's the most complicated thing in the universe. Best of all are places that give us a sense of yourself like who we are and also give us a sense of time and space outside, And if you reduce the blood supply to these areas, people can do that by meditating, being specially calm - they lose the sense of space and time and feel like they're in heaven, all blissful and smiley. Not really much is known about what being conscious is, which is not like in boxing where you can be knocked unconscious to the ground and black out. We need not fear about looking inwards, the inside universe; that's just as important as discovering the outside universe.

But then Bess learnt that extra curious people in these things, called scientists were now definitely finding that animals have feelings and personalities - she knew that already 'cos they'd got a dog at home called Buzz as he was always sniffing around this and that, with whirring tail wags, and he had expressions and feelings and was different to their next door neighbour's dog in his personality. And that animals can show kindness to animals in trouble like one dog who licked a poorly cat friend as he passed by. There was no reward of survival there; and that elephants show they are kind of sad when one of their herd dies - they keep going back to the place where he died and respectfully and quietly touch the bones of their dead mate. Chimps can do that too. There doesn't seem a reward of survival in that. We might think we are top of the tree, and we are in words, art, music, science and making complicated machines, but a dog can smell thousands more than we can; and can even smell when a person is going to have a fit before it happens; and a bee can hover over a flower and know by its hidden waves that another bee has been there before to collect nectar, so don't bother going there. We can't do all these things so that means we are all special in different kinds of ways. Maybe there are many trees to be top of.

Bess now felt she needed a rest from all this exciting but confusing stuff so she was often off playing with her mates, greeting them as was customary as 'Hi matey' and 'hi babes', 'hi guys' and enjoying much fun and DVD's and movies and trips to town and wearing the same style clothes as her mates. And 'wicked' and 'cool' and 'stuff' were great. And cos it's the fashion when you're trying to find words, to say often, 'like' and 'you know' and make hand shapes at the same time. One lad could even beatbox with hand shapes and different drumming grunts.

Then she met a nice older person called Jim who was learning stuff about the universe, all those stars and planets and galaxies which you could see on a good night in a place with little light pollution from all the peoples' houses and streets, so the sky was 'like' black 'like' near her home on the sea-shore. The planets are all given names of ancient Greek and Roman gods and goddesses, as if those who named them still believed in many gods - except our earth, which just means ground or soil. Jim and Bess came down to the rock pool and looked at all the tiny creatures and fishes, those were her favourites, and the sea-weeds. They're not really weeds 'cos you can use them to make your soil better and one is even a food.

Jim then told her how the universe and all this might have begun, the best tested current story was called the Big Bang. That sounded good. 'Tighten your seat belt and we'll blast off in a space-craft to see it' Jim said. 'But you needn't 'cos it happened right here and everywhere and all over and it happened many billions of years ago (she knew some lucky people could win a quarter of a million pounds on the TV show 'Deal or no Deal' but billions was so large, it was hard to imagine). And at an enormous temperature of millions of degrees. She had once been ill and her mum had taken her temperature - it was only 38. And on top of that it began as a tiny point, much much smaller than a pin point, and it expanded and grew bigger millions and millions of times in a few seconds. 'Wow wow wow' she said at such mind boggling stuff. 'That's real cool, well hot really' she added.. It was not an explosion like a bomb blast on tele, but like you blow up a big balloon very fast. This pin point contained the potential, like a bud becomes a rose, to form the whole universe - from tiny to 'ginormous'.

And in this kind of cloud of steam were little things smaller than an atom, an atom used to be the smallest indivisible bit ever, it can't have smaller bits, but they did find smaller, Jim called them creatures, called quarks - not exactly quacking though, but that sounds good, and querky, and it makes it more interesting. And the word was first made up by an famous Irishman who wrote famous books and it was meant to mean like 'a cry of a gull' and the man who found out about quarks, when wondering what name to give them, first heard the sound in his head, then read the Irishman's book with the word, and so named it that. 'So you can see what imagination can do' said Jim.

You can't see them, a bit like ghosties, but you discover them by experiments done by clever people with big titles like astrophysicist and quantum physicist, and by those who love maths and scribble funny squiggles all over blackboards. A quantum is supposed to be an indivisible portion but so was an atom once. 'Perhaps quarks can have indivisible portions in them too' said Bess. 'That's a new idea' said Jim. 'And perhaps these quark portions have even littler bits and these littler bits have even more tiny bits and so on forever, or else down to the end which is lovely peaceful Nothing - no busy bits, no energy, no space, no time, before the very beginning' said Jim. His thinking had gone a bit too far for Bess but she got the drift.

Anyway this blowing-up-balloon's temperature was due to all the rapid movings of these little things - 'wow, they must be moving very very fast' she said 'to be that hot'. All this happened at fractions of a second later. Stuff kind of comes from ghostly nothing. 'It's like a cloud of steam you see when you boil your kettle' Jim said, then the same-all-over steam cools and forms formed water on the side of your kettle and if you collect lots of that and put it in the freezer it forms different shapes of icicles or like snow flakes. Bess remembered forming and drawing shapes on a blank piece of paper and also how beautifully shaped snowflakes fell from nowhere in a winter sky; so cooling (and heating) seems to make things.

Well these quarks, there are only six kinds of them, love joining up in pairs and they are called 'up and down' quarks, 'top and bottom' quarks and 'charm' 'ing ones' Bess added, to give them personalities, who pair up with 'strange' quarks. They all just love getting together like people do. Then they form hadrons which are stable kinds of protons and neutrons in the atom's nucleus; a nucleus is like a small solid nut inside a shell. Jim then drew a sand circle whirling round and round all over the place; that was an electron (or more) with negative minus charge, buzzing around the nucleus nut blob in the centre made of a little proton who weighed something and what's more had a positive, plus charge. This little proton was kept company by another little thingy who also weighed something but he didn't have any charge at all; he was neutral, a neutron. So now we have hydrogen (with 1 proton and 1 neutron) and he joins up with another hydrogen to form helium, like the gas they blow up party balloons with and it makes you talk in squeaky voices - that's 2 protons and 2 neutrons, and they gain mass, then, hurray, light begins to shine - so for thousands of years all this was going on, like in the dark womb of the universe, but that was still soon after the Big Bang Birth happened. 'Wouldn't that be fun if we had lots of free helium inside us, then we could float and have high voices' said Bess. 'Well sound travels 3 times faster in simple helium than in complicated air' said Jim smiling.

Later more proton joinings happen to form all the element bits in the universe - that's 92 naturally occurring ones like carbon and oxygen and nitrogen.

The simplest way to see all this is like blowing a soap bubble from one of those little bottles you can get at the corner shop and then more bubbles, and some join up in different numbers and different ways; that's instead of doing sums of what's got what and who joins with who. In case you're keen on sums - water is 2 hydrogens and 1 oxygen which is 1 helium and a carbon which is 6 protons and 6 neutrons; and nitrogen which is 2 carbons which is 12 protons and 12 neutrons. A very simple set-up making more complex things in a mind-boggling underneath complication. The sun has got hydrogen and helium and it makes hundreds of tons of it in one second. And the sun has got billions of years left before it runs out of fuel and collapses and returns all its stuff back to the universe, like we recycle our rubbish bins. We have had it, when that happens as we depend so much on the sun. Not so long ago we didn't recycle our rubbish but our earth has been calling out for us to do it and to take more care of her, perhaps 'cos there's too many people, but they should share more.

Also, like we grow old and can't see or hear like we used to, like the very old lady who goes to the corner shop with her walking-thing on wheels with a seat in front for getting tired and a basket to carry her shopping. She's got a very bent back and a sore knee so she has to hobble and take pills and keep warm to help the pain. Then when she dies 'and I'll miss her a lot' said Bess, she gets cremated, like being burnt in a very hot fire, like at the beginning of the universe, and her ashes scattered which is very helpful to the universe to make new stuff. All things, stars and people run down and get recycled for making more. So our stardust goes back to the stars. 'I remember looking up at the night sky and seeing a bright star and that was Grandad when he died' said Bess quietly.

But physics hasn't yet been able to tell us more of these subatomic little thingies' inner natures - just charge and weight or not, and joinings, energy, force and not much more. That's why Jim likes to call them little creatures to make them come alive in our imagination. 'There are other little particles called muons which mew and gluons which glue' - he teased Bess with that. 'Well if us and animals have different personalities, why can't the little thingies have personalities too' said Bess.

Also in the beginning there was a joined-up force which split into the 4 forces found, called gravity, electromagnetism (you might have heard of them) and strong and weak nuclear forces. But never mind that. A spacecraft has taken photos of this early stage and it shows coloured spots and specks which are the seeds where stars and galaxies are forming. And you can actually hear that when someone tunes an older radio to find a station. It sounds like crackles or chuckles. Amazing.

Well large clouds of all this form galaxies and smaller clouds form our stars. And the stars use up lots of energy to form all this stuff then run out of energy and collapse under gravity, 'you know that force which makes apples fall down to the ground' said Jim. 'It would be funny if things fell up' said Bess. Then they explode like a popped balloon and die into dust and that's our stardust which made our place and from then on life could very slowly begin to take shape 'cos the conditions slowly became right. 'So we really are made from sparkling stardust' said Bess, Dancing on the Edge of the pool. 'Yes' said Jim, ' even like all the stuff in your skin comes from that stardust and so long ago'. She lifted up a skin fold in her arm and felt astounded. But she also felt sad that stars had to die for us and was that evil or just the insistence in the universe to keep on making shapes and stuff at the cost of things dying.

But what is very important is energy, like you feel, like when you're rearing to go for a run and what keeps you running. At the beginning of the universe energy was set at a given, no more, no less - that's it, 'like mum makes one big cake, no more' said Bess. It 'cannot be either created or destroyed' said that famous original man called Einstein, with twinkly eyes, who thought outside the usual boxes. 'And we should trust our hunches and imagination more and jump outside the boxes' said Jim 'while learning what's in the boxes - like Eve picking the fruit of the tree of knowledge'. And on top of that, mass or stuff and energy are the same physical thing and can be changed into each other. The mass of a thing or set-up is a measure of its energy inside. Big exciting ideas. 'So when we die, a big leap to let happen, our massstuff is changed to our energy and recycling dustash. That means that's still a new something of us around and is that spirit? Bess wondered. Jim was honest and said he didn't know, except that spirit meant something like the essential principal in something; that life is precious 'cos it has to end.

And also, all this space is not empty; it's full of energy and forces and sparking charges and gravity. If you took all the world's people and squashed out their spaces in their atoms you would be left with a sugar cube sized shape. So there is an incredible amount of space filled with the most lively force and energy. 'Is this spirit' Bess wondered, going quiet in amazement, drawing a small square sand shape.

Before Bess got too tired Jim wanted to share with her a few more bits then they could rest by the pool and doodle shapes in the sands.

Jim said there were other little thingies, little creatures called photons 'you know like in the word photography for cameras which use light. Well believe it or not they only exist when observed. 'So they don't exist when not looked at, or they hide until someone wants to meet them, then they come out of hiding 'cos they like being seen' Bess said. 'So energy, spirit only comes out of hiding when someone wants to talk to it'. 'Perhaps, I don't know' said Jim. He was the first to say he didn't know so much, not like some know-alls. But then Jim said more, that when you watch something you actually change it. 'Like when you watch me, so I sit up and take notice when I wasn't concentrating before' said Bess. On top of that these little photons have two kinds of personalities - they can either be waves or little particles. They carry a lot of energy but don't have any weight, 'perhaps like ghosts only they are light ones' Bess thought. Something having no mass or weight was too much for Bess. 'Perhaps a thought can't have weight, or can it?', she wondered.

Then she asked him what time was, or is. He just said 'it isn't'. 'We only have like different clocks in our heads to help us make decisions on what we've learnt and how to deal with making future choices. Like how does a frog know when to shoot out its tongue at the right time to catch a fly. It's learnt by trying before'. Bess knew that time passes quickly when you're enjoying yourself and slowly when it's boring. Jim said that Eastern belief is that time is an illusion - an idea we think is, but isn't. The more we look at things the more we find we're not sure but that keeps us going on and on to try to find out. Clocks just have hands to count time, 1 to 2 and so on.

Then he told her of our old friend, the proton, proton means first; remember it's in the centre of the atom's middle, its nut, and it has a positive charge and it weighs. Well it can do amazing things like be in two places at once. 'Wouldn't that be good if we could do that but we can't cos our protons from the stardust are all bound up in our other stuff like our water. But more than that it can go right through matter, ghost-like, like a ball passing through a brick wall. We can't do that' said Jim. That left Bess dumbfounded and amazed. So they both rested and doodled shapes and patterns in the sand, thinking how these humble lively little thingies have godlike qualities.

Finally Jim told what might seem common to the universe and us, in all these stories, of which we are part. Both like joining up and making things; both like then separating, creating and giving birth and growing and understanding; both cross critical changing points, making big leaps, like Eve and the Big Bang, which was like Adam and Eve being sharply born out of the special garden called Eden, Jahweh pushing them out mightily, 'cos everything was supplied except freedom, knowledge and what good is; both have become large from being small; both have an inner urgency to just be and to become; an urgency to understand; and grow old and die to be recycled and give their stuff for something else; all the stories don't deal with what happened before time and the first ghostly stuff; and they all have an inbuilt propensity, 'I can't think of another word, perhaps talent ' said Jim; and all want to come out of the fertile but difficult darkness into light, like when first being born, and when first light was made so long ago, or like coming out of a dark sad place.

'Wow' said Bess and they both squiched up the dunes to her home.

As for Jake, Bess had heard, in school rumours, that he had got caught up in gang stuff, had been in court for street fights and for several ASBO's, that he cut his arms with razor blades, had run away from home and the special school to the big city where he hung about in the back streets which were dark and scary and full of uncollected rubbish and that he slept rough in a cardboard city begging for money. Bess's heart sank. In his life everything was decaying so young, so soon. But fighting was the only way he knew to survive. She held his little carved fish.

He had a good school counsellor for a few months then that service was cut then he had a very good social worker with whom he could really feel in touch but that was only for a short time as she had so many different troubled people to work with.

Then he was involved in a bad street gang fight with knives, remember he had carved a little fish for Bess. So now he got stabbed many times. It was like he had been stabbed in his inner heart many times since he was little.

An ambulence took him to hospital and at last he was warm and cared for by nice nurses and doctor with blood transfusions and stitchings.

He remembered Bess so they managed to phone her mum and dad who rushed her round to see him but he was in a bad way 'cos of losing lots of blood. Both were more grown up now. He had been stabbed in the chest as well, and his heart had been nicked, cut and stolen, and he was losing consciousness, gliding through and above light clouds, flying like a gull, drifting off, but he could see and feel Bess with him in a hazy kind of way. It was so good. It was then as if he was coming to rest on the edge of this Dancing circle of care at last. Then he entered the very centre of the circled pool at its deepest quiet place, the heart, surrounded by a warm glow. Then he died. Bess wept, in her dark sad place. 'Is it that energy, spirit of space; maybe Elohim' she cried, her hand holding Jake's. His turbulent surface torrent had stopped to a quiet depth.

'And the end of all our exploring
Will be to arrive where we started *'What will survive of us is love'*
And know ***the place*** *for the first time.'* *Phillip Larkin: An Arundel Tomb*

T.S.Eliot. Little Gidding, Four Quartets.

Owl (where is wisdom water?)

just that we are, everything is -
carried into it.
Moon grazes down the night
quietly; cow-soft,
her warm breath misting white

the hallowed haloed night;
a pivot of need, the being-womb,
placenta attached,
the rage of its loss over fragile snow
in gusts of tenderness
undeciding, melts, which is the foundation rock.
Our brow furrows with an easy yoke -
a bond made good, plough-cut detached, burden-light.

(That rare gold ingot flame of peace).
Showered souls - their faces up, eyes closed
toward the waterfall of given love,
The quanta of trust.
The atlas of the world.
Sacrum of born civilisation.
The arched foot of sprung inspiration.
Branches tendril asking to the sky in hope
But we tread heavy, bent, over rough stones,
pained slow steps in the dry desert crags.

The essential oils of love trust hope - balm,
aromatic, scenting the air we breathe
and are inspired by, when lost;
against the stench of discipline drive pace will
duty and obedience - rotting our guts,
a thickening and hardening of the arteries of being;
the quick thin edge between by a length thrown
into the dark unknown.
Footfalls of the path stir golden autumn leaves
rustling with decay for new growth.

Hot resolve slips drained under the shower
of water-cooling-rest
Shading from the parched heat and dry desert dust,
a tumbleweed of wanting inclusion,
wanting to know only a concealed
rolling windblown unknown revealed
which remains unknown, then shivers
with cold thought and intellect, in a gust.

That quaint word love so overused when gone
snow melting to water, evaporated to nil, blown south
I can see the sound of silence. It roars
  as thunder divides the sky in a flash.
Peace rarely comes - wrapped in wet cloths,
  and evening days grow longer
    and lengthen lenten spring.
The candlewick burns, singeing a carcassed moth.
   How we are. I am.
Language flickers and its shadows distort in the dark.

I can hear the small weed grow -
  creaking the pavement crack.
This - how we are - pain in the cracking
  as a nutshell splits
the white tendril stem tender - upshot.
The intention to keep steady, muted
  in unpious simplicity -
wordless at the kitchen sink, washing up.
 Unceasing glimpses of fading hope
as candlewax drowns the last faint glow - but
 it turns to a shining white stone, fossiled cold touch.

The owl in my eyes blinks his big eyes
 alight with a smile and a hoot of hello.
There is a response from this silent world.
He flies soundless within the soft moon mist
white-faced as moonlight, a ghost -
no wing beat heard; just as love and peace may quietly appear -
    winging low; the still small voice -
        over the swaying grass.
But he drops, stopped, on our tiny mouse-soul,
 claws plummet down, wings and tail brake;
     how easily we are, if open, hurt;
        the torn shredded heart.

  The rich brown ploughed adjacent soil
 of being loved, constancy, acceptance -
  that tiny shoot may just survive. We are.

Count The Hours; the time of being held is
gentle strength
bundling dry faggots together -
then we are more what we truly are,
resolving fire-warmth for the heart's hearth.
But they in the street devour our deep self soul.
and a road cuts and gulps the contours of the land in front.
I have a name and I am strings which vibrate to a pluck;
a psalm - our life
so easily shrieking-snapped by harsh discord.
Owl disappears in the still night.

Mar.2004

'Dactylic' Parsimony of Form Only Broken whole
(A relentless transformation process)

Generous uterus -
capacious vacuous.
Stridulous animus -
amorous querulous.
Marvellous nucleus -
numinous cankerous.
Tortuous unconscious -
tremendous perilous.
Stupendous genius.
Blasphemous consensus.
Curious colossus -
wondrous rigorous.
Nocuous stimulus -
sensuous tortuous.
Ridiculous famous, thunderous, humorous, anomalous anonymous.
Multitudinous bonus, boisterous vivacious, scandalous marasmus.
Voluminous rumpus, vociferous chorus, cacophanous opus.
Vertiginous, heinous, desirous ravenous, miraculous clonus.
Ludicrous syllabus -
serious spurious.
Dangerous tetanus -

tremulous gangrenous.
Odorous vomitus -
copious hideous.
Arduous exodus -
righteous, riotous.
Ominous terminus -
barbarous slumberous.
Ruinous tumulus -
spacious vacuous.
Glorious hibiscus -
fabulous frivolous.
Luminous cumulus -
numerous mountainous.
Incredulous Icarus -
audacious, disastrous.

Christ Icarus - spiralling, whirling.
Incredible. Sun-held. Risen. Magnanimous.

May 2003

Better read from below up.
(earth is below!)

Incredible. Sun-held. Risen. Magnanimous

Icarus, audacious disastrous. Icarus - spiralling, whirling -
Luminous cumulus, numerous mountainous. Incredulous
vacuous. Glorious hibiscus, fabulous, frivolous.
barbarous slumberous. Ruinous tumulus, spacious
exodus, righteous, riotous. Ominous terminus,
Odorous vomitus, copious hideous. Arduous
Dangerous tetanus, tremulous gangrenous.
Ludicrous syllabus, serious spurious
ravenous, miraculous clonus.
Vertiginous, heinous, desirous
chorus, cacophanous opus.
Voluminous rumpus, vociferous
vivacious, scandalous marasmus.

Multitudinous bonus, boisterous
humorous, anomalous anonymous.
Ridiculous famous, thunderous,
stimulus, sensuous tortuous.
wondrous rigorous. Nocuous
consensus. Curious colossus,
Stupendous genius. Blasphemous
unconscious, tremendous perilous.
numinous cankerous. Tortuous
querulous. Marvellous nucleus
Stridulous animus, amorous
capacious vacuous.
Generous uterus -

(A relentless resurrection process)
Parsimony! - Broken whole.

Partners
One Minute in Time in Greyfriars Gardens

In hope, I prune clustered rose hips
to encourage a second flower crop
from a low bush by a path
round a wild flower meadow
in the middle of a town.
A Bumble Bee joins me
large and furry and fat,
sartorial, in his mustard and black
He's done well with his striking stripes
to ward off birds with a beady eye
for snapping up a juicy quick snack.

The dog-rose blossoms - satiate,
bend low to his chunky weight
as he bumbling lands, as if inebriate;
and like a helicopter
lazily wobbling
above the sea of green waves

drops dunked
on their pollen and nectar
stamen-fluffy island decks
And he does a little dance
among the fragrance
in circles anti-clockwise
to gather up all the goods -
such happily offered delicious foods
in abundant essence.
He lifts off, humming,
hovering for the next -
and the done bloom
springs back in radiance.

The blossom and bee relate,
neither worry about the future or the past -
both a part, partners, in romance
of the happy Whole at last.
And I'm drawn in a trinity -
with a Sparkle and a Smile
that made my day alight without -
yes, without a shadow of a doubt.

Sept 2010

Broken is Beautiful. Simple Pebbles

They own nothing
and neither are they owned -
they are the divine's Own
beached toys in his world sandpit;
waves help them whisper together,
tinkling in quiet sound -
fresh - in million upon million,
each single one is not the same
as any, anywhere else;
each an identity of its own.
Flint chips, shells, stones -

corners rounded, flaked, cut;
I like the ones with central holes
or the smooth St. Peter's thumb prints;
colours mute - tan, cream,
pottery blue and white, black,
and ferrite iron rust.
Now sad sea waves
hurl them crying awash -
the moon makes their tides
ad infinitum and so on - back
to the God before the Big Bang
before the beginning of time.
So many bruised, so like us
chipped scarred by war
each unique, alive but dead -
starvation, earthquake -
the turmoil of survival -
and our inner turmoil dark.
We kill to stop the killing - storm tossed!
And loneliness - the worst poverty
as mother Theresa said.
I have seen the wounds of Christ
in the wounds of many.
but is there a God in bad and good?
in simple bread and the wine cup.
His compassion, love amongst us
in the raised arm robes - concern awash
and in the care of a friend - close.

This untidiness of reality.
But everyone, everything has a within God?
in the broken-transformed Christ.

The pebbles are not alone.

Aug 2010

Laughing Perfume or Fragrant Nonsense
Un Odorant Absurdites Parfum de Elize Vielle d'autodefense
(Poking Fun at Perfume)

Black and white tele ads to show 'lust' without love's colour.
'Pure Poison' perfume - a woman with snarling wolf face
crawls along a long passage escaping on all fours - Dior's Elixir
from frightening things zooming down in chimeric chase.
She reaches a stand where a bottle alone stands, spellbinds
dissolving the beasts in thin air with a swift scent whiff.
Her poison scatters the dark in the mirage of our minds.
but, unbeknown, how to terrify a pursuing lover off.
'J'Adore' by Dior where a model lolls along a catwalk
as only models can, with that extraordinary walk - gaunt faced -
one foot placed, not in front but across the other leg, slow paced
with down-slung shoulder the same side and long curved neck
discarding items of minimal vogue dress with a quick pluck
eyes glinting, mouth puckering for a juicy lip-flesh snack.
She's supposed to be alluring and full of passion and lust,
rounding up and cornering her sexual object mate.
It seems you manipulate compete win devour discard
you use the other without respect and love and regard.
Ralph Lauren's 'Romance' - a scent for 'him',
advertising a flashing tempting plaything, trunk and limb trim.
'Aqua di Gio' by Giorgio Romani - water splashing 'strong' men,
major muscles dripping with half shut focussed eyes, hunting
though no pouting lips. I wonder at that, wildcat musk format -
the insurgence of pretence in the presence of intense advance
the compliance of connivance in the prominence of pursuance.
No nuance of romance in 'Hypnose,' Lancome's fragrance -
and I didn't know that's what you're supposed to do!-
hypnotise, hence the mesmerising glinting hungry eyes.

Duped in seriousness though a flicker of truth ignites -
no - it's amusing, ridiculous - I have to laugh;
it's supposed to be high fashion passion in vogue;
yes - it's the fragrance of nonsense, pathetic sad;
it obviously sells to confused folk, duped -
hypnotised to copy and not be themselves

This is the way now and it obviously fails
(like current religions) - the high separation and divorce rate.
Perfumes made to mask in ages past - foul smells
decay excrement, dirt - like incense, thurifer-whisked
round the altar - as 'perfume' means to thoroughly smoke -
in dry climes with scarce washing water, natural, sweet -
but now to exaggerate the ferromones of nature and us
in the interest of fast money and leering lust.

'Insolence', 'Sublimage', 'Dior Homme', 'Dior Captive'
'Cherie', 'Dior Addict', 'Crystal Holiday', 'Eau Sauvage'.
'Miracle Forever' and also 'Fahrenheit Heat'
'Dolce Vita', 'Energy', 'Chanel Allure', 'Homme Sport'.

Insolent poisoning savage addictive, wild -
alluring, muscular, miraculous, in heat -
versus loving dear, eternal endearing sweet -
now here's some hope. All these in the glitzy shops sold.

Have you walked around a garden or in a wood
and a woman daubed, whiffing, passes in high scent;
it's repugnant repellent masking, foul and false.

Love uses little and discreetly without all this fuss
but primordial carnal impulse is a creative source.
Old fashioned, a spot of 'Old Spice' is still nice.

Silver and purple snowballs in Whitefriar's merchandise
whiteflakes replaced nonetheless in the winter showcase
I wonder if now, nature will copy, and that will suffice.

Canterbury Dec 2006

Perhaps In the storm Who are We? Some Excavations

The fundamental principle which provokes, counsels,
urges to hold to the difficult, formidable

in what seems most alien, thicket-thorn-torn painful -
which can then become what is most trusted and essential
through living towards an answer or none, in exile -
        like nailing water or netting the wind.
Words spring from interest and need, determined.

That integrity will not let us forget death in the midst of life;
to accept death, not as a foreign stranger, but as central
and very manifest, palpable, inevitable, visible -
the silent enigmatic partner in the twisting dance unsaid -
wheat sheaves reaped are scythed, struck-cut dead
by that Black blade, to life-giving stone ground bread.
Why should we be deeply different from all that is made.

We need the mindgodheart more than ever now; immense -
it is too much to distance him in solemn reverence;
as god is nearer than God - in warm people, the good.
and even moreso as no name absolute
as one of nothing, not even silence - the empty plenitude;
to feel back to paths in forgotten places, to childhood
pricked back to life, death, seeing a babe and motherhood
                in quietude, understood
as unknown, to days of pain and hurt still unexplained, disturbed -
to minutes of laughter and delight; to little things, small words;
to have been at the bedside with hovering death, the last gasp heard
and the first at birth; to forget when memories flood and to wait
and remember when they emerge or are deep, lostinsensate;
it is not the memories alone but shared, turned to living blood
in true steady compassion that is with understanding and ruth
        now, if never before - open in indecent truth
    honesty and trust - in the, at last, home-altared-hearth.

Soon we will be moving on air - the engineering of
tracks, suspended trains - christ walks on water. In physics
things can be made to disappear in invisible cloaks -
  maybe we will be able to as well and reappear -
christ on the road breaking bread with his friends after death.
There are more things in heaven and earth than imagined yet,
        yet he never told of a literal virginal birth -

all conception of whatever kind is a marvellous event. It is new,
fresh, the manifold into one in insight, sudden idea, surprise clue.
Much work begins, then torn
to a birth - crying kicking, never laughing, or aborted stillborn.

Gurgling smiling come later between two pairs of eyes resonant -
(measuring time in fresh toilet rolls spent)
words calling - spring from interest, need and concern -
('interest' inter esse to be between) when eyes are unmet or absent.

Particle physics is looking for the origin of the universe
a fraction after it was born, not in a whimper, but the Big Bang-
explosion-expansion, but not yet how nothing became
simple central something in the first place; just the something's
penultimate beginning - all this for a 'theory of everything'
hoping for a conjunction of Einstein and Quantum in one.
I and all are derived from the simple particles and before, from
Nothing itself in its fullsome plenitude bursting with potential form;
pregnant with nothing, no babe yet - in pregnant silence the nothing,
void, being full of hidden child.
God himself impregnated his-herself in Love - the beginning
of the silent pregnant nothing till the big birth bang
where the babe universe was born -
the violence of conjugal creation in love's spark
and out of - like a literal birth from a mother's labour and work.
The child is expelled down a dark canal out of the dark
and, at first, saw it was light, harsh. Then together they rest.
Particle collision needs the speed of light not dark.
Nothing is where-is-no-is, before matter, space, time
before existing, being, form - an unimaginable non-place
where is not where not-God is-not. Language fails.
Maybe Nothing (is!) (where!) Love Know Create (are!).
'Is, are, am, be, where' all exist in being and form and place.

Eyelids open and shut; the mind unseen behind controls
so with life and death, open and shut; the unseen god.
The winds of black change rush through hushed leaves, dying down,
clattering pain, fright, which shudder, dead-brown, crisp-blown,
shrouding sad earth; scarred trees stand stark bare, alone -

in myriad wounds against the grey sky, ominous confused thrown.
Yet spring comes again.
That thunderstorm battleground clash of warm rising air
against the higher cold - the tumult of our opposites, bare;
extreme air current lightning storms - of rage against pain, fear;
this unseen elemental inner force. It happens in the atmosphere.
and in us. Now here turns to nowhere and nowhere to now here.
christ like the crackling of a crystal set which ceases, stops clear
when found tuned - the cat's whisker; but when, where?

Even now we see a pagan God who desires his son cross-dead
to pay for our 'sins'- in unknowing confusion, chaos, led unfed;
suicide is a way out of being disgraced - words slashed unsaid

- an ancient God, merciless, violent, sacrificial -
in a monolith of church identity institutional
not homely ordinary but liturgical nonsensical
with off-pat thoughtless fearsome discordant chants;
and cannabalistic, parasitic - living off the body and blood of Christ.
Being hung drawn and quartered was worse than the 3 day cross -
it is Gethsemane that is the worst worse
as is long starvation or pain of body and heart withal in exile;
those who suffer severely have no luxury at all
of saying 'there is no God' or 'there is a God'. It is both, cruciform -
'my god why hast thou forsaken me'. He died then transformed.
Both died then, not in likeness, becoming at-one.
Hate drains; our idea of god evolves;
suffering, death in whole or in part seem what change involves.
To a babe, absence is non-existence, absence is 'is not'
till the proof of mother's actual return ....and if not....?;
as everything is interwoven - his suffering was also ours shared,
likewise theirs - for somehow the presence of a renewed heart.

Young families have more movement discord chaos
than the settled more rigid routined old, yet within - is what?

To increasingly know even as also I am known - now face to face
as I rarely was before to another's dark mask in a dark glass.
The Ultimate words - Love Create Know.

In the beginning and before and now, it was and is -
lasting Energy in and around everything;
Energy which is disturbing intriguing astonishing
causing astounding happening unfailing unending.
Love impells creating-knowing-joining out of and in Nothing
Can you help float my boat or not
before I pop me'clogs?

Sept 2008

Etymology in 'forsaken', a strong highly active verb.
for = (intensive) away.
sake = strive, dispute, crime, fault, to contend, rebuke, (strongly against).
ruth - concern.

Petrarchan type Sonnet 2
Even Worse
A Gash

On one defined enlightened happy day,
a lambling, dappled black and white, was born;
she struggled bravely, shaking legs. Forlorn -
enticingly she slumped into the hay.
The sun was shining bright and warm. A ray
of light reflected off the glowing husks of corn,
collected, reaped, and stacked that very morn.
The sudden shaft of light enriched the growing grey

of looming clouds and mist, increasing fog;
the atmosphere - an eerie curdling hush,
encircling gloom now pierced by lightning flash
as then there dashed at speed a vicious dog
who split the lambling's throat and blood did gush.
The little beast was sacrificed for us, aghast. A gash.

Canterbury Dec 2002

John Whitworth's 'forky' in his sonnet is a nice word but the dictionary doesn't list it. Hence my word 'lambling', like duckling. A lambling is even smaller than a lamb! And it has mystical connotations. But there is no room to resolve the issue of it's death, such is the limiting nature of this sort of writing. I have kept extra words in 'cos I want to and have to. The rhyming words ending in -ay, -orn, -og, -ush, -ash, dictate the content. Perhaps some other animals could have been used instead of a lamb or dog.

Pigeon Drinking

Carrying messages, pigeons saved lives in WW1. They can fly 600 miles a day.
Gentle White Wing drops down about 11 o'clock
from her roof top perch for regular bits -
bits pinched off the corners of my toast -
in winter twelve in all; morsels from the table top
not 'crumbs under the table' dropped to exist
from an unworthy 'sinners' Eucharist.
Now she has a husband, her cocky assertive mate
able to get pieces first unless I see to it, not -
like bumper cars they shove each other over and out
in the fairground, competing for food got;
he's a handsome marble-grey dapple white
and 'thicker' off the mark and not so bright.
In winter they loose most of their shiny greens, blues
and put on fluffy cosy coats for the bitter cold
doing a lot of walking for short trips to warm up.
Food is scarce as folks now eat indoors
and flying uses up fast more precious fuel
in those great muscle-breast pectorals.

They also get four thumb size torn sugar lots
from little brown envelopes. I think they can taste like us.
Sugar bowls, cubes are now history in cafs.
And they give me some relationship, such interest.
Perhaps their tiny pulses of warm breath

cannot make snorting spray-mist plumes like us in frost

After all that, White Wing flies up
to a gutter in the sun on the edge of the roof
and if it's not turned to solid slabs of ice -
water undrained is there to sip up.
Buttered toast has to be washed down -
like we do too with coffee or tea replete
but not by swallowing upside-down.
Yet the sight of her sipping was so sweet
I chuckle soft and dull people turn to look.
She had up-ended her tail feathers
and there were her two little stick legs
furry tops, but so knock-kneed and splayed.
Pigeons have 'false' knees but they angle back
not forwards like ours, meant bent.
And there, present, her white V triangle vent.

She flew to a corner sheltered spot
of sunned lead flashing, tanned bricks
and dozed, a full fluffball, head sunk in her neck,
warmed and well and watered and fed.

Jan 2009

Pigeons in St. Margaret's Street

A flock of twenty or more
gang up above a fish and chip shop
for scattered chips and bits
dropped by the folk below.

They zoomed down on the crowds beneath
annoying shoppers with the whiff of their wings.
Two Chinese girls giggled along
zappy, Western fashion smart.
But a pigeon flew low past

and scuffed their hair and in fear
one lass swivelled scared
eyes screwed up, she screamed
but no morsel for the pigeon there.

I am like that.
I have doom and gloom pigeons
that swoop low and scare.
If I feed their gloom with more doom
it will attract a whole flock.
But if there is no morsel about
they will fly off.

I can welcome one
with a gentle crumb
in acceptance and compassion
but not dwell on the whole lot
in the rumination of doom.

Perhaps the one
will fly up
a white peace dove
with an olive branch
to dry firm land
from the turbulent sea
underneath.

Mar.2012.

Doughnut Donut Do-not Dunked

Anarkos - without beginning I see
my pug marks in the Snow, within the secret folds of nature.
The Spark that through the burnt fuse drives Death.
God is more than God and less than All.
Anarkos - without beginning and 'In the beginning was the Word,
and the Word was with God, and the Word was God.'.

'What God is, we do not know'
'When love goes wrong, then nothing goes right'.

In Praise of Pigeons and others

Sip coffee on a bench near the Donut caravan in the High Street watching people pass with their christmas shopping. Well, at least I don't have to worry about that - Christ mass on my own probably. An old lady comes to feed the pigeons and I watch them scurry for the bread scraps. I notice one who is thin and hobbling - one leg damaged and mostly curled up under his chest. He stops and tries to swallow but can't. He stretches up his neck in an attempt to clear it. It looks as if something is stuck in his throat. Then he huddles close to a pole - fluffed out, trying to get warm. Dishevelled. His damaged leg pulled up and shaking tremulously. I feel as if he is in pain. He can't get at the scraps before the others do. They seem unconcerned. This is survival of the fittest. I can't bear it and look away. I cannot. I swear at God as a bastard. Pain and suffering is life. And what fucking does He do. I think to ask the Donut man for any scraps as I haven't any - and to feed that pigeon specially and ward off the others but he can't swallow easily. He flies off low a small distance and lands at the feet of a Japanese couple talking - no fear, he is desperate and they might throw down something - some scraps and 'crumbs under the table' (and 'we are not worthy so much as to gather up the crumbs under thy table'- the holy communion!). They just continue talking, not noticing him. I can't stand it. But if he can fly a bit then, is there hope? ... Pain and suffering and a slow death are shreaking at me. I cannot prolong his dying by feeble attempts at scraps from the Donut man. I have to leave.

I write of him. He is worthy of being remembered and valued. That is all I can do. He is me also ...

I have a bacon stick and cheap coffee in the chair outside homely Wingham Bakery in Iron Bar Lane off Burgate. Mostly the Serco street cleaners like it there after they have hosed down their whiskery caterpillar brush-wheel suction motors. One looks like James Stewart. The little serving ladies can't see well over the high counter and they peer at you through their glasses. Frau gets her Bloomers bread there and sometimes when she can't - I do for her.

Have you ever looked at a brown and white pigeon - it's jewelled with colours. My one had ruby eyes and aquamarine blue cheeks and a mauve heather lilac neck with darker grey, slashed with emerald green. His white-tipped wings were cinnamon and light brown . His tail feathers - sheer white. His chest - mauve and grey. Such a very fine pigeon. And all, and that's all that pigeon means is a young bird, a chirper, a piper. When he strutted fast, his little head bobbed forwards and backwards rapidly too - I wondered what he could see with all that motion. Humans are upright so their heads don't jut back and forth. Try turning your head fast and see what you can see.

The hosed down water trickled past in the gutter smelling of dettol and a tiny piece of polystirene merrily floated along out of sight to Burgate street. Pigeon strutted sedately after it and disappeared - the best painted gnome in the concrete garden of Iron Bar Lane.

The purring fibres of my soul sipping thick hot tomato and basil soup and big broken chunks of bread - my holy communion.

Where is the soft underbelly of culture amongst harsh frost words?

Mind your own mind (not business) - the flashes of lashes - eyes - to flog - to bind firmly together - a snare.

I love little round people - short and fat in old long coats and bochel* rocker bottom shoes; their tiny feet walk twinkling. Chuckley, they belong to the kingdom of god. The smart sane sanitized same set have no character and are worthy only of a fast glance. Underneath they are killer whales surfacing and heaving up massive bulked hulks of water. A seal to be eaten jawed - I retreat up the shore of silence and lowered eyes. I am them too.

Seeing hearing touching tasting - these are the sensibles. Sensible. They make sense - them. Tense.

Perceptibles - well - conceive deceive perceive; conception deception perception.

Without soma feeling - there are no words.

Receiving is the same as giving - no better, no worse. Not lessor.

Canterbury Dec.2003

*Bochel - well worn, 'shoddy' shoes. Shod - shoed! (? Scots origin).

A Piper's Message to the Master
and
A Salute for a Tutor

This 'Unjust Incarceration' -
Of overwork and now 'MacDonald's Sweetheart' lost
Where is no 'Kiss of a King's Hand' -
'Nameless' - the beginner piper,
'Too long in this Condition'
Profoundly thanks the master
For his message hidden
But given also to the two
Judged great behind the Glaziers table
Whose glance concerned
Came straight through space to
This hiding sad sinner!

This pipe is the unpredictable
But one love remaining
Yet a 'Desperate battle'
In the harsh desert
Of learning piobaireachd -
Where is no sweet wayside water.

Will 'Lachie's Lullaby' soothe?
Fraoch Eilean (island heather).

7.11.83 London.

The words in inverted commas are the names of piobaireachd - classical music for the great Highland bagpipe. In old times messages were sent by pipe from hill top to hill top. The Glaziers Hall London - the place where piping competitions are held.

Monday, June 2nd 2003 at 8.30ish
John Whitworth, established poet
and my creative writing tutor,
pointed to me and my papers
and said adamantly, twice -

'You are a poet,
You are a poet'.

I have a name now.
I have a name.

June 2003

Poetry is not

People write lovely stuff
And don't call it poems.
Poetry can be inflated
And 'important' and false.
Real poetry is that
Which is said in a way
That evokes 'Ah' and 'Yes, yes'
And new eyes and ears
And maybe help us
Change and evolve.

I can't call mine poetry -
Only someone else can.

Oct.2015

Poor A Woman Eating Fish

Etymology of meek - supple pliable soft; not as we now know the word!

I came out of a book shop and
wriggled and wangled my way
through the crowds in the street
and across to the fish and chip shop,
all bustling and busy at Xmas
with the logistics of just-living uppermost -

from here to there and what next;
the many steps to achieve one thing.
For Christmas I'd like one thing -
gravity low down in my feet
not wobbling high in an anxious chest -
a true Russian doll with a steady lead base.
All over town, the unending shops'
sales, reductions - the recession credit crunch;
buskers being dropped a few coins in caps
and a beautiful saxophonist, his sound in his heart.
And sitting quietly and close and stark,
it was freezing cold, a bitter painful frost -
most wrapped in scarves and parcels and coats,
a woman and her sight struck me sharp.
She had poor little shivering shoes -
no stockings, socks - her legs blotched with cold
and further up as my eyes concerned, scanned -
a small summer flimsy-faded, flower-print frock
and an old grey cardigan, shabby, on top
but she was wrapped round her purchase -
a take-away paper cone of a piece of batter fish -
the little wooden fork delicately feeding her
an O so welcome white flake piece - calmed anguish -
which, so pure so simple, she so relished;
firing up her empty furnace with food, steaming fish -
her eyes sad but her face alight with delight.
Moving on, I cracked-choked in the fading light.
This should not be - such poorness plight.
A sentence struck from her true full, not false meekness -
'Blessed are the poor for they shall see God' in warm gentleness.

I hope God sees her instead first. But how?
In her hunger through the hot fish here and now?
Is that sufficient? and not more? allowed anyhow?
Quite a few around had money, warmth, food -
but deprived, empty inside, buying to fill the vacuum -
walled off, complex, a diminished residuum -
scouring sad shops, toppling like skittles
from the ball shot of the credit crunching upheaval

- throttling the little people, brutal.

Jan 2009

The Pope in Cuba on TV

Has the Pope early Parkinsons -
walking - his arms stiff by his side?;
he's treated as a puppet
and lifted down steps
by his two aides -
elbow held -
his feet dandling in red shoes
as he pretends to down-step
each step in the air down the stairs;
a puppet on strings.
        Poor man.
        Vulnerable.
        Fragile.

May 2012

A simmering rushed non-poetic reply

to Mr. Alexander Pope correctly writing to his Physician
Dr. Arbuthnot
of his vicious state of mind in reply to the 'Sporus' slandering poem
of Pope.

Let Popery shiver. What? That slime of filth
Pope of popes, a purveyor of lies,
wizened, shrunken and extremely odd;
slit-eyed, virulent, foul-mouthed.
A writhing viper with hissing tongue,
vicious, venomed, a killer of men.
Maybe you have found and realize

this pumped up snake turns tail
and 'coupling' bites on himself
with poisonous spit -
he writhes and dies
in front of our listening eyes
to a sublime vile slug squashed.
Is backstabbing a cure for being back-stabbed?
Tit for tat, it has backfired.
I too am in guilt.
But is poetry no more
then clever coupling and rhyme?

A warty gossiping old woman shrew, malicious slandering,
vituperous, virulent victimizing and vain.
A vehement vengeful vandal, a vestige, full of vice.
A vampire, verbose verminous, swollen varicose, a veneer.
Vulgar villainous, vindictive violent vitriolic, a void.
The V's have it - thumbs down!

Elizabeth = Hebrew, Oath of god.
I have since discovered that Arbuthnot wrote to Pope that he was terminally ill. Pope replied to him with his vicious poem on 'Sporus'! Arbuthnot died 6 weeks later.
Pope felt that his poem was the 'best memorial of friendship'! (appalling) and his own character in reply to Arbuthnot's letter to him that he was terminally ill.
Where is compassion? ('Sporus' was Emperor Nero's male concubine).

A Sidewalk Poppy

A small toil
squeezed up
in dry ground
near a concrete path
among bare stump grass
and stone, poor soil.
Being crushed a threat -
unseeing people, giant grown;

or mown, machine down.

We stood amazed;
it's personhood -
a tiny wonder plant,
who blest our
simple seeing -
our seed sight sown.
They love to bloom
in crowds, we said -
joyful company over fields
in sheer bursting red floods.
But he, now, dares to offer
a few yellowed leaves,
a delicate bloom -
so threatened - on his own
in the then big world.

It doesn't matter now
so much - it did then -
it gripped my heart -
if he dies, is killed.
This imprisoning capacity
to know coming time.
His work is done,
like theirs in Flanders fields.*
He brought our bigness
to being little, with us -
mediation immediate.
His strife shines,
in glory he is lifted up;
no trumpets sound
but a soft ascending flute -
a feather.
Even less than a sparrow
falling to the ground - he;
the sound of a light breeze

*World War I.

gently weaving rustling leaves.

July 2002. Canterbury

Poppy Week

It's a hundred years since WW1 -
scenes everywhere over the air -
old shots of destruction, death,
trenches, the guns of wars.
And 'over the top' shot -
a real man falls dead
just like that - in front of our eyes,
amongst barbed wire thorns -
the act of murder alive -
chilling tears and chilled hearts.
The grief, agony, violence of it all
so much so that we go numb-dead inside.

Yet on the High Street
less than 5% of people
wear the blood red flower
of Flanders fields long ago -
to commemorate -
remember together now.
They have forgotten or don't know
or don't care at all or anymore.
So 'the war to end all wars'
is sunk denied, dead
and as such can again arise
in more done blood shed.
I fear the worst in shopping's blind rush -
with desire, mouths agape, wide eyes.

And yet, is it better to forget
such human horror mind-blown?
inglorious, the mud plugged mouths
and clotted shot holes

in poppy red lakes of blood
grown dark and cold.

And yet, Christmas is not far off
and less than 5% of street folk
remember or know
what that originally meant -
the birth of a human God-child
to be like us -
amongst straw and strife
to die on a cross strung bold
and to arise transformed.
The old story repeats itself.

Nov.2014

Porcupines and Crimes
(with thanks to D J Enright)

They curl up tight and shoot darts but my mother said 'eat sheeps brains and you'll be brainy'. That's why I baa-aa now and have overdud it!

Crimes:
Flesh oozing out of corsets
soggy poppadums
crinolined thoughts
litter louting gainers
cabbage ear listening.
Prattling priests
hawking snot bogeys
doublebind duffled talk and knit picking.
Spinning the doctors
mendicant doubleglazers .
Vacant beauty plucked eyebrows
macho men bragging lunch boxes.
Broad brimmed hats with false flowers
and gloved pink arms to keep them on.

Pontificating gridlocked parents
pink orange and purple together
perfumed women in the woods
spitting on the pitch
grouting chewing gum on the pavement.
Boring yapping mouths
unresponsive gits.
Skilling counsellors
the short straw
gushing silence.
Parading mobile phone self non-talk.
Pressing the star button, hash button 0,1,2,3,4,5,6.
Globulating warbling wobbly opera singers.
Leaving frightened children alone.
Antennae arms waving in a church
the words sin and sins.
meandering in zig-zag lines in the High Street.
Violation of UN security resolution 1441.
Floccinaucinihilipilification* *estimating things as if they are worthless
False water and food
Abuse of children.

the porcupine squeeked in delight and shot his squills
in Punishments.
'I like it, I like it' - he cried.

Push a toe up the nose
football gobstopping
quadratic equations
Gilles de la Tourette.
Shopping for necessaries
pessaries impaled.
balderdash quango
bare jean midriff in snow with belly button rings
quintessential cartwheeling.
Inhaling petrol
drowning in scent.
Hone down to the bone.

A splosh in the face.
Eczematous exfoliation
learning the telephone directory
eating others bogeys.
Wire brush skin scrubbing
Anencephaly.
Stuck in drying concrete
No laughing at all.
Bankruptcy per urethra.
Hair shirt combinations
tight shoes all day
be eaten by a whale.
Masticate stones.
Conjunction with the Iron Lady.
Tongue gritting black ice
licking dirty feet.
Mesenteric dysentery.
Millstone round the neck.
Getting to know you.
Deglutition of grubs.

'Yeah, wicked' - he said.
'Spin the world in spider webs and lay it gently in mothballs'.

Canterbury Feb 2003

He said there were no words to rhyme with 'orange' and 'silver'. So I'll have a bad go.

Romans pilfer silver on a site at Reculver
but there's only a flange of an orange arranged at Stone Henge
and an in situ quack said 'derange' so she squashed the silly
old orange!
Which, of course, stood for the quack as a monster.

And, of course, there aren't any.

Pork Scratchings

The sun is a manifestation of the supreme God
Pyramids have slit windows that the indestructable
soaring soul can reach the stars. Aten. So the
eyes - the lights to you, you switch on and off
(the steel visor helmet snaps shut) and not -
through the sharp sparks of your speech.
Seeing sometimes has nothing to do with anything -
reverie. We train our children to look out
instead of both - battering their brains and heart
with demand - to stop our frenzied collapse. But
a seeing-in strength, the crown post and tie beam
from solid oak. The weaving spindle
of choice where it can exist, if at all.
A flood foam of song - the pure bond loam
of our heart - sometimes rabid froth. Who we are takes
age to block - and find out - in our dry sand hour glass.
Lightning spasms in dark conjunctions form, primordial.
We must not be led by the compulsion thrust, (as we are),
of our past - or the tinsel now. Unstriving rest can be fertile.
Names words hold and reject. Are we more than
our obvious - windows moisture condensed?
Tender is tender and legal. But china ornaments of style
and dress and celebrity are broken easy. Though not now -
being made of concrete fast. Hope walks on red
hot coals already determined; living goes on
in temporary nil spurts as we cannot bear a nothing look.
I hold my unrest behind bars - emptied hands.
The hours are taken quietly out of the days
a fountain rise of yearning faith falls, the gripped suffocation
of trust in the throat within a crumbling home heart
as hope detracts from what already is - now.
(In paradise there is no hope, all is in light shown).
Words gurgle in the gutters, wedding petals thrown
fall trodden - but they floated in the air once.
We judge by the attractive paper wrapped
ribboned front, noble in our dreams and wants
scattered on the compost heap dump but

a butterfly trembles on a there giving tiny weed bloom.

He yawns after a good fiddle with his prickle -
while Rome burns - alone. Clubbing to chase the chicks
yelling to be heard above the pub din crowd -
and with voracious speed to chill out. Why?
The crunch of our scratchings here and now is
nothing like the sound trod on mussel bed rocks.

Canterbury April 2004

Sex in the City

A secret garden, private sanctuary
open for the public to share;
the centre heart of the city -
under the washing line there
a standing pair
near the rubble and monk's conservatory -
a grey-haired man,
flies undone
gropes her crack
up the crack folds
of her floral skirt, long;
she's middle-aged,
plump fair-haired, red faced,
looking at the unseen sky, dazed
in ecstasy, eyes closed
as she fly-fumbles his poke-firmed-flesh
while they cling with the nuptial pads of Natterjack toads.

I feel assaulted at this indecent exposure;
I am angry at this pornography
in the serene garden sanctuary -
an exposing exhibitionistic
lusting after parts of body parts
and not loving entire and whole
meant for love in a secret shared home,

warmed and transformed, two in one.

The garden was raped by a rape
under scented corner shrubs
by two deprived adolescents
under hormone bursts
unable to control
some six months past -
their past cursed.

The garden will survive
long after they are dead,
unless it transforms
to a rubble concrete jungle -
no choice but to go to die
to the centre of the circle -
under human neglect
with scorn sown.
When we discover where our enemy cries -
the rose offers it's scent to all who stop or pass
without regard or curse or sigh or fuss.

June 2007

Prawns
or How the Moon Got Bald -
a bedtime story for little Liz

Nonsense doggerel on the set words given of grandmother, never, buttons, bald, morning, sandwich.

Her grandmother (but never payed)
sewed buttons on his suit each day
each morning just at five she stitched,
each morning just at five she did -
pop this, pop that, snap far and wide
because he was so fat, he was

so fat he was, indeed so fat
he also popped his hairs so white
each one by one and everyone
till bald he did, enhanced, become
indeed so bald his pate became.

A sandwich on a plate lay light
so neatly cut of bread so white
with ham and prawns and sauce and egg -
a snack for gran between the thread
to munch at ease between the snaps.
But then one day she sickened mad
the Doctor he was called so fast.
It was the sandwich prawns she had
it was the sandwich prawns so bad
they made her mad they made her sad -
she tore her hair so vast, so fast
she pulled her locks so hard in haste
that none was left. So bald. At last.

They both were made as one
by the light of the silvery moon
and moon, now bald as well, did smile
till all the earth was one.

Canterbury Oct. 2002

Prayer

Let me throw my weight
Tonned, full force
Hurled caught
Strength withstood
To Thee - not them;
Let me know
Lifeline clasped, grasped
Mine - deep, secure.
Your love, concern

Arrow pointed, sad
In need of me
At my rejection -
'Why hast Thou rejected me?'.
In part I know rejection
That the reason
I trust Thee - if poor.
It's this -
Steel needle wavering
Between nought and
A hundred miles an hour;
Trough and crest
Pinnacle and pit
At such rapid rate - shot.
Now permanent pit
I hate you - God;
You deny that which I crave
A human god, a lap
A mother - on which
To lay my head.
You take he who was close
Priest in me
Cross speaker, Christ.
Confuse, conflict
Cauldron stirred up
Once more.
Pulled from these I know -
These leagued in
Surface, glib and joke
Gibed, anaemic mice
In holy huddles;
Pulled apart to two poles
He for me
Sincere, solid flesh
No jargon, depthed;
Breadth of mind and shoulder
hair newly cut
Tired, admired
Driven, consumed by One
Close yet infinite, remote

In trust such as I have not;
Trust experienced in flesh
Easier then in spirit got.
Rejected - again approached
Thrown out, short of word.
This all brought to God.
God, God
Accept me
Need me, value this
Friable finite
Fractioned, shivering
Mind split, cold -
Twisted, inverted
Thrown in on itself.
Yet because You take -
A cry reverberate
Stabbing - convulsed
At the Christ.

date, late '65 Cape Town

Prynne notes.

loose rein on quite the wrong horse
killed steel still curved at a glance
points failure
sweet vernal abcission.
averting trembled fermentation
be gentle be just
tree, - tunes
scan, quantum, absconding, lazy
affection is a kind of fruitfulness arranged around a core
morning estuary
ruin (rains down)
polar bear packs propped on the escalator
vertex, good grief
the air flip icing at sunrise
those who see what they can't eat
scale of colours

axes are ground back (swords ground down)
natural flavour
take what you get, go anywhere and strictly come back with nothing
false danger triggers waste fear
jittered like spring water
nerve and verve broke for lunch and were gone (
good green things
the first anvil of entry
the blue line of mental illness
lime slurry
buttered the throat
wait to lick the spoon
all the hedges are paid for (streets)

Psalm 151.Cantate. To The One
(with apologies to King James and to those past and present; after those who have said it before).
'Sing unto the Lord a new Song' (Psalm 149).
'Make a joyful noise unto the Lord' (Psalm.100).

1. Our Father which art Nourisher Guide Protector,
beyond and before and In all gender
Incarnate, immanent, immense, the Now eternally forever;
the Beginning in the Now and in every now, without before or after.
The Being above and in all being, being before becoming and time.
The toward and with and in and inbetween all creation.
The thingness Thouness essence of all essences.
The I Am of all our I ams. Thou art therefore we are.
Thou art so I am. Without any journey or ascension - we are.
2. Protect us from all minishment, diminishment
Who was and is now, and is forever; who both is and is not.
Who shuts and opens the door of our understanding
according to his desire; who is unitedly diverse - the universe -
as a body is one yet many its parts.
3. Behold uncreate Him who creates the theatre cosmos
for his and our amazement, interest and delight;
the director-producer Alpha and Omega, the cast - angel comets,
asteroids, shooting stars, the flaming fire of sun and Son

fractals, galaxies, infinitesimal particles; matter because it matters.
The shining ones - costumes designed by Light.
4. The replenishing terror of volcano, magma magnificent -
and awesome storm; nebulae, space and time, so immensely grand;
the changing quakes of earth's fearful crust,
ceaseless unchanging change with no end.
Incomprehensible - He garments it all with dark and light
and showers us with songs symphonies and lullabies,
rippling streams and white water rivers. O see - ah.
Even the tiny cased pupa metamorphosing to a butterfly, lifted up.
In nature's most secret folds - the God plays. Everything is God.
5. And more magnificent than all these - our consciousness
before and in the convolutions of the brain(which receives our mind)
and its galaxies of neurones, millioned - above all angel splendour;
the small spiral of a snail, helical DNA somersaulting.
And in our slow snail spirit in our littleness, feeling, spiralling -
resonating the evolution of the universe slowly becoming.
6. Bless the Lord O my being, who answers my turmoil
with the slow response of his patient people;
who understands my roaring rage of a lion
and impetuous haste of an unreined horse.
Who hears my cry of desolation in silence.
His tender mercy comes like the Samaritan - and as gentle dew -
and not that of a false judge. He gives thoroughly in pardon,
and in forgiving - gives before. Not the experience - but the Event.
7. Who hast the power of thunder, the speed of lightning
and the grace of flowing water - superabundant;
behind and in all bubbling, laughing and moving,
the twinkling of an eye; in all sadness and weeping magnanimous.
The music in all things resonating in Thy people -
their resonance between - of sweet sounding strings,
singing bowls, rippling flutes and thunderous drums.
The wind in our face, that very wind which blows where it desires
and cooled the countenance of Christ - the same, the Spirit -
in the parched desert sandaled dust. Divine disclosure revealed.
The very wind who brushes the grass hair
on wild dune tussocks and moorland slopes.
Who is the soft innocence of morning sunshine
and the evening sunset of evensong wisdom - blood red.
8. Our God is Comfortable in the temple of man's soul,

the ground of existence, Prompting us to be free
of fear - hidden or open - as naught is free,
Nice Naught, as nothing is, and God in his Something
with his hands outheld to hold, safely and gently enfolds, holds
as Christ clears the clutter of fear of our strange within guests;
the labour not ours alone but shared in the meeting of people -real.
9. The Father who came down to meet us, His family,
when we were far, far off. And we who are made in his Image.
Who loves us before we ever loved him - as Friends not servants.
Whose delight is In us, who bends down to feed us and takes us up In
his arms and lifts us up as a little child to His cheek;
who crowns us with his soft mercy and lifts up the light
of his countenance for us - In the very same of people good.
10. He takes our yoked burden when we stumble and fall.
The Inbetweeness of the Spirit between people.
The Betweeness between the smiling eyes of mother and child.
And In our fragile soft weakness and rainbow tears
before our true strength and power. We are not known to ourselves.
Who is the Word, who is Truth which is one,
who is Light and DeLight and Life and Love.
11. The redeemer of the past through the present presence
of love, trust, faith and hope in and for us - of good people.
Before we loved He loved us. The Eloi* - a vulnerable God
and In the very Cry of crucified Christ on the cross, horror, Nought-
the purity of untransformed horror - absolute;
and In our cry. The Christ - the only incarnate
passionate living God, the only bound God.
The only vulnerable nailed killed God - who knows Ours;
the soothing Balm to our pain - healed; and through
his decreed Resurrection, so our Transformation - ours.
12. Our weakness is as the still reed bending in the breeze,
pliable with vulnerable strength; and woven strands
together are rope - strong.
The straight still lithe bamboo - waiting for the wind
to touch and enkindle among its leaves and stems - whispering song.
After such Love and Truth and Beauty and Goodness
and Light and Delight and Life and beyond all understanding -
with no end to the things to be said
He is and was and shall be the only ultimate Peace and Rest.
The All in all. Real. Free. Profoundly Simple.

The One.

*'Eloi, eloi, lama sabachthani?' - 'My God, my God, why hast Thou forsaken me?
Mark 15:34

Canterbury Jan 2003.

In Honour of My Puddy Pudding Cat
What the Queen taught him.
apologies to the nursery rhyme
All are worthy of honour which means respect and worth

Puddy cat Puddy tat where have you been?
I've been to London to visit the Queen.

Puddy cat Puddy tat what did you there?
I was met at the entrance and climbed palace stairs.

Puddy cat Puddy tat where is the Queen?
Right there before me giving me cream.

Puddy cat Puddy tat what happened then?
I was lifted and cosied, purring again and again.

Puddy cat Puddy tat what happened next?
Home in heaven I am honoured, treated with respect.

Puddy cat Puddy tat who is now your Queen?
Lady Elizabeth of Spirallings on whose pillow I lean, preen
or kneel on the window sill, content with friends serene
then such greetings all round on her homecoming keen.

Puddy cat Puddy tat how does that feel?
Ever so lovely, happy, thrilled and real.

Puddy cat Puddy tat - such a tall tale to tell;
simple, homely and down to earth as well.

Me for she, lovable soft revealed.
And yes, she for me, gracious healed.

Apr 2008

Puddy is my pudding shaped round toy cat - 8 inches in diameter - with stumpy paws and a soft tail and an expressive changing face.

The Puppeteer

Acknowledging fragility, vulnerability
to what, to whom - the vacuum-
burning fear like scalded skin;
this alienation, isolation of being alone -
walking the streets tensed
and head down.

But there in the square
with autumn leaves on the ground -
a little older man, simple and sound -
floppy hat, old loose clothes,
bright smiling face -
twinkles in his eyes abound -
played the two busker puppets
with their violin and drum
to background fiddle tunes around
set in a farmyard scene.
Children, magnetised, draw in
watching wide-eyed -
hands out, reaching for the scene,
prams and parents behind.

Their simple curiosity and delight
alighted mine.

For a moment I was with them, not alone.
Yes, being simple in the moment gave peace
and I walked tall and proud then on.

I took 'winning' for granted before
but I'm not good at it now.
It's refreshing to find others the same -
a shower of relief
dowsing the insistent achievement
drum beat.
Not to do but nobler to be.
I am that I am, now.

Nov.2014.

Quatrain in 5 minutes

Where now the bath is empty
and ne'er a tub tap flows,
in an abandonned bathrobe
a naked she arose.

Canterbury Nov 02

A Question 2?

'Doesn't everything die at last, and too soon?'
asked Mary Oliver in her poem 'The Summer Day'.
'Yes' I say, dying scared now already
but relief at being dead.
How so? As when I'm dead I won't know relief
but I may in the arms of God?
And again - 'yes'
with ruminations of how I'll die -
the worst horrors
gnawing away

like a locust swarm.
What anti-dote to all this doom and gloom?
        Learning how to let go, patience
                and simple trust.

Oct 2013

A Quick Lesson

A young priest, white collared - in black
beamed around with sanctimonious smiles
at the waiting Cathedral crowd -
humming with happy communion talk

His shoe toe caught clicked
in the cobbled forecourt cast.
He forward lurched at thirty degrees
and nearly face fell.
The silly smile became -
a serious care.

Who's at work here?

Canterbury Mar.2004

Raw Fractured Reality to Raw Rage. damn you - can't you see I exist

As the Buddha proclaimed - all unhappiness stems from desires,
needs and wants?

Blast mere existence, a shit-life bastard
born by some god who's absent - guilt, gilt-glazed -
who never was present; ugliness' acrid daze;
who inbuilt in all - heaven's azure gaze
yet we only exist to die - if at all,
a fantasy prevalent - seeing a prison garden far,
the prisoners only see behind bars.

Analysis' vision is worse than blindness -
time and time again rubbing my face
in that common seen experience I never had at base
or had little and now discover first
and at this stage will never have. In thirst
I keep open doors in case, in trust, in interest -
yes, I go out to find - and find swamped
thickness hardness dullness stamped;
a community absent yet pretending it, up-pumped.
The old abandoned to sludge in beaten chairs
between the slats, between ribs racks wracked - afraid
Shut your shit, fuck your gobs with your lips
of scarlet and puckered plastered pasted faces;
die down in shrunken shrivelled fragments.
Enough is sufficient; the best suffer bent
to dream of some homeland huddled place
shielded safe from destiny's fate.
Idiots fools - yeah-yeah-bang-break
on your base enhanced speakers in heat -
an unconnected absurd response pulse beat,
party clubbing in booze and drugs -
wicked cleavages, cool brill to drool; thugs
let your trousers fall off your arses;
buy consume natter litter, money-mad excesses.
In furious curiosity entire, I must preserve
in private, people absent - my unknown assets
in imagination's sparkling streams serene made
and green leafed cool glades and shades, unafraid
within this concrete people-jungle - the herd
whose fracturing talk reverberates; nerds
yelling pleading drumming booming
heavy metal, rock, pop goes the weasel
like their music of metal. 'It so is' - ruin, wreck
all twisted of steel mind muscle, violence, sex.
This litter of scorn - decisions close the gates.
Made by the gods, destroyed by the same in hate.
A paper scrap is the same in any city in any street -
flotsam I am - swirled in dry sand, no roots in scorched heat,
searching for a home, lame, maimed without a name.

This quicksand desert where strange bright-eyes flame

July 2008

Rainstorm

What's messing my emotions? -
feel the downstorm of fear
and carry on with it anywhere
even if we get lost and drenched;
and sometimes we may lose as well -
but accept that too.
It's time to say hello
to the destructive tapes in my mind -
of inferiority, being abnormal, deficient,
guilty, dying unfound isolate,
disabled or dead of a heart attack;
toothless, sightless, deaf,
friendless, without kin or kith;
fear is at the bedrock base
of all this in this dark dank room.
But these are just fearfull tapes
of muddy, confusing thought, widely agape.

Under this I stand
no shelter at hand;
head high-held;
I am of value valued, I hope -
I am whole me
as I watch these tapes -
thoughts as clouds storming across.
I once chose to run in a rainstorm -
thunder and lightning around -
and gloried in the drench and floods
with the scent of soaked earth
long ago in London's Primrose Hill.

But one can't do this all the time

or concentrate on current chores.
I need to find shelter in what I have learnt
and find any good - to balance -
and some firm, no-nonsense words
in the distraction of 'time-out'
as well as tuning in,
in the awareness of 'time-in' now
and to notice any ease and content
however small
which is usually rapidly drowned out.

July 2012

Red Red-emption

Crimson pools of blood
passion congealed iridescent,
velvet dark-wine ground-grapes
deep down the dark gourd well,
dense rage clots red -
in rage - gelatinous, viscid.

I swelled my bunged lungs,
inhaled inspired fire
which fire-balled fast
and shot to my crackling heart
till I had ashed the split night-sky.

'This is my body and life' -
dough-white brain bread
dipped in the wine blood
crusts and crags of my heart -
Given .... vulnerable helpless
in individuating tenderness.
My eyes have seen
too much dying and dead.

Learning again to belong -
I need a small warm language
for the little me which died,
stoppered, dunked down dead.

Stinging rain tears,
a wellspring to healing well,
drenched the rage out
to sodden soil mud
autumn iron red
Was it fruitful at last - a fallen windfall?

Temporality that ticks in age's warp on the backs of every minute.
That old infinity of freedom against fractured finitude -
the former in dreams conjunction oneness resonance
like a ring dove easily flows, not flies, blown in a west wind flight
or the unimpeded circling of soaring thermalled birds in delight.
There is no abstract transcendence, idea, thought first. Insight -
homely bread and wine convey the abstraction 'community'
shared in essence. It's the body and things physical - first.
Skin hunger's comfort in touch contact. We are risen 'touched'.
Seeing, listening, creating, the 'word' the 'sound' -
Sanskrit -'I cause to be performed', I- in the hands of the living god.
Only 'love' and 'art' can liberate.

July 2008

Redemption

Quite often the young are all alike
but age with its chiselled face is carved.
Undoing the done to -
the taking atoned acquired back
making whole again at one.
Long in the tooth youth.
Not the blasphemous 'original sin' and guilt induced
'he died to forgive our sins' done and done again -
elevated by angelic indifference; but - he lives

and died to aid us in the way - now known -
the benefit of his passion.
And a child held the right way -
not up side down by disaster, blind mal-intent
and old, so cold before its years grown spent -
appalling loss. Acid in the eye.
Our feeling is oxygen to the heart
which can be an impossible
fanned flame ignited, blown
or the rain slanting with wind
the pupil moist; or the heart encased in ice.
And a breathing warm light stronghold
under the cloak of delicious tenderness
a homecoming repast with music - the sound of the soul;
a safe sounding order steadfast -
though stenched and sunblind
as a miner trapped found
out of a collapsed coal face - done to, not done.
That aweful image of abandonment
dereliction despair - fixed immaculate,
with no cry no word. Air-brushed out of life.
Time tears at us as the sound of torn tissue, shred.
We draw blood, blood the seeping soul
when we talk. Toxic gits insensitive to the frail -
both starved of real love - wounds -
the only marks those eyes - deep hidden scars.
Most children cruel-chase street pigeons
scrapping for scraps - something smaller
than themselves to intimidate as they have been done to so.
How the years fog the now
as you wrench open our
delicate oyster flesh, firm shelled
with a blunt short knife gripped
and down it - in an upturned gulp
with bread and wine celebrant! Theology.
Instead, he simply said 'This is me for you'.
Living gently holds
the skull rise of dying -
that last horrible journey
which may be an exciting adventure

if it led to a love-ly place.
'Dying to live...' as I wander
among their bare bold bones.
I will not be polite now.
To those harmed, 'he died to forgive sins'
are empty hollow horrible telegram words
Instead - it is a long hard work.
The matter is serious. Salt.
And rind squirts oil from zest;
ionic poles of those hated now loved
by a rare new one other alongside blest -
an immanent intimately close place with secret space
unforced pace - for gestation - destruction and growth;
a sour spasm where the past sloughs off -
a new raw delicate trust - embraced. No disgrace.
The search for the magnetism of bliss caressed -
distress duress repressed retraced embraced
a dream in the eye realised, regressed,
returned, fertile rest, redressed, carekissed -
commonly masquerading as drugs violence and sex -
with our tectonic plates, seismic basic faults
earthquakes interfaced transgressed - manifest.
The earth is borderline psychotic
breaking apart with inner tumult -
a macro microcosmic base. Like us.
Lava is rich but dangerous - unsafe.

As *Yeshua descended into hell to 'be with ..'
Judas - (his friend) without whom, what then?
Mostly the real deep search
is equivalent to breast-fed, bosom-held grace
blest, but cusps and straps bind them up tight
as we skim over the milk of paper tits thrust out -
a breastplate of false power and might
People have clothes, little skin is real to air, fresh.
Naked the nipple to the mouth unclothed - 'naive need'
basic, open, gentle, simple-fed, honest. Held
Peace - where the soul is light. Shown essence.
The grand pyramid, golgothan hellhill, bosom-rise;

the ascension place -
forwards from the within tombwomb,
a new present from an old past.
Get the felt drift?
A great troublesome task.

*Yeshua- the Aramaic name for the
hard contaminated word 'Jesus'

Canterbury April 2004

from 'Remember' by Joy Harjo

'Remember that you are this universe and that this
universe is you'.

C.G.Jung when asked if he believed in a god
replied 'I don't believe I know'
so I too know that I am of this universe
with such deep delight done
and the philosophy theology psychology physics
that is my inscape.
Yes I have deeply known all along
despite religion's cry that 'I am not worthy
to eat the crumbs under Thy table'.
I am in You and You in me -
made in the image of God
not in foul 'Original Sin'
This Big Bang universe
formed so long long ago
forming the forces and elements formed -
universal laws.
My iron magnesium manganese, and all
photons and forces have come from that
first explosive unimaginable 'bang' -
such a little word, such a big sound.
WOW.
The grunt of language before the Word.

Respite

It's very still - sitting on the stoep
Sitting for some hours now
In sunset at seven
It was even then - a Greecian heat
Drinking golden apple juice in sparkling glass
With chunks of cheese and fruit
Aglow and vibrant - tanned
Tracing the tributaries
The veins of my hand are full
Blue and hot.

The shrubs are green, the stoep red
The grass a green carpet
With jacaranda splash -
They are still falling
In breeze
Sprung slight and soft -
At an angle. Deep
In those trees there's cool black -
The walls and sky blue -
It really should be painted.

You see - I'm trying to extract
Maximum to what is there
Quiet Buddhist intensity - leaf looking
I haven't got the capacity
To know this experience for myself
And remain content.
By myself - yes easier
Incongruous company loud voiced
Shatters and distracts.
Others must share
But they are caught up
Icelandic islands alone
In their own unique experience -
paradox
Unbalanced a hundred to one

It works both ways
As I - quiet - upset and disturb
Their spirit of good cheer.

The corner street lamp has been repaired
So it is not as black
As night was the night before.
The two cats are with me
And in part we share -
One is near -
Incomplete in whole
His black merges with the night
Dividing night from the white in sight
In just curling tail and paws,
Face, whiskers and dinner jacket front.
Sense organs flickering intense
Alert for strike or defence.

The scene one of movement now
And colour tone
In every lilting tone of black.
Little sound to distract.
I light a match
Snatch a breath
And puff it out
Then blindness for a second.

The street lamp tingles
With light the leaves silver
And the trunk in front
Tries to hide its straight iron post.

Nothing in nature is straight - it flows
And curves in rhythm;
My living is wrong here
It has no sine wave of season -
Hesitant - yet it will.

There are shadows too

But these tonight are more significant
Than shadows past
A whisper of wind teases the leaves,
There's some sheet lightning
In Eastern infinitude
And three large fruit bats flit
Circling the lamp
Staccato like in vision and out
No form visible - not solid
Light lash alone, second settling in
The wild plum tree across the way.
No passer has noticed
A secret shared between cat and I.
So an old man passes
And hawks at his throat -
I expect him to spit
But he doesn't
Continuing his way.
Humans and machines intrude
And shatter the scene -
Another problem now
Of how
To weave this thread
In now the night's cool
Depth of experience.
A pair of boots - metal clipped
Of duckie boy passing
His boots not him.
A chiton coated beetle buzzes
Dazed, crashed to the white light
On the wall behind
And has fallen on his back
Buzzing, trying to right.

Queenie cavorts in circles
On the lawn - chasing
Falling flowers.
Pixie disappears, later to return
With a grasshopper

For me at my feet
And I leap
As it lunges toward.
Tranquility tossed
heart beat increased
But also amused.
It whirrs sluggishly, drunkenly
For height.
Two pairs of eyes - corneal glints
White whiskers up - follow
But gone.
Silence in movement there.

Sea tang comes up -
Wind whistling freshens
To rain tomorrow
From sun and heat.

65 Rondebosch Cape Town shared flat

P.S. Wish I had some of this now and the many years past.

Life Giver, A River Heart

'I behold London - a human awful wonder of God' W. Blake 'Jerusalem'

London's name, obscure origin, no surety of known meaning like that of the divine

Great strength - the river Thames
a holy noble, lusty regal river
greater than London was, ever
unwordable uncontained
glowing face eyes aflame -
exuberant exhilarant, shining current
impetuous pace magnificent presence
the rhythm of unrelenting flow in abundance;
splendid immediacy, full of light and dark
and life and world, Word and heart.

In the beginning the river was
and the river was with God
and the river was in the heart of God;
with no river, no city ever was;
All great cities were born near water shores
the root and flower of culture, civilisation and word;
scuttling thronging hurrying faceless crowds
intent on futures or on the night bridges despairing from the past
with no inner life-water, water was and is life -
water was of the divine, to people a gift enough.
This great rolling river, ignored in the illusion of time
fast flowing pulsing, welcoming allowing
flooding, life-loving, the spring of life sublime;
aortic arterial magnetising mesmerising,
flamed like sheets of gold reflecting the gold of sky.
River music of flow, engines, scaffolds, buildings poking the sky -
of millionaire apartments bank-lining by flooding money-minds,
built up banks, asthmatic, the river wheezes froths and coughs,
mighty monarch flood troubled breast strapped, bound.
Our Father who art in old father Thames also
who used to be in part one mile wide
and in winter, heavily iced over.
A long liquid story, birthing little lives
who try to tame and train the Thames
polluted him, blocked up his sides;
just as, without respect, we block our lives,
heart tributaries hard walled -
and now rainfall is unreaborbed
and who put barrier valves in his mouth -
those glinting steel helmets come down
and the great tonned visors rise
kingdom's beacons to hold back the sea tide
as the world warms and sea levels rise
and England's south east corner tilts down
following the last Ice-Age long ago gone.

Yet this great heart where again life-alive, strives, survives -
graced swans and glinting salmon revive, rise and thrive -
the river releasing with relief, distilled at last

rich brown torrents high flowing fast
and the floods of the plains around ease -
just as folk need the same in their lives - these
the fast flooding worlds of heart and mind.

But still and in stillness dark stick-figures leaning
on the twenty bridges spanning our inner living -
tiny blobs of a few people daze, dreaming -
water-birth meditating, our ebb and tide flowing,
lost and found in another world of essence, quiet -
being found in our unknown rich brown silt end heart -
our blood coursing as the river blood runs.
And Great Parliament on Westminster bank won
democracy's first, the pacemaker pump of the country's heart.

Strong Thames flow swiftly to ease our flood plain pain -
the river carries that which is and ever was -
the transcendent found in the ordinary Now to ordain
the recognition of That which gently calls to be known in us.

at the time of the floods 2007-2008

The River's Sermon

Hope is a state of tension
unresolved, a yet ungiven,
a waiting in confidence
which means absent with.

Greed is really a gr(eat n)eed -
a weed eat'n by expiring want.

Peace is hope fulfilled in love
I hesitate with that felt latter word
- the conduit for it. It's a word right,
right in the centre-heart of the altar
altering all.

Peace is ultimate, the litmus paper indicator
of all that has gone before and the now
and of confidant dreams
aspiring inspired together.

The great willow tree waxed stiff-frozen, its
drooping fronds symmetric at 15 degree angles
unmoved under the East wind.
(I swear it was like that last winter)
But the fronds in water-air ripple free now -
in mustard Spring yellow;
'Clocks change - Spring forward' - spring;
then green in summer.
That great river Canterbury Stour
wandering dreaming wondering
flowing full under the little bridges
of communion between its peopled sides,
arching stick-like up the white horizon against the light;
bridge under bridge under bridge receding
as hope is diminished and undone.
And under the weir locks great hunks
of black-chocked, cog-wheeled metal
of our defence and control - part open -
bulks turbulent torrents - jowled corpulent
and chowked - bellies of silver water -
the mass of our overwhelming passion and hope
for all the blue-print aspiration unrealised
towards the good created in us God-wise!
Music water - sometime serene and gentle, sometime urgent
overflowing turbulent tumultuous longing desolate.

Jammed logs, sticks, water weeds needing to be cleaned
lest the banks flood as our closure opens.
A stately mallard duck, sartorial splendour in his emerald cap
- he takes on the river's might under lock
as he trusts his inherent buoyant float -
to the still side-water by the bank for rest and a snack.
I laugh. Can we be like that - decisions confidant in letting go?
Flotsam - trusting our water to keep us up.

In the park 3 massive tree stumps have been carved
from the Great Storm of 1987 dead done -
a face, flowing hair, mouth and fish appear
ghostly out of the wood - forms inbuilt.
That is what we aspire to become - simply carved
out of destruction without too much effort
- what under, truly is.

And there, secretly down a yew conduit hedge opposite
rests a quiet sunfilled old brick nook, warm bench
and blossom trees so delicate and light.
Perhaps we have also such within, out of the torrent life.
I sit quiet in reverie and rest - a blue plastic bag
eases slowly to greet me in the gentle chuckling breeze -
so disturbed by a refuse man's claw metal hand killing it
in his deep black bag. Cruel life. The wrench hurts
as I greeted blue bag's approach - 'hello and...
.
There is no straight line riverflow except
at the flood water man-made side-step locks.
We learn to flow and are flowed - sometimes wandering
wondering waiting, sometimes stagnant -
sometimes joining confluent concordant resonant -
fast, quiet or slow.
The river does not know where he goes. He just is -
a myriad state - like us.
And I am dazzled by the sun on the fast ripple sounds
scintillating shimmered symphonic quartet notes -
my eyes naturally with ease with them unfixed flow.
I am dizzy when my eyes stop fixed and stare straight
at the quavered quiver sparkles straight ahead
on top of the fast flickering water bulk.
There is no stopping in life except at the edge.
Flowing days will end the pain somehow.

But here's a faint flash feeling glimmer -
I might be other remembered and felt -

also a quiet water.

Canterbury Mar.2004

R.M.S. Edinburgh
Castle line

The day we left the other behind
And acceleration to 808
And one's guts on the ground floor
And those first steps round the corner
To your warmth and little book, wise man and flower
And the kiss you gave
And my arms laden in a brown cloak, excited and fear.
I talked to the taxi driver, determined -
A big man with dandruff, an old car and time meter
We laughed of diamonds and hidden gold.
I want to remember - why - that agony
Underplaying in exaggeration
The word is not right, word water, water word
But it hurts very much - underplaying unemphasised
because I know you know and you understand
My lack of trust.
People looking at the sea for words at writing tables.
The baggage man at the docks was Afrikaans and old
Among pine wood boxes. He had been kind by 'phone
And work mates at Groote Schuur -
people were separately important
Close - as they had not been before
And this tonned steel bolted hull
Heaves in Cape rollers
The Table grey, sad and gulls reel
And those words heave and lurch and pitch and roll
Great sea cuts and swerves
And curves blue black foam topped
That this monster can be swayed
And metalled - object.
The split of apple skin teeth cutting white on deck

Varicose veins and bunyoned sandalled toes
Browning in oil.
Get out of my forceful sight
The cut and curve
Of wave and tern swerve
And sun - wind piped.
There's a time and a place
For broken tongues and memories past
But not this
And the urge of word upon word
Wrung from a piece - a jagged fragment cut.

I met two Cockney chums, the one with no neck
His tie curved out as a consequence
'You must saw through the crust
Before you reach sweet dough' he said
And I tried on my Mae West and blew my whistle attached.
Decisions must float on their backs
As you open both hands in informed assent
So I talked to a missionary philosopher
Trained in the quadrangles of ancient halls and Thomist incense.
Of the Mountains of the Moon
And ninety nine people fit in one life boat
As he offered sugar lumps.
A quiet voice said
Don't lose yourself in sherry
And lemonade cigarette stumps.
The little clerk in checked hacking tweed
And facial tick said he couldn't meet girls
With a mouth of grey teeth
And the engineer became glass eyed
As he travelled in many ships to many places
And his soul throbbed to the heart of turbo engine props
In the bellies of ships.
And Bristol cream tones
Tittled across the front of mouths.
The full fleshed, lacquered, eye lashed
Raven black haired, fluorescent, lipped
Over stitched, easy sexed

Sang songs and was a buyer for a boutique
And Robert, her Yank, rolled up drunk
Among silver spoons, threw glasses
And tried sipping his soup
And Bob was a sky diver with Irish words.
Big Bob gave brandy and champagne, black witch -
Rather my stomach a grinding pit.
I can play no part - no fancy dress
As the steel ribs groan and crack at night
And engine shafts turn
And I turn alone in a bunk of 4 in vacant lots
While they dance behind masks.
And your orchid at the porthole
And bee and green flask
Sip sea spray, twice signed.
With age this pain may calm, it creates and destroys.
Crepe susette classics treacle out
And the horizon goes up and down
And I have fallen for the bearded engineer
And people live on memories in the corner of the lounge.
The crew watch and no one knows
How to talk among many words
The lacquered lady stuffs a banana
Down the coat of the Yank as he shouted blue murder
Before not after and evil became rank.
He lectured, went to dark Africa
Talked of war, lived for pleasure
And teased your system of thought
Which you then found unsystematised and unthought
At the University of Minehaha or something.
A cathedral goes down in the sea
And a girl smokes a pipe.

Forced to play this game of words between mouths
My unspoken speech and people laugh unlaughing
Full of despondency and sickness and no longer
They have thrown themselves knowing
And I have thrown myself into living too much.
This tendency to terrorise

And I would wish to throw up and live in riot
And seven more days in this ship hole at twenty two knots
And so many fathoms and so many faces too close.
Entertainment organised
As if authorities feared for total disintegration.
And two old ladies unstopping talk
With black ribbons round their throats.
I saw a paederast at the pool
And big fatherly Bill turned down my collar neatly
And Cynthia too, infertile from secondary tubercule
But fertile in anxious words
And her absent husband with a passion for yachts
And bearded Big Bob, hypomanic at times
With a flow of amusing, at times poetical words
And Chris grey toothed and ticking
Is divorced with three blond kids and a vintage Rolls
But the bearded engineeer was the one for me
And he shaved his beard for my infertile friend
And sky diver Bob, bald and sunburnt.
They converge as a spittoon for their purulent words.
The Rev. and Mrs. over triangle sandwiches and lettuce
With two months leave every five years and dark eyed.
The insight and outsight without acceptance.
I've come to a prescription - a concoction of permitted rot
Taken help, no fusion, written word and routine tasks
Four times daily in divided doses.
You and he cannot possibly entertain
The idea of possibly missing me
Prevent the pill, wear a blown up condom on your hat.
The ships shopkeeper plopped
A fat cold hand on the engineers
Who could never forget.
I bite my thumb staring
The sun orb blows as an orange wind balloon
The stewardess told of her brother drunk to death
And of human animals below in the bilges
And the Captain, the Supreme at ports.
Dong dong dongle ding - two children sing
The disher-outer and dispenser of dreams
The docks with people - dirty washing bleaching in the sun.

I sit in a corner chair listening
A suck of cigarette
'Cocked up are ya' - a bar steward and giggling youth
And the paederast has his pool trunks pulled
By tearing friends with growing groins.
Browned, the steward said he'd fetch her
Wide and high from the dance.
'How are the white holes in your stomach dear?'
The platinum blond with coloured curlers in her hair
Netted like the inside of a transistor set.
The sea wind is with us
And the davits crack above
And flying fish fly in spurts
And the engineer - a temperature of 136 F.
'I don't want to remember it'
Calloused hands, crude treacle oil
Grained and scarred
'The sweat dripping off your bum in pools'
My head cooled in spray, very close, lapelled
Big chest. The nicest thing he ever said to me
Retching clear, he kissed me
Tasting acid which he said was sweet
Tender and I as I am and was and ever shall be.
Las Palmas and sea legs, pesetos
Fried prawns and octopus tentacles
Wine and rum cracked pavements and carapace
The lighthouse at flash per seconds, veins blood heavy
No content unless the inside matches the outside. God.
This conflagration in the groin with a thought
Then I wrote no more lying long hours in dark
And Bill opened the porthole on blue.
Coming up the Solent was my first England on either side.
From the South to the North and land was brown and green here too.
I thought there was no land
Just cities and towns crowded close
As plovers piped overhead.
Take my soul sir, I am - not broken
But the Thomist on deck talked of God and perfection
While the sun rose
And my soul flapped in my brown cloak -

Wind stirred.

7-19 August '68, Atlantic Ocean

RRH Children's Court
in the middle of the forest

Prosecutor Tuff Jo. (17 years).
'State your full name and address to this court, gathered together for the small people'.

Defendant Old Wolf. (infinite years).
'I am the ghost of Old Wolf in Red Riding Hood Valley and I hold my cut head in my arms. I am of no fixed abode. I long to be fixed but that is unghostly. Little Red Riding Hood's father axed my head off when I was about to gobble her up after eating her Granny'.

Prosecutor Tuff Jo.
'Why did you eat up Granny in her bed, in her very own house so near the woods when she trusted you with your false squeeky voice and told you how to get in by pulling the door bobbin which lifted the latch? Speak your case.'

Old Wolf.
'I 'had eaten nothing for a long time and was very hungry..' I was too 'old' and weak of limb to be able to hunt and catch mice, rabbits, lizards and beetles. It was too good a chance to miss and a good thing Red Riding Hood dallied picking flowers and nuts in the forest and made posies and chased butterflies. I watched her for a bit from behind a dark tree then limped off to Granny's cottage. If she hadn't dallied, she would have been eaten too - before her father later came and saved her. And Granny was 90 years old and bed ridden and far too trusting; and I was starving - so I ate her. She is now in heaven and safe at last, not alone in her bed at the edge of a dark wood. And Red Riding Hood has learnt a sharp lesson - not to trust false appearances. She has grown in wisdom and stature.
Now I wander, and appear as a reminder, whenever a child gets into

near danger'.

There was a murmuring amongst the younger gathered children but they felt safer together. (There were some mums and dads there too.) They were afraid of this old ghost and his appearance but they remembered how he had helped jog their memories and alert them to impending danger.

Judge Jenny (20 years).
'Do you think that is a just dessert for your crime?'

Old Wolf.
'yes M'Lud. I killed and I was killed but more than that, I now serve a useful purpose. All should know that any old, weak, meat-eating animal turns on weak or little people out of starvation and despair. And something similar happens in principle with humans. The worm can turn in deprived folks. But you should know not to be deceived by false sweet words. Even now, these very words maybe sweet. I say - you must put down firm, strong roots in the gathering of a warm, understanding family - as strong as the strength delivered to me by that axe. Though I doubt the validity of capital punishment. I must have been a very ferocious beast for that, killed in self defence.'!

The court adjourned - real justice still unknown as it can never be known; but lessons learnt. And although the littler 'uns didn't understand a few of the bigger words, they knew at heart that the older ones and mums and dads cared. So they went away feeling safer. 'Nature is red in tooth and claw'. Fear is sometimes appropriate but better balanced by stronger company of good heart!

7.2.02 Canterbury

the heavy yoke of dying old past dogma -
Recycling Mental Rubbish

the mind's compass magnetised at every juddering onslaught,
wavering wild in the happenstance of history past wrought

in fate/destiny's dark night of frenetic flickering talk-thought
wired into the hard lines of repetitive rumination, clutter-caught
distraught - in mood's white searing lights taken as the uncouth truth
contorted by fear and the fear of fear and in this paradigm brought
asundered suffering as first, not sins; the first sin in origin bought -
in a mother's absence, loss, abuse; lack of ultimate love unsought.

Confused haphazard mouse-clicks crash in the brain's sea storm;
forced idols of anxiety as computer cyber-space gigabytes swarm
splutter sneeze, deform, a stuck needle on a vinyl record born;
of inner noise, cacophony clatter debris static radio hiccups untuned;
flashing disco lights and drumming forced video repeats again rerun
of being an alien not a person, beyond the pale, out of bounds,
dying alone, death of him, death dumb within the leaden skull found
A hurt reject, surplus to any requirements as body bits shutdown.
Longing fulfilled, a new wise heart, honour is the deepest ground.

It's not to judge, strive to survive, condemn - diminished, drained;
creation has no care for common convention - not taint contained;
it is triadic, the basic unit, kairos the real shared heartful moment,
not the Fall, original sin sent but original given primal worth meant;
not chronos' chaotic mind-filled world-speeding fragment-time bent.
Replace the earnest in the cause of the serious - the still small voice
lost in tortuous mind muscles, tendon sheen-spun taut knotted ropes.
Do I have the right to righteousness' penultimate communion?
and everyone is entitled to my opinion! Celebrities haven illusion.
Longing for right-relatedness. Crosstianity's guilt-pride restriction.

'Where are you' the first garden God, us-searching, careful calls
in the second garden tomb where in renewed life he faithful came
to calm, console us in our distress and, quiet, calls our unique name.
He came to meet us when we were yet far off, small, withal
lost in the swirling litter of deprivation poverty veiled in violence;
finding the lost chasm-crackstuck-us-coin, unable to move, cry out;
who finds and shoulder-lifts the one entangled in the mind's briars;
who rushes to greet the returning despairing desolate child entire.
Our name called out - as well pleasing, beloved, as the person M -
and as a mother cosies and comfies her babe - the first God known.
The vulnerable strong divine, praising worshipping worthful-us first,

before we can respond as specially made In his image immersed.
This the first love gracious given, the full inherited inherent concord
of shining meeting eyes. Gospels err, hint, warp but can't bind God.
A cold snap does put colour in ripening tree apple-cheeks -
the orchardman's true folklore seen - simple practical, unique.

Apr 2008

Sand and Grit

White beach sand, brown-tanned with mud and age
and the sustained shift-wave, pounding surge;
hillock dunes mist top blown, trillion grains wind whistling
tussock strong sedge, fair grass-hair wisping waving
my bare footsteps infilling, gentle waves touching and outing -
the tree of my heart heavy with fruit unpicked and rotting
sight clearing, hearing wave on shore and rock flowing;
gulls wheeling world-turning shifting erupting.
    Spawn spat settles on the stones and old shells
cultch-broken to grow in four full years.
The oyster shell clams-shut on an iridescent pearl heart,
not to be wrenched open with a gouging knife -
of great beauty built on pain round a sand-grain grit -
in the same way he gave our own true life-self
so protected by hard husk, - both variously arise, can surprise;
few oysters have found pearls - we likewise;
some so closed, denied, mostly insensitive hard
but all have a tender hidden heart-soft-flesh.
My seeming is only an outer garment - roughshod
rough-spiked, broken and covered in weed and mud.
    Two children build sand castles, fragile made
then break them in glee with colourful spades -
the ocean brings more gifts of brown sugar sand
more castles built - which the waves creep in, invade -
waves and children play, splash and laugh together.
Thirty angels keep watch - offshore windturbines, ever silver
grey in the light grey mist - evanescent eerie mysterious moreover;
ninety metre glass-fibre trinity feathered-humming wings, an enigma

set on a seventy meter tubular steel trunk, strong, out further.
I give them names - Angel Billy is not working today, but
the five men in their boat must go fix him, tend to his rays, that
'Celtic Storm', the service vessel specials for the Kentish Flats.
A warm sheltered coffee indwelling, crab sandwich oozing,
crisp lettuce, raspberry wheat beer, a window-day-dreaming
out to the klinking-shingle pebble beach sown;
groyned wood-pile breakwaters in neat rows down;
gulls wind-dipping slanting spiralling spun around.
The Dredgermens caf - old timber seafront eating place
the Royal Native Oyster Company, now trendy nonetheless.
Iron wood-fire, sepia photos, old smocked fisher-folk;
(working sail boats turn directly into wind, brake-stop).
A raspberry danish oozing jam, alone on a glass shelf cabinet -
my glass shelf days end. I ask for it and he dryly says
'put it out of misery'. 'It's going to a good home!' I say.
My hour-sand-glass is top emptying, base filling dismay; at bay -
I turn myself directly into the storm-wind and tideway,
no headway in the grey spray this day.

Sept 2006

A Scared Bird's takes Flight

rest in the Father.
Ruach. Pneuma.
The breath.

You've seen a bird startle -
stretching, he thins up
as tall as he can on reaching legs,
his beady eyes scanning
for danger below or above.
And then, shoulder muscles braced
his rapid scattering take off
on fluttering reaching wings.
His flight in fright -
shoulder propelled

So likewise I find
my shoulder muscles tight
most of time's time.
Am I a bird tensed
about to take off
in fright's flight?
But can't.

Relax down. Drop.
What is the danger inside?
'Hello fear. It's ok'.
Rest in the Father
whom I never had.
Ruach. Pneuma -
the breath always gentle,
like the Father - always here.
The breath of life;
my breath sighed out.
My shoulders drop at rest.

The breath.

Feb. 2012

A Sea Shore

And the wind
Whisking white sea tops
Whistles soft spray scatters;
Sheet backwash seeps and meets
Full swaying surge.
Each wave breaks to
White tripping surf
Sending a hove of plover scuttling
In centipede steps;
And a lone gull swerves
As I foam leap and scatter the surf at speed.
The sun burns my brown

And tingling skin-salt crusts
Each crystal drop out;
And the loneness goes - alone
At a clear pool
Refracting ripples of coloured gem -
Tickling anemone with toe.

A bubble bursts from a stalk-eyed crab
Spying - and I laugh.
Mussel clusters crowd close
As sea awash trickles in gutters
Off a domed rock;
And slime green weed frays and sways
To every wind and wave tossed.
Children cry afar; stick figures dart
In every posture thought
Clamorous in ecstatic freedom -
Frisking at jellied parents
Who fry in oil and swearing squirt.
And plastic products discard never die
But proclaim man's reign
Crisp crunching - supreme,
Stumbledly shouting
That we die - used and thrown
Yet somehow live on,
In Spirit - forever.

2.4.67 Houtbaai Cape Town

A Seaview

'On the seashore of endless worlds, children play' - Rabindranath Tagore

An open sky-blue slatted wide window
white lacewing curtains wind whispers ripple
the gentle breeze soft gauze billows
deep sea slanting-light sun dappled
fine peppered cream sand jostles

the long green dune grass rustles.

Blue blobbed hydrangea, pine table
azure jug, white milk froth
terracotta bowl, clear water
buttered words on toast.
'Good morning Morning'
we pucker our eyes into the light
rubbing the sleep off, knuckled
as all things pass on between hands bundled.

Silver glint splinters dance on the sea surface
sun shot for a calm peace inverted
hot slanting fear melts and dribbles
a few bouncing clouds converse converted
turning the eyes of this and that and there
and nowhere - but here now.

Sea birds call - anointing diving, gliding stalling
weaving as one, twisting skewing, dying living.
Fishes sing in a drone song unheard -
a low humming heart - the tide out;
born brightness ringed hallowedness
the bright water rings and sings
coming into the distance of nearness,
the nearness of distance.

All - 'loved into life' - the Wind whispering.
Razor edge salt of the earth. Salt tears
as sweet as a crunched nut munching
Axis. The sea of ourselves appears.

Canterbury October 2004

A Seed Falls He Drawing the Sting Out

('Except a corn of wheat fall into the ground and die, it abitheth alone; but if it die, it bringeth forth much fruit.' Jn 12:24).

Hidden he appears - constant relentless insistent
solemn step, burdened grave abundant
scything the wild meadow grass, the harvest reaper -
of his before measured engraved path nearer
in the white night of burnt umbral shadow clearer,
not black dark despair - but a stranger
within the sudden steel splinters of terror.
'I loved you before you yet feared me so, as a foe -
and tenderly gather you to my cheek as a little child low
beyond understanding, and at last' - remembered;
the seed falls to the ground from full courage, joy embers.
So she took his offered hand - a shuddered thing life releasing,
the dot and seal stamped hard, her body to ashdust giving,
a furnace, burnt burnished bright afire, entropy the flower
He gravely lifts her gently, drawing the sting out slow.
A closed, seed-shell songscape, burst its confined coffin-case
ascending life - gravitating to - nirvana-paradise -
heart's needle, into the body of Christ bite the communion wafer -
He had died dark before and knew before ours.
Royal crimson, deep sound dark thunder;
a black case shell the negation of all colour
encasing and affirming within, bursting light-life night asunder.
And cloven-hoofed grim fear is accepted now, understood.
Graven, gravid-laden so grave, grieved, before so feared, subdued.
The ground grain pearl, tear-grief watered, curled, unfurls births;
a buried protected earth-hole dug deep - winter bulb rest
in ease, recess; silence absence, patience to presence
bursting in spring a fresh life-full, of meaning substance;
honey out of stone rock cut, gravity roots deep; experienced essence.
The cup runs over, opened the brim fills bright eyed
making the soil soft with the drops tear torn; mourned
that what was, is not what is and what is, is not the second later.
Dark death is dunked dead, transfigured transformed.

He calls all the stars by their names and one expires,
radiating a gamma light burst and at the last
body breath I have heard the spirit rush past.
Our life the full breath blown - he the one reed
then the song full falling, spiralling rising -

to Silence, beginning containing all.
(I am too small to be so grave but I light his candle).
In pain, wrought ends this nought through shock anger despair.
So ashen, little, knowing she is loved by God -
he is coming to fetch her - the last hugs depart -
all is meaningless otherwise. The healing heart.
Going home - the new world, welcomed to belong well, whole -
blood light red sunset spills through the dappled leaf shoal;
a tender bud from under a massive rock beside the spring river -
water music washing discord from frightened fears.
And from our cheeks, he shall wipe away all tears.
'And our eyes at last shall see him' gently, face to face.

Canterbury early Dec 2004

Seven Attitudes for health

Not judging self or others - stepping back, being aware.
Patience.
Beginners mind.
Trust.
Not striving.
Accepting.
Letting go.

July 2013

Shadows

Cats, gas points
Shillings in slots
Dog shit on pavements
Spittle on the steps.
Dented dustbins
dead on their sides -
their heads blown off -

rubbish, their guts.
Sleet, ice wind in gusts
The smell of paraffin lamps.
It seems urine steams
from drain holes.
Am old now, nowhere, no thing
tombed in a sleeping bag
in an attic room.
Lifetide ebbing
Dreaming -
no wilderness
eastern salt marsh.

Conjoint components of a part in words,
The juxtaposition of sounds that strike -
Tuppence hapenny off the recommended price -
Cauterising brain cells, cutting out words.

No cicada sings
No horizon not jarred
by skeleton of steel and stone.
No crackle of yellow grass
and clean brown dust
on a dark red sun
slung low over orange hills.

At this height the wind soars
as Big Ben tolls over chimney tops
and Thames tugs in the New Year moan.
I remember. I remember no thing -
turning in the whirls of my roundabout mind
watching ant people weave their way home.
The wind wraps and curls round itself
and slaps each furl in a crack -
It likes the sound of its voice.
An invisible attraction
of a stone cut face
which won't let go
at the corners of dark streets.

And you lean a warm cheek
on a numb hand - fibrillating
Fibre and muscle strung taut.
A porcupine. Antarctic. I.
There's a time to understand
which means a capacity for an identity
which can stand alone with its shadow.
A reflection in a dark lake.
A man is an island. And a time not -
climbing the ninth turn of the stairs
to where you sit like clay in your chair
and your grey eyes pierce.

No cicada sings here -
only television hums
an ear drum roll.
And jets run shadows
in the depths of tall streets.
Fluorescent lights make ghosts
who are ghosts of themselves.
No shadow flickered firelight
in the veldt at dark.
No widow bird scythes
its flight across grass.
Here - no cicada sings.

I'd make a worthwhile citizen
they said with some reserve.
A zen of the city. A zomb.
My most productive time
is in the dark
when my word children come
and tell of planktonic forms
and oceans encased
in my pearled sea shell.
Brain pearls crack and decompose.
Are we demented yet?
I protest and slam my fist
on the desk.

I am not a production line in Fords.
The rain touches me. Soft.
I cannot touch the rain
as I say one word
in ten thousand cloistered hours
and not the thunder of my thoughts.

If there is nothing more -
I would like the sound
of my name - windblown.
Tell me about one flower.
I grow warm from a central point.
The sun gods shout
and echo earthround -
an explosive moment without explosion
And I am the light of my world.
This experience in moments
hasn't words -
the inexpressable is the essence
as I ask for reasonable reflection.
I can pick a portion
of crisp green grapes
and live on sweet and sour sauce
mushroomed rice and light bitter ale.

There are sun sword ...
RA. Christ. I am.

It's silent and still.

1.1.72 London.

She

She is old with dropping dewlaps and neck folds. But she has a grace and dignity borne of hard times - the velvet neck piece, strings and odd bits tell of that.

She is in her garden gently coaxing the phlox to flower and she ties up the sweet peas with carefully collected string bits. She loves different plants and they love her.

Her joints are clicky and stiff from long years wear; pain killers are her friends. She supports her local action group to save the Kent and Canterbury hospital and, with help, managed a demonstration march in Canterbury not long ago. An African bead bracelet tells of long treks in distant lands and I like to imagine one such was over the Blue Mountains in her youth. Only she would know. She is one of those dying breed of eccentric, hardy Englishwomen that roughed it and forged the way for others in unusual travels.

Her heart has seen deep and wide. On wet cloggy days she embroiders jug covers with dangly beads and day dreams. Old browning photos remind her warmly of her past love life in that old Austin in 1937.

She grew up in sparse conditions and still carefully collects any bits and pieces that may come in useful - an old plastic pen tray (the first plastic ever made) and folder name holders, an odd junk piece pierced ear-ring, a little plastic pastel coloured ball her grand-daughter had given her with that bouncy metal spiral ringed piece - those reminded her of happy times.

She is not without an interest in the present and is something of a photographer - the towering flint Kent ruined pillar on Kodak film against the blue sky is one of her better takes.

And yet there is that pair of slim pliers - no mate alive to do those small tasks about the house - but she has learnt how. He died some years back. She has lived alone since.

*****

Her name was Rosemary - for remembrance. And I, at the British Red cross shop sort her few belongings for sale and discard the apparent 'junk' with respect. It has been loved. The old photos may possibly fetch a collector's price.

She is helping others to survive now.

23.3.02

Shotokan Karate

A synchronous set of
ten black belts
surged towards me - watching -
with kias - yells of the spirit.
The hair on the back of my neck
stood up on end.
My spirit revived.
I had been found and saved.

Courtesy above all - the beginning and the end
in basics, kumite and kata -
those ancient solo choreographic forms
of great beauty -
interweaving thunder lightning and waterflow -
of power speed and grace.
Never to instigate a street fight. To predict;
first to focus with that gleam of meaning and power
in the eye - to shrivel and deter
and if running away is of no avail
to stand and counter defence fight -
with minimum effort.
Shaolin monks tell
of thirty killing points.
Smashing bricks with ones body
is only for brutes.
The thirty or so kata are the ultimate.
Chinte - funny fingers, Bassai Dai
storming the fortress.
Gangaku - crane on a rock.
Empi - a flying swallow.

At sixty five this year awarded
a black silk belt after seven years,
embroidered with my name and
Shotokan - the place of billowing pines;
empty hand - karate
It has given me some peace.

Hara - the place of breath and power.
Zazen - meditate.

Canterbury Sept.2002

Sibelius 150th Anniversary Concert, Marlow Theatre

Perhaps words are the daughters of music.

Sibelius' 2nd symphony -
'momentous, beautiful, inspired
changing, majestic, magnificent'.
Words are so little -
language primitive, it has ground to a halt -
only as yet knowing how to construct a chord
which is a word - as yet far from a symphony of the within deep;
we only just get by but not much for profound things;
yet revealed, the body knows -
riveted, utterly absorbed enthralled. Music heals -
all common feelings are transformed.
Words can destroy, wound as attempted notes.

A hundred musicians in final as one, in tremendous accord -
this creative force -
intensely here and now, one in our true self
Ashkenazy impels players, gives life and play to lifeless ink notes.
In the beginning was the note, the sound -
notes - like the alphabet evolving
which is the sound for the later word.
Words have run out -
sound remains - this nameless symphonic Event.
I write to try to give ordinary things their glow
like a firefly glimmering in the forest of night
to repel predators but to attract, draw-to, a like-hearted note.

Perhaps the universe is the son's sound -

in awe, I had heard God! a stop, blocked name, inherited;
saying that name I am always hesitant.
Hidden under that Name - this music is the Event;
that taken-for-granted Name said, the cause of much shed blood.
Music beyond and hidden within all religions - blocked,
a religionless religion released.
What maybe coming is a new Name
but if there's an Event - this music,
there is no need for a Proper Name - Allah or God.
As the lilies of the field flourish
and know not their Name or the name of God.
But becoming conscious - is language, is the word!

'It is good, good... very good' in Genesis said 7 times within time -
that God said as He saw his creation work.
Ruach.
My thanks to John Caputo 'The Weakness of God'

June 2015

Silence

Drug guttered search for comfort, love and word
Loss, nothing and dark appear to where You are; as much
The faint blossom on the plum tree. Singing.
Or a wood flute in the hills rippling.

My breath is in You
But you blew my mind.
My pulse is in you
And my heart burst.
You gave hunger and thirst
And left me burnt
Till ripped in pain
Beyond limit or word
You held me - dark peace
A moment. Then shrapnelled blown
You gave a moment of calm
After the storm.

Nameless You withdrew
esse qua esse, esse ipsum
As the You was in I
And the I in You.

    Absence, silence, abstinence
    Autistic. Alone.
        Thou.
        Father...

20.5.79

Simples
Decay transforms
The Tortoise and the Deer

Between the quiet lavender flair
and soft red scent of rose
a sounding out small tortoise moves -
image of the real us, a home-shell,
hard husk, crust carapace to world cope -
danger threats, harbour sharks - to hide curl.
The white harvest ready, being reaped and cut.
He plods between two towering giants -
hapless frenzied, tragic and manic hares.
Two dangers - avoiding one risks the opposite
(the foundering whirlpool and jagged rock -
Scylla and Charybdis - to between steer).
Little tortoise - your dream hopes held
within your house around you felt
and a load on your plaqued domed back -
sometimes a burden to running free
as wild as a wide eyed leaping deer
who has no shell-shield to safe save.
I forget me-you in dense white pain
you forget me not untangling dark knots
of old wounds, white scars
as you nuzzle round the rubbish dump

where limp lettuce leaves are thrown
and the best flowers can grow.

seeing now enkindling this now; a trust to survive
a trust in dying that will be good, pupa to butterfly;
letting go, resting down, smooth muscles loose;
one congruent - 'few associates';
little goods, less decay;
our 'alienated majesty' hidden there;
doing only the next thing; pottering; -
fearful tenderness.

so you would confine the divine
to quietude? The sun does not rise.
No - midnight is the point
of the beginning of sight
as the earth opens to turn
toward the blinding light.
Is - is now. When it was, a was, once.
Let all that is me - be, now -
cutting through concrete frozen fear.
I am a stricken deer that left the herd -
the darts are gently forced, drawn forth -
sore, tender, raw.

Canterbury June 2004

A Hidden Song
'wild thing I love you,' in the town

Poets often escape to the easy celebration of wild nature -
as people, from that, seem apart, but there *is* sparkling song
where most of us are, if we're open, in the veiled drab city or town -
in the forest of buildings growing out of earth, bare brown.
It's not really singing, just seeing and hearing clear spun -
the 'stars' here, too numerous to 'see' so I cease to sing;
just quiet awareness under the inside vacuum of a cry.

I sing for the pebble glasses on her nose-tip, haloed by light,
the hand elegantly poised, delicate fingers, rising cigarette smoke.
Her bent knees buckled when she lays the brimmed beer-glass down
as bending her waist would spill the cream thick froth blown.
I sing for glunk globby tubbies who sail schooner-sedate along -
heads held high aloft, billowing clothes like sail-cloth.
No two people the same in all the world except rare twins -
divine generosity, ingenious profusion to ensure wide choice.
I hum for steaming leak soup in the clinking white bowl
between their intimate talk; and the buff melting butter-blob spread,
moistening the brown-seeded-crusty-munching soft bread.
And reluctant men-folk pulled into shops to look at this and that
by their lasses dithering eager - though no stopping them at pubs.
I chuckle at young folks talk 'wicked'='wkd' text, 'it so is', 'brill'.
'I aint bovverd', mobile phone hunched, 'like..?', 'yu know..? Cool'.
I sing for the cobbles on the streets that shadow, shine and trip.
For the iron swinging shop sign, squeaking in the wind, bleak.
The tight hip jeans that wrinkling smile on the cheek behind butts,
in their sway-swaggering walk, tacticalmuscles tight packed;
those tattooed flesh gaps between trouser and top; nose, belly rings;
medieval point tassel boots, stockinged mini skirts, jewelled bling,
little soft key-ring toys dangling on bags and rucksacs hanging.
And there a posse of happy prams, chubby babes out peaking -
streaming abreast across the tight street, joyful yahoo, yippee young.
Nothing's new except dull colours, once bright centuries before -
mourning purples and blacks are all the rage now,
colours in meaning have become up-side-down.
But there's crock-pots pans bins, spoons and brooms
in rainbow shades at the land-locked Steamer Trading Cookshop -
bristling 'buy me' proud; never was such a joy to sweep in thought;
orange is really orange, shining yu' know! and reds glow sun-fire
if we only look now. Just as much as the tiny 'weed' flower
squeezing courageously between some corner concrete cracks.
But nothing grows in the new Whitefriars 'post-modern' hell-hole;
elsewhere under the few brown lime trees that give the city heart -
wind-tossed winter's leaves of yellows, reds and dancing golds.

I sing for my fingers - blind, they tell of the difference between
soft paper and cloth and what coin in my pocket is what.

As ever, the cathedral looms high behind hiding stone walls -
and, burning their last candles, the idle idols of tarnished christs
die under the merchants of faith in the opulent temples versed
in putting dying unlove where before simple living love was first -
unfriendly religions masking and tearing the Image of God
like the mess and crap received of being badly brought up -
and from ash, the New Christ, among a few, rising silent, quiet -
the Lost Coin being slowly found in love and insight;
and yearly a fresh finding chance, the unborn god, God born Christ.
Impelled, I have woven words to somewhat satisfy
my satisfaction in symmetry, the nativity of the trinity
in community and in the family - newborn, incarnating ourselves.
We ache for a few sweet kindnesses, multiplying manifold -
becoming the person we were not before allowed
(through the dull thud of silence or abuse);
trying to hold essential central love, remembered, close -
like the scent of incense from an embered stick
of smouldering herbs.

It's not easy to be thankful for little common things in fear, lost;
to see what to sing and cry, to see to see in the city I sing
but to see them now, fresh for the first second's springing time
like a child in father's lap, being vulnerable with, the strong song -
after being warmed, fed, loved within a mother's arms around.

Canterbury Dec 2006

Some Little Sketches of Some Little People
the familiar is not known because it is familiar; the present is eternity now

Wilkinson's
A tall till Lady of a bargain basics shop
with everything under the sun, shelf stacked -
a lass with three double chins, rolly plump
and an ochre-paste face, thick make-up
the line ending at her lily white neck;
her long black hair pulled back

and her lacy dress, smart black;
there was something flamenco there
or of a receptionist at the Hilton
or London Dorchester bespoke hotel
or organising the count down launch
to a space rocket strategic lift-off -
so confidant important assured,
a flam-buoyant two-finger concert pianist
pressing the till buttons in sole charge
for consumers cash or credit cards -
her head held high and proud;
this, her ongoing long day job -
and they say 'It's cool to be hot'.

The Security Man at M & S.
Proud in his smart uniform and epaulettes
with belt-hung important intercom phones ready, set
but for hours on end he waits, to misdeeds spot;
all he has to do is walk and watch and lean
and he does, dead-pan, without fuss or groan.

Little Old lady in M & S
Round and tubby and sweet
a twinkle sparkle smile, and neat -
her content inbuilt not forced;
the new collection, she touches and strokes -
of blue-green fashion tops and frocks
for youngsters slim - but she wanders on,
quite happy to release the desire to own.

Lady Reading a Book at Fenwick's outside Caf
Hunched over and totally absorbed
amidst all her coats, bags and clothes
among the corner din and noise
of commuters traffic and buses bustling;
something exciting was happening
in her book. And I admired, walking on.
All these said it's ok to be me in this present. I am not dying nor young. Things just as they are - nothing more, nothing less. I am.

Feb 2009

An Iona Skylark
(Alauda arvensis)
(laud and praise)

Not to fake a Christian mask.
The arrow must shoot home to its mark.
Will He bandage up the hurt?
Unless I touch and see
and be with in all time -
not the moment of the lark,
ascension in song and flight
above bleak moor and rock,
hidden in cloudgod - tor abba light,*
above the depth of grey mist
and circling gull-sight.

Unless I am -
that bird unbeing
shot in quivered song, burning.
I cannot - incrying.
Did Christ ascend singing?
Here. Now?
leaving us bereft below.
Bird broken body transformed
to an absent resurrection song
above the grey raincloud.

*tor ab - the hill St. Columba climbed to pray near the present abbey.
abba - father.

Iona. Saturday 11am '84

Slippers

An old tan
moccasin pair -
foot-holed from wear

and hand repaired -
not thrown
rubbished in a bin.
Faithful loving, loyal -
they huddle
doorway crosswise.
Vulnerable, used, old
waiting patiently for me -
And loved well.
Once barefoot
I crack.
And gather them up
with care.

22.2.02 Canterbury

A Slow Return

The sequence of events grew in jagged moments
out of the sun, white ahead and imperceptible -
and flies circling, coned down stung dark, a halo spun -
Cringing laser shot to offshade an eclipse of wing-ed monotones.

We scarce knew any truth or justice,
diminished with intent
in diphthonged tongues thin whipped
by kyphosed, concave men -
striving at exaltation
and uncertain doctrined reason
with unsmiling minds.
Taking advantage of authority and age.
And wiser ones not knowing either -
attempting with an accepting boot
to resolve co-operation with diplomatic hurt.
Our anger would be but is returned
in pieces from pyramid hands and reclining chairs.
Named potato eaters of a worm ridden earth.
Is our anger unjust, our creation in vain?

Threatened in extreme by three events,
which probably were not
or were but could not be. Neither
withstood as a swarm of lancinate force.
We could not open our protest -
there was none in the circumference
and so we lay down in glazed peace.
It was strange how the tremor eased -
and felt ourselves unworthy and exiled.
The potential of intense, vaulted pain
funelled to an emmergent interim flux,
while we waited for the sun focussed years to pass -
of a tired acceptance of our rotting disorder.
And in our delirium saw a spectre of wisdom
haze in the dry heat of the world,
while the swarm stung within
and the parched sun stared
at our pain and impotent words.

The confined projection in infinite nothing
Evaporated depth blown South
Sun gently, a song wrapped
in a smoking dream. A search -
Hung heavy over tiled wet roofs
and chimney tops.
A cripple of crackled leaves
whirled in blue coppered smoke.
And rainbow spheres lashed
from eyes egg-yolked.
And the lines of limbs relaxed
in an axis.
A slam cut sigh
brained apexed
in a blast impulse
hurled out by a gale behind
a thermalled bird swung sharp
soaring high.
A released dimension
shot riddled in relentless migration

from hot granite rock.
Our Fahrenheit force
cracks compassed in frictioned current
from a molten creative core.
There is this word, risen up -
a magnetic relevance, unsaid;
white retinal heat reflects
a staggered slow blind daze -
in an apraxic complexity
of dark and light,
of repulse and grasp -
A facet of questioned quartz.

I have this to offer -
a gentle perhaps, a tender hour.
An other, the discrepant tension
of seen things and I and unformed worldless words.

12.5.68 Cape Town

Snow

Snow Igloo
Inuit Eskimo.
Blown snowdrift rows
thrown, grow in furrows.

Seasons of the pole
ice, ice-floes;
huskies scamper close
sleds in tow.
Giant white bears know -
follow after seals below -
rear up high
slam down
to break their
breathing holes low
in ice shallows.

Glistening glinting aquamarine green
azure, cobalt, blind white, blue seen
silence, then, low ice cracks show - and echo.
Sliding whales blow below
curving, largo, massive dark forked, slow.

The profound Animal Shadow
hovers - a sacred soul halo.
The divine rules now, and long ago.
Sheer snow-ice glows
and Northern lights colour-sounds throw
scintillating shimmering flows -
credo bestowed, adagio -

so I take my child sled
across the road instead -
dark woods, white hills prance
alive, silent speak, and dance then
three snow huskies - I make until
evening falls, skidding down thrilled,
bumped out spilled, I am summarily dismissed;
I laugh down-rolled.
Hushed - hazy grey - and snow fast falls.
All are one and one in all
a simple life in touch, the best.
I thank the hovering spirit, eerie quiet.
The still three, watch on guard - on high.

Canterbury Mar 2005

So What
Not what if or why not

So what - M is going away,
losing his memory at times
as in the aging of older folk -
no more a counsellor to tell all and lean.
So what - I, an old black belt

was beaten in a kata by a red belt -
my legs, balance and fire weak.
So what - an old neighbour
has just died, in the past, truculent and blunt
her world famous magnolia gardens
and old house development ripe;
which she called 'The Haven'- her own home,
rejecting the sparcity of a care home;
a coffin hearse has just passed.
So what - Greyfriars bridge is rotting
and has closed - where I routinely parked.
So what - the brother friars might have to leave
so no more gardening there in voluntary work.
So what - there is little work to do
now at the Red Cross shop.
So what, so what, so what -
how little control we really have
though it frightens and hurts
and how will I cope, empty and tensed -
an orphan, as if kicked in the guts.
So what - the banks may go bust
so I live in poverty, disabled, dying -
so what - will I take my own life?

Be robust - feel all this,
it's neither wrong nor right
and breathe it in and out.
It may not be true and fixed, it maybe a fact
but the aversion thought-opinions around it
are just mental events passing by, based on the past.
A thought creates a drama out of and around facts -
the two are quite separate but now thought
wants them to join in confusion and mess.
So then say, so gently, 'so what!.'

The only certainty is uncertainty - hard;
accept the rainstorm, get drenched -
the anchor - breathe into it and breathe it out.

Breathing is a fact - uncertainty becomes soft.

July 2012

after 'This Quiet Place'
the best find on our journey is an honest friend -
that great difference between 'friendly' and a 'friend'

An Old Soldier

Short, strong - as they were then
in both World Wars long gone -
freedom's lintel slab support -
like old cottage low door beams
wood-wormed, death watched -
that, taller now, as commonplace
you bang your head as you underpass.
He shuffles along, bent out of breath
his wide eye scans for a passing seat -
time and things pass by fast in slowed old age -
wizened in the wisdom of experience;
gnarled knobbed hands - like old oak,
he still caries a heavy back-pack,
his stick, a rifle once -
driven by an order
blasted in blood
in the fields of France
to keep on the going
as to stop is certain death.

His caring daughter finds this place, stops at this spot,
brings a tray, white tinkling cups, a honey-tea pot
and butter croissant; this wayside comfy-seat coffee place;
he offers to pay from his little blue pension purse.
'No Dad - it's ok.' so he rests with a sigh as he shuffling-sits
and cares slip off his back and face in drips;
his shakes - old horrors buried, nameless, of the past.
He finds a gentle flower to interface

among the colour plump-pudding hanging pots
and heavenly rests in this garden place, an intimation -
at centre settling heart, a walled garden paradise
hinting unimpeded flow, still timeless space,
a fore-taste, without stop or start
where clear waters glint in that ultimate primal Place
and Kingfishers dart-dive, catch fire-light, flash bright.

The infinity of freedom dreamt
against fractured finitude meant.
So burdened - this fragile delicate world -
so easily crushed, turning to dust.

July 2008.

Heaven - a canopy; paradise - a walled garden; images of an oasis in the desert.

Some Clothes in Winter in Butchery Lane

Skin tight stretchy jeans
with slits in the knees smiling at the world -
the knees cry out, crying
'we're freezing, cover up'.
Trainers luminescent red
against black slacks -
puffing out proud -
so stop and admire
'look at us, we're the best'.
Colours on kids dance
full of promise and hope -bold and full in your face.

Sept.2015

A Song of Writing

In the beginning was the word
And the word was life
And the word was the word
In whom was God.

They know I'm a word catcher
They trickle and dodge,
Flirting chilled reason
Hiding in sulcal cracks
Hurling to the wind, lost.
Till a lanced thought
Penetrates the unformed fired depth
Copulate in one agonal birth, in death.

It can be very grey
Up amongst the Betz cells
Mountain misted
Sheer crystalled
Calculate, cerebrate.
But the word says
I am alpha and omega
In whom was life
That was no life.
The beginning and the end.

Pierced quintessence in geometric design
Space in line curved straight;
Thundered
In precision phrased -
Triumphant.
An earth end echo - reverberate;
Anarchic agony - expressed.

2.3.68 Cape Town

*Betz cells - giant pyramidal motor cortex neuronal cells.

Shakespearian type *Sonnet 1.Discipline

(In the beginning was the word?
'Whose service is perfect freedom' or
'Whose freedom is perfect service').
But Sound Matters

Oh sonnet, little sounding git, witheld,
so strict and tight, thin lipped and lawed to kill.
The might of peoples gift in word unweld
that dwells supreme in every heart, now nil.

How can we love your starving bones so bared,
how can we flesh your obsessioned neuroned brain.
Was such strict structure ever much adored?
But flawed, so feared, ignored. Unheard such pain.

The cruel sound is now that harsh and shrill;
a sonnet screaming, strident tyrant. Disciplined hells.
A juggling, drilling, tricking, searching grill:
words lost in chasmed void, in cerebrate cortex cells.

My heart so cramped has now no warm true play;
imprisoned, slammed, clamped, - it shrinks, no light of day.
(The price to pay?)

Canterbury Dec 2002

*Sonnet = little sound; - but at this price? There are the usual departures from strict iambic pentameter and I have kept extra words in 'cos I want to!

*

Elizabeth - Behave Yourself (c.f. Shakespeare's Sonnet 130)
Sonnet 3..

My lover's face is nothing like the moon

the sky is far more blue than his eyes blue
if hay be stacked why then his hair be strewn
if hairs be fine his beard is thick to do
We know that shells are sculpted coils and flutes
but no such shapes see I in his blob ears.
And in some scents there is more pursuit
than in the foot-stench that from my lover rears.
I love to see him smile, yet well I know
that old paintings have a greater pleasing show.
admitting I've not seen a fine god beau.
My lover when he sits, slops on a chair.
    And yet, by paradise, I feel my man as scarce
    as any he disproved with fake contrast.

    And now I am utterly in despair.

SPACE

STOP. OPEN up. SOFTen. SPACE -
soften to your real self unbraced.
It's to stop getting in our own way,
it's to give up stirring the mud in the mind
and making it cloudy and opaque;
the stirring being the doing mind
in could ought would should haves
and in thinking planning
wanting worrying judging
dooming and glooming
and obsessively ruminating.
Just breathe breath -
sense it in and out.
Let the breath breathe itself.
A condition of pure simplicity -
the hardest yet easiest
thing of all and -
all may become well
not by searching
but just by being

in this moment now
in the breath -
in compassion
with myself -
being kind to yourself.
This is wisdom itself.
Stop striving, fixing,
just let be and let go,
of this fearfulness of fear,
in the given Space.
Let fear, that inner bellowing bully,
that irrational tyrant from the past
that may have served a need then
but not now - dissipate.
I do not need to be happy
or be better or fixed;
just let go.
Give that Space.

'Listen O my Child
and have no fear.'

April 2013

A Spanish Hat

A crotched erect young man
rubbed his pectoral nipples squared,
haired - in the cold waters of a pool.
And asked my number, I - angled
under a spanish hat.
Spasmed, his veined bulk arched
and stroked gulfing and undulent.
Sun specks flecked his watered
brown guttered, rhomboid back -
and quickened hot
I streak shot
Quivered

To cold
Green
Depths.

You fling naked to feel
the soft sheets and cool patches
woven white on hilled slopes.
Without imposition, witheld.
One speaks softly in urgent words.

1.4.68 Rondebosch South Africa

Causation in Seconds!
(the butterfly theory of relationship)

A sparrow sneezed
a tiny fine gust of mist -
a flea had first kissed
its nose in jest -
the morning air
zest-blest, sunburst;
and over the far horizon
round the earth's curve thereon
to boundless space and on
a star was born observed and shone;
and a babe unplaced,
careworn, new-born
cried in chaos foregone
- caesura.
A second later
a blast went off
bursting somewhere.
Horror.
It was
an 'act of god' - a tornado.
The seconds simmer
and boil over
bubble froth.

And pennies on Big Ben's
pendulum.

Canterbury Dec. 2004

Stones and Correlation

Pebbles, heaved and tossed by every wind and wave and froth
washed up broken-naked, spume raked, sea-puked, dead-baked,
basic elements traced, delightful beach shelled, muted gems with
- stones - each single one on countless shores, wave smashed
thrashed, back-lashed dashed crashed, gashed shining wet -
trillions of billions millions, each matchless in colour, set;
each telling a unique Grounding trek from the world's beginning
and so unseen by us except with tender bare feet, care-treading;
still, silent till the next tinkle together in tide lines clinking.
Broken like us, Creator's tumbled creatures, unique playmates
and like us, earth's volcanic centre shifts with colliding plates.
A Stone's essential inner nature to be still, quiet at rest based -
if it falls it does so to be at ease as that function cannot be erased;
one only sounds when striking against that to which it falls -
it takes two to tango talk together in relationship called;
it is stone's dense mass that gravity G pulls towards itself -
that universal unseen spirit, steady, deep quiet, a law to itself
so both wait; if stone becomes insecure, imbalance acts -
insecurity - the condition in which God has also placed himself,
the vulnerable potential of truly being and always becoming -
imbalance the great leveller and certain changer - so Stone drops
to its primary balanced, still place, to the holding Ground forseen;
the three, a trinity in trapeze, catcher, flying-faller, power between.
Gravity pulls, Ground waits as stone falls then sits calmed, quiet;
the father ground, the stone son, gravity that unseen free spirit -
three dance, gravity's glee, stone's smile, ground's grave presence;
Stone held in its weight by the unceasing G force partnership
with firm constant Ground; everywhere and All is relationship.
Not one only is, one is not, only more are - is the essence.
Not I, not you, but we are also special stones of the Rock,
our born irremovable good symmetry and essence.

Badness is not made, create - it is the stark absence
or hiding, of created good, for this reason or that locked -
the fertile mud, or polluted gravel on stone and rock.

The ancient Greeks carved their marble gods state
in the splendour of full human form - history's first;
later, the Divine also became Rock man, the Realist -
through the unseen Bond to together relate -
together the three in the one Whole, the ground -
ground to a perfect pitch, fine tuned, smooth honed ;
I believe this, I don't believe that,
and tumbled about, mumbling, I know not.
But the solid sanity in Stone, once liquid lava, remaindered -
remains

Canterbury Dec 2007

Stopping the rot of a muddy mind!

Peace is only present in the present moment -
no fixing, no doing just being aware
in times of green pastures -
in times of cracked drought.
Acceptance and self compassion -
not pre-living the future
or dwelling on hard times of the past;
not on autopilate but aware
in detachment from thinking,
planning worrying doing -
aware of direct bare experience
of the present as best as we can.

Let it be, let it be
whatever it is; it's ok

Forced stirring of muddy water
allows no patient settling of the mind

to clear water times.
We get in our own way
with self blame -
the mud is stirred with
'could's, ought's
would's, should haves';
likewise forcing thinking
to doing, to fixing,
to control things
to get our own way -
just provokes an agitated, stirred up
ruminative doom and gloom mind.

Let it be, let it be, let it settle.
Whatever it is, it's ok.

July 2012

The Street Gaits of Passers by -
of all ages - with glasses braces colours strides guises sizes
civvies hoodies tramps gals geezers pensioners toddlers -
and follow your feet. Humdrum pedestrian? - none
as I munch mouth-melt, my fizzle teasele scrumptious
'Lizzie's sticky lemon drizzle' tickling my taste buds cake slice

The Easy - letting go to gravity.

Most walk - living enthusing supple-moving,
limbs freely swinging sizzling
bouncing running hurrying worrying;
even the elderly slower hobbling
and trammelled by age
but within their bounds engaged
not rigid masked caged;
even a few with Parkinsons
still have an inner glint and shine
within their shaky stopped confines.

The Robot - in fear; severe gravity - the grave.

Just a mechanical aim
from A to Z to trundle along -
a frightening flat dead pan
paste of her face; a machine
in a bulbous coat and jeans -
her body a full fleshed skeleton.
No zip zest fizz buzz zing
worrying, puzzling -
nothing easy assured, none;
a short corpse walking -
and where was the life living
behind that rigid steel mask?
Was it made by heavy drugs?
to deaden the within chaos
or her way of survival unasked?
from first birth to the last end
in one so young, so deadened.

Feelings come first
even for the brain to form;
love, affection
not not, never nor last.

Feb 2009

Strict Haiku
Crumbs to jewels

	syllables
I saw a sick man	5
in winter sleet, creep low slung;	7
His sad, slow eyes - teared.	5
My red breast robin	5
flits fast to my feeding spot.	7
His kind eye looks deep.	5

Little snowdrops burst 5
white baubles, the first life sign 7
as my heart rises. 5

The forsythia 5
has suddenly burst 7
yellow. And I sleep! 5

The Sahara, sand blown 5
in ripples over low dunes - 7
cries out my dried soul. 5

A moth flutters stuck - 5
gutted in candle light wax. 7
Life ends in death - dunked. 5

Yahoo Internet 5
surfing fast, flips the wide world 7
for me - to find zilch. 5

Fish moth, why do you eat 5
my woollen kilt, round holed? 7
Shall I leave you there? 5

Crockery pots sit 5
well used, proud, ancient, serene. 7
I have feet of clay. 5

A blank paper page 5
is better than useless words. 7
I like clean white snow. 5

A little boy chucked 5
a hunk of bread at a duck 7
who turned full turtle. 5

Tiny ladybird 5
being bounced 'oooh' on a leaf 7
by falling rain drops. 5

Gales rip my roof ridge. 5
Phalanx winds hurl gusts at me. 7
I reel and stutter. 5

Sartorial bird - 5
immaculate green-sheen-black; 7
big crow, flying low. 5

The name of my house 5
is Chiang - angel seagull. 7
Thai elephant luck 5

Canterbury bells
Cathedral peel, ringing clear. 7
Old Harry - low, deep. 5

25.2.02 Canterbury

Unstrict Haiku

Autumn leaves
In a high wind
My choked cries falling.

Loss, nothing and dark appear to where You are; as much
The faint blossom on the plum tree, singing
Or a wood flute in the hills, rippling.

The mockery of life
hits in death; speaking in a
cocktail cup of opiate.

Jerked open
are the sluices of my
dammed up longing.

Two birch trees in the concrete street -

Their winter leaves falling
like yellow snow flakes.

God grounded, Cathedral earthed.
And Christ in the womb heard the beat
of his mother's heart.

It's over. Because the sine wave of season
protects against time - itself a part. Because the depth of grief
is never sounded. And tears dry quick.

The morning square is empty
and a shop sign squeeks -
wind hanging.

The street lamp tingles with light
the leaves silver. And the trunk in front
tries to hide its straight iron post.

Workers dad, steel-eyed mate
Wheel push chair
Chubbing child, cobbled street.

Pigeons settle on crumbs -
They clatter, skit-skeet,
flick-fly fast.

A long coat lady, old; twinkles her little legs;
A pudding hat pulled down -
firm above her nose in the street..

I sip my coffee at the round caf pavement table.
And my cigarette smoke rises -
incense.

25.2.02 Canterbury

Styles

Winter trousers ascendant and
jeggings - leggings, tight stretchy jog jeans;
I bet folk have a tug of war
to get them on mornings before the rush hour;
flared jeans are out except on a few middle aged.
Now old ladies keep up with the drift
of trouser stockings which are black tights
beneath a short skirt (not as short as in the young)
atop a long vest under coats which are very short even for men.
In summer and winter too layers of clothes are so in.
Posh young executives in silky suits -
'bum-freezer' jackets, tight trousers
with ankle wrinkles and long pointy shoes.
'It so is', 'cool' are slit holes in knee jeans, cold for winds.
Tights can come in multi-coloured swirled designs -
trousers in their own right, medieval-like
with wrinkled floppy tassled boots
or 'UGGS' if you can afford them at £200.
Big blousy bags are shoulder slung
only for shoulders level and straight hung
to stay on as they fall off slopes.
'Animal' and 'Superdry Jpn' T shirts and skimpy jackets are in
and one leg skateboards with a long handle are a must for kids.
Shaven or half shaven sandpaper or full beards abound
with hair very cropped short back and sides
and long ontop, creamed glistening smooth
or floppy in a one-eye-covering 'quiff'
with a toss of the head to clear the view.
And men can be head shaven shiny, polished, glossed;
women too have quiffs and very uneven chewed hair cut
all up and down to match their waterfall shawls.
Black and blue the predominant colours, bruised
but with Christmas a day away there's a flourish of reds.

Oh - just to fox me, a man in Bermuda shorts
made of a union jack with sandals passes by.
It is dead winter but mild for that but not that mild.

I sit at the City Arms sipping coffee watching.
I am annoyed as just next door near me
the silversmith shop is in full swing selling
much to men as gifts for their partners and wives.
The door never seems to stop loudly banging
as buyers escape with tiny parcels pocketed out.

Dec 2014

A Suicide

A dead body
Two days old
Two days old
In a cupboard
Blue bloated
Amongst shoes
Fumed foetus
Curled.
Curled in a cupboard
Womb dark
And bathed in her desolation
Extreme regression
Dead and stark.

A youth enfurled
Thanatos whirled,
With all the impression of vigorous earth.
Walking alone
With insidious Satre
Singing at a night club
For pocket cash.
Learning disease, drug
And her own diagnosis
Perverted to death.
Destiny governed
In a fist of pills
Incontinent

Denied in death.
Reeling at the desperation
And torment felt
That stretched out a hand
In help -
And found
Barbiturate.

Youth shall weary and condemn
It's god-filled parasitic parents -
Crucified for them.
Part of us dies
Saddened, frightened
At our own inevitable end.
Inside, we stand still -
Still as the heat
And scented oppression of Spring;
Still, with omission.
And the sun sets.

28.10.67 Medical student's death

Sun Shafts

Within an ice ball vulcanising deep magma within. Who melts - you and I.

Hurling up into the dead black sky the ember shower spray of lost loves hidden. She stood immobile in glazed eyes, staring resolute into death. Does the world end in a whimper. The sky said that and the still sea mocked the storm within.

The handbag of all women hung at her side - an emblem of servant hood. Tight shoes pinched squeezed feet as that was what was required by the rest. Her soul sped skyward high as a spiralling bird above sea and burnt like Icarus in the hidden sun.

He was old and smitten with care, spine curled and hips fat flabbed; creased trousers relaxed in the standing from his amble promenade. Before that he sat often, staring sad.

The past of separation father dying - and desolation annihilation despair. Mind swirled and the little girl within sobbed in hunger and neglect. Little hands reached out to be held in vacuum. So she retreated to hide where no children play on the seashores of time and delight.

The older man lived in a back street bed-sit. He walked to shake the snow fear flakes of aloneness and the finger of death - to see people pass. They moved, alive. But here was one heavy and still and he saw the white bird of her soul soar behind cloud and her blind gashed gaze seared .

The white bird sang to him to hold her safe so his wing enfolded her and the sun burst through in shafts.

27.10.01

The Town Supermarket

Regimented - shelf upon shelf
stacked with battalions of food -
oranges displayed in neat rows
angled at forty-five degrees -
stalk-docking pits uppermost
as if 'eyes right' - an army in salute.
Bread loaves of every sort -
staple food plastic packed,
their fresh baked scent blocked.

Oranges and Bread talk -
they want to be bought -
not to rot but
to give peace, delight.

But we grab at them, blind
to their uniqueness, beauty, good
and rush to the next overweight want -
confused at so much;
a third of all food bought
is unused, thrown out
while forests are slaughtered
and silent, scream out - cut;

while deserts blast sand
and people starve, hands out.

Aug 2010

A Swarm of Poppy Seeds Blown. Nunc Dimittis
(that world peace which the world cannot give, and neither can heaven)

Wasted concern blunt returned
triassic tedium empty churches echo
blind, blind to human need burnt
harm to hearts hurt. Servants - void
hollow with old dull gilt off-pat
cultivated egotism of guilt
credal dogma wear the right hats
at the proper times stand and sit
frozen mid-air incense fast fogs
the freedom of uniqueness bogged
on the shore the tide goes out
clutching flotsam bits of hope.
Of falling autumn leaves
he narrows his eyes to slits
and picks his teeth to bits
her corsets whale bone straight laced
buttress and hold her oozing encased
face like dough apart. The tongue protrudes
to the tip of my fear forehead beads of sweat
the pollen count soars upshot
doves and pigeons water-sip
heads-down, hopping sparrows can't.
words pickle over tea cups
running - the timid stop abrupt
and knock on the door shut,
throbbing with open fear
tears stream down cheeks
furrows in the soil clefts
'He wept' tear drops halo the universe.

Not refuse dumped - that refused
but re-fused sparked
passion bypassed in the past.
His real self wastes in each step
the air redolent with chaos
falling in a cone of ash
fear is no sin but the litmus
of danger, danger looms and booms reverberate
outwitting texting e-mailing downsizing evaluing
appraising conferencing fast tracking monitoring -
I can only afford nothing -
we part not caring - each alone. Pug faced.

Gripping the rail up the chapel steps
the dove's lament curdles triads of honey tones
a young sparrow trembles to be fed
his words fur with warmth in his throat
music strokes my fiery head
wounds heal with scabs picked off -
as plums secrete resin in tear drops.
A sign of wisdom - dependence, the blood of hope
scars, broken sap the marks
not of shame but life's honour dark.
Poppies fire in blood shelled soil holed
their bloated dead body pods with choirboy ruffs
old, white opium pain dulled
and the little hills skip like lambs
let my people go - he said
and it was done so, shattering the glass.
Grotesque entropy demeans renews
myrrh oiled feet tear-washed hair-dried
behovely sin nibbles frozen wings free
trust woven to passion, descent into hell.
My eyelids from closing Thou dost hold

Thinking of you as a dream hope scent ascending
of the pasture bedstraw spikes honey rancid in hot sun
wafting amongst the wild waving wind grass
they think slow in wise lethargy

what they say is nothing - as
being right is not being now
truth waddles like a wood pigeon
from side to side, blinkered by his nostril bumps
to see either side, and not the binocular vision
in two depth dishes whole as an owl who sees
forward at night in the dark

Stress illness an all time high
rocketing suicide rates in the young
children on anti-psychotic pills
the divorce rate, teenage pregnancy the highest in Europe
endemic alcohol and drug abuse
religions fight, praying places for the insider elite.
empty fast. Abuse of under-involvement neglect
guilty by omission - the pain held firm sway
within the glint of reaped grain, wheat and tares,
we see slowly the little house who cares
where hands can be warmed, hearts held
buzzing bees plonk down on the flowers
nuzzling easy on clover low. Asking tilts to receiving
a piece of silver paper tilts the unbalanced scale back
a piece of paper is the same in any city, in any street.
Dried, the pepper-pot pods split grape-shot shaken and sling -
a seed speck shell breaks, the heart in pain takes wing.
Very quietly now - Nunc dimittis.

Canterbury July 2004

Sweet Chestnut

Hello leaf. Have I chosen well?
Mustn't reject you 'cos you're brown and olding
and wet with tears with a dead snail sludge.
This balmy day and some freedom from pain
leaving little tinged blips.
Spear shaped assegai leaf - a fighter
but now time to lay down your spear

in autumn before winter's age.
Like me you are. I lift you to the light
which shines through and like me too perhaps
as I have inherited those same light photons
from the Big Bang birth of the universe
trillions of years ago - and still here.

2013

Sweets

A plump person
dawdles past
a patisserie shop -
No. 10 Butchery lane
followed by
her patient spouse.

Seeing the window
sweeties and bonbons -
gaudy, handmade,
she turns and pushes
the gilt lettered door -
(they have old leather books
and an ancient bell gramophone) -
and enters the treasure trove
in anticipation.
And hubbie follows
with a smile on his rotund face.

The juices are dripping
and the cellulite piggies
squeal in delight.

I love it chuckling.

Feb.2015

Sainsvery's Safe-reserve Animal Vegetable Mineral
Symphony Orchestra
('Bare Bones Bumpily' limerick song
in G major. Allegro Maestoso*)

Elegant elephants honking
zillion kangaroos thumping
platypi plop
jellyfish slop
pattering porcupines grumbling.

Clattering cauliflowers bugle
happily, cucumbers giggle
lettuces rap
aubergines tap
flatulent broccolis gurgle.

Amethysts, emeralds tumble
silicates, sodalites grumble
carbonates bob
arsenates sob
malachites, microlites mumble.

Busily, bumble-bees nuzzle
anxiously, anchovies frizzle
crocodiles snap
butterflies flap
garrulous grasshoppers guzzle.

Reddening radishes ring
chicory, celery sing
coconuts clash
pineapples bash
cabbages, artichokes ping.

So animal, vegetable, mineral
rang definitely finally musical.
They banged on the beat
and jumped on their feet,

then flowed down the scale as they're whimsical.

Canterbury Feb 2003

*allegro - sprightly }
maestoso - majestically } !

Symptom Substitution

People can frighten me sometimes
as I, identity lost, become them.
But unique I am - I am me
so no need to feel deficient,
so no need to compare.
The word 'special' is better -
less isolating than 'unique'.
Now the repetitive tune within flares -
obsessive intrusive pervasive -
a new pain and fear.
Ruminative doom and gloom
has become a base three note tune
maybe to be seen as a boon -
as a primitive voice calling for true sound.
But I have learnt to substitute
a compiled CD-tune list to relieve -
to click on within my loose-lost mind.
Must see this as a minor pain
and maybe the tunes are lullabies -
soothing company in music's sound.

And now I have IBS pain,
pummelled from all sides
white-knuckled
I am.

Now that has gone -
replaced by sheer fear.
The only certainty is uncertainty.

I have to inwardly work
    on all this
    and work
to keep that work alive.

June 2012

Old Frayed Tapestry

The deep wound zooms past the pin-point of recall
but double valued, divine; a photosynthetic cry -
though I was loved before time was
and met when yet far off then
and even now if my stormed centre will allow
but that my real 'sin' - separate from my God
through those who bore me
in separation abuse death and fractured pain;
being genuine while there is yet time
and time goes fast and dies before I
and i who have little time left,
bewildered isolate, learning how to learn
and accommodate - homeless
in this homeless house.
True human pain so sharp we hit the ampoule
and braked to a false full stop
in the hive of too many sounds and words.
And yet is not yet - not quite the ripe seed split
or too ripe well before time;
old, encasing a left, dark child
and we get by, by fumble jumble guess-work -
the new-born still damp in the dark tunnel of fear,
still trembling to settle in peace in a mother's safe hold.
Our lips spill streams of words.
No more my name seems right, and never was -
with my eyes scanning hidden for a welcome smile;
the thin end edge of this wedge keeps us primed
and across the wooden floor, light settles
like a sword-struck shaft - sun melting the glue dark

and a Jenny Wren sings sharp, stark;
everything is here and is being ashed slowly enough
and so I care just correctly little and horribly more;
fatuous prayer and serenity is dispelled in tears.
A rising vertical and horizontal trust
a bruising event - the cross.
A furious storm then sun shot-spliced the dark
and the seed shell splits, sudden - apart -
soul sours reborn within the pain of the crack;
the singing flow - I wish it were.
The default click of no return, struck dumb
causing the forest to fail by watching leaves fall
with no more coming spring.
Where else can I care more? -
and yet with my heart deep...
Still?

Oh.
on taste

written from the top of my mouth (and head),
the tip of my tongue,
my tongue in my cheek etc

Zangy zest zings sweet scent squits and sings
oily orange orbs fresh round pristine glow
little tingling pimple pits ooze and ping
peeling in delight with a squeak and a bite
teared eyes shine as I tear the thick skin low
white pith cloth coat-off, blest undressed now
mouth waters, juices in abundance flow
crescent curve segments crack and ring
yellow liquid bursting in wide sharp squirts
popping tiny globule capsule bits apart
of ripe meat soft flesh seeds flat squashed;
so, sucked dry, the pith spat out fast
and the dour sour earth sweetens, lights.

No good company here now, as before
I sat on a low wall dangling swung legs
in the thirsty sun high hot, high and far.
But I once saw touched smelt tasted heard
and danced. And it was good. Not now.
O.!

Haiku

Crisp green grape strung taut
I bite once and crack sweet juice
My firm flesh bursts forth.

Canterbury Jan 2005

'Tell me what it is you plan to do with your one wild and precious life?' (Mary Oliver)

I will fly into heights unheard of
as an eagle soars sublime
or a falcon falling diving
two hundred miles an hour
rocketwise down
to a rat on the ground.

I would leap like a leopard
down to kill a deer below the tree
spotted dappled silk-smooth

or a lion lazing in the shade
purring after a huge meal.

No locust or grasshopper I.

Oct 2013

Britain's Ten Commandments Now

1. Treat others as you would have them treat you.

2. Take responsibility for your actions.

3. Do not kill - except in euthanasia, abortion and war.

4. Be honest.

5. Do not steal - except in order to eat to survive.

6. PROTECT AND NURTURE CHILDREN.

7. Protect the environment.

8. Protect the vulnerable.

9. Never be violent.

10. Protect your family.

Draft of mine.

Trust the wisdom of your guide and if not - why?
Love yourself - as unique and special
Understand your past and its darkness and its affects on you now
Help the hungry starved of love (and yourself) and starved of food
Be aware sensitive considerate firm understanding
Enjoy your life and what you have in small things. No need to compare others
Let creativity take you
Respect children as little persons and that within you.
When snow falls, drop everything and go to it.
You may then 'see' God within you and outside in others and things
and may then feel love

Tenderness
A Breaking Taboo

The quality of Tenderness is not strained -
as a soft breeze, it breathes, goes and comes -
it condemns not, neither does it judge;
it waits patient - its roots spring from first being loved
like a tender child within mother's smile and arms
and so, who loves in welcoming contact return;
it holds - in the soft aura of understanding concern -
empathic intuitive, not put on like a garment, assumed.
Its ultimate nature is from Love, fresh or warm
and is tendered, offered for our acceptance with open hands.
It is given by the generous grace of heavens sunshine and
thus it creates out of love and waits to be received to amend
as nature abhors the vacuum of barrenness intoned alone -
and in togetherness, communed, it can bud blossom fruit bloom,
watered by its rippling music stream; attuned -

it twinkles, strengthens, suffers and soft melts;
in congruence, it can burst the wineskins of hardened hearts
and its cup runs over, calm quiet, waiting to be sipped or quaffed.
It goes out to meet - delicate spirit, authentic real, secure sure
and tenuous fine slender; so feared as so betrayed unadored before -
once bitten we are twice hardened sore-steeled to wall a tender core.
In its vulnerability lies gentle strength, firm reliant -
easily bruised but remaining costly courageous constant.
Its rainbow colours are delicate soft, or radiant resonant -
bursting as the sun through the fragments, stark unknown
of stained glass, melting the iced dark - atoned.
It is Colour's palette - not the then superimposed idea, form.
It has few still words - simple ordinary, often unheard -
its smile, the eyes ...in compassion encompass, warmed.

When damaged with distrust, can we have feared courage
to begin to risk to trust and the little gifts receive, thirst assuaged.
This fragile trust within fire ice, gathered tenderly in its arms -
of 'make My healing touch your home', a home found first.
Before the beginning it was, is and shall ever be, sunburst -

faithful given Tenderness - rarely seen, received
in this 'far off' broken embattled world, violent parched
crying out for its tender touch to slake starved thirst -
bridging living paradox opposites, warp and weave, cruciate,
spinning through companions friends, oneness consummate.
Tenderness, as music, is the food of love - touched on.
We are born to be loved to love or else die shrivelled, fleshless bone.
Tenderness, the fertile soil where growth sown inspired, must at one.
And upon the face of the waters, the spirit of God moved.

April 2007

The Desert
Water

The U.K. in September is cold at 14 degrees C
and wet most of the time. Green. In N. Africa it's 44 -
a sweltering sun, parched arid land
with patches of green - crops and trees,
olives, oranges, pomegranates and vines
where the rich can afford a bored well.
Dry river beds, eroded brown earth.
The people wear long loose light clothes
often white, reflecting heat -
djellabahs with peaked hoods for shade, some black like monks.
The church here wears desert clothes cassocks, albs -
long remnants of the eastern desert days.
The affluent West - the church here cannot fathom
biblical stories where water is central, rare -
like Christ by the well, waters of lfe,
the vineyard, baptism, community life
still so strong in desert life now.
Here the old are left to die by themselves. Isolate.
Sandals are worn, not shoes.
No wonder the bible is not understood -
it's not written for the west
unless wells and water and deserts

are taken to mean inner states.
Water as the source of life -
3 days without it and you're dead.
not so without food. The desert is wilderness
where no people are; isolation, abandonment.

Christ walking thirty miles trying to explain his purpose
to his disciples - unlistening
and bragging about their good works.
That is - Christ, often in the desert, is lonely, isolate
in the midst of company - his 'deaf' 'friends' -
so he took up a child to show them
that his God values qualities of the child;
children were insignificant in those days
except for their work done and inheritance.
'No man is free who will not dare to pursue
the question of his own loneliness'. His too
in the secret chambers of the heart, shared.

Where water is, there also is the exotic -
dates herbs spices grapes sultanas couscous,
mint tea poured from on high
from a curvy graceful hot water pot.
Almonds figs honey lamb. Manna. Beggars, the crippled.

Nov.2012

?The Disabled Enable a holy dying?
finding a homeland where you are not yearning, dying to live for something else
yet dying to life for ?a new life

Unable to sit walk talk
a seizured six year old
24 hour in home care - died
and Parliament recessed in respect -
the first time ever for a child,
the first time for a long time

the real personal unites where politics divides -
the eldest son of the family of Cameron
leader of the opposition, the shadow PM.
The PM and him have now both lost a child -
in the House of Commons, in common.

The boy gave a sense of peace
to all in his serene presence
with large deep eyes and a smile -
the rest of him immobile

Through the haze, it dawned -
this the way to die - reborn
in complete rest and quiet
resting in the arms of the divine
held safe within the father's arms -
with no more fight - struggle and fear gone;
the emergency escape hatch.

But the disabled have 24 hour care;
at the end, usually alone - would I?
Will the Homeland find me instead?-
a history of - it doesn't -
but I don't know. It may.
The foundation
of the house of personality
is laid in life's first year -
worn out through torn war -
eating your own liver in stress -
self-ending is an escape
from being disgraced.
This the dying echo -
the stillness of intense silence
booms and reverberates;
zenith - the point of the heavens
directly overhead. A twilight.
The uncertainty of love hurts -
eating humble pie -

putting love in where love isn't.

Mar 2009

The First Part

And the scritch of skiffed nylon
As she leavened her way from the chair
The rosewood unfelt door aching
In finger tip to smoothe and silk touch.
I saw two pictures of a young pale boy
with Indian hair lying cornered
by a rising club. My aim is wisdom.
The other a mosquito net veiled white
Pouring golden coins
On a brown coffin with brass clasps;
And anger as a boy fondled jutting
brown pipped breasts of a young girl across lust.
Radio one I said. Vaguely I said
How personal this all was and others said
how justly wrong the writing of it.
There are things we observe and find words for
Which are lost.
When we say die, meaning what?
And I have seen many deaths before.
You are playing chess with my mind -
And the sound of sweeping
And short harsh breathing
up the carpet stairs. Shells.
Shells cutting down the time of unspent depth
Which would consume and fuse.
In my country things are young, urgent.
This plaster pip is your nipple
And this garland phallus on the wall -
'I'd like one' I have heard them say
Thrusting powerful hips.
I cannot stay at these levels
among mumbled unprofundities

and expensive words.
I have the unwanted answer
from corner eyes
across the dinner tables
Between
        flamed
            silver
                dark
That warm womb cannot open again
The shell remains - and others -
And if the light is wet
We occasionally see pearled colours.
And that is the unwanted answer
They have said many times.
A stretch of wild coast in the South
Where the wind mourns blowing grass -
Running free - I - a thousand flamingo
pink flight arrow shot.
That was mine inside -
It had to be walking
round round.
I only sit down when people come.
And sonorous tone echo
of tugs in the river fog.
English pennies are heavy
And make purses fat -
Have you noticed each
in wear and colour and width?
I have one 1894 thin smudged and burnt -
Brittania's right breast
is always the first to go.
Beside the waters of Zion
we sat down separate at tables,
sipping coffee in a shop
and hung our harps on weeping willows
and scaffold pipes as she asked deep thoughts.
I said no, seven later years -
They have said it many times -
But I have never liked the sound

The sound of my spoken words.

3.12.68
Beginning analysis - London

The Journey

This journey? I'm stuck -
butterflies in my stomach -
do I journey or not?
The inevitable end -
Damocles sword
swings high and wide
immanent.
They say its good
to have death's face confront.
But I long to be young
and thoughtless
and extravagant.
Jesus I'm not.
A journey - what's that?
Hate the word flat.

July 2014

The Library Meeting Room

The room and the table wait -
expectant for us to give birth to the word
under the care of a wordsmith midwife;
to then build blocks and knock them around
or on the anvil to forge and hammer steel shapes
under the sparks of laughter and hidden tears.
Creation is always violent in its birth
pushed and pulled in sweat and pain
and blood and tears; in ice, in thirst.

But, near bubbling streams
there's a smile as well.

Feb 2013

The Praying Mantis God

In the beginning of the world when the word was god, millions of years ago - fire and wind and water and earth alone lived peacefully together. One day there was an earthquake, storm, tornado and volcanic eruption all at once and out of these elements, in one second in time, god was begat. He was also the devil. His attire was that of peace and war. His mantis face scarlet gashed, his eyes angry and vengeful. His fine cow hide shield was never needed for none could overcome him; and his staff of office and power - a cross - and his sainthood hung as a crossed halo kept up by his golden ear-rings and his ears heard all things and God knew all things. His right hand was held in false greeting, ready for benediction in the name of the father, son and holy Ghost and he wore a ring of marriage to himself. Fine jewelled beads circled his neck, ankle and wrists which the people gave in expiation of their sins but his hand was ever ready to halt and crush flesh which was thrown to his cavernous throat. He was a fine powerful god and knew all things in Heaven and Earth - because by this time there was a separation into the two.

And he arose out of the earth and shat upon the earth - and Phoenix the golden eagle appeared, whose wings were torpedoes and pieces of shit. And Phoenix thrust his beak into the cunt of god, for god was man, woman and child and holy Ghost. And god thrust his phallus into the throat of the bird, and the eye saw all things and it was good. And god's testes burnt in ecstacy red, from which two leopards drank, guarding a cave inside. Out of this union was begat mary, the mother of god, who was god's unborn child. And water-robed mary begat a white christ rat in the womb of god which was a dark cave lined with guardian angel rocks. And an everlasting fire kept the cave warm. And god's umbilical stump was gnawed by two sea fish which gave him continuous belly ache. His groans sprang thunder and his umbilical stump was joined to rat christ's cord. And christ rat was albino still-born. And god's phallic eye spewed forth pink sperm mixed with the blood of christ crucified. And a white nation was born. And god's moon mountain breasts 'nyanga', were filled with pus and pumpkin pips which grew melons and pregnant people with no bones. And the eyes of his breasts saw all things and were sad. And his belly shook and the earth trembled with his crying. But he was a wrathful god and gouged out persons with his blood dripped horns and he gnawed his prey to pulp. His destiny was everlasting hunger and his belly would rumble and shake the earth.

But he was a fine powerful god and knew all things in Heaven and Earth. Thus god lives forever. Amen. Aaaih.

Ngulube. (which means pig). (the name of our car when I was little).

? date early Cape Town

The Nativity - a local native birth

Yes, the God-Child is being born -
symbolic native and real in all -
ordinary people, shepherds the apostles;
bishops popes now just richly dressed up;
Christ - the bridge between people and God;
angels - persons with depth contact.
All can give birth within to the God -
if receptive aware - as Mary was
and Mary's birth pangs in all, torn -
the work of giving ultimate Essence
which can be so obscured, dense but immense;
and Mary's hand in pain stretched up to the God
met by the absent man, Joseph's present hand -
'present' both as a gift and the now in presence -
who, despite the stigma, came to come alongside -
the hidden Christ in his hand.
The divine works through his creation man
borne in us through our animal simple nature -
in the sheep, donkeys, manger cot. The journey long

just also as that of the wise men
who balanced immanent blood and life's natural muck
with the universal transcendent song
with energy in God, unseen, the 'process'
and seen the 'object' in Christ - interwoven, involved -
now in a form - mathematics, physics in this age
in the amazing principles and unknowns of science, sung;
just as waves seen are not water but energy unseen within.
And a song is not that unless sung by someone.

What did the holy family do
with the given gold myrrh and frankincense? -
perhaps to help the poor around
and a support in times, ground down, of hardship
and to set up home and a carpentry shop.
But just as much -
an indication, dormant or discovered -
of the rich gifts and talents
given us
among the pain and muck.

Standing under -
I am trying to understand
the relevance now
of that remote
event.

Feb 2011

The Task
Describe a place in a single 200 word sentence

The Place The Universe
What's On Shooting Stars
A True Story

A first showing will be held in the Celestial Universe Cinema Monday

18th November in the year two thousand and two, at 11.30pm of a star performance of thousands of Shooting Stars - so reserve your seats outside, wrap up warm and scan the sky with emphasis on the North East but, be assured, further performances and encores will occur though Cloud Curtains may obscure the shows, even though the best seats will cost Simple Delight and the cheapest - Complicated Thinking but those exhibiting denigration, false intellectual snobbery and snootiness will experience a sharp flash of thunder and be evicted henceforth by the doorkeepers - as the Universe is, as you know, everywhere and nowhere, though non-dual, is yet diverse in its unity - so you may therefore also be interested to know that the Director and Producer is Alpha and Omega, the Cast are Angels and the Costumes are designed by Light; - this information was relayed to the announcer of Classic FM radio, though not in this manner - and Patrick Moore with his monocle and one raised eyebrow confirmed the message so they hope you will have an exhilarating experience - though later, I am now sad to say, that indeed, the Cloud Curtains obscured all performances with consequent sighs of disappointment from the gathered audiences, as God was either a spoil-sport or more probably, nay indeed, feeling very tired and near cloud-tears after a busy day dealing with his wandering, confused, troubled, lost peoples.

Canterbury Dec.2002

Notes.
? he will mind me sort of taking the mickey.
Better heard read than seen read.
I'm a believer in dashes.
A semi-colon ; is that 'marking a point greater
than the division of a comma'.

The Spiral

Dying is giving one's whole life back
to other life - to give it sustenance -
to make more space; a letting go -
fragile vulnerable, with a whole heart -
at the end without bitterness, fear.
This passion of deep gut fear

which can be a catalyst is hard to bear -
points failure of body parts and love -
at profound loss a good grief
and gain of possible wisdom, depth, belief
to death programmed for timeless life.
Dying is in all - little and large; it comes
borne as a bag of pebbles, stones or rocks -
round the corner, now or miles away; it mocks;
but who knows - maybe it could be safe.

Meanwhile recapture the sheer delight
as if a toddler
discovering walking for the first time
which is only possible
if he knows he is surrounded
by big ones caring for him and safe.
And when he stumbles and falls
they are there to calm his cries in fright.
A fresh new day each day
one day at a time -
no before no after
but here, Now.
A God watching over.
Just to trust. But how?

The wild flower meadow blooms
and after is curved-steel-scythed,
the ground then harrowed for new life
heavily gouged and scarred.
Poppies, daisies, sky-blue cornflowers die,
their seeds wind-blown, broad-cast wide arced.
The old to a compost heap of death -
heavy harrowing grief
enriching poor soil for young growth.

I have waited long to be free of fear.

Sept.2010

The Starved…

are my gold standard;
those who I have - to think of -
not celebrities, not athletes,
not olympians, not professionals,
not families, not couples,
not whatever

but the poor and hungry
the neglected, abused
and the lonely.
These are the greats -
these have courage.
These the golds

So when my cup feels empty -
remember who they are.
And help.

Aug 2012

The Table (What do we put on it?)

Simply.

I put nothing on the table
as Nothing can give
the possibility of All.
So I put God on the table
and he didn't like that -
dissected and confined
but he liked it
in the bread and wine,
broken - and others shared;
as he was broken

like us - it is said.

July 2014

In All
The Thesaurus

The dominion within
little words, gifts given -
such obvious creatures,
their presence, structures
taken for granted, even.
Solid small glue words,
holding together unheard
the loud long words of different size
and guise but not small, common
and replaceable often likewise.

Little words, no substitute - some,
except in a sentence - long.
Like, but-in-the-is-not-done
if-he-to-she-it-us-on;
for-a-yes,-both-by-an-at
my-be-I-am,-does-me-not ;
and-with-our-some,-we-be-do
was-of,-now-does,-or-can-so
up-who-are,-what-did-that-oh.

Tiny buds come slow,
survive in frost, hard snow;
incredible, bract wrapped
tender weak, exposed trapped
in bitter bleak - but capped.
You find another name for 'the' or 'that'!
there's not even one for 'bract' -
meaning a precious leaf of gold.
crowning the little heart-fold.

It's all by an All -
that I am.

Lent 2006

They
Editors

they want you to write fast lines
they want you to think of many words
they want you to be superficial
or intellectually abstruse
they want you to write what they want, not you
they don't like what you write
and don't understand what you do.
They keep you waiting months and months
and send you rejection slips.
They want you to write 40 lines only
and most of all
it's your money they want.

Canterbury Feb 2003

Those Eyes
The Hours

Metaphor is a luxury language in starving countries

Sand veers and sears in eyes, lungs phlegm -
from harsh scrub flatland seen through dust;
their bank cash - as penned goats condemned,
their water bugged with filth and thirst
behind a thorned, rood-fenced requiem.

The young for the old - investment shrouds,
mothers die fast before and giving birth;

flies zoom down dark, quick stung, in clouds,
but war has stopped; loud tanks quiet rust; bare earth;
kids shit and vomit parched, wounds rot; language - bed rock.
Scrap. Folk count as little worth.

They walked three days for hospital help -
the child screams tears - his compound fracture realigned -
tortured, ligatured, sutured - without drugs.
Those eyes. Bright burn. And shine.
White bone through dark skin - bloodcrust fear.
How can you not crack and cringe
at such shuddering hurt - unhinged?
Under windflood - gusts thud.
Those eyes - sear through - as winds sheer.

To survive, to accept, to go on - proud.
He makes a spade from tank tin rust,
she makes charcoal, hallowed load,
he works till he slumps in deserted desert dust,
she gives spare wound swabs and crusts.
A baby is born.
And we give scorn.
And small concern.
An aid forlorn
from our full bellies - robust
and carping mouths unjust.

In this - (vertiginous rage) -
to us who wait and assuage -
and unsharing fiddle, and fractured flutter
while simple unbowed people die and suffer?
But the essence of us knows and can restore -
The hours. Those eyes. They're also yours.
They're ours.

Canterbury Mar 2003

Threadbare Cloth

The hound wound zooms
past the pin-point of recall
but double valued, a divine reply;
fractured, unfound, a hell-hole,
a photosynthetic sun-eclipse cry -
though I was loved before time
and met when yet far off then, fine
and even now if my stormed centre will allow
but that real 'sin' - god-separate the sign
through those who birth-bore me sour
in separation death and abuse, malign,
marked unasked on an ashed, gashed brow.
Being genuine while there is yet time
and time goes fast and dies before I -
and i who have little time left, am left
learning how to learn, bewildered isolate
to accommodate this homelessness, adrift,
situate in this homeless house until
the pain so sharp we hit the pill -
cracked the capsuled silver paper pack
and braked to a false stop back
in a within hive of buzzing sounds and words;
with congealed phlegm snot,
wax-glued, opaque viscid -
that, - the thick silence without, set.
And yet is not yet -
not quite the ripe fruit, seed-secret-split
or too ripe well before the target time ratchet;
old, encasing a left, dark child here hit.
We get by, by jumbled guess work -
the new born still damp, dear
in the dark tunnel of fumbled fear,
still trembling to settle in peace, bare -
at one in some mother's safehold withheld; rare.
Our lips spill streams of spit words.
No more my name seems right -
with eyes scanning sight hidden bright

for a welcome smile, light;
the thin edge of this wedge might
keep us jammed tight, armed bereft.
And across the wooden warped floor, cleft
light slits and strikes like a sword struck shaft -
sun melting the dense solid dark;
and a Jenny Wren sings sharp, stark;
then and now, in Belsen no bird sings.
Everything is here and is being ashed slowly before
and so I care correctly small and fearfully more.
Defensive serenity, prayer unfelt across
a rising vertical and horizontal trust
a killing event - the cup which did not, not pass
in beads of blood sweat before the cross.
A furious storm, then the sun,
splice-shot the dark
and the seed-shell splits apart -
soul sours reborn within the pain of the crack,
the singing-freeing flow. I wish it were;
undoing a default click of no return dumb struck
causing the harvest to halt,
with spring coming no more.

Where else can I care more
at all - and outcall, outpour
and yet my heart, hidden deep, sore ...

He is in all, all for me, me in all
in the chalice cries crumbs crusts
the craves and crises, the gaps
that crown the cruxcross.
In pigeons, profane passion, people passing, scrap
panic, scaffolding, parable, pavement cracks
prayer, chaos, pebble-puzzle-patch;
a picture - the pieces shut
puzzle-placed, snap.

outcast obedience
a listening to acceptance
what is - is, the voice -

no more no less.
The Little House, humble - lovable
cosy quiet, patient personal
snuggled essential, sincere special
dell-deep, sheer steep. Now, vital;
hid high down Summer Hill - tranquil
where the sun-fire sets low and level
below rowed fields of fruit, still, rural
'til cupped hands warm pick -
gentle.

2005-06

The Throstle(the crucifiction)
The Thrush's Thinging Throngsong
(threshed thyme - to th... Thou the divine)

Thou thinkest that this thin thief-thing
thirsts thy thought thrust through thick
and thin, though thrashing themed theory
that thronged those thirty thicket thorns
threaded through thy thermalled thundered throne.
That thorax throbbed,
thereafter the three thumped thuds thawed.
Than that this throat thrilled,
that then thou thoroughly threw
thyself through their threatened thin,
thonged theology theme.
Thrombosed thanatos thugs they,
their theist thoughts, throes,
theories, theses - throttling thorned.

Thence Thou thrived that theatre -
there thrown - thwarted them thus -
that this thin thing, that thither thereby therein,
this third thief, therefore thrice thanks thee,
thousandfold - thanks thine.

These, Thy Thee Thou
Thyself Thine.

Canterbury June 2002

Apologies for ‘to’, ‘divine’ and ‘and’ as non-th... words.
A throstle is the older word for a song thrush.
‘Thinging’ refers to singing the ‘thingness’ (Heidegger) of a thing!
‘Threshed thyme’ smells sweet.
Apparently the Sanskrit tat.h for that and similar english words have divine implications. The th... words found seemed to dictate a ‘christian theology’.
It is about the obfuscation of r/Reality by theory, preconception, paradigm etc.
The three thuds refer to the sound made by the three nails of the cross.
It is neither ‘evangelical’ nor ‘liberal’ nor ‘catholic’.
In Yorkshire folks still address another as ‘thou’.

Working Through (mourning the losing of former life)

Does it really matter - no.
Does anything really matter -
Detachment - yes.
Drop thy still dews of quietness
Drop shoulders, chest
Deep breath in and out - quietly is best
Acceptance - with patience wait.

my soul is exceeding sorrowful even unto death -
take this cup from me but not my way but thine -
with no-one here to be with. And days on end.

this before me now - a cup and plate - vital sight
each small thing - that before my ears, eyes ;
cutting a pear - slowly and with care -
no need for speed passing over fast

no chores - instead, every little thing the crux to life
and no-one here; just a voice within
and perhaps being held by Him as an idea.

in Africa - a dehydrated starving child -
awful. It cracks. Wracked by tears.
the child within dies. Bodiless substance -
perhaps being held by Him, Ideal, as an idea.

Sin - falling short of the mark, not wide -
falling short of one's true essence -
of succumbing to the impact of one's negative past
engulfing anything positive and good.
Yet I'm not sure. But I say the confession. Broken inside.

M, Tracy, Jon, Amy
Ruth, Valerie; Lizzie - yes;
(and maybe Sarah, Sue though I doubt -
in this I was right!).

I need to be content with what I have
and who I am - and learn to wait;
to go inside for the things that count
except I feel there is none now except distress.
A fearful life goes on, mundane -
am I precious, loved? yes - sane.

Inner karate discipline required.
I am a white belt in life.
Change - a new life desired - a painful birth.
Thy way and will be done.

June 2011.

Ticking Time Bomb - Intimations of Mortality

get the hell out of me - infected, cancerous in fear;

peace begets peace but fear begets fear.

the fear of future dying lonely, stewing in shit, paralysed
except in imprisoned awareness, tortured, incised -
without community where there is loving and love
in meaningful relating - authentic, soft, moved.
Where an old close 'friend' might die
and in fear of that I die inside.
The child inside is dying. That's the cross, the crux.
The siren song of imprinted distress.

unable to cope, but coping doing
not being - as being alone is hell;
perhaps seen as abnormal in many ways
from low self respect, gut riddled fear.
Sparked off by the diagnosis of CKD -
chronic kidney disease grade three,
the minor type. And attempts to sell and move house
to God knows where - nearer a shop, a bus - in case
and moving people moving outside - not still and dead.

And should it be ended now but how.
I envy those with a terminal sentence. At least they know.
But M has survived one kidney out.

Yet a loving caring dying might be best -
maybe it should be trusted to happen -
can I wait? - the last hope and faith.
And where all death is an explosion to the universe -
transformed to an unimaginable unspeakable way -
maybe to that of a true child - but this time held.

Yet rage at this onslaught and when that lulls
the ordinary little things and people's good signs -
a smile. a hello, a laugh shared
at their own time, place and pace unforced, cared.

And it's me - Elizabeth - precious in essence, good.
'It's you, Elizabeth', 'talk to me' says God.

When I was little 'they' moved a lot and died a lot
hence the me now, without control - as then.

This is ordinary anxiety and lots of people feel it a lot.
This is growing older to a new age
and the only thing peculiarly proper is whatever is going on now -
not before, not later. A difficult task.

June 2011

Time

Gulls are working the wind-gushes
while marine skies stay silent,
quiet in the clear blue glare;
small adjustments to feathers in tail or wing
while black bead eyes scan below for a snack
then dark clouds crowd and rumbling confer
and white waves slash the shores below.
Relentless change, action, motion, flow -
if not the gulls would drop flopped to the rocks
like a peregrine falcon plummets to the kill -
this time stone dead and still.

And time and
nothing never ever stays forever the same.
But something will as
eternity is where time has stopped
to timelessness leavened within,
inspanned, the Name.

May 2010

Ref. Notes (addendum to Time, Water, Wild and Wind. etc.

The early **foetus is sexually ambiguous**, ambivalent, neither male nor female, then at about 7 weeks it differentiates, the female being the basic default state, as in computers, (not faulty) with no gonad descent externally. The male foetus undergoes further development under the influence of the SRY gene in the Y chromosome producing DHT (dihydroxytestosterone) and gonad descent to the testes.

One might therefore say that the male is secondary to the female. But that means to ignore the blueprint maleness inherent in the Y chromosome at fertilisation not yet evident till after 7 weeks. Or even that the male is more advanced than the female!

It is suggested that **recognisable humans** are about 40,000 years old - that is showing recognisable human behaviours - artefacts, burial sites. Neanderthal man 500,000-200,000 yrs old.

Their art shows they have thought and maybe were aware of time. But c.f. also Orangutangs, Chimps, Capuchins.

Mesopotamian Babylonian (now Iraq) pagan (Etym - rustic, villager) = polytheistic creation myths said to be from 5000 yrs. BCE to 1600 yrs BCE. - possibly the earliest written creation myths. The epic of Gilgamesh and the Enuma Elish story. The change from polytheism to monotheism was gradual. Most Israelites were initially polytheistic hence a slow change was made but allowing 'in our image' to allow slow accommodation to the monotheistic idea.

There seems to be an **evolutionary progression from polytheism originally, to the idea of a chief god, to monotheism's one god**. Ancient Egypt's sun god Ra 3000yrs BC and Ancient Greece's Zeus (Jupiter Roman) 800 yrs BC whose lesser gods made the first woman. In the Mesopotamian myths the lesser gods made humans to help them. They needed humans in their work.

In Botswana Africa evidence of **Snake ritual worship** 70,000 years ago from cave paintings and carbon dateings.

It is posited, though with no empirical evidence that **language** must have arisen 360,000 to 150,000 years ago. The task to find out about this is said to be 'the hardest task that science has ever had to undergo' - study of primate behaviours and vocalisations. ?inbuilt genes for grammar infant studies.

Of yore, **Jewish boys at 3 years** of age started studying the Hebrew alphabet encouraged by being given wooden blocks dipped in honey. Now all children are taught. Previously vowels were excluded from writing but they are now included. It's the Aramaic Hebrew alphabet (there are others e.g Yiddish) now.

Quarks - a sub-atomic particle carrying a fractional electric charge; the building blocks of **hadrons** which form protons and neutrons. They have not been observed but their existence has been confirmed on experimentation. 6, 3 pairs (up/down, top/bottom, charm strange.

Other sub-atomic particles/creatures **Muons** - mew! **Gluons** - glue! **Quarks** - quack! They're cute.

Post-modern Perhaps. Skipping on a new edge of the circle.

Writing a paper is like an infant being formed in utero; the time comes when it needs to come out, be born with midwives/husbands urging 'push' or 'stop'.

I have also felt as if I am playing with re and upcycled old toys made new, brand new toys from new books and some toys I have made by hand. Toys being ideas. It enlarges ones being. We have all come before all the great studies, they came after us, from us. T-shirts tell us something like 'Play outside not online', 'Dream on', 'Be-You-tiful' or like watching a young girl cupping her hands collecting rain drops. It's not just playing. It is playing.

(Indebted to NRSV Bible, Armstrong, Caputo, Levinas, Zizek and Cox, Al-Khalili)

I am neither an astrophysicist, nor biblical scholar - just a mundane retired medic. with a basic degree in Science, curiosity, questioning and my experience and wonder.

Time and Water and Wild and Wind (Caputo). **Poetry and Image/ Imagination.**

There are some similarities in Genesis (1-3) Rabbinic monotheism stories with the Mesopotamian polytheistic creation epic poems.(the earliest written creation myths - 5000-1600BC) - polytheism slowly gave rise to monotheism (see end notes).

The writers of both Genesis stories are not divorced from their peoples conditions.

Imagine them writing the stories by firelight.

1. E/P Elohim, Priestly (by convention) story Genesis 1+, 600 yrsBC. to encourage the suffering downtrodden Israelites in Babylonian exile in slave labour

In the beginning was something, there was already time and formless lifeless stuff.

'In the beginning when Elohim God created'- he was high above, (not down below in Eden as in the 2nd.Y/J story) and omniscient - here are two time words - 'beginning' and 'when' so time was already present. He took the desolate barren wilderness of earth (Hebrew tohu-wa-bohu), (Marduk the chief god in the epic poems) which was already there - an empty place but not void or chaos, and the lifeless waters of the salty deep ocean, also to hand, Hebrew tehom - a feminine noun, (originally Tiamat, the mother goddess. She was murdered by Marduk and hence the feminine was obliterated and so montheistic Gods were male and father and remained such) over which his breath wind spirit swept (**Ruach**) and light was created right at the start out of the unknown unknowing darkness, then he created the rest. And mankind, male and female, nameless, was made in **'our image'**, **'our likeness' said 4** times - from all his personalities, a plural of majesty or a polytheistic culture remnant. The 'Israelites' were originally polytheistic. The change was gradual No ribs are mentioned. What a tremendous compliment for us. A story full of majesty.

The caring loving Elohim God works quietly (not like the tantrums of Yahweh in the Y/J story) with the materials at hand - the wild and the water. He separates them off and names them - earth/sky, dark/light unnamed sun, (1000 yr. old word) named stars (but the sun is a star), day and night lights (no light pollution then) ocean, lifeless made to life, a 'beautiful risk' (Levinas) - a becoming - **all was good, very good, said 7 times**. 'Good', a most ancient and aboriginal word also seen in the 2 epic poems. The omniscient Almighty then needs a rest! I love that, as if to say 'Whew, I just love what I have made but I'm now tired; I'll sit down, put my feet up then have a cuppa' - a relatable-to God. We need to say 'good' more of ourselves instead of only being sinners! Let alone accept the idea of Original Sin and the Fall which the churches made dogmas (etymology dogma = opinion) in the 5th C. AD. (or was it Irenaeous in the 2nd C.?) There is no concept of this in Judaism. Dominion mentioned is 'stewardship' - the act of caring for not superiority. The only thing subdued was the earth.

Yes, yes. (Caputo). All is harmonious order/structure now.

The Torah Bet/Bereshit for Genesis- the Hebrews love the importance of their alphabet; (Hebrew for genesis, pronounced bereysheet) doesn't open with the 1st alphabet A alpha/aleph sacred letter but with the 2nd B beta. Beginning is B - bet/bereshit. God the Artist A working with materials present - lifeless formless clay and water made to a pot. Genesis does not begin with the Absolute beginning, the Godhead beyond God (hence bereshit B) of I Am Alpha and Omega (Greek) (aleph and taw - Hebrew)- before the beginning and time. Elohims job description, which he has given himelf is the separator, namer and creator, joiner, maker of lifeless to life. Even the sacred 'a' is left out of YHWH.

In the beginning life was small, plants seeds creepy-crawlies and the end was large -sea monsters, cattle, man. Now it's from the planktonic bloom of life through the food chain and plants to large. Did you know plants are clever - conifers can live for 4,000 yrs; plants make food from CO2 and their excretion O2 for us; we can't. No plankton, plants - no us. Simple to complex, small to large. A beautifully crafted, creative story.

2. Y/J Yahweh/Jaweh (by convention) (later Jehovah) story-Genesis 2-3, 1000 yrs BC to 'a settled agricultural people with imperial ambitions'.

To me it is about the freedom from mindless dependency / desire for wisdom/insight.

A dream of lush (in desert conditions).'spoiled' /altered by 2 peoples' mindedness and awareness resulting from being made as in Yahweh's likeness. The snake simply pointed out that fact and a bit more. Yahweh Jehovah Lord gets down to earth and walks in the garden among Adam and Eve all dusty dirty.(no names yet, later Adam which is Hebrew for earth = soil, ground - gives Eve her name - 'Mother of all', his name only appears in Chap. 5 by the way). He created man out of dust and breathed into his nostrils then out of Adam's rib, a crafty kind of stem-cell woman as a second rate citizen, giving them a chance to know (by temptation) as He does (the fruit of the tree of wisdom) but when they do eat (he has told them not to and that they will die if they do) - but they don't die, he banishes/expels them in anger, a massive critical transition point,(like the Big Bang in the origin of the Universe) from a childlike immature paradise, as if they were being born, to grow to mature adulthood - the Fall, I call it the **Inlightenment**! (?Fall - using gravity to bring to birth, not like on your back). He gave them temptation, the forbidden tree of wisdom. Adam the first man is alpha and both are vegetarians. It was Eve's initiative, curiosity, 'free will' to take the fruit, possibly tired of being treated as second rate - only a piece of old rib. She crossed a critical point. It is mainly a mother's task to promote her infants maturing with her husband's backing however much she loves their adorable infancy. Was this Yahweh's hidden agenda under his rage?

In this story there is no 'good', and 'very good', but guilt and difficulty. A No, No. story. Yahweh gave Adam and Eve temptation - the forbidden fruit. They succumbed ? the origin of 'and lead us not into temptation'.

The snake told Eve if she ate the fruit of the tree of wisdom/knowledge of good and evil or touched it her 'eyes would be opened' and she would be like god knowing. Eve was kind of aware it would make her wise but she seemed to go first for the 'pleasing' food and that it was a 'delight to the eye', the senses came first but not deeper good perhaps; then 'free will'/curiosity kick in - the wisdom idea came last - she didn't yet know what good or wisdom were. She seemed to have no fear in picking the fruit? The snake countermanded god's statement that she would die. She didn't die. The snake was right and 'their eyes were opened' Maybe that made god furious. So why did god tell a fib. Didn't Christ say 'be ye wise as serpents and harmless as doves'; He must have disagreed with the interpretation put on the snake - well versed as he was in his Torah bereshit. I think yahweh is more infantile than them - dictatorial, tempting, fibbing and he had a tantrum (chucked out his 2 toys - the man and the woman, who he had made from his play-pen (the garden of Eden) and unfair (shouldn't have put the tree there, perhaps better to have hidden it in the backwoods, not obvious in the garden centre - like a sweetbowl placed in the kids central play area; and merciless, unforgiving, commanding, ticking off but mainly unjust. I emphasize that this is not the Absolute God beyond God that is before time and matter and the writer of the Y/J story does not claim it to be. Meister Eckhart 'I pray God that I may be rid of God'. This story is bereshit not aleph. The only said 'good' thing in this story was materialistic gold, 'and the gold was good' (? money, precious ornaments), and onyx to be found in the land of Havilah at one of the 4 branches of the Eden river which watered the garden. Reminds me of Dickens Fagin!

On top of that Yahweh expelled them as he was worried that they might then eat of the 2nd tree - of Life and so not know death, living forever like he and so challenge his authority and power as the only one knowing and not dying (remember this was written to a settled agricultural people with imperial ambitions, like saying 'don't you get above your station'). But why tempt them?

And he's also not that omniscient as he goes walking in the garden trying to find them and calling out 'where are you?' after they discovered they were naked and so hid. (Why this shame of nakedness?) If he was omniscient he would know where they were.

Also he naively then first made animals and birds as a helper, partner for Adam's loneliness (? knew that by empathy) and Adam was given the task of naming them. That's good of him. But it fails; he should have known that it would fail. So he then made acceptable Eve as she was 'bone and flesh of my flesh' Adam said, now pleased - sounds narcissistic, incestuous and not good for the gene pool and healthy offspring; perhaps resulting in the murderous Cain. Eve was created from one of Adam's ribs while he was anaesthetically asleep (? a 12th short rather redundant rib at the back and easier to get to there - retroperitoneal and no need to go through frontal body cavities!) or as rib stem cells which are multipotent but not totipotent that can differentiate to form organs and tissues (they can't make everything). It's not cloning as that would produce an exact Adam male replica. After the op. Yahweh 'closed up the flesh'. It sounds like an operation.

But to his credit he did make them garments of skins (he killed and skinned cattle) for their life outside of Eden (fig leaves didn't last) - a parting gift and au revoir! That's encouraging them to make a go of it, willing them on their way; that's surprising.

Before they ate the forbidden fruit Adam said interestingly 'a man leaves his father and mother! and clings to his wife and they become as one flesh'. It seems that Adam was already thinking of leaving god as father/mother (he had no other parents) and setting out on his own with his wife. So there we have it. The separation/individuation idea was already there - given by Yahweh.

After the expulsion the couples relationship with Yahweh and vice versa continued to some degree but then Yahweh regretted the conflicting violent humans he had made later, and murdered them all in the Flood apart from Noah the only one 'blameless' and who 'walked with God'. Violence met by violence but Yahweh was more violent than Cain. Isn't evolution violent and murderous too to our eyes but it's all about survival? Anger is ok but not murderous violence in humans. We don't need to eat each other for food now.

Imagine what it would be like if they hadn't eaten the fruit of knowledge of good and evil. Both, before, did not know GOOD and WISDOM (that's astounding) and evil. How did they live with onopened eyes? (c.f. 'eyes to see, let him see NT')- like robots not knowing especially good - just walking about, eating, talking, swimming in the river, milking the cattle everything materially provided, like children (what about an inner life). Did good and **evil knowledge only exist in Yahweh's awareness** before it became apparent. Evil virtually present before all time. Astounding. Is evil being naked or more - ? tempting lust. But Yahweh had already offered temptation in the fruit. Good/evil go together it seems and were already there from the word go like the virtuality in physics (in God's knowledge).

The banishment is a critical point like Eve's eating the fruit. Something new happens. And being expelled in god's anger equivalent to the Big Bang at the origin of the universe - critical events in creation, in the Universe and the formation of humans.

Although a very difficult story for all - **I am glad of it** otherwise we would remain unformed childlike robots, eyes closed, with no Wisdom of GOOD - a kind of birth story from the uterus of the garden of Eden. So this 'bad' story has become GOOD. Also a chance, perhaps, for the lonely God of Love to have real company with the responding, responsible 'Other', 'walking with God', (not being carried), the I Thou, freely given (or withheld.). That is GOOD. Love cannot exist on its own. God is Love, needs love, maybe Care is a better word) and creates out of it - the whole impetus of creation. ? bad is necessary in order to know Good. First the second encouraging magnificent good Elohim God story, then the merciless, unfair Yahweh Lord as the second, which is the first story of harsh reality. One doesn't tell bad stories to suffering people.

But we would like to remain infants in Eden in times of great trouble where it would be good to be comforted, fed, lulled to sleep and decisions made for us.

Astrophysics model of the Origin of the Universe Physics and Mathematics

leaning on Quantum theory.(Quantum =something indivisible! Physics is more and more finding divisions).

Hold onto your seats, we're ready for blast off to space-time, ghosties and the 'real'! The origin occurred 13.7 billion years ago. We too have billions of brain neurons with miles of brain blood vessels. The Events cannot go before their names.

An Event is a reframing, a critical turning point which is, in its true dimension unseen

(Zizek) and unexpected. Events break out and break in and interrupt the course of things - like :-

The Big Bang theory - the current acceptable best explanation one, claims that the universe began very early at the onset of the first fractions of a second (10-43 = a decimal point followed by 42 zeros then 1) at 1,000 trillion, trillion degrees C. (and heat is a measure of sub and atomic motion - wow) - from an initial point or singularity expanding over billions of years to form the current universe. A singularity means a point region in space-time where gravitational forces cause matter to have infinite density so that the laws of classical physics are suspended and become meaningless and the subsequent behaviour of the system cannot be predicted. A point gave rise to the universe. Wow. People often ask where did the Big Bang happen and where's the centre of the Universe? It's right here and wherever allover everywhere. So we don't need to blast off!

So already we have space-time and ghost matter, sub-atomic quarks (see note) forming hadrons (then protons, neutrons without mass) (Quarks quack!, muons mew, gluons glue!). There are 6 forms of quarks who love to pair up; 'up/down'top/bottom' and 'charming/strange'. One cannot really measure the infinite. It was not an explosion but an expansion of a 100 million million million million times in 10 seconds. Amazing.

All future matter in the universe was concentrated into a single incredibly small point which enlarges rapidly into a hot expansion and is still expanding. The echo of the original expansion has been detected in photo by a spacecraft in the form of the colder Cosmic thermal Microwave light afterglow radiation in the universe Background (CMB) occurring 400,000 years after the Big Bang - that's still soon after the Big Bang. You hear that when you tune your analogue radio - the background crackle/I call 'chuckle'. Amazing. This CMB contains the seeds where stars and galaxies will grow.

Microwave ovens are different in that they have magnetrons that take electricity and convert it to short electromagnetic radio waves. Ovens may seem harmless but aren't.

Several Broken symmetry stagesfollowed a millionth of a second later - less hot stages. How something comes from 'nothing'. The quantum vacuum state is not an absolutely empty 'void' but it contains fleeting electromagnetic waves and particles that pop in and out of existence; originally quarks and anti-quarks (see end notes)and negatively charged electrons and they begin to coalesce and quarks begin to gain mass then combine to form hadrons then protons, neutrons; electrons combine with these to form hydrogen and helium; and light can then begin to shine. (see also Genesis). Hurray. Small inherent in large and vice versa. The symmetry is broken because the transition brings the system from a virtual homogenous symmetrical disorderly state into definite states. Everything is less than nothing, not fully existing, virtual. So there is identity between virtual nothingness 'void' and the infinite wealth of potential. Nothing in physics means having no mass (? like thought!) - ghostly electromagnetic waves and ghostly particles. Space

is not nothing/empty, it has energy and force. If you took all the earths' people and extracted all their atom space you would be left with an object the size of a sugar cube! So we and here, the world and Universe is mainly space amassed with masses of energy but we can only sense mass/matter not energy.
So this single infinitesimal point contains the universe, like a fertilised egg to embryo, to foetus to baby which is inherently an adult.

Being derives its features from joining then separation and individuation - like a baby being born, or like the toddlers' 'terrible twos' of 'no' to everything and their defiance establishing 'I am me' after being an infant, like Adam and Eve thrown out of paradise, god separates himself from them (I give god the responsibility for that) so they have to then know how to survive and grow as themselves, as individuals. 'Subjective existence derives its features from separation'Separation is the very act of individuation, the fact of starting from oneself as equivalent to separation' as an I (Levinas); only an I can respond to the other - the I Thou. I say therefore a chance for the lonely God of love to have responding company! - 'walking with God' (the **Inlightenment).** Love requires the Other. The second reason that the No, No of the Y/J story turns out 'GOOD'. The growing Adam and Eve together outside Paradise with very fraught punishing parent Yahweh.

Mother Theresa said the worst suffering is isolation. Jahweh knew Adam was lonely (maybe by empathy!) so eventually made a companion, partner from him in common, not with another sea monster; and Adam found no company in theYahweh's trial run with cattle and birds as a partner, Yahweh should have known that - it had to be another person where 2 become one as in the creation of the Universe elements.

Just after the Big Bang all the forces of nature and all elementary particles were the same, then in the instants, at the critical transition points, their symmetry was broken - phase transitions. Infinitesimally small fluctuations acting on a system which crosses critical points decide the systems' fate, by what path a bifurcation is taken - like Eve picking the forbidden fruit. (picture her seeing the fruit then stretching out a hand). A system in a homogenous disorderly state into one or more definite states. e.g an unformed steam cloud cooled to formed water cooled to formed icicles/snowflakes.

So a unified force had separated into the final 4 as now (electromagnetism, gravity, the strong and weak nuclear forces) and from sub-atomic nuclei hydrogen and helium obtained mass, no longer virtual. Hurray. To me sub-atomic particles are little creatures. Physics tells us nothing of the intrinsic nature of atoms and pre-atoms - what they are like in themselves. (remember atoms have a proton, neutron nucleus with an buzzing around electron)

Energy is what causes things to happen.

The energy of the universe, fixed since the Big Bang, given as 'that's your lot - no more no less' by 'Someone', has a strong tendency to clump (forming hydrogen molecules to helium, the first social communities!) as it crosses critical points. The fluctuations take place at the level of not fully existing virtual entities (like Adam and Eve before eating the fruit) which are in a way, less than nothing/something! The insight from this idea of broken symmetry lies in the identity between relative nothingness ('void', vacuum) and the infinite wealth of potentialities.

Extremes of infinitesimal and infinite.

Einstein's E=mc2 (E-energy, m-mass, c2- the speed of light squared) is that, to quote him 'energy can neither be created nor destroyed. It can only be changed from one form to another'. Mass and energy are the same physical entity and can be changed into each other. The mass of an object or system is a measure of its energy content.

I think perhaps our matter at death, the transitional critical point, is transformed to energy - ? what form and our chemical elements recycled to the Universe - how much of each, energy and recycled matter? Amazing. (Being cremated and scattered is the most helpful for the Universe). Physics does imply that there is life (energy) after death. Also to me Death requires Justice and Love - 2 of the qualities of God! This going beyond our death - this relationship with the Infinite ('walking with God') cannot be limited in time and stop at death; that makes no sense, that would be clearly unjust/unloving ('that's it, I'll just get rid of you now'); it is not measured by duration and finite being. The courage of dying is also the fear of the loss of the I with the fear of gaining a new unknown I in continued relationship - for those who want ongoing relationship, called life after death. To me, there need not be 2 worlds of heaven and earth- just a unified condition/state of transcendence/immanence combined here now

but we don't know it yet 'cos of our matter/mass!

There is a frantic shifting back and forward of energy and momentum occurring perpetually in the universe of infinitesimal distance and time intervals. Small gives rise to large. I think like an unformed whisper, something virtual simmering, (this is fascinating as we all have a 'stream of consciousness' of many fleeting images which then alight on/

focus on one or a couple and then a word/s form then these are spoken as a word/s. ('in the beginning was the Word'). To me 'in the beginning was the Sound **Ruach**' - breath, wind, spirit - after all words are sounds. This is how in the 'empty' space, physicists say, a particle emerges out of nothing, borrowing its energy from the future and paying for it with annihilation (death inbuilt in life - the crucifixion) before the system notices the borrowing. Words are singing the world (Merleau-Ponty).

We are derived and have, from the Big Bang, hydrogen and helium (see later) dust, and several other broken symmetry stages have occurred - an original unified force splits into the 4 we know today, gravity (the weakest of the 4 forces - the Infinite has chosen the weakest) makes hydrogen and helium coalesce - great clouds becoming galaxies (all the planets are named after Greco-Roman ancient gods, that's significant, except Earth - Hebrew Adam!- it's still like us needing gods, a polytheistic remnant)and smaller gas clouds collapse to form the first stars, 100 million years after the Big Bang - that's not long after. The Sun (is also a star) (by the way the Sun doesn't rise or set but it's poetic to say so; it's the earth moving round the Sun (Galileo/Copernicus) considered heresy by the R.C. hierarchical church/also Martin Luther; sorry mates - get off our egocentric high horses again, we're not the centre of the Universe or the Solar system!) and stars are powered by fusion of hydrogen and helium - 600 million tons of helium is made from hydrogen in the sun/second, then via dying and dead stars - stardust is formed, they have run out of fuel and collapse under gravity then explode - not expand as in the Big Bang; (He 'formed man from the dust of the ground') where stars are nuclear reactors capable of nuclear fusion, [like **Cern's Large Hydron Collider** where hadron particles are made to collide at speeds near the speed of light 186.000 miles/sec.(186,282.397) miles/sec. and the elusive unfound Higg's or ' the God particle' was at last found this year. (not nuclear fission as in the atomic bomb)] an amazing human achievement, copying an early stage of the Big Bang.

So in the stars there is the fusion of neutrons and protons - hydrogen (1 proton, 1 neutron) to helium (2 protons, 2 neutrons) and on to form carbon (6 protons and 6 neutrons), nitrogen (2 Carbon atoms), oxygen (a helium and Carbon together), iron, sulphur etc. along the 92 naturally occurring chemical element chain. (There are more than 92 but they are man made). Helium (2 protons and 2 Neutrons) - which we don't have (a floating gas for kids' party balloons). Imagine if we did have uncombined helium on its own - we maybe floating about and talking in high pitched voices!).Someone wise left it out. Aah! It would be good to float sometimes!

Meteorites from stars apparently contributed to our amino acids - containing C. H. N. O. which we cannot make but which we get through plants and animal proteins. Amino acids are the basis of all life through DNA deoxyribonucleic acid (double helical paired chains of chromosomes full of genes; 4 such amino acids in pairs - Cytosine with Guanine, Adenine with Thymine and protons bind the pairs together. Things love pairing up and being paired). Stars die and their chemical elements are returned to the Universe and recycled. Death (nothing to do with the crucifixion as a 'sacrifice paid for sins' Augustine) gives rise to life - resurrection. This preceded the crucifixion. Its in all things. An inescapable fact of the Universe. As also its love of recycling which we have only relatively recently seen the importance of; so reflect when the bin man comes!

Caterpillar to pupa-death to butterfly. In the pupa there forms a massive molecular soup which totally reorganises to a butterfly (incredible). The Absolute/Infinite is thoroughly fragile and fleeting and appears to us in fleeting moments, like a welcome/welcoming smile given genuinely by a so called rude hard person; 'the face as a source from which all meaning appears' (Levinas). The Absolute must be treated as carefully as a butterfly - it can disappear before it can even appear; like a thought which disappears going to another room to do something then forgetting what it was.

The symbolic order, the universe of the Word, can only emerge from the experience of abyss/darkness. And God said let there be light in the darkness. Remember when light first appeared when Hydrogen and helium first formed. This night, this darkness - this empty 'nothing' contains everything in its simplicity, especially energy though it may not feel good ('dark night of the soul'). Light requires dark for itself to appear.

The Infinite can be small, weak, vulnerable, like 'and Jesus wept', like 'the kingdom of heaven is like a child', the weakness of God needing rest, - not 'omnipotent' as 2nd century AD theological doctrine would have it. 'The divine life is incarnate in us and the weakness of God requires that we do all the heavy lifting' (Caputo). Christ had to do it (crucifixion) and 'take up your cross'.

This idea of 'omnipotent' leads to an all powerful patriarchal deity, (the feminine has always been excluded since time immemorial in all the monotheisms)and to hierarchical systems resulting in religions fighting each other as to who has the true god, who owns the holy places and lands, violent religious wars, inquisitions, crusades, jihadis etc. It can be helpful to drop the name 'God' (although the name of God calls forth the best and the worst)('I pray God that I may be rid of God' Meister Eckhart) as that would appear not to be the true God and to search for what is under that name - the Event, the Call, the Insistence (after Caputo).Caputo has 'an unconventional idea that God is not really and truly God without us' that the insistence of God requires our existence and so depends on us; (you find that in the epic poems - the gods needed help so made humans, and in the underlying 'reason' for Adam and Eve's expulsion I think - needing the Other to 'walk' with). And I could say, as we are made in his likeness, the vice versa!. i.e. our insistence to him; our pleading the same liturgical prayers, supplications week in week out (I love the Jews and their unabashed honest haranguing of their God) - our insistence to him requires his existence. Its no good insisting to the ether - a 'Presence' needs to be there! But 'the insistence of God means that we insist on God existing'.

The weakness, vulnerability of god can be the power of powerlessness (crucifixion).

God did not prevent the Holocaust, Hiroshima, starving children or the devastation of tsunamis, volcanoes, earthquakes which are not man-made. Where is the power of powerlessness in these? This is the inescapable weak god, doing nil about it if he's omnipotent. Is this where we do all the heavy lifting? 'The Almighty all powerful', strong words - might or might not - **perhaps**; may or may not - weak words.

The origin of the word god is not clear. I have difficulty in saying that word. Possibly from 'gud' earliest Germanic tribes with a gothic bible, 'godan', in the 4th century AD - so a relatively new European invention possibly. Hebrews are hesitant to say their God word too.

Aramaic, Christ's language, preceded Hebrew; and Aramaic words for god are Elaha, eli, eloi 'Eloi, eloi lama sabachthani' - my God my God why hast thou forsaken me. And Jesus' name was not that but Yeshua - not the hard J's of Jesus, Jehovah Jahwah. J's tend to be germanic in origin. I have difficulty in saying the word Jesus which has been presented so unattractively in the past. I prefer Yeshua. Caputo said he's interested in Yeshua not Christianity. Hurray.

So this astrophysics model is beta/bet not alpha/aleph as also the creation myths - that is it is not in the Absolute beginning which requires a before space-time, energy and matter!. Big Bang and Broken Symmetries, in the Beginning - all are B's, beta/bet. There are other less accepted models of the origin of the universe - like the Multiverse and String theories.

Matter and spirit are intertwined (particles/mass, energies). A thing is a result of the process (event) of its own becoming and this process desubstances it. Clay, water are desubstanced by the potter to a pot. Spirit isn't a positive counterforce to nature, not a dichotomy, a split, a binary, a half or a different which shines through natural stuff. It is nothing but this process of freeing-itself-from. It is the very nature of spirit to be this absolute liveliness, this process to proceed forth from nature, to leave its nature, to come to itself and to free itself, as such a product of itself; its actuality being merely that it has made itself into what it is. (After Hegel and Zizek). 'Spirit is the cause of itself'. Here physics and philosophy and post modern theology coincide - perhaps.

To me, 'worshipping in spirit' is in the all united, not dualistic - not just that which is minus nature/flesh. Physics and mathematics have given back mystery.

My eyes hear! (There's a man whose ears see - he's blind and uses echolocation by emitting tongue clicks like bats to ride around on a bicycle without collision) Wow. Seeing persons, especially kids can train themselves to echolocate - sound echoes are usually suppressed by the brain. Yes. Meister Eckhart 'The eye in which I see God is the same eye in which God sees me'.

In quantum physics photons only exist when observed!. What happens to them when they're not observed? Just not there? ? So I think Spirit may only exist when related to! **Relating** to seems to be so marked and widespread in the Universe - the basis of all. Observation alters what is observed. You alter me when you watch me. See also Eastern religions - 'all is illusion' (see MRI scans later). Photons have 2 personalities, existing either as waves or particles. A photon can be a particle representing a quantum of light or other electromagnetic radiation. It carries energy but has zero mass.

A Proton can be in 2 places at once!, we can't. Amazing. A proton can go through matter (as can neutrons! as could Christ!). Amazing. We can't as they're bound in our e.g. water - and as we've seen protons bind the pairs of amino acids in DNA.(C-G, A-T)- the basis of life. Particles love to pair up, and they're clever. We're not the egocentric pinnacle of creation; egocentricity in kids is necessary for survival but not so much in adults.

Science leans on its factual value which, to me, can give its perspective and a wholeness-propensity and even moreso, mystery, surprise and strangeness.

The universal principles I see from both Genesis and Astrophysics are something like:-

Critical transition points; in Broken Symmetry as also in Genesis 1-3.

Small to large;

Separation-individuation; birth, unformed to form. An inner restlessness in things.

Relating/Community/joining - love cannot live in isolation and so particles can't.

Matter and energy/spirit are interchangeable

Death throughout the Universe with recycling to life to others, in particles, people NT. - crucifixion. Doesn't occur in Genesis 1-3

Both don't deal before time = the Absolute, Godhead, Infinite (Call, Event, Insistence

The Insistence of it all - dogged, compelled, impelled (in the earth/ Universe) - the spirit of evolution - at whatever cost. If there is no adaptation there is no survival - so theology needs to take note.

The inbuilt propensity of things within - like singularity point, sexuality (see end notes), subatomic and atoms, foetus. Everything.

Being in the world (Heidegger)..

This is the becoming of all. The Insistence of it all.

The basic 'bringing to light' (Heidegger).

The bringing together.

All betas. The b's are busy.

Perhaps there is no heaven up there; no mind/body distinction

Perhaps there is only one world; no duality of life/death but unknown by us who have mass.

Time is an illusion experienced in hallucinogen (psilocybin) drug tests/prayer meditation of nuns, buddhist monks in MRI scans with resultant reduced blood flow in the brain's posterior cingulate and medial prefrontal cortices when there is a sense of floating away from space and time. These brain areas give us awareness of our space and time surroundings and our sense of self. As space and time no longer have meaning here I could say 'so a before-time Godhead is possible' - perhaps.

Perhaps in here is 'the after life', 'eternity', 'heaven' already here now.

I suggest a new evolutionary theological study, as all things evolve and change; call it Quantum theology! like a chrysalis opening to a butterfly. Or a kind of gene mutation change Event

The current fruit of the tree of knowledge ?wisdom, of good/evil is synthetic biology, computer spare human parts printed in 3D, computer altered yeast cells producing mass quantities of diesel (+ CO2) not the natural alcohol; IVF, stem cells, cloning, robots, nano technology. A nano is 1 billionth of a meter. 1 nano is about the length that a fingernail grows in 1 second. Future nano chips are planned to be small enough to travel in the blood to perform complex ops at the cell level e.g repair damaged brain cells in stroke and Alzheimers. Do we pick the fruit and proceed or not? (Perhaps human nature is a work in progress.) It's commonly called 'playing God'. Eve provided the first initiative/curiosity ?without fear for the first advance and now occur advances in Medicine and the Sciences. !without her there would be none!(still in the stone age without medicines etc., phones - you wouldn't be able to phone for the ambulance and there would be no ambulance etc.). The Y/J story and women are at last now relevant. The public/early humans fear new stuff (dangers lurking). 'The fear of the Lord is the beginning of wisdom' the first OT appearance of the word 'fear' (?awe, ?trust (Gen 22:12).Abraham told to murder his son as a burnt offering to god.

To me I alter Meister Eckhart's 'I pray God that I be rid of God' to

I pray God that I may understand and try to recycle, this lesser god. - perhaps.

Compiled and extrapolated August 2015.

A Thin-skin Tin Can in the Wind

the inanimate becomes alive - inspiring some words with 'in' born!*
In physics particles change their behaviour when observed, watched
- they relate
All is alive, personal, even stone There is no such thing as inanimate

Gale-wind gusts hum and the cold slanting rain cuts -
a busy bus commuter corner one stop coffee shop -
a solitary trash small bruised tin can, yellow green -
a goblin named 'V' on an atomic background theme
V - 'inVigorating' - a small fizzy rushed snack drink
rattling, annoying me at the jarring junk din;

but then to my delight it danced for me in the wind,
skipped merrily high on the gusts, a lame urchin -
circling and circling, it ran up and round and down
clanking, and grinning kicking it, thick-skinned yob assassins
but it laughed - wheeling and jumping and chuckling.
I sparkled with its bubble and fizz and spin.
Like me, akin, bruised but unbroken, and bent
it had defiant spirit and fizz and glint, innocent.
Yes.
At last, tired tamed, he came to rest spent flung
next a broad pillar of a top shop overhang
and sighed with relief, long harangued, pain-wrung.
I finished my coffee, got up, wandering along
wondering - and gently picked him up, intent meant
carrying him safely home maimed, bent
to a safe sheltered black trash street bin
and laid him comfy in the dim coffin
in the warm soft papered nest within
in the inside orange plastic hammock, thin,
with friends brethren discarded as rubbish, among some kin.
He will be resurrected recycled as perhaps a top class tin -
Pimm's No.1 Cup 1840 or Scrumpy Jack Cider, Premium
or Dark Red Rum or Gordon's Tonic Dry Gin
and top of the list 'this is my blood given for you' of full red wine.
All things counter common reject strange foreign, genuine
whatever is discard cracked, who knows how the origin -
He fathers forth whose brokenness surrects, sovereign.
Imagine - 'I thirst' and he slaked the thirst of someone
then his last dance to new life from his death begun -
the tin can in the bin, won from the spun wind in fun.
Now I fondly remember this hectic place when I sip or pass
where he gave such life and such fun amidst the chaos.
Fin.

Feb 2009

*Now some 45 'in' words. Etymology of coffin - from a case or basket.

To a Cushion

Loosening my concrete
Cortical shell
In the unhurried waters
Of reflection -
An apertif -
I chanced upon a thought -
A snail -
An ode to a cushion.

Feathered soft
Dumped fat, a tuft
Happy sits -
Humptied, puffed.

I sigh and smile
Like a child
Loose limbed
Flaccid, sprawled.
The curtain behind
Chuckles my cheek
And the sun seeps
In the soft wind
At the window drawn.

7.11.67. Cape Town

To Paul Tillich

A clean cold room -
high hospitalled
where the truth is.

Stuttered contact -
islanded.
other waves froth my shore

and likewise reverse.
Continuum of solid earth
reefed and surfed.
Doubleness in emotion;
deep tears turned
to laughter
tear sprayed.
Straddled on the bed
with mug and spatula spoon;
crisis crescends
Fear
And descends to -

You must exist -
You must exist.

The eventual life theme.
perfect, full, warm and soft.
Will I never unchain -
deepest concern -
and flow and grow.
Andante cello
mellow
to clarinette close
converse.
That's perfect. It is it -
To reach and touch.

People who know and don't -
owl eyed, opacified;
organised ants
in a hierarchy
of system - pretending
space and freedom;
confined by chromosome,
culture and custom
to conform in confusion
of children
tearing the wings off a fly.

An egg box age of atom,
avulsion and area act.
Spluttering - a moth gutted
in candle light wax.
Of three blind mice
and see how we run.
Yet it is and we are.
Contact walled concrete -
for the cruelty of people
does not permit
their own concord - walled.

What I say
Must be that, that I say
and not, I think,
what I think
others want.
I am an integer
not thrown
fractioned to form
others whole form.
Perhaps we have
a part of truth
untrapped.
Well, these grapes were good
and the common things matter.
But the bitter remains
in the dregs of draught -
the top bubbling sweet.

We know so much out
so little in.
Because the object
us watched
is the observer.
'Gracious, her seems
are straight.'
Cynic - well
The feelings

trying to thrust
were not.
You cannot contact
even self - let alone -
The pursuit of truth
must cut -
destroy in ways
and try to construct.
I must believe that -
else not to exist
Essential.
And nothing is;
An empty flask.

But the orange sun
rises the Flats
And the low mauve mist
mourns for Jan in pain.
The oaks are green
and there's that whole sky arc
left for sun; the mist spinning
lose and light, the soft
of my guitar soul.

17.3.67 Cape Town

Tobogganing and Meister Eckhart
(a light ditty - with apologies and thanks to him)

A clear crisp day of soft white snow.
Calling, called to call out - 'don't waste it. Enjoy.
Take your cheap plastic merchandise sled - and go.
Run to the little hills below'.
Old and in old clothes I go.
It was many, many years ago
I first felt the flying Spirit of speed -
so, scared, I set the sacred sled
at the hilltop, gully strewn, rocks below.

Mindless, I ease down old bones and sit;
lean back, legs in, balance with winged arms;
finger tips zip light in light snow -
just a slight touch to steer.
My 'I' has windflown.
I am a nothing Naught.
Without after or before -The Eternal Now -
The same as snow, wind and speed-
icing universe. No words.
No idea of the word god.
We are one - free - off this earth flown
and all the heavens ring.
We are one. Attached. Who? No matter.
We fly over bumps and leap in the air.
Just one. Simple in the child innocence -
in old and any age. Sheer exhilaration, dear delight.
Often I am detached thrown -
and skid and roll and bottom-bounce down
and crash to brambled bushes blown.
In a few sacred seconds heaven is Here.
A slow slog back up - obedient for what? -
flushed with light and the eye-glow.
Ascension and descension, up and down -
the first hard, the second brilliant -
but neither up nor down, neither here nor there.
And my sled is sacred - all and both.
And in that - the unknown is sown,
the Naughtness is held
by the God sitting so Comfortable
in the temple of the soul.
The ground of existence.
And I am wise and sit bruised!

Naughtiness - on trespassed ground!
The hazy lazy sun, smiling shines -
so hot foot home to a bubbling bath.

Jan. 2003 Canterbury

'Today' for the Dung Beetle

This day, this very day
and only this - no other
but more than that, or perhaps less -
this hour set down, down to
this moment in time blest.
Now and now and now -
no before or after
of isolation's hell or eternity's bliss.
Because this moment
can be neither, either or both sent.
Chug chug chung
hummed the dung beetle
dum dum zunk zung
across the desert sands' song.
Chug chug kadunk
with his mouth full of
sweet bits of dung
rolling it backwards
up dunes
to a place he can't see
tumbling down.
On and on he urges
scuttling in reverse -
his hind legs holding the precious
pure-perfect camel-dung ball.
Only this moment set down -
his whole life force shining
in that moment set down.
Just a beautiful black beetle
loving carefully the shit that we spurn -
in this round round ball.

Being this, this and only this -
now.

Feb 2013

Today

A Process through -
This - a vine to be pruned of dead branches -
destructive self-absorption is dead wood.
This new word 'Father' unknown before.
And their joy and content over there
so neglected in you can be yours now;
their suffering and fear is yours
that you know so well.

So 'let it be', 'let it be' the song sings;
and tears are better than fears.
'Looking for love' as a cure all -
you have mine the Father says.

The waves and storms come and go -
in patience, just ride them out.
Come on England - the Euro footie
and the 1p is found in tele's 'Deal or no deal' -
raise a fist in hurrah - and left on my doorstep
someone left me yellow roses in a vase.

The Process proceeding -
Awareness Poetry God - my path.

June 2012

Tortoise

everything has to hide sometimes
and everything needs to come out of its defence

I wish you could walk with me out into the small world
right here, now, - a sparkling blessing, as jenny wren has called;
but loved and understood, then to understand and love, grown -
no easy celebration, - as a babe in mother's before arms.

Here down on the ground where He is - not up in the gods
        of truth and thought where only God is also
        and little by little to love our sole life self.
To find a place down in the folk-forest humming streets -
        but first to go apart to a secret place held, ourselves to meet
as everywhere there seemed none in my form, none resonating
        to my singing string - theirs unplucked or harsh,
grasping at beaded-wet spiders webs which broken, disappear fast;
the cacophonous discord erupting in the concrete echoing city
as street people surge in torrents of broken logs, block boulders
        which we zig-zag between in the crevasse high ravine;
the wasteland of our wit, the bedlam babble of our brain,
        dry and arid thought;
the child growing hidden in crouched corners between,
        filling the cramped shape to survive in a flood hot, dry world.

But he, the little one, camouflaged, ground bound,
crooked front legs, hind elephant leg stumps -
plaqued tortoise-shell plates, polygonal scute-skin scales
which so inspired the Roman legions in conquering defence -
a spectrum rainbow of different greys and browns,
scrawny unlovely neck and back leg skin, powerful beak
front-paw-rowing-walk on his flat surfboard base
with uptipped front over slow ground sods, no haste -
his dome house-hut on his back - at home with himself.

In spring he comes out of the crackling winter leaves
under the shining honey-drip of the sun's petal rays
warmed and held by the sunrise to move and rise -
so also we need to be held to let go, warmed to allow going slow;
the drowsy dawn morning, in the diamond dew teardrop grass -
we go rusty within, if we don't sometimes cry as the dew does.

He is ponderous slow, determined, surety not speed -
his only danger, being flipped by a lethal fox or curious dog
as he cannot roll over, turn turtle back up -
so he quickly withdraws to his safe hidden shell, easily scared -
hunkering down, waiting in time's dark hug to safe emerge.
Leafy food in his path, cheeky chappies of sparrows hop round,

a young mottled throstle after a slug or snail found.
White as a splatter of milk - shy daisies on the grass -
the days in hand to together string; a slime shining worm
in the sunshine recoiling under soil moist,
as brilliance without a shadow is blinding to us - now.
Dying is a slow slithering snake, unnoticed by most till the last -
and we don't know what we're searching for, driven by fear, lost.

He has no future-distant vision - not for ever, only now,
the hazy horizon, wherever and whatever that is, recedes;
he doesn't feel what he is destined to do, take control -
doesn't know heaven, paradise, endlessness, eternal;
he's drawn by other than himself, through himself
and allows himself to be what he is in his small around world.
His still soft self, unblinking bead of an eye aware -
and we have our grown-hardened imprisoning shell
necessary somewhat in a rivalling harsh, reviling world
around a soft together-tender communing heart child
with 'few associates' to share.

So, solid slow and sure
he beat the charging exhausted hare -
that fire within the straw twig-nest of our imagination
needing only a small spark to quickly alight.
Simple clear-eyed, wise innocence, bright.

Canterbury Nov 2006

Toward the Unknown

Without sounding absurd -
A new nudity
of flame and flower -
orange red ash
shot in fantasy
smouldering curved;
whirled on a rise of curve
mount served soft.

Orange flame
brown, rises and dies -
A need swells
from my urgent depth
and rhythmed - simmers
in a sine wave of season
engorged and parched.
This cracked my veneer.
A jewelled body
draped unknown and feared
toward the unknown,
swaying antiphonal
fugal fantasia.
A strange new force,
a deep green surge
of strength and
Profound peace.

I needn't accept my lot.
That cracked my defence
and left me shivering
on the verge of resurrection.
So I must go back
though I have in seven years.
A journey to deeper origon and meaning -
down labyrinthine ways
through misted humid swamps
shrouding the spirit dark and sick;
up mountain face
down cracked crevasse
across desert and ocean vast.
Wildness and murmuring veldt
of rock and sun baked strength.
Eagle spanning spirals
thermalled fired
in blue blazing vision.
And I, a rider
shade my eyes
against blinding perception;
coning vision down

to an amazing burst
of energy, strength and hope,
and the beauty
that within me lies -
though lashed
in the harsh wind
of a thorned desert.

I will always have you -
my muse of mystery and word
and the beauty that lies within.

1.10.67 Cape Town

Toys

and toys in the empty two pillow cleft next -
wise Bagpuss, Big Bear, welcoming arms out
and to him, little Honey Bear snuggling soft,
rare Panda and his bamboo shoot -
panic if it's not there, in his black-eyed snow suit;
and Pudding - a round cosy cat; on my return,
sad sometimes and 'where have you been?'
and Gruffy puppy-dog keeping guard
with a look of 'don't mess with us' assured.
There beside the tele is smiling Pumpkin -
he's a toddlers cap - he's for Tortoise, frightened
in his soft shell - rescued, scared of touch, being abandoned
but special behind them both
is a photo, faithful, of M.
To them all, I can talk unbowed out loud
without being mid-sentence cut in reply
and they tell me many things with their eyes.

I am W and they are W - I am them and they are me.
Simple Wise Bagpuss with penetrating eyes
and 'What's really up, by the bye?';
arms out, a strong Welcome Big Bear

with such a direct look 'for you, I'm here' -
and Wulnerable little Honey Bear
and Wary Wandering Torty full of care
now snuggling next Panda and Honey Bear.
He's had affirming affection in Pumpkin's smiling eyes there
and Woolly always eating Panda filling his gaps
and 'What's up Doc?' from Warm Pudding cat -
and Woofing puppy Gruffy, safe, firm.
And behind all these is a photo of M.

They are not just toys but real alive;
they maybe just to play with to a grown-up
and just a transitional passing phase.
Toys, toy with, to play with, enjoy
but also to dally with and relate.
Yet, dashed, with my rational limited adult brain
that 'just toys' they are, the same in name -
imagination numbed by hard fact, lamed, tamed.
For me 'transitional' to where, what?
At my age - to dying and death - out?
Mostly adults think of that. How, indeed, about that!
so I'd rather be a child. Yet -
it would be nice to hear a voice about -
'cos the toys have gone flat, silent like God. But ...

Jan 2009

Town Tribes

Mobile phones head-bent-glued, high tech gear
cord dangling iPods and MP3's from ears
wide angle LED, plasma TV, HD at home
each with a language of its own;
Some 'dysfunctional' bravado gangs
swagger booted and tattooed along;
some as groups of lasses - the same styles -
black tights, shorts over with easy slipper shoes
or tottering on the new six inch heels

with bouffant ruckled skirts
or with raggedy ends clinging like vests;
some with the same uneven chewed hair styles
tinted blue or orange or red or pink
and lads with jeans half way down their butts
A few bravely wear their Muslim masks
long dresses and head scarves
lead by their man in front, the boss.
Young college groups coming out
from their Uni warrens and books -
to coffee latte americano expresso
panninis and mutifarious baguettes.
The same supermarkets, fashions, faces, shops
yet the homeless bedraggled crouch.
Suited up businessmen focus intent, fast.
Older women face painted in young clothes,
sunglasses so 'cool' atop their heads;
the elderly in pastel lycra ironed slacks
limp along, predominantly beige, in coach packs.
Hair dressing for all these 'battleship blues'
must be a profitable job and, dreadlocks for blacks
and spiked glued-up hair for some lads.
And the power of terrorist groups disaffected -
they now belong attached.
All 'shout' me, me - assertive of self
but it's not 'me' - it's belonging
the same as the tribe - the individual is lost.

Where is my tribe - I long to belong
with persons' essence to essence
the hidden song.

May 2010

Trite Words are not Trite
a List

Courage. Feel the fear and do it anyway.

I can do it because I do it
and I do it because I can.
Let go, let go, let go.
We have little real control.
and every little helps - I have done well.
Patience. Wait.
Change is life. To be sensible -
think outside the box as well.
Peace is only in the present not future or past.
Whatever it is, it's here, it's ok.
It's not as bad as it seems
and abnormal, I am not.
And to give, not to want all the time.
After all, this is your life - take it as it comes.
Simplicity - small things as every little helps.
It's ok to say 'I don't know'.
Being comfortable with where one is -
with where and who I am.
Be a friend to myself - I starve myself it not.
I am professionally retired - I am.
We have our allotted time, no more, no less -
Someone somewhere is in control, perhaps -
like the sparrows who fall to the ground
and the lilies who toil not.
Be not so seriously self-absorbed ruminant.
We are our own worst enemy
in the propaganda of grindstone worry
of depressive doom and gloom.
Not pre-living the future -
being, not doing, not fixing.
I do not need to be happy,
always clutching at it from afar,
always rushing to get to the next moment.
Painful feelings of fear, greet them with
'there you are, I see you, little monsters'
and they tell me I need to give them
kindness and gentleness and space, space -
airy space around, simple and light
in the mere awareness of their presence uncramped.
Breathing is a true uncluttered holding simple fact.

Thoughts are not facts.
JUST TRUST - unbraced.
Perhaps there are no monsters under the bed.

July 2012

Trying

What do you know of pain - Jenny?
people can unwittingly inflict.
Coffee for four where five are present.
And choice of many thoughts
Like the rainbow reflection on the record,
blue label going round and round;
peoples incapacity to help -
because they have not experienced.
Rejection by one of me
and my unresolvable dependency,
but keeping me on
tantalising a rat
caught in a trap
with a morcel of cheese
which she eventually eats -
the rat still left clamped
in the vice like grip
of her own internal claws.
If you can't get out and sort out
this boiling brew of you -
strength yet unexperienced
by you and most others
yet far away and where achieved
still cut off as before.
Below others before - after above
not one of the lot.
The other girls out
as usual at flick -
two and two and two to one cast
back into the turmoil

of her own thoughts -
thinking of a solitary drink
then attempting to make
this episode of pain
constructive and creative
by writing it down.
Valueless to the community;
afflistion to herself alone
and then at that
a jumble of junk;
getting to no clear cut
conclusion at all.
Rage and frustration
at the natural order of things
in that you can't get
what you want -
close, comfortable company
which you want and don't want.
Attempting to write poetry
turning out confused junk.
Beethoven to Bartok.
Valueless, valueless -
Oh God - not.
When you leave - Dr.B
you asked me what
I would feel. It's this -
a great gap.
Something precious lost.
The cycle repeats itself
of malignant premeditated acts.
So withdrawal to dreams
to what cannot be supplied
in destructive reality.
Then that stopped
in a numb frozen chasm
without hope.

Tomorrow a Monday -
lectures till six,

ward duties
cooking week again
and a June exam.
Too many demands
and alone and weak.
This episode provoked
by the pairing of my friends
gone out and my fantasies
of being close to a Valkenburg Dr.-
wanting him in certain respects
to provide wisdom, stability, tenderness.
And not in others -
because he is a man and
his small head, peaked nose
and why is he a psychiatrist -
what makes him so?
Two days gone
without saying much -
alone with psychiatric books
which dig and gouge
at my weakness.

And yet in now a
more constructive mood
after a visit from Pierre
in need of him and he of me;
to discuss our common ground
of inability to cope;
group therapy consisting of two.
A glimpse in between
his sentences which
are rather verbose -
that you're not lost
even when gone;
some of you
incorporated in me.
That - perhaps
I can worship - no,
depend on -

myself yet you.
A you - me
A new me.

early '60's Cape Town.

The Lost Children of the Great Wave - 26.12.04

The Divine omnipotent - a mass made mistake?
an aweful awful, terrible tsunami quake -
or he is his creation done with, denied enraged?
150 thousand killed and a rising unnumbered wake -
the rotting bloating stench, burning flesh pyred
bodies to pits bulldozed, raw pain dazed.
No more suffering for the dead.
Disease starvation destitution a secondary event
throbbing disaster fault bursting pus.
10 ravaged countries 2 continents 5 million poor
without shelter and food and water pure.
A seaquake - Richter scale a high nine
from a buckling tectonic plate far below - felt far
shifting the earth's axis one inch
the earth spinning faster for a time
(and one island moving a hundred feet.)
A 60 foot wave at near central point
travelling at a jet speed wall front.
Appalling devastation - slaughtered innocents dumped.
God's way of culling the earth in a smashed hump?

And He is born the day before - manger safe
the church demanding highest praise as we pray
to him to 'lead us not into temptation' and he does.
The killer wave God - this 'natural' to him.
An unnatural natural disaster - a legal 'act of God'
insurance denied! 'I am the way and the truth..'
and the death. His Book growls, His soul torn shreds
'Gloria in Excelsis' - no way said. With no precedent.
If not, and incomprehensible still -

do tectonic plates freewill
or not, to buckle and collide?
Does the Lord of the Universe -
creator lover, destroyer -
ever repent?

The enraged lion of thus the wound mind -
no difference between birth and death.
The worlds' silent people stunned, give, rally round
becoming one, together in loss, and in worth.
Compassion - a still small voice. God is love too.
And He became one within us. Within innocence.
In the little heart's healing niche. And Jesus wept ...

Late Dec. 2004

Two Old Women

pure feeling is good, requiring little if any thought, a gift received in surprise. 'Bad' 'feeling' is no gift - or a tarnished one that needs much thought to be understood

a). Glad The Face. The Sun.

She caught my glance
the next table down
an Irish lilting sound -
an old woman her face
like the gold glad sun;
van Gogh's sunflower strokes -
massed with wrinkles swirls
around her blue eyes, red mouth -
in beautiful lines flaring out
symmetrical, even, care-full;
like the photos of sun-spots
radiating whirls of curled fire shot
churning, curving wisps of flames out;

like a Catherine wheel spun in sparkle, delight.
She has soft pink radiant skin - bright,
some freckle spots and pure white hair
lifted lightly, halo-fluffed there.
She listened well, encouraged and
supported her younger troubled friend.
Being old - from her to me a gift
is now beautiful, good; not the ugly fixed mask of a botox face-lift.
An amazing extraordinary, track-stopping, eye-catching face
against the sun-light and her sky blue dress with lace.
Together they rose and left, nourished refreshed -
gathering up their bags, flowers - new and fresh.

b).Bad Mad Sad Then the old Grumpy Gonk, Fat Tump Croc.

I came out of the loo, content, relieved
and waiting her turn, she looked peeved.
I came out, she passed in
with a muttering mumble
of 'Ladies only!' a hobbling stumble.
Stunned - Am I a man? - again blotted out
    I know I'm not. But she hurt -
superficial crap, tinsel surface yaps,
judging a parcel by its paps and wraps
To her 'Ladies only!' - I said 'I'm one' -
should have also said, and more, 'You're not'.
Her bastard pastel lycra slacks and clothes -
so corseted-common in gangs of the old.
'The Sun, the Face' spoiled and cold.

Sept 2008

Transformation of 'Uglies'

Those who accept and build on
their given idiosyncrasies
become beautiful and lovable.
    They shine.

A little roundy woman
with fuzzy splayed, ginger hair
and a summer dress -
fullsome and billowing
and gathered curving
like a balloon into her calves -
with little fat legs, black socks
and a pair of large white trainers
so thick at the heal that she could sprint off.
She didn't but walked proudly
down the cool street. I chuckled sweet.

Another little roundy woman
in tight jeans and plump yellow shirt
stopped to look at the sweeties
in the window of the coffee shop;
sweeties are universal, attracting all nations
like bees to nectar flowers
transformed to honeyed smiles.
She held a little paper bag
with the label - 'Fatface'
the name of the high street shop.

O - I love them both.

Another tiny plump woman
in black jeans with slits
above the turns-ups
bedecked with sparkly diamond glits
and shoes with big name labels
on the backs of her heels
stopped to read the menu -
so very proud of herself and I was too.

I learn that even trainers can be given new life
in the washing machine by a wash!
And only English men and women
wear shoes, sandals, trainers -
and longer socks up to their calves with bermuda shorts.

Is there such a thing, a category, class
as ‘ugly’ - shackled and boxed?

July 2015

The Unexpected

An expensive caf -
coffee £3 a shot -
a teenage courting couple
in the current fashion gear
properly sit in the sun -
the art deco table and chairs.
The waiter brought a tea-pot
and two delicate cups
then two plates of cream
and jam and scones
which they delicately spread
looking coyly at each other
with smiles and shy eyes -
quiet.
They had entered an adult world,
though still unsullied, baby faced.

A copper dawdles past
amused, perhaps amazed -
to this kind of youth, unused.

Nov.2014

Unknown Communion

Autumn leaves in a high wind
My choked cries falling;
Attack the black hole, back,
Reach out, outreach flailing

The farthest point of uncertainty finding.
And take this sphere crossed
And to thy comfort cup-this
Encircled in the unknown binding.
The dark candleglow curve
Rose window wheeling winding -
Bounty of vacant nothing.
A soft mist swirl of sundance dawn
Incense rising.

Inreach your dazed hand open
Unheld, no return - with no meeting;
Then in a gone glazed moment
As a starved child lay -
The soft sphere mouth-melts,
Heartholds, stillholding.

London 29.12.79

Unlaboured Spin
(A Bad Effort)

The sun is blue,
the earth is square.
We walk on air
and breathe the dust.

Trees up side down
flail roots around
and stones are soft
and streams don't run.

The sea is rock
and lies are truth;
time has no clock
and false is true.

Billions are 'spent'
on health and crime
yet where's the dent
of our full tax?

All this is true
so think it so -
a better State,
believe it true.

This is a fact
as this is that,
that they'll increase
our Council tax.

Canterbury Sept. 2003

Adventure Update Notes. 'Quantum hanky panky'
taken as improper, mischievous behaviour.
And the problem of non-human evil

[Genesis 1 - 'made in the image of god'. The first physical image is a reflection from a dark still pool of water or in a water pot (human ancestors). 6,ooo BC obsidian volcanic glass mirrors Turkey. 4,000BC, polished copper mirrors Mesopotamia, 3,000 BC mirrors Egypt. Genesis 2 written about 1,000yrs BC. Genesis 1 600 years BC].

Quantum hanky panky.

Protons and neutrons are made up of 6 kinds of quarks in 3 pairs in 3 families with fractional electric charges which make electrons zoom off in different directions. They've never been seen. They have 'colour' and 'flavour' unseen, untasted. (Physics struggling with limited scope of current language like religion's difficulty in talking of experiences of God except in stories and myths of their forefathers). They contribute to quantum particles extraordinary behaviour as 'weird', 'spooky'. Quarks make up protons, neutrons and electrons. These are all 'fundamental particles'. A gluon does actually glue quarks together.

'Fundamental religion' is not fundamental. It is surface literal myth.

An electron-neutrino interacts weakly with surrounding matter so passes through the earth. Every second 1 million of them pass through

every square centimetre in your body. Are in 'Dark matter' and have tiny mass.
Top and bottom quarks were previously called 'truth' and 'beauty' quarks. The aurora borealis is made up of protons, a result of electrons and protons from sun's flares reacting with atmosphere O2 and N2.
Laser - light amplification by stimulated emission of radiation. Uses coherent monochromatic light by stimulated emission of photons from excited atoms and molecules. Use in CD's, surgery and other cuttings.

Quantum tunnelling - particles e.g hydrogen protons can pass thru' matter like a ball passes through a brick wall. Electrons also do this.

Quantum spin - the direction electrons spin round a nucleus, the singlet type, (where 2 electrons spin in opposite directions and so cancel out) and the triplet spin type (where 2 electrons spin in the same direction). An electron can spin in both clockwise and anticlockwise directions at the same time when not being watched or measured. They're not like ping pong balls as they have no size. Without their spin there would be no universe and no us - all dependent on spin.

Quantum superposition - a particle can be in millions of places at the same time - the ability of a quantum particle to be in a superposition of 2 or more states at once. The 2 slit experiment where 1 particle is fired to a partition with 2 slits in it and the result 'photographed' on a sensitive plate behind. The 1 particle shows up as 2 light points on the plate. Or an electron beam of particles can be fired and show up as a series of dark and light lines on the plate as it has now become a wave. Or an electron could be spinning both ways at once. The same goes for a pair of electrons which can spin in the same direction and in opposite directions simultaneously. Electron bonds between atoms are often formed by the sharing of a pair of electrons. They 'sniff' out, recce, their surroundings

Quantum entanglement - electrons originally paired then become separate. If one is nudged the other instantaneously jumps even at either ends of the observable universe. (Phenomena of identical separated twin simultaneous experiences no scientific evidence). The diameter of the observable universe is 92 billion light years. Light travels at 186,000 miles/second. So nothing to do with the speed that light travels. If the universe is flat it is infinite - a postulate.

This instantaneous connection between 2 particles across space Einstein called 'spooky action at a distance'
In the quantum computer world what is now important is not space-time, matter and energy but 'information' and information is physical, is reality. The observable universe is seen as having a skin where all information is passed down as in a computer model. Picture a cut fig - where it grows from the green skin and white pulp inwards to form the purple flesh and eventually the pips with a central gap. The information to do that is in the skin.
Information theory, quantum theory and thermodynamics are intertwined in a way that suggests a new theoretical framework of the Universe is possible.

Nowadays it has been shown that quantum theory is behind everything, not only in electronics, but everything in the whole universe. In the way phones work, it creates our bodies, it makes stars shine and it fills empty space with particles that fizz in and out of existence. And this power has no need of time.

Hydrogen - 1proton
Hydrogen - 1 proton + 1 neutron =deuterium isotope. As in the sun.
Hydrogen - 1 proton + 2 neutrons = tritium isotope.

Einstein when asked if he believed in god said 'there must be something behind the energy' (neither created nor destroyed),

It's like physics has 2 gods - classical physics for the macro-world and quantum physics for the micro-world. A Theory of Everything which is a unified one law, evades. But see the possible above.
'A photon (or you or I), if we set the experiment up right has no independent existence. It is not a wave or particle. It is neither or both in a mysterious way that depends on its interactions with its environment. Looking at the experiment, or working at a certain temperature, brings a particle into existence. Other conditions make it behave as a wave.' - hinting at no subject/object split. 'The laws of nature are information about information and outside of it there is just darkness. This is the gateway to understanding reality. Information is a far more fundamental quantity in the universe than matter'.
Richard Feyman, Nobel laureate - 'Everything that living things do can be understood in terms of the jiggling and wiggling of atoms'. Living

cells are crammed full of complex molecules in a state of constant random agitation and turbulence and molecular noise vibrations. This is the 'normal' state of molecular decoherence/chaos 'evil' (not about primary quantum particles which are coherent unchaotic and primary) - equivalence of 'evil'original sin' but this is about the molecular state as secondary. Classical physics depends on it. And it can disrupt/wash away quantum systems which are primary. But quantum behaviour is coherent, choreographed not random. Without this the universe and us e.g.enzyme catalytic activity would not exist.

We're not sitting on chairs but on space. But our brain tells us we're on chairs. ?brain has evolved only to feel chairs hardness - survival mechanism e.g primitive man's hand throwing a stone tipped spear at the optimum angle for a strike for food.

Physics is forced to use conventional current language to describe quantum phenomena as there's none other. As also religion - NT embedded in OT books and liturgy and OT had no reference but made up their own from culture of its people and the previous first Epic of Gilgamesh and Enuma Elish creation stories.

Polarisation e.g sunglasses and the N. and S. poles. To do with photons in light which come with all sorts of polarisation angles - sunglasses filter them.
Massless photons in electromagnetic radiation do not experience time. Quantum particles and theory - the power behind the universe and life have no need of time. Apparently there is no time in the quantum universe. Time isn't a fundamental part of the universe. Take the photon, the particle we associate with light. It simply does not experience time. How could it, when it travels at the speed of light? The closer you go to the speed of light, the slower time flows. To a photon travelling at the very speed of light, time is 0; it simply does not exist. So quantum particles are eternal, (as energy is eternal) - amazing; something like eternity is here but isn't - depends on the environment, the temperature, measuring and even observer presence. ? Link with prayer!

Well a quantum particle in its quantum state points in many directions simultaneously. But when its polarisation state is measured it is instantly forced to forget its quantum abilities and has to take on a conventional classical physics property such as pointing in 1 direction only. From being cheeky it has to now behave itself!

Quantum coherence, entanglement and tunnelling are involved in a whole range of biological systems - photosynthesis, enzymes, smell receptors, DNA splitting and magnetoreception in birds etc, respiration. All involve a small number of particles. 'Life on the Edge' Profs. Al Khalili and McFadden page 431 show how vital are biological quantum phenomena in all their unusual ways. European robins migrate 2,000 miles to N. Africa 200 miles/day using magnetoreceptors to migrate by an inclination (not usual polar) compass from light activating eye cryptochrome involving electron entanglement and superposition of electrons. If a mini pirate eye patch is put on a robin's right eye she can't migrate. Life began 3.8 million years ago as microbes. Migration is common to a wide range of life - birds fishes turtles insects by magnetoreception - electrons in pairs in entanglement and superposition spin - so an early ancient phenomenon that evolved and which is so complex.

Exciton = electron (-ve charge) gone AWOL! out of atom + the hole it has left behind!(+ve charge) = a tiny battery.
Electrons get 'excited' - that is they have more energy as when boxed in they get frantic - as if 'claustrophobic.'

'I do not know what I appear to the world, but to myself I have been only like a boy playing on the sea-shore, and diverting myself in now and then finding a smoother pebble or a prettier shell than ordinary, while the great ocean of truth lay all undiscovered before me'. **Isaac Newton.** (founder of classical physics - macro stuff - gravity, thermodynamics for steam engines, cars, fridges, planets, footballs etc.). c.f. Shrodinger - founder of quantum mechanics - microcosmic level.

'Quantum walking/strolling' - a photon's wave-like exciton energy is transferred to the photosynthesis reaction power centre following multiple pathways all at once coherently choreographically despite decoherent molecular noise of jigglings and wiglings which can destroy quantum activity. But they don't try to avoid the noise - they 'dance' to its beat - 'quantum beat'. But only to specific types of optimum noise - the Goldilocks zone. 'White noise' low energy josslings of water and metal ions. 'Coloured noise' of higher energy limited to certain frequencies of larger molecular structures of amino-acid string vibrations that are flexible and bendy. Both these noises shepherd the exciton to the reaction centre. The oscillations of the exciton and the oscillations of the surrounding molecular proteins beat to the same drum. Good vibrations keep us all alive.

Close and continuous observation and measurement can prevent quantum events from happening e.g. a radioactive atom will never decay if observed 'the watched pot never boils'. Heisenburg pointed out, in the quantum realm, the act of watching/measuring alters the state of the thing being observed.
He was interested in position/velocity. If the position of a moving object is determined the velocity of its moving cannot be determined at the same time; and vice versa. Perhaps that shows more our limited knowledge and lack of suitable measuring instruments!
'Energy can neither be created nor destroyed' that is by us, this universe - Einstein. Amazing statement. ? Therefore from where does it come before time and space, the universe origin. ?It was there all along. A given amount. And is never destroyed.
'Energy is eternal' Prof. Brian Cox. Also quantum particles are not dependent on time so too are 'eternal'..

Electrons actively 'hop' from one atom (becoming oxidised) to another.

Quantum 'hanky panky', Einstein's 'spooky action at a distance', 'weird' behaviour. To me 'weird' is derogatory.

'Perhaps physical death represents the severing of the living organism's connection with the orderly coherent choreographed quantum realm (of entanglement tunnelling and superposition) leaving it powerless to resist the randomizing forces of thermodynamics (molecular storms, disorder chaos and jiggling and wigglings). (where white noise and coloured noise of molecular vibrations can't be used). So the fundamental quantum disconnected cell will sink beneath the thermodynamically turbulent waters becoming an entirely classical object'.
We cannot only live in classical physics. Life would not be possible.
The second law of thermodynamics is that the disorder of the universe is always constant or increasing.
'Can our new understanding of life replace the soul with a quantum vital spark?' Profs. Jim al Khalili and McFadden.

'The remarkable ability of life to harness the forces of chaos to sail the narrow edge between the classical and quantum worlds'.

The problem of non human evil

Genesis 2:17 'but of the tree of the knowledge of good and evil you shall not eat for in the day that you eat of it you shall die'. The writer of this **story had hit on something astounding as myth** (apart from Adam and Eve not dying after eating it!) This means that both had no knowledge of both good and evil up till they ate! Evil was therefore already in existence in God's knowledge before humans came (and his later evil practise in the flood). To my knowledge no-one has yet explained this pre-existent non human evil except in near polytheistic terms as Satan, the devil, Lucifer. Hence my attempt through Quantum Physics. Evil needs classification - utterly vile as in god's murder of all people except Noah and family in the flood, and commanding Abraham to slay his son etc. And ISL/Daesh decapitation of victims, Hitler Holocaust. Bad, etc - not gross.

Remember the chaotic disorderly decoherent (incoherent!) 'evil' molecular and atom cellular activity in classical thermodynamics harnessed for useful means in steam, petrol engines, fridges planetary motion etc.- classical laws of physics. 'Order from disorder'.

Decoherence can kill off the coherent orderly quantum micro level behaviour.

But quantum activity can even use white and coloured vibration noise of this molecular chaos to life-giving-ends in the quantum beat.

Chaos 'evil' thus has a function. It's not there for nothing. Out of dark and chaos comes light and life. And creative and self replicating activity. Life consists of highly complex cells with masses of interactions between molecules, atoms and quantum particles and waves - with organisation; 'order from disorder' and 'order from order'. A social system as in human society. The clash between theism and a-theism gets nowhere. A new understanding is now evolving - see Caputo and Spong.

Hence perhaps I understand 'evil', darkness, black, chaos in terms of the origin of the universe and in terms of quantum phenomena.

And remember Einstein's 'energy can neither be created nor destroyed'. It was there as a given before creation began.

Trying to understand the divine by understanding life and origins has to me only 1 way - from the roots.

A balance between disorder and order ('evil' and 'good') (decoherence/chaos and coherence).

This the reason why both were present in god's knowledge as the tree of wisdom before life and humanity occurred. Even god is evolving (violent/evil OT to compassionate NT). 'God is working his purpose out as year succeeds to year' hymn - his evolution, or more probably man's understanding of the divine is evolving, also helped somewhat by Richard Dawkins a-theism, countering a 'creationist', supernatural, theistic supreme being/object, though his boxed god is Darwin and Natural Selection. c.f. Spong and Caputo's 'The Folly …'. - no subject/object, but the Unconditional, Event, Call under the name (of) God.

Antimatter is the opposite of natural matter but the electrical charge is reversed. Antimatter and matter were both created after the Big Bang But there was more matter than antimatter. They annihilate each other and release large quantities of energy (so from destructive'evil' comes creative energy) but as there was more to start with of matter it continued to form galaxies and stars.etc. Antimatter is much less now in today's universe (as in 'good' wins over 'evil'!).

A Positron is an antielectron-antimatter and is used in body scans in PET (c.f MRI scans) - positron emission tomography made by man. Anti-matter ('evil') put to good use. It is done by an injection of radioactive sugar. The radioactive element gives off positrons, that is the antimatter equivalent of an atom's electrons. When these positrons meet electrons in body tissue the result is annihilation with a gamma flash of energy which is picked up by the scanner. So you have a 3 dimensional map of the body.

Darkness - origin of universe in darkness. Light came out of dark.

Black hole is a place in space where gravity pulls so much that not even light can escape and everything near it is sucked in. It can swallow billions of stars and perhaps planets too. Gravity is so strong that matter is squeezed into a tiny space e.g.when a star is dying. Stars close to black holes behave differently. A black hole the size of 1 atom has the mass of a mountain. Black holes were present in the origin of the universe. A 'supermassive' black hole, the largest, Sagittarius A-star, can have the mass of around 4 million suns together in our Milky way galaxy. No-one knows what happens to the sucked in stuff.

Dark Matter can't yet be seen but accounts for most of the matter of the universe! Its existence is inferred from the gravitational effects on visible matter, on radiation and on the large scale universe structure. It is still very much a mystery. It doesn't emit or absorb light or any other electromagnetic radiation. It is estimated that it is 84.5% of the total matter of the universe and posited to be made of subatomic particles (our quantum little friends hiding!). Just how little we know.

Dark Energy said to be behind the expansion of the universe.

Dark Flow flows in the direction of 2 other universe constellations and in the direction of the Great Attractor, the closest massive galaxy cluster to our own Milky Way that has enormous mass concentrated there with consequent massive gravitational attraction, therefore being known as the Great Attractor and it dominates our region, pulling our Milky Way towards itself at 14 million miles per hour but it can't be pinpointed as to where or what it is.

Dark Fluid is a combination of dark matter and dark energy outside the Earth and Solar system.

So Dark things and Anti things, black hole things, chaos, annihilation are going on in the universe from its origin and all part of it - non-judgementally but are described as evil, gross where people are concerned. And inherent in the knowledge of god before space-time and matter.

Dark in astrophysics can mean hidden and it is little understood.

Concepts in physics - chaos, dark, decoherence, anti stuff, black stuff, annihilation are inbuilt in the Universe and can be put to transforming means. Chaos is the 'normal' state capable of being transformed ('order fom disorder'. The quantum state is coherent 'order from order'.

Concept in religion - 'evil'. Equivalence. Can be put to inner and outer transformation, 'resurrection'. 'Evil' and chaos are par for the course, whether we like it or not, and are inbuilt before the origin, creation of the universe as is energy which is 'eternal' in both.

Physics is evolving. Everything changes, evolves. The question is can religion also evolve? now stuck in literalism, theism and supernaturalism. Survival of the fittest, so ?survival of religion.

Suffering 'evil', whether non-human e.g tectonic plate shifts - earthquakes, tsunamis, volcanoes, death of a child or young - or human violence, war, and all the more minor forms - can feel and is horrible - an inner tumultuous experience. That tumult/chaos/suffering is pure profound energy and energy is the force that drives the universe or is the deep spirit of Elohim. - transformable and transforming!

'The laws of physics and consciousness (mainly the ability to see

touch smell taste hear) should be seen as complementary' Pauli, Nobel laureate.
Others posit 'thought (consciousness/observation) creates reality' in the quantum world.. Subject/object become blurred - also Caputo 'Folly'p.14
Maybe our observations are limited. 'There is more than meets the eye'. Certainly we have limited colour perception. The light spectrum has more colours in it than we can see of infrared and ultraviolet. Dogs, bats etc hear more than we do. Bees see ultraviolet light etc.

So, finally, our little quantum friends in general can hop, pop and fizz in and out of existence, sniff around, walk, stroll, get excited, claustrophic, bubble, have flavors and colours, dance to a beat, (atoms and molecules jiggle and wiggle and are chaotic), tunnel through matter, spin in different direction all at once, be in many places at once, and if a pair are separated can react instantaneously to what's happening to the other, and their polarisation angles point in different directions all at once. They prefer doing all these things in secret as when observed or measured these things sometimes don't happen or change. They are real lively, lovable-to-me, characters, vital for life, the 'vital spark'. These descriptions are all from quantum physicists except 'lovable' as they pose perplexing, frustrating questions for physicists and mathematicians - therefore are called 'weird' or 'queer'. See separate Belavkin Equation complexity.

Even a perfect vacuum 'bubbles' with quantum particles! They're up to their 'hanky-panky' again. 'Right now a particle and its anti-particle are 'popping' into existence in a tiny fraction of a second, then annihilating each other which releases energy - to leave their little region of space empty once again'.

In conclusion we may partake in timeless eternity here - in our energy, but importantly in the timeless quantum particles of which we are made. Our imagination, knowledge and reason are under-equipped to cope with tiny things that behave outside the realms of our limited evolution and common sense. We have yet to evolve much more. Common sense lets us down in such micro levels of 'behaviour', as common sense deals with the macro world as we know it or have been helped to know it. That's where our brains are not developed enough. J.B.S.Haldane

- eminent biologist 'Now my suspicion is that the universe is not only queerer than we suppose, but queerer than we can suppose. There are more things in heaven and earth than are dreamt of in any philosophy'.

Dec.2015

'Life on the Edge' by Profs. Jim al Khalili and McFadden.

'At the Edge of Uncertainty' Dr. Michael Brooks - consultant New Scientist. 'The Folly of God' - Prof. John Caputo.

'The Elegant Universe' - Prof. Brian Greene.

'Jesus for the Non Religious' - Shelby Spong.

And we are 'Dancing on the Edge'. Maybe the Big Bang is a Big But yet the Big Bang's high temperature and pressure create turbulent vortices and eddies where galaxies and stars seed out. So it is a likely possibility. Richard Feynman 'If you think you understand quantum theory, you don't understand quantum theory' - as also God! Right now our bodies are in the 'eternal', that is our energy and our quantum particles.

Some of my 'favourite things' are dugongs, kakapo birds, bumblebees, hedgehogs, pandas, penguin chicks, owls and especially quantums! What are yours?

An Upmarket Supermarket (Spoilt and Spoiled for Choice)

Some items of the Pastries, Biscuits and the Bakery aisle

Puffs, swirls, waffles, truffles, bourbon cookies, brandy snaps,

dunkers, digestives, fingers, rounds, curls, cereal bars, chunks,

florentines, Biarritz, marquisette, Italian cantuccini, shortbreads,

crispies, crackers, crunches, Jaffa and short and cup cakes,

water biscuits, ginger and flatbreads, spelt bits, choc croissants,

breakfast amaretti, caramel cremes, crepes, hot cross buns,

stollen, sponge rolls, sandwich cakes, maple pancakes, yule-logs, eccles cakes, loaf and Welsh cakes, shorties, drizzles, bakes,

fondant fancies, flap jacks, rocky roads, sticky toffee, scones,

shortbread millionaires, pikelets, pains, Marlborough buns,

bagels, oat and teacakes, crispbread, iced buns, spiced buns,

baps, focaccia, ciabatta, cholia, soda breads, choc rwists,

posh dog and posh chip brioche rolls, richtea, Battenburg cakes,

submarine, chia rolls, muffins, tiffins, cornflake bites, yumyums.

And best of all Kouign Amman - pronounced what? query what -
of Brittany butter, demerara, caramelised - ooh, back home baked.
But on the tele, a starving child
who has no plain bread - the staff of life -
lies emaciate on the tarmac road
  dying in the blistering sun.
We guzzle while Rome burns.

Dec.2014

Folk fodder of Flanders Field guns.

Touching on - the relentless, intermittent deep
(in V), a Within Central Voyage, (with l's)
words now first found, before preverbal,
for the lessened unwordable unimaginable upheaval

1. A vagrant rebel victim unthinkable vulnerable -
wandering between watering holes in concrete city dust,
Trying to contain a volcanic void upsurgeprimordial
total incompatible impossible pressured infernal
tangible palpable inexplicable unmanageable,
gut chasm central, gut chasm central, first known
imprisoned in a within prison, fixed, abyss abysmal,

and pre-erupting, vast voracious predictable,
volted vortexed violent, critical near-fatal,
liquid unstable electrical universal
vacuumed vacant, a void, unlovable -
threatening very being itSelf , terrible intolerable;
vicious exploding vandalising - damnable untouchable;
a 'bad-is-good' defence release, habitual unavoidable
virulent veering maggot-ridden variable,
vehement inflexible vitreous, screen-glassed insoluble
coping vivified valiant, sheer-thin veneer, fallible.

2. The Void from that vital early non-relationship discernable;
no-one was there - vanished into thin air, unreachable unavailable
but now hand held vanquishing victorious, the damage incalculable.
Some-one is here, dependable loyal real special
holding on either side remediable, life-vital
this horrific incompatible *volcanic void* of the lava past formidable -
then seen as primary causal definable bearable.

3. Now an ordinary *emptyburnt pressure cooker*
as over the stove, someone is at last tending,
finally, secondary but a first - in these last old years
and first 'food'-filling - and off the boil, containable
in this little starved, scared, sacred, simple repairing bundle
still now preverbal.

June 2007

Over the top. Under the bottom

If you don't understand this -
Go there for yourself to your own.

void

Yes - that's it (now IT)

Volcanic ---Void

Vortex Pain

Confined by tongued ears
to conform
in jellied quietness
And churl up
the snarls
and drooping mouths -
all infinite weakness
and -
O god
my soul;
barred
tombed in
concrete.
To let rip
vomited gut
and hit.
And let my pulse
and breath beat
in vertiginous hate
in the magnitude
of Sibelian release
Immense
and deep
and what i am.
A paraesthetic whirl
of hurt words -
Word water.
Rather the burnt ends
of severed nerves
than this -
shot - a vortex
of crushed death;
i cannot share;
it belongs - take -
not this muse
of singing pain
discord unsaid

and tunelled gloom
inflicting nuclear pain
atomed. Drummed
i cannot - detonate. I -
disintegrate.
Tympanitic
it warns and splits
and takes me along
the canyoned rapid.
Gangrenous - I
can express
perhaps - Triumphant
the shattered depth
in word.

Let them dilate and die -
the quack of
duck death.
The visioned revelation -
it wells again
from coiled alpha
thermalled high;
a flight
of tornadoed peace.
Urgent, feared -
can extreme hate
Blasted?
coned, spiralled
from paralysed
worldless
hurt.
The tears clot
fear thuds -
the fist is next
Inverted.
Disciplined again
I cannot contain
and can none other?
Nothing -
a disintegrate

derelict.
O my god
Not my agony
the bleat of humanity
to scorn or dissect.

Beth Bew. 8.12.67

Instruction to write on 'Feeling Warm'

'Glow' said the glow-worm
in the forest dark;
'tingle' said the embers
dying in the grate.
The god said
'there shall be neither hot nor cold
but just nice'
then He said
'it is good' for some
as we wrap up warm
with long scarves
woolly caps
furry boots
and long socks.

Then the fire is lit at home
and I said
'Oooh'
all safe and snug.

Dec.2013.
The only decent word here is 'oooh'!

Who's the Wasp?

A couple perhaps fresh
from a Costa del Sol break -
from english fish and chips -

and their fat frying in oiled sun-tan,
order 'all day breakfasts'
at Morellis family caf -
with down-turned mouths and bermuda shorts;
with self-serve salt packets and tomato sauce.
They settle outside in the sun
then compulsively wipe down
their tissue-wrapped
clean knives and forks with frowns.
Dismayed at her fork seen as 'unclean'
she rushes in to complain to the counter staff team
then settles again and notices a young lad
taking coffee who is the managers son
with gel spiked hair and jeans falling down
and not at all 'bad'and schooled at Eton!.
Tight lipped, she scowls and mutters to her mate;
two pecking people pecking holes in all in hate.
They eat fast and often pausing -
hold their knives and forks pointing
skywards, every now and then.

I feel irritation but then delight
when two wasps buzz them
to jump up fluttering,
their arms scared in fright.

Natural justice but not yet stung back!

not yet, but wait for a counterattack!

Canterbury Oct 2010

The Week's Shopping

a.)

Mum dragged her two kids to Tesco's; Dad had left the 'home' long ago after he'd beaten her up; and Nan had no truck with her family at all.

Tempers amongst all three got worse. 'I want this water gun' screamed Jan.

'No - your're not having that fucking gun' yelled Mum as she snatched it from her

Jan cried wretchedly 'I want it, I want it' between tears. Mum, her face red with rage, slapped her hard over the earhole. People turned and stared in concern and fear.

Jan ran off and couldn't be found behind all the shelves stacked with ungetatable goodies. I'll smash these things to the floor, she impulsively felt. Something had to take the brunt of her pain.

Jimmy jumped up and down shouting repeatedly 'I want this Action Man'.

'No screamed his Mum 'you can't have it' and she grabbed it back. 'All you think of is yourself, you selfish bugger'. A shop attendant brought Jan back to her mum. And Jan was whacked. 'No sweets anymore for both of you' and she dragged them 'home' and slammed the front door hard and gave them the hiding of their lives.

b.)

'Time to go to Tesco's' said Mum to her two kids; Dad was at work. 'Jimmy and I will go and Jan can stay with Nan - you can play with your favourite game while we're away'.

'Aah Mum' said Jimmy; 'can't I stay and play too?'.

'Well' said Mum, 'there might be a surprise for you'. Jimmy jumped up to get ready and Jan ran to join Nan in the living room to get the game out.

'I love this too, it's fun' said Nan as she nestled herself in her cosy armchair.

At Tesco's the trolley was for Jimmy to wheel and Mum got all the necessary food for the week. 'I want this Action Man' demanded Jimmy.

'Well - no, we can't afford that' sighed Mum; but she showed him a simple toy from the top shelf knowing in her heart what he liked. He did and jumped for joy.

'Oh thank you Mum' and he hugged her legs and off they went back home.

18.11.01

Westie Terrier

a bundle trots past proud
white coat, compact
neat and roundy plump;
on a leash, obedient.
He's curious scanning wide-arced;
a soft human face
and button black eyes
looking at me straight in the eye.

Then he abruptly pulls up
for a lift-leg pee
against a bollard post.
But no pee comes
so he trots on -
a bouncy backside -
tail held high aloft.

A roundy old lady follows -
same sweet face
same cropped white hair awry -
same firm limbed, curiosity,
same quick steps
but now she doesn't leg-lift,
just jauntily walks gaily on.

Dec.2014

'What If ....?'

'What if' it had been this way or that;
this had not happened or that had -
imagining the bad or hoping for the good -
then the past, now the present
or in future time's ascent.
But then all this thought and regret and hope

might well be seen as dark, sometimes white clouds
passing as fluffs in the mind or as stirred up muddy water
or as bubbles in a stream where floating leaves abound
or mind as a cinema screen
flashing at us diverse sights and sounds.
They are mental events and not the real us.
They become habits of feeling and thought, continually stirred up
and like a scratched record hiccupping -
stuck in a deep groove. A chatterbox mind,
tunnel vision; a dog mind gnawing a dry bone -
crunching, stuck in concepts seen as true
when they may well be not -
creating imaginary repeated scenes
that become adhesive, tempestuous, toxic -
with prolonged mental pain bullied by fear.
Unknowing, we get in our own way, are our own worst enemies.
'What ifs ...' are not accurate or really significant, they destroy -
the more we struggle in tunnel vision the more we sink swamped
trawling in the past or future, continually stirred up - and not Now.
Doing, judging, comparing, fixing,
dooming, glooming, ruminating, striving.
All of these the going away from Being
then maybe, in acceptance, the coming back
but now through the breathing breath
which happens this moment, not the future or past.
Nod and smile to - 'Hello fear, let me bodily feel who you are
over there in here' then let the dark cloud pass
'What ifs ...' I am not them - there there.
How we feel after all - it's not as bad as it seems, was.
This new thing - it's Life leading me by the hand.
so don't dam the river or push the stream,
let it flow turbulent or calm as neither right nor wrong
and breathing aware - in compassion Watch,
centring down, ground firm
sensing, accepting, letting go in the Now - here here.
Straws in the wind pass, turbulence drops, muddy water clears;
the mind settles to maybe deep gut peace at last.
Not ruled by fear, shrunken, but I am me, con-fidant, in trust.

Gentle living Now. Take a treat. Whatever - it's OK.

Aug. 2011

What's in a face , a name?
I remain the Same

Machines in my head
to help me to see, hear and eat.
Teeth rotten, surgically removed
sunken mouth, gums stitched;
now a near toothless old hag
with infilling plates to chew.
Eyes with cataracts removed
and plastic lens implants improved
and glue-ear hearing aids placed.
Machines all over my face.

What's in a face, a name -
do I remain the same?

Apparently I do

early 2009

White Moon Waits The first White

the sound of our voice hollow in white skull
white pain rebounds, feeling advent, virgin snow
out of stone thought toy words etch
clothes congeal curdled with sweat
toward a child's broken arm bent -
bone gleaming in white plaster locked
feeling stunned white voltage shock
to keep pearls from swine rampant
through gadarene gethsemene golgotha.

I move when i move and not before, snail pace
here, now, the thrush cries
step down the glinting river
white asylum shines inside
tarry awhile if we knew when to;
wait for the flood to pass
when to wait wait for ever
waiting under the white moon, always wait
arriving forever by the child
down the black tunnel underpass
waiting alone bag set down
learning to melt, no name round its neck,
waiting for the train run that never comes,
distraught by patience, dazed on the station platform.
Waiting is nothing to what comes next.
For centuries preaching judgement sin -
a charade, in a moment open wounds grin
the altar crumbles incense jells darkness spins
the priest becomes ash a new stillness rose then
from peoples hunger tolled again and again.
White noise white lymph white light
locked in the heart white blind cataract
the days glide under night light
the quiet turn of your prayer insight
tilting down plight - doze through the morning
careworn child. O my child wet with tears
holding the folded white dove near -
prism white - 'hate thy mother and father' far
and take up thy cross my yoke is hard
burnt burnished by blanched light dared.
Rest your head on the white pillow offered lap
nursing the lost smile, the first hurt,
as white sound singes the seventh nerve.
I live in surgent dialogue within my brain
the voice we hear is our own
granite ground white grown grain.
That ancient echo of love cauterised.

Moon cow - dappled cow

grazes down
the dark night now,
quietly swallowing the stars then sinks low.

Canterbury July 2004

Seriously - Why Write?

I was impelled to write to survive then. I did not chose to, words seemed to chose me. I cannot say more here but I have said more in what I have written before.

But those events now are Grit in the Oyster - the title for an unpublished collection - to build and create something of value amidst brokenness - numerous bits of which submitted for publication or competition are apparently only worthy of repeated rejection.

So now I write for me and another - to discover more. I think we are impelled to make, build, create. I can only compare it in a nutshell like being pregnant, in labour - maybe miscarriages, abortions or sterility - then sometimes something is born. There's intercourse, seminal ideas - something may impress or catch or strike us from inside or out; beginning conception which may grow or not; the work of forming and giving birth. We may prefer to rest quiet and not bother with all that - and rest is necessary. And maybe all this is too grand a metaphor.

But there are pearls somewhere.

It has been good to share with you all and I'll miss coming here.

Canterbury Mar.2003

Some Winter Whys? Unlocking the Blocks

Why does a wagtail wag its tail

in the midst of a town square,
even-lilting, even at rest -
conserving energy has gone out the door
with its permanent parkinsonian twitch -
so that language can give it its name

and twitchers twitch with delight
to add it to their lists - accurate?

Why does a youth all in black,
in shirtsleeves, in snow and ice
wear rings in his nose ears and lips?
He's trying to 'say' something
but what, basically, is that - concise?

Why does a lad rise up on the tips of his toes
with each jaunty continual step he takes.
Perhaps in an exuberant mood -
but what happens when he is downcast sad?

Why does an old man wear
a woolly cap over his ears
with silly woolly worms
sprouting from its top? -
because he likes it. Full stop!

Why does a man walk like a pigeon -
his head jutting forward and back?
He is a man not a pigeon, at that.

Why do lumps of people
slump in entrances to shops
to block others getting in and out? -
blind to others except those in their clump.

Why do I wear a hearing aid
when there's mostly meaningless
babbling talk? - in the hope not?

Why do third world people starve
when the West is bulging obese
with food, everything under the sun, excess?

'Cos unequal something is better than Nothing I guess;

as we're only half way there, as yet, to redress -
to progress to a Shared Earth blest the best.

Dec.2010

Wings - flight BA 2666 to Morocco

Gatwick plane window seat.
Taxi for take off - tarmac,
manoeuvre easy, slow.
Stop to line up - up speed fast
then engine roar, Rolls Royce;
wing ailerons not out, flat.
I'm pushed back in my seat
sudden thrust and sudden
ascent. Take off,
spine tingling exhilarate
to the point of tears.
Oh, the superb mind of man
the designer and engineer
in the image of God.
The wings upper curved
to create this lift to keep
the plane and I aloft
from that simple physical fact -
that ordinary becomes extraordinary -
that small fact becomes huge.
Tremendous. Amazing grace.
We rise and rise above
English green fields,
the coast, the Isle of Wight,
Bay of Biscay, the boundary
between Portugal and Spain,
Gibraltar, tiny millimetre ships
and their little wakes, North African coast,
Casablanca and down to Marrakech -
the desert and tiny terracotta house blocks
never taller than a mosque minaret;
the take off and landing

are controlled by the pilot -
but mid flight is automatic
so speed goes right down, just floating -
the wings rolling, wobbling -
we bump down and suddenly, with reverse engine thrust
the wing ailerons shoot down and up.
and we brake fast - now down safe.

On the way back BA 2667
there's those clouds over thirty thousand feet up -
two layers of them and different shapes;
earth people only see the first.
The sunset, the curve of the earth
and the crescent moon red.
Oh - the mind of man and God.

Nov 2012

A Winter Smile

I think his name is Martin
but I don't really know -
he came with his urgent steps
for a usual coffee and fast fag - so
anxious and innerly impelled
and frowning serious, sharp, unheld.
I left my seat warmed by the heater above -
gestured 'this is more cosy' and left
whereof, he surprisingly broadly smiled
but in his cold seat he stayed put while
still adrift in the stiffening draught
fragile, immobile.

In him - is this the given grace of God?

Feb 2012

Winter
on the way to the Library meeting

The white stuff -
when walking on it,
really is talking
crunchy and crisp.

If you stand still
harsh outlines of this and that
soften - smoothe -
this, the mute snow.
Fluffy duvets clean-white-covering
but punishing
on ice hiding ice
in a sudden slip fall.
Ice sheets frighten silencing
the dead dark-glassed below.
But see new grass shoots,
glazed in clear black ice glass -
yet life can spring rise;
yet fragile buds
survive severe states -
and it seems we can too.
Sprinkling soft snowflecks of whitefleece -
soft kinding
a child's cry of landing
sprawled in delight.

Feb 2013

Just Womens' Talk
a quick ditty

No - for those curious dangly 'bits'
That surprisingly rise to greet you;
And that flat pectoral'd chest
With full stops on either side -
Set firm and proud to meet you.

Unlike us, a man has no waist incurving
So his trousers tend to descending

To that rock hard, round builders'-butt
glistening thighs, thrusting calves - inside;
That gleam in the secret eye
Powered penetratingly by
A dominant linear determined mind
Knowing to first - caress you.
Pray - no; Praise - yes. Yes-You!

Jan. 2002

Sermon on Words of Sensing
Supersensory Words

Words are secondary or concurrent with the sense.
The classical senses - of touch, vision, hearing, taste and smell - Aristotle's 'windows to the soul'. Others are of spatial, balance, pain, temperature, vibration sense.
Secondary words are abstract or joining like - 'but' - this is a stopped change word, in itself beautiful.
Thoughts are mind secretions, the interior landscape and words bubble up and words alter thoughts. 'Thought' has no sense connection in itself - only in what it points to.
Words are labels - sound and smellscapes, eyescape, hearscape, touchscape.

Take OWL, ROCK, SALT, PIG, MOON, SWEETS, BITE, CRUNCH, LEMON, STING, WOBBLE, HOT - the sense connection is clear.
We can see/hear/touch/smell/taste/feel one of these words immediately because of one or more of the senses. 'Love' - a 'lovely' feeling, memory, longing but still with a primary sense as well say of touch.

Let our imagination take off with one word then describe the sense it invokes - our filtered words. Words are secondary to sense.
'LEMON' immediately is saliva and 'ugh' and a screwed up face and sight of shape and yellowish colour and tangy smell - all from memory, imagination.

Look at a picture by an old master - everything is supplied, there is not much room for imagination. We are spoon fed. Left brain function is mainly being used - the linear story rational thought.
Look at a Picasso disjunction, or a cubist piece - these allow free ranging imagination, even if it's simply on form, shape alone (if not explosive rejection or confusion indicative of a conjoined mix of sensation memory imagination thought) using right brain function predominantly - lateral splash thinking, intuitive. Poetry can be like these two types as well.

For the deepest things of our inner life - music so far is the highest deepest form of communication. Words become difficult when trying to speak/write of spiritual experience and the experience of turmoil, desolation, joy, peace, anxiety, fear - gut feeling, sixth sense - interoreceptors, tensions in muscles, breathing, gut, heart beat. We tend to ignore these under the word e.g. 'discomfort'. But in detail what is this? So suppressed are we. But words have to evolve. So I say let us be aware of our externally orientated senses as well as our interior landscape. The pace of living tends to block them out.

April 2015

A New Worry

Say I suffer a cerebral bleed or clot
or severe accident - whatever?

An image -
there i lie
in a hospital bed
with the 'locked in syndrome' -
totally paralysed
and utterly conscious
and utterly unable to speak.
Imprisoned -
and 'they' force me to live
when I would probably want to die
Maybe I could blink

to somewhat communicate.

It seems a future fact
but it's just
a feared thought -
accept it, don't fight -
there are thousands of things
that could happen to me but don't.
Breathe into it and out.
Breath is a fact.

Aug 2012

Lightly - Why Write?

I sometimes like making squiggles in the dust when I see it somewhere and best of all in sand - lovely smooth fine-grain light sand - so soft like velvet to the fingers - all sorts of squiggles - anything.

It's my mark 'I am' on the face of the big universe. 'I am here'. And sea can come in and smooth it over for a fresh lot like turning the pages. So I can write anything I like - unexpurgated truth!.

Call it grafitti if you want. Yobos do it in ugly places and it can make it better and bright. They're saying 'I am' too. Often we are seen as faceless but our mark made with a finger or a tool says 'I am', 'we are'. We have made something fresh.

Sand loves being touched. He squeaks little squeals of delight and the Nile Rosetta Stone rests happily with his Man marks. 'I am first' he says.

So I can now write this that it was good to share our squiggles and I'll miss coming here.

Canterbury Mar.2003

Yesterdays far Gonebye

The difficult to remember small gains, delights -
the always forefront known dereliction but

glimpses, spot beacons, candlelights light -
in the dark past, washed out - yet despite
that mass of knots, galls in the stunted grained oak-
with effort and rest hidden growth can revive.
Still a mighty oak unknown and great because of that -
formed from an acorn nut, abused neglected deprived;
in the storm, an oak snaps yet an ash bends.
Too often talked of, no more for this time - these galls and knots,
just the green hiding spark that lit despite ... transcends.

That long past gone - squatting moulding mud cakes in the sand;
fairy sand pit homes which really were ant-lion traps;
a tree house; hiding in dark cupboards candle-lit
no grown up about; making tents with chairs upturned
carpet covered, hurriedly restored before IT returned;
a cart on 4 wheels, a camel-caravan on the Silk Route to Samarkand;
all these to find a corner of safe warmth not found;
the slim paw-paw tree, yellow globules of sweet fruit, black pips;
to do the impossible, 'The Ascent of Everest' - books;
on first hearing 'Eroica'- heroes honoured, win, survive.
Charlie Ndiweni, our black cook, sheltering us against IT
A holiday on a bundu farm in Rhodesia's rock granite hills,
exploring caves - dangerous leopard hide-outs;
two horses bareback for three kids and thrown off;
brilliant bishop, paradise flycatcher birds, hoopoes massive nests
bilharzia's untouchable water where scarce water was -
yet one cold river in the high Inyanga mountains of the Moon
where we swam and cascaded down slimy rock slopes.
Swung around hanging on to heifers tails, tall haystacks;
a python crawling in the window, malaria mosquito nets,
mattresses on the floor for beds and good Bona
who ran the farm on her own; her smile and laugh.
The Victoria Falls and rain forest - hippos baboons giraffe.
That strange big water at Port Elizabeth called the sea
which rolled you over but allowed you to breath
down under - wave tossed, drowning but alive.
Truanting from school to watch birds by the river of mud;
guide camps in the bush, night fires under star spangled skies.
Top school swimmer, hockey trips, top in biology chemistry physics

despite being dull; University degrees medal bursaries scholarships.
Zoology trips to S.W. Africa - flamingos, seining, skate
darts. Climbing Table Mountain often, proteas - hairy, bright, hard;
humming birds gem-flashed. Made a tutor of the residence
to say, before hall meals at high table - 'Benedictus Benedicat' -
crockery, cutlery clinking, the scuffle-chuckle of sat down chairs;
a bright mind, and as there was no primal 2, dull at Physics Maths.
Medicine - much laughter learning, 'I love you' written on my white
coat! - someone did. Healing curing comforting killing. Sun tanned.
Surgical hands amputations sub-dural taps TB spines picked clean -
paralysed - they rose and walked; needed, of value at last.
Lovely African kids, black faces large white eyes -
cardiac tamponades, pleural taps, jugular drips, kiddies smiles.

Struggle, suffering - to England for the mind and frozen heart -
deteriorate, sunless, dark, yet survive under a professional shield
now a Consultant and ass. director in a clinic for Jung
and an invited member in a mysticism university course.
Retire, not valued needed, redundant now.
An Alien trying to find her real deep self - broken, deaf
but shared with a special person, slowly shown
that she is precious known cared - before unknown.
Volunteering at a Red Cross shop - window displays;
gardening, growing in a monastery garden patch;
driven to write and in old age - a Karate Black belt.
Lessened need to gain and achieve and strive -
the real deep, before unknown, is tenderness in quiet rest -
an odyssey, sharing with another the now and then,
far more essential than competing to frantic win, fast.
Making my house a home, still not yet;
a first predictable another, a real person first -
accepted and understood just as I am -
a new good unknown utterly surprising experience.

March 2007

Youth and Age in Shorts

A young man passes
tweaking his winkle of an itch

tanned in shorts
thrusting and strong, the whole of life panning out.

A middle age man
sports extremely tight thigh white 'underpants' -
his tackle bulging ugly and big,
the size of a coconuts.
To be like this he must be in crisis, mid-life;
balls of a bull in a field, snorting for cows to mount.

An old man sparse of hair and bald
with light green shorts and dirty shirt
dashes past stained behind -
he has shat himself
in incontinent diarrhoea.
He's at the library a lot; I hope they clean the seats.

A tall elder man weighting on an NHS stick
in shorts and long elasticised socks
with holes cut for the toes
hobbled along, each sandaled step in pain
then to the museum back again.
He talked to the ticket girl
and she looked up with respect;
that was his day's dose of human touch
rationed by God and he alone
had pushed himself to the edge
just to keep going and not give up.
He emerged from the museum dark
and glanced up to the sky, the bit of it left;
his face haggard and drawn and eyes dark-lined.
The eyes pleaded relief and got none -
'My yoke is easy and my burden light' said Christ.
I guess he longed to lie down at the last.
Once handsome, a leader of men now sunk to this -
where was his God? And I swore.
At least I can walk.
The town's folk cope and go their ways
but there's a deathly deadly undercurrent force beneath

which is too much. Then compassion calls out.

Oct. 2014

Brahms' First Symphony

(approaching the absolute, heaven's mystery - on St. John's gospel 1:1)'In the beginning was the Word and the Word was with God and the Word was God'

In moments of great dark, a core profound. The eye of a hurricane -
Relentless and sustained; drummed gunned sound at the encounter.
I Affirm.
You shall know who I am at the first knock on the door
And beyond is leavened within - inspanned annihilation.
Not within, not without, beyond and both
In the time between point light and dark
Pointing reaching - with a cry, a shout
There, Thouhere
The Unseen impending, Infant cross rending
The Transition
Fermenting, And sound was the word, the cry, the shout

Here peace is not. Energy.
Point infinite source. Urgent
The impulse within the universe.
And we are strong before disintegration
In the infinity of felt annihilation
Where is no faith, no hope, no word.
dark is not Dark and this not Depth -
It only becomes in transformation and transition.
I am what I am, and to know - stumbling, falling
Before I'm forgiven in unknowing doing.
And that is the profound in a time transcending
yet not I - but through the I
The eye of a hurricane
And the sound was the word.

Untouched inthis time point, unmade unbegun

Torn from the cord, borne. I am.
Despair-wrenched, affirmed: an instrument after, sharp fine -
Tearing and searing at the incision lanced line
Bisected by a cross through the central point
A dialogue of ChristGod in One on a hill
between absolute Weakness and Absent allness.
Between the end and beginning of the world.
Hill-domed dialogue in dark Godquaked
Unkingdomed Christcanyon catalysed, atoned.

The veil is rent, the stone rolled
And I soar released
Where gashglint of heavenhint
The Sword of the humming Sun, resonant -
The two-edged blade of truth and concern
Swings crossglint in a sharp arc round
And sound was the sword swung sundered, singing Son.

In full and magnitude -
The longbow bent, the arrow shot.
When others sleep - awake burnt -
The infant instorm deintegrate has transformed
And men are islands in that unformed state
But not - out. Aware that this is not the last echo, reverberate
Sound must come before the still-coming word,
Resonance from a sevenfoldphonic universe.
In the beginning was the sound and the sound was with God
And the sound was God, Soundword.
The last last movement of the first, the first and last
Raw rung triumph, shivered silence.

And the sound was within.- soundGodword.

London '78

Contents

Grit in the Oyster Explained. 4
8 5
Modern Speke 6
Music Sound Word 7
A Wild Garden – a continuing environmental saga 8
The Meeting Room 9
1 & 2 letter Words 9
'16 Tons' 11
A Child, The Universe and Time, 12
A Couple 13
A Dive In 14
A Little Dog 15
Just Bubbily Doodeling 16
A/Cross Dressing 17
More Info. on Ants 18
An Apple Bit 18
Basset Hounds. Bodies of Beauty 19
Beachy Head Cliff Deaths 20
Black Holes 21
Blackbird 22
Blue Tit on a Flower 23
A Blue tit 24
Ordinary 24
Brexit. Since the Referendum Unsolved 25
Bzz. Thump 26
Cadbury's Chocolate Ad 26
Christ!! ??IT? Wait 27
Clock 28
The observable Universe update Dec. 2021 29
Cosmical Waking 30
Some Cheeky Potted Scrambled 'Counter-intuitive' Creation Quantum Noteicles 31
The Creeping Crab Sentencing to Death 37
Silly/Simple/Stupid/Wise Delight 38
Cystoscopy K and C Hospital 39
Death 40
Destruction of Dinosaurs 41
Disorder 42
A Dog and Bare Bones. The Horror 43
The Streets of Yore 45
Gravity and Time. A Conundrum 45
Smiles or Yuks? Finding your Way 46
Draft Dying and Death 47
Electrons in Touch Sight Smell and Hearing 48
Final Marathon Run. Cancer 49
Flash Camera Shots 50
'Flu Silence. To Clear the Air 51
Dammed Up 52
Two Forgotten Heroes 52
Fur and Things 53
Pigeons and Town Steps to the Citi Terrace Caf 54
Gliding 2 54
Graduation Noise 55
A Drab Grub 56
A Jumble of Mumbles 57
Unstrict Haiku 58
'Have a Nice Day' - 59
Have you Noticed. Micro-'observation' 60
Attitudes to Health, Illness 62
Hearing Sound Yes Observing No. Macro-'observation' 63
Heat Wave Drought 64
'Let there be Light' 65
I am an Old Woman Now – not When I am one 66
Here and There. West and East

– under the influence of deafness 66
'Home is so Sad' 68
Home is so Glad 69
An Outburst. Humans and Animals 69
I am a Particle! 70
It is as It is 71
Legs and Things 72
Legs 74
Tumbling Dandelion Seed 74
Letter in the Post. Sudden News 75
Life seemed new for a few moments 76
Little'uns and Old'uns 79
A Lockdown Prudent Lift. A Risk 80
Logistics of Living 80
1 Item for Example 81
Looking Forward to ? 82
The Lost Cap and Death 83
Luscious Lady 84
Me and Nonsense An Exercise and I apologise 85
A Merry Midday Buffet 86
My Fridge Freezer 87
Near the End if not at -...In Limbo 87
Night Driving 89
On Off Things 89
Our Profligate Language 90
Pandemic Ads 90
A Pot Plant on the Coffee Table 91
Parody 92
Pre the Big Bang which was not a bang 93
In Prison 94
A Question? 95
A Story in the Repair Shop 96
I Vote the Best Shop Window in the U.K 97
Soul 98
Special Animals 99
Steam Engine 100
Strange Encounter in Butchery Lane 101
Summer High Street 102
Smart Mobile Phones 102
Surprise Delivery 103
Teeth 104
A Determined Toddler 104
The Alien in Butchery Lane 105
The Gym 106
The Muse! 107
The Woman behind the Bar 108
The Word 109
Record Thirst Ever 110
Those Eyes The Hours 110
Time, Change and the Acorn 112
Time. Note Sketches T,T,S,S,H 113
Time? 115
Town Oddities 116
UltraSound Scan 117
Up There 118
Warms 120
Waves 120
What to Write? 122
When will it Stop? 123
Wondering And Some Whys 124
A Few Special Word Sounds 126
Crazy Fun Blurb Words - 127
Conversion of Microsoft Works WPS old poems in Poems 1 128
World Word – Update 129
Worthy 130
YgUDuh 131
A Gift 132

A Little Gem 133
A Quiet Vacuum. 134
A Side Street 134
?Abstract Nothing in Winter 135
Our African Cook 136
Age 137
Ageing Growing Old 138
'Amputee' 139
'Beauty' 140
Open Behind Bars Broken 141
Believing in Oneself 142
Best of Britain 142
Mahatma Gandhi - ‘a nation can be judged on how it cares for its animals’ 142
Bits and Bobs 143
Bits and Bobs 143
A Smart Woman 144
A Bonny Graduate 144
A Bubble Bath 145
A Winter Leaf 146
Winter Buds 146
Butchery Lane Canterbury 147
A Cantonese Ivory Fan 148
Change 149
Celebrating the Coccolith Story. Over 250 relevant c words distilled to 130 149
Cosy Things 152
Waiting a CT Scan 153
The CT Scan (abdomen and pelvis) 154
Dark Matter and Energy in the Sea Hell Deep 155
Dog Trots 157
Face with a Cold 158
Fatness 158
Fashion 158
FIRE 160
Foreign Foods in a Food Hall Canterbury. (over 170 of them) 161
Catching the Air. Gliding in a Sailplane. A First 163
God and his Kenosis. (his self-emptying/altruism) 164
Hacked 165
Honoring Hannah Hauxwell of Low Birk Hatt Farm, Baldersdale 167
Head on 169
The Honey Pot 170
I am 171
Images 171
Little Things 172
Manchester Suicide Bomb 173
March 174
Substance Soul 174
Metaphysics 175
More Clothes 176
Muscles 177
The Brain 177
My Heart 178
My List of Attitudes for Health 178
My Mundane Tooth – A Current Preoccupation 179
My Tree 180
Natural History Museum London 181
New fresh Thoughts 183
Newborn 183
The Lord Oak 184
Overlooked 185
Stopped in my Tracks 186
Poetry 186
Polly 187
Poppy, the Book, Simon 187
Proud 188
Puddles 189

Putting Off 189
Q and A Spong 191
Quantum Fundamental Particle Noteicles 192
Rendevous with Death 194
Roots in Brexit 195
She Rests 195
Shoes 196
Simply 196
Yes 197
Snapshots 197
Town Street Snapshots 198
? Stupid Humans; Us 200
Surprised 201
Taking myself in hand 202
Tele and Current Cool Kids Speke 203
The Body 204
The Call 205
'The Cloud' 206
The Farm For Fun 207
The Anatomy Class For Hard Work 208
At Café Rouge 209
A Sudden Meeting in the High Street 210
WATER 211
Breakfast 212
Don't We Often Do This? 213
The Throstle's Song in th … notes 213
Thumbs Up 215
My Toe 216
Transients 217
To W.B.Yeats 218
Walking Round the Earth in Time. From the book of Revelations 219
What to do Today 220
Winter Warms 222
Words 222
HRH's Visit to Riding for Disabled School, S.Augustine's, Canterbury 224
Evil hides and They Bomb Red Cross Huts in Kabul 224
A Small Story of the 104th Archbishop of Canterbury 225
A Mother 226
The Cold 226
A New Voice 226
Psalm 151, Cantate 227
A Question 230
A Time Past 231
A First Abseil for Kids Cancer Charity 232
Trilogy 233
The Sorting in ABCD 233
The Place. with a.b.c.and d. 234
Addendum to Creation Evolution Mystery Question Mark 236
Adonai Prism 236
Afghan Women 237
Age? Redeemed 238
Alan - a lesson 239
The Alien 240
It's Hard being Allah 241
Amber - Pause 241
An Appalling Event in Spring 243
What is an Angel? 244
Anxiety 245
Anxious about Anxiety 248
Inscape Inspace in Apollo 12 249
2 Separate Seconds 250
The Astounding before Christmas 251
Baby A & - beginning and the end. Blinds on the Unthinkable,

Drawn or Opened. The Ordering principal - 252
Baptism 259
A Grotto Bath 259
To write on 'Be Here Now' – (as we're trying to create!) 261
Beauty Spoiled 262
Bedevilled. Discovery. Lions and a Lamb 262
Before and After 265
Beginning Again. 265
That Bird Dying 267
A Flavour of Busy Boho's Caf-Bar Eating-place 268
Coxed, Boxed and Foxed 269
A Loaf of Bread 271
Breakwater 271
A Breughal-Within ButterMarket Mass of People. 273
Broken Beauty 274
Broken Bridge 275
A Broken Reed 276
Bzz. Thump 277
English Buses 277
Buttermarket 1 278
Buttermarket 2 279
Buttermarket 4 280
Summer in Cafe Rouge
Longmarket Square 281
A Navy Woollen Cap in Pantellis caf 283
Casualty 283
Magnifi-Cat on Cathedral Spring Grass 285
Cathedral 287
Cern and Particle Physics And 'Perhaps' 288
A Chant for Advance in Retreat 290
Love Warmed 291
Cinquain Fugue in B flat Minor 292
Suggested tune in B flat minor with your rhythm – 293
Clearing Out 293
A Closing Day - the Touch 295
Coffee by the Wayside in Butchery Lane 295
The Common Touch 296
'Communication' 297
Compassion 302
A Small Simmering Compost Heap 303
A Compromise 303
A Concept 304
Confusion - from, to pour out together 306
Connie 2 307
A Fictional Character 308
Contrast 309
Hymn to Creation, Evolution, Mystery ?Question Mark 310
A Game of Canterbury Cricket 311
Feed the Children First 312
Crumbs and Tit-bits 312
The Current Eucharist 315
D and D 316
A Dark Place - She not I 317
Dialogue of 2 Inanimate Dead Objects 320
Middle Ear Deafness. Sound-Drowned and Sound-Starved 321
Deformed Life 322
Design 323
Dialogue of 2 Inanimate Objects 323
'Fog Everywhere' 324
'I Stood...' A Dilemma of which Path to Take 325

Discard 326
Doom and Gloom 327
The Dove 328
Dress 328
A Drive 329
The Drumchasers and Dancers 330
Dud Avocado 332
'Doesn't Everything Die at Last, and Too Soon?' 333
Dying - to Live 334
Dying to Live 335
Clay Modelling 337
Conflict 339
Farm Life 340
A Game of Squash 341
My Gift 342
Optimism 344
On Specialling a Plump P.E.T. Patient 346
A Rare Adventure 348
Eckhart 29 358
E.C.T.Echo - from 1960 359
Eggs 361
The Either Side and the I of us Is 362
The Established Office 365
A Gaunt, Starved, Wide-eyed Child in Ethiopia* 367
Evolution 368
Exercises 368
Exile in the Desert It's 369
2 Person Post card Dialogue 370
Extremes and betweens 371
Warming Up 372
In honour of the Allegorical Faery - a divine Chuckle 372
A Morelli's Family Tea 376
Cheap High Street High Fashion Now 377
A Father's Funeral 378
Instructions to write on 'Feeling Warm' 379
Feet 380
Fever 381
Fire 384
Fertile Flames 386
Flying. British Airways Boeing 777 BA 5 and 6 flights 387
Flying 389
Mother Teresa - 'Loneliness and the feeling of being unwanted are the greatest poverty' 390
Fragments as they Fall 395
All of This has Possibilities 400
A little French family 401
Double Dactyl form 402
The Gargoyles around New Year 403
A Gathering Moment 406
'In the Gift Box of Darkness' 406
Girly Fashion and new Words 407
Gladiatrix 408
Glimpses of Shapes 409
Gnomes 410
Gnomes in Dead Winter 411
Good Things 413
The Grace of God? 415
The Great Flood 416
It's all Greek to me 417
The Grey Clan. Grosvenor Hotel 417
The Theme off Music. 419
Hassled by High Street Tunnel Vision 420
Hats Off, Hats On 421
The Hearth 422
'Heavy' Beauty 423
'Give two true things about you

and one which is a lie' 425
Heifers, Horses and Haystacks 425
A Babe's Terror 427
Under the Feathers of Hen 428
Chuckles 429
A Little Scene with no Apologies 430
Hitting the Ground Running 431
Meditations on the Holocaust 433
Holy Week 435
Home is so Glad 437
A poor piece - to G. M. Hopkins 437
To Jim.(Hopkins seminar leader) 438
Monologue of an Inanimate Object written in 5 minutes 439
A Nursery Rhyme without e's written in 5 minutes 439
Hymn to Orange. 439
I am Done ... and there are still those ... 441
I am 442
I - ego 443
I Have 444
'I Will Find Time to...' what? 445
An Icon Experience 446
Real Identity Virtualed Do-u-do Yahoo? 447
An IDS Apology* 448
Impatience 450
In Definition Indefinite 451
The Sudden Incident 452
Indefinition 453
What has happened to the Inner City? 455
Intellect 457
Is Dying Done? 458
IT 459
Exile in the Desert 460
Flighty Shaft-light Beauty 461
'Germinal' - by George William Russel (AE) 463
'The Transfiguration' - by Edwin Muir 464
Karate 464
Killing Wasps 465
Lass with a Pram 466
Leaving Cape Town 467
Legs and Feet of Passing Folk 470
Lent 471
Lesotholand Lost 472
Less is More 474
Let it be in the Fresh Air 475
Letter 476
Lilies of the Field 479
Listen O My Child and have No Fear 480
Llandudno Point 481
London by Coach 483
London Steps Retraced 484
The Lost Mite of a Coin 487
The Gardener in the Burial Place 491
Love Divine 494
'Love is in the Air' in the side street 495
MAbba 496
Mach II after Church! 497
Made in the Image of God 498
Magnification 499
A Meeting 499
A Mental Hospital 501
Christmas Rush 505
Middle and Side States 507
and the place where we are 509
More Fragments 511
More Strict Haiku 513

This Quiet Place - a Watering Hole Oasis 514
Early Morning 516
Morning 517
Soft Mouse Moments 518
A simmering rushed non-poetic reply to Mr. Alexander Pope correctly writing to his Physician Dr. Arbuthnot 519
Jean, 14 years, Meets Mr. Tayer 520
Mudlarks 521
Multiculturalism 523
Negative Thought and Emotion 523
Rest in Bed 524
My Flame 526
My room 527
My Three in One 528
A Simple Mystical Question in St. Margaret's Street 529
A True Tale of a Near Death on a City Tube 531
The Needle's Eye and NOT 532
Negative Automatic Minds 533
New to the Trendy 534
The New Born Pristine Babe.
What I'd like! 535
Exile Jug 537
Some Nonsense Stuff. True stories 538
NOTES 538
Nothing (White Teeth) 542
Nought The price of peace 543
Oh They're All Glorious 545
Odds and Sods 547
Ode to a Lost Cap 549
Old Zimbabwe 550
Olympics - London 2012 551
On 'U'. Grossity Atrocities 552
One Skittle Down 553
Orange Flow 555
Our Journey An Adventure 557
Owl (where is wisdom water?) 571
'Dactylic' Parsimony of Form
Only Broken whole 574
Incredible. Sun-held.
Risen. Magnanimous 575
Partners 576
Broken is Beautiful. Simple Pebbles 577
Laughing Perfume or Fragrant Nonsense 579
Perhaps In the storm Who are We? Some Excavations 580
Petrarchan type Sonnet 2 584
Pigeon Drinking 585
Pigeons in St. Margaret's Street 586
Doughnut Donut Do-not Dunked 587
In Praise of Pigeons and others 588
A Piper's Message to the Master 590
Poetry is not 591
Poor A Woman Eating Fish 591
The Pope in Cuba on TV 593
A simmering rushed non-poetic reply 593
A Sidewalk Poppy 594
Poppy Week 596
Porcupines and Crimes 597
Pork Scratchings 600
Sex in the City 601
Prawns 602
Prayer 603
Psalm 151.Cantate. To The One

606
In Honour of My Puddy Pudding Cat 609
The Puppeteer 610
Quatrain in 5 minutes 611
A Question 2? 611
A Quick Lesson 612
Raw Fractured Reality to Raw Rage. damn you - can't you see I exist 612
Rainstorm 614
Red Red-emption 615
Redemption 616
from 'Remember' by Joy Harjo 619
Respite 620
Life Giver, A River Heart 623
The River's Sermon 625
R.M.S. Edinburgh 628
RRH Children's Court 633
the heavy yoke of dying old past dogma - 634
Sand and Grit 636
A Scared Bird's takes Flight 637
A Sea Shore 638
A Seaview 639
A Seed Falls He Drawing the Sting Out 640
Seven Attitudes for health 642
Shadows 642
She 645
Shotokan Karate 647
Sibelius 150th Anniversary Concert, Marlow Theatre 648
Silence 649
Simples 650
A Hidden Song 651
Some Little Sketches of Some Little People 653
An Iona Skylark 655
Slippers 655
A Slow Return 656
Snow 658
So What 659
An Old Soldier 661
Some Clothes in Winter in Butchery Lane 662
A Song of Writing 663
Shakespearian type *Sonnet 1.Discipline 664
Elizabeth - Behave Yourself (c.f. Shakespeare's Sonnet 130) 664
SPACE 665
A Spanish Hat 666
Causation in Seconds! 667
Stones and Correlation 668
Stopping the rot of a muddy mind! 669
The Street Gaits of Passers by - 670
Strict Haiku 671
Unstrict Haiku 673
Styles 675
A Suicide 676
Sun Shafts 677
The Town Supermarket 678
A Swarm of Poppy Seeds Blown. Nunc Dimittis 679
Sweet Chestnut 681
Sweets 682
Sainsvery's Safe-reserve Animal Vegetable Mineral Symphony Orchestra 683
Symptom Substitution 684
Old Frayed Tapestry 685
Oh. 686
Haiku 687
'Tell me what it is you plan to do 687
Britain's Ten Commandments

Now 688
Tenderness 689
The Desert 690
?The Disabled Enable a holy dying? 691
The First Part 693
The Journey 695
The Library Meeting Room 695
The Praying Mantis God 696
The Nativity - a local native birth 697
The Task 698
The Spiral 699
The Starved… 701
The Table (What do we put on it?) 701
In All 702
They 703
Those Eyes 703
Threadbare Cloth 705
The Throstle(the crucifiction) 707
Working Through (mourning the losing of former life) 708
Ticking Time Bomb - Intimations of Mortality 709
Time 711
A Thin-skin Tin Can in the Wind 727
To a Cushion 729
To Paul Tillich 729
Tobogganing and Meister Eckhart 732
'Today' for the Dung Beetle 734
Today 735
Tortoise 735
Toward the Unknown 737
Toys 739
Town Tribes 740
Trite Words are not Trite 741
Trying 743
The Lost Children of the Great Wave - 26.12.04 746
Two Old Women 747
Transformation of 'Uglies' 748
The Unexpected 750
Unknown Communion 750
Unlaboured Spin 751
An Upmarket Supermarket (Spoilt and Spoiled for Choice) 762
Folk fodder of Flanders Field guns. 763
Over the top. Under the bottom 764
Vortex Pain 765
Instruction to write on 'Feeling Warm' 767
Who's the Wasp? 767
The Week's Shopping 768
Westie Terrier 770
'What If ....?' 770
What's in a face , a name? 772
White Moon Waits The first White 772
Seriously - Why Write? 774
Some Winter Whys? Unlocking the Blocks 774
Wings - flight BA 2666 to Morocco 776
A Winter Smile 777
Winter 777
Just Womens' Talk 778
Sermon on Words of Sensing 779
A New Worry 780
Lightly - Why Write? 781
Yesterdays far Gonebye 781
Brahms' First Symphony 785